NATIONAL GEOGRAPHIC
Reach
for Reading
COMMON CORE PROGRAM

Program Authors
Nancy Frey
Lada Kratky
Nonie K. Lesaux
Sylvia Linan-Thompson
Deborah J. Short
Jennifer D. Turner

NATIONAL
GEOGRAPHIC

Hampton-Brown

Meet the Artist

Joel Sotelo grew up in Tijuana, Mexico and began coming to the United States with his mother as a young child. He now lives in San Diego where he works as an artist and designer. Sotelo loves to travel and integrates elements of many countries and cultures into his art.

Acknowledgments

Grateful acknowledgment is given to the authors, artists, photographers, museums, publishers, and agents for permission to reprint copyrighted material. Every effort has been made to secure the appropriate permission. If any omissions have been made or if corrections are required, please contact the Publisher.

Lexile®, Lexile Framework® and the Lexile® logo are trademarks of MetaMetrics, Inc., and are registered in the United States and abroad.

Cover Design and Art Direction: Visual Asylum

Cover Illustration: Joel Sotelo

Text Credits: "The Letter" and "The Lunchroom" by Nikki Grimes from *Thanks a Million*. Copyright © 2006 by Nikki Grimes. Reprinted by permission of HarperCollins Publishers.

Excerpt from *Facing the Lion* by Joseph Lekuton. Copyright © 2003 Joseph Lemasolai with Herman Viola. Reprinted by permission of the National Geographic Society.

"Trees" by Harry Behn from *The Little Hill*. Copyright © 1949 by Harry Behn, renewed 1977 by Alice L. Behn. Used by permission of Marian Reiner.

Photographic Credits: IFC (tl) Design Pics Inc./Alamy, (cl) Blend Images/Alamy, (bl) Washington Post/Getty Images, (tr) ZSSD/Minden Pictures, (cr) Glow Images/Getty Images, (br) Paul Nicklen/National Geographic Images Collection; iii, BP1, BP4, BP7, BP10, BP13 (t), BP16, BP19, BP22, BP25 James Godman; BP13 (br) Thomas Perkins/iStockphoto; BP31 Jacek Chabrazewski/Shutterstock; BP32 Jupiterimages; BP36 (b) cardiae/Shutterstock; BP40 (b) Monkey Business Images/Shutterstock; BP42 Jacek Chabrazewski/Shutterstock; BP47 (b) Shutterstock; BP49 Ariel Skelley/Blend Images LLC/Jupiterimages; BP51 Getty Images; BP55 Tim Pannell/Corbis; T1g, T27h, T33p, T55f (bl) flab/Alamy; T1h (br) Leland Bobbe; T33l (bc) J J.D. Griggs/USGS; T55h (bl) Bruce Dale/National Geographic Stock; PM1.28 Images of Africa Photobank/Alamy; PM1.29 Feije Riemersma/Alamy; A1.43 (tl) Jacek Chabraszewski/Shutterstock, (tc) paulaphoto/Shutterstock, (tr) Andy Dean Photography/Shutterstock.

Illustration Credits: All PM and RT illustrations by National Geographic Learning; A1.9, A1.20, A1.26 National Geographic Learning.

Acknowledgments and credits continued on page Ack1.

Visit National Geographic Learning online at www.NGSP.com

Visit our corporate website at www.cengage.com

Printed in the USA.

RR Donnelley, Menasha, WI

ISBN: 978-07362-96526

B

12 13 14 15 16 17 18 19 20 21

10 9 8 7 6 5 4 3 2 1

Program Authors

Nancy Frey
Professor, San Diego State University

Lada Kratky
Author and Curriculum Consultant

Nonie K. Lesaux
Associate Professor, Harvard University

Sylvia Linan-Thompson
Associate Professor,
University of Texas at Austin

Deborah J. Short
Senior Research Associate,
Center for Applied Linguistics

Jennifer D. Turner
Associate Professor,
University of Maryland

Literature Review Panel

Carmen Agra Deedy
Author

Grace Lin
Author and Illustrator

Johnda C. McNair
Associate Professor, Clemson University

Anastasia Suen
Author

Reviewers

Kristin Blathra
Lead Literacy Teacher
Donald Morrill Elementary School
Chicago, IL

Irma Bravo Lawrence
Director II, District and English Learner Support Services
Stanislaus County Office of Education
Turlock, CA

Vicky Brioso-Saldala
Director of ESOL
Broward County Public Schools
Fort Lauderdale, FL

Blanca L. Campillo
Reading Coach
Chicago Public Schools
Chicago, IL

Sandy Cano
Bilingual Special Education Teacher/Case Manager
Pasteur Elementary School
Chicago, IL

Sina Chau-Pech
Elementary ELD Lead Teacher
Folsom Cordova Unified School District
Sacramento, CA

Carla Chavez
Language Arts Specialist
Galena Park Independent School District
Houston, TX

Anna Ciani
Teacher
PS 291X
Bronx, NY

James M. Cleere
Teacher
Donald McKay School
Boston, MA

Judy H. Cole
Teacher
Southwestern Randolph Middle School
Asheboro, NC

Jonathan Eversolll International Baccalaureate
Curriculum Coach
Park Center Senior High
Brooklyn Park, MN

Aimee R. Finley, Bilingual Teacher
C.A. Tatum Jr. Elementary School
Dallas, TX

Griselda E. Flores, Bilingual Instructional Coach
Chicago Public Schools
Chicago, IL

Julie Folkert
Language Arts Coordinator
Farmington Public Schools
Farmington, MI

Barbara Ann Genovese-Fraracci
District Program Specialist
Hacienda La Puente Unified School District
Hacienda Heights, CA

Norma Godina-Silva, Ph.D
Bilingual Education/ESL/Title III Consulant
ESL-BilingualResources.com
El Paso, TX

Vanessa Gonzalez
ESL Teacher/ESL Specialist
Rhoads Elementary
Katy, TX

Laura Hook
Elementary ESOL Resource Teacher
Howard County Public Schools Central Office Building
Ellicott City, MD

Leonila Izaguirre
Bilingual-ESL Director
Pharr—San Juan—Alamo Independent School District
Pharr, TX

Myra Junyk
Literacy Advocate and Writer
Toronto, ON, Canada

Lisa King
District Lead ESOL Teacher
Polo Road Elementary School
Columbia, SC

Keely Krueger
Director of Bilingual Education
Woodstock Community Unit School District 200
Woodstock, IL

Lore Levene
Coordinator of Language Arts, NBCT
Community Consolidated School
District 59
Mt. Prospect, IL

Estee Lopez
Professor of Literacy Education and ELL Specialist
College of New Rochelle
New Rochelle, NY

Susan Mayberger
Coordinator of ESL, Migrant, and Refugee Education
Omaha Public Schools
Omaha, NE

Annena Z. McCleskey
ELA Consultant/Regional Literacy Training Center
Director
Wayne RESA
Lathrup, MI

Michelle Navarro
Teacher
Orange Unified School District
Orange, CA

Janie Oosterveen
Bilingual Teacher Specialist
San Antonio Independent School District
San Antonio, TX

Theresa Proctor-Reece
Teacher
Windy River Elementary School
Boardman, OR

Sashi Rayasam
Director of ESL Services K-12
Durham Public Schools
Durham, NC

Robin Rivas
Curriculum Specialist ESL/FL
Milwaukee Public Schools
Milwaukee, WI

Shareeica Roberts
Teacher
Carroll Academy for International Studies
Aldine, TX

Cynthia Rodrigues
Bilingual Teacher
Brill Elementary School
Spring, TX

Cristina Rojas
MS.Ed., District Program Specialist, EL Programs
Hacienda La Puente Unified School District
Hacienda Heights, CA

Ana Sainz de la Pena
Director, ESOL and Bilingual Programs
The School District of Philadelphia
Philadelphia, PA

Julie Sanabria
Teacher
Mamaroneck Avenue School
White Plains, NY

Stephanie Savage Cantu
Bilingual Teacher
Stonewall Jackson Elementary School
Dallas, TX

Jennifer Skrocki Eargle
Elementary Language Arts Specialist & Contract Employee
Galena Park Independent School District
Houston, TX

Terri L. Sailors-Chartier
Teacher
Fremont Elementary School
Alisal Union School District
Salinas, CA

Jennifer Slater-Sanchez
Educator
Palmdale School District
Palmdale, CA
Adjunct Professor
Brandman University
Antelope Valley, CA

Georgia Thompson
Literacy Coach
Esperanza Hope Medrano Elementary School
Dallas, TX

Dr. Annette Torres Elias
Assistant Professor School of Education
Texas Wesleyan University
Fort Worth, TX

Sonia James Upton
ELL Consultant, Title III
Kentucky Department of Education
Frankfort, KY

Kathy Walcott
Spanish Immersion Specialist
Rockford Public Schools
Rockford, MI

Christine Kay Williams
Teacher
Baltimore County Public Schools
Baltimore, MD

Michelle Williams
ELL & Migrant Programs Director
West Ottawa Public Schools
Holland, MI

Bonnie Wiseman
Coordinator K-12, ELA & ELD
Pajaro Valley Unified School District
Watsonville, CA

Rebecca Wood
Teacher
Henry F. Kammann Elementary
Salinas City Elementary School District
Salinas, CA

Reach all students with this innovative, new common core reading program

Empower every classroom to reach for reading success through

- Content-based instruction
- Reading for every learner
- Structured and flexible teacher support

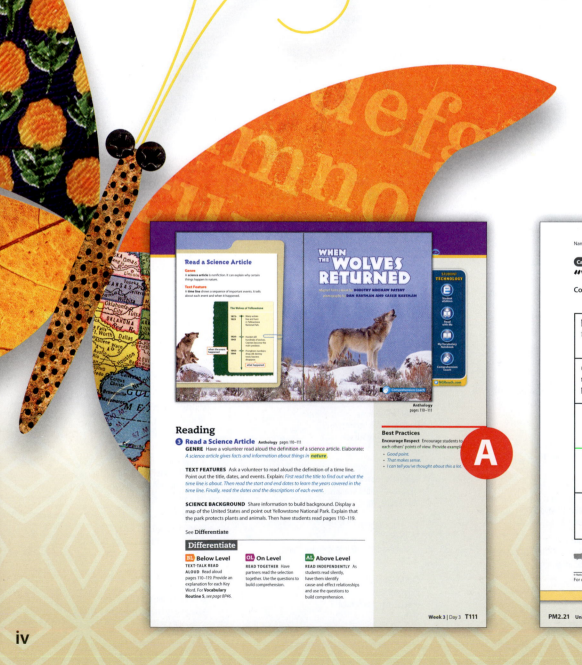

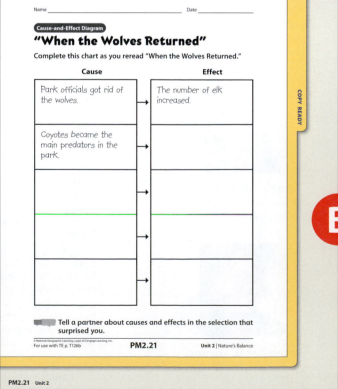

Everything you need for the unit is in one book

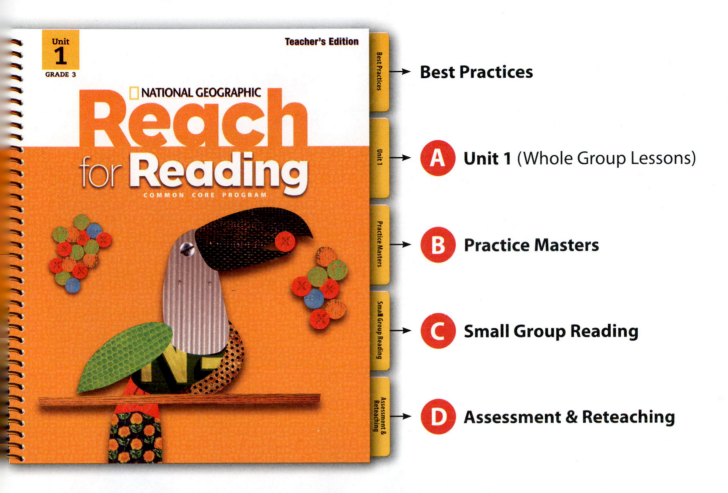

→ **Best Practices**

A **Unit 1** (Whole Group Lessons)

B **Practice Masters**

C **Small Group Reading**

D **Assessment & Reteaching**

C

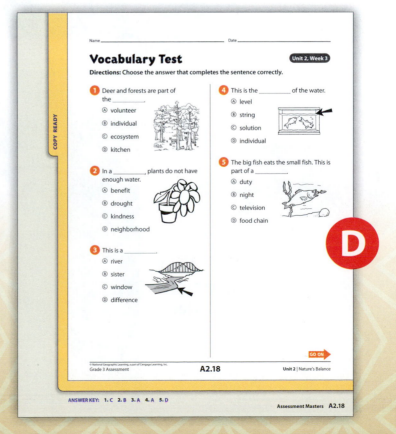

D

Engage students with exclusive National Geographic content and authentic texts

Unit at a Glance
▸ **Language:** Tell an Original Story, Express Opinions and Ideas, Science Words
▸ **Literacy:** Synthesize
▸ **Content:** Forces of Nature

Unit **7**

Blast! Crash! Splash!

BIG Question

What forces can change Earth?

Share What You Know

Do It!

❶ **Think** of a force of nature, such as an earthquake or a storm, that you have read about or seen on TV.

❷ **Draw** a picture of it.

❸ **Share** your picture with the class. Explain your drawing.

I saw a tornado on TV.

Build Background: Watch a video about forces of nature.
NGReach.com

412

Build Background Videos

Selvakumar Knew Better
by Virginia Kroll
illustrated by Xiaojun Li

Comprehension Coach

A Better Way
by Juan Quintana

NATIONAL GEOGRAPHIC EXCLUSIVE

Comprehension Coach

Authentic, multicultural literature

Amazing visuals

Life Returns to
Mount St. Helens
by Andreas Pilar

On a visit to Mount St. Helens today, you see a quiet volcano and green forest. But what if you been there on May 18, 1980? You would have heard a powerful bang as the volcano erupted. You would have seen the entire north face of the volcano suddenly collapse. You would have seen hot gas, ash, and steam moving across the landscape at 200 miles an hour. The forest would have disappeared before your eyes.

▲ Mount St. Helens erupts.

Interactive Whiteboard Activities

Reading for Every Learner

Learn skills and strategies with an accessible anthology

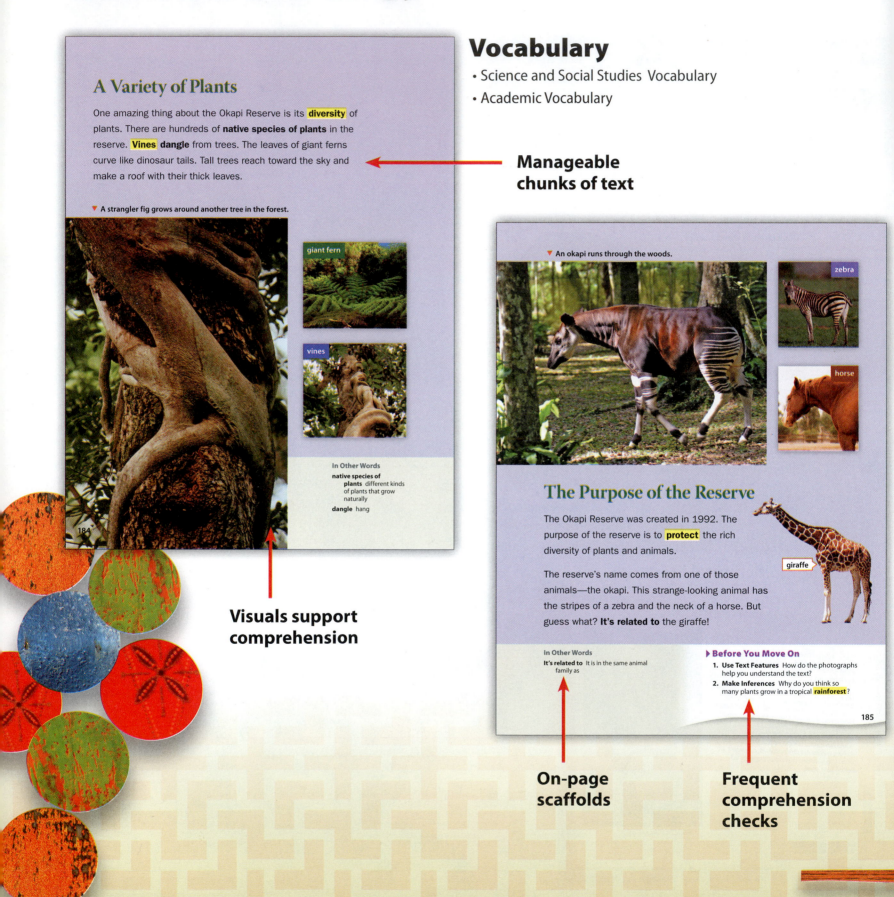

A Variety of Plants

One amazing thing about the Okapi Reserve is its **diversity** of plants. There are hundreds of **native species of plants** in the reserve. **Vines** **dangle** from trees. The leaves of giant ferns curve like dinosaur tails. Tall trees reach toward the sky and make a roof with their thick leaves.

▼ A strangler fig grows around another tree in the forest.

giant fern

vines

In Other Words
native species of plants different kinds of plants that grow naturally
dangle hang

184

Vocabulary
• Science and Social Studies Vocabulary
• Academic Vocabulary

Manageable chunks of text

Visuals support comprehension

▼ An okapi runs through the woods.

zebra

horse

The Purpose of the Reserve

The Okapi Reserve was created in 1992. The purpose of the reserve is to **protect** the rich diversity of plants and animals.

The reserve's name comes from one of those animals—the okapi. This strange-looking animal has the stripes of a zebra and the neck of a horse. But guess what? **It's related to** the giraffe!

giraffe

In Other Words
It's related to It is in the same animal family as

▶ **Before You Move On**
1. **Use Text Features** How do the photographs help you understand the text?
2. **Make Inferences** Why do you think so many plants grow in a tropical **rainforest**?

185

On-page scaffolds

Frequent comprehension checks

Apply skills and strategies with differentiated reading

Accessible books for struggling readers

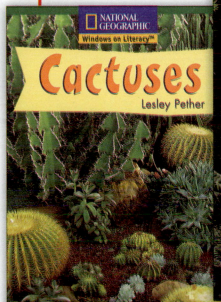

BL Below Level

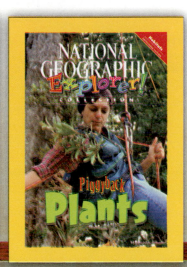

BL Below Level

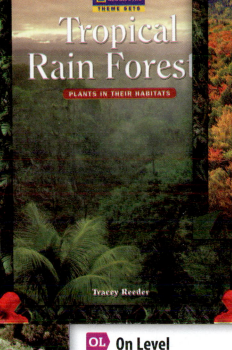

OL On Level

AL Above Level

Challenging books for above-level readers

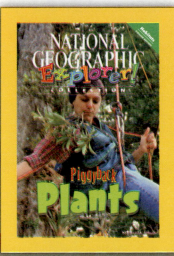

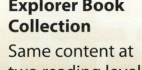

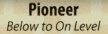

Explorer Book Collection

Same content at two reading levels

Pioneer
Below to On Level

Pathfinder
On to Above Level

Structured and Flexible Teacher Support

Follow the lesson path or tailor your plans to meet instructional needs

Online Lesson Planner

Clear time allotments

Grouping options

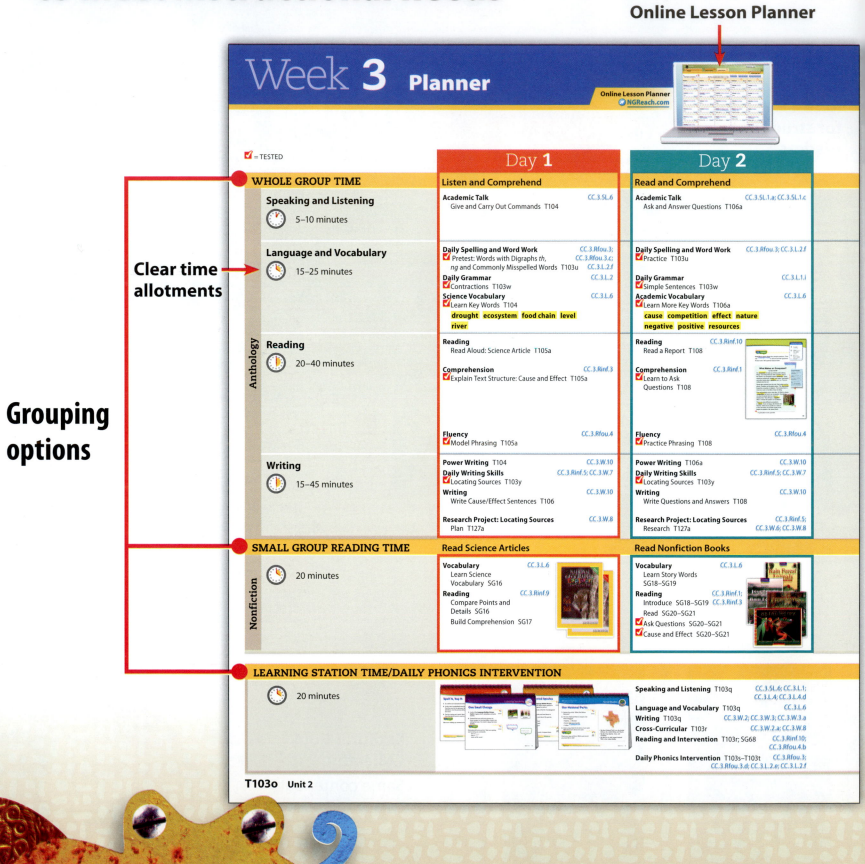

Week 3 Planner

Online Lesson Planner
NGReach.com

✔ = TESTED

		Day 1	Day 2
WHOLE GROUP TIME		**Listen and Comprehend**	**Read and Comprehend**
Speaking and Listening 🕐 5–10 minutes		**Academic Talk** CC.3.SL.6 Give and Carry Out Commands T104	**Academic Talk** CC.3.SL.1.a; CC.3.SL.1.c Ask and Answer Questions T106a
Language and Vocabulary 🕐 15–25 minutes		**Daily Spelling and Word Work** CC.3.Rfou.3; ✔ Pretest: Words with Digraphs *th*, CC.3.Rfou.3.c; *ng* and Commonly Misspelled Words T103u CC.3.L.2.f **Daily Grammar** CC.3.L.2 ✔ Contractions T103w **Science Vocabulary** CC.3.L.6 ✔ Learn Key Words T104 drought ecosystem food chain level river	**Daily Spelling and Word Work** CC.3.Rfou.3; CC.3.L.2.f ✔ Practice T103u **Daily Grammar** CC.3.L.1.i ✔ Simple Sentences T103w **Academic Vocabulary** CC.3.L.6 ✔ Learn More Key Words T106a cause competition effect nature negative positive resources
Reading 🕐 20–40 minutes		**Reading** Read Aloud: Science Article T105a **Comprehension** CC.3.Rinf.3 ✔ Explain Text Structure: Cause and Effect T105a **Fluency** CC.3.Rfou.4 ✔ Model Phrasing T105a	**Reading** CC.3.Rinf.10 Read a Report T108 **Comprehension** CC.3.Rinf.1 ✔ Learn to Ask Questions T108 **Fluency** CC.3.Rfou.4 ✔ Practice Phrasing T108
Writing 🕐 15–45 minutes		**Power Writing** T104 CC.3.W.10 **Daily Writing Skills** CC.3.Rinf.5; CC.3.W.7 ✔ Locating Sources T103y **Writing** CC.3.W.10 Write Cause/Effect Sentences T106 **Research Project: Locating Sources** CC.3.W.8 Plan T127a	**Power Writing** T106a CC.3.W.10 **Daily Writing Skills** CC.3.Rinf.5; CC.3.W.7 ✔ Locating Sources T103y **Writing** CC.3.W.10 Write Questions and Answers T108 **Research Project: Locating Sources** CC.3.Rinf.5; Research T127a CC.3.W.6; CC.3.W.8
SMALL GROUP READING TIME		**Read Science Articles**	**Read Nonfiction Books**
🕐 20 minutes		**Vocabulary** CC.3.L.6 Learn Science Vocabulary SG16 **Reading** CC.3.Rinf.9 Compare Points and Details SG16 Build Comprehension SG17	**Vocabulary** CC.3.L.6 Learn Story Words SG18–SG19 **Reading** CC.3.Rinf.1; Introduce SG18–SG19 CC.3.Rinf.3 Read SG20–SG21 ✔ Ask Questions SG20–SG21 ✔ Cause and Effect SG20–SG21
LEARNING STATION TIME/DAILY PHONICS INTERVENTION			
🕐 20 minutes			**Speaking and Listening** T103q CC.3.SL.6; CC.3.L.1; CC.3.L.4; CC.3.L.4.d **Language and Vocabulary** T103q CC.3.L.6 **Writing** T103q CC.3.W.2; CC.3.W.3; CC.3.W.3.a **Cross-Curricular** T103r CC.3.W.2.a; CC.3.W.8 **Reading and Intervention** T103r; SG68 CC.3.Rinf.10; CC.3.Rfou.4.b **Daily Phonics Intervention** T103s–T103t CC.3.Rfou.3; CC.3.Rfou.3.d; CC.3.L.2.e; CC.3.L.2.f

(row labels on left side: Anthology, Nonfiction)

T103o   Unit 2

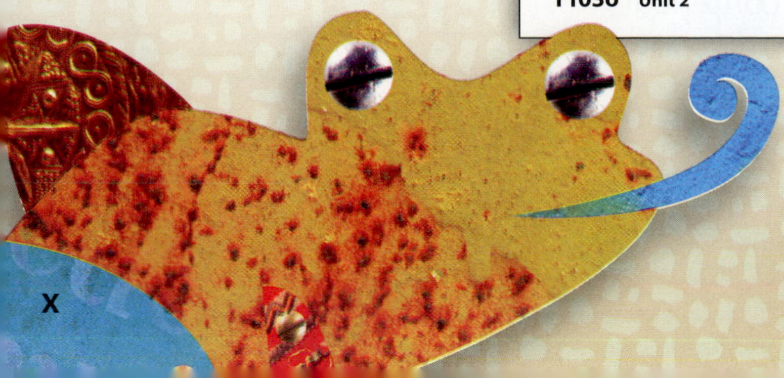

Daily writing, spelling, and grammar

Thematic Connection
Profile of an Ecosystem

BIG Question What happens when nature loses its balance?

Day **3**	Day **4**	Day **5**	
Read and Comprehend	**Read and Comprehend**	**Review and Apply**	
Academic Talk CC.3.Rinf.1; CC.3.SL.1 Preview and Predict T110	**Academic Talk** CC.3.SL.1 Summarize Reading T120	**Academic Talk** CC.3.SL.1.d; CC.3.SL.4; Talk About "When the Wolves CC.3.SL.6 Returned" T126	← **Common Core Standards**
Daily Spelling and Word Work CC.3.L.2; CC.3.L.2.f ✓ Practice T103v	**Daily Spelling and Word Work** CC.3.Rfou.3; CC.3.L.2; ✓ Practice T103v CC.3.L.2.e	**Daily Grammar** CC.3.L.1; CC.3.L.1.i; CC.3.L.2 ✓ Review T103x	
Daily Grammar CC.3.L.1.i ✓ Compound Subject/Compound Predicate T103x	**Daily Grammar** CC.3.W.5; CC.3.L.1.i; CC.3.L.2 ✓ Grammar and Writing T103x		
Vocabulary Practice CC.3.L.6 ✓ Expand Word Knowledge T110	**Vocabulary Practice** CC.3.L.6 ✓ Share Word Knowledge T120	**Vocabulary Review** CC.3.L.6 ✓ Apply Word Knowledge T125a	
Reading CC.3.Rinf.10 ✓ Read a Science Article T111–T119	**Reading** CC.3.Rinf.10 Read a Science Article T120–T125	**Reading** CC.3.Rinf.10 Reread a Science Article T111–T125	
Comprehension CC.3.Rinf.3; ✓ Identify Cause and CC.3.Rinf.1 Effect T112–113, T116–117 ✓ Ask Questions T112–113, T116–117 Identify Sequence T114–115	**Comprehension** CC.3.Rinf.3; ✓ Identify Cause and CC.3.Rinf.1 Effect T121, T122–123 ✓ Ask Questions T122–123	**Comprehension** CC.3.Rinf.3 ✓ Cause and Effect T126b	← **Focused reading skills and strategies**
Fluency CC.3.Rfou.4 ✓ Practice Phrasing, Accuracy, and Rate T112–113	**Fluency** CC.3.Rfou.4.b ✓ Practice Phrasing, Accuracy, and Rate T121	**Fluency** CC.3.Rfou.4.b ✓ Check Phrasing, Accuracy, and Rate T127	← **Daily fluency activities**
Power Writing T110 CC.3.W.10 **Daily Writing Skills** CC.3.Rinf.5; CC.3.W.7 ✓ Locating Sources T103z	**Power Writing** T120 CC.3.W.10 **Daily Writing Skills** CC.3.Rinf.5; CC.3.W.7 ✓ Locating Sources T103z	**Power Writing** T125a CC.3.W.10 **Daily Writing Skills** CC.3.Rinf.5; CC.3.W.7 ✓ Locating Sources T103z	
Writing CC.3.W.10 ✓ Write a Sequence of Events T118–119	**Writing** CC.3.W.10 Write as a Wolf T124–125	**Writing** CC.3.W.10 ✓ Write About "When the Wolves Returned" T126	
Research Project: Locating Sources CC.3.Rinf.5; Research T127a CC.3.W.6; CC.3.W.8	**Research Project: Locating Sources** CC.3.W.6; Organize T127b CC.3.W.8; CC.3.SL.5	**Research Project: Locating Sources** CC.3.W.6 Present T127b	
Read Nonfiction Books	**Read Nonfiction Books**	**Read Nonfiction Books**	
Vocabulary CC.3.L.6 Expand Vocabulary Through Wide Reading SG18–SG21	**Vocabulary** CC.3.L.6 Expand Vocabulary Through Wide Reading SG18–SG21	**Vocabulary** CC.3.L.6 Expand Vocabulary Through Wide Reading SG18–SG21	
Reading CC.3.Rinf.1; Read and Integrate CC.3.Rinf.3 Ideas SG20–SG21 ✓ Ask Questions SG20–SG21 ✓ Cause and Effect SG20–SG21	**Reading** CC.3.Rinf.1; Read and Integrate CC.3.Rinf.3 Ideas SG20–SG21 ✓ Ask Questions SG20–SG21 ✓ Cause and Effect SG20–SG21	**Reading** CC.3.Rinf.10 Connect Across Texts SG21 **Writing** CC.3.W.2 Choose a Writing Option SG20–SG21	← **Substantive differentiation**

ASSESSMENT & RETEACHING

Assessment and Reteaching T127c–T127d
✓ Reading Comprehension Test A2.16–A2.17 CC.3.Rinf.3
✓ Reading Strategy Assessment SG57–SG58 CC.3.Rinf.1
✓ Oral Reading Assessment A2.1–A2.3 CC.3.Rfou.4
✓ Vocabulary Test A2.18–A2.19 CC.3.L.6

✓ Spelling Test: Digraphs th,ng and CC.3.Rfou.3;
Commonly Misspelled Words T102u CC.3.Rfou.3.c;
CC.3.L.2; CC.3.L.2e; CC.3.L.2.f
✓ Writing, Revising, and Editing Test CC.3.W.10;
A2.20–A2.22 CC.3.L.1.i; CC.3.L.2
Reteaching Masters RT2.7–RT2.8

← **Assessments inform instruction**

Week 3 | Planner **T103p**

Engaging Technology Tools

Bring content to life at NGReach.com

Student Technology

- My Assignments
- Digital Library
- Build Background Videos
- Build Background Interactives
- Read with Me Selection MP3s
- Fluency Model MP3s
- Practice Masters
- Teamwork Activities
- Other Student Resources

Vocabulary Games

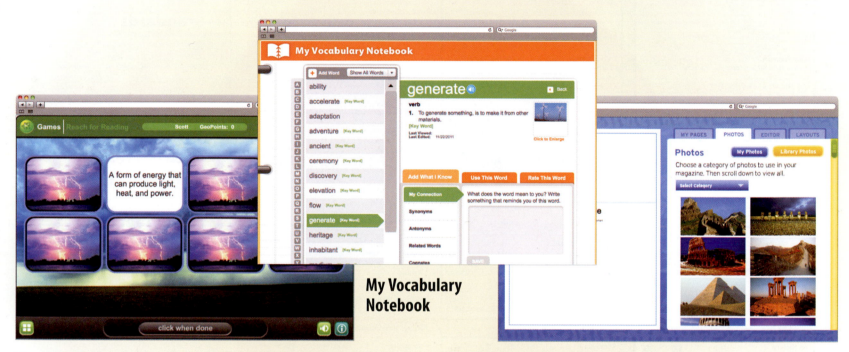

My Vocabulary Notebook

Magazine Maker

Student eEdition

Comprehension Coach

Teacher Technology

- Build Background Videos
- Build Background Interactives
- eVisuals
- Family Newsletters
- Teamwork Activities Teacher's Guides
- Test-Taking Strategies Teacher's Guides
- Other Teacher Resources
- Online Professional Development

Interactive Whiteboard Lessons

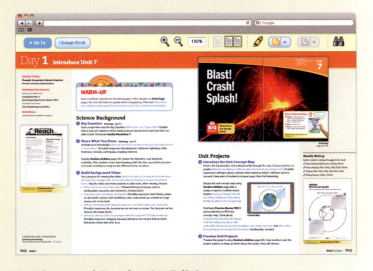

Student and Teacher's eEditions

Digital Library

Online Lesson Planner

Frequent and Varied Assessments

Inform instruction every step of the way

Teacher's Edition Assessment Resources

- Weekly Tests
- Unit Tests
- Oral Reading Assessments
- Rubrics and Answer Keys

Additional Resources

Benchmark Tests

ExamView® CD-ROM

eAssessment™

Week 3 — Assessment & Reteaching

☑ = TESTED

Assess

OBJECTIVES	ASSESSMENTS

Reading

☑ Explain Text Structure: Cause and Effect
☑ Ask Questions to Comprehend Text

Reading Comprehension Test
A2.16–A2.17

Reading Strategy Assessment
SG2.30–SG2.31

Fluency

☑ Phrasing
☑ Accuracy and Rate

Oral Reading Assessment
A2.1–A2.3

Use these passages throughout Unit 2. Work with Below Level students this week.

Vocabulary and Spelling

☑ Use Domain-Specific Words
☑ Use Academic Words
☑ Spell Words with the Digraphs *th, ng*
☑ Use Commonly Misspelled Words Correctly

Vocabulary Test
A2.18–A2.19

Spelling Pretest/ Spelling Test
T103u

Grammar and Writing

☑ Use Contractions
☑ Use Simple Sentences
☑ Use Locating Resources

Writing, Revising, and Editing Test
A2.20–A2.22

Research Project Rubric
A2.38

T127c Unit 2

Happy to Help

? BIG QUESTION

How do people help each other?

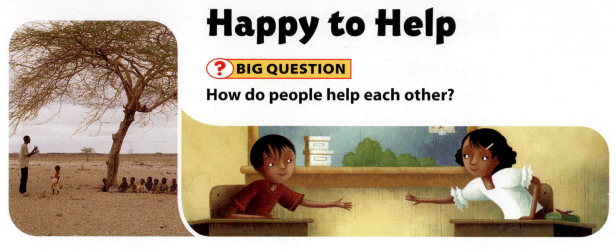

Unit 2

Nature's Balance

? **BIG QUESTION**

What happens when nature loses its balance?

Life in the Soil

? BIG QUESTION

What is so amazing about plants?

READING SKILLS

RESOURCES

Practice Masters PM3.1–PM3.39

Small Group Reading SG1–SG68

Assessment Masters A3.1–A3.45

Reteaching Masters RT3.1–RT3.13

Unit 4

Let's Work Together

? BIG QUESTION

What's the best way to get things done?

RESOURCES

Practice Masters PM4.1–PM4.40
Small Group Reading SG1–SG68

Assessment Masters A4.1–A4.44
Reteaching Masters RT4.1–RT4.14

Mysteries of Matter

? BIG QUESTION

What causes matter to change?

From Past to Present

? BIG QUESTION

How can we preserve our traditions?

Blast! Crash! Splash!

?) BIG QUESTION

What forces can change Earth?

RESOURCES

Practice Masters PM7.1–PM7.39

Small Group Reading SG1–SG68

Assessment Masters A7.1–A7.48

Reteaching Masters RT7.1–RT7.14

Unit 8

Getting There

? BIG QUESTION

What tools can we use to achieve our goals?

☐ = National Geographic Exclusive   🖥 = Interactive Whiteboard Selection

Best Practices

Download author podcasts

Contents

Nancy Frey

Lada Kratky

Nonie K. Lesaux

Deborah J. Short

Sylvia Linan-Thompson

Jennifer D. Turner

Jennifer D. Turner, Ph.D.

Deborah J. Short, Ph.D.

Building Comprehension for All Students

by Jennifer D. Turner and Deborah J. Short

As teachers, we have all worked with students who can read any text placed in front of them, but they simply can't comprehend what they've read. When we see these students struggle, it reminds us that comprehension is more than just reading a text; when students comprehend they are able to make meaning from the text, and equally important, they are able to critically think about and transform those meanings for their own purposes (Au, 2006; Hammerberg, 2004).

Why don't all students "get" comprehension?

There are a number of reasons why students may have difficulty with reading comprehension. Some readers do not have some of the "basic building blocks" of comprehension, including phonemic awareness, phonics, fluency, and vocabulary. Students of non-English language backgrounds may also have to learn our alphabet system. Such skills are the vital foundation for constructing meaning from texts.

Some students have started to develop these foundational skills but struggle in other ways. They may decode words successfully but not know the meaning of an unfamiliar word, or they know an alternate meaning for a multiple-meaning word. They may not have the background schema to activate key concepts or themes in a text. Without broader vocabulary and background knowledge, students struggle to comprehend what they read.

Other readers may not have acquired comprehension strategies because they had limited access to explicit strategy instruction. In today's schools, this may sound a bit unbelievable, but it does happen. Students from culturally and linguistically diverse backgrounds are often placed in low-level reading and writing groups which over-emphasize beginning skills. Although some students may need these skills, a problem occurs when instruction in these groups overemphasizes literal recall and other lower-level skills, and at the expense of building higher-order thinking skills and teaching comprehension strategies (Au, 2006).

A related and equally significant impediment happens when teachers do not believe that students of color are capable of building and using complex comprehension strategies (Hammerberg, 2004). By waiting too long for introduce comprehension strategies to students, we do them academic harm as they get further and further behind their grade-level peers.

Finally, some students, especially those who have severe reading difficulties or have been placed in special education, may need additional scaffolding to acquire comprehension processes and strategies. Some may need additional in-class support, while others might need targeted interventions.

What can teachers do to promote comprehension for all students?

Many students benefit from an explicit approach to teaching comprehension strategies, including clear teacher modeling and explanation, extensive practice and feedback, and opportunities for application across a variety of literary and informational texts that span topics across the content areas (Pearson & Duke, 2002; Duffy, 2009; Villaume & Brabham, 2002).

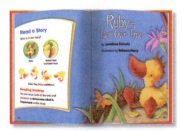

▲ Decodable texts and authentic literature selections provide literary and informational texts that span the content areas.

According to Fisher, Lapp, and Frey (2011), comprehension is dependent upon the interaction of four sets of critical variables:

- reader variables
- text variables
- educational-context variables
- teacher variables.

We would add a fifth set as well, support variables—oral and written discourse supports for making meaning of text.

To consider, plan, and implement effective comprehension instruction, teachers need to become *orchestrators* (Turner, 2005). Orchestrators carefully and thoughtfully bring together these five variables in ways that support students' comprehension and develop their lifelong love of literacy. Finding and using appropriate materials can assist teachers and students in this endeavor.

Reader Variables

No two readers are the same. Children enter our classrooms with a variety of backgrounds as literacy learners. They have different strengths in reading and writing, different genre preferences and interests, and different areas of challenge. All of our students have their own cultural and linguistic backgrounds, and participate in a multitude of literacy practices embedded within their families, friendship networks, and communities (Au, 2006; Turner & Hoeltzel, 2011). Research shows that comprehension instruction is most effective when it is responsive to the varying needs and interests of individual readers and builds upon their cultural and linguistic resources (Au, 2006; Hammerberg, 2004).

Fortunately, *Reach for Reading* can help teachers to learn more about their students and use that knowledge to their pedagogical advantage. First of all, the units and lessons feature high-quality fiction and informational texts that reflect the diversity in our classrooms. In these pages, students read about people and places within a wide variety of cultural, racial, ethnic, and global communities. Primary languages are often incorporated into the selections in ways that affirm students' linguistic backgrounds, and multiethnic characters and storylines build on students' cultural knowledge (Moll, 1992). As children discuss these varied texts, make personal connections, and share their family and community experiences, teachers gain insights about their students' cultural backgrounds.

Second, affective diagnostic assessments in the *Reach for Reading* program, such as interest surveys, also provide multiple opportunities for teachers to gather information about students' reading preferences in and out of school. All of this information can help teachers to be more responsive to the diverse strengths and needs of their students.

Text Variables

Increasing literacy demands of the workplace and a globalized society require that our children know how to consume, comprehend, and critique the texts they encounter in their schools, their families, their friendship networks, and their communities (Au, 2006). Now more than ever, students need to start learning to read a wide range of texts and then reading to learn from them. The Common Core Standards as well as the National Assessment of Educational Progress put a premium on different genres.

Students therefore benefit not only from exposure to various text types but also to explicit instruction in genre study and in selecting appropriate comprehension strategies according to the genre. This type of instruction helps students anticipate the type of information to be delivered and offers schema for constructing meaning.

Reach for Reading offers students a wide variety of fiction and nonfiction texts. While children from all cultures enter our schools with knowledge of narrative, because story-telling is a universal experience, not all children have been exposed to informational and expository text, or poems and biographies for that matter. Yet we know that the ability to make meaning from all types of text is critical for success in school. *Reach for Reading* highlights a wealth of genres including realistic fiction, science articles, photo essays, poetry, folktales, and digital texts (e.g., blogs). Students are given tools for attacking these types of text, first recognizing unique features of the genres and then applying step-by-step comprehension strategies in guided, then increasingly independent, ways.

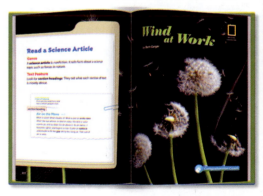

▲ Students are given tools for working with informational and literary texts.

▲ Anthologies and libraries feature a diverse array of literature and informational texts.

Educational-Context Variables

Comprehension should be woven into all aspects of classroom life. Teachers must be purposeful about the "creation of the social contexts and situations that shape children's cognition" (Smolkin & Donovan, 2002). Whether teachers are working with the whole class, in small groups, or one on one, comprehension is a key literacy goal. This is easier said than done, given limitations on instructional time and the daily distractions that arise. *Reach for Reading* provides teachers with numerous research-based practices, such as cooperative learning strategies, small group and learning station resources, and technology-oriented activities that maximize instructional time, address learning styles, and facilitate deeper understanding of texts.

Highly-motivating classroom communities are designed with active, inquisitive children in mind. To become strategic readers, students need multiple opportunities to interact with peers and meaningfully respond to tasks that support text comprehension. Just as students need practice reading and making meaning of texts from different genres, they also need to respond to a range of literal, inferential, and critical thinking questions. *Reach for Reading* includes engaging learning activities that help students to build the kind of comprehension competencies emphasized on standardized tests (e.g., stating the main idea, making inferences) as well as more authentic tasks that encourage students to apply and extend their critical thinking skills and communicative skills.

Teacher Variables

Teachers play a significant role in developing skilled readers "who actively read and automatically construct meaning as they read" (Fisher, Lapp, & Frey, 2011, p. 259). Although there is no "magic bullet" for teaching comprehension, the gradual release of responsibility model is a useful framework. Fisher, Lapp, and Frey (2011) outline five critical steps within this model:

1. Establishing Purpose
2. Teacher Modeling
3. Guided Instruction
4. Productive Group Work
5. Independent Student Practice

Through these steps, teachers build skilled readers by explicitly modeling comprehension strategies and coaching students to collaboratively practice using strategies with a variety of texts. Then they step away to allow students to independently apply strategies.

Reach for Reading is built upon this model of systematic instruction, with units and individual lessons designed to support the release of responsibility from teacher to students through multiple opportunities for practice, feedback, and the "trying out" of new skills. By focusing instruction on one strategy over the course of a unit, students spend time "getting good" at each strategy. Strategies that arise naturally out of the text's demands are consistently included to ensure strategies are employed in the service of reading comprehension.

Support Variables

While much of this monograph has focused on the process of reading, research shows us that investing time in student-generated oral and written discourse can support the development of comprehension skills (Cazden, 2001; Holliday, 1994; Saunders & Goldenberg, 2007). By creating structured opportunities for students to engage in academic talk and academic writing, we can build their reasoning skills, their background knowledge, their vocabulary, and their ability to use discourse markers and subject area registers to share ideas and relate experiences. Talking about a text before, during, and after reading it builds comprehension. Talking with partners lets students confirm or clarify their emerging understandings of a piece of text. Writing about a text gives students time to reflect on what they read and convey their impressions, formulate an argument, or condense details into a summary.

One major support that *Reach for Reading* provides is explicit teaching with language frames. Sentence starters and other types of language frames help students articulate their thoughts, orally or in writing. When a student wants to give an opinion, the program helps them say not only "I believe that…" or "I disagree because…" but increases the sophistication of the discourse, showing them other options such as "In my opinion, _____ should _____" and "_____ claims _____ but I found that _____." These language frames offer students ways of thinking about and applying higher-order comprehension processes and reading strategies. As they learn to use them, they will also learn to recognize and comprehend them when encountered in text.

Conclusion

We know that young learners do not always learn at the same rate as their classmates. And when reading and language arts instruction are considered, we know that some skills and language domains may develop more rapidly than others. We also know that our students enter our classrooms with varying reading abilities already in place—some accelerated, some on grade-level, some below-level, and some having no success yet. Our job as educators is to help all students become skillful readers. We do that best by knowing our students' cultural and linguistic backgrounds, topics they might be interested in reading about, skills they have acquired, and those they need more instruction and practice on.

The *National Geographic Reach for Reading* program gives us tools to make our work with young learners more effective, more meaningful to them, and more fun overall. Students learn to read and learn how to talk about and write about what they have read. If we do our jobs well, students will be on the path to a lifelong love of reading.

For **research citations** see page R27.

Silvia Linan-Thompson, Ph. D.

Lada Kratky

Building Foundational Skills

by Silvia Linan-Thompson and Lada Kratky

Learning to read can be a very easy one for some students, while for others, reading will be one of the most difficult tasks they will undertake. Typically, a classroom is made up of students with varying strengths and backgrounds, and the teacher will have to orchestrate instruction to meet the needs of all.

The report of the National Reading Panel in 2000 identified five key components of reading instruction: phonological awareness, phonics, vocabulary, comprehension, and fluency. These components are inter-dependent and mastering them all will lead to reading success. The foundational skills—phonological awareness and decoding skills—are critical for reading success.

Foundational skills do not, however, function in isolation. As students are building foundational skills, they must also attend to word meaning and comprehension. Strong instruction in foundational skills and consistent connections of these skills to all areas of reading is a key to building long-term reading success.

Phonological awareness

Phonological awareness is the ability to hear, identify, and manipulate sounds in words. It is an essential skill for emergent readers: children must be able to distinguish sounds in words before they can link the sound to the letters that represent them. Explicit instruction in phonemic awareness improves students' reading (National Reading Panel, 2000). For very young learners with little awareness of the sounds they articulate when speaking, Yopp (2000) recommends starting with activities that focus on rhyme. Playful poems and chants, as well as songs, will naturally engage young learners and encourage them to focus on sounds in words.

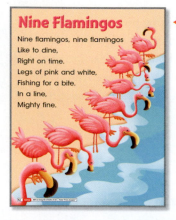

◀ Sing with Me Phonics Songs engage students with rhymes.

Phonological awareness then continues developing sound awareness tasks like isolating and substituting initial, medial, and final sounds, as well as segmenting and counting sounds in words. These activities, at the phoneme level, are the most predictive of later reading success.

Through activities at the phoneme level, children begin to recognize the sequence of sounds in a given word. An effective way for learners to develop this skill is through Elkonin—or sound—boxes. Elkonin was a Russian psychologist who devised the practice of showing a picture and a series of boxes corresponding to the number of sounds in the word the picture represents. The task of the learner is to say the word slowly while pushing a chip into each box as its corresponding sound is being said. By this method, the learner becomes aware quite graphically of the initial, medial, and final sound in a word. Eventually, children will be able to segment words without the support of the Elkonin boxes.

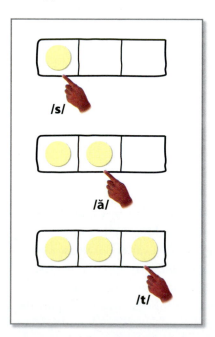

Children's phonemic awareness skills will continue to develop as they acquire knowledge of the alphabet. Phonemic awareness begins but does not fully develop until children learn to read and spell. It is learning the correspondence between sounds and printed letters that allows children to develop and automatize the full representation of sounds (Goswami, 2006).

Phonics

Explicit and systematic phonics instruction is an essential part of a successful classroom reading program (National Reading Panel, 2000). Phonics instruction teaches students sound-symbol correspondence and then teaches to blend sounds to decode words. To read, children must learn to map sounds to print. As they learn grapheme-phoneme correspondences, children are building an alphabetic schemata, or map, into which they fit and store the letter/sound relations they encounter.

National Geographic Reach for Reading includes consistent routines for phonics. Using these routines, children are taught first to blend using the sound-by-sound blending routine; additional routines (vowel-first blending, whole word blending) are included for children needing additional support. Consistent, systematic classroom routines are provided to help students acquire knowledge and automaticity in reading and spelling words.

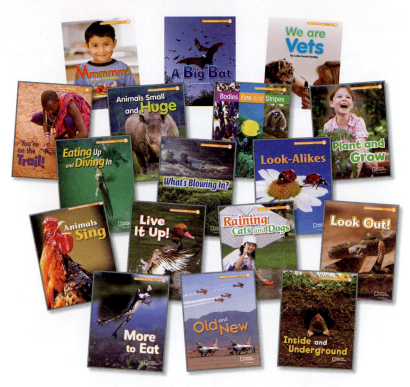

Typical English texts include a large number of High Frequency Words. These are common words that appear very frequently and are often phonetically irregular, such as *a, are, one, of,* and *the.* Children must learn to read these words, as well as write them. To achieve this most efficiently, students use a High Frequency Word routine and a variety of review and practice games that provide multiple opportunities to read as well as write those words.

After learning and practicing phonics skills and High Frequency Words in individual words and sentences, children read the Read On Your Own Books, which have decodable informational texts and stories. Accurate reading of words is only the first step in efficient reading. In order to develop automatic recognition of words, students must have multiple exposures to words in a variety of contexts. Read On Your Own Books have been designed with the idea that children can learn content even as they are learning to read, debunking the traditional thinking that in kindergarten through second grade, students learn to read, and not until third grade do they start to read to learn content.

Research shows children love science, and the books in this program abound with science stories, illustrated with outstanding National Geographic photographs. Children practice new phonics skills as they learn all about animal look-alikes, animals huge and small, bodies, fins and stripes, and so many other wonders of nature and culture.

Read On Your Own Books are not simplistic decodable texts. They present grade-level science and social studies concepts, topics that relate to real life, and texts that are worth reading and are interesting to students. Beginning readers read for meaning and are then asked to think about their reading. They give opinions, hold discussions, ask questions, and answer them. With National Geographic photographs, texts can be both decodable and content-rich.

In third grade and beyond, the Common Core Standards indicate that students have acquired most foundational phonological awareness, decoding, and spelling skills. In *Reach for Reading*, Daily Spelling and Word Work helps reinforce and build automaticity for all learners. Additionally, resources are provided for older learners who may need to build any prerequisite skills. An intervention kit, *Reach into Phonics* for grades three through five, provides age-appropriate lessons and texts to build foundational reading skills. To help students transition from the primary grades to this more rigorous intermediate-level expectation, additional games and activities are provided in the grade three Teacher's Edition for daily phonics intervention.

Fluency and comprehension

All children should learn to read accurately and without effort. Fluent reading, the ability to read with speed, accuracy, and prosody, is essential to reading comprehension. Students' oral reading provides insight into their fluency. If they are still developing decoding skills, their reading will be labored as they sound out words, and their reading of text may resemble reading a list of unrelated words—reading in a monotone.

If students pause appropriately, use correct phrasing, or change their intonation and expression in response to the text, they may not need fluency practice. Furthermore, we can usually assume that they understand what they are reading. Their response to the text is a reflection of their processing of the text as they read. These students may not need additional fluency practice. However, to be sure, assess students' oral reading fluency to ensure they are meeting grade-level benchmarks. Oral reading assessments focus on accuracy, rate, and comprehension to reinforce the importance of reading to understand, rather than simply calling out words.

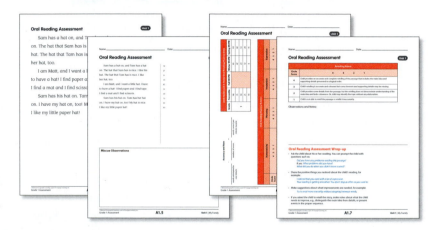

▲ Oral reading assessments include resources for measuring accuracy, rate, and comprehension.

Reach for Reading has high-interest books at various reading levels to ensure that students have numerous opportunities to read text at their independent levels. Additionally, there are several activities every week that focus on building fluency in addition to activities that build decoding skills, language, and automaticity for students that also need that support. Consistent fluency practice routines and practice passages provide support for building fluency and comprehension. The Comprehension Coach is an interactive software resource that provides a risk-free and private individualized opportunity for repeated reading. Literature selections from the anthology and Read On Your Own decodable books are included in the program. Students can read silently or listen to a model of the selection being read fluently. They can also record and listen to their own reading of the selection. After reading a section, the software automatically calculates and graphs their reading rate in words correct per minute

(WCPM). This frequent and individualized opportunity for repeated readings helps students build fluency in a risk-free environment. The inclusion of rich texts and comprehension questions supports the connection between smooth reading and understanding.

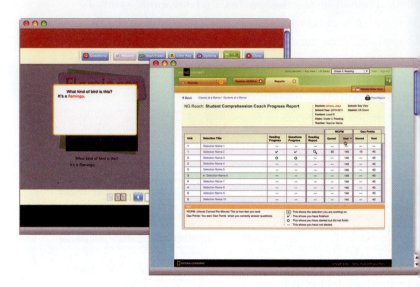

▲ Speech recognition technology is built into the online Comprehension Coach so individual students can record multiple readings and track improvement in their words correct per minute (WCPM).

Conclusion

It is important to see the five components of reading instruction as being interdependent, and that mastering them will lead to reading success. Through poems and chants, students are naturally engaged, focus on sounds in words, and learn that words are made up of a sequence of sounds and that you can manipulate those sounds. Through explicit phonics instruction and multiple exposures to words in a variety of contexts, students learn to read accurately and without effort. Students are given engaging, content-rich text to help them continue to learn to read by reading for information. Fluent reading is essential to reading comprehension, and providing reading material that is worth reading and high interest to students will ensure that they read for meaning and think about what they are reading.

For **research citations** see page R27

Nancy Frey, Ph.D.

Developing Young Writers *by Nancy Frey*

The ability to read and write to convey information, provoke thought, and inspire others has long been considered a hallmark of an educated person (Manguel, 1996). More importantly, reading and writing are tools for empowerment—they provide a voice and a forum for those who would otherwise be silent (Freire, 2000). The importance of being heard, both verbally and through writing, is especially vital.

Writing instruction across dimensions

Writing instruction has lagged behind reading instruction in both its scope as well as its depth. While educators recognize that reading requires carefully crafted experiences to promote phonemic awareness, mapping sounds onto letters, building vocabulary knowledge, and fostering comprehension across longer pieces of text, writing lacks the same fine-grained approach. Writing instruction has been confabulated with causing writing (Cutler & Graham, 2008; Gilbert & Graham, 2010), with comparatively little attention dedicated to building skills, establishing a variety of purposes for writing, and building motivation for doing so. Even worse, writing occurs infrequently and for short durations, leaving students without the stamina they need to engage in sustained writing.

Reach for Reading seeks to alter the way writing occurs in the classroom by promoting instruction across dimensions. Dimensions include project-based writing and writing in response to authentic questions; writing to reinforce comprehension; developing writing fluency; and building writing skills.

First and foremost, the need to write begins on the first page of the unit when a true purpose is established. Students confront meaningful Big Questions such as "When do harmless things become harmful?" as they explore the world of insects and competition for habitats. Students also write daily in lessons that focus on specific skills. They learn about the grammar of the language through writing as well, and incorporate vocabulary and grammar in generative sentences. Importantly, they build their writing fluency through daily power writing. Weekly project writing allows students to answer these Big Questions across a variety of genres and forms as they apply their knowledge of conventions and build their capacity to engage in skilled production. Taken together, these instructional components consolidate to form systematic, scaffolded writing instruction that mirrors the purposeful teaching of reading. Let's look further at the research base on programmatic implications of each of these principles.

Motivating writers with Big Questions

As with all people, children are spurred to discovery by questions that require investigation. Ask a child "What is the difference between then and now?" and then give her the resources and experiences she will need to address the topic, and wonderful things can occur. She might learn about how communication technologies have changed, but the need to communicate has not. She can compare and contrast similarities and differences between past and present, view a video about invention, and develop visual literacy skills to examine photographs and illustrations of transportation across time. The question can even spur on investigation about space exploration and changes that have occurred as women have become astronauts and scientists. This is intriguing content for anyone. And, in *Reach for Reading*, the content is presented in a way that is accessible to young students. With information, ideas, and opinions swimming in her imagination, the student can use writing as a natural outlet for sharing with an audience.

Motivation in writing is essential in the development of this complex skill. Young writers are motivated to write when they have an audience and purpose (Wilson, 2008). As well, knowledge of content and writing forms has been found to have a significant positive impact on the writing performance (Olinghouse & Graham, 2009). It is also significant that even primary writers find self-expression to be a motivation for writing in school (Nolen, 2007).

The spirit of inquiry in *Reach for Reading* serves as a catalyst for spurring the act of writing. But the willingness to write can be muted by a lack of skill. Therefore, writing instruction needs to be scaffolded to build competence and confidence.

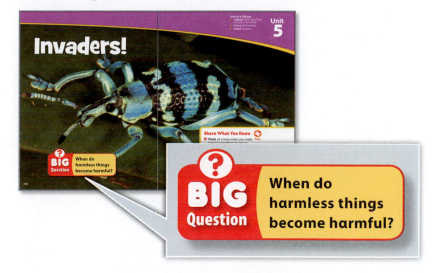

Scaffolded instruction builds writing skills

Scaffolded instruction is a principle of teaching dating back to the early 20th century. Vygotsky's (1938/1978) observations of the interactions of children who were learning together gave him insight into the possibilities of what could occur when a competent other (teacher or peer) was present to offer support. Over time, Vygotsky's insights about a learner's zone of proximal development were reinterpreted as the teacher practice of scaffolding (Wood, Bruner, & Ross, 1976). Scaffolding in turn has been further explained in reading as a gradual release of responsibility model of instruction (Pearson & Gallagher, 1983). More recently, this model has been expanded for reading and writing instruction to include a collaborative learning phase where students engage in productive group work in the company of peers (Fisher & Frey, 2007, 2008).

Effective teachers deliver writing lessons designed to scaffold student learning using a gradual release of responsibility model of instruction (Pearson & Gallagher, 1983). Scaffolded instruction in writing includes opportunities for students to witness the act of writing by their teacher while he or she uses a think aloud approach to explain the decision-making used by a writer (Davey, 1983). *Reach for Reading* provides examples of modeled writing to support teachers as they implement scaffolded writing instruction.

Think Aloud	Write
I'm going to write about the Great Wall of China. When I visualize *the wall, I think about its stone walls. They are bumpy and remind me of a tortoise's shell, so I'll make that a simile.*	The Great Wall has stone walls that are as bumpy as tortoise shells.
The wall is long and twists like a snake. I'll make that a metaphor.	The wall is a snake. It twists through the mountains.

At various times, students also benefit from writing together through the guided instruction offered by interactive writing. In addition, students regularly experience skill-building exercises such as generative sentences, daily writing skills, power writing, and close examination and replication of writing models (Fisher & Frey, 2007). Schleppegrell and Go (2007) examined the writing of fourth and fifth grade English learners who had generated lists of possible academic language and vocabulary prior to writing and found that the young writers utilized these lists to strengthen the structure and content of their writing. In addition, the children whose teachers used writing models were able to transfer these linguistic structures effectively.

Daily writing builds fluency

Systematic building of writing skills within a supportive environment that includes scaffolded instruction is essential if students are to become accomplished writers. However, the issue of writing fluency is also critical to their development. As with reading instruction, where it is understood that a steady daily diet of texts nourishes young readers and contributes to fluency, so it is with writing. In addition to the scaffolded writing instruction noted above, additional daily writing instructional activities are provided in *Reach for Reading* including power writing, generative sentences, and daily writing skills.

Power writing (Fearn & Farnan, 2001; Fisher & Frey, 2007) builds the writing stamina of young writers. These brief, timed writing events encourage children to put their ideas down on paper in order to build writing fluency. Students are encouraged to write for both volume, and with effort, for a minute at a time and then count words and circle errors. This can be repeated, and students can chart their best result to gauge their own progress over time. By engaging in these short timed writing exercises, students build stamina similar to results of daily training for a physical activity. In addition, students can track their own growth, set goals, and discuss their progress with their teacher. All of these practices are found to be essential for maintaining motivation (Bong, 2009).

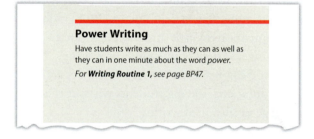

Power Writing

Have students write as much as they can as well as they can in one minute about the word *power*.

For **Writing Routine 1**, see page BP47.

The purpose of generative writing is to draw the student's attention to several key features of effective writing, including vocabulary, syntax, and semantic meaning (Fisher & Frey, 2007). Inspired by the work of Fearn and Farnan (2001) on given word writing, students are challenged to incorporate a vocabulary word or specific part of speech into a sentence. Unlike convention writing exercises, several conditions are provided to constrain their work. For instance, students might be instructed to use the word *weather* in the third position in a sentence that is at least seven words in length. Responses include the following:

- The cold *weather* caused me to go back to get a coat.
- I like *weather* that brings sunshine after a rainstorm.
- Meteorologists study *weather* so they can make predictions.

The attention to position and length causes the writer to simultaneously consider the grammatical and semantic elements required, giving them a time to consolidate this knowledge authentically. By integrating grammar instruction into a progression of more extended writing, students move from learning basic skills in isolation toward making decisions about grammar at its point of use.

Daily Writing Skills provide focused instruction, practice, application, and assessment resources that target specific skills such as using transitions or supporting ideas with sufficient and relevant details. These focused activities help develop the craft of writing to support students as they participate in extended writing projects.

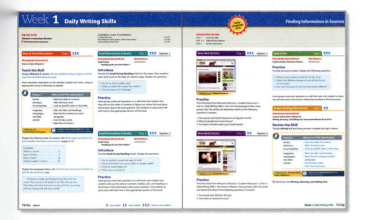

Writing projects extend writing opportunities

The view that recognizes that writing is a social act, not just a strictly cognitive one (e.g., Au, 1997; Dyson, 1989) is a central tenet of *Reach for Reading*. These social acts are fueled by the conversations that occur between writers. The weekly writing projects in the program capitalize on the interaction of oral language development and writing development. Students regularly experience research-based instructional routines that invite them to compose orally in the company of their peers (Lapp, Flood, & Tinajero, 1994). They meet to discuss their writing with peer responders who are supported with language frames to shape their collegial discussions.

Time is devoted at the end of each week to publish and share their writing with an audience, thereby further reinforcing the purpose of the writing as a way to answer a compelling question. These writing projects do double duty, as each spotlights a writing trait as well as a format or genre. These projects provide further opportunity to consolidate complex writing behaviors, develop self-awareness, and build community in the classroom. After all, isn't that what writing is for?

While writing is often viewed as an independent activity, the research on the importance of collaboration before and after writing is compelling. Writing is ultimately about audience, so conversation and response is integral to the process. As noted earlier, writers typically begin to compose orally before they put pencil to paper. Therefore, it is essential for young writers to convey their own ideas, listen to the ideas of others, and dialogue about both. Children also need opportunities to discuss what they have written with fellow writers in order to obtain peer responses. Students meet the authors of many of the readings in the *Reach for Reading* program and learn how these professionals approach their craft. These author conversations are intended to model the kind of thinking that writers of all ages engage in.

Conclusion

The act of writing is far too important to leave to chance. We know that merely "causing" writing through writing prompts is not enough. Young writers must be taught about the structures and conventions of the language, as well as the craft. Purposeful attention to building the fluency, content knowledge, and art of writing are woven together into a compelling program. Using a scaffolded approach to writing instruction, children learn not only what and how to write, but most importantly, why we write. In discovering the art of writing, they also discover themselves.

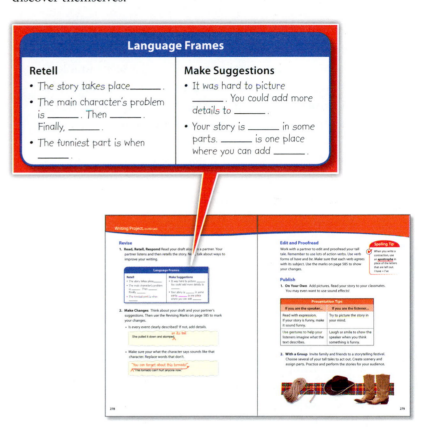

For **research citations** see page R27.

Nonie K. Lesaux, Ph.D.

Beyond the Word List: Comprehensive Vocabulary Instruction *by Nonie K. Lesaux*

Across generations of schooling, vocabulary instruction has started with a list of words—often words from a particular story. And in many classrooms, to teach these words, a familiar scene unfolds: the teacher introduces the words and posts the list. As part of this vocabulary instruction, students might match words with their dictionary definitions, and, at some point, they might read a story containing the words and answer a set of comprehension questions. After these kinds of instructional activities, it's often time for assessment.

In this traditional scenario, the time and attention devoted to vocabulary learning are limited. But to meet the needs of today's readers, and the literacy demands that are part of today's Common Core Standards, research tells us that this instructional paradigm is going to have to shift. We need to focus more carefully on the words we're choosing to teach, reconsider the duration and overall approach to vocabulary instruction, and investigate the types of opportunities we're giving our students to learn any given word.

For all learners, vocabulary and reading comprehension have a reciprocal relationship—while greater vocabulary leads to greater comprehension, better comprehension also leads to learning more vocabulary words (Stanovich, 2008). Yet vocabulary learning is an enormous task; in order to be academically successful, students must leave high school with a working understanding of about 50,000 words. And at the core of the role of vocabulary in reading comprehension is the relationship between vocabulary and a child's knowledge about the world—their background knowledge.

Thinking about vocabulary instruction as a vehicle to building up a child's background and conceptual knowledge, though, has major implications for how we go about the instructional task (Heibert, 2005). And that means a paradigm shift—in at least four ways. We need to

- focus on the words that matter most
- use a deep, interactive approach to build word knowledge
- follow research-based routines
- build strategies for word learning.

Focus on the words that matter most

We can't possibly teach students the roughly 50,000 words they need to know to be academically successful—we just don't have the time. So we need to make sure that we're making the absolute most of that time. That means a focus on building up students' vocabulary and background knowledge for reading success in *all* content areas.

As in the opening scenario, traditional vocabulary instruction practice tends to focus on low-frequency or rare words, or to focus on the concrete nouns that are part of children's everyday lives (e.g., *furniture, foods)* (Heibert, 2005). But these words can be relatively unimportant when we stack them up against all of the words that our students need to know. To be effective, we must more strategic about the words we are teaching as part of vocabulary instruction.

In every classroom, we can focus on the words students need to be academically successful and then use them as a platform for a number of important learning goals, including 1) increasing academic talk (e.g., dialogue, debate); 2) promoting more strategic reading of narrative and informational text; and 3) supporting students' research and inquiry—all skills that make up what we call "advanced literacy" and all key anchors of the Common Core Standards. We call these words *high-utility, academic* words (e.g., *analyze, characteristic, observe)* because if learned deeply, they support overall academic success, not just the comprehension of a specific text or reading lesson. They are words that show up far more in print than they do in conversation, even between educated adults.

A focus on academic words is especially important when teaching students with underdeveloped vocabularies, who need to know them in order to access the content-specific words they encounter. In *Reach for Reading*, we have been very strategic about what words are taught during the precious instructional time spent on vocabulary instruction (high-utility, academic words).

Use a deep, interactive approach to build word knowledge

Knowing a word is not an all-or-nothing affair—we all have *degrees* of knowledge of any given word. Degrees of knowledge range from no knowledge at all to a general sense of the word, all the way to an understanding of the abstract concept that underlies the word. As is the case for many students in today's classrooms, we might understand a word when *someone else* uses it in a specific context, but we don't use the word in our own writing or speaking, and we might struggle with its meaning when we come across it in print when we are reading on our own and don't have the benefit of interaction with another person. And this compromises our comprehension in that instance. But for many of our students, lack of deep word knowledge compromises not just their reading comprehension, but their academic success. These students have *some* understanding of a whole lot of words—but it's not accumulating for academic success.

The goal of vocabulary instruction, then, is for students to gain an understanding of the concept that a word represents, to acquire its multiple meanings, to understand its relationship to other words, and to understand how it is used figuratively or metaphorically. But getting to deep knowledge of a word takes time and a much more interactive, comprehensive approach than what has been standard in our classrooms. This means an instructional plan that builds in opportunities to learn these words over an extended period of time, providing multiple exposures across the lesson cycle, and in different ways—drawing on and developing students' reading, writing, listening, and speaking skills.

Word learning must be anchored in rich content. Students need to learn *how* to think about language and how words work—and this takes time and multiple opportunities across different instructional contexts. It especially means the benefit of discussion and dialogue to clarify one's knowledge and grapple with new learning. And there is consensus that this deeper, more sustained approach to vocabulary instruction means focusing on fewer words. This contrasts with the more common practice of teaching a large number of words starting with a list or workbook, a practice that might get us to Friday's vocabulary test but not to deep knowledge that is maintained over the long-term.

Reach for Reading includes academic and content words that are very tightly connected to content under study—to build up background knowledge. Students using *Reach for Reading* gain multiple exposures to each word and are given myriad opportunities to hear, read, and use the word in reading, writing, listening and speaking.

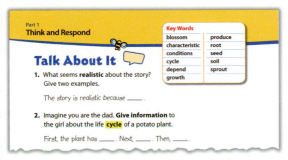

Follow research-based routines

In spite of the fact that gaps in reading performance are often associated with gaps in vocabulary knowledge, instruction in this area occurs infrequently and inconsistently in most classrooms across the U.S. and Canada (Foorman et al. 2001,: Lesaux et al., 2006; Scott, Jamieson-Noel, & Asselin, 2003; Watts, 1995). Estimates suggest that in kindergarten through second grade classrooms, only between 10 percent and 28 percent of academic time focuses on explicit instruction to support oral language development; by the middle school years, this number is about 10 percent. And when it does happen, much of this vocabulary instruction is what we would call "incidental" in nature. Instruction is often not part of a long-term plan, nor does it provide students with multiple, varied opportunities.

Take, for example, what research finds to be one of the most common scenarios for vocabulary instruction: The class is gathered around for a read aloud and the teacher starts reading. As she moves through the pages, she comes across a word that she is fairly certain many of the students will not know. She stops, provides a definition (with example) for the word, in passing, and continues through the pages. In this way, the students are really only exposed to the word once, and there is just one teaching method (i.e., a verbal explanation). This instruction is not part of a long-term plan, nor does it provide students with multiple, varied opportunities as part of a comprehensive routine to build up deep knowledge. Whether deep teaching and learning has occurred is questionable, even unlikely; we know from important research on vocabulary instruction, especially that which focuses on the number of exposures, across contexts, that a child needs to learn a word, that a much more planful, comprehensive approach is needed.

Guided by a long-term plan for vocabulary learning, *Reach for Reading* features a weekly research-based vocabulary instructional routine. The routine recognizes the importance of repetition in deliberate and strategic ways to provide students with multiple, varied exposures to the words (and their concepts) and to practice their word learning. Across the cycle, instructional tasks draw on and develop students reading, writing, listening and speaking skills.

▲ My Vocabulary Notebook is a digital resource to support the Reach for Reading vocabulary routines.

Build strategies for word learning

As mentioned earlier, we can't possibly "cover" all the words students need to learn for academic success. But while reading, students constantly come up against words that they don't know—and readers need tools to figure out the meaning these words. Therefore, as part of deep, interactive vocabulary instruction, we need to equip students with strategies to try to figure out the meaning of an unfamiliar word they encounter while reading. Without these tools, readers might skip the words repeatedly and potentially lose overall meaning, or they may get "stuck" on those words and lose their train of thought that is central to the meaning-making process. What the students do at a crossroads while reading depends in large part on the word-learning strategies they have in their toolkits.

To become advanced readers, students need to be able to pull apart an unfamiliar word (e.g., *is there a root or suffix that might help to signal its meaning?*), dig deeply enough to find a helpful context clue (e.g., *does something in the prior paragraph signal what this might mean?*), think of a related word that looks the same (e.g., *is it a cognate?*), or think about when they heard the word prior to this reading (e.g., *what is the connection to background knowledge?*). With direct and explicit teaching of word-learning strategies, students are better able to work through more challenging text and get closer to that goal of acquiring the thousands of words needed for academic success.

Instruction in word-learning strategies is systematic and incorporated into the instructional pathway presented in *Reach for Reading*. Students connect strategies to key words and have multiple opportunities to apply word-learning strategies.

Conclusion

Research finds that well-developed vocabulary knowledge—the often specialized and sophisticated language of text—is an important tool for making meaning while reading. It is also a common source of weakness for students who don't understand deeply the text they've read, even when they might have read it fluently. In fact, these same students might answer a set of literal comprehension questions accurately, but when they move to more complex literacy tasks—including drawing inferences, producing a written composition, and engaging in academic debate and dialogue—lack of deep vocabulary knowledge impedes performance.

To equip today's readers with the advanced literacy skills that are needed for post-secondary success (and full participation in society) and that are part of today's Common Core Standards, research tells us that there are key shifts to instructional paradigm for promoting word learning. Within our literacy blocks and across classrooms, we need to focus more carefully on the words we're choosing to teach, reconsider the duration and overall approach to vocabulary instruction, and investigate the types of opportunities we're giving our students to learn any given word.

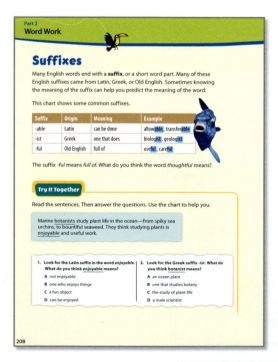

▲ Instruction and practice in word-learning strategies equip students to extend vocabulary beyond the words taught in *Reach for Reading*.

For **research citations** see page R27.

Nonie K. Lesaux, Ph.D.

Academic Talk: A Key to Literacy *by Nonie K. Lesaux*

To develop stronger readers in classrooms across the country, we need more productive noise—the sounds of students talking and working together on academic tasks. Talk is, in fact, one of the most crucial tools in the classroom to promote critical reading and thinking. Consider the following statistics that clearly demonstrate we must strengthen our reading instruction for *all* students:

- On one International Student Assessment, only 30 percent and 12 percent of U.S. students scored in the highest category on the reading and problem solving sections, respectively (Wagner, 2008).
- According to the National Center on Education Statistics, over 40 percent of students in community colleges and 20 percent of students in four-year institutions require remedial instruction (NCES 2004b).
- Educators in colleges and universities, including elite institutions, report a steady decline in students' critical thinking, reading, and writing skills (Baum & Ma, 2007).

So why focus on academic talk? Well, we know that reading words is necessary to support comprehension, but it's only a first step. While the reader must be able to successfully decode, he or she must also recognize the meaning of the words themselves and especially the concepts those words represent. To do this, the reader draws on his or her background knowledge, constantly applying what he or she already knows about the text's topic while making his or her way through the word-covered pages. But if the words or the topic are completely unfamiliar or just too difficult to grasp independently, then sounding out the words may look like "reading," but it is simply an exercise, unsupportive of learning.

The specialized, sophisticated language and abstract ideas featured in text prove challenging for many readers—not just those who are struggling. In fact, we may have a false sense of security that students who reach proficiency in early grades are inoculated against later difficulties and destined for success.

The following guiding principles will help teachers design effective academic language instruction to promote students' academic reading and writing skills:

- Provide daily opportunities for academic talk.
- Go beyond comprehension questions.
- Facilitate rich discussion.
- Connect academic talk to academic writing.

Provide daily opportunities for academic talk

Despite national calls for instructional frameworks that focus on *Reading, Writing, Listening,* and *Speaking,* and although talk is one of the most powerful tools for comprehending and analyzing text, research tells us very clearly that speaking is the neglected standard. For hundreds of years, students have been taught to listen quietly as the teacher talked, so that they would learn; still today teachers dominate classroom talk (Cazden, 1988; Heath, 1978; Snow, Tabors, & Dickinson, 2001). When attention to developing oral language does occur in most classrooms, it tends to be in preschool and kindergarten. So, ironically, as the texts and the language needed for academic success become more difficult, less instructional time, if any, is devoted to academic talk and oral language development. For students to succeed as readers and writers, we need to focus on developing their sophisticated language skills.

And if speaking is the neglected standard, listening is the misunderstood standard. *Passive* listening, like following directions, is the norm. *Active* listening is needed. Teachers can help students develop *active* listening and speaking skills through structured dialogue and debate activities that center on rich concepts. These practices also build the reasoning skills and background knowledge that are at the core of strong reading and writing.

Reach for Reading is designed to infuse reading time with significant opportunities for students to develop their academic speaking and listening skills. In every unit, and across the lesson cycle, students are presented with

- Big Questions that focus on interesting cross-curricular topics to talk about
- interesting ways to engage in academic discussion (cooperative learning structures, book discussion groups, and more).

By placing academic talk at the core of good literacy instruction, *Reach for Reading* not only builds students' speaking skills, but their active listening skills also. Teachers are guided to support students to participate in academic talk effectively with structured opportunities to do so.

◀ Big questions provide interesting, cross-curricular topics for reading, writing, listening, and speaking.

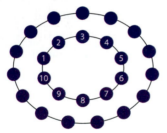

◀ Cooperative learning and partner work facilitate active engagement involving every student.

Go beyond comprehension questions

When students are given opportunities to speak during reading instruction, they most often answer low-level questions with one or two word replies, and usually during the whole-group lesson. Consider the read-aloud: the teacher reads a story, pausing every now and again to pose a question to the group. Some students raise their hands, and the teacher calls on one to respond. This practice is widespread. Researchers have found that questions about the here and now or questions with answers easily found in text are used between 50 percent and 80 percent of the time in classrooms (Watson & Young, 1986; Zwiers, 2008). But these questions serve primarily one purpose—to evaluate students' understanding about something relatively concrete and literal. It's our strongest readers who can engage effectively with the question-answer format. Overall, however, very few students benefit from this.

To promote academic talk, we can't just have whole-group settings, and we can't rely almost exclusively upon teacher questioning as our tool to do so. Effective instructional practices to promote academic talk in the service of reading comprehension and writing development focus very seriously on *dialogue*—engaging conversation about rich topics and ideas featured in text—in order for students to develop their ideas and informed opinions.

When they engage in academic talk, students make claims and justify them with evidence, articulate causes and effects, compare ideas. They work as a whole class and in pairs or small groups. Students may have roles to play so they consider perspectives other than their own, or they may share opinions and work to build consensus. In classrooms focused on academic talk for improved literacy, teachers model good academic discussions. Teachers might also work with students on turn-taking or constructive disagreement with another's opinion.

In *Reach for Reading*, instruction to broaden academic talk centers on a Big Question featured in every unit and is anchored in rich text, which is key to building comprehension skills. Instruction draws significantly on the teacher's and students' personal connections to topics. At the end of each unit and throughout the course of study, students take a stance and debate a point of view, or do some research as part of a collaborative project, and report out to their peers as experts. In conjunction with a high-quality literature and nonfiction selections, students pose questions and find answers or apply their knowledge to new situations.

In structured discussions, we ask students to learn from their peers by observing and listening, exposing them to rich and engaging text that features academic language. *Reach for Reading* also teaches and provides repeated exposures to cross-curricular and academic language registers and vocabulary words to improve their academic language skills. The scaffolded instruction on language frames moves students from forming basic sentences to making comparisons, giving opinions, and justifying choices to their peers. Students pull together their emerging skills and practice academic talk in all of the unit projects as well. Overall, the instruction is dynamic and engaging. It qualifies as much more than basic communication and prepares students for the rigorous academic environments in middle school, high school, and beyond. Academic language frames scaffold students to promote participation at all levels.

Facilitate rich discussion

If our students are going to advance to the next level, they need to actively construct their own knowledge. This means we need a paradigm shift in the role and actions of the teacher. If students are to deeply understand new texts and topics and generate new conceptual knowledge, lessons need to be designed accordingly. This means much less stand-and-deliver or step-by-step instruction to show students how produce the "right" answers, and more lessons designed around an open-ended question or big idea, connected to a long-term plan for content learning, and student collaboration. As a facilitator of students' own active learning, the teacher leads discussions on topics and texts. She is skilled at managing the process of inquiry—which doesn't always go in the direction planned—and, over time, supports students' unpacking of difficult text and big ideas (Goldenberg, 1992).

Reach for Reading supports this shift in roles through the gradual release of responsibility. Its design was guided by the principle that teachers are facilitators of student learning, guiding students on how to construct their own knowledge through in-depth interactions with text and abstract ideas. For this reason, the program supports teachers in leading fertile discussions about big ideas. Teachers model what good conversations look like and how one builds on the ideas of others. Rich discussion is fostered by enabling students at all levels to engage with authentic fiction and nonfiction texts that extend social studies and science questions beyond the shared reading in the anthology. After reading, heterogeneous groups meet to share and compare knowledge and insights gained from the different books. Cross-text sharing enables students to apply reading in authentic ways in a context that facilitates contributions by all participants.

▲ Students at varied reading levels explore different content-rich texts and novels. Heterogeneous groups share and compare thematically-related books creating an authentic context for academic discussion.

The *Reach for Reading* teacher's edition offers effective whole-group and small-group lessons to increase academic talk in our classrooms, encouraging teachers to take advantage of built-in opportunities for peer scaffolding to push students forward, while paying careful attention to groupings. Every unit features numerous occasions for teachers to foster academic language, including the end-of-unit collaborative projects that focus on the Big Questions.

Connect academic talk to academic writing

Recent research is very clear that writing is a significant weakness for many students in our classrooms. For example, in a recent study in urban middle schools, participating teachers agreed that writing a paragraph is a difficult exercise for 6th graders (Kelley, Lesaux, Kieffer & Faller, 2010). How does increasing academic talk relate to promoting students' writing skills? It does so at least three ways:

1. Effective pre-writing work begins with teacher direction and modeling and encourages structured academic talk as students generate and organize ideas with the help of a classmate.

2. Effective writing assignments provide a platform for developing students' academic language skills; when students can accurately use new vocabulary or sentence structures in writing, clearly they have a sound understanding of the meaning and mechanics.

3. When writing instruction is embedded into the overall unit of study, and therefore linked to texts, it's another chance to have students grapple with academic language. Students gain the scaffolded support they need to generate and organize ideas, incorporate appropriate academic words and sentences, and move from notes or a graphic organizer to a flowing paragraph.

The *Reach for Reading* writing approach provides opportunities for increased academic talk and peer-learning. This is especially the case during the prewriting and editing phases when students share ideas with a partner and when students edit each other's work and learn how to give feedback constructively. In addition, all writing instruction is embedded in the unit of study and connects to rich text, providing further opportunities to develop academic language.

Language Frames	
Tell Your Ideas	**Respond to Ideas**
• Something in nature I know about is _____.	• How would you turn _____ into a tall tale?
• One tall tale I know is _____. I could write something like that.	• _____ sounds funny. What will make your tale different?
• The problem could be _____.	• What will _____ do to solve the problem?

Conclusion

If we are to support all students' literacy development, prevent reading difficulties, and close achievement gaps, our classrooms should be filled with academic talk—talk that centers on big ideas and complex concepts worthy of discussion and debate and is engaging for our students. To do this we need to increase student talk and decrease teacher talk (Cazden, 2001; Fisher, Frey, & Rothenberg, 2008; McIntyre, Kyle & Moore, 2006; Saunders & Goldenberg, 1992). We need to expand teachers' repertoires to go beyond questioning to get students speaking. The dialogue that promotes reading comprehension and writing skills engages students to work and think together about a complex problem, to see others' viewpoints, and to better understand the knowledge and experiences they bring to the issue.

For **research citations** see page R27.

Deborah J. Short, Ph.D.   Jennifer D. Turner, Ph.D.

Reaching Your Reading Potential

by Deborah J. Short and Jennifer D. Turner

Our classrooms are very diverse across a range of variables: income, culture, first language background, learning styles, and more. Children enter our classrooms with different early literacy backgrounds—strengths and weaknesses in reading and writing, varied personal experiences that could be activated as prior knowledge, ranges of vocabulary knowledge, Roman or other alphabetic/graphic systems, and perspectives on print. Even with similar backgrounds, students learn to read at different rates.

Nonetheless, all students have the potential to be effective readers, writers, and thinkers. They need more than basic skills instruction to reach their potential, however. They benefit from meaningful, generative activities that ask them to analyze and apply what they are learning, make connections and compare ideas, solve problems, and create new products. The call for college and career readiness standards now being instantiated in many state standards and for deeper learning (Alliance for Excellent Education, 2011) demonstrate that many educators are ready to shift away from rote learning and standardized testing of facts to promote instruction that can lead students to be successful in school and beyond.

While the thought of high school graduation may be far from the average first or third grader's mind, these thoughts should be front and center in their teachers' minds. We want all students to start on the path to postsecondary learning and we want to give them critical tools to move forward. Unfortunately, many students from lower income or language minority families are not in classrooms that focus on challenging, creative learning (Au, 2006; Snow, Griffin & Burns, 2005; Edwards, McMillon & Turner, 2010). Sadly, research has shown that these classrooms often focus on basic skills instruction with decontextualized worksheets and memorization drills. If these students start to struggle with reading, they receive more of the same, perhaps with more intensity. This is not a winning solution.

Reach for Reading has been designed to break this cycle. It provides rich, robust instruction for all students with relevant and engaging literature that gives students satisfaction when they reach the conclusion of a story, article, or poem. Moreover, the series has connected reading instruction to the content areas—giving students tools to access the content and fostering higher-level reading skills across all subjects encountered during the school day.

Differentiated instruction is the underpinning of all lesson activities. As we discuss below, whether the class is working on vocabulary, post reading responses, unit projects, or another task, *Reach for Reading* gives teachers multiple approaches for delivering new knowledge to the students and for enticing the students to practice and apply that knowledge.

Content-based reading

How will *Reach for Reading* move students along the pathway to reading success? The move begins with content-based units centered around a Big Question that connect to science or social studies. These are not questions with simple, factual answers, but questions that require both facts and analysis. Students can think about questions the way one might in the real world, a college course, or a workplace. The Big Question thread is pulled through the unit. *Reach for Reading* holds fast to the thematic plan and addresses grade-level content standards in addition to foundational skills development, grade-level reading, and language arts standards.

Oral language

Big Questions are written to promote academic talk among students, giving them an opportunity to consider the topic from their personal perspectives and read the selections. But if we want to generate more productive talk in classrooms, we also have to ensure students have the skills and knowledge to participate in academic discussions (Fisher, Frey & Rothenberg, 2008).

To facilitate academic talk, *Reach for Reading* involves students in a range of vocabulary development activities focusing on subject-specific words and general academic words which have been carefully selected to convey conceptual knowledge. Lessons incorporate many opportunities for students to learn and practice using the words through discussions, sketches, brief writing tasks, role plays, and hands-on activities. Technology supports learning with resources including online photographs, video clips, and a student's own personal vocabulary notebook.

Linking discussion with reading and writing strengthens all skills. *Reach for Reading* systematically taps all language domains for student activities. For instance, oral language practice is not just fluency work. We know that competent readers can talk about what they have read, make predictions as to what will happen next in a story, and express an opinion about a character or action. Yet to do so orally, they must have structure for their utterances.

Many students have rich oral language backgrounds, but they may not have developed the academic language proficiencies that advance literacy and content learning in schools. So students will benefit from *Reach for Reading's* academic language frames. According to the purpose of their statements, students learn how to start a sentence or how to organize their thoughts effectively. Teachers can help students make statements with increasing levels of sophistication, too, so their oral language development grows. Plus, these academic language frames help with reading and writing. Structures students use orally they learn to recognize in print and employ in writing.

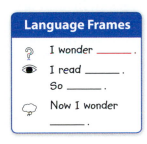

Language Frames

- ? I wonder _____.
- 👁 I read _____.
- So _____.
- 💭 Now I wonder _____.

Authentic literature libraries and anthology selections

While the Big Question can whet the students' appetite for reading, good literature seals the deal. *Reach for Reading* includes Caldecott and Newbury winners as well as National Geographic exclusive articles and interviews with scientists and explorers. The rich multicultural selections and the assortment of genres entice the students. When they have something in front of them that they want to read, they are motivated to learn how to read well. And *Reach for Reading's* leveled libraries will help ensure that students have access to high-interest fiction and nonfiction texts at their appropriate reading levels. Pre-reading supports, such as video clips from National Geographic and summaries of the selections in multiple languages, coupled with the vocabulary development work, set the stage for reading success.

If students struggle with comprehension, differentiation is available, particularly with flexible reading groups that can accommodate varied reading levels, English language proficiency, and genre preferences. Some of the supports built into *Reach for Reading* include specialized collections of leveled readers. One set has thematically linked books for each unit at different reading levels. Another set has content-related readers for independent reading and fluency work. Young learners can partner read with Read with Me Big Books. For students who are working on decoding, Read On Your Own decodable texts are also included.

- ☐ *The Great Wall of China*
- BL *Sitti's Secrets*
- BL *Miss Rumphius*
- OL *Everest: The Climb*, Part 1
- AL *The Cay*, Part 1

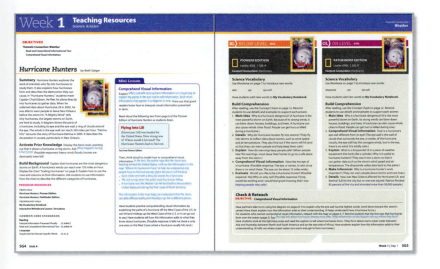

Explicit, systematic instruction and assessment

Furthermore, the building blocks for reading, phonemic awareness and phonics, are present in the grade-level books. In the primary grades students experience daily lessons on these elements. In the upper grades for the small percentage of students who still need help decoding or for the recent immigrant students new to English, a supplementary kit, *Reach into Phonics*, is available. At any grade, online phonics games can supplement the regular instruction. Teachers have flexibility in choosing the amount of support to provide students based on their needs.

Explicit instruction in reading comprehension strategies, another critical piece of the reading puzzle, is also present throughout the units. With step-by-step instructions and practice with a portion of the selection to be read, students experience a consistent introduction to each strategy. These strategies are the focus of the comprehension checks while they read texts at their level and the post-reading activities that link the topics to the Big Question.

Reach for Reading offers teachers and students multiple ways of demonstrating understanding. Students respond to reading through writing activities designed for their reading and language proficiency levels. *Reach for Reading's* informal assessment tools, including running records and comprehension strategy checklists, help teachers to monitor students' progress and tailor instruction to meet their needs on a daily basis, while unit tests and projects allow teachers to gauge their learning over time.

A major concern for all teachers is what to do when children struggle. What if they can't read well despite one's best efforts? Before moving students to intensive interventions, we encourage teachers to try the monitoring and reteaching techniques built into *Reach for Reading*. Students can use online games, Comprehension Coach, and other technology resources for extended practice.

An extensive array of scaffolding features helps teachers to readjust instructional tasks so that students are challenged at the appropriate level. Cooperative learning activities anchor each lesson so that students support one another as they are learning the subject matter, and practice their oral language skills as they interact verbally. Additionally, on-the-page text supports, including Before You Move On and In Other Words, scaffold students' vocabulary knowledge and reading comprehension. Writing activities are designed to guide students through the process of authoring and editing texts in print (e.g., stories, essays) and online formats (e.g., blogs, emails).

Conclusion

By 2050, demographers predict the U.S. population will be majority-minority. In many of our school districts, this trend has become a reality. We have to reach all our students with core reading instruction that will move below-level students to on-grade level and on-grade level students up to an advanced level. Our advanced readers, who may be in these classrooms as well, need to be challenged so they make progress, too. With *Reach for Reading* we will help all students—below-level, on-level, and above-level—become better readers, writers, and thinkers.

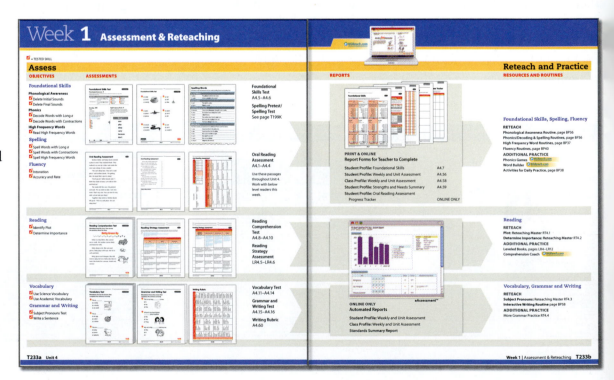

For **research citations** see page R27.

Sylvia Linan-Thompson, Ph.D.

Monitoring Progress to Reach Reading Goals

by Sylvia Linan-Thompson

In today's heterogeneous classroom, monitoring progress is more important than ever. Research has long shown that teachers need to use assessment data to inform their instructional planning and decision making (Afflerbach, 2007; Edwards, Turner, & Mokhtari, 2008). With today's focus on Response to Intervention, or RtI, this principle of using assessment to inform instruction has been more formally defined and organized in a system to help connect this critical research finding to the complex logistics of classroom teaching. Response to Intervention (RtI) describes a framework that promotes the use of successive cycles of assessment, instruction, and decision-making as a means for preventing the development of learning difficulties.

Multi-tier instruction

The cycle begins with benchmarking. The data provides the teacher with information about students' reading skills. All students receive core reading instruction or Tier 1. The classroom teacher provides the first tier of instruction to all students. This does not mean that all students get the same instruction, however. In this first tier, instruction is differentiated and scaffolded, and flexible grouping is used to maximize learning.

Students who do not meet benchmark are also provided Tier 2 instruction, and their progress is monitored with formative assessments. Assessments are used on a regular basis. If students have made adequate progress and meet benchmark, they exit from Tier 2 instruction. If they have not made adequate progress, they continue to receive Tier 2 instruction in addition to Tier 1. In most models, the first two tiers of instruction are provided in the general education classroom. The second tier of instruction is provided to students, usually 15–20 percent, who do not meet grade-level benchmarks. Targeted instruction meant to "catch them up" is delivered to these students in small, homogeneous groups.

Students who continue to exhibit difficulty in acquiring reading skills after one or two cycles of Tier 2 receive Tier 3 instruction. While there might be some variation in terms of the length of Tier 2 or who provides instruction, the sequence is standard. The third tier is the most intense. Because very few students (5–7 percent) need this level of instruction, students receive instruction in groups of one to three students. In many models, the third tier of instruction is provided outside the classroom

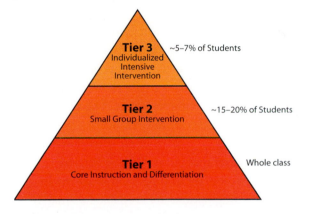

Characteristics of effective Tier 1 instruction

Tier 1 reading instruction and core reading instruction are synonymous. For Tier 1 to be effective for all students, attention must be paid to both the content and delivery of instruction. Furthermore, it has to meet the literacy needs of all the students in the class. To accomplish this, *Reach for Reading* has ensured that the instruction is explicit and systematic, is differentiated, and that there are sufficient materials to ensure that all students have multiple opportunities to read every day regardless of their reading level.

There is consensus in the research field about what constitutes effective reading instruction. Effective reading instruction builds students foundational reading and decoding skills, develops their vocabulary knowledge, teaches strategies and builds knowledge needed to comprehend and analyze text, and focuses on fluency instruction that includes increased exposure to vocabulary and print (National Reading Panel, 2000). *Reach for Reading* includes instruction in all of these areas with interactive and integrated lessons.

Additionally, because *Reach for Reading* is built around content area topics, students as early as first grade are engaged with both narrative and expository text and acquire not only new content but also the vocabulary, language, and text structures associated with a variety of texts. This enables students to apply core reading knowledge in all subjects throughout the school day.

The content of instruction is only one part of effective instruction. *How* instruction is delivered is equally important. Well-delivered and supported instruction helps to create a safe environment in which students can acquire new knowledge. The lessons in *Reach for Reading* are structured to provide several layers of support. The first level is the structure of the lessons. They provide a clear introduction, with modeling to make the task explicit for children. Guided practice is included so the teacher can ensure that children learn the task, and then there is independent practice to solidify learning. Additionally, guidance in providing corrective feedback and opportunities to check for understanding are included.

Differentiation and Tier 1 instruction

As noted earlier, Tier 1 instruction includes differentiation. To become successful readers, students need opportunities to read different types of text every day. To ensure all students have access to text they can read during Tier 1 instruction, the *Reach for Reading* program gives students a variety of reading resources. The rich, authentic literature and informational texts in the student anthologies are scaffolded with on-page supports, frequent comprehension checks, and pre- and post-reading activities that build skills, strategies, background knowledge, and vocabulary to support all learners. In addition, a range of leveled reading options are available for small group reading. In addition to providing reading practice, content-based reading at varied levels builds students' content knowledge and allows them to participate in and contribute to discussions.

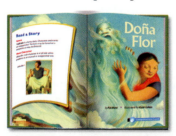

◀ Scaffolded anthology selections provide an entry point for all learners in Tier 1.

▲ Differentiated small group reading—with Explorer Collection books and trade books—matches readers and texts over a range of reading levels.

Finally, across lessons, flexible grouping formats are used to provide students with additional opportunities to practice what they are learning. Homogeneous and heterogeneous small group formats are used in addition to purposeful pairing as appropriate for the learning objective.

Multiple measures

Frequent assessments are critical to monitoring progress and identifying opportunities for reteaching for all students. A variety of assessment tools, including both formal tests and embedded informal assessments, are provided to gauge student progress and identify students who may require reteaching or students who would benefit from additional practice to build automaticity. Using a range of measures is critical to capture the multi-dimensional range of skills required to read, write, listen, and speak.

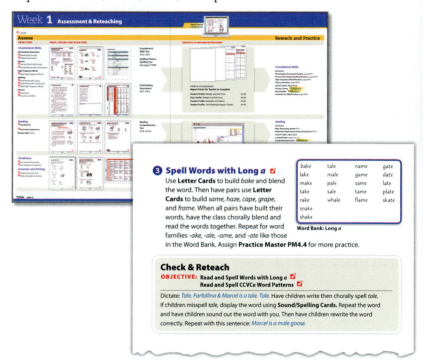

▲ In addition to formal assessments at the end of each week, every tested skill includes point-of-use ideas for informal monitoring of progress and reteaching.

Providing Tier 2 instruction

Who needs Tier 2 instruction? Students who do not meet benchmarks benefit from Tier 2 instruction. There are a variety of factors that inhibit students' reading progress including

- limited early literacy experiences
- lack of instruction or practice
- failure to develop phonemic awareness
- failure to develop the alphabetic principle
- failure to master basic decoding skills
- ability to read accurately but not automatically
- very slow learning.

When planning Tier 2 instruction, use data to determine what students need and group them homogenously. When children can't decode, we focus on basic word-level skills and ensure that students learn the skills needed to read words. They need to know letter sounds, how to map those sounds to letters, and blend them to read words. They also need to practice reading the words until they can read them automatically. It is also important to ensure that students are also learning language. Building students' listening and speaking vocabulary will also help them in reading words automatically. When words are known well, both the pronunciation and meaning are accessed automatically.

Reach for Reading has several components that can be used to support these students as they develop the code, including routines and resources for reteaching foundational skills identified for the early grades. For intermediate grades, a complete phonics intervention kit, *Reach into Phonics*, is provided for students who struggle with foundational reading skills. In addition, a range of digital resources provide opportunities for repeated practice for automaticity development.

▲ Comprehension Coach and *Reach into Phonics*

When children can decode but are not fluent, Tier 2 instruction focuses on building fluency in text reading. But children who are not fluent may also need to develop language and automaticity. They also need opportunities to read text at their independent reading level.

For this group of children, the *Reach for Reading* trade books are a valuable resource. Materials in the program's leveled library extend to reach students who are two years below the grade-level reading targets. These books can be used to provide students practice reading at their independent level while they build content knowledge. Further, there are several opportunities for students to practice additional independent reading. Time is allotted in pacing for the leveled library for teacher work with Tier 2 students and to conduct conferences with all students.

Some children will develop adequate decoding and fluency skills but will not comprehend what they read. These students need to learn to monitor their comprehension and to use comprehension strategies. However, to understand text, students must also know the meaning of the majority of the words they are reading:

- Pacing includes reading and rereading texts to enable the students to read once for literal comprehension and then read a second time to deepen comprehension.
- Background knowledge and vocabulary lists are provided for anthology and library reading to help students at all levels.
- Writing options provide options for all students to respond to reading in level-appropriate ways.

Building students' background also aids in comprehension. The words we can associate with topics we know about and the depth of our knowledge of specific topics facilitate our understanding of texts on those topics. Therefore exposure to a wide range of topics provides students with opportunities to develop vocabulary associated with various topics in an engaging and embedded context and thereby build their world knowledge in the process.

Conclusion

It is not enough for us to assess for accountability purposes. Teachers not only need to know how to collect pertinent data on students' learning and development, but to use it in an easy-to-implement way to make appropriate instructional decisions about grouping, reteaching, and more. The range of measures, teaching resources, and reteaching resources in *Reach for Reading* help teachers respond to individual needs and grow as capable and confident readers, writers, listeners, and speakers.

For **research citations** see page R27.

Lada Kratky

Jennifer D. Turner, Ph.D.

Orchestrating Instruction *by Lada Kratky and Jennifer D. Turner*

Our classrooms are made up of students with a variety of interests, strengths, and personalities. Some are shy while others are outspoken; some are afraid to take risks, while some are bold; some have been read to, others have never held a book. In the classroom, one of the challenges a teacher faces is grouping these diverse personalities in such a way that they will all flourish. It has been shown that small group instruction is more effective for students than simply doing whole group instruction during the entire day (Taylor, Pearson, Clark & Walpole, 2000). And so, how do we group students?

We know that the best literacy teachers don't simply organize their instruction; they *orchestrate* learning within their classrooms (Turner, 2005). Heilman and his colleagues (2002) note that "Implementing reading instruction in a class requires careful orchestration of time, materials, and instruction to satisfy the needs of individual children" (p. 508). This means that teachers must be thoughtful and purposeful as they make grouping decisions.

Reading groups

Although there are many grouping formats that teachers may use for reading instruction in their classrooms, we focus on two primary types—homogeneous groups and heterogeneous groups. Homogeneous groups are formed when students of similar reading levels come together to read a text. The purpose of homogeneous reading groups is to provide explicit instruction to groups of four to six students at their instructional levels (Fountas & Pinnell, 1996; 2001) and to scaffold students' understanding of texts (Frey & Fisher 2010). Importantly, homogeneous groups should not be static, or students will remain in the same reading group for the entire year (Fountas & Pinnell, 2001; Iaquinta, 2006). Rather, homogeneous groupings must be flexible and allow for individual growth and continued challenges.

Heterogeneous groups are formed with students of varying strengths, needs, and interests as readers. According to Heilman et al (2002), heterogeneous groups "have the potential to increase students' academic engaged time and achievement by promoting active learning, with students talking and working together rather than passively listening" (p. 502).

Which grouping format is best? A primary consideration for making this decision is identifying the task at hand, and the question becomes if students should be placed in homogenous or heterogeneous groups to provide the best setting for the given task.

When learning and practicing a skill, students will work best when grouped with others of similar skill levels. Instructional levels are determined by observation of student strengths. Reading means deriving meaning from print. To that end, teachers should be aware if students are purely decoding or if they are using phonics and language skills to arrive at meaning. Teachers of emergent readers, in addition, should be aware if students control concepts of print, have letter knowledge, and can identify High Frequency Words. The best tool for assessing student strengths in reading is the running record.

Running records

In *An Observation Survey,* Marie Clay (2000) states that running records help teacher in

- the evaluation of text difficulty
- the grouping of children
- the acceleration of a child
- monitoring the progress of children
- observing particular difficulties in particular children.

A running record of student performance can be carried out with any introduced text and at any time. It consists of following the student's reading by making markings, which will be used to analyze strengths and difficulties. The teacher jots down a tick, or check mark, for each word read correctly. A miscue is recorded. If a child corrects an error, the correction is recorded as well. A struggling reader should be observed frequently in order to track his or her progress and inform his or her instruction. On-level readers can be observed on a regular basis.

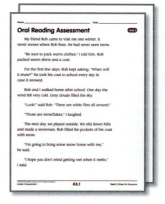

▲ Oral reading assessments provide running records of reading progress. Measures are provided for accuracy, rate, and comprehension.

Flexible grouping

Using running record scores and other measures, the teacher will create homogeneous reading groups. Reading groups are formed to provide explicit instruction to a group of four to six students at their instructional levels. These groupings must be flexible and allow for individual growth and continued challenges.

The most important and continual consideration has to be that groupings are flexible. Students grow at different speeds. Flexible groupings are essential to avoid frustration and keep kids engaged by keeping them appropriately challenged and meeting individual needs. Running records and conferences must become part of routine and constant observations of each student's growth, which will guide continual and necessary adjustments between groups.

As Iaquinta (2006) observes, flexible groups "avoid the traditional problems of grouping, because teachers change the composition of groups regularly to accommodate the different learning paths of readers" (p. 414). In order to maintain flexibly, it is necessary to assess students' strengths and needs on an ongoing basis. Thus, constant observation of each student's growth, as well as periodic adjustments within groups, are vital in order to allow each student to advance at his or her own rate.

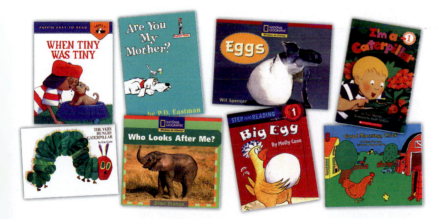

▲ Leveled books provide opportunities for students to explore science and social studies content and apply reading skills and strategies at their individual instructional levels.

Once groups are formed, there are a variety of different instructional approaches that classrooms take to implement small group reading. Guided reading involves teacher-supported discussions in small groups (Fountas & Pinnell, 1996). Literature circles are heterogeneous, student-lead groups of four or six children who read the same book. They prepare for discussion by taking on particular role e.g. Discussion Director, Connector, Illustrator. (Daniels, 2002). Many other reading routines exist and can be effective once groups are formed. Regardless of the format used, homogeneous group reading is just a first step in reading. It's also important to have students share and extend learning through heterogeneous group discussions.

After students work with texts at their level, *Reach for Reading* provides the opportunity for all students to share the knowledge gained about the different stories and informational texts they have read through heterogeneous group discussions. The "Connect Across Texts" part of the small group and leveled reading routines provides opportunities for all learners to transform facts and ideas gleaned from their books into knowledge, ideas, and opinions about the core content topics and questions that form the center of each unit.

Selecting the right book

Among the many baskets of books that are made available in a classroom, students will find books that are easy for them, those that are at instructional level, and those that are difficult. It is important to know which books are appropriate for each learner. Fountas and Pinnell say, "Easy readers…allow children to focus on the meaning and enjoy humor and suspense. [They] give children "mileage" as readers and build confidence." However, it is not enough for children to just read easy texts.

Instructional-level books are those that allow readers to learn more and progress little steps at a time. They provide practice of known strategies and go a step beyond, allowing for fluent reading and opportunities to problem solve. Hard texts will more than likely discourage the reader. The reading will be choppy, punctuation will be ignored, perhaps there will be sounding out of individual letters, all of which will result in little or no comprehension and the message that reading is difficult and frustrating.

Reach for Reading provides a large range of texts to meet the diverse levels of today's heterogeneous classrooms for every one of the

- 32 content-based decodable readers are provided in the primary grades
- over 100 thematically-connected trade books carefully selected to span across the range of below-level, on-level, and above-level readers
- 64 Explorer Books featuring articles from *National Geographic Explorer* magazine written at two different reading levels.

Grouping for cooperative learning

Generally speaking, when involved in cooperative learning activities, heterogeneous groupings will engage students most effectively. These groups mix language abilities as well as personalities in order to combine talkers with non-talkers, the shy with the bold. The purpose of this type of grouping is to share ideas, discuss, talk, brainstorm, or build together. By having heterogeneous grouping, talkers become role models, and non-speakers slowly build up enough confidence to speak. These activities allow students to learn from each other as they work together.

The teacher is the most informed person with regards to student strengths in language and participation and is the best person to match up different students for mutual benefit and growth. *National Geographic Reach for Reading* offers a wide range of cooperative learning activities. An example of such an activity is "Corners." Each of the four corners of the classroom is assigned one aspect of a discussion. At their seats, students think and write about one of those aspects. Then they go to the corresponding corner to discuss their ideas. At the end, one student from each group shares the thoughts of the group with the class.

Corners

Cooperation, discussions, listening to others' opinions and sharing of ideas are behaviors that are desirable and have to be learned. When students work together in heterogeneous groups, those behaviors can be nurtured and made to develop.

Independent reading

In addition to selecting texts according to students' reading levels, teachers should also select texts based on students' interests and preferences. For example, students generally choose the book that they would like to read during independent reading time. Teachers may also encourage students to select topics of interest in science and social studies and support students in using a wide range of informational texts, which promotes content learning and literacy development (Bergoff & Egawa, 1991). Finally, recent research suggests that students respond enthusiastically to texts that mirror their cultural, linguistic, or ethnic backgrounds, and teachers should select books which are relevant to students' lives and interests outside of school (Louie, 2006; Turner & Kim, 2005).

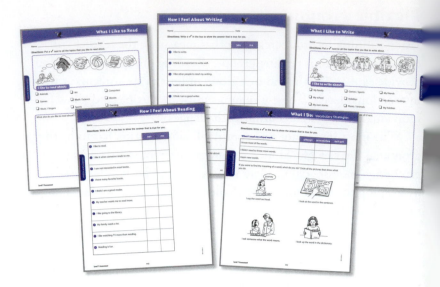

▲ Affective and metacognitive assessments are provided at NGReach.com.

Independent reading time is a time in the day for readers just to explore reading. Whereas leveled reading takes place in homogeneous groups and texts are selected primarily for their appropriate instructional level, independent reading can happen when students are grouped heterogeneously and texts are selected based on personal interests of the reader. Book baskets are leveled, so students can select easy or instructional-level texts and read to each other. In addition, students can explore book baskets that might contain selections to entice diverse interests. These might be catalogs, how-to manuals, magazines on motorcycles, cars or airplanes, cookbooks, or any other type of texts that might not otherwise be available to students. It is exploration time, a time readers confirm the fact that reading is fun.

Conclusion

Small group instruction has been proven to be most effective when teaching students of different backgrounds and strengths. In activities where the focus is learning a skill, such as reading, homogeneous groups are more efficient because they group students by ability and instruction is aimed at each specific ability level. Constant observation of student participation and progress is required for teachers to be informed about their students. Finally, it is important for teachers to remember that small group instruction is critical, but it is just one part of a balanced literacy program. Small group instruction provides opportunities for students to work closely with their peers and with texts, yet it should not be the only instructional feature of the literacy block. Participating in small instructional groups, as well as accessing literacy events within the whole community (e.g., read alouds, shared writing experiences) and opportunities to read independently, enhance children's development as critical readers, writers, talkers, and thinkers.

For **research citations** see page R27.

Nancy Frey, Ph.D.

Using Technology to Foster Learning for a New Century *by Nancy Frey*

Peer over the shoulder of an elementary-aged child who is working on a computer and prepare to be amazed and a little intimidated. The children in today's classrooms have never known a time when the Internet did not exist and have been raised in an environment where information is just as likely to be presented digitally as it is in print. When confronted with an interesting question, they are as likely to turn to a computer, or other device with a Web browser, as they are to look in a book. This shift in learning is not confined to school-aged children. Increasingly, teachers of these same students have themselves experienced curriculum development as a process that occurs within digital spaces.

Professional organizations have united in their calls for a 21st century approach to education that broadens our approach to teaching, learning, and literacy. The International Reading Association in 2009 called for literacy curriculum that emphasizes use of print and digital technologies in learning, and further stated "students have the right to… teachers who use ICTs (information and communication technologies) skillfully for teaching and learning effectively" (IRA, 2009). The Partnership for 21st Century Learning Skills, a consortium of education and business organizations, states that the 21st century content must include "global awareness, financial, economic, business, and entrepreneurial literacy, civic literacy, and health and wellness awareness" (Partnership for 21st Century Learning Skills, 2009). The digital divide still exists, and there is enormous disparity in access to technology in homes, classrooms, and communities. A survey by the Kaiser Family Foundation reported that schools play a key role in providing access to those students who lack access to technology in their homes and communities (Rideout, Foehr & Roberts, 2010).

However, the development of 21st century learners who are also learning to be literate is complex. Hobbs (2010), in her testimony to the United States Congress, noted that there are three kinds of possible risks: *content risks* that expose students to harmful material; *contact risks* that may result in online harassment or bullying; and *conduct risks* that include misrepresentation and misinformation. The troubling nature of access to 21st century learning experiences is confounded by access to hardware that is connected to the Internet.

According to the Pew Internet and American Life Project, access to broadband is significantly lower in poorer households, among Hispanics, and in homes where English learners live, and that the rate of access has declined in the last several years among this population due to cost (2008).

The fact is that preparation of students for learning in a new century means that the curriculum they use must focus on building the types of critical literacy needed for global communication. It presents a unique challenge for elementary educators who need to balance the development of the kinds of skills needed for becoming digitally literate with the very real concerns about shielding young children from risk.

Reach for Reading is designed to build students' capacity for learning with technology, and to support teachers' efforts in utilizing technology in a safe environment. In addition, the curriculum design of the program accentuates the content knowledge needed by 21st century learners.

Literacy 2.0: learning in the 21st century

Literacy and learning in the 21st century is shifting from an emphasis on the tools (e.g., computers, smartphones, podcasts, networks) to processes. In other words, we know that the tools teachers and students use will continue to change at breathtaking speed. In fact, it is likely that by the time you read this white paper, there will be new tools that did not exist when it was written. Instead, educators understand that the focus needs to shift to the processes used by learners when utilizing technologies. All learners need the following technology literacy skills (Frey, Fisher, & Gonzalez, 2010). Students must be able to

- search and find information
- use information
- create information
- share information.

Reach for Reading is designed to promote searching for information across both print-based and digital texts through online reading experiences focused on topics and issues that impact the social, biological, and physical world. Students view video clips to build their background knowledge and listen to both the teacher and others to build their language skills. They use information from printed texts and digital texts to formulate answers from an inquiry-based curriculum. The Digital Library provides a media-rich search resource and access to National Geographic texts, videos, and images is available online.

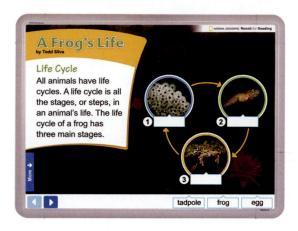

▲ In addition to traditional printed texts in anthologies, Big Books, and trade books, interactive texts are designed for whole-class reading.

Each day, students create information through writing. Importantly, writing genres include those needed for digital communication, such as writing emails and blogs. Many of the writing projects utilize Magazine Maker which focuses students on using technology to produce writing. The digital nature of these resources brings the most current information about the world to the classroom. As always, students are consistently challenged to be discriminating consumers of information.

◀ Students create writing projects using the Magazine Maker.

MAGAZINE MAKER

Social learning in the 21st century

Noted literacy researcher Paul Gee (2007) states that learning is socially constructed between people and requires them to probe, hypothesize, reprobe, and rethink and that this occurs in both face-to-face and digital environments. The Web 2.0 revolution has made digital spaces interactive, and people expect to be able to dialogue, confer, and debate on any topic of interest. Whether in a classroom or a digital environment, students need the skills to ask questions, form opinions, ask more questions, and draw conclusions. Therefore, a curriculum designed to prepare 21st century learners must include ample opportunities for students to converse with their peers, ask questions, disagree, and formulate their own opinions.

In *Reach for Reading*, communication is located at the heart of the program. Students engage daily in verbal and written discourse about ideas and information that impact their local communities and the world at large. Rest assured that these environments are constructed to reduce the content, contact, and conduct risks that might otherwise lead to restriction of such experiences due to these concerns.

Reading and writing in the 21st century

Leu et al. (2009) state that the "self-directed text construction" of online reading experiences represents a shift from traditional print-based literacy. Students in an online environment move freely between texts to form understandings. Students need ample experiences with moving among a group of texts in order to develop the ability to synthesize information. Therefore, each unit in *Reach for Reading* is organized around a Big Question that prompts students to move among a set of informational and narrative texts to construct understanding.

The Big Questions are designed to defy easy answers, and learners are prompted to use both their background knowledge and what they have learned from their readings to draw conclusions and formulate answers. Research activities in the program include traditional print-based research and online research. This organization encourages students to engage in the kinds of nonlinear multi-text explorations needed when reading and researching online.

◀ Web research activities help students use synthesis skills using printed resources in the program and text and media resources online.

Communication in the 21st century

Both on- and offline experiences are necessary for students to become thoroughly literate in the 21st century. *Reach for Reading* emphasizes the communication and collaboration skills necessary for students to engage in these practices in both face-to-face and digital environments. In particular, the language frames present in every lesson cause students to focus on both the academic language and academic vocabulary needed in verbal and written communication. As Leu and colleagues (2009) note, "[o]nline reading and writing are so closely connected it is not possible to separate them; we read online as authors and write online as readers" (p. 266). The ability to do so requires that learners are immersed in the rich oral and written dialogue with others that is critical for online learning.

Digital resources like phonics games, vocabulary games, and the Comprehension Coach provide options for additional practice.

Let's not forget literacy learning!

Reading, writing, and communicating in digital environments is essential for learners in a new century, but let's not forget that our primary job is to induct children into the world of literacy. Therefore, the resources available to the teachers of these students must be similarly cutting edge. Because the *Reach for Reading* program features both print and digital tools, teachers are able to draw from a rich catalog of materials that would otherwise be prohibitively large to store in a classroom. These include instructional support tools such as online letter cards that can be manipulated to form words for use in phonics instruction, vocabulary cards that bring meaning to life when providing reading comprehension instruction, and graphic organizers that make it easy to show students how information is sequenced during writing instruction.

Even better, digital resources make it even easier to provide the necessary alternative materials needed for Tier 2 Response to Intervention programs to supplement quality core instruction. In the past, students who struggled to read and write often did so because their teachers were not able to supply them with enough repetition and practice of skills. However, the digital resources make it possible to provide struggling students with meaningful reteaching and practice opportunities to accelerate their progress.

Conclusion

It is imperative that we prepare students for their future as members of a global community where information is shared, produced, and understood across space and people. It is clear that the challenge is great, especially because the past decades have taught us that we are not able to predict the tools they will be using as adults. Rather, our best approach is to ensure that students know how to communicate and collaborate with one another in both face-to-face and digital environments. They must be provided with daily opportunities to read, write, speak, listen, and view using many kinds of visual and written texts. Students must become increasingly comfortable searching for information, storing it, sharing it, producing it, and presenting it to a variety of audiences. Learners who are able to do these things are well prepared for a new century.

For **research citations** see page R27.

Reading

Research Basis: Research demonstrates the importance of teachers providing support for comprehension skills as students read text at their instructional level. Working with leveled text helps students negotiate increasingly difficult texts (Pinnell & Fountas 1996)

Small Group Reading Routine 1

Introduce

- **Assign books.** Use the summaries of the books in the Teaching Resources for an overview of content. Analyze the **Assessment Masters** and your conference notes to assign books according to students' interests and reading levels.

- **Introduce books.** Activate prior knowledge and build background for the books, using the Teaching Resources. Remind students that all of the books connect to the Big Question.

- **Introduce vocabulary.** Use **Vocabulary Routine 1** to teach the story words for each book.

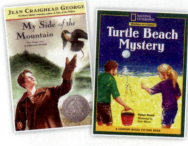

Small Group Reading Routine 2

Read and Integrate Ideas

- **Have students read independently.** Circulate to observe students as they read. Ask individuals to read sections aloud. Note any miscues as they read, and encourage students to self-correct. Model by asking questions like: *Did that make sense in the sentence? Does that sound right?*

- **Monitor students' understanding.** As students read, have them complete the Graphic Organizer **Practice Master** for their books. Prompt them to show you where in the books they gathered the information to complete their organizers.

- **Form homogeneous discussion groups.** Group students who have read the same book. Distribute the Discussion Guide **Practice Master** for that book to each member of the group.

- **Monitor group discussions.** Have students discuss the book they read, using the questions on the Discussion Guide. Use the Build Comprehension questions in the Teaching Resources to develop higher-order thinking skills. See the Discussion Guide Answer Keys:

  - Week 1: SG60–SG61   Week 3: SG64–SG65
  - Week 2: SG62–SG63   Week 4: SG66–SG67

- **Provide writing options.** Have each student complete one of the writing options from the Teaching Resources. Encourage students to share their writing with their group.

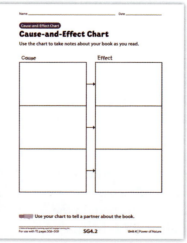

Small Group Reading Routine 3

Connect Across Texts

- **Form heterogeneous groups.** Group students who have read different books. Include at least one representative for each book read that week.

- **Introduce the activity.** Distribute the Connect Across Texts **Practice Master** for the week. Explain to each group that they will share the books they read, talk about their themes, and discuss what the books say about places in the world.

- **Have students summarize.** Ask students to summarize the books they just read, including new story words that helped them understand the themes and content. Have them refer to their graphic organizers as they share their books with the group.

- **Have students connect across texts.** Have groups use the questions provided on the Connect Across Texts **Practice Masters** to guide discussions. See the Discussion Guide Answer Keys for possible responses.

- **Monitor groups.** Use the Speaking and Listening Observation Log **Assessment Master** to assess students' participation in discussions.

Small Group Reading Routine 4

Conduct Conferences

- **Assess reading.** Have each student select and read aloud from a section of the book that connects to the Big Question. Listen for fluency. Ask: *Which strategies did you use to help you understand this section?* Use the reading strategy rubrics **Assessment Masters** to assess how well the student uses the reading strategies. Then have the student complete a Reader Reflection **Assessment Master** to assess his or her own reading fluency.

- **Assess writing.** Have the student share a completed writing option. Say: *Tell me about what you wrote.* Monitor responses to gauge how well the writing relates to the book. Ask: *How did your writing help you understand the book?*

- **Plan intervention or acceleration.** Ask the student to summarize what he or she has learned. Plan for further instruction:

  - If the student needs additional support with asking questions, identifying problem and solution, identifying cause and effect, or identifying and explaining figurative language, use the Assessment and Reteaching resources provided.

  - If the student successfully applies the focus skills, use the Recommended Books on page SG68 to guide the student in choosing books for independent reading.

Research Basis: Research confirms the importance of all students being exposed to grade-level text for concept and vocabulary development. These routines provide support for students who are not yet able to read grade-level selections on their own. Listening to a recording of the selection provides the most support.

Echo reading has been shown to contribute to the reading growth of low-achieving readers (Mathes et al 2001). Echo reading, choral reading, and paired or partner reading provide increasingly lower levels of support and encourage students to develop toward independent reading of grade-level text. In addition, the added comprehension focus that teachers provide before, during, and after reading provide additional opportunity to rehearse reading skills and strategies. Observe students as they read, with the goal of providing the lowest level of support that will enable students to access the text being read.

Learning Station Routine 1

Listening Center

1. **Choose a space.** A good space is a quiet corner, where students using the center will not be distracted or disturb others.

2. **Gather resources.** Resources can include MP3 or CD players, headphones, books recorded onto a computer, audio CD, or other electronic device, and one or more copies of books students will listen to. You may also want to provide response sheets, pencils and markers, and baskets to hold books and materials.

3. **Assign text.** Students can listen to books on their own or in groups, depending on interest and reading level. Encourage students to follow along in the text as they listen.

4. **Provide ways to respond.** Have students illustrate their favorite part of the story, complete a response sheet, write about what they heard, or respond in some other way.

Learning Station Routine 2

Echo Reading

1. **Select a text.** The text can be a complete selection or a portion of text. Passages for echo reading are best when they are short and motivating for students.

2. **Select students.** Echo reading can be used with a small group or an individual student. It is most appropriate for students who are not yet able to process the text on their own but can track the print as you read aloud and as they repeat the sentences after you.

3. **Have students listen and repeat.** The teacher reads a sentence aloud, modeling good intonation and rhythm. Students then read the sentence aloud following the teacher's model. Encourage students to track the print as they listen and repeat.

4. **Correct errors.** The teacher provides immediate feedback to correct student mistakes.

5. **Have students reread.** After reading aloud with the teacher, have students reread the text in pairs until they can read it fluently.

Learning Station Routine 3

Choral Reading

1. **Select a text.** The text can be a complete selection or a portion of a text. Passages for choral reading are best when they are short and motivating for students. Predictable text works well for choral reading.

2. **Select students.** Choral reading is most appropriate for students who are hesitant to read aloud independently but can join in reading the text in unison with other students with the teacher leading. Choral reading helps build students' motivation, confidence, and fluency.

3. **Read the text aloud first.** Model fluent reading and good intonation.

4. **Read the text in unison with students.** Have all students in the group read the passage aloud in unison with you. Encourage them to use good intonation.

5. **Have students reread.** After reading with the teacher, have students reread the text in pairs until they can read it fluently.

Learning Station Routine 4

Paired Reading

1. **Select a text or portion of text.** Passages for paired reading are best when they include strong emotions or dialogue.

2. **Pair students.** You may wish to pair students of similar reading ability, or pair a higher level reader with a lower level reader.

3. **Explain the procedure.** Tell students if you want them to:
   - Read the passage aloud in unison.
   - Take turns with each person reading a sentence, paragraph, or page.
   - Have one student listen while the other reads.

4. **Model error correction.** Demonstrate how students should support each other by rereading misread words, and asking for and giving help when needed.

5. **Encourage fluent reading.** Partners should practice good prosody (phrasing, expression, and intonation) as they read.

6. **Encourage discussion.** Have the reader pause at the end of a paragraph or section. The listener can then summarize or make a connection. Pairs can ask each other questions about what was read, such as:
   - *What was your favorite part of the story?*
   - *What was your page about?*
   - *Were there any parts that were hard to read?*

Research Basis: Within a good instructional program, independent reading can help students develop fluency, vocabulary, comprehension, and background knowledge. However, reading independently is not a substitute for key skill instruction in decoding, vocabulary, comprehension, and fluency. Teachers can support students as independent readers by assisting with book selection and encouraging students to share information about what they have read (Cunningham & Stanovich, 1998).

Independent Reading Routine

Purpose: Support students in making effective and successful use of independent reading time.

1. **Select topics.** Provide a rich collection of books to choose from. Books may include known texts, classroom favorites, or picture books. Support students in selecting books of interest for independent reading. Discussing books in advance with individual students or groups can motivate readers and help them determine what they want to read. Use the Small Group Reading Books at a Glance on SG1 and the Recommended Books list on SG68 of every Teacher's Edition for book suggestions.

2. **Share.** Bring students together to share their reading experiences. Students who have read different books can summarize what they read, and share what they found most interesting in their reading. Students who have read the same or similar books can share what they have learned about the topic and what more they would like to learn.

3. **Extend.** Encourage students to extend their understanding of the book with an activity such as one of the following:
    *   Rewrite the story with different or additional characters, a new ending, or other changes.
    *   Create a short play or pantomime based on the book.
    *   Write a letter to the author or to one of the book's characters.
    *   Research and report on something mentioned in the book.

Use the **Leveled Book Finder** to find more books.

Fluency Routine 1

Choral or Echo Reading/Marking the Text

1. **Select a passage.** Choose an appropriate text and provide copies for students. Keep passages short and use a variety of texts: narrative, expository, poems, songs, student writing. Choose text that is motivating.

2. **Provide a model.** Have students listen to a fluent reading of the text. This can be read aloud by the teacher or a recorded version. Use the fluency models provided on the selection recordings audio CD or in MP3 format at **NGReach.com**.

3. **Have students mark the text.** As they listen to the model, have students mark the reader's phrasing (/ for a short pause; // for a longer pause) or intonation (rising or falling inflections) on a copy of the text.

4. **Have students read the text.** Students can echo or choral read the text with you, following markings for phrasing and intonation. Coach phrasing and intonation as needed.

5. **Have students do repeated readings.** Have partners practice reading the same text in its unmarked version until they can read it fluently.

Fluency Routine 2

Paired Reading

1. **Select a passage.** Choose an appropriate text and provide copies for participants. Paired reading works best with a selection that contains strong emotions.

2. **Establish pairs.** Pairs can be peer-to-peer or student-adult groupings. Note that performance tends to be better when students read aloud to an adult as opposed to a peer.

3. **Read alternate sentences.** Have partners alternate reading sentences, checking each other's readings as they go.

4. **Monitor fluency.** Encourage students to attend to prosody (phrasing, expression, and intonation).

Fluency Routine 3

Recording and Tracking ▐ Comprehension Coach

1. **Read and record.** Have students use the **Comprehension Coach** to record and analyze their readings.

2. **Re-record as needed.** Encourage students to repeat their recording until they are satisfied with their reading and rate.

3. **Note progress.** Have students note their accuracy and rate as measured by the **Comprehension Coach**. They should see increases in both rate and accuracy over time.

Fluency Routine 4

Timed Reading ▐ Comprehension Coach

Use this technique to help students develop an appropriate reading rate with good accuracy. Research suggests this technique is highly motivational if students have a clear target for words read correct per minute (WCPM) and then chart their progress.

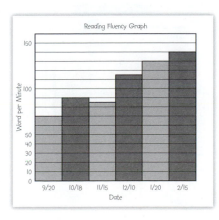

1. **Read and record.** Have students use the **Comprehension Coach** to record their readings. The Comprehension Coach encourages students to read carefully and thoughtfully, repairing miscues, thinking about vocabulary, and actively comprehending.

2. **Graph results.** Have students record their WCPM on a graph or chart each time they use the **Comprehension Coach**.

Vocabulary

Research Basis: Decades of research have confirmed the important role that vocabulary plays in reading comprehension and in students' overall academic success (Hiebert & Kamil 2005). Immersing students in rich and varied language experiences permits them to learn words through listening, speaking, reading, and writing. In this view of robust, explicit instruction, vocabulary is introduced using consistent, predictable routines (Beck et al. 2002). Follow these steps to help students make words fully their own, so that vocabulary can be accessed at will in a variety of situations.

Vocabulary Routine 1

Introduce the Words

Purpose: Students engage in learning concepts and acquire background knowledge as they learn new key words and develop a deeper understanding of the words.

1. **Pronounce the word.** Model the pronunciation of the key word and point to the accompanying picture; have students pronounce the word.

2. **Rate the word.** Have students hold up their fingers to show how well they know the word.

 I can use it in a sentence or give a definition   **I have seen the word before but I can't use it in a sentence**   **I have never seen or heard this word before**

Ask: *What do you know about this word?* Encourage students to share their ideas about the word.

3. **Define the word.** Use a student-friendly definition to explain the meaning. (Definitions are provided in the Picture Dictionary at the back of the Anthology.)

4. **Elaborate.** Generate discussion of the word. Use one or more of the following strategies:
   - Relate the word to your personal experience.
   - Encourage students to use the word as they talk about their own experience.
   - Using questions or comments, motivate students to engage in discussion about the word. Extended discussion will help all students understand the word and how it is used.
   - Point out word parts and spelling patterns that will help students recognize the word.
   - Challenge students to connect the word across content areas.
   - Post the words on the Word Wall.

Have students add words to
My Vocabulary Notebook.

Vocabulary Routine 2

Expand Word Knowledge

Purpose: Students use graphic organizers, illustrations, and writing to expand their knowledge of the meaning and usage of new words.

1. **Form pairs.** Explain that each pair will become experts on one vocabulary word.

2. **Display the graphic organizer.** Use the graphic organizer or three-dimensional graphic organizer specified in the Teacher's Edition lesson, or another graphic organizer from the examples in Vocabulary Routine 4.

3. **Select a key word.** Display the vocabulary word and model for students how to locate information about the word and complete the graphic organizer.
   - Find the word in the Picture Dictionary in the Anthology or in another dictionary and read the information about the word.
   - Write the word.
   - Add a definition, context sentence, and picture.

4. **Assign key words.** Assign a word to each student pair and have them create a similar graphic organizer for their word.

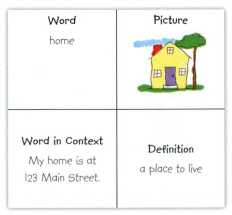

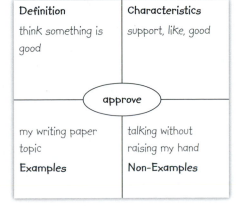

Fold-Up Tab

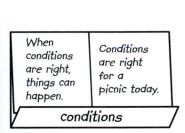

4-Corner Vocabulary

Frayer Model

Vocabulary, continued

Research Basis: Talking about words and sharing their knowledge of words provide additional opportunities for students to use new words in different contexts and to become increasingly familiar with how the words are used. Taking the role of the class expert on a word motivates students to continue exploring words and their meanings (Beck et al. 2002; Blachowicz et al. 2005).

Vocabulary Routine 3

Share Word Knowledge

Purpose: Students deepen word knowledge by sharing their deeper understandings of words for which they have become class experts.

1. **Form pairs.** Pair each student with a partner who studied a different vocabulary word for Vocabulary Routine 2 (Expand Word Knowledge).

2. **Share.** Partners take turns reading to each other their graphic organizers from Vocabulary Routine 2.

3. **Discuss.** Partners discuss and create sentences using both vocabulary words. If needed, give students sentence starters.

4. **Write.** Students write their sentences in their journals or **My Vocabulary Notebook** and draw a line under each vocabulary word.

5. **Repeat.** Repeat steps 1–4 above until each student has an entry for each vocabulary word.

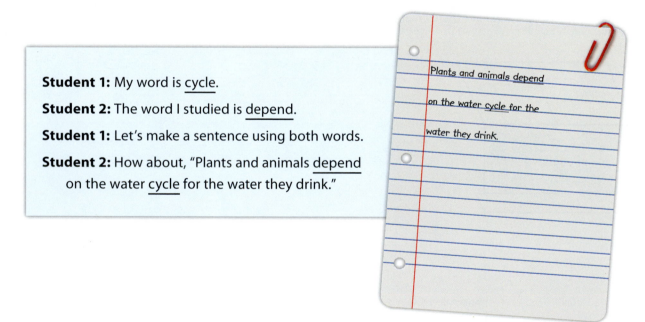

Student 1: My word is cycle.

Student 2: The word I studied is depend.

Student 1: Let's make a sentence using both words.

Student 2: How about, "Plants and animals depend on the water cycle for the water they drink."

Plants and animals depend
on the water cycle for the
water they drink.

Research Basis: In addition to learning key words that are important for selection comprehension and understanding content area concepts, students are often exposed to many new words used in classroom directions, explanations, and discussion. Examples are words such as *classify, clarify,* and *routine.* Research demonstrates that graphic organizers are an effective tool for introducing these words and giving students experience in using them and exploring their meanings (Hiebert & Kamil 2005).

Vocabulary Routine 4

Review, Extend, or Reteach Vocabulary

Purpose: Provide instruction and practice with vocabulary words and other important words used in classroom directions and discussion.

1. **Display the word.** Write the word on the board or chart paper.

2. **Display the graphic organizer.** Use the graphic organizer specified in the Teacher's Edition or select another graphic organizer from those shown below.

3. **Model.** Think aloud as you model partially completing the graphic organizer.

4. **Involve students.** Encourage students to create their own graphic organizers and add information about the word to the graphic organizer. Information can include a picture, examples and non-examples. Have students use the graphic organizers to talk about the word and concept.

Three-Dimensional Graphic Organizers

Portrait

Window

Upright

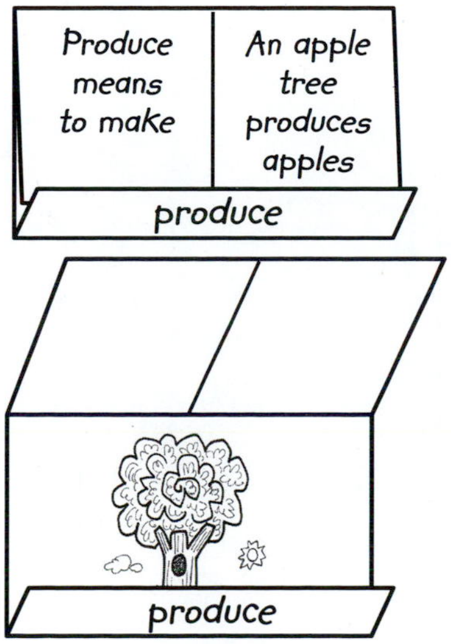

Fold-Up Tab

Three-Quarter Book

Other Graphic Organizers

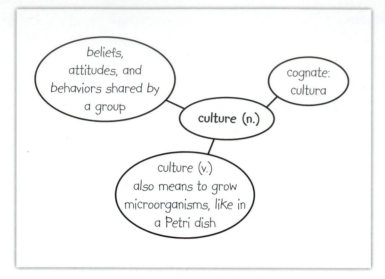

Word Web

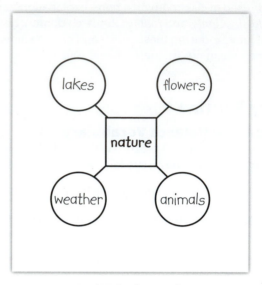

Word Web of Examples

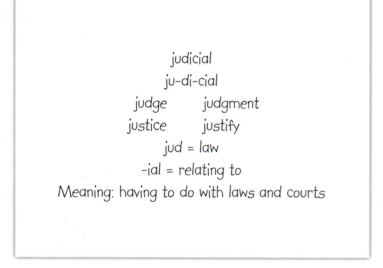

Wordbench

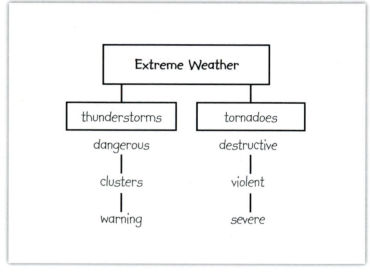

Semantic Web

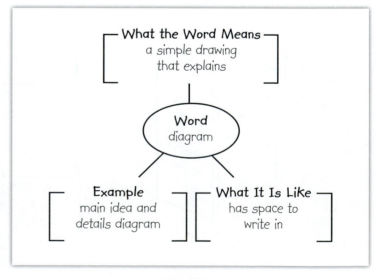

Word Map

Word	Definition	My Example
strategy	a plan	my football team's plan to win

Example Chart

Research Basis: Research demonstrates that reading aloud to students is most effective when the teacher engages students in discussion about words, concepts, and events in the selection both during and after reading aloud. The text-talk method provides a framework for guiding discussion and focusing on important key words (Beck et al. 2002; Gambrell et al. 1996).

Vocabulary Routine 5

Text-Talk Read Aloud

Purpose: The text-talk method teaches text-specific vocabulary after a selection has been read aloud to students.

1. **Display the key words.**

2. **Read aloud.** As you read, pause to provide a short explanation of each key word as you come to it. For example, if you are teaching the word *otherwise* you might say: *You can use the word* otherwise *when you are explaining what might happen. For example, I hope I catch the bus today after school, otherwise I might be late.*

3. **Elaborate meanings.** After reading, activate prior knowledge: *What do you know about this word?* Explain the meanings of the key words more fully, using the steps of Vocabulary Routine 1.

4. **Discuss.** Create discussion prompts that encourage students to use the words together. For example, for the word *otherwise,* you may display the following frame and ask students to use the word as they tell about an upcoming weekend activity, holiday, or school event.

   I hope _____ otherwise _____ .

5. **Extend.** Encourage students to think about and use the key words at other times in classroom discussion, and in their lives beyond the classroom. Invite them to tell about how they have used the target words outside of class and to tell about how they have heard friends and family use the target words.

In July, when the plants were as tall as my waist, we picked potato beetles off the leaves. I dropped them into a pail of soapy water.

"Gross."

"We have to do this," Dad said. "**Otherwise**, the bugs will eat the leaves and the potatoes won't grow."

potato beetle

In Other Words
Otherwise If we don't

156

Otherwise, the bugs will eat the leaves and the plants won't grow. In other words, if we don't, the bugs will eat the leaves..."

Vocabulary Routine 6

Reteaching Vocabulary

Purpose: Review or reteach vocabulary that has been previously introduced.

1. **Form groups.** Group students who did not master vocabulary, or who will benefit from reviewing the words. Follow the following steps for each word to be retaught or reviewed.

2. **Focus on the key word.** Point out the word on the Picture Dictionary page of the Anthology.

3. **Pronounce the word.** Say the word and have students repeat it after you.

4. **Teach the meaning.** Read the definition of the word, and then elaborate the meaning using different words and giving additional examples. For example, for the word *depend* you might say: *You depend on something when you need it to live or to do something. Some students depend on the school bus to get to school. We all depend on each other to make our school a healthy, happy place.*

5. **Make connections.** Discuss with students when they might use the word. Model an example. Then have students use Think, Pair, Share (BP46) to make connections.

6. **Write and remember.** Have students record each word on a separate page in their journals or review the word's entry in **My Vocabulary Notebook**. Ask them what they note about the word's sounds and spelling. Then have them do one or more of the following:

   - Make a Word Map to help them remember the word. (See Word Map, page BP38).
   - Add a drawing or photo to illustrate the word's meaning.
   - Write a definition in their own words.
   - Write a context sentence.
   - Write their connections to the word.
   - Write the translation of the word in their home language. Go to **NGReach.com** to find translations of key words in seven languages.

Picture Dictionary in Anthology

Activities for Daily Vocabulary Practice

Purpose: These routines can be used to give students additional experience in a variety of contexts with vocabulary introduced during lessons.

Whole Group Games

Vocabulary Bingo

1. **Distribute cards.** Hand out Bingo cards. (Go to **NGReach.com**).

2. **Fill out cards.** Have students write the key words in random order on the card.

3. **Give clues.** Provide oral clues or questions about the key words. For example, for the word *produce* you might say: *This word means to make.*

4. **Mark the words.** Have students place a marker on each word as they identify it.

5. **Bingo!** When a student has a complete row of markers, he or she calls, "Bingo." Ask the student to review his or her answers and pair answers with the clues.

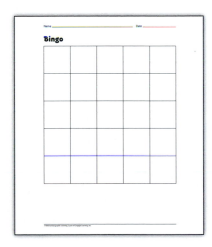

Stump the Expert

1. **Name the expert.** Designate one student to be the expert.

2. **Challenge the expert.** Another student (the stumper) presents a definition. The expert has 10 seconds to produce the term.

3. **Continue the challenges.** If the expert responds accurately, the next stumper offers a challenge. This continues until the expert is stumped or answers a set number of challenges and earns applause.

4. **Name a new expert.** The student who stumps the expert becomes the new expert.

Whole Group Activities

Yes or No?

1. **Ask questions.** Pose yes or no questions using two vocabulary words. You or your students can make up the questions. For example, the following questions might be asked using words to do with plants: *Do roots grow in the soil? Are blossoms a characteristic of rose plants?*

2. **Students respond.** Students can respond orally, in writing, or they can use thumbs up or thumbs down. Have students compare responses and pair their answers with the clue. Remind students to use complete sentences and restate the question. For example: *Yes, roots grow in the soil.*

Around the World

1. **Choose a traveler.** A student designated as the traveler moves from his or her seat to stand by a neighboring student, the challenger.

2. **Provide a definition.** The teacher gives the traveler and the challenger a definition; whoever responds first with the correct word becomes the new traveler and challenges a new student.

3. **Continue the challenge.** A traveler who continues to respond first and returns to his or her own seat has gone "around the world."

Rivet

1. **Select a key word.** For this variation of the game Hangman, choose a key word.

2. **Write a blank for each letter.** On the board, write a blank for each letter of the word. For example, for *ecosystem,* write _ _ _ _ _ _ _ _ _ .

3. **Fill in letters one by one.** Fill in the blanks one letter at a time: e c o _ _ _ _ _ _ .

4. **Have students guess the word.** Pause briefly after you write each letter. Encourage the class to guess the word.

5. **Complete the word.** When someone identifies the word correctly, have that student fill in the remaining blanks.

Vocabulary, continued

Small Group Games

Picture It

1. **Write the words.** Display several vocabulary words.

2. **Group students.** Arrange students in small groups, each with chart paper and a marker.

3. **Teams plan.** Have each group:
   - Choose a key word (without telling what the word is)
   - Decide how they can show the word's meaning in a drawing
   - Choose one member of the group who will create the drawing.

4. **Students create drawings.** Call on a group, and allow the drawer 15 to 30 seconds to complete the picture.

5. **Students identify the word.** Have other groups talk quietly about the picture. When they agree on the key word, they designate one member to raise his or her hand and give their answer.

6. **Award points.** When a group guesses the key word correctly, award 1 point to the group and have that group's drawer take the next turn. Continue until one group has collected 3 points.

Vocabulary Concentration

1. **Prepare pairs of cards.** Write each key word on two cards or slips of paper.

2. **Spread the cards.** Turn the cards over and spread them randomly on a table.

3. **Students look for matches.** Students take turns turning over two cards. When a student turns over two cards that have same word, he or she keeps the cards and uses the words in a sentence.

4. **The winner!** The student with the most cards is the winner.

Small Group Activities

Multiple Key Word Skit

1. **Group students.** Organize students in small groups and give each group a list of five or more vocabulary words.

2. **Brainstorm.** Allow time for groups to brainstorm how the words relate to each other and to create a skit with dialogue that includes all the words.

3. **Discuss.** After students present their skits, discuss with them which skit was most original, most humorous, or used the words most accurately.

Word Sorts

1. **Students write words.** Have students write the words on index cards or strips of paper, one word per card or strip.

2. **Establish categories.** For a closed sort, provide the category of how the words should be sorted, such as:
   - Related meanings or concepts
   - Synonyms
   - Part of speech
   - Connotation
   - Formal or informal
   - Spelling patterns
   - Words with multiple meanings
   - Words with Spanish cognates

   For an open sort, have students work together to determine the sort categories.

3. **Explain sorts.** When students have sorted the words, have them explain their sorts. Have them create a chart or web to record the word relationships they found.

4. **Sort again.** Have students sort the words again using different categories. Have them record the information in a graphic organizer.

Part of Speech Sort

Nouns	Verbs	Adverbs
abstract (n.)	adhere (v.)	ethically (adv.)
dilemma (n.)	advocate (v.)	desolately (adv.)
	reinforce (v.)	deliberately (adv.)

Number of Syllable Sort

2	3	4	5
ab-stract	ad-vo-cate	des-o-late-ly	de-lib-er-ate-ly
ad-here	di-lem-ma		
	re-in-force		
	eth-i-cal		

Individual Activities

Word Poems

1. **Diamante Poems.** Diamante poems are 7 lines long. To begin, have students think of two words that are opposites (antonyms).
   - Line 1: Write a noun
   - Line 2: Add two adjectives that describe line 1
   - Line 3: Add three action verbs that relate to line 1
   - Line 4: Add two nouns that relate to line 1, and two nouns that relate to line 7
   - Line 5: Add three action verbs that relate to line 7
   - Line 6: Add two adjectives that describe line 7
   - Line 7: Write a noun that is the opposite of or contrasts with line 1

2. **Cinquain Poems.** Cinquain poems have different patterns. Have students use key words to complete the pattern below.
   - Line 1: A noun
   - Line 2: Two adjectives
   - Line 3: Three related words ending in –ing
   - Line 4: A related phrase
   - Line 5: Another word for the noun

3. **Concrete Poems.** Students draw a meaningful shape or object and write words along the outline of the shape, so words look like the physical shape. For example, a student may draw a volcano and along the outline write: *lava, magma, cone, flow, ash, erupt.*

Structured Response

Research Basis: Structured response formats are instructional practices that can be incorporated into daily lessons and allow all students to participate productively (Heward, 2006). Carefully planned structured response routines can ensure that every student participates in a lesson, and that participation remains focused and on task. They also allow for immediate feedback to support correct answers and to address incorrect ones.

Structured Response

Purpose: To support all students in participating actively in daily lessons.

Choral Responses

Choral responses allow students to join in on important academic words, expressions, or ideas. They allow the teacher to determine immediately which students understand a presentation.

1. **Cue students in advance.** Use an established spoken cue (e.g., *Everybody; Look at me; Eyes up*) to focus students' attention.

2. **Give a prompt or ask a question.** Use prompts or questions that can be answered with one or two words or an academic phrase.

3. **Allow wait time.** Use a visual cue (e.g., holding up a hand as a "stop sign," then dropping it quickly) to provide wait time for students to think before they answer (and to keep some students from blurting out the answer). This use of wait time allows students to think about and form their answers and increases their confidence to join in class interactions.

4. **Provide feedback.** Acknowledge correct responses. For example: *That's right. Good work, everyone!* If some students give the wrong answer or say nothing, provide immediate corrective feedback. For example: *The correct answer is _____. Let's all say that together.*

Response Cards

Response cards can be used to ensure participation by every student. Response cards work best when the answer is short; for example, students are asked to change a verb in a sentence from present to past tense. Response cards can be index cards, small white boards, or small pieces of paper.

1. **Use simple prompts.** Give students a prompt or ask them a question that can be answered with one or two words, *yes/no,* or *true/false.*

2. **Allow wait time.** Tell students to think about their answers. Silently count to 5, then say: *Write your answer.*

3. **Students display their cards.** After students have had time to write, say: *Hold up your cards.*

4. **Give feedback.** Quickly check all of the cards and provide feedback, such as: *Good work! Almost everyone wrote* true, *which is the correct answer.* If some students give an incorrect answer, provide immediate corrective feedback, such as: *I see some of you wrote* Sammy, *which is the name of the main character in the passage. The correct answer is _____.*
Say it with me, _____.

5. **Continue with other prompts and questions.**

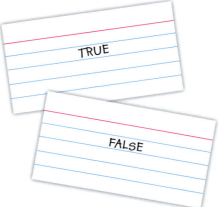

Cooperative Learning

Research Basis: Cooperative learning routines take advantage of classroom diversity and make it a vital resource for helping all students acquire challenging academic content and language. These routines promote active engagement and social motivation for all students. For English language learners, they also create opportunities for purposeful communication. Regular use of such routines has been shown to be effective (Johnson & Johnson 1986; Kagan 1986; Slavin 1988).

Purpose: These routines provide consistent opportunities for students to work together and learn from one another.

STRUCTURE & GRAPHIC	DESCRIPTION	BENEFITS & PURPOSE
CORNERS	• Corners of the classroom are designated for focused discussion of four aspects of a topic. • Students individually think and write about the topic for a short time. • Students group into the corner of their choice and discuss the topic. • At least one student from each corner shares about the corner discussion.	• By "voting" with their feet, students literally take a position about a topic. • Focused discussion develops deeper thought about a topic. • Students experience many valid points of view about a topic.
FISHBOWL	• Part of a group sits in a close circle, facing inward; the other part of the group sits in a larger circle around them. • Students on the inside discuss a topic while those outside listen for information and/or evaluate the discussion according to pre-established criteria. • Groups reverse positions.	• Focused listening enhances knowledge acquisition and listening skills. • Peer evaluation supports development of specific discussion skills. • Identification of criteria for evaluation promotes self-monitoring.
INSIDE-OUTSIDE CIRCLE	• Students stand in concentric circles facing each other. • Students in the outside circle have one role; those inside have another. • On a signal, students rotate to create new partnerships. • On another signal, students trade inside/outside roles.	• Talking one-on-one with a variety of partners gives risk-free practice in speaking skills. • Interactions can be structured to focus on specific speaking skills. • Students practice both speaking and active listening.
JIGSAW	• Group students evenly into "expert" groups. • Expert groups study one topic or aspect of a topic in depth. • Regroup students so that each new group has at least one member from each expert group. • Experts report on their study. Other students learn from the experts.	• Becoming an expert provides in-depth understanding in one aspect of study. • Learning from peers provides breadth of understanding of over-arching concepts.

Cooperative Learning, continued

STRUCTURE & GRAPHIC	DESCRIPTION	BENEFITS & PURPOSE
NUMBERED HEADS TOGETHER	• Students number off within each group. • Teacher prompts or gives a directive. • Students think individually about the topic. • Groups discuss the topic so that any member of the group can report for the group. • Teacher calls a number and the student from each group with that number reports for the group.	• Group discussion of topics provides each student with language and concept understanding. • Random recitation provides an opportunity for evaluation of both individual and group progress.
ROUNDTABLE	• Seat students around a table in groups of four. • Teacher asks a question with many possible answers. • Each student around the table answers the question a different way.	• Encouraging elaboration creates appreciation for diversity of opinion and thought. • Eliciting multiple answers enhances language fluency.
TEAM WORD WEBBING	• Provide each team with a single large piece of paper. Give each student a different colored marker. • Teacher assigns a topic for a web. • Each student adds to the part of the web nearest to him/her. • On a signal, students rotate the paper and each student adds to the nearest part again.	• Individual input to a group product ensures participation by all students. • By shifting point of view, students develop broad and in-depth understanding of concepts.
THINK, PAIR, SHARE	• Students think about a topic suggested by the teacher. • Pairs discuss the topic. • Students individually share information with the class.	• The opportunity for self-talk during the individual think time allows the student to formulate thoughts before speaking. • Discussion with a partner reduces performance anxiety and enhances understanding.
THREE-STEP INTERVIEW	• Students form pairs. • Student A interviews student B about a topic. • Partners reverse roles. • Student A shares with the class information from student B; then B shares information from student A.	• Interviewing supports language acquisition by providing scripts for expression. • Responding provides opportunities for structured self-expression.
MIX AND MATCH	• Prepare cards that can be matched as pairs, such as a word and its definition. • Hand one card to each student. • Students mingle and talk about their cards. • Teacher calls "Match," and each student finds the partner whose card matches with his or her own. Students exchange cards and mingle again.	• The mixing process encourages students to have multiple conversations with an academic focus. • Discussions provide each student with language and concept understanding. • Cards can be traded, so students don't know who their partner is until the end.

Writing

Research: Research shows that expert writers write longer strings of words before stopping to think than less skilled writers. Power writing practice helps students learn to get their words down on paper quickly. It also helps them overcome the tendency to stall before starting to write (Fisher & Frey 2007). While power writing can focus on any word or concept, this routine is most effective when key words and ideas relate to the topic or theme of a unit.

Writing Routine 1

Power Writing

Purpose: Develop students' writing fluency; provide an opportunity for students to record their progress in writing fluency.

1. **Display a word or picture.** Choose a word or picture that will be motivating for students to write about. Invite them to think about the word or picture and what they know about the word or concept. Activate prior knowledge or experiences: *What do you think of when you hear/see _____?*

2. **Set the timer.** The timer is usually set for one minute. In some cases you may want to vary the amount of time.

3. **Have students write.** Ask students to write as much as they can, as well as they can in one minute.

4. **Check work.** Have students check their spelling and grammar and circle any mistakes.

5. **Count words.** Have students count the number of words they wrote and record the number on their papers.

6. **Repeat the procedure.** If time allows, have students create more than one passage. Repeat steps 2–5 one or two times.

7. **Record results.** Have students record their best result and create a writing fluency graph. Over time, the graph will show students' growth in fluency and help motivate their progress as writers.

8. **Adjust the time.** To develop fluency further, vary the amount of writing time from 30 seconds to two minutes or more in separate Power Writing sessions.

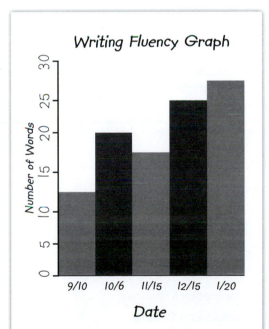

Research: Many students may not understand the process of recording their thoughts or conversation in writing. Modeled writing demonstrates the process of how language is represented in written form. Modeling the process often is effective in improving students' attitude towards writing as well as their writing skills (Fisher & Frey 2007). Modeled writing also helps deepen vocabulary, language, and concept development through frequent exposure to clear models and think-alouds.

Writing Routine 2

Modeled Writing

Purpose: Model the process of composing to help students learn the writing process, writing strategies and writer's craft.

1. **Model thinking about the first sentence.** Think aloud as you decide what you will include in your first sentence.

2. **Write the first sentence.** Read aloud what you have written.

3. **Continue thinking aloud as you write.** Think aloud to model how you plan and write additional sentences.

4. **Involve students.** Encourage students to help write additional sentences. Discuss their ideas with them, and add the new ideas to the writing as appropriate.

Think Aloud	Write
I want to tell about some new puppies that were born last week. I'll write a news article to tell about the puppies. I'll begin by telling the most important facts.	Last week, six new puppies were born on Davis Street.
Next I'll tell what the puppies looked like.	The puppies were brown and white and had soft fur. Their eyes were closed.
What else do people want to know about the puppies?	They were born under the porch of the Marino's house. Mrs. Marino fixed a bed for the puppies and their mother in the hall.

Puppies Born

Last week, six new puppies were born on Davis Street. The puppies were brown and white and had soft fur. Their eyes were closed. They were born under the porch at the Marino's house. Mrs. Marino fixed a bed for the puppies and their mother in the hall. Mrs. Marino said she would look for new homes for the puppies in a few weeks.

Writing Routine 3

Generative Writing

Purpose: Provide specific practice for structuring grammatically-correct sentences.

1. **Provide a prompt.** Give students a directive about the position of a word or part of speech in a sentence. For example: *Write a sentence with the noun* magma *in the third position*.

2. **Have students write.** Ask students to write their sentences and underline the word that addresses the prompt.

3. **Respond to writing.** Check students' work. If the word is in the wrong position in the sentence, guide the writer to rework it to meet the prompt. If the word is used incorrectly in the sentence, reteach the grammar skill to help the writer understand the concept.

4. **Provide additional prompts.** For further practice, give directives that have students use the same part of speech in different positions in different sentences.

5. **Have students write independently.** Encourage students to use their generative sentences as the beginning of paragraphs they write independently.

The bubbling magma exploded from the volcano.

Research: Most elementary students need continued support as they become independent writers. They are most successful when the teacher provides effective prompts, a collaborative context, and effective coaching (Fisher & Frey 2007).

Writing Routine 4

Independent Writing

Purpose: Provide support to help students achieve success as independent writers.

1. **Provide appropriate writing prompts.** Make sure that writing prompts are motivating and appropriate. Prompts should:
   - Encourage a variety of responses
   - Allow for a range of writing abilities
   - Be appropriate for the writers' experiences
   - Include topics that interest students.

2. **Use RAFTs.** Have students use the RAFT structure to make sure writing assignments have a clear purpose and authenticity. Students should understand their Role, Audience, Form, and Topic before they begin to write. Here is a sample RAFT:

   Role: A student who wants to clean up a vacant lot

   Audience: Neighbors who could help clean up the lot

   Form: An email message

   Topic: A gathering on Saturday to help clean up the lot

3. **Support peer response.** Teach students how to be effective peer reviewers of each others' writing.
   - Use the language frames from the Writing Projects to scaffold conversation.
   - Have writers invite responses from peers, but don't compel them.
   - Encourage students to talk with each other as readers, not as critics. If something makes them laugh, or feel sad, or catches their interest, they should tell the writer so. If something isn't clear, they should tell that, too. However, details of word choice, organization, sentence structure, etc. are best dealt with in teacher-student conferences.

4. **Conference.** Confer with students about their writing. Conferences should be short and focused. Include the following steps:
   - **Inquiry:** Ask about the topic, how the work is coming, and areas of difficulty.
   - **Decision:** Based on student responses, decide on the focus for the conference.
   - **Instruction:** Choose a point for teaching. This may be any of the writing traits, writer's craft, grammar, usage, spelling, capitalization, and punctuation. Refer to records of student performance on grammar, revising and editing, and spelling lessons and assessments. Writing Rubrics for conferences are provided in the Assessment section of each Teacher's Edition.
   - **Recording:** Record anecdotal notes of the conference for follow-up. Include next steps for the writer.

Research: Expert writers make many decisions as they write. Students may not understand all of the decisions involved. Interactive writing makes these decisions part of the conversation between teacher and students. It also demonstrates for students how expert writers think about word choice and constantly review to maintain syntax and meaning as they write (Fisher & Frey 2007).

Writing Routine 5

Reteaching Writing

Purpose: Use a collaborative composition to reteach a writing skill or trait.

1. **Introduce the activity.** Provide a RAFT that allows for focused practice of the skill or trait being reviewed.

2. **Review the skill**. Give a brief overview of the writing skill or trait. For example: *Writing has fluency when the sentences are varied. It also sounds natural when read aloud.*

3. **Talk through the text.** Lead a discussion with students about how to word each sentence, and then support individual students as they write sentences on the board or chart paper. For example: *How will we begin?... Good, Alana. Can you come up and write that for us?* Continue the discussion having different members of the class take turns writing.

4. **Practice.** Use questions or prompts to help students practice the skill or trait as they write. For example: *Let's read the first two sentences we've written aloud. We want to vary our sentences so how should we begin the next sentence?... Good idea, Duwayne, let's start with an adverb... Can you come up and write the next sentence?*

5. **Reread frequently.** Reread the entire message after each sentence is added. This will help students see how a skill or trait is being applied in each sentence.

Anita Wheeler is the youngest mayor in Danville history. She was elected just after she graduated from college. Now, at age 24, she is making decisions about the town budget and schools.

Foundational Skills

Dictation Routine 1

Sound-by-Sound Spelling
Purpose: Students segment sounds to spell words with the target sound/spelling.

1. **Review sound/spelling.** Review the target *Reach into Phonics* Sound/Spelling Card. Tell students that they will be spelling words with (identify sound).

2. **Say the word.** Say the first word.

3. **Segment sounds and identify sound/spellings.** Model how to segment the sounds in the word. Have students say the first sound in the word, match the sound to a **Sound/Spelling Card**, and identify the spelling.

4. **Write spelling.** Have students repeat the spelling and then write it. Repeat for the remaining sound/spellings in the word.

5. **Check and correct spelling.** Write the word. Have students check their spelling. If a word is misspelled, students should circle it and write it correctly.

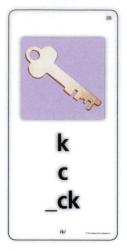

Dictation Routine 2

Whole Word Spelling
Purpose: Students spell words to write sentences with the target sound/spelling.

1. **Say a sentence.** Have students listen as you read the sentence.

2. **Spell words.** As you read the sentence slowly several times, have students write it.

3. **Check and correct spelling.** Write the sentence. Have students check their spelling. Students should circle any misspelled words and write them correctly.

Word Work Routine 1

Word Building
Purpose: Students use *Reach into Phonics* **Letter Cards**, magnetic boards and tiles, or **Write-On/Wipe-Off Boards** to build and transform words. In the beginning of the year, you may want to limit the number of **Letter Cards** students work with at once.

1. **Build a word.** Say a word and ask students to make or spell it. Students should say the word slowly and place or write the spelling for each sound they hear.

2. **Self- check.** Circulate and check for accuracy. Then display the word and ask students to self-check.

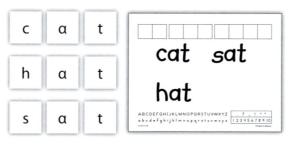

Word Work Routine 2

Word Sorts
Purpose: Students sort words into categories based on sound and/or spelling patterns.

1. **Prepare.** Create word sort charts by drawing column lines on blank paper and making copies. Distribute and have students write key words or sort categories at the top of each column.

2. **Sort words.** Provide a word list or have students choose words to sort into the categories. Students write each word in the appropriate column.

3. **Read words aloud.** Have students read each group of words aloud. Ask them to tell what is the same about the words in each group.

Variations: Students can sort *Reach into Phonics* Phonics Picture Cards by beginning, ending, or middle sound. They can sort words by sound or by spelling pattern. Once students are familiar with sorting, they can do open sorts. In an open sort, students decide how to group the words.

Activities for Daily High Frequency Word Practice

Whole Group Practice: Word Wall ★★★

Post Words
After introducing new High Frequency Words, post the **High Frequency Word Cards** cut from the **Practice Masters** on a classroom Word Wall. Organize words by the sound of the first letter.

Sound Sort
Students take turns saying a sound, other students name the words on the Word Wall that start with that sound.

Random Reading
Point to words at random and have students read them aloud. Increase the pace as students gain familiarity with the words.

Word Sorts
Have students sort words by beginning letter, numbers of letters, rhymes, rimes, onsets, vowel sounds, or other categories.

Create Sentences
Post sentences with High Frequency Words. Read them aloud or have volunteers read them. Underline the High Frequency Word and have students place the matching High Frequency Word Card in the Pocket Chart.

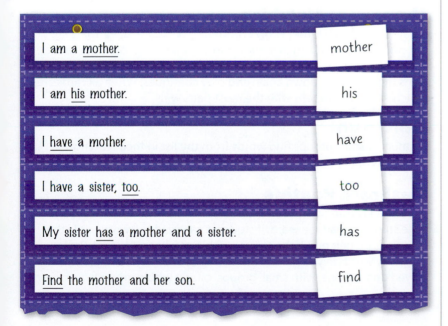

Whole Group Games ★★★

Word Clues
Begin spelling a word from the Word Wall one letter at a time. Pause after placing each letter, give a clue to the word, and see if students can guess the word you are spelling. Students can respond with the correct answer orally, in writing, or by holding up individual **Word Cards**. Continue adding letters and clues until students guess the word. Clues can include number of letters, meanings, antonyms or synonyms, or sentence frames. This activity can be done with **Word Builder** or with **Letter Cards** in a pocket chart.

> It has three letters.
> It begins with *n*.
> It rhymes with *blue*.
> It completes the sentence:
> *I want to buy some* _____ *shoes.*

> *new*

Bop!
Organize students into two teams in front of the Word Wall. Give the first student on each team a cardboard tube. Read a word. The first student to bop the word with the tube spells and reads the word to score a point for that team. Play continues until all students have had a turn.

Build, Mix, Fix
Write or display a High Frequency Word. Have students build the word with **Letter Cards**. After all students have spelled the word, have them mix up their letters. Cover the displayed word and have students fix their word by putting the letters back in the correct order. Uncover the word and have students check and correct their work. Then chant the word's spelling. Continue with remaining words.

Toss and Spell
Use a bean bag and sit in circle. The first student says a High Frequency Word and its first letter, and tosses the bean bag to next student. That student says the next letter. Tossing continues until word is complete. The student who says last letter also uses the word in an oral sentence.

Whole Group Games, continued

Wordo

Create blank grids by drawing a grid like the one below and making copies. Distribute grids and game chips. (Depending on the number of words you are using, you may want to fill extra spaces with stars to show that they are bonus spaces.) Have students write the target words in random order on the grid. Shuffle the **High Frequency Word Cards** for the same set of words. As you call out each word, chant the spelling together and have students mark their boards. The first student to mark a 4-word row horizontally, vertically, or diagonally says "Wordo!" and play begins again.

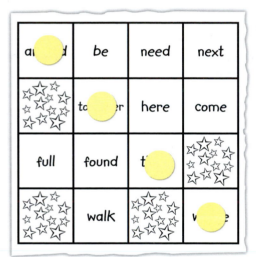

Hopscotch

Make a hopscotch grid on the classroom floor with tape. Choose a Word Wall word and write one letter in each box of the hopscotch and the whole word at the top. Students hop and say each letter to spell the word and then say the word at the end. Repeat for additional words.

Small Group and Partner Games

Bang!

Place **High Frequency Word Cards** and three or four cards that say Bang! in a container. Have a small group of students pass the container and choose a card. If they can read the word and use it in a sentence, they get to keep the card. If they get a Bang! Card, they return all of their cards to the container.

Clues and Choose

Lay several **High Frequency Word Cards** face up on the floor. Have a small group of students sit in a circle around the cards. One student mentally chooses a word and gives a clue about it: *This word begins with a* b. The student can continue to give clues until another student selects the correct card. He or she gets to give the next set of clues.

Guess the Missing Word

Write sentences with the target High Frequency Words. Cover up the target word in each with a stick-on note. Work with a small group of students. Have students guess the word with no letters showing. Write 5 reasonable guesses out to the side. Uncover the onset and cross out any guesses that are eliminated. Make additional guesses if necessary. Show the whole word and help students confirm which guess makes sense and has the right letters.

Memory or Matching

Create two of each target **High Frequency Word Card.** Partners lay the cards face down and take turns turning up two cards. If the cards match, the student keeps the cards. If the cards don't match, the student turns the cards face down again and play continues. When all cards are matched up the student with the most pairs wins.

Word Hunt

Partners or small groups find words from the list in their reading selections or in print around the school or classroom.

Flashcard Routine

Use **High Frequency Word Cards** as flashcards. Show each card and have students read the word. If students can read the word easily the card goes in their pile. If they have trouble you keep the card. Review the tricky words in your pile at the end of the activity. (This game can be played one-on-one, with small groups, or as a whole group.)

Technology

Research Basis: When readers engage with a text more actively, they comprehend it more deeply (Harvey, 2000). Marking a text is one method for facilitating this deeper, more active comprehension. Teachers can more effectively model abstract thinking processes by annotating as they think aloud. Students can then have focused opportunities to follow the teacher model by adding their own highlights and making their own notes about questions, important parts, opinions, connections, and so on. Annotating texts is a strategy that not only supports retention and synthesis of information, but can also be used by teachers to provide insights into students' thinking (Harvey, et al. 1996).

Mark-Up Text Routine

Purpose: Having students interact with text reinforces their comprehension and acquisition of reading skills.

1. **Preview the text.** Download the appropriate **Mark-Up Model** file from NGReach.com.

   - If you are working on an interactive whiteboard, ensure that the appropriate interactive whiteboard software is installed on your computer. Then download the Notebook file for a SMART™ board or Flipchart file for a Promethean board.
   - If you use a computer and projector, you can project the PDF file onto a board or paper where students can mark up the text.
   - If you use an overhead projector, copy the PDF file pages onto acetate to create transparencies. Project them onto a board or paper for students to mark.

2. **Prepare your tools.** Preview the lesson to see what tools you will need for the **Mark-Up Model.** For example, on an interactive whiteboard, make sure that the highlighters are set to the colors needed for the lesson.

3. **Read aloud the Mark-Up Model.** Display the lesson and read the selection text aloud.

4. **Conduct the lesson.** Involve students in a variety of ways:

   - Assign a different student to mark each step of the lesson.
   - Have one set of partners mark up one screen and then have different partners mark the next.
   - Assign highlighter colors to different students. Have the class offer answers while the student with the appropriate color makes the marks.
   - Have the student marking the text choose the next student to mark the text.

Regularly remind the class to copy the marks onto their **Practice Masters** to serve as a model for their independent work.

Mark-Up Text Routine, continued

5. **Have students mark the Mark-Up Reading.** Have students read the remaining **Mark-Up Reading** on the **Practice Masters** independently. Then have them work with partners to follow the model and mark up the reading.

6. **Close the Mark-Up Model file.** If you are using the Notebook or Flipchart file, choose how to close the file.
   - To save the marks the students made during the lesson, save the file with a different name.
   - Close the file without saving to keep an unmarked version of the file.

   If you need a clean file for future lessons, download it from **NGReach.com**.

7. **Review students' notes.** Look through the **Mark-Up Reading** to determine if students comprehend the skill. If students are highlighting too much text or the wrong text, offer the **Reteaching Masters** that align with the skill.

   For more technical assistance, see the user guide on **NGReach.com**.

Find **Mark-Up Reading** Masters and a technology guide here.

Find **Mark-Up Model** files and an interactive whiteboard user guide here.

Whole Group Time

TEACHER	STUDENTS
▪ Introduce Anthology	▪ Read and Respond to Fiction and Nonfiction
▪ Conduct Reading Lessons	▪ Build Content Knowledge
▪ Teach Daily Language Arts	▪ Develop Reading Skills
Daily Spelling & Word Work	▪ Engage in Language Arts Activities
Daily Grammar	▪ Collaborate on Writing Projects
Daily Writing Skills	▪ Complete Assessments
▪ Differentiate Instruction	
▪ Guide Writing Projects	
▪ Assess Progress	

Small Group Reading Time

TEACHER	STUDENTS
▪ Introduce Books	▪ Read and Discuss Books
▪ Conduct Mini Lessons	▪ Extend Content Knowledge
▪ Monitor Small Group Reading	▪ Apply Reading Skills
▪ Guide Discussion	▪ Connect and Compare Texts
▪ Assess Progress	▪ Demonstrate Comprehension

Learning Station Time

TEACHER	STUDENTS
▪ Suggest Books for Independent Reading	▪ Read Independently
▪ Introduce Learning Stations	▪ Complete Learning Station Activities
▪ Meet with Small Groups or Individuals for Intervention, Reteaching, or Acceleration	▪ Meet for Intervention, Reteaching, or Acceleration
▪ Guide and Redirect as Needed	▪ Work on Assigned Skills Practice

Happy to Help

BIG Question How do people help each other?

Helping Others

Week 1	Week 2	Week 3	Week 4
Individual Responsibility	Heroic Deeds	Heroes Then and Now	Heroes Then and Now

WHOLE GROUP TIME

Student eEdition

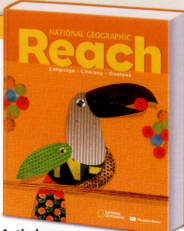

Anthology

Build Background Video

Interactive Whiteboard

Mark-Up Models 1.1, 1.2

Student Technology
- Student eEdition
- Digital Library
- Build Background Video
- Other Student Resources

SMALL GROUP READING TIME

Fiction Books

Nonfiction Books

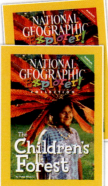

Explorer Books

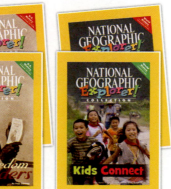

Leveled Book Finder

Small Group Reading Masters
SG1.1–SG1.32

LEARNING STATION TIME

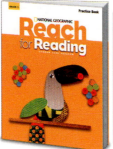

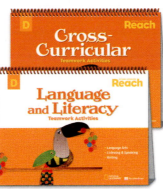

NGReach.com

Comprehension Coach   **Digital Library**   **My Vocabulary Notebook**

Student Technology
- My Assignments
- My Vocabulary Notebook
- Vocabulary Games
- Comprehension Coach
- Read with Me MP3s
- Fluency MP3s
- Practice Masters
- Teamwork Activities
- Other Student Resources

ESL Kit

Practice Book
PM1.1–PM1.31

Practice Masters
PM1.1–PM1.31

Teamwork Activities

Reach into Phonics Kit

PLANNING RESOURCES

NGReach.com

Teacher Technology
- Student and Teacher eEditions
- Lesson Planner
- eVisuals 1.1–1.39
- Family Newsletter 1 (in seven languages)
- Teamwork Activities Teacher's Guides
- Test-Taking Strategies Teacher's Guide
- Professional Development
- Other Teacher Resources

Teacher's eEdition

Online Lesson Planner

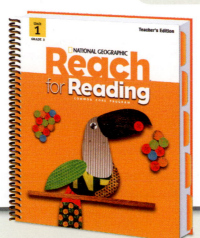

Teacher's Edition
- Whole Group Lessons
- Practice Masters Small Group Reading
- Assessment and Reteaching Masters

ASSESSMENT & RETEACHING

eAssessment™

ExamView®

Assessment Masters
A1.1–A1.46

Reteaching Masters
RT1.1–RT1.13

Unit 1 Skills at a Glance

BL = BELOW LEVEL   OL = ON LEVEL
BL = BELOW LEVEL   AL = ABOVE LEVEL   ✔ = TESTED SKILL

Introduce Unit 1	BUILD BACKGROUND VIDEO • INTRODUCE THE BIG QUESTION		
	WHOLE GROUP TIME		
	Speaking and Listening	Language and Vocabulary	Reading
Week 1 	Retell a Story Tell a Story	✔ Daily Spelling and Word Work: Short *a* and Short *o* and Commonly Misspelled Words ✔ Daily Grammar: Nouns ✔ Social Studies Vocabulary action difference gift problem receive solution ✔ Academic Vocabulary kindness need plot prediction preview understand value want	Read and Comprehend Realistic Fiction ✔ Comprehend Plot ✔ Learn to Plan and Monitor ✔ Fluency: Practice Expression, Accuracy, and Rate
Week 2 	Read Poetry Aloud Relate Readings to the Big Question	✔ Daily Spelling and Word Work: More Short *a* and Short *o* and Commonly Misspelled Words ✔ Daily Grammar: Pronouns and Sentences ✔ Alphabetical Order	Read and Comprehend a Poem ✔ Learn to Plan and Monitor ✔ Identify Elements of a Poem Read and Comprehend a Poem ✔ Identify Elements of a Poem ✔ Analyze and Compare Characters ✔ Fluency: Practice Phrasing, Accuracy, and Rate
Week 3 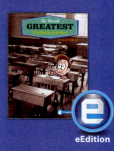	Make Comparisons Discuss Photographs	✔ Daily Spelling and Word Work: Short *i* and Short *u* and Commonly Misspelled Words ✔ Daily Grammar: Subjects and Predicates, Phrases and Clauses ✔ Social Studies Vocabulary improve individual neighborhood offer volunteer ✔ Academic Vocabulary benefit clarify comparison duty identify impact learn point of view narrator	Read and Comprehend an Autobiography ✔ Make Comparisons ✔ Learn to Plan and Monitor ✔ Fluency: Practice Intonation, Accuracy, and Rate
Week 4 	Discuss Points of View Relate Readings to the Big Question	✔ Daily Spelling and Word Work: Words with Digraphs *ch, tch;* Commonly Misspelled Words ✔ Daily Grammar: Subject-Verb Agreement, Compound Subjects, and More Subjects and Predicates ✔ Determine Meanings	Read and Comprehend an Autobiography ✔ Determine Point of View ✔ Learn to Plan and Monitor Read and Comprehend a Biography ✔ Identify Point of View Identify and Compare Events ✔ Fluency: Practice Expression, Accuracy, and Rate
Unit 1 Wrap-Up	ANSWER THE BIG QUESTION • UNIT PROJECTS		

Question **How do people help each other?**

Writing	SMALL GROUP READING TIME	LEARNING STATION TIME	ASSESSMENT & RETEACHING
Power Writing Write to Retell a Story Write About a Prediction Write a Prediction Write About Characters Write about It ☑ Daily Writing Skills: Develop a Plot Sequence ☑ Writing Project: Write Realistic Fiction	☐ *The Children's Forest* **BL** *A Chance to Shine* **BL** *Tomas and the Library Lady* **OL** *The Quiltmaker's Gift* **AL** *The Quiltmaker's Journey*	**Speaking and Listening** Talk About Kind Acts; Being Responsible **Language and Vocabulary** Games; My Vocabulary Notebook **Writing** Volunteer; Write a Helping Story **Cross-Curricular** Study Feet and Shoes; What Size Is Your Shoe? **Reading and Intervention** Comprehension Coach; Helping the Environment; Phonics; ESL Kit	☑ Plan and Monitor ☑ Plot ☑ Fluency: Expression, Accuracy, and Rate ☑ Social Studies and Academic Vocabulary ☑ Spelling: Short *a* and Short *o* and Commonly Misspelled Words ☑ Grammar: Nouns ☑ Writing: Develop a Plot Sequence ☑ Writing Trait: Organization
Power Writing Write a Poem Write a Response Write to Reinforce Grammar Write a Poem Write About Characters ☑ Daily Writing Skills: Use Colorful Details to Elaborate ☑ Writing Project: Write a Poem	☐ *To the Rescue* **BL** *New York's Bravest* **BL** *The Snow Walker* **OL** *Passage to Freedom* **AL** *Mercedes and the Chocolate Pilot*	**Speaking and Listening** Mother Teresa; Record a Poem **Language and Vocabulary** Games; My Vocabulary Notebook **Writing** Person to Person; Write a Helping Poem **Cross-Curricular** Lost and Found; Discuss an Article **Reading and Intervention** Author Study; Additional Reading; Phonics; ESL Kit	☑ Plan and Monitor ☑ Elements of a Poem ☑ Fluency: Phrasing, Accuracy, and Rate ☑ Alphabetical Order ☑ Spelling: More Short *a* and Short *o* and Commonly Misspelled Words ☑ Grammar: Pronouns and Sentences ☑ Writing: Use Colorful Details to Elaborate ☑ Writing Trait: Word Choice
Power Writing Write About Comparisons Write About Monitoring and Clarifying Write a Prediction Writer's Craft Write About It ☑ Daily Writing Skills: Choose and Narrow a Topic and Develop Interview Questions ☑ Research Project: Write a Biographical Sketch	☐ *Freedom Readers* **BL** *Harriet Tubman* **BL** *Helen Keller: Courage in the Dark* **OL** *Louis Braille* **AL** *Mary McLeod Bethune*	**Speaking and Listening** People in the Community; Interview **Language and Vocabulary** Games; My Vocabulary Notebook **Writing** Beating a Disease; Write a Friendly Letter **Cross-Curricular** Heroic Athletes; Dyslexia **Reading and Intervention** Comprehension Coach; Author Study; Phonics; ESL Kit	☑ Plan and Monitor ☑ Make Comparisons ☑ Fluency: Intonation, Accuracy, and Rate ☑ Social Studies and Academic Vocabulary ☑ Spelling: Short *i* and Short *u* and Commonly Misspelled Words ☑ Grammar: Subjects and Predicates; Phrases and Clauses ☑ Writing: Choose and Narrow a Topic; Develop Interview Questions
Power Writing Write with Third-Person Point of View Write a Response Write to Reinforce Grammar Write a First-Person Account Write to Compare Events ☑ Daily Writing Skills: Use Formal and Informal Language ☑ Writing Project: Write a Personal Narrative	**BL** *Martin's Big Words* ☐ *Kids Connect* **BL** *Roberto Clemente: A Life of Generosity* **OL** *Franklin D. Roosevelt* **AL** *Nelson Mandela*	**Speaking and Listening** Making a Difference; Holiday Helping **Language and Vocabulary** Games; My Vocabulary Notebook **Writing** Discover the Difference; Write a Letter **Cross-Curricular** The Long Road Home; Research Kenya **Reading and Intervention** Kakenya's School; Additional Reading; Phonics; ESL Kit	☑ Plan and Monitor ☑ Point of View ☑ Fluency: Expression, Accuracy, and Rate ☑ Determine Meanings ☑ Spelling: Words with Digraphs *ch, tch* and Commonly Misspelled Words ☑ Grammar: Subject-Verb Agreement; Compound Subjects; More Subjects and Predicates ☑ Writing: Use Formal/Informal Language ☑ Writing Trait: Voice

Online Lesson Planner
NGReach.com

 = TESTED

	Day 1	**Day 2**
	Listen and Comprehend	**Read and Comprehend**

WHOLE GROUP TIME

Anthology

Speaking and Listening
5–10 minutes

Day 1 — Listen and Comprehend

Social Studies Background — CC.3.SL.2
Introduce the Big Question;
Preview Unit Projects T2–T3

Academic Talk — CC.3.Rlit.5; CC.3.SL.4
Retell a Story T4

Day 2 — Read and Comprehend

Academic Talk — CC.3.SL.4
Tell a Story T6a

Language and Vocabulary
15–25 minutes

Day 1

Daily Spelling and Word Work — CC.3.Rfou.3;
✓ Short *a* and *o* and — CC.3.L.2; CC.3.L.2.f
Commonly Misspelled Words T1l

Daily Grammar — CC.3.L.1; CC.3.L.1.a
✓ Nouns T1n

Social Studies Vocabulary — CC.3.SL.4; CC.3.L.6
✓ Learn Key Words T4

action difference gift problem
receive solution

Day 2

Daily Spelling and Word Work — CC.3.Rfou.3; CC.3.L.2;
✓ Practice T1l — CC.3.L.2.f; CC.3.L.4.d

Daily Grammar — CC.3.L.1; CC.3.L.1.a;
✓ Common and Proper Nouns T1n — CC.3.L.2

Academic Vocabulary — CC.3.L.4, 6
✓ Learn More Key Words T6a

kindness need plot prediction
preview understand value want

Reading
20–40 minutes

Day 1

Reading
Read Aloud: Realistic Fiction T5a

Comprehension — CC.3.Rlit.5
✓ Comprehend Plot T5a

Fluency — CC.3.Rfou.4
✓ Model Expression T5a

Day 2

Reading — CC.3.Rlit.10
Read a Story T8

Comprehension — CC.3.Rlit.10
✓ Learn to Plan and
Monitor T8

Fluency — CC.3.Rfou.4
✓ Practice Expression T8

Writing
15–45 minutes

Day 1

Power Writing T4 — CC.3.W.10
Daily Writing Skills — CC.3.W.3.a; CC.3.W.3.c;
✓ Develop a Plot Sequence T1p — CC.3.W.3.d

Writing — CC.3.W.10
Write to Retell a Story T6

Writing Project: Realistic Fiction — CC.3.W.3
✓ Study a Model T27a

Day 2

Power Writing T6a — CC.3.W.10
Daily Writing Skills — CC.3.W.3.a; CC.3.W.3.c;
✓ Develop a Plot Sequence T1p — CC.3.W.3.d

Writing — CC.3.W.10
Write About a Prediction T8–T9

Writing Project: Realistic Fiction — CC.3.W.3; CC.3.W.3.a;
✓ Prewrite T27b — CC.3.W.3.b; CC.3.W.5;
— CC.3.W.10

SMALL GROUP READING TIME

Fiction & Nonfiction

20 minutes

Read Social Studies Articles

Vocabulary — CC.3.L.6
Learn Social Studies
Vocabulary SG4

Reading — CC.3.Rinf.2;
Determine Main — CC.3.Rinf.10
Idea SG4

Build Comprehension SG5

Read Fiction Books

Vocabulary — CC.3.L.6
Learn Story Words
SG6–SG7

Reading — CC.3.Rlit.5;
Introduce SG6–SG7 — CC.3.Rlit.10
Read and Integrate
Ideas SG8–SG9
✓ Plan and Monitor SG8–SG9
✓ Analyze Plot SG8–SG9

LEARNING STATION TIME/DAILY PHONICS INTERVENTION

20 minutes

Speaking and Listening T1h — CC.3.SL.1; CC.3.SL.4; CC.3.SL.5
Language and Vocabulary T1h — CC.3.L.6
Writing T1h — CC.3.W.3; CC.3.W.10
Cross-Curricular T1i — CC.3.W.8
Reading and Intervention — CC.3.Rlit.10; CC.3.Rinf.10;
T1i; SG68 — CC.3.Rfou.3; CC.3.Rfou.4.b
Daily Phonics Intervention T1j–T1k — CC.3.Rfou.3.d;
— CC.3.L.2.e; CC.3.L.2.f

BIG Question **How do people help each other?**

Day 3

Read and Comprehend

Academic Talk CC.3.SL.1
Preview and Predict T10

Daily Spelling and Word Work CC.3.Rfou.3; CC.3.L.2.e;
☑ Practice T1m CC.3.L.2.f

Daily Grammar CC.3.L.1; CC.3.L.1.a; CC.3.L.1.c
☑ Concrete and Abstract Nouns T1o

Vocabulary Practice CC.3.L.6
☑ Expand Word Knowledge T10

Reading CC.3.Rlit.10
Read a Story T11–T20

Comprehension CC.3.Rlit.2;
Analyze Characters CC.3.Rlit.3;
T12–T20 CC.3.Rlit.5; CC.3.Rlit.10
☑ Comprehend Plot
T12–13; T20
☑ Plan and Monitor T14–15

Fluency CC.3.Rfou.4;
☑ Practice Expression, Accuracy, CC.3.Rfou.4.a, b
and Rate T12–13; T18–T19

Power Writing T10 CC.3.W.10
Daily Writing Skills CC.3.W.3.a; CC.3.W.3.c;
☑ Develop a Plot Sequence T1q CC.3.W.3.d

Writing CC.3.W.10
Write a Prediction T21

Writing Project: Realistic Fiction CC.3.W.3; CC.3.W.3.a;
☑ Draft T27b CC.3.W.3.b; CC.3.W.5;
CC.3.W.10

Read Fiction Books

Vocabulary CC.3.L.6
Expand Vocabulary Through
Wide Reading SG6–SG9

Reading CC.3.Rlit.5;
Read and Integrate CC.3.Rlit.10
Ideas SG8–SG9
☑ Plan and Monitor SG8–SG9
☑ Analyze Plot SG8–SG9

Day 4

Read and Comprehend

Academic Talk CC.3.Rlit.2, 5; CC.3.SL.4
Summarize Reading T22

Daily Spelling and Word Work CC.3.Rfou.3; CC.3.L.2;
☑ Practice T1m CC.3.L.2.f

Daily Grammar CC.3.W.5; CC.3.L.1; CC.3.L.1.a;
☑ Grammar and Writing T1o CC.3.L.2

Vocabulary Practice CC.3.L.6
☑ Share Word Knowledge T22

Reading CC.3.Rlit.10
Read a Story T23–T24

Comprehension CC.3.Rlit.3;
☑ Comprehend Plot CC.3.Rlit.5;
T23; T24 CC.3.Rlit.10
☑ Plan and Monitor T24

Fluency CC.3.Rfou.4.a, b
☑ Practice Expression, Accuracy, Rate T23

Power Writing T22 CC.3.W.10
Daily Writing Skills CC.3.W.3.a; CC.3.W.3.c;
☑ Develop a Plot Sequence T1q CC.3.W.3.d

Writing CC.3.W.10
Write About Characters T25

Writing Project: Realistic Fiction CC.3.W.3; CC.3.W.3.a;
☑ Revise; Edit and Proofread CC.3.W.3.b; CC.3.W.5;
T27c–T27d CC.3.W.10; CC.3.L.1; CC.3.L.1.a; CC.3.L.3

Read Fiction Books

Vocabulary CC.3.L.6
Expand Vocabulary Through
Wide Reading SG6–SG9

Reading CC.3.Rlit.5;
Read and Integrate CC.3.Rlit.10
Ideas SG8–SG9
☑ Plan and Monitor SG8–SG9
☑ Analyze Plot SG8–SG9

Day 5

Review and Apply

Academic Talk CC.3.Rlit.5; CC.3.SL.1;
Talk About "Those Shoes" T26 CC.3.SL.1.d; CC.3.SL.4

Daily Grammar CC.3.L.1; CC.3.L.1.a; CC.3.L.1.c; CC.3.L.2
☑ Review T1o

Vocabulary Practice CC.3.L.6
☑ Apply Word Knowledge T25a

Reading CC.3.Rlit.10
Reread a Story T11–T24

Comprehension CC.3.Rlit.5
☑ Comprehend Plot T26a

Fluency CC.3.Rfou.4.b
☑ Check Expression, Accuracy, and Rate T27

Power Writing T25a CC.3.W.10
Daily Writing Skills CC.3.W.3.a; CC.3.W.3.c;
☑ Develop a Plot Sequence T1q CC.3.W.3.d

Writing CC.3.W.10
Write About It T26

Writing Project: Realistic Fiction CC.3.W.3
☑ Publish and Present T27d

Read Fiction Books

Vocabulary CC.3.L.6
Expand Vocabulary Through
Wide Reading SG6–SG9

Reading CC.3.Rlit.2, 5, 10;
Connect Across Texts CC.3.SL.1.a
SG9

Writing CC.3.W.10
Choose a Writing Option
SG9

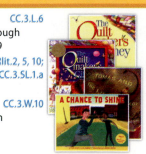

ASSESSMENT & RETEACHING

Assessment and Reteaching T27e–T27f
☑ Reading Comprehension Test A1.7–A1.8 CC.3.Rlit.5
☑ Reading Strategy Assessment CC.3.Rlit.10
SG1.30–SG1.31
☑ Oral Reading Assessment A1.4–A1.6 CC.3.Rfou.4
☑ Vocabulary Test A1.9–A1.10 CC.3.L.6

☑ Spelling Test: Short *a* and *o* and CC.3.Rfou.3;
and Commonly Misspelled CC.3.Rfou.3.c; CC.3.L.2;
Words T1l CC.3.L.2.e; CC.3.L.2.f
☑ Writing, Revising, and Editing Test CC.3.W.3; CC.3.W.3.a;
A1.11–A1.12 CC.3.W.3.c-d; CC.3.L.1.c; CC.3.L.2
Reteaching Masters RT1.1–RT1.3

Speaking and Listening

Option 1: Talk About Kind Acts

PROGRAM RESOURCES & MATERIALS

Speaking and Listening Teamwork Activities: Card 6

Teacher's Guide on NGReach.com

colored markers or crayons

Discuss Topics, Expressing Ideas Clearly	CC.3.SL.1
Add Visual Displays	CC.3.SL.5

Option 2: Being Responsible

"I can help you with that."

Display the prompt:

> Tell a partner about a time when you helped others. Tell the events in proper order and use words like *first, next,* and *last* to talk about what happened.

Recount an Experience	CC.3.SL.4

Language and Vocabulary

Key Words

action · difference · gift · kindness · need
plot · prediction · preview · problem · receive
solution · understand · value · want

Option 1: Vocabulary Games

NGReach.com **Online Vocabulary Games**

Acquire and Use Academic and Domain-Specific Words	CC.3.L.6

Option 2: My Vocabulary Notebook

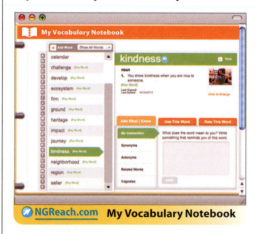

NGReach.com **My Vocabulary Notebook**

Have students expand word knowledge.

Under Add More Information > Use This Word > Write a Sentence, have students use the vocabulary word to write a sentence about helping others.

Acquire and Use Conversational, Academic, and Domain-Specific Words	CC.3.L.6

Writing

Option 1: Volunteer for Community Service

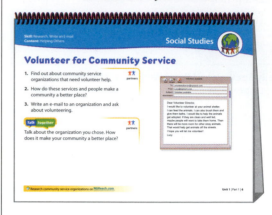

PROGRAM RESOURCES

Cross-Curricular Teamwork Activities: Card 6

Teacher's Guide on NGReach.com

Write over Shorter Time for Specific Purposes and Audiences	CC.3.W.10

Option 2: Write A Helping Story

PROGRAM RESOURCES

Digital Library: Key Word Image for *action*

Display the image and the writing prompt:

> Look at what the kids are doing in the photograph. Why are they doing this? What will happen next? Make up a story about what is happening.

Write Narratives	CC.3.W.3

= one student   = two students   = three or more students

Cross-Curricular

Option 1: Study Feet and Shoes 🏃🏃🏃

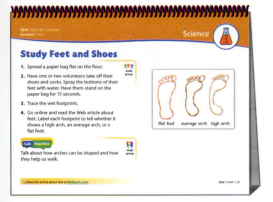

PROGRAM RESOURCES & MATERIALS

Cross-Curricular Teamwork Activities: Card 5

Student Resources Directory

Teacher's Guide on 🔵 NGReach.com

brown paper bags • spray bottles of water

Gather Information	CC.3.W.8

Option 2: What Size Is Your Shoe? 🏃🏃

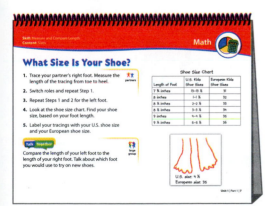

PROGRAM RESOURCES & MATERIALS

Cross-Curricular Teamwork Activities: Card 7

Teacher's Guide on 🔵 NGReach.com

ruler that shows inches

Reading

Option 1: Comprehension Coach 🏃

🔵 **NGReach.com**   **Comprehension Coach**

Read and Comprehend Literature	CC.3.Rlit.10
Read Orally with Accuracy and Appropriate Rate on Successive Readings	CC.3.Rfou.4.b

Option 2: Helping the Environment 🏃

🔵 **NGReach.com**   **Student Resources**

To read the article, have students go to Resources > Unit 1 > Learning Stations > Week 1 > Coastal Cleanup.

Have students read the online article and write a short summary of how Cammy helped clean up the environment.

Read and Comprehend Informational Text	CC.3.Rinf.10

Intervention

Phonics Games 🏃

🔵 **NGReach.com**   **Online Phonics Games**

Apply Phonics and Word Analysis Skills	CC.4.Rfou.3

For Reteaching Masters, see pages RT1.1–RT1.3.

Additional Resources

ESL Kit 🏃🏃🏃

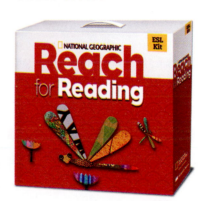

ESL Teacher's Edition pages T2–T27

OBJECTIVES

Thematic Connection: Individual Responsibility

Recognize High Frequency Words

Develop Phonological Awareness: Isolate Sounds

Associate Sounds and Spellings /ă/a; /ŏ/o

Blend Sounds to Decode Words

Teach   Day 1

PROGRAM RESOURCES

High Frequency Words:
  Teaching Master 1

Sound/Spelling Card 6

Word Builder: Transparency 11

Decodable Passage: *A Lap, a Cat Nap, and a Pal*

Practice Book, page 92

Reach into Phonics

Lesson 1, page T2

Lesson 3, pages T4–T5

High Frequency Words

Follow Lesson 1 to present High Frequency Words:

from	home	new	go	there

Short Vowel /ă/a

Follow Lesson 3. Use **Reading Routine 1** and **Sound/Spelling Card 6** to teach sounds and spellings /ă/a. Guide students through **Transparency 11**. Use **Reading Routine 3** to guide students as they read Decodable text.

*For **Reading Routine 1**, see Reach into Phonics, page vi.*

*For **Reading Routine 3**, see Reach into Phonics, page ix*

NGReach.com   **Word Builder: Transparency 11**

Teach   Day 2

PROGRAM RESOURCES

High Frequency Words:
  Teaching Master 2

Sound/Spelling Card 16

Word Builder: Transparency 12

Decodable Passage: *Jan Has Hot Dogs*

Practice Book, page 93

Reach into Phonics

Lesson 2, page T3

Lesson 4, pages T6–T7

High Frequency Words

Follow Lesson 2 to present High Frequency Words:

many	first	next	then	one

Short Vowel /ŏ/o

Follow Lesson 4. Use **Reading Routine 1** and **Sound/Spelling Card 16** to teach sounds and spellings /ŏ/o. Guide students through **Transparency 12**. Use **Reading Routine 3** to guide students as they read Decodable text.

*For **Reading Routine 1**, see Reach into Phonics, page vi.*

*For **Reading Routine 3**, see Reach into Phonics, page ix.*

NGReach.com   **Word Builder: Transparency 12**

👤 = one student   👤👤 = two students   👤👤👤 = three or more students

COMMON CORE STANDARDS

Use Conventional Spelling	CC.3.L.2.e
Use Spelling Patterns and Generalizations	CC.3.L.2.f
Read Irregularly Spelled Words	CC.3.Rfou.3.d

Oh, No! — Day 3 — Option 1

MATERIALS

index cards, 16 per pair of students • timer

Prepare

- Arrange two pairs of students in a group of four.
- Have each pair collaborate to write each word from the word bank below on a separate card and then write "Oh, no!" on the two remaining cards.

from	home	new	go	there	glad	cat
many	first	next	then	one	stop	hot

Play a Game

- Have groups shuffle all the cards, including the *Oh, no!* cards, and place them face down in a pile.
- Set a timer for 10 minutes. Players take turns selecting a card and reading it aloud to the group.
- If the player reads the word correctly, he or she keeps the card. If not, it goes back in the pile. Play then moves to the person on the right.
- If a student draws an "Oh, no!" card, all of his or her cards go back in the pile.
- When time is called, the player with the most cards wins.

Word Hunt — Day 3 — Option 2

PROGRAM RESOURCES
Sound/Spelling Cards 6, 16

MATERIALS
timer

Prepare

- Arrange students into groups of 3.
- **Display Sound/Spelling Cards 6** and **16**. Have students use them as a reference during their word hunt.

Play a Game

- Have groups go on a word hunt. Set a timer for 15 minutes. Have groups look in books and other classroom print materials for words with short a spelled *a* and short o spelled *o*.
- Have one group member assigned the role of recording the words.
- When time is called, have groups read their words. The group with the most words wins.

Word Scramble — Day 4

MATERIALS

index cards, 14 per student • timer

Prepare

- Have each partner write the vowels *a* and *o*, and the consonants *b, c, d, g, l, m, n, p, r, s, t,* and *x,* on a separate card.

Play a Game

- Set a timer for 5 minutes. Partner 1 arranges the letter cards into a word and reads the word. Partner 2 writes the word.
- The partners continue to make, read, and write words until time is up. At the end of 5 minutes, Partner 1 reads all the words.
- Have partners switch roles and repeat. The player that makes up the most words wins.

Word Sort — Day 5

PROGRAM RESOURCES
Sound/Spelling Cards 6, 16

MATERIALS
index cards, 16 per pair of students

Prepare

- Have partners work together to write each word from the word bank below on a separate card.
- Have partners place the 16 word cards face down.
- Set out **Sound/Spelling Cards 6** and **16**.

mask	hat	jam	camp	fan	brag	cab	dad
cost	hot	fox	drop	pond	hog	sob	nod

Play a Game

- Set a timer for five minutes. Have Partner 1 select a card, read it aloud, and sort it by placing it with the **Sound/Spelling Card** that has the same sound. Continue until time is called.
- Have Partner 2 award one point for each word that is sorted correctly.
- Have partners switch roles and repeat. The player with the most points wins.

OBJECTIVES

Thematic Connection: Individual Responsibility

☑ Spell Words with Short *a* and Short *o*
☑ Use Commonly Misspelled Words Correctly

SUGGESTED PACING

DAY 1	Spelling Pretest
DAY 2–4	Daily Practice Options
DAY 5	Spelling Test

Spelling Pretest	Day 1	

Spelling Test	Day 5	

Spelling Words

Use these words and sentences for the weekly Spelling Pretest and Spelling Test.

Words with Short *a* and Short *o*

1. action	Walking your dog is an **action** that shows responsibility.
2. bonds	We have strong **bonds** because we love one another.
3. chance	When you volunteer, you have a **chance** to help others.
4. confident	I am **confident** that we will do well on the test, because we took responsibility for studying every day.
5. doctor	A **doctor** is responsible for helping people who are ill.
6. example	Cleaning up your room is an **example** of being responsible at home.
7. follow	Will you line up behind me and **follow** me to the park where we will clean up litter?
8. grand	The kids in the hospital have a **grand** time when Ms. Simms brings her dog for a visit.
9. happen	The race to raise money for charity will **happen** soon.
10. humanity	**Humanity** is a word that stands for all people.
11. longing	Todd is **longing** to be a teacher when he grows up, because he loves teaching others.
12. outstanding	Mr. Taylor won an award for his **outstanding** service.
13. possible	Our bake sale will make it **possible** for the school band to buy new uniforms.
14. talent	If you have a **talent** like painting or singing, you can and should help other people learn new skills, too.
15. tasks	One of my **tasks** at the animal shelter is walking dogs.

Watch-Out Words

16. a while	I know you have volunteered at the shelter for a **while**.
17. awhile	I waited **awhile** before deciding to volunteer, too.
18. accept	I hope you'll **accept** my offer to help you.
19. except	I can help after school every day **except** on Mondays.

Short *a* and *o*	Day 2		Option 1

MATERIALS

index cards, 17 per pair of students

Teach

Display and read *bonds* and *grand*. Explain, stretching the vowel sounds slightly as you say the words: *Listen for the vowel sounds in these words:* graaand /a/; booonds /o/. *The short* a *in* grand *is spelled with the letter* a, *and the short* o *in* bonds *is spelled with* o.

Point to the vowels as you pronounce each word again, having students read them with you.

Prepare

Arrange students in pairs, and have partners collaborate to write each of the first 15 spelling words on a separate index card. Tell them to write the labels *Short a Words* and *Short o Words* on the remaining two cards.

Play a Game

- Have partners shuffle all the spelling words and stack them face down. Tell partners to place the two label cards face up on either side of the stack.
- Have Player 1 turn over the top card and say the spelling word aloud, listening for short *a* or short *o*. He or she places the word under the appropriate label card.
- Then have Player 2 take a turn, repeating the process. Play alternates between partners until cards are sorted.
- Direct students to check their word sorts and then to shuffle the cards together. Tell them to see how quickly they can sort under Short *a* and Short *o* again.

Apply Phonics Skills	CC.3.Rfou.3
Use Spelling Patterns and Generalizations	CC.3.L.2.f

Troublesome Words	Day 2		Option 2

Homophone Hints

- Have partners create drawings to help them remember the differences between each pair of Watch-Out Words.
- Before drawing, have partners use a dictionary to be sure they are illustrating the correct meaning.
- Have partners label each drawing with a sentence that uses the Watch-Out Word in context.

Please accept my gift, Aunt Maya.

Use Glossaries and Dictionaries	CC.3.L.4.d
Consult References	CC.3.L.2.g

Ⱥ = one student   ȺȺ = two students   ȺȺȺ = three or more students

Short *a* and *o* Syllables — Day 3 — Option 1

MATERIALS
index cards, 8 per pair of students

Teach
Display the words *action* and *longing* with a line between the syllables: *ac/tion*, *long/ing*. Say each word, emphasizing the short vowel sounds. Point to the first syllable in *action* and explain: *When a syllable ends with a consonant, the vowel is usually short.*

Prepare
- Display these syllabicated words: *hap/pen, con/fi/dent, hu/man/i/ty, bonds, tal/ent, pos/si/ble, tasks, doc/tor.*
- Have pairs of students collaborate to write each word on a separate card (showing syllable breaks) and then stack them face down.

Play a Game
- Have Player 1 pick and display a card. Partner 2 points to the syllable with *a* or *o* followed by a consonant, names the consonant, pronounces the word, and spells it aloud.
- Player 1 decides if Player 2 has pronounced and spelled the word correctly. If so, Partner 2 keeps the card. If not, the card goes to the bottom of the stack.
- Players switch roles and take turns playing until they have displayed all of the cards and spelled all of the words correctly. The partner with more cards wins.

Apply Phonics and Word Analysis Skills   CC.3.Rfou.3
Use Spelling Patterns and Generalizations   CC.3.L.2.f

What's Missing? — Day 4 — Option 1

MATERIALS
index cards, 15 per pair of students • scissors, one per pair

Prepare
- Have partners collaborate to write each of the first 15 spelling words on a separate index card. Tell partners to print the letters *a* and *o* on separate pieces of paper and cut them out so that each is on a small square of paper.
- On the back of each index card, have partners write a short phrase using the word and draw a blank line in place of the spelling for /*a*/ or /*o*/.

Play a Game
- Tell partners to shuffle the word cards and stack them with the phrases facing up. Have them place the small letter squares above the stack.
- Have Player 1 choose a card, read its phrase, and hold up the card with the *a* or the *o* to show the missing letter. Then have him or her say the word and spell it aloud. If correct, the student keeps the card.
- If a student misspells the word, his or her partner picks up the correct letter and respells the word. Have students confirm the spelling on the back of the card. Continue playing until all cards have been used.

Apply Phonics Skills   CC.3.Rfou.3
Use Spelling Patterns and Generalizations   CC.3.L.2.f

Trace Letter Shapes — Day 3 — Option 2

MATERIALS
markers, one per student

Visualize It
- Have students print each spelling word on a separate sheet of paper. Tell them to print letters far enough apart to allow tracing around each letter.
- After students outline each letter of the first word, say:
  1. Close your eyes and visualize the shape of the word.
  2. Look at the word again and name each letter.
  3. Read the word aloud softly.
  4. Close your eyes and visualize the word's shape again and then write the word on the back of the paper.
- Have students repeat the steps for each word.

Use Conventional Spelling   CC.3.L.2.e

Group Writing — Day 4 — Option 3

MATERIALS
colored pencils or markers

Write a Short Tale
- Arrange students in small groups and have each write a very short tale about a good deed or other act of individual responsibility, using five spelling words.
- Invite groups to illustrate their tales. Have them underline each spelling word, and suggest that students display their tales or compile them in a class book.

> My classmates had a *longing* to learn soccer. My dad had *talent* and was *confident* since he's an *outstanding* player. He volunteered to coach them. Wasn't that *action* a good deed?

Demonstrate Command of Spelling   CC.3.L.2

OBJECTIVES

Thematic Connection: Individual Responsibility

☑ Grammar: Use Concrete and Abstract Nouns

☑ Grammar: Use Common and Proper Nouns

COMMON CORE STANDARDS

Edit Writing	CC.3.W.5
Demonstrate Command of Grammar	CC.3.L.1
Explain the Function of Nouns	CC.3.L.1.a

Day 1

PROGRAM RESOURCES
Nouns: eVisual 1.2

MATERIALS
crayons, markers, or colored pencils for drawing

Teach the Rules

Use the suggestion on page T6 to introduce nouns. Then use **eVisual 1.2** to teach and provide examples.

> **Nouns**
>
> - A **noun** names a **person**, **animal**, **place**, or **thing**.
>
>   A **friend** needs you.
>
>   She has a **dog**.
>
>   She took it to the **park**.
>
>   The **leash** broke and he ran off.

🔵 NGReach.com   Nouns: eVisual 1.2

Play a Game 👥

Have partners play "Label It!" Explain:
- *First, draw a scene that includes pictures of persons, animals, places, and things.*
- *Then, trade drawings with a partner. Your partner will label your nouns and you will label your partner's nouns.*
- *When you are finished labeling, compare your drawings with another pair of students. The pair with more nouns wins.*

Differentiate

EL English Learners

ISSUE Students lack the English vocabulary to label nouns.

STRATEGY Create a chart of cognates. For example: *bicycle/bicicleta; family/familia; flower/flor.* Have students use the chart to label pictures and encourage them to add to the chart throughout the week.

English Nouns	Spanish Nouns
bicycle	bicicleta
family	familia
flower	flor

Day 2

PROGRAM RESOURCES
Common and Proper Nouns: eVisual 1.7

Teach the Rules

Use the suggestions on page T9 to introduce common and proper nouns and **eVisual 1.7** to teach the concept.

> **Common and Proper Nouns**
>
> - A **common noun** names any **person**, **animal**, **place**, or **thing**.
>
> - A **proper noun** names a particular **person**, **animal**, **place**, or **thing**.
>
> - All important words in a proper noun start with a <u>capital letter</u>.
>
>   Our **teacher** is worried.
>
>   The **hamster** is not in its **cage**.
>
>   Our **school** is a big **place**.
>
>   ---
>
>   **Ms. Sims** is our **teacher**.
>
>   **Hammy** is the class **pet**.
>
>   **Jana** and **Mik** find **Hammy**.
>
>   **Hill School** is a caring **place**.

🔵 NGReach.com   Common and Proper Nouns: eVisual 1.7

Generate Sentences 🧍

Prompt students to write sentences.
- Describe how you showed responsibility for a person or pet. Use a proper noun in the third position in your sentence.
- Write a sentence about people who help others. Use a common noun in the fifth position.
- What is one rule at your school? Use a proper noun in the second position. Use a common noun in the sixth position.

For **Writing Routine 3**, see page BP49.

Differentiate

SN Special Needs

ISSUE Students struggle to determine a word's position in a sentence.

STRATEGY Provide a numbered sample sentence. For example:

1 2 3 4 5 6
I helped Sarah with her homework.

🧍 = one student   👥 = two students   👥👥 = three or more students

Use Abstract Nouns — CC.3.L.1.c
Demonstrate Command of Capitalization — CC.3.L.2

Day 3

PROGRAM RESOURCES
Concrete and Abstract Nouns:
  eVisual 1.9
Game: Practice Master PM1.3

MATERIALS
paper clip or small object for game piece,
one per student

Teach the Rules
Use the suggestion on page T21 to introduce the concept of
abstract nouns. Use **eVisual 1.9** to teach and give examples.

Concrete and Abstract Nouns

• A **concrete noun** names something you can see, hear, smell, touch, or taste.	clouds thunder flowers kitten salt	crocodiles (see) drums (hear) spice (smell) scarf (touch) mint (taste)
• An **abstract noun** names something you can think about, but cannot see, hear, smell, touch, or taste	childhood beauty strength love courage	knowledge health weakness anger fear

NGReach.com Concrete and Abstract Nouns: eVisual 1.9

Play a Game 👤👤👤
Distribute **Practice Master
PM1.3**. Have small groups
play the game.

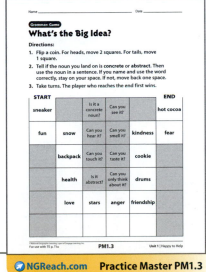

Grammar: Game
What's the Big Idea?
Directions:
1. Flip a coin. For heads, move 2 squares. For tails, move 1 square.
2. Tell if the noun you land on is concrete or abstract. Then use the noun in a sentence. If you name and use the word correctly, stay on your space. If not, move back one space.
3. Take turns. The player who reaches the end first wins.

START				END
sneaker		Is it a concrete noun?	Can you see it?	hot cocoa
fun	snow	Can you hear it?	Can you smell it?	kindness	fear
	backpack	Can you touch it?	Can you taste it?	cookie
	health	Is it abstract?	Can you only think about it?	drums
	love	stars	anger	friendship

PM1.3 Unit 1 | Happy to Help

NGReach.com Practice Master PM1.3

Differentiate

BL Below Level

ISSUE Students have difficulty with abstract nouns.
STRATEGY Give examples: *You can feel a hug, but not kindness itself.*
Have students use the hints in the gray areas of the game board.

Day 4

PROGRAM RESOURCES
Grammar and Writing: Practice
  Master PM1.4

Grammar and Writing 👤
Distribute **Practice
Master PM1.4**. Have students
use editing and proofreading
marks to correct errors
with nouns.

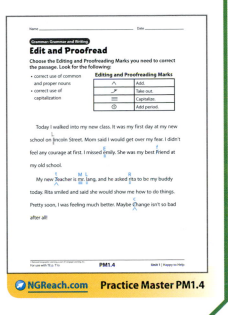

Grammar: Grammar and Writing
Edit and Proofread
Choose the Editing and Proofreading Marks you need to correct the passage. Look for the following:
• correct use of common and proper nouns
• correct use of capitalization

Editing and Proofreading Marks	
∧	Add.
✄	Take out.
≡	Capitalize.
⊙	Add period.

Today I walked into my new class. It was my first day at my new school on lincoln Street. Mom said I would get over my fear. I didn't feel any courage at first. I missed Emily. She was my best Friend at my old school.

My new Teacher is mr. lang, and he asked rita to be my buddy today. Rita smiled and said she would show me how to do things. Pretty soon, I was feeling much better. Maybe Change isn't so bad after all!

PM1.4 Unit 1 | Happy to Help

NGReach.com Practice Master PM1.4

Day 5

PROGRAM RESOURCES
Writing, Revising, and Editing Test:
  Assessment Masters A1.11–A1.12

MATERIALS
timer

Review and Assess 👤👤
Copy and display the chart and have partners copy it. Allow
partners ten minutes to complete the chart with explanations
and as many examples as they can. Then have each pair of
students trade charts with another pair, choose one example
word from each category, and write a sentence with each.

Type of Noun	Explanation	Examples
common noun		
proper noun		
concrete noun		
abstract noun		

☑ Administer the **Writing, Revising, and Editing Test**.

OBJECTIVES

Thematic Connection: Individual Responsibility

☑ **Develop a Plot Sequence**

COMMON CORE STANDARDS

Organize Events in a Sequence	CC.3.W.3.a
Use Temporal Words or Phrases	CC.3.W.3.c
Provide Closure	CC.3.W.3.d

Introduce Plot Sequence   Day 1

PROGRAM RESOURCES

Plot Sequence Passage: eVisual 1.3
Story Map #1: eVisual 1.4

Teach the Skill

Display **eVisual 1.3** and have volunteers read it aloud.

Plot Sequence Passage

It was a bright spring morning. Hakeem glanced up as the moving van pulled into the driveway. He already missed his friends back home. He wondered if they had forgotten about him already.

Hakeem's father opened up the back of the van. He motioned for Hakeem to grab a box labeled "Hakeem's books." As Hakeem reached for a big box, he heard a voice say, "Do you need help?"

Hakeem looked up. A boy his age stood in the driveway. The boy pointed at the box.

"Hey! You must like to read." the boy said. "I like to read, too. Let me help you with the box. Then we can look at some of your books!"

Hakeem smiled as the boy grabbed the other end of the heavy box. Maybe I can make new friends, after all, he thought.

🌐 **NGReach.com Plot Sequence**
Passage: eVisual 1.3   📋 **INTERACTIVE WHITEBOARD TIP:** Highlight the beginning, middle, and end.

Explain: *When you tell a story, you usually tell the events in the order they happen. The order in which things happen is called the sequence. Every story has a beginning, a middle, and an end.* Display **eVisual 1.4**.

Explain: *The writer of the story about Hakeem used a story map to plan the story's beginning, middle, and end.*

Story Map #1

Hakeem rides to his new house.	A boy offers to help Hakeem.	Hakeem and the boy share an interest.

🌐 **NGReach.com**
Story Map #1: eVisual 1.4   📋 **INTERACTIVE WHITEBOARD TIP:** Label the boxes '1,' '2,' and '3.'

Develop a Story Idea   Day 2   Option 1

PROGRAM RESOURCES

Story Map #2: eVisual 1.8

Introduce

Display and discuss **eVisual 1.8**. Explain that the 'Why' in this kind of story map is the problem to be solved.

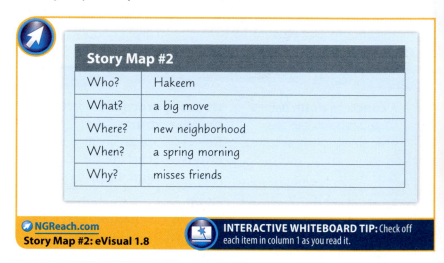

Story Map #2

Who?	Hakeem
What?	a big move
Where?	new neighborhood
When?	a spring morning
Why?	misses friends

🌐 **NGReach.com**
Story Map #2: eVisual 1.8   📋 **INTERACTIVE WHITEBOARD TIP:** Check off each item in column 1 as you read it.

Practice

Form groups of three. Have students brainstorm a story to write together. Then have the group work together to fill in a 5 W's story map for the story they could write. Have them save their story map for Day 3.

Develop a Story Idea   Day 2   Option 2

Practice

Copy and display the story map below. Have partners fill in the map for a story to write together. Have them save their story map for Day 3.

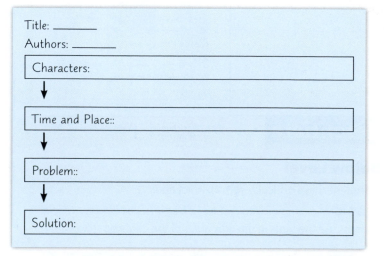

Title: _____
Authors: _____

Characters:

↓

Time and Place::

↓

Problem::

↓

Solution:

 ✶ = one student   ✶✶ = two students   ✶✶✶ = three or more students

Develop a Plot Sequence Day 3 Option 1

PROGRAM RESOURCES

Story Map #1: eVisual 1.4

Introduce

Display **eVisual 1.4: Story Map #1** from Day 1. Tell groups who worked together on Day 2 to think about what will happen during the beginning, middle, and end of the story they planned on Day 2.

Remind students that when they retell story events in the order in which they happen, it is called relating events *in sequence*.

Practice

Have students create and complete a story map like the one in **eVisual 1.4**. Tell groups to relate the story events in sequence as they fill in the chart.

If time allows, have students share their story maps in small groups. Have them save both story maps for use on Day 4.

Develop Your Story Day 4

Introduce

Tell students that they will use the story maps they created on Days 2 and 3 to write and illustrate their stories. Tell them to think carefully about how to end their story. Explain: *A good ending shows how the main character solved his or her problem or shows how the main character changes. It satisfies the reader.*

Tell students that as they develop their story, they can use words and phrases that help readers follow the sequence. Display examples such as: *In the beginning, It was a Monday when…, The next day, After that,* and *In the end.*

Practice

Suggest that students divide the tasks, with one or two students performing the role of writer and one student taking on the role as illustrator. As students write and illustrate, have them collaborate to see that the artwork fits the story as it evolves.

After each task has been accomplished, have students combine their art and writing and share them with another group or pair of students.

Develop a Plot Sequence Day 3 Option 2

PROGRAM RESOURCES

Story Map #1: eVisual 1.4

Introduce

Display **eVisual 1.4: Story Map #1** from Day 1. Remind students that when they develop a plot sequence, they list events in the order they happen.

Practice

Have partners who worked together on Day 2 use the story map they created on Day 2 to plan what will happen at the beginning, middle, and end of their story. Tell groups to relate the story events in sequence as they fill in the chart.

Have students fill out a story map like the one shown in **eVisual 1.4: Story Map #1**. If time allows, have students share their story maps with another pair of students.

Have partners save both of their story maps for use on Day 4.

Review and Assess Day 5

PROGRAM RESOURCES

Writing, Revising, and Editing Test:
 Assessment Masters A1.11–A1.12

Review the Skill

Have small groups discuss the kinds of story maps they used during the week. Tell them to choose the one they think helped them most.

Tell students to write a few sentences telling why they like that story map best. Then have them draw a blank copy of the story map they chose.

Mix up the groups so that students who worked in groups join with students who worked in pairs. Have students share their story map and sentences about it so that all students can see examples of all three kinds of story maps.

☑ Administer the **Writing, Revising and Editing Test**

OBJECTIVES
Thematic Connection: Individual Responsibility
Preview Content

PROGRAM RESOURCES
PRINT & TECHNOLOGY
Family Newsletter 1
Unit Concept Map: Practice Master PM1.1
TECHNOLOGY ONLY
Unit 1 Build Background Video

MATERIALS
markers and colored pencils

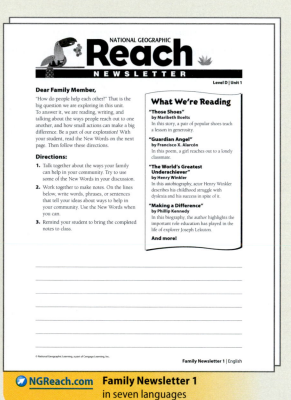

NGReach.com Family Newsletter 1
in seven languages

COMMON CORE STANDARDS
Speaking and Listening
Determine the Main Ideas and   CC.3.SL.2
Supporting Details of Information
Presented Visually and Orally in
Diverse Media

WARM-UP

Point to **Anthology** pages 2–3. Explain: *This photo shows a boy helping to fix a house.* Ask: *What are ways that you help at home? How do you help at school?*

Social Studies Background

1 Big Question Anthology page 2
Have a volunteer read aloud the Big Question. Explain that this unit is about helping others. Students will be reading about many ways that people's actions make a positive difference in other people's lives. Distribute **Family Newsletter 1**.

2 Share What You Know Anthology page 3
Activate prior knowledge: *What are ways to help someone?* Display **Student eEdition** page 3, read aloud the instructions, and distribute materials. Have students describe how their pictures show them helping someone.

3 Build Background Video
Set a purpose for viewing the video: *Watch the video to find out ways to help others.* Play the video and invite students to take notes. After viewing, discuss the video:
- *What are some examples of people helping others in the video?*
- *How do the images help support what the narrator says?*

Mini Lesson

Analyze the Message
Explain: *Videos can present important messages. A narrator makes key points and gives details about the message. Photos, recordings, interviews, dramatizations, graphics, and animation can support the message.* Replay the video and pause after details about helping classmates.

Think aloud: *The narrator and the images present ways to help others, like talking to a lonely person or carrying groceries for someone.* Replay video segments, pausing to have partners discuss how acts of responsibility, or kindness and respect, help others.

NGReach.com Build Background Video

Ask: *What is the main important idea of the video?* (Everyone can help others.) *What examples does the video show?*
Have students identify details that support the main idea.

Unit 1

Happy to Help

BIG Question
How do people help each other?

Share What You Know

Do it!

1. **Think** about the people you know. Who could use some help?
2. **Draw** yourself helping the person.
3. **Tell** the class your idea. How does it make you feel?

I can read to my little sister.

Build Background: Watch a video about helping.
🌐 **NGReach.com**

2

STUDENT TECHNOLOGY

e Student eEdition

🔍 Interactive Exploration

🌐 Resources

🌐 **NGReach.com**

Anthology
pages 2–3

Unit Projects

4 Introduce the Unit Concept Map

Review the Big Question. Ask students to flip through the unit, and prompt them to predict: *What do you think you will learn about helping others?* Responses should include specific examples from the unit.

Display the unit concept map using **Student eEdition** page 68, or provide a bulletin-board version of the concept map. Explain: *As you go through this unit, you will read about ways that people help others. Use the concept map to organize your answers to the Big Question.* Distribute **Practice Master PM1.1** and model how to fill in a concept map. Ask: *What ideas can we add from the video?*

Concept Map

How people help each other

5 Preview Unit Projects

Point out the projects, using **Student eEdition** page 69. Have students read the project options so they can think about which one they will choose.

Weekly Writing

Gather students' writing throughout the week:

✓ Daily Writing Skills Practice (T1p–T1q)
✓ Power Writing (T4, T6a, T10, T22, T25a)
✓ Writing (T6, T9, T21, T25, T26)
✓ Writing Project (T27a–T27d)

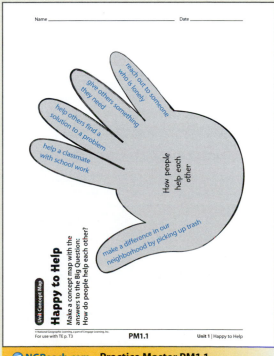

Name _____ Date _____

Happy to Help

Unit Concept Map

Make a concept map with the answers to the Big Question: How do people help each other?

- reach out to someone who is lonely
- give others something they need
- help others find a solution to a problem
- help a classmate with school work
- How people help each other
- make a difference in our neighborhood by picking up trash

© National Geographic Learning, a part of Cengage Learning, Inc.
For use with TE p. T3

PM1.1   Unit 1 | Happy to Help

🌐 **NGReach.com**   **Practice Master PM1.1**

OBJECTIVES

Thematic Connection: Individual Responsibility

☑ **Use Domain-Specific Words**

☑ **Comprehend Plot**

PROGRAM RESOURCES

PRINT & TECHNOLOGY

Family Newsletter 1

Story Map: Practice Master PM1.2

TECHNOLOGY ONLY

Sing with Me MP3

Digital Library: Key Word Images

My Vocabulary Notebook

Read Aloud: eVisual 1.1

Power Writing

Have students write as much as they can as well as they can in one minute about the word *gift*.

*For **Writing Routine 1**, see page BP47.*

COMMON CORE STANDARDS
Reading

Refer to Parts of Stories and Describe How Successive Parts Build	CC.3.Rlit.5
Read with Fluency to Support Comprehension	CC.3.Rfou.4

Writing

Write Over Shorter Time for Specific Tasks	CC.3.W.10

Speaking and Listening

Tell a Story	CC.3.SL.4

Language and Vocabulary

Determine Meaning of Words and Phrases	CC.3.L.4
Acquire and Use Academic and Domain-Specific Words, and Use Words that Signal Spatial and Temporal Relationships	CC.3.L.6

Academic Talk

① **Retell a Story** Anthology page 4

Read aloud the introduction and play the **Sing with Me Language Song**: "A Friend Helps Out." Explain: *After you read or hear a story, you can retell the most important parts of the story in your own words. To retell the chant, I will think about what happens in the beginning, middle, and end.*

Model retelling the story in the chant:
- *In the beginning, a puppy ran away.*
- *Later, the two friends searched for it.*
- *In the end, they found the lost puppy.*

Point out how the use of signal words and phrases such as *In the beginning, Later,* and *In the end* helped clarify the order of events. Then ask: *What other details from the song can you include in the retelling?* (the girls' names, where they found the puppy)

Say: *Now tell a story about a time that someone helped you.* Have students work in pairs. One partner tells an original story. The other partner listens carefully and then retells the story. Then have partners trade roles. Remind students to speak clearly and at an appropriate pace.

Social Studies Vocabulary

② **Key Words** ☑ Anthology page 5

Explain and model using **Vocabulary Routine 1** and the diagram on **Student eEdition** page 5 to learn the Key Words.

> **Key Words**
> action · difference · gift
> problem · receive · solution

- ***Pronounce the word** and point to the first picture:* **problem**.
- ***Rate the word.** Hold up your fingers to show how well you know the word. (1=very well; 2=a little; 3=not at all) Tell what you know about this word.*
- ***Define the word:** A* **problem** *is something that needs to be fixed or solved.*
- ***Elaborate:** Relate words to knowledge and experience: A broken bike can be a* **problem** *when you are trying to get home.*

*For **Vocabulary Routine 1**, see page BP34.*

*For more images of the Key Words, use the **Digital Library**.*

Have partners take turns repeating the routine for each word using page 5. Have each student add the words to **My Vocabulary Notebook**.

See **Differentiate**

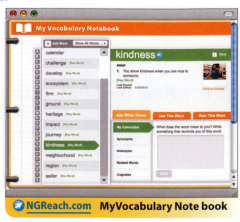

NGReach.com **MyVocabulary Note book**

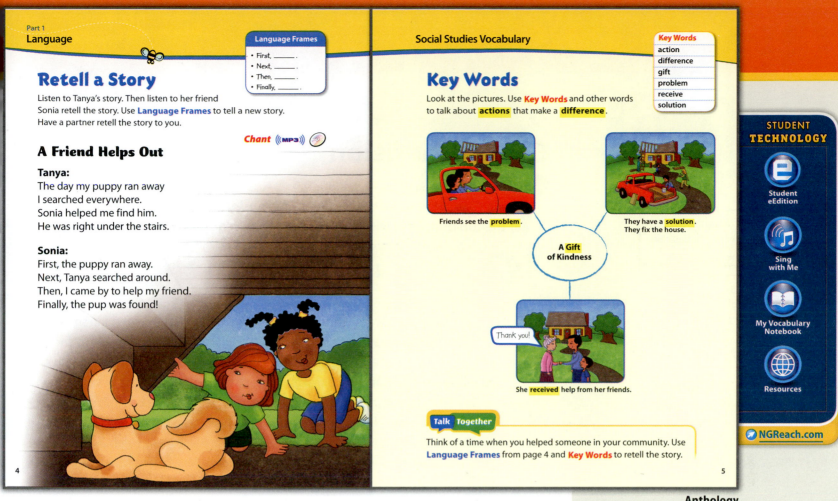

Language Frames
- First, _____ .
- Next, _____ .
- Then, _____ .
- Finally, _____ .

Retell a Story

Listen to Tanya's story. Then listen to her friend Sonia retell the story. Use **Language Frames** to tell a new story. Have a partner retell the story to you.

Chant ((MP3))

A Friend Helps Out

Tanya:
The day my puppy ran away
I searched everywhere.
Sonia helped me find him.
He was right under the stairs.

Sonia:
First, the puppy ran away.
Next, Tanya searched around.
Then, I came by to help my friend.
Finally, the pup was found!

4

Social Studies Vocabulary

Key Words
action
difference
gift
problem
receive
solution

Key Words

Look at the pictures. Use **Key Words** and other words to talk about **actions** that make a **difference**.

Friends see the **problem**.

They have a **solution**. They fix the house.

A Gift of Kindness

Thank you!

She **received** help from her friends.

Talk Together

Think of a time when you helped someone in your community. Use **Language Frames** from page 4 and **Key Words** to retell the story.

5

STUDENT TECHNOLOGY

Student eEdition

Sing with Me

My Vocabulary Notebook

Resources

NGReach.com

Anthology
pages 4–5

---

③ Talk Together   Anthology   page 5

Have one partner tell an original story about a time when he or she helped someone in their community. Then have the other partners retell the most important parts of the story. Then have partners change roles. Remind students that they can use signal words to make the order of events clear.

Provide an example that includes Key Words, such as: *Last week, Julia's neighbor had a big* **problem**. *She was in the hospital for a couple of days. She needed someone to care for her cats. Then Julia had a* **solution**. *She could take care of the cats until her neighbor got home. Julia's* **action** *made a big* **difference**.

Check & Reteach

OBJECTIVE: Use Domain-Specific Words ✓

As students tell and retell their stories, listen for correct usage of the Key Words. If students use words incorrectly, provide sentence frames for them to complete orally, such as:

- *Something you give to someone is called a _____ .* (**gift**)
- *When you get something from a person, you _____ it.* (**receive**)
- *When you make something better, you make a _____ .* (**difference**)

Differentiate

EL English Learners

ISSUE Students do not understand definitions.

STRATEGY Provide translations of the Key Words. Access **Family Newsletter 1** for translations in seven languages. Use cognates for Spanish speakers:

action/acción	*difference/diferencia*
problem/problema	*receive/recibir*
solution/solución	

BL Below Level

ISSUE Students cannot think of definitions for the Key Words to use for part 3 of the vocabulary routine.

STRATEGY Have students refer to the definitions in the **Picture Dictionary** on **Anthology** pages 605–627 to help them complete step 3 of the routine. They can use the sample sentences as models for how to elaborate.

Word Map

```
┌─────────────────────────────────┐
│        What It Means             │
│  the events that happen in the   │
│  beginning, the middle, and the  │
│  end of a story                  │
└─────────────────────────────────┘
              │
        ┌───────────┐
        │   Term     │
        │   plot     │
        └───────────┘
         /          \
┌──────────────┐  ┌──────────────┐
│   Example    │  │ Non-Example  │
│ First, she   │  │ The story    │
│ woke up.     │  │ takes        │
│ Then, she    │  │ place on a   │
│ brushed her  │  │ farm in Iowa.│
│ teeth.       │  │              │
│ Finally, she │  │              │
│ got dressed. │  │              │
└──────────────┘  └──────────────┘
```

Comprehension

④ Plot ☑ **Anthology** page 6

Use a Word Map to teach the literary term ***plot***. Then read aloud the information at the top of page 6. Display **eVisual 1.1** and read aloud "Tanya's Helping Hand."

 **Read Aloud**   **Realistic Fiction**

Tanya's Helping Hand

Last week, Tanya was playing in the park when she noticed something small and red on the bench. It was a wallet! A missing wallet would be a big **problem** for someone. Would Tanya be able to come up with a **solution**? She knew her quick and responsible **action** would make a huge **difference** to the wallet's owner.

"Look, Mom!" Tanya called. "Someone left this wallet on the bench."

"Let's look inside," her mom suggested. "Maybe we can find some information."

When Tanya opened the wallet, the first thing she saw was an identification card with a picture of her neighbor. "This wallet belongs to Mrs. Lorenz!" said Tanya. "She must be so worried about it!"

"Let's walk over to her house now and return it to her," Tanya's mom said.

Together, they walked to their neighbor's house. Miss Lorenz looked happy and relieved to see Tanya holding the red wallet.

"Thank you, Tanya," Mrs. Lorenz said. "This is the best **gift** I could ever **receive**!"

 **NGReach.com** **Read Aloud: eVisual 1.1**   **INTERACTIVE WHITEBOARD TIP:** Underline sentences or phrases that tell the main events of the plot.

⑤ Map and Talk **Anthology** page 6

After students read about how to make a story map, ask questions, such as: *What happens in the beginning of the story?* (Tanya finds a wallet.) *What happens at the end?* (Tanya returns the wallet to her neighbor.) Then ask students to suggest more events from the **Read Aloud** and determine where they belong in the map.

⑥ Talk Together **Anthology** page 6

Read aloud the instructions and explain that students may choose to create a story about a fictional character instead of a real person. Have students use **Practice Master PM1.2** to make story map for their partner's story.

Check & Reteach

OBJECTIVE: Comprehend Plot ☑

As students share their stories, listen for a clear beginning, middle, and end.

If students have difficulty presenting a clear plot, have them name the story problem.

Ask: *What do the characters do after that? What happens in the end?*

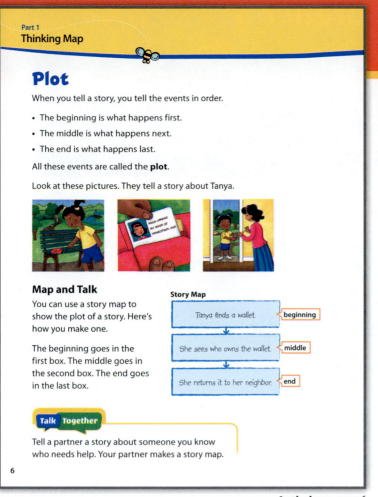

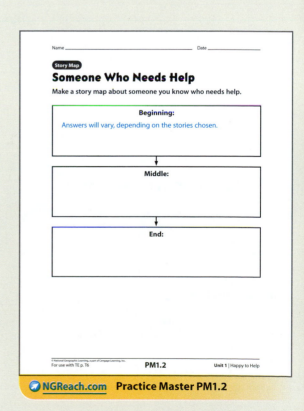

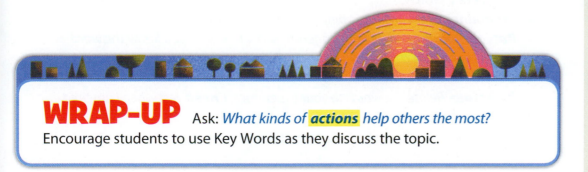

Plot

When you tell a story, you tell the events in order.

- The beginning is what happens first.
- The middle is what happens next.
- The end is what happens last.

All these events are called the **plot**.

Look at these pictures. They tell a story about Tanya.

Map and Talk

You can use a story map to show the plot of a story. Here's how you make one.

The beginning goes in the first box. The middle goes in the second box. The end goes in the last box.

Story Map

Tanya finds a wallet. — beginning

She sees who owns the wallet. — middle

She returns it to her neighbor. — end

Talk Together

Tell a partner a story about someone you know who needs help. Your partner makes a story map.

6

Anthology page 6

Writing

7 Write to Retell a Story

Introduce: *Now you will write a paragraph that retells the story your partner told about someone who needs help.* Model the process using "Tanya's Helping Hand."

Think Aloud	Write
First, I write what happens at the beginning of the story.	First, Tanya finds a lost wallet at the park.
Then I write about events that happen next.	Next, Tanya finds out that her neighbor owns the wallet.
Next, I write what happens last.	Finally, Tanya and her mother return the wallet.

For **Writing Routine 2**, see page BP48.

Have students use the story maps they prepared in **Talk Together** to retell their partner's story. Have students add their stories to their Weekly Writing folders.

WRAP-UP Ask: *What kinds of actions help others the most?*
Encourage students to use Key Words as they discuss the topic.

Name _____ Date _____

Story Map

Someone Who Needs Help

Make a story map about someone you know who needs help.

Beginning:
Answers will vary, depending on the stories chosen.

Middle:

End:

For use with TE p. T6   **PM1.2**   Unit 1 | Happy to Help

NGReach.com Practice Master PM1.2

OBJECTIVES

Thematic Connection: Individual Responsibility

☑ **Use Academic Words**

☑ **Preview and Predict to Comprehend Literature**

PROGRAM RESOURCES

PRINT & TECHNOLOGY

Family Newsletter 1

Unit Concept Map: Practice Master PM1.1

TECHNOLOGY ONLY

Digital Library: Key Word Images

My Vocabulary Notebook

MATERIALS

timer

Power Writing

Have students write as much as they can as well as they can in one minute about helping others.

*For **Writing Routine 1**, see page BP47.*

COMMON CORE STANDARDS

Reading
Read and Comprehend Literature   CC.3.Rlit.10
Read with Fluency to Support   CC.3.Rfou.4
   Comprehension
Writing
Write Over Shorter Time for   CC.3.W.10
   Specific Tasks
Speaking and Listening
Tell a Story   CC.3.SL.4
Language and Vocabulary
Determine Meaning of Words and   CC.3.L.4
   Phrases
Acquire and Use General Academic   CC.3.L.6
   Words, and Words that Signal
   Spatial and Temporal Relationships

WARM-UP

Ask: *What are some **problems** you can help fix?* Have partners brainstorm a list. (Possible response: I can pick up trash to make the playground clean.)

Academic Talk

❶ Tell a Story

Explain: *When you tell a story, be sure to include relevant facts and descriptive details. Always speak clearly and at an understandable pace that isn't too fast or too slow.*

Model telling a story, using words that signal beginning, middle, and end:

- *Early this morning, my dog Sasha chased a squirrel out of our yard.*
- *Then I jumped on my bike to chase Sasha, but both tires were flat. I ran down the street, but it was too late. There was no sign of Sasha!*
- *Finally, almost an hour later, my neighbor brought Sasha home. He had found Sasha in the park, barking at a squirrel in a tree.*

Have students create their own stories to go with the pictures on **Anthology** page 5. Organize a **Fishbowl** for students to share their stories.

- Have students on the inside tell their stories. Remind them to use signal words and to speak at an appropriate pace.
- Have students on the outside listen for a beginning, middle, and end, as well as signal words such as *first, next, then, last,* and *finally.*
- Have groups switch places and continue the activity.

*For **Fishbowl**, see page BP45.*

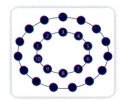

Fishbowl

Academic Vocabulary

❷ More Key Words   ☑ Anthology   page 7

Say: *Let's learn some more words to help us communicate effectively.* Explain and model using **Vocabulary Routine 1** and the images in the **Student eEdition** to learn the Key Words.

- ***Pronounce the word*** *and point to its picture:* **need** .
- ***Rate the word.*** *Hold up your fingers to show how well you know the word (1 = very well; 2 = a little; 3 = not at all). Tell what you know about this word.*
- ***Define the word:*** *When you* **need** *something, you must have it.*
- ***Elaborate.*** *Relate the words to your experience: I* **need** *rest when I am tired.*

*For **Vocabulary Routine 1**, see page BP34.*

*For more images of the Key Words, use the **Digital Library**.*

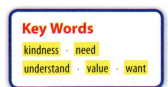

Key Words

kindness · need
understand · value · want

More Key Words

Use these words to talk about "Those Shoes" and "Guardian Angel."

kindness
(kĭnd-nus) *noun*

You show **kindness** when you are nice to someone. Teddy shows **kindness** to his mom.

need
(nēd) *verb*

When you **need** something, you cannot live without it. People **need** to drink water.

understand
(un-dur-**stand**) *verb*

When you **understand** something, you know what it means.

value
(**val**-yū) *verb*

When you **value** something, you care about it. The girl loves and **values** her dog.

want
(wawnt) *verb*

To **want** something is to hope or wish for it. He **wants** to get a guitar like this one.

Talk Together

Make a Vocabulary Example Chart for the **Key Words**. Then compare your chart with a partner's.

Word	Definition	My Example
Kindness	a nice act	My friend helped me fix my bike

Add words to My Vocabulary Notebook.
NGReach.com

7

STUDENT TECHNOLOGY

Student eEdition

My Vocabulary Notebook

Resources

NGReach.com

Anthology page 7

Have partners take turns repeating the routine for each word using page 7. Have each student add the words to **My Vocabulary Notebook**.

See **Differentiate**

3 Talk Together Anthology page 7
Have partners make and compare a Vocabulary Example Chart that includes entries for the five Key Words. Call on volunteers to share a word, its definition, and an example.

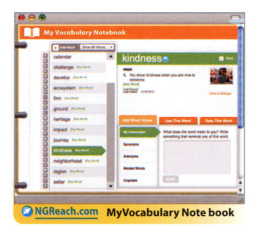

NGReach.com **MyVocabulary Note book**

Check & Reteach

OBJECTIVE: Use Academic Words ✓

As partners share from their Vocabulary Example Charts, listen for correct usage of the Key Words.

If students use words incorrectly, ask questions about the words. For example:

- *Which word means "to hope or wish for something"?* (**want**)
- *Which word describes being nice to someone?* (**kindness**)
- *Which word means "to care about something"?* (**value**)

Best Practices

Model Academic Language If student discussions reflect too much informal speech, model an academic conversation with or between two students. Then have the group echo the model to role-play academic discussions in small groups.

Differentiate

EL English Learners

ISSUE Students do not understand definitions.

STRATEGY Provide translations of the Key Words. Access **Family Newsletter 1** for translations in seven languages. Use a cognate for Spanish speakers: *value/valorar*

AL Above Level

ISSUE Students have already mastered understanding of words in the lesson.

STRATEGY Have students add related words for the Key Words to **My Vocabulary Notebook**, such as *kind* or *kindly* for the Key Word *kindness*. Then have students use some of the words in sentences.

Wordbench

prediction
pre-dic-tion
Other words in this family:
predict   predicting
Meaning: an idea about what
will happen in the future

Fluency

Practice Expression As partners read aloud Tanya's story, circulate and listen for expression.

Comprehension

④ Learn to Plan and Monitor ☑ Anthology pages 8–9

Use Wordbenches to teach the terms **preview** and **prediction**. Then project **Student eEdition** page 8 and read aloud the introduction. Model previewing and making a prediction about the illustration:

- *I read a store sign that says "Grocery."*
- *I see a man dropping his groceries.*
- *I read that the girl asks: "Can I help you?"*
- *I predict that the girl will help the man pick up his groceries.*

⑤ Talk Together   Anthology page 9

Read aloud the instructions on page 9. Guide students to preview the story by looking at the pictures and reading the title. Then work through the sample prediction. Explain that students can read on to confirm the prediction.

Ask: *How does making **predictions** help you understand the story?* (Possible response: It helps me decide on a purpose for reading.)

Have partners read the rest of "A Puppy Problem" together, pausing to make and confirm predictions. Circulate and monitor their conversations.

Check & Reteach

OBJECTIVE: Preview and Predict to Comprehend Literature ☑

As students make and confirm predictions, check that they base them on the text. If students have difficulty supporting predictions, point out the picture of the dog and reread the second and third paragraphs. Then prompt a text-based prediction: *What will happen next? What in the text or picture supports your **prediction**?* Have students review the remainder of the story and identify whether their prediction was correct.

Writing

⑥ Write About a Prediction

Introduce: *We are going to write sentences about the **predictions** we made while reading "A Puppy Problem."* Model the process.

Think Aloud	Write
*First, I write my **prediction** and what it is based on.*	I read that Tanya takes Riley to doggy school. I see Tanya holding Riley. I predict that the puppies in the class will make Riley bark more.
*Then I tell whether my **prediction** is correct or not.*	My **prediction** is not correct. Riley learns to bark less instead of more.

*For **Writing Routine 2**, see page BP48.*

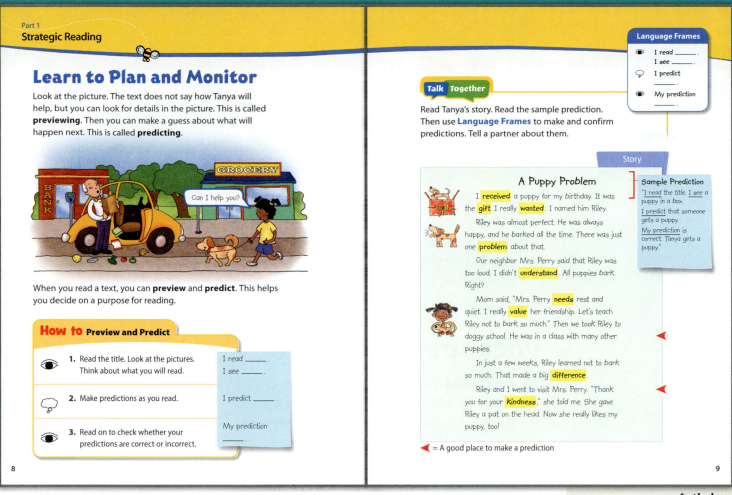

Have partners review the predictions they made together. Then have students work independently to write sentences about one of the predictions. Remind them to describe how they support their predictions. Students should use details from the story to confirm whether their predictions were correct.

Have students share their sentences with partners before adding their writing to their Weekly Writing folders.

See **Differentiate**

WRAP-UP Have small groups discuss the difference between *want* and *need*. Ask if they agree with the statement: "We don't need to have everything we want." Students can add ideas to their unit concept maps.

Daily Language Arts

Daily Spelling and Word Work ✓
Practice page T1l

Daily Grammar ✓
Point to the nouns "gift" and "Riley" on **Anthology** page 9. Then use page T1n to teach common and proper nouns.

Daily Writing Skills ✓
On **Anthology** page 9, point out the beginning, middle, and end of "A Puppy Problem." Then use page T1p to practice plot sequence.

Differentiate

BL Below Level

ISSUE Students have difficulty expressing their predictions in writing.

STRATEGY Display a word web. Label the circles: "I see," "I read," and "I predict." Guide students in filling out the web for the beginning of "A Puppy Problem." Model how to write the information from the web into sentence form.

OBJECTIVES
Thematic Connection: Individual Responsibility
☑ Comprehend Plot
☑ Preview and Predict to Comprehend Literature

PROGRAM RESOURCES
TECHNOLOGY ONLY
My Vocabulary Notebook
Read with Me: Selection Recordings:
    MP3 or CD1 Tracks 1–2

MATERIALS
timer • markers

Power Writing

Have students write as much as they can as well as they can in one minute about the word *kindness*.

*For **Writing Routine 1**, see page BP47.*

COMMON CORE STANDARDS
Reading
Recount Stories	CC.3.Rlit.2
Describe Characters and Explain Characters' Actions	CC.3.Rlit.3
Refer to Parts of Stories and Describe How Successive Parts Build	CC.3.Rlit.5
Read and Comprehend Literature	CC.3.Rlit.10
Read with Fluency to Support Comprehension	CC.3.Rfou.4
Read with Purpose and Understanding	CC.3.Rfou.4.a
Read Orally with Expression on Successive Readings	CC.3.Rfou.4.b

Writing
Write Over Shorter Time for Specific Tasks	CC.3.W.10

Speaking and Listening
Discuss Texts, Building on Others' Ideas and Expressing Ideas Clearly	CC.3.SL.1

Language and Vocabulary
Acquire and Use General Academic and Domain-Specific Words, and Use Words that Signal Spatial and Temporal Relationships	CC.3.L.6

WARM-UP

Say: *Think about a time when you **wanted** something that someone else had.*
Ask: *Did other people **understand** its **value**?* Ask volunteers to respond.
Explain that students will read about a boy who wants something very much.

Vocabulary Practice

❶ Expand Word Knowledge ☑
Students will practice Key Words by creating 4-Corner Posters. Use **Vocabulary Routine 2** to model how to make an organizer for the word ***kindness***.

- Write the word.
- Add a picture.
- Add a definition.
- Add a context sentence.

*For **Vocabulary Routine 2**, see page BP35.*

Key Words

action · difference · gift
kindness · need · plot
prediction · preview · problem
receive · solution · understand
value · want

Assign a Key Word to each set of partners. After students complete their organizers, have them add the context sentences to **My Vocabulary Notebook**.

Academic Talk

❷ Preview and Predict
REVIEW *What can you do when you **preview** a story?* (You look at the pictures and read the title before you read the story.) Remind students that when you make a prediction about a story, you guess what will happen.

Model: *On pages 10–11, I see a boy who looks like he **wants** the same shoes all the other children are wearing. I read that the title of the story is "Those Shoes." I predict that the boy will get a pair of those shoes by the end of the story.*

Display these Key Words: *gift, kindness, need, prediction, understand* and *want*. Have students use a **Think, Pair, Share** to make and share their predictions about "Those Shoes."

- Students preview the illustrations on **Anthology** pages 10–21 independently.
- Students form pairs and discuss their predictions. Encourage students to use Key Words and to convey ideas precisely.
- Individuals share their ideas with a person from another pair.

*For **Think, Pair, Share**, see page BP46.*

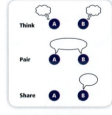

Think, Pair, Share

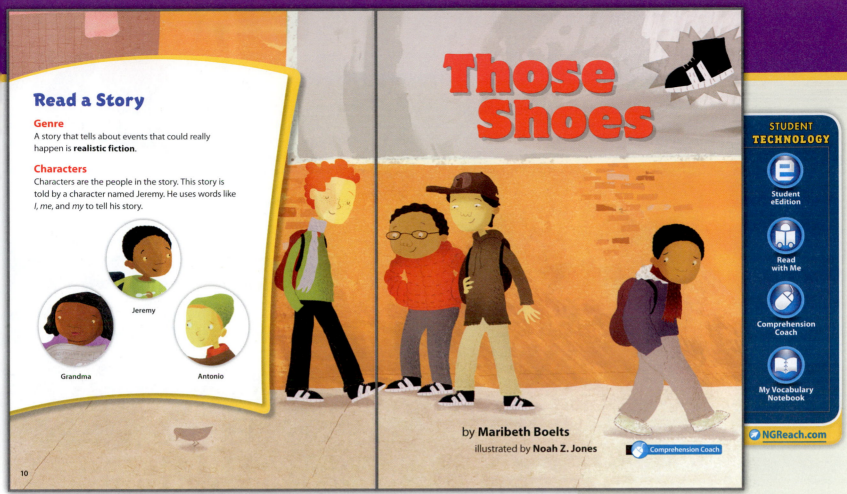

Read a Story

Genre
A story that tells about events that could really happen is **realistic fiction**.

Characters
Characters are the people in the story. This story is told by a character named Jeremy. He uses words like *I*, *me*, and *my* to tell his story.

Jeremy

Grandma

Antonio

10

Those Shoes

by **Maribeth Boelts**
illustrated by **Noah Z. Jones**

Comprehension Coach

STUDENT
TECHNOLOGY

Student
eEdition

Read
with Me

Comprehension
Coach

My Vocabulary
Notebook

NGReach.com

Reading

③ Read a Story Anthology pages 10–11

GENRE Have a volunteer read aloud the definition of realistic fiction. Elaborate: *This story is not about real people and events, but they seem like real people and events. Some details remind you of real life.*

CHARACTERS Ask a volunteer to read aloud the definition of characters. Reinforce the concept: *In this story, a boy named Jeremy tells about himself, his grandma, and his friend, Antonio.* Connect to the genre: *As we read the story, think about whether the characters and events seem real.*

SOCIAL STUDIES BACKGROUND Share information to build background: *Thrift stores are places that sell used clothes and shoes at lower prices.* Have students read pages 12–21. See **Differentiate**

Differentiate

BL Below Level

FRONTLOAD Preview and discuss the illustrations. Then read the story aloud and use the questions to build comprehension.

OL On Level

READ TOGETHER Have students whisper read the selection in pairs. Use the questions to build comprehension.

AL Above Level

READ INDEPENDENTLY As students read silently, have them take notes about the story's plot. Use the questions to build comprehension.

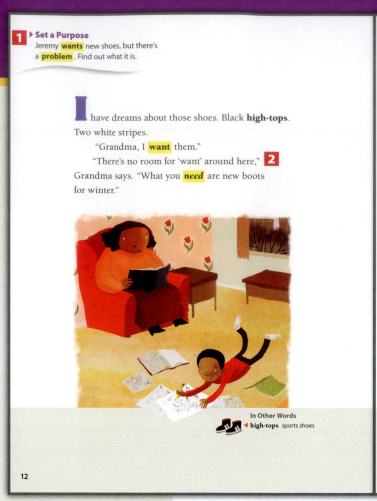

Anthology
pages 12–13

Fluency

Practice Expression, Accuracy, and Rate
As students read, monitor their expression, accuracy, and rate.

Read and Build Comprehension

1 Set a Purpose Have a volunteer read aloud the purpose statement. Then discuss what Jeremy's problem could be.

2 Analyze Character's Motive *Why does Grandma say, "There's no room for 'want' around here?"* (Grandma reminds Jeremy that they only have enough money to get what they **need**. They do not have extra money for things they **want** but don't really **need**.)

3 Describe Plot ☑ Guide students to tell what happens in the beginning of the story: *What does Jeremy want?* (black high-top shoes) *What are other kids coming to school wearing?* (the shoes he **wants**)

Differentiate

EL English Learners

ISSUE Students have difficulty identifying the story events.

STRATEGY Have students use the illustrations to retell key events in the story. Ask questions, such as: *What does this illustration show? What happens in the next picture?* Encourage them to use sequence words such as *First, Next, Then,* and *Last.*

BL Below Level

ISSUE Students have difficulty summarizing the important plot points in order.

STRATEGY Have students list the story events for the first two pages. Then have them summarize the plot so far using a language frame: Jeremy wants _____, but _____.

In Other Words
comes apart tears
guidance counselor adult who helps students solve **problems**

14

In Other Words
turn my back turn away

▶ **Before You Move On**
1. **Clarify** Why can't Jeremy get the new shoes he **wants**?
2. **Character's Motive** Why does Jeremy **want** the black high-tops?

Anthology
pages 14–15

4 **Predict** ☑ *Based on what you have read and seen so far, what* **prediction** *can you make about what will happen next?* (Possible response: I read that Jeremy wants black high-tops. I see blue high-tops on page 14. I predict that he will get blue shoes.) Remind students to read on in order to confirm or adjust their predictions.

5 **Analyze Character's Feelings** *How do you think Jeremy feels when the kids in class laugh?* (Possible response: He feels embarrassed and upset.) *How do you know?* (Possible response: In illustration, Jeremy's slumped shoulders make him look ashamed or embarrassed. At home, Jeremy stops himself from crying, which tells me he's trying not to show how hurt he feels.)

Differentiate

BL **Below Level**

ISSUE Students have trouble making predictions based on previewing the story.

STRATEGY Have students reread **Anthology** page 12. Ask: *Do you think Jeremy will get the shoes that he* **wants**? Guide students to look at the illustrations on page 13 and give details from the pictures to support their prediction.

EL **English Learners**

ISSUE Students struggle with words and phrases, such as *comes* apart on page 14.

STRATEGY Direct students' attention to **In Other Words** at the bottom of the page. Model how to reread the sentence from the text, substituting the phrase *comes apart* with the suggested statement: *tears*. Explain that students can use the **In Other Words** feature to find restatements for many unfamiliar words or phrases in each selection.

Best Practices

Link to Experience As students answer questions, prompt them to discover their own connections to characters, for example: *Almost all of Jeremy's classmates are laughing at him. Have you ever felt like people were laughing at you? How did it make you feel?*

Answers Before You Move On

1. **Clarify** Jeremy can't get the new shoes he **wants** because his Grandma only has enough money to pay for things he **needs**.
2. **Character's Motive** Jeremy **wants** the black high-tops because many of his friends have them. He wants to be like the other kids.

Week 1 | Day 3 T14–15

1 ▶ Predict
What will Jeremy do to get the new black shoes?

On Saturday Grandma says, "Let's **check out** those shoes you're wanting so much. I got a little bit of money **set aside**. It might be enough—**you never know**."

In Other Words
check out look at
set aside saved
you never know you might be surprised

16

At the shoe store, Grandma turns those shoes over. She **checks the price**. When she sees it, she sits down **heavy**.

"Maybe they wrote it down wrong," I say. Grandma shakes her head.

In Other Words
checks the price looks to see how much the shoes cost
heavy in a sad way

17

Anthology
pages 16–17

Mini Lesson

Analyze Characters

Introduce the concept: *You can learn about characters by finding examples of what they say and do. They give clues about characters' traits and feelings.*

Project **Student eEdition** page 12 and remind students that the story is told from Jeremy's point of view. Model how to analyze the character's feelings: *Jeremy says, "I have dreams about those shoes." This shows that Jeremy really* **wants** *a special pair of shoes. He thinks about them so much that he even dreams about them at night.*

Point out the following on page 13: "I was always the fastest runner before those shoes came along." Ask: *What do Jeremy's words tell you about him and his feelings?* (Jeremy is fast, but he worries that the shoes make others faster.)

To check understanding, ask students how Jeremy feels on page 15 when he turns his back and explains, "I'm not going to cry about any dumb shoes."

Then have partners find examples on **Anthology** pages 12–17 of what Grandma says or does and then tell how she thinks or feels, for example:
* page 12: *"There's no room for 'want' around here"*
* page 15: *"How kind of Mr. Alfrey"*
* page 17: *Grandma shakes her head*

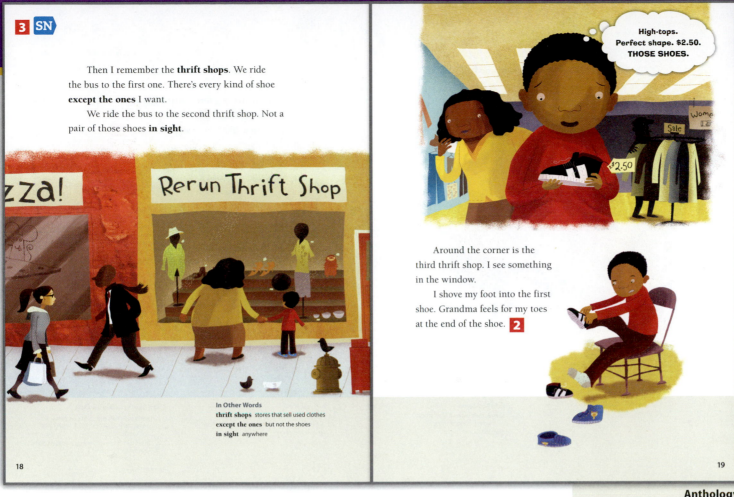

Then I remember the **thrift shops**. We ride the bus to the first one. There's every kind of shoe **except the ones** I want.

We ride the bus to the second thrift shop. Not a pair of those shoes **in sight**.

Around the corner is the third thrift shop. I see something in the window.

I shove my foot into the first shoe. Grandma feels for my toes at the end of the shoe. **2**

In Other Words
thrift shops stores that sell used clothes
except the ones but not the shoes
in sight anywhere

18

19

Anthology
pages 18–19

Read and Build Comprehension

1 Predict ☑ Read aloud the predict question on page 16 and ask: *What do you see in the pictures?* (Possible response: I see Grandma looking at the newspaper.) *What do you think Jeremy will do?* (Possible response: I predict Jeremy will find a sale in the newspaper, so they can afford the shoes.) Remind students to read on to find out more.

2 Analyze Character's Feelings *Study the illustrations on page 19. How is Jeremy feeling?* (Possible response: He feels hopeful when first holds the shoe, but he becomes frustrated when he tries to put it on.)

3 Confirm Predictions ☑ Have students confirm predictions they have made so far. Mention that they may need to read on or revise their predictions.

Differentiate

SN Special Needs

ISSUE Students have trouble keeping track of their predictions.

STRATEGY Have students write their predictions on self-stick notes. After finishing each page, have them review the notes to see if any of their predictions have been confirmed.

AL Above Level

ISSUE Students read so quickly that they miss details to confirm their predictions.

STRATEGY Have students pause at regular intervals to check their predictions using a two-column note-taking technique. In the left column, have students record their predictions. In the right column, have them record details from the story about the prediction. Have students place a check mark by predictions that have been confirmed.

Best Practices

Link to Experience As students make predictions, prompt them to think about how their own experiences are similar to characters' experiences. Ask questions such as:

- *Have you ever **wanted** something as much as Jeremy **wants** the shoes?*
- *Did you have to save up money to buy it?*
- *Do you know any ways to get something at a lower price?*
- *What could Jeremy do that has worked for you?*

"Oh, Jeremy," she says. "I can't **spend good money** on shoes that **don't fit**."

"They're okay," I say, curling my toes. Then I buy them with my own money.

In Other Words
spend good money use money I worked so hard to save
don't fit are too small

20

A few days later, Grandma puts a new pair of snow boots in my closet. She doesn't say a word about my **too-big feet shuffling around in my too-small shoes**. **1**

"Sometimes shoes **stretch**," I say. **2**

In Other Words
too-big feet shuffling around in my too-small shoes shoes that are too small
stretch get bigger

▶ **Before You Move On**
1. **Confirm Prediction** What **actions** did Jeremy take to get the black shoes? Was your prediction correct?
2. **Character** How do Jeremy's **actions** show what kind of person he is?

Anthology
pages 20–21

Read and Build Comprehension   Anthology pages 20–21

1 **Analyze Character's Motives** *Why doesn't Grandma say anything about Jeremy's too-small shoes?* (She knows how much he **wants** them.)

2 **Describe Plot** ☑ Guide students to tell what happens in the middle of the story: *What does Jeremy find at a thrift store?* (the shoes) *What happens next?* (Jeremy buys the shoes even though they are too small.) *Then what happens?* (Jeremy begins to accept that the shoes he bought are too small.)

Check & Reteach

OBJECTIVE: **Comprehend Plot** ☑

Ask: *What event happens a few days after Jeremy buys his shoes?* (Possible response: Grandma buys Jeremy a pair of snow boots that he **needs**.)

If students can't recall or identify key events, prompt: *How does Grandma help Jeremy get shoes that fit?* (She buys him new boots.) Provide sentence frames for students to complete as they describe the plot: At first, _____. Later _____. After that, _____.

OBJECTIVE: **Preview and Predict to Comprehend Literature** ☑

Have students explain how they previewed the text and illustrations to make predictions. If students have difficulty, reread page 21 and ask: *What will Jeremy do next?* (Possible response: He will wear the boots that fit.) Draw out details: *What clues from the text or illustrations helped you make that **prediction**?* (Possible response: Jeremy calls his feet "too-big.") Remind students to confirm their predictions as they read on.

Answers **Before You Move On**

1. **Confirm Prediction** ☑ Jeremy finds the shoes at a thrift store and buys them even though they are too small. He tries to stretch them so they will fit. Answers about predictions will vary.
2. **Character** Jeremy's **actions** show that he is very determined to have the same shoes as the other kids.

Writing

④ Write a Prediction

REVIEW Ask: *What is a* **prediction**? (a guess about what will happen in a story) Explain that you can make a prediction based on:

- what you already read in the first part of the story
- previewing the text and illustrations in rest of the story
- what you know about a character.

Introduce the activity: *Now, we will use what we know to write a prediction about the rest of the story.* Model how to write a prediction about what Grandma will do next in the story.

Think Aloud	Write
First, I write some things I know about Grandma's character.	I read that Grandma takes Jeremy to four stores to find the shoes. This shows that she is hopeful and **wants** to help Jeremy get his shoes.
I write a **prediction** *about what Grandma will do.*	I predict that Grandma will find a way to buy the shoes for Jeremy as a surprise.
Then I describe how I can find out whether the **prediction** *is correct.*	I will read the rest of the story to find out whether Grandma buys Jeremy the shoes.

*For **Writing Routine 2**, see page BP48.*

Have students write a prediction about something that Jeremy will do or learn at the end of the story. Remind them to support their predictions using details about the plot or his character from the text. Have students add their sentences to their Weekly Writing folders.

See **Differentiate**

WRAP-UP Have student groups discuss stories they've read, heard, or seen about a problem someone needs to solve. Then ask: *How are the characters similar to the characters in this story?*

Daily Language Arts

Spelling and Word Work ✔
Practice page T1m

Daily Grammar ✔
Reread the first sentence of "Those Shoes" on **Anthology** page 12. Point out that "shoes" is a concrete noun because it is something you can touch or feel. Then use page T1o to teach the differences between concrete and abstract nouns.

Daily Writing Skills ✔
Point out the text on **Anthology** page 12 and explain that these events take place in the beginning of the story. Then use page T1q to practice plot sequence.

Differentiate

EL English Learners

ISSUE Students lack the language skills to write predictions.

STRATEGY Provide sentence frames: I read that _____. I predict that next, _____. To check this **prediction**, I can _____.

AL Above Level

ISSUE Students satisfy the minimum requirement for the assignment.

STRATEGY Challenge students to add details and use Key Words in their sentences.

OBJECTIVES

Thematic Connection: Individual Responsibility

☑ Comprehend Plot

☑ Preview and Predict to Comprehend Literature

PROGRAM RESOURCES

PRINT & TECHNOLOGY

Unit Concept Map: Practice Master PM1.1

TECHNOLOGY ONLY

My Vocabulary Notebook

Read with Me: Selection Recordings: MP3 or CD 1 Track 3

Comprehension Coach

Power Writing

Have students write as much as they can as well as they can in one minute about the word *value*.

For **Writing Routine 1**, see page BP47.

COMMON CORE STANDARDS

Reading

Recount Stories	CC.3.Rlit.2
Describe Characters and Explain Characters' Actions	CC.3.Rlit.3
Refer to Parts of Stories and Describe How Successive Parts Build	CC.3.Rlit.5
Read and Comprehend Literature	CC.3.Rlit.10
Read with Purpose and Understanding	CC.3.Rfou.4.a
Read Orally with Expression on Successive Readings	CC.3.Rfou.4.b

Writing

Write Over Shorter Time for Specific Purposes	CC.3.W.10

Speaking and Listening

Tell a Story	CC.3.SL.4

Language and Vocabulary

Acquire and Use Academic and Domain-Specific Words, and Use Words that Signal Spatial and Temporal Relationships	CC.3.L.6

WARM-UP

Ask: *What act of* **kindness** *have you* **received** *from someone else? How did the person's* **gift** *make you feel?* (Possible response: I **valued** my sister's help getting ready for my big test. I was thankful she took the time to help me.)

Vocabulary Practice

❶ Share Word Knowledge ☑

REVIEW Have students use the 4-Corner Posters they made on Day 3. Review what the organizers show.

Group each student with a partner who studied a different Key Word. Have partners follow **Vocabulary Routine 3**.

- Have partners take turns reading their organizers.
- Encourage partners to talk about how the pictures show the meanings of the Key Words.
- Have partners create sentences using both Key Words.
- Have each student add the sentences to **My Vocabulary Notebook**.

For **Vocabulary Routine 3**, see page BP36.

> **Key Words**
>
> action · difference · gift
> kindness · need · plot
> prediction · preview · problem
> receive · solution · understand
> value · want

Academic Talk

❷ Summarize Reading

REVIEW Remind students: *When you summarize the* **plot** *of a story, you tell the most important story events in the order they happened. Think about what happens at the beginning, middle, and end of the story you have read so far.*

Write these Key Words: *action, need, understand, value, want.* Use a **Fishbowl** to help students summarize what they have read so far in "Those Shoes." Remind students to use Key Words as they summarize.

- Have students on the inside summarize pages 10–15.
- Have students on the outside listen for Key Words and the most important events.
- Have groups change roles and positions. The new inside group summarizes pages 16–21.

For **Fishbowl**, see page BP45.

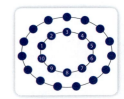

Fishbowl

Anthology
pages 22–23

Reading

3 Read and Build Comprehension

1 Predict ✓ Read aloud the predict question. Have students preview the illustrations and review what they have read in order to make their predictions. (Possible response: I see that Antonio needs new shoes. I read that Jeremy thinks, "I'm not going to do it!" I predict that Jeremy will give Antonio his too-small shoes. I will read on to find out what happens.)

2 Analyze Character's Motives *Based on what you know about Jeremy, why does he run after ringing Antonio's doorbell?* (Possible responses: I know that Jeremy is too proud to talk about how he feels, so I think he doesn't want to explain why he is giving Antonio a gift .)

Differentiate

EL English Learners

ISSUE Students do not understand the term *glanced*.

STRATEGY Provide a restatement and demonstration. Explain that Jeremy *looks quickly* at Antonio's shoes. Model how to glance at someone's shoes.

AL Above Level

ISSUE Students forget to check for confirmation of their predictions.

STRATEGY Have students review their predictions. If the prediction is not correct, have students revise their predictions based on new story events.

Fluency

Practice Expression, Accuracy, Rate As students read, monitor their expression, accuracy, and rate.

At school, I feel happy when I look at Antonio's face and mad when I look at my Mr. Alfrey shoes.

Later, snow is everywhere.
Then I remember what I have in my backpack. New black boots.

24

Standing in line to go to recess, Antonio leans forward.
"Thanks," he says.
I smile and give him a **nudge**. "Let's race!" ❖ **1** **2**

In Other Words
nudge friendly push

▶ **Before You Move On**
1. **Confirm Prediction** What did you think Jeremy would do with the small shoes? Was your prediction correct?
2. **Character** How does Jeremy help Antonio? How do you think Jeremy feels about this?

Anthology
pages 24–25

Read and Build Comprehension

1 **Analyze Character's Motives** *Why does Jeremy ask Antonio to race?* (Possible response: to make friends, to show he can still run fast in his boots)

2 **Confirm Predictions** ☑ Have students check their Weekly Writing folders for their predictions about what Jeremy would learn or do at the end of the story. Ask: *Was your prediction correct?* (Possible response: My prediction wasn't correct. Jeremy did not find a way to buy the shoes he wanted.)

Check & Reteach
OBJECTIVE: Comprehend Plot ☑

Check for accurate responses to all of the comprehension questions about plot.
If students have difficulty, ask questions about story events: *What happens after Jeremy notices that Antonio's shoes are falling apart? What do Jeremy and Antonio do at the end of the story?*

OBJECTIVE: Preview and Predict to Comprehend Literature ☑

As students make and confirm predictions, listen for evidence that they have previewed and reviewed the text and illustrations.
If students have difficulty, ask them to restate a prediction they made while reading the story. Have them point to illustrations and story clues that helped them make the prediction. Then have them point to evidence that helped them confirm or revise the prediction.

Answers Before You Move On

1. **Confirm Prediction** ☑ Answers about predictions may vary. (Possible response: My prediction was correct. Jeremy did give his too-small shoes to Antonio.)
2. **Character** Jeremy gives Antonio something Antonio needs—new shoes. Jeremy is happy that he can do something nice for Antonio.

Writing

⑤ Write About Characters

REVIEW Ask: *How do you learn about characters in a story?* (Possible response: by considering what the characters say and do)

Introduce the activity: *Today we will write a paragraph that describes one of the main characters in "Those Shoes."*

Explain: *When you describe a character, ask yourself:*
- *What does the person* <mark>want</mark>, <mark>need</mark>, *and* <mark>value</mark>?
- *What does the character do and say?*
- *What words best describe what the character is like?*

Display **Student eEdition** pages 12–13 and model writing about the character of Grandma:

Think Aloud	Write
First, I describe Grandma's character.	Grandma is thoughtful and caring.
Next, I give examples that support my description of Grandma.	Grandma thinks about what her grandson <mark>needs</mark>, like warm snow boots for winter.

Have students suggest additional sentences that support your description of Grandma. (Possible response: She saves money to buy Jeremy some shoes.)

For **Writing Routine 2**, *see page BP48.*

Have students work independently to write a description of Jeremy. Remind them to support their descriptions with details from the text. Then have students compare their descriptions before adding them to their Weekly Writing folders.

See **Differentiate**

WRAP-UP Remind students that the boy in "Those Shoes" gives his too-small shoes to someone in need. Ask: *In your reading today, were you reminded of a time you helped someone in need? How did the author help you* <mark>understand</mark> *how it feels to help others?* Have students add ideas to their unit concept maps.

Daily Language Arts

Daily Spelling and Word Work ☑
Practice page T1m

Daily Grammar ☑
Have students find proper nouns on **Anthology** page 15. Then use page T1o to practice using nouns.

Daily Writing Skills ☑
Point out the text on **Anthology** pages 24–25 and explain that these events take place at the end of the story. Then use page T1q to practice using plot sequence.

Differentiate

SN Special Needs

ISSUE Students have difficulty writing coherent sentences.

STRATEGY Invite students to write their descriptions of Jeremy using words and phrases. Then have students work with partners to revise the descriptions into complete sentences.

EL English Learners

ISSUE Students lack the vocabulary to describe the character.

STRATEGY Have partners use translations tools and English dictionaries to brainstorm a list of adjectives that describe Jeremy. Then provide sentence frames to help them use the adjectives: Jeremy is _____. When he _____, it shows that he is a _____ person.

OBJECTIVES

Thematic Connection: Individual Responsibility

☑ Comprehend Plot

☑ Read with Fluency

PROGRAM RESOURCES

PRINT & TECHNOLOGY

Unit Concept Map: Practice Master PM1.1

Test-Taking Strategy Practice: Practice Master PM1.5

Story Map: Practice Master PM1.6

Fluency Practice: Practice Master PM1.7

TECHNOLOGY ONLY

Online Vocabulary Games

Comprehension Coach

Read with Me: Fluency Models: MP3 or CD 1 Track 1

MATERIALS

timer

Power Writing

Have students write as much as they can as well as they can in one minute about the word *solution*.

*For **Writing Routine 1**, see page BP47.*

COMMON CORE STANDARDS

Reading

Refer to Parts of Stories and Describe How Successive Parts Build	CC.3.Rlit.5
Read and Comprehend Literature	CC.3.Rlit.10
Read Orally with Expression on Successive Readings	CC.3.Rfou.4.b

Writing

Write Over Shorter Time for Specific Purposes	CC.3.W.10

Speaking and Listening

Discuss Texts, Building on Others' Ideas and Expressing Ideas Clearly	CC.3.SL.1
Explain Ideas and Understanding	CC.3.SL.1.d
Report on a Topic	CC.3.SL.4

Language and Vocabulary

Acquire and Use General Academic and Domain-Specific Words, and Use Words that Signal Spatial and Temporal Relationships	CC.3.L.6

WARM-UP

Display the Key Words. Then set a timer for one minute and have students quickly write sentences about "Those Shoes" that use one or two Key Words. Have pairs share their favorite sentences.

Vocabulary Review

❶ Apply Word Knowledge ☑

Write: ***plot***, ***prediction***, ***preview***. Point out the other Key Words on **Student eEdition** page 26. Then have students apply their knowledge of the Key Words to create and perform a Multiple Key Word Skit. Explain:

- *You will work together with a small group.*
- *I will give each group a list of five Key Words.*
- *Your group will brainstorm how the words relate to each other and then create a skit that includes all the words.*
- *The groups will take turns presenting their skits while people in the audience listen for the five Key Words.*
- *After all the groups present their skits, we will give awards for the skits that are the most original, most humorous, or use the most Key Words accurately.*

Have students work together to plan and present their skits. Encourage students to be creative, reminding them that their skits do not have to realistic.

*For **More Vocabulary Routines**, see pages BP41–BP43.*

For additional practice, have students play the **Online Vocabulary Games** in pairs or individually.

Key Words

action · difference · gift · kindness
need · plot · prediction · preview
problem · receive · solution · understand
value · want

NGReach.com **Online Vocabulary Games**

Part 1
Think and Respond

Talk About It

Key Words

action	receive
difference	solution
gift	understand
kindness	value
need	want
problem	

1. Name two **realistic** events that happen in the story.

   One realistic event in the story is _____.
   _____ was also like real life.

2. Listen to a partner's story about a friend. Then **retell the story**.

   First, _____. Next, _____. Then, _____. Finally, _____.

3. Name one thing that you **want** and one thing that you **need**. What is the **difference**?

   I want _____. I need _____.
   When you want something, _____. When you need something, _____.

Learn test-taking strategies.
🌐 NGReach.com

Write About It ✏️

Imagine you are Antonio. Write a sentence to tell how you felt when you **received** Jeremy's **gift**. Use **Key Words**.

> When Jeremy gave me the shoes, I felt _____ because _____.

26

Anthology page 26

STUDENT TECHNOLOGY

- Student eEdition
- Comprehension Coach
- Fluency Model
- Assessment

🌐 NGReach.com

Academic Talk

2 Talk About It Anthology page 26

Have partners use the Key Words as they discuss the **Talk About It** questions on **Student eEdition** page 26. Remind students to use signal words *First, Next, Then,* and *Finally* when they retell the plot events for question 2.

Then use the test-taking strategy lesson from **NGReach.com** and **Practice Master PM1.5** to ask more questions about the selection.

Writing

3 Write About It Anthology page 26

Read aloud the directions on page 26. Point out the sentence frame and remind students that it includes the pronouns *me* and *I* because it is written from Antonio's point of view.

Model using Key Words as you write sentences:

- *When Jeremy gave me the shoes, I felt thankful because I really* **needed** *a new pair of shoes.*
- *When Jeremy gave me the shoes, I felt excited because I* **wanted** *a pair of black high-tops with white stripes.*

Have students add their sentences to their Weekly Writing folders.

Daily Language Arts

Daily Spelling and Word Work ☑️
Test page T1l

Daily Grammar ☑️
Point out a proper noun and a common noun in the last sentence on **Anthology** page 17. Then use page T1o to review and assess nouns.

Daily Writing Skills ☑️
Have students tell what happened in the beginning, middle and end of "Those Shoes." Then use page T1q to assess students' understanding of plot sequence.

Answers Talk About It

1. **Realistic Fiction** One realistic event in the story is when Mr. Alfrey gives shoes to Jeremy at school. Classmates laughing at him was also like real life.
2. **Retell a Story** Students should retell the beginning, middle, and end of their partners' stories in correct order using the sentence frames.
3. **Compare and Contrast** Possible response: I **want** a video game to play with. I **need** a coat to stay warm. When you **want** something, you hope to have it. When you **need** something, you cannot easily live without it.

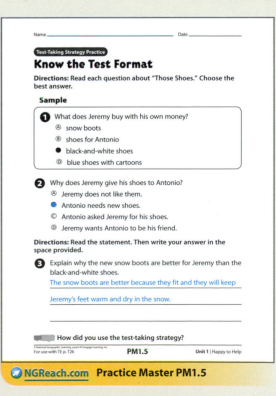

🌐 NGReach.com **Practice Master PM1.5**

Differentiate

SN Special Needs

ISSUE Students have difficulty completing their story maps.

STRATEGY Focus students' attention on the box they need to complete and the box before it. Cover the other boxes and ask guiding questions, as necessary.

EL English Learners

ISSUE Students lack the language skills to identify and record plot events.

STRATEGY Allow students to create a visual story map to represent the plot of the story. Have students draw pictures of the key events and label them with words and phrases that tell about each event.

AL Above Level

ISSUE Students have included more events than their story map can show.

STRATEGY Remind students that unimportant events can be removed without affecting the main story. Then have students share their story maps with partners and review each event to see if any can be removed or combined with another.

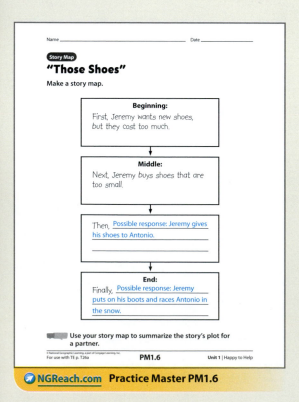

NGReach.com **Practice Master PM1.6**

Comprehension

④ **Plot** **Anthology** page 27

REVIEW Display **Student eEdition** page 27. Read aloud the instructions and review the meaning of plot: *The* **plot** *of a story tells what happens in the beginning, middle, and at the end of the story.*

Point out the sample story map and explain: *The story map shows events that happen from the beginning to the end of the* **plot**. Read aloud the first two events in the story map and ask students to think about what happens next in the story.

Have partners work together to complete **Practice Master PM1.6**. Remind them that each section of the plot can include more than one event, as long as all the events are listed in sequential order. Circulate and use the questions below to guide students in discussing how each event influences the next.

See **Differentiate**

Plot Point	Guiding Question	Event Description
Middle	*What happens after Jeremy buys shoes that are too small?*	(Then, he secretly gives them to Antonio.)
End	*What is the last important event that happens in the story?*	(Finally, Jeremy and Antonio race.)

Check & Reteach

OBJECTIVE: Comprehend Plot

Listen for the most important events as students summarize their stories.

If students have difficulty, help them identify the important events by asking: *What happens in the beginning? What happens in the middle? What happens at the end?* Then ask: *What word signals the beginning event?* (First)

Have students replace the word *First* in their sentences with "At the beginning of the story." (Possible response: At the beginning of the story, Jeremy **wants** new shoes, but they cost too much.)

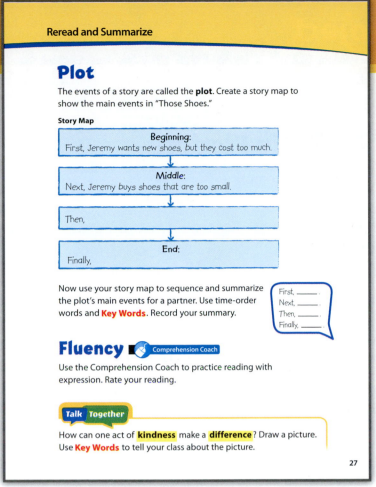

Plot

The events of a story are called the **plot**. Create a story map to show the main events in "Those Shoes."

Story Map

> **Beginning:**
> First, Jeremy wants new shoes, but they cost too much.

> **Middle:**
> Next, Jeremy buys shoes that are too small.

> Then,

> **End:**
> Finally,

Now use your story map to sequence and summarize the plot's main events for a partner. Use time-order words and **Key Words**. Record your summary.

> First, _____ .
> Next, _____ .
> Then, _____ .
> Finally, _____ .

Fluency 🔵 Comprehension Coach

Use the Comprehension Coach to practice reading with expression. Rate your reading.

Talk Together

How can one act of **kindness** make a **difference**? Draw a picture. Use **Key Words** to tell your class about the picture.

27

Anthology page 27

5️⃣ **Fluency** ☑️ **Anthology** page 27

Have students read aloud the passage on **Practice Master PM1.7** or use the **Comprehension Coach** to practice fluency.

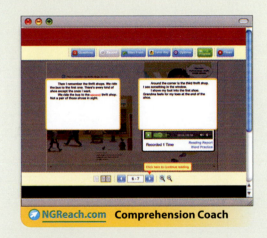

🔵 **NGReach.com** **Comprehension Coach**

Check & Reteach

OBJECTIVE: Read with Fluency ☑️

Monitor students' oral reading.

If students need additional fluency practice, have them read along with the **Fluency Models**.

6️⃣ **Talk Together** **Anthology** page 27

Have small groups discuss examples of kindness. Point out Key Words on **Anthology** page 26 and remind students to use them as they share their pictures.

WRAP-UP Have students think about and discuss the acts of kindness they discovered in "Those Shoes" and the Small Group Reading books. Ask: *How have this week's readings changed the way you think about helping others?* Then have students add ideas to their concept maps.

Name _____ Date _____

Fluency Practice

"Those Shoes"

Use this passage to practice reading with the proper expression.

I have dreams about those shoes. Black high-tops.	8
Two white stripes.	11
"Grandma, I want them."	15
"There's no room for 'want' around here," Grandma says.	24
"What you *need* are new boots for winter."	32

From "Those Shoes," page 12

Fluency: Expression

1 ☐ Does not read with feeling.	3 ☐ Reads with appropriate feeling with most content.
2 ☐ Reads with some feeling, but does not match content.	4 ☐ Reads with appropriate feeling for all content.

Accuracy and Rate Formula
Use the formula to measure a reader's accuracy and rate while reading aloud.

_____ − _____ = _____		
words attempted in one minute	number of errors	words correct per minute (wcpm)

© National Geographic Learning, a part of Cengage Learning, Inc.
For use with TE p. T27   **PM1.7**   Unit 1 | Happy to Help

🔵 **NGReach.com** **Practice Master PM1.7**

OBJECTIVES

Thematic Connection: Individual Responsibility

☑ Write Realistic Fiction: Organization

PROGRAM RESOURCES

PRINT & TECHNOLOGY

Writing Rubric: Assessment Master A1.41

TECHNOLOGY ONLY

Sample Realistic Fiction: eVisual 1.5

Organization: eVisual 1.6

Magazine Maker

SUGGESTED PACING

DAY 1   Study a Model

DAY 2   Prewrite

DAY 3   Draft

DAY 4   Revise/Edit and Proofread

DAY 5   Publish and Present

COMMON CORE STANDARDS

Writing

Write Narratives	CC.3.W.3
Organize Events in a Sequence	CC.3.W.3.a
Use Dialogue	CC.3.W.3.b
Plan, Revise, and Edit Writing	CC.3.W.5
Write Over Extended Time Frames for Specific Tasks	CC.3.W.10

Language and Vocabulary

Demonstrate Command of Grammar	CC.3.L.1
Explain the Function of Nouns	CC.3.L.1.a
Use Knowledge of Language and Conventions	CC.3.L.3

Write Realistic Fiction

Display and read aloud the prompt.

> Write a short realistic story about helping someone. Make sure it has a beginning, middle, and end.

Study a Model

Read Realistic Fiction

Explain: *Let's read one student's realistic fiction.* Display and read aloud **eVisual 1.5**.

Sample Realistic Fiction

The Groceries

Nate sat by the kitchen window eating his cereal. Outside, a cold rain fell.

Through the window, Nate saw a small figure shuffling slowly down the street. It was Mr. Walters, his neighbor. He was carrying two big bags full of groceries. Mr. Walters leaned on his cane to make sure he didn't slip and fall. Nate grabbed his jacket and an umbrella and raced out the door.

"Do you need help, Mr. Walters?" Nate asked.

"Yes, thank you," Mr. Walters said, smiling. He accepted Nate's help.

Nate took the grocery bags in his arms, handing Mr. Walters the umbrella. Nate carried the bags to Mr. Walters's apartment, walking slowly beside him. Nate felt as glad as Mr. Walters about what he had done.

🌐 **NGReach.com** **Sample Realistic Fiction: eVisual 1.5** **INTERACTIVE WHITEBOARD TIP:** Label the beginning, middle, and end of the story.

Teach the Trait: Organization

Introduce the concept: *The plot of a well-organized story tells events in order. It tells what happens in the beginning, the middle, and the end.* Display and read aloud **eVisual 1.6**.

Writing Trait: Organization

A story that is organized

- has a clear beginning, middle, and end
- has a plot made up of events that flow smoothly from one to the next

🌐 **NGReach.com**   **Organization: eVisual 1.6**  **INTERACTIVE WHITEBOARD TIP:** Underline key words: *beginning; middle; end.*

Display **eVisual 1.5** again. Ask: *What happens in the beginning of the story?* (Nate looks out the window while eating cereal.) *What happens in the middle?* (Nate sees Mr. Walters carrying groceries in the rain. So he runs outside to help him.) *What happens at the end?* (Nate carries the groceries to Mr. Walters's apartment.)

Prewrite

Choose a Topic

Reread the first sentence of the prompt. Ask: *What is your role?* (writer of realistic fiction) Continue with the remainder of the prompt in order to determine the Role, Audience, and Form for the RAFT.

> **Role:** Writer
> **Audience:** Classmates
> **Form:** Realistic fiction

Help students choose a topic for their realistic stories. Students can brainstorm topics with a partner, or they can look through the Small Group Reading books for ideas. Have students choose a topic and complete a RAFT.

Get Organized

Review the sample: *When you tell a story, you tell the events in order. The beginning tells what happens first, the middle tells what happens next, and the end tells what happens last.* Display a story map and say: *You can use a story map to help create the plot of a story.* Model using the events from "The Groceries" to complete the story map.

Have students use story maps to plan their realistic fiction. Tell them to make sure their stories have a beginning, middle, and end.

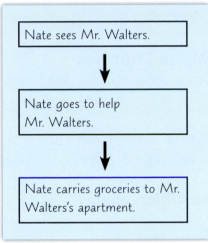

Story Map

Draft

Write Ideas

Show sample layouts in **Magazine Maker** and have students select one. Then have students draft their realistic fiction using their story maps. Remind them to focus on organizing the events in their story in sequence.

See **Differentiate**

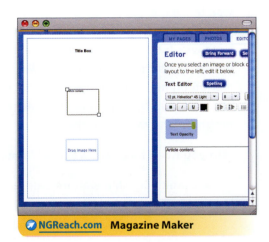

NGReach.com **Magazine Maker**

Differentiate

BL Below Level

ISSUE Students have difficulty understanding the organization of a plot.

STRATEGY Have students number the boxes in the story map with *1*, *2*, and *3*. Then have them tell what happens in the story first, second, and third. Point out that they are telling the story events in order.

Daily Language Arts

Daily Spelling and Word Work ✓
Practice Pages T1l–T1m

Daily Grammar ✓
Point out the nouns *Nate, window,* and *cereal* in the first sentence of the student model. Then use pages T1o–T1n to have students practice using nouns.

Daily Writing Skills ✓
Point out the beginning, middle, and end of the story in the student model. Then use pages T1p-T1q to have students practice using elements of plot.

Differentiate

AL Above Level

ISSUE Students easily organize a plot sequence.

STRATEGY Challenge students to add more dialogue to their drafts to better illustrate the story events.

Revise

Read, Retell, Respond

Have students read aloud their drafts to partners. Have listeners retell the events and offer ideas to improve the organization. Use language frames to guide the discussion.

Language Frames	
Retell	**Make Suggestions**
• In the beginning, _____. • Next, _____. • At the end, _____.	• The sentence about _____ sounds realistic. • Changing _____ would make your story more realistic. • I am not sure what happened first: _____ or _____. Can you make the order of events clearer?

Make Changes

Have students revise their realistic fiction. Remind students to focus on organization. Their stories should have a clear beginning, middle, and end.

Explain how to insert a title in **Magazine Maker**: *Press the Layout tab and drag the Article Title box to the page on the left.* Then demonstrate how to type in a title.

See **Differentiate**

Student Sample: Revise

Sample Analysis

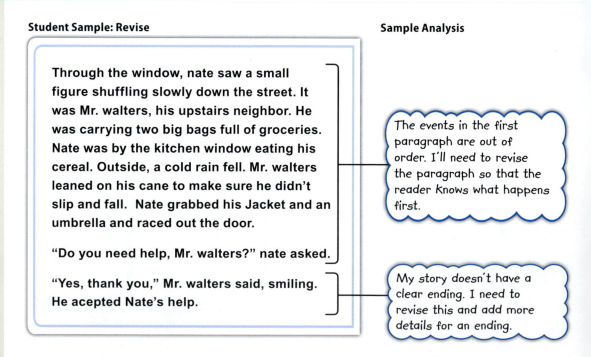

Through the window, nate saw a small figure shuffling slowly down the street. It was Mr. walters, his upstairs neighbor. He was carrying two big bags full of groceries. Nate was by the kitchen window eating his cereal. Outside, a cold rain fell. Mr. walters leaned on his cane to make sure he didn't slip and fall. Nate grabbed his Jacket and an umbrella and raced out the door.

"Do you need help, Mr. walters?" nate asked.

"Yes, thank you," Mr. walters said, smiling. He acepted Nate's help.

The events in the first paragraph are out of order. I'll need to revise the paragraph so that the reader knows what happens first.

My story doesn't have a clear ending. I need to revise this and add more details for an ending.

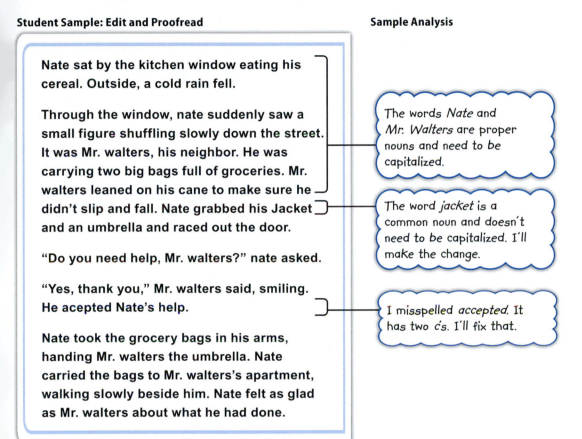
Edit and Proofread

Check the Realistic Fiction

Have students check their grammar and spelling, focusing on the Week 1 spelling words and the proper use of nouns.

Student Sample: Edit and Proofread

Nate sat by the kitchen window eating his cereal. Outside, a cold rain fell.

Through the window, nate suddenly saw a small figure shuffling slowly down the street. It was Mr. walters, his neighbor. He was carrying two big bags full of groceries. Mr. walters leaned on his cane to make sure he didn't slip and fall. Nate grabbed his Jacket and an umbrella and raced out the door.

"Do you need help, Mr. walters?" nate asked.

"Yes, thank you," Mr. walters said, smiling. He acepted Nate's help.

Nate took the grocery bags in his arms, handing Mr. walters the umbrella. Nate carried the bags to Mr. walters's apartment, walking slowly beside him. Nate felt as glad as Mr. walters about what he had done.

Sample Analysis

The words *Nate* and *Mr. Walters* are proper nouns and need to be capitalized.

The word *jacket* is a common noun and doesn't need to be capitalized. I'll make the change.

I misspelled *accepted*. It has two *c's*. I'll fix that.

Publish and Present

Make a Final Copy

Tell students they can lay out their text on a page in **Magazine Maker** to allow space for images. Students can also adjust the size of photos in their layouts. Model how the image editor appears by clicking on Photos. Show that moving the Scale Image bar up and down resizes a photo.

Share with Others

Have volunteers read their stories to the class. Tell them to speak clearly at an appropriate pace. Display stories. Have students make additional copies for their Weekly Writing folders.

Use the **Writing Rubric** to assess each student's story.

Student Sample: Publish

The Groceries

Nate sat by the kitchen window eating his cereal. Outside, a cold rain fell.

Through the window, Nate saw a small figure shuffling slowly down the street. It was Mr. Walters, his neighbor. He was carrying two big bags full of groceries. Mr. Walters leaned on his cane to make sure he didn't slip and fall. Nate grabbed his jacket and an umbrella and raced out the door.

"Do you need help, Mr. Walters?" Nate asked.

"Yes, thank you," Mr. Walters said, smiling. He accepted Nate's help.

Nate took the grocery bags in his arms, handing Mr. Walters the umbrella. Nate carried the bags back to Mr. Walters's apartment, walking slowly beside him. Nate felt as glad as Mr. Walters about what he had done.

Best Practices

Review Each Pass Use **eVisual 1.6** to review students' stories after each step in the writing process.

Writing Rubric

NGReach.com **Assessment Master A1.41**

☑ = TESTED

Assess

OBJECTIVES	ASSESSMENTS	

Reading
☑ Comprehend Plot
☑ Preview and Predict to Comprehend Literature

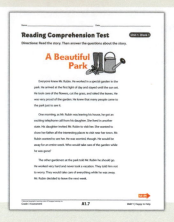

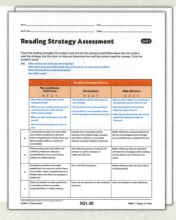

Reading Comprehension Test
A1.7–A1.8

Reading Strategy Assessment
SG1.30–SG1.31

Fluency
☑ Expression
☑ Accuracy and Rate

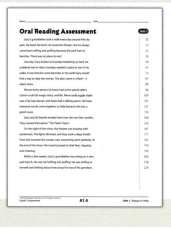

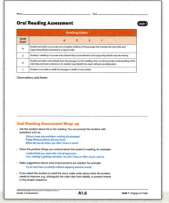

Oral Reading Assessment
A1.4–A1.6

Use these passages throughout Unit 1. Work with Below Level students this week.

Vocabulary and Spelling
☑ Use Domain-Specific Words
☑ Use Academic Words
☑ Spell Words with Short *a* and Short *o*
☑ Use Commonly Misspelled Words Correctly

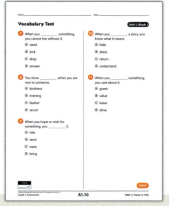

Vocabulary Test
A1.9–A1.10

Spelling Pretest/ Spelling Test
T1l

Grammar and Writing
☑ Use Concrete and Abstract Nouns
☑ Use Common and Proper Nouns
☑ Develop a Plot Sequence

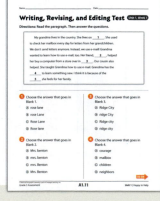
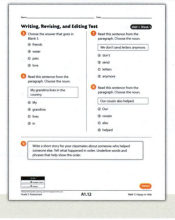

Writing, Revising, and Editing Test
A1.11–A1.12

Writing Rubric
A1.41

ExamView®

Reteach and Practice

REPORTS

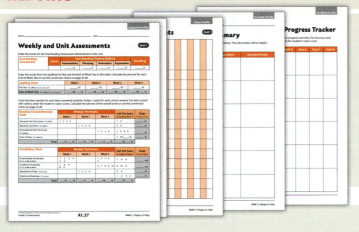

Student Profile: Weekly and Unit Assessments

A1.37

PRINT & ONLINE
Report Forms

Student Profile: Weekly and Unit Assessments	A1.37–A1.38
Class Profile: Weekly and Unit Assessments	A1.39
Student Profile: Strengths and Needs Summary	A1.40
Student Profile: Oral Reading Assessment Progress Tracker	A1.3

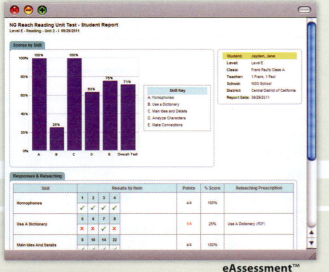

eAssessment™

ONLINE ONLY
Automated Reports

Student Profile: Weekly and Unit Tests

Class Profile: Weekly and Unit Tests

Standards Summary Report

RESOURCES AND ROUTINES

Reading

RETEACH

Plot: Reteaching Master RT1.1

Plan and Monitor: Reteaching Master RT1.2

ADDITIONAL PRACTICE

Comprehension Coach NGReach.com

Fluency

RETEACH

Fluency Routines, page BP33

ADDITIONAL PRACTICE

Comprehension Coach NGReach.com

Vocabulary and Spelling

RETEACH

Vocabulary Routine 6, page BP40

Spelling and Word Work Routine, page BP52

ADDITIONAL PRACTICE

Vocabulary Games NGReach.com

Daily Spelling Practice, pages T1l–T1m

Grammar and Writing

RETEACH

Common and Proper Nouns: Anthology Handbook, page 583

Writing: Reteaching Writing Routine, page BP51

Writing Trait: Organization: Reteaching Master RT1.3

ADDITIONAL PRACTICE

More Grammar Practice PM1.8

Daily Writing Skills Practice, pages T1p–T1q

☑ = TESTED

	Day 1	**Day 2**
WHOLE GROUP TIME	**Listen and Comprehend**	**Read and Comprehend**

Anthology

Speaking and Listening
🕐 5–10 minutes

Day 1 — Listen and Comprehend

Academic Talk CC.3.SL.1; CC.3.SL.1.b;
Discuss the Big Question T27s CC.3.SL.1.c

Day 2 — Read and Comprehend

Academic Talk CC.3.SL.1
Preview and Predict T28c

Language and Vocabulary
🕐 15–25 minutes

Day 1

Daily Spelling and Word Work CC.3.L.2
☑ Pretest: Words with Short *a* and Short *o* and Commonly Misspelled Words T27m
Daily Grammar CC.3.L.1; CC.3.L.1.a
☑ Pronouns T27o
Vocabulary Strategy
☑ Alphabetical Order T27s

Day 2

Daily Spelling and Word Work CC.3.Rfou.3; CC.3.L.2;
☑ Practice T27m CC.3.L.2.f
Daily Grammar CC.3.L.1; CC.3.L.1.a
☑ Complete Sentences T27o
Vocabulary Strategy
☑ Alphabetical Order T28c

Reading
🕐 20–40 minutes

Day 1

Reading CC.3.Rlit.5
Read Aloud: Poem T28a
Comprehension CC.3.Rlit.5
☑ Identify Elements of a Poem T28a

Fluency CC.3.Rfou.4; CC.3.Rfou.4.b
☑ Model Phrasing T28a

Day 2

Reading CC.3.Rlit.10
Read a Poem T29–T30
Comprehension CC.3.Rlit.3;
☑ Preview and Predict CC.3.Rlit.5
T29
☑ Elements of a Poem
T29, T30
Analyze Characters T30

Fluency CC.3.Rfou.4; CC.3.Rfou.4.b
☑ Practice Phrasing, Accuracy, and Rate T29

Writing
🕐 15–45 minutes

Day 1

Power Writing T27s CC.3.W.10
Daily Writing Skills CC.3.L.3; CC.3.L.3.a;
☑ Use Colorful Details to Elaborate T27q CC.3.W.3.b
Writing CC.3.L.3.a
Write a Poem T28b

Writing Project: Poem CC.3.W.10
☑ Study a Model T33i

Day 2

Power Writing T28c CC.3.W.10
Daily Writing Skills CC.3.L.3; CC.3.L.3.a;
☑ Use Colorful Details to Elaborate T27q CC.3.W.3.b
Writing CC.3.W.10
Write a Response T31

Writing Project: Poem CC.3.W.3.b; CC.3.W.4;
☑ Prewrite T33j CC.3.W.5; CC.3.W.10

Fiction & Nonfiction

SMALL GROUP READING TIME
🕐 20 minutes

Day 1 — Read Social Studies Articles

Vocabulary CC.3.L.6
Learn Social Studies
Vocabulary SG10–SG11
Reading CC.3.Rinf.2
Identify Supporting CC.3.Rinf.10
Details SG10
☑ Build Comprehension SG11

Day 2 — Read Fiction Books

Vocabulary CC.3.L.6
Learn Story Words
SG12–SG13
Reading CC.3.Rlit.10
Introduce CC.3.Rlit.3
SG12–SG13
Read SG14–SG15
☑ Plan and Monitor SG14–SG15
☑ Analyze Characters SG14–SG15

LEARNING STATION TIME/DAILY PHONICS INTERVENTION
🕐 20 minutes

Speaking and Listening T27i	CC.3.Rfou.4.b; CC.3.SL.1; CC.3.SL.5
Language and Vocabulary T27i	CC.3.L.6
Writing T27i	CC.3.W.10
Cross-Curricular T27j	CC.3.Rinf.2; CC.3.Rinf.10
Reading and Intervention T27j	CC.3.Rlit.10; CC.3.Rinf.10; CC.3.Rfou.3
Daily Phonics Intervention T27k–T27l	CC.3.L.2.e; CC.3.L.2.f

BIG Question **How do people help each other?**

Day 3

Read and Compare

Academic Talk CC.3.SL.1
Talk Together T32

Daily Spelling and Word Work CC.3.Rfou.3; CC.3.L.2.e
☑ Practice T27n

Daily Grammar CC.3.L.1; CC.3.L.1.a;
Generate Sentences T27p, T32a CC.3.L.2
Vocabulary Review CC.3.L.6
Review Social Studies and
Academic Vocabulary T31a

Reading CC.3.Rlit.10
Reread a Poem T31a
Comprehension CC.3.Rlit.5;
Compare Genres CC.3.Rlit.10
T31a

Fluency CC.3.Rfou.4; CC.3.Rfou.4.b
☑ Practice Phrasing T31a

Power Writing T31a CC.3.W.10
Daily Writing Skills CC.3.L.3; CC.3.L.3.a;
☑ Use Colorful Details to Elaborate T27r CC.3.W.3.b
Writing CC.3.L.1; CC.3.L.3
Write to Reinforce Grammar T33

Writing Project: Poem CC.3.W.3.b; CC.3.W.4;
☑ Draft T33j CC.3.W.5; CC.3.W.10

Read Fiction Books

Vocabulary CC.3.L.6
Expand Vocabulary Through
Wide Reading SG12–SG15
Reading CC.3.Rlit.10
Read and Integrate CC.3.Rlit.3
Ideas SG14–SG15
☑ Plan and Monitor SG14–SG15
☑ Analyze Characters SG14–SG15

Day 4

Read and Comprehend

Academic Talk CC.3.Rfou.4.b
Read Poetry Aloud T33d

Daily Spelling and Word Work CC.3.L.2; CC.3.L.2.g
☑ Practice T27n

Daily Grammar CC.3.L.1; CC.3.L.1.a; CC.3.L.2;
☑ Grammar and Writing T27p CC.3.W.5
Vocabulary Practice
☑ Alphabetical Order T33c

Reading CC.3.Rlit.10
Read a Poem T33a–T33b
Comprehension CC.3.Rlit.5;
☑ Elements of a Poem CC.3.L.4
T33a–T33b

Fluency CC.3.Rfou.4; CC.3.Rfou.4.b
☑ Model and Practice Phrasing T33b

Power Writing T33c CC.3.W.10
Daily Writing Skills CC.3.L.3; CC.3.L.3.a;
☑ Use Colorful Details to Elaborate T27r CC.3.W.3.b
Writing CC.3.W.10; CC.3.L.3.a
Write a Poem T33d

Writing Project: Poem CC.3.W.3.b; CC.3.W.4; CC.3.W.5;
☑ Revise; Edit and Proofread CC.3.W.10; CC.3.L.1;
T33k–T33l CC.3.L.1.a; CC.3.L.3

Read Fiction Books

Vocabulary CC.3.L.6
Expand Vocabulary Through
Wide Reading SG12–SG15
Reading CC.3.Rlit.10
Introduce CC.3.Rlit.3
SG14–SG15
Read and Integrate Ideas
SG14–SG15
☑ Plan and Monitor SG14–SG15
☑ Analyze Characters SG14–SG15

Day 5

Review and Compare

Academic Talk CC.3.SL.1
Relate Readings to the Big Question T33h

Daily Grammar CC.3.L.1; CC.3.L.1.a; CC.3.L.2
☑ Review T27p

Vocabulary Practice
☑ Alphabetical Order T33e

Reading CC.3.Rlit.10
Reread a Poem T33f
Comprehension CC.3.Rlit.3
Analyze Characters
T33f
Compare Characters T33g

Power Writing T33e CC.3.W.10
Daily Writing Skills CC.3.L.3; CC.3.L.3.a;
☑ Use Colorful Details to Elaborate T27r CC.3.W.3.b
Writing CC.3.W.10
Write About Characters T33h

Writing Project: Poem CC.3.Rfou.4.b; CC.3.SL.5
☑ Publish and Present T33l

Read Fiction Books

Vocabulary CC.3.L.6
Expand Vocabulary Through
Wide Reading SG14–SG15
Reading CC.3.Rlit.5;
Connect Across Texts CC.3.Rlit.10;
SG15 CC.3.SL.1.a
Writing CC.3.W.10
Choose a Writing Option
SG15

ASSESSMENT & RETEACHING

Assessment and Reteaching T33m–T33n
☑ Reading Comprehension Test A1.13–A1.14 CC.3.Rlit.5
☑ Reading Strategy Assessment CC.3.Rlit.10
SG1.30–SG1.31
☑ Oral Reading Assessment A1.4–A1.6 CC.3.Rfou.4
☑ Vocabulary Test A1.15 CC.3.L.2.g

☑ Spelling Test: Words with Short *a* and Short *o* CC.3.L.2
and Commonly Misspelled Words T27m
☑ Writing, Revising, and Editing Test CC.3.W.3.b;
A1.16–A1.17 CC.3.L.1-1.a; CC.3.L.2; .3.CC.3.L.3; CC.3.L.3.a
Reteaching Masters RT1.4–RT1.6

Speaking and Listening

Option 1: Mother Teresa

NGReach.com **Student Resources**

To view the online video, have students go to Resources > Unit 1 > Learning Stations > Week 2 > Mother Teresa

Remind students that they learned about Mother Teresa in the Build Background Video.

Have small groups watch the video. Then have them discuss what they learned from it, and how it helped them understand a bit more about Mother Teresa.

Discuss Topics, Expressing Ideas Clearly   CC.3.SL.1

Option 2: Record a Poem

> When I felt so sad...

MATERIALS
recording device

Students rehearse a poem and then record it.
- Have students practice reading the poem "Guardian Angel" aloud, paying attention to phrasing.
- When students are ready, have them record themselves reading the poem.

Read Orally with Accuracy and
  Appropriate Rate and Expression on
  Successive Readings   CC.3.Rfou.4.b
Create Audio Recordings   CC.3.SL.5

Language and Vocabulary

Key Words

action · difference · gift · kindness · need
plot · prediction · preview · problem · receive
solution · understand · value · want

Option 1: Vocabulary Games

NGReach.com **Online Vocabulary Games**

Acquire and Use Academic and
  Domain-Specific Words   CC.3.L.6

Option 2: My Vocabulary Notebook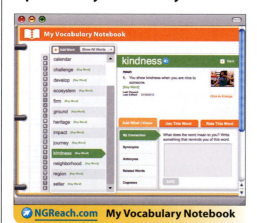

NGReach.com **My Vocabulary Notebook**

Have students expand their word knowledge. Under Add More Information > Add What I Know > My Connection, have students write what the word reminds them of.

Acquire and Use Conversational, Academic,
  and Domain-Specific Words   CC.3.L.6

Writing

Option 1: Person to Person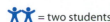

PROGRAM RESOURCES & MATERIALS

Language and Literacy Teamwork Activities: Card 7

Teacher's Guide on **NGReach.com**

Write Over Shorter Time for Specific
  Purposes and Audiences   CC.3.W.10

Option 2: Write a Helping Poem

PROGRAM RESOURCES

Digital Library: Language Builder Picture Cards D1–D10

Have students write a short poem.
- Students select a picture card and write a poem about the helpful act shown.
- Remind students to use colorful descriptions in their poems.

Write Over Shorter Time for Specific Purposes   CC.3.W.10

= one student   = two students   = three or more students

Cross-Curricular

Option 1: Lost and Found

PROGRAM RESOURCES & MATERIALS

Language and Literacy Teamwork Activities: Card 5

Student Resources Directory

Teacher's Guide on NGReach.com

atlas, globe, or world map • colored markers and crayons

Determine the Main Idea of Text	CC.3.Rinf.2

Option 2: Discuss an Article

NGReach.com **Student Resources**

Have students read an article about kids helping to stop a deadly disease.

Go to Resources > Unit 1 > Learning Stations > Week 2 > Kids Fight Malaria. Have partners discuss ways kids contributed to the project.

Read Informational Text	CC.3.Rinf.10

Reading

Option 1: Author Study

Francisco X. Alarcón

	Theme
Title of Poem	
Title of Poem	
Title of Poem	

MATERIALS

books by Francisco X. Alarcón such as Animal Poems of the Iguazú, From the Bellybutton of the Moon, *and* Poems to Dream Together

Have students select a book to read over the course of a week.

After students have read their books, have them choose three poems and create a chart listing each poem's title and theme.

Read and Comprehend Literature	CC.3.Rlit.10

Option 2: Additional Reading

PROGRAM RESOURCES

Week 2 Small Group Reading Titles, page SG1

Independent Reading Recommended Books, page SG68

Leveled Book Finder

Have students choose a book they haven't read before from the Week 2 **Small Group Reading** titles, the Independent Reading Recommended Books, or the Leveled Book Finder.

After reading, have students write a sentence about something new they learned. Students may also wish to take books home for additional reading.

Read and Comprehend Literature	CC.3.Rlit.10
Read Informational Text	CC.3.Rinf.10

Intervention

Phonics Games

NGReach.com **Online Phonics Games**

Apply Phonics and Word Analysis Skills	CC.4.Rfou.3

For Reteaching Masters, see pages RT1.4–RT1.6.

Additional Resources

ESL Kit

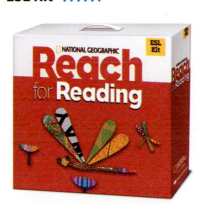

ESL Teacher's Edition pages T28a–T34h

OBJECTIVES

Thematic Connection: Heroic Deeds

Develop Phonological Awareness: Listen for Rhyming Words; Blend Onset and Rime

Associate Sounds and Symbols: short *a* phonograms; short *o* phonograms

Blend Sounds to Decode Words

Teach Day 1

PROGRAM RESOURCES

Lesson 5, pages T8–T9

Word Builder: Transparency 13

Decodable Passage: *A Dog and a Cat at Last*

  Practice Book, page 94

Word Builder: Transparency 14

Phonograms

Follow Lesson 5 to teach short *a* and short *o* phonograms. Guide students through **Transparency 13** and **Transparency 14**. Use **Reading Routine 3** to guide students as they read Decodable text. *For **Reading Routine 3**, see Reach into Phonics page ix.*

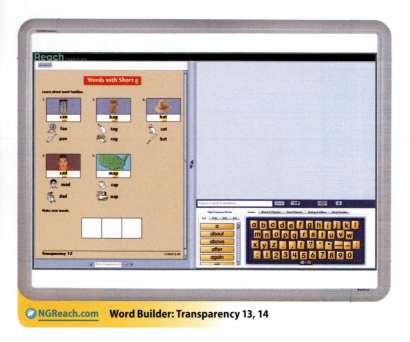

NGReach.com Word Builder: Transparency 13, 14

Practice Day 2

PROGRAM RESOURCES

Reach into Phonics

Lesson 6, pages T10–T12

Decodable Reader: *A Bad Day!*

  Practice Book, page 131

Build Reading Fluency

Provide students with the **Decodable Reader,** *A Bad Day!* Use **Reading Routine 3** to guide students as they read Decodable text. Then follow Lesson 6. *For **Reading Routine 3**, see Reach into Phonics page ix.*

T27k Unit 1

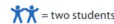 = one student  = two students = three or more students

COMMON CORE STANDARDS

Use Conventional Spelling	CC.3.L.2.e
Use Spelling Patterns and Generalizations	CC.3.L.2.f

Match Phonograms   Day 3   Option 1

MATERIALS

index cards, 20 per pair of students

Prepare

- Have partners collaborate to write each word from the word bank on a separate card. Ask partners to check each other's spelling.
- Have partners place cards face down in four rows of five cards.

cap	hat	ham	bag	cab	cop	hot	job	nod	dog
map	cat	jam	tag	tab	mop	cot	sob	rod	jog

Play a Game

- Have Partner 1 turn over two cards and read the words. If the words are rhyming words, Partner 1 identifies the matching letters that end both words. If no match is made, Partner 1 returns the cards, and Partner 2 plays.
- Play continues until all matches are made. The winner is the player who has more cards.

Mystery Words   Day 3   Option 2

MATERIALS

index cards, 8 per student

Prepare

- Write and display each word from the word bank.
- Assign one word as a "mystery word" to each pair of students.
- Have partners work together to create three clues to help other students identify the word.

from	home	new	go	there	many	first	next
then	one	cat	log	mad	dog	bag	dot

> Mystery Word: *can*
> Clue 1: The mystery word has a short a vowel sound.
> Clue 2: The mystery word rhymes with man.
> Clue 3: The mystery word will complete this sentence: I opened a _____ of soup. (can)

Play a Game

- Have each pair of students read one clue at a time to the other pairs.
- After hearing Clue 1, other pairs collaborate to list all the relevant words. As players hear Clues 2 and 3, they cross off irrelevant words.
- When a pair has the answer, the partners call it out.

Phonogram Brainstorm   Day 4

MATERIALS

index cards, 10 per pair of students • timer

Prepare

- Have students write each phonogram on a separate card: _an, _ag, _at, _ad, _ap, _ob, _og, _ot, _od, _op.
- Then have them place the cards face down in a pile.

Play a Game

- One partner picks and displays a card.
- Players have one minute to write as many words as they can that end in the letters shown.
- After time is up, Player 1 reads his or her list of phonograms. Player 2 listens for any repeats. Players receive 1 point for each word that ends in the letters shown on the card.
- Have partners take turns choosing cards, reading lists, and listening for repeats. Partners continue to brainstorm words for each phonogram.

Review   Day 5

PROGRAM RESOURCES

Word Builder: Transparency 15

Reach into Phonics
Lesson 7, page T13

Review

Follow Lesson 7 to review words with short *a* and short *o*. Guide students through **Transparency 15**.

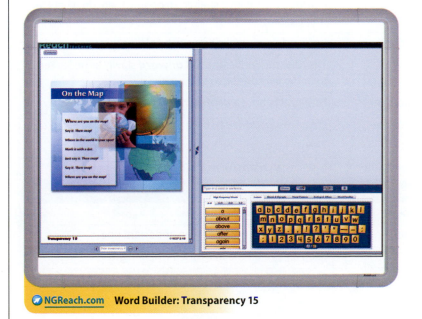

NGReach.com   **Word Builder: Transparency 15**

OBJECTIVES

Thematic Connection: Heroic Deeds

☑ **Spell Words with Short *a* and Short *o***

☑ **Use Commonly Misspelled Words Correctly**

SUGGESTED PACING

DAY 1	Spelling Pretest
DAY 2–4	Daily Practice Options
DAY 5	Spelling Test

Spelling Pretest — Day 1 🧍🧍🧍

Spelling Test — Day 5 🧍🧍🧍

Spelling Words

Use these words and sentences for the weekly Spelling Pretest and Spelling Test.

Words with Short *a* and Short *o*

1. advice	People give **advice** on how to remain calm in the face of danger.
2. bothered	I am upset and **bothered** that so few people helped clean up after the big storm.
3. busybody	That **busybody** wants to know everyone's business!
4. common	Police officers going beyond the call of duty happens every day here; it is a **common** sight in our town.
5. conference	Our firefighters are going to a **conference** in a big meeting hall with other local heroes.
6. dollars	When Haylie saw two **dollars** drop out of a man's wallet, she told him about the money right away.
7. honest	He is always **honest**, so he must be telling the truth about saving an eagle.
8. jobless	My big sister is **jobless**, so she might babysit for working moms.
9. manage	I **manage** an animal shelter, so people there do what I tell them to do.
10. model	His good deeds make him a **model** for others.
11. onward	The tow truck driver moved **onward** slowly as he looked for more cars off the road.
12. problem	Firefighters have a **problem** when a fire is very hot.
13. promise	We gave a **promise** to help clean up, so we'll do it.
14. satisfy	Thanks for giving me food to **satisfy** my hunger.
15. transform	A smile can **transform** a sad face into a happy one.

Watch-Out Words

16. you're	**You're** new to our ball team.
17. your	**Your** role as our catcher is an important one.
18. eye	Keep an **eye** on the ball to see where it goes.
19. I	Since **I** am the coach, **I** try to help you play better.

Short *o* and *a* Syllables — Day 2 🧍🧍 — Option 1

MATERIALS

index cards, 15 per pair of students

Teach

Display the words *bothered* and *transform* with lines between the syllables: *both/ered*, *trans/form*. Say each word, emphasizing the short vowel sounds. Point to the first syllable in *bothered* and review the rule: *When a syllable ends with a consonant, the vowel is usually short.* Circle the *th* in *bothered* and the *ns* in *transform*. Explain: *Sometimes there is more than one consonant after the vowel. It still makes the short vowel sound.*

Prepare

- Display these syllabicated words: *ad/vice, bus/y/bod/y.*
- Have partners check a dictionary and collaborate to write each of the first 15 spelling words on a separate index card, displaying the syllable breaks. Then, have partners stack the cards face down.

Play a Game

- Have Player 1 pick and display a card. Player 2 points to the syllable with *a* or *o* followed by a consonant, names the consonant, pronounces the word, and spells it aloud.
- If Player 2 pronounces and spells the word correctly, Player 2 keeps the card. If not, it goes to the bottom of the stack.
- Players trade roles and take turns until all cards have been displayed and all words spelled correctly. The partner with more cards wins.

Apply Phonics and Word Analysis Skills	CC.3.Rfou.3
Use Spelling Patterns and Generalizations	CC.3.L.2.f

Comic Strips — Day 2 🧍 — Option 2

Make a Drawing

Have students use spelling words to create comic strips for the classroom. Encourage students to use one pair of Watch-Out Words.

Apply Word Analysis Skills	CC.3.Rfou.3
Demonstrate Command of Spelling	CC.3.L.2

🧍 = one student 🧍🧍 = two students 🧍🧍🧍 = three or more students

Daily Language Arts

| Syllable Sort | Day 3 | ★★★ | Option 1 |

MATERIALS

index cards, 15 per pair of students

Teach

Display and read *conference*. Say: *Each part of a word has a vowel sound.* Read again, pausing between syllables: *con fer ence. How many vowel sounds do you hear?* (3) Underline *o, e,* and *e. How many syllables?* (3)

Prepare

- Have partners collaborate to write each of the first 15 spelling words on a separate index card.
- Have partners write *Syllables* at the top of a sheet of paper and write *Two* in one column and *Three or More* in the other.
- Have partners softly read aloud each word in unison and tap a finger lightly as they pronounce each syllable.

Play a Game

- Tell partners to mix up 14 of the 15 words and place them face down.
- Have partners choose seven cards each. At a signal, all players race to place their words in the correct column on the chart.
- The first person to correctly place his or her words wins two points.
- Have students play a few rounds, mixing up cards and changing out the unused card in each round. The player with more points wins.

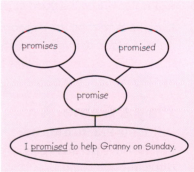

Syllables
Two — Three or More
advice — busybody
bothered — conference

| Apply Word Analysis Skills | CC.3.Rfou.3 |

| Concentration | Day 3 | ★ | Option 2 |

MATERIALS

index cards, 19 per student

Prepare

Pair students. Each partner writes each spelling word on its own card.

Play a Game

- Have partners shuffle both sets of cards together and place them face down on a table. Students take turns turning over two cards.
- If the cards match, the student spells the word aloud without looking and, if correct, keeps the cards.
- If the cards do not match or if the player misspells the word, the player replaces the cards face down.

| Use Conventional Spelling | CC.3.L.2.e |

| Alphabetize | Day 4 | ★★★ | Option 1 |

MATERIALS

index cards, 19 per student • dictionaries, one per group

Prepare

Have each student write each of the 19 spelling words on its own card.

Play a Game

- Have each player turn his or her cards face down and mix them up. At a signal, students turn over the cards and arrange them alphabetically as quickly as they can.
- At another signal, students count the number of words alphabetized correctly. Assign a point to each correctly alphabetized word.
- Encourage groups to use a dictionary to confirm the correct order of those words that require alphabetizing beyond the first letter. Tell them they can underline the letters: *bothered, busybody, common, conference, manage, model.*
- Have students remix the cards for another round. After a few rounds, the player with the most points wins.

| Word Webs | Day 4 | ★★ | Option 2 |

Use Graphic Organizers

- Have partners make a word web for each of these words: *bothered, manage, model, promise, satisfy.* Tell students to write each spelling word in the center circle.
- Tell students to use their own knowledge along with a dictionary to find additional forms of the word. Direct them to look for spelling changes and to place the new word forms in circles that extend from the center circle.
- Under the web, have students write an original sentence using one of the added forms of the spelling word.
- Extend the activity by having students use a word processing program to create the webs electronically.

promises — promised
promise
I promised to help Granny on Sunday.

Word Web

| Demonstrate Command of Spelling | CC.3.L.2 |
| Consult References | CC.3.L.2.g |

OBJECTIVES

Thematic Connection: Heroic Deeds

☑ Grammar: Use Pronouns

☑ Grammar: Use Sentences

COMMON CORE STANDARDS

Edit Writing	CC.3.W.5
Demonstrate Command of Grammar	CC.3.L.1
Explain the Function of Pronouns	CC.3.L.1.a

Day 1

PROGRAM RESOURCES

Pronouns: eVisual 1.11

Game: Practice Master PM1.9

MATERIALS

index cards, 8 per student

Teach the Rules

Use the suggestion on page T28b to introduce pronouns. Explain: *Pronouns take the place of a noun. We use pronouns so we don't have to repeat the same noun over and over.* Display **eVisual 1.11**.

> **Pronouns**
>
> - A **pronoun** takes the place of a **noun**.
> - Some pronouns are:
>   **I you he she it**
>   **we you they**
>
> **Martin** is a good person.
> **He** helps people.
>
> **Ana** is kind.
> **She** helps people too.
>
> The **dog** is friendly.
> **It** comforts the cat.
>
> 🌐 NGReach.com Pronouns: eVisual 1.11

Point to the nouns in the examples and the pronouns that replace them. Read the sentence pairs without pronouns. For example: *Martin is a good person. Martin helps people.*

Explain: *When you use a pronoun, tell about the right person, animal, place, or thing. I, you, he, she, and it take the place of one noun. We, you, and they take the place of more than one noun, as in: "The firefighters rescue the cat. They rescue it."*

Play a Game 👥

Distribute **Practice Master PM1.9**. Have partners play the game.

Differentiate

SN Special Needs

ISSUE Students have difficulty focusing on cloze sentences.

STRATEGY Have students highlight the blank in each statement to draw attention to the part that is missing.

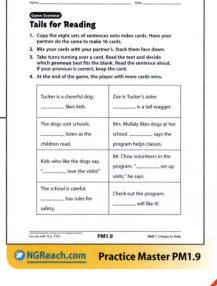

Game: Grammar
Tails for Reading

1. Copy the eight sets of sentences onto index cards. Have your partner do the same to make 16 cards.
2. Mix your cards with your partner's. Stack them face down.
3. Take turns turning over a card. Read the text and decide which **pronoun** best fits the blank. Read the sentence aloud. If your pronoun is correct, keep the card.
4. At the end of the game, the player with more cards wins.

Tucker is a cheerful dog. _____ likes kids.	Zoe is Tucker's sister. _____ is a tail-wagger.
The dogs visit schools. _____ listen as the children read.	Mrs. Mullaly likes dogs at her school. _____ says the program helps classes.
Kids who like the dogs say, "_____ love the visits!"	Mr. Chou volunteers in the program. "_____ set up visits," he says.
The school is careful. _____ has rules for safety.	Check out the program. _____ will like it!

PM1.9   Unit 1 | Happy to Help

🌐 NGReach.com **Practice Master PM1.9**

Day 2

PROGRAM RESOURCES

Complete Sentences: eVisual 1.17

Game: Practice Master PM1.10

Teach the Rules

Use the suggestion on page T30 to review parts of a sentence. Then use **eVisual 1.17** to teach sentences.

> **Complete Sentences**
>
> - A complete sentence has two parts.
> - A <u>subject</u> tells whom or what the sentence is about. It is usually a **noun** or a **pronoun**.
>   A <u>student</u>
>   **She**
> - A <u>predicate</u> tells what the subject is, has, or does.
>   <u>has many crayons</u>
>   <u>shares them with others</u>
> - Use a <u>subject</u> and a <u>predicate</u> to make a complete sentence.
>   A **student** <u>has many crayons</u>.
>   **She** <u>shares them with others</u>.
>
> 🌐 NGReach.com Complete Sentences: eVisual 1.17

Play a Game 👥

Distribute **Practice Master PM1.10**. Have partners follow the directions.

Name _____ Date _____

Game: Grammar
Putting It Together

Rules for Playing "Putting It Together"

1. Take turns spinning the spinner.
2. Read the sentence part you land on. Add a subject or a predicate to make a complete sentence.
3. Write your sentence on paper.
4. Take five turns each.
5. Choose your three favorite sentences. Read them to another pair of students.

(spinner: We / filled the room with laughter / the perky puppy / discovered a strange thing / tumbled across the floor / At last, it / The whole class / imagined a big surprise)

Make a Spinner
1. Put a paper clip over the center of the spinner.
2. Touch the point of a pencil on the middle of the wheel and through the loop of the paper clip.
3. Spin the paper clip to make a spinner.

PM1.10   Unit 1 | Happy to Help

Differentiate

BL Below Level

ISSUE Students lack a solid understanding of the definition of a complete sentence.

STRATEGY Have students create a color-coded diagram to use as they play the game. Encourage them to keep it as a reference for other activities.

> Who | what is,| has | does.
>   Subject   predicate

🌐 NGReach.com **Practice Master PM1.10**

👤 = one student   👥 = two students   👥👤 = three or more students

Daily Language Arts

Demonstrate Command of Capitalization   CC.3.L.2

Day 3

Review the Rules

Use **Anthology** page 33 to review complete sentences. To reinforce the concept, copy and display the chart.

A complete sentence has two parts.	
A sentence always begins with a <u>capital letter</u>.	
Subject: <u>Who or What</u>	**Predicate:** <u>is, has, or does</u>
<u>T</u>he new girl	is sad.
<u>M</u>ia	has the seat next to her.
<u>S</u>he	smiles at the girl.
<u>H</u>er teacher	is very glad.
<u>W</u>e	want to help, too.
<u>E</u>veryone	makes a welcome card.

Remind students that the subject tells who or what the sentence is about, and that the predicate tells what the subject is, has, or does. For each sentence, ask: *Who or what is the sentence about? What do we learn about the subject in the predicate?*

Generate Sentences 🕺

Prompt students to use subjects and predicates as directed as they write complete sentences. For example:

- Describe one of your heroes. Include a two-word subject.
- Tell about a time when someone did something heroic. Include a three-word subject.
- Tell how you can be a hero. Include a five-word predicate.

For **Writing Routine 3**, see page BP49.

Differentiate

BL Below Level

ISSUE Students have difficulty following the prompts.

STRATEGY Prompt students with questions as they write sentences. For example: *Who or what is your sentence about? This is the subject. What does this subject do or have? This is the predicate.* Have students underline the subject and double-underline the predicate. Then have them check the position of each subject and predicate.

Day 4

PROGRAM RESOURCES

Grammar and Writing: Practice Master PM1.15

Grammar and Writing 🕺

Distribute **Practice Master PM1.15**. Have students use editing and proofreading marks to correct incomplete sentences and capitalization.

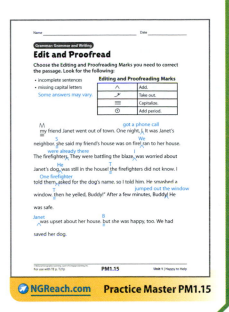

Practice Master PM1.15

Day 5

PROGRAM RESOURCES

Writing, Revising, and Editing Test: Assessment Masters A1.16–1.17

Review and Assess 🕺🕺🕺

Assign partners. Group two pairs together. Challenge each pair to write what they have learned about complete sentences. Have pairs trade papers and add anything that might be missing from each other's explanation. Then have each pair start a sentence and then trade to complete it.

A complete sentence has two parts.
It starts with a capital letter.
The subject tells who or what. It is a noun or pronoun.
The predicate tells if the subject is, has, or does something.

☑ Administer the **Writing, Revising, and Editing Test.**

OBJECTIVES

Thematic Connection: Heroic Deeds

☑ **Use Colorful Details to Elaborate**

COMMON CORE STANDARDS

Use Description	CC.3.W.3.b
Use Knowledge of Language	CC.3.L.3
Choose Words for Effect	CC.3.L.3.a

Introduce Colorful Details — Day 1

PROGRAM RESOURCES

Colorful Details: eVisual 1.12
Details Chart: eVisual 1.13

Teach the Skill

Display **eVisual 1.12**.

> ### Colorful Details
>
> Jeff was hiking through dense woods when he suddenly heard a shrill cry for help. His feet froze on the muddy path. He glanced around nervously.
>
> There it was again! Jeff sprinted down the path, listening as the cries grew louder and louder. Up ahead, he saw that part of the trail had broken away. All that was left were tree roots holding slimy chunks of clay. Jeff inched forward, his heart pounding.
>
> Jeff slowly peeked over the edge. To his surprise, a man stood on a ledge below him. He smiled up at Jeff.
>
> "Can you give me a hand?" the man asked.
>
> Jeff felt relieved. He unzipped his backpack and pulled out a long silk rope. He would pull the man up safely in no time.

NGReach.com
Colorful Details: eVisual 1.12 — **INTERACTIVE WHITEBOARD TIP:** Underline each colorful detail.

Read the passage. Explain: *You can easily imagine this story. because the writer used colorful details. The writer also used details to show how he or she feels, or what he or she thinks about the topic.*

Display **eVisual 1.13**. Use the passage above to fill out the chart. Explain how the writer chose colorful nouns, verbs, adjectives, and prepositional phrases to make the story more descriptive.

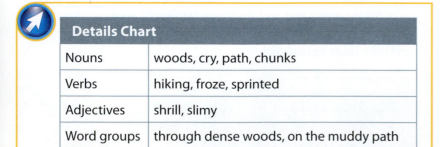

Details Chart	
Nouns	woods, cry, path, chunks
Verbs	hiking, froze, sprinted
Adjectives	shrill, slimy
Word groups	through dense woods, on the muddy path

NGReach.com
Details Chart: eVisual 1.13 — **INTERACTIVE WHITEBOARD TIP:** Have students offer more details for each row.

Write Descriptions — Day 2 Option 1

PROGRAM RESOURCES

Digital Library: Language Builder Picture Card D5

Introduce

Display the photograph of the firefighter. Tell students that they will brainstorm colorful details to tell what is happening in the photograph.

Practice

Have partners work together to brainstorm colorful nouns, verbs, and adjectives that tell what is happening in the photograph. Tell students to create a three-column chart and fill it in with colorful details based on the photograph.

Then, have each student pick one noun, one verb, and one adjective from the chart. Have them write one sentence using each detail.

Write a Description — Day 2 Option 2

Introduce

Arrange students in pairs and have partners visualize an animal shelter or a wildlife sanctuary.

Practice

Have students imagine they are working in the animal shelter or wildlife sanctuary. Have them brainstorm colorful nouns, verbs, and adjectives to describe the scene and what they do there to help out.

Then have them write a narrative paragraph of three or more sentences about their work at the animal shelter or wildlife sanctuary using as many colorful details as they can.

Have each pair read their paragraph to another pair of students. Have listeners identify the colorful details that help them visualize the scene.

🕴 = one student   🕴🕴 = two students   🕴🕴🕴 = three or more students

Use Colorful Details to Elaborate

Choose Words for Effect   Day 3   Option 1

PROGRAM RESOURCES

Digital Library: Language Builder Picture Card D5

Introduce

Display the photograph of the firefighter from Day 2. Tell students to think about how it might feel to be the firefighter or to watch the firefighter in action. Ask: *How can you get across your feelings as you write about the picture? Would words like "fearlessly climbs," "rickety ladder," and "devouring flames" help to get your feelings across?*

Practice

Have partners brainstorm and write down additional colorful nouns, verbs, and adjectives to describe the scene and the firefighter's actions. Then have students use the details to write three sentences. Tell students their sentences need to show how they feel or think about the firefighter and his or her actions.

Have partners trade sentences with another pair of students. Have each pair describe how each of the other two students feels or thinks, based on the sentences they wrote.

Choose Words for Effect   Day 3   Option 2

PROGRAM RESOURCES

Digital Library: Language Builder Picture Card D9

Introduce

Display the photograph of wildlife rescuers. Have students imagine being one of the rescuers and ask themselves: *Which person am I? How do I feel? What do I notice? Do I think I have the skills I need to help?*

Practice

Have partners list colorful details that they might use to describe the situation and their feelings about it.

Then, have each partner use some of their details to write a paragraph about the scene. Afterward, have students compare paragraphs and point out details that express what the writer felt or thought.

Revising for Colorful Details   Day 4

Introduce

Tell students they will revise a piece from their Weekly Writing folders.

Practice

Have students select a fiction piece from last week's Weekly Writing folder to revise. Have students add colorful details, such as descriptive nouns, verbs, and adjectives to express their own feelings about what is happening in the story.

If time allows, have volunteers read their revised pieces in small groups.

Review and Assess   Day 5

PROGRAM RESOURCES

Writing, Revising, and Editing Test:
    Assessment Masters A1.16–A1.17

Review the Skill

Display the following purposes and sentences. Have partners point out details that reflect the writer's purpose for choosing them.

> 1. Details to communicate the writer's feelings: Sam shivered with horror at the scary sound.
> 2. Details to communicate the setting: Lily's boots crunched in the hard snow.
> 3. Details to tell how fast things felt: Without hesitation, Sarah ran hastily down the apartment steps, taking them two at a time.

Have partners write an additional sentence to add details to each scene.

☑ Administer the **Writing, Revising and Editing Test**

PROGRAM RESOURCES
TECHNOLOGY ONLY
Read Aloud: eVisual 1.10

MATERIALS
timer

Power Writing
Have students write as much as they can as well as they can in one minute about the word *want*.

For **Writing Routine 1**, *see page BP47.*

COMMON CORE STANDARDS
Reading
Refer to Parts of Poems — CC.3.Rlit.5
Read with Fluency to Support — CC.3.Rfou.4
    Comprehension
Read Orally with Accuracy and — CC.3.Rfou.4.b
    Appropriate Rate on Successive
    Reading
Speaking and Listening
Discuss Topics, Building on Others' — CC.3.SL.1
    Ideas and Expressing Ideas Clearly
Follow Rules for Discussion — CC.3.SL.1.b
Link to Others' Remarks — CC.3.SL.1.c
Language and Vocabulary
Choose Words for Effect — CC.3.L.3.a

WARM-UP

Have students review the readings from Week 1, including "Those Shoes" and *Freedom Readers*. Have them tell about the problem and solution in each text. Ask: *What would you do if you had a similar* **problem**?

Academic Talk

❶ Discuss the Big Question

Tell students that they will discuss acts of kindness. Remind students of the following rules of discussion: *Take turns speaking, acknowledge what others say, and then state your own ideas.* Model: *If Dirk says that he saw an act of* **kindness** *at school, I wait my turn and say that I agree that what he saw was an act of* **kindness**. *Then I tell about a different act of* **kindness** *that I have seen.*

Explain that students should also think about how other people's ideas connect with their own. To model the process, ask: *What act of* **kindness** *have you seen at school?* Invite a volunteer to answer and ask: *Where did that happen?* After the volunteer responds, say: *That reminds me of another act of* **kindness** *at school.* Tell about a similar act of kindness you have seen at school.

Use a **Fishbowl** to have students discuss the question: Can one act of kindness make a difference? Remind students to build on what others say, state their own ideas clearly, and connect their ideas to those of others.

- Have part of each group sit in a closed circle, facing inward and the other part of the group in a larger circle around them.
- Have students on the inside discuss the question while those on the outside listen for new ideas they can build on.
- Have groups reverse positions and continue the discussion.

For **Fishbowl**, *see page BP45.*

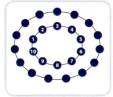

Fishbowl

Vocabulary Strategy

❷ Alphabetical Order ☑ **Anthology** page 28

To have students share prior knowledge of dictionaries, ask: *What is a dictionary? Why do you use a dictionary?* Project **Student eEdition** page 28 and read aloud the introduction. Have students look at page 605 of the Picture Dictionary in the **Anthology**. Point out the letter *A* at the top of the page. Then have pairs find the rest of the letters in alphabetical order.

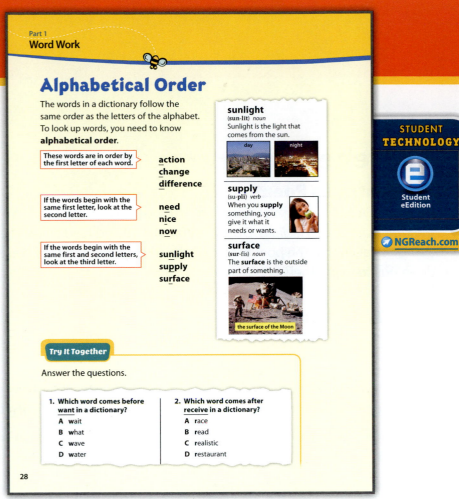

Anthology page 28

Read the first explanation. Explain: *To look up a word in a dictionary, you need to know how to use alphabetical order.* Model how to alphabetize to the first letter: *I name the first letters of* **action** , change, *and* **difference** . *I know that* a *comes before* c *and* c *comes before* d. *This tells me that, in a dictionary,* **action** *comes before* change *and* change *comes before* **difference** . Read the second and third explanations and have volunteers help you model how to alphabetize to the second and third letters.

❸ Try It Together **Anthology** page 28

Read the directions aloud and have partners work together to answer the questions. (question 1: A; question 2: D)

See **Differentiate**

Check & Reteach
OBJECTIVE: Consult References: Dictionary ☑️

As students answer the questions, determine whether they are able to use alphabetical order to find words in dictionaries.

If students have difficulty, help them break down the process into steps. Display *wait* and *what.* Ask: *Are the first letters of the words the same or different?* (same) *Look at the second letters. Are they the same or different?* (different) *Which letter comes first,* a *or* h*?* (a) *So which word comes first in the dictionary?* (wait)

Weekly Writing

Gather students' writing throughout the week:

✓ Daily Writing Skills Practice (T27q–T27r)
✓ Power Writing (T27s, T28c, T31a, T33c, T33e)
✓ Writing (T28b, T31, T33, T33d, T33h)
✓ Writing Project (T33i–T33l)

Differentiate

BL Below Level

ISSUE Students have difficulty understanding how to determine which letters in a word to use when alphabetizing.

STRATEGY Have students use small pieces of paper to cover all but the first letters of the words in the Try It Together. Have them determine if the visible letters are the same. If they aren't, then students can put the words in the correct order. Have students repeat this process for the second and third letters in the words.

AL Above Level

ISSUE Students are ready for more complex word work.

STRATEGY Have students put all the words from both questions into alphabetical order and explain why they put them in that order.

Fluency

Model Phrasing Explain the concept: *Fluent readers read groups of words together. You can use the punctuation in the poem to help you group words as you read.* Model phrasing by reading aloud stanzas from "Trees." Have students practice phrasing by taking turns reading aloud two or more stanzas.

Comprehension

❹ Elements of a Poem ☑

Introduce: *A poem is a text that uses colorful words, phrases, and details to express the writer's ideas and feelings.* Display **eVisual 1.10** and read aloud the title and author. Explain that the poet of "Trees" describes trees as if they were people who do things to help others.

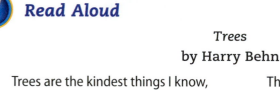

> **Read Aloud**   Poem
>
> ### Trees
> #### by Harry Behn
>
> | | |
> |---|---|
> | Trees are the kindest things I know, | They are the first when day's begun |
> | They do no harm, they simply grow | To touch the beams of morning sun, |
> | | |
> | And spread a shade for sleepy cows, | They are the last to hold the light |
> | And gather birds among their boughs. | When evening changes into night, |
> | | |
> | They give us fruit in leaves above, | And when a moon floats on the sky |
> | And wood to make our houses of, | They hum a drowsy lullaby |
> | | |
> | And leaves to burn on Hallowe'en | Of sleepy children long ago… |
> | And in the Spring new buds of green. | Trees are the kindest thing I know. |
>
> 🌐 **NGReach.com** **Read Aloud: eVisual 1.10**    **INTERACTIVE WHITEBOARD TIP:** Add accent marks above the stressed syllables.

Explain that poets plan their poems very carefully so their ideas are clear. Elaborate:

- *Poets usually plan to arrange their ideas in lines of specific lengths. Each line expresses a different idea.*
- *Sometimes poets use rhyme. Each pair of lines in "Trees" ends in words that rhyme.*
- *Poets often group certain lines together to form stanzas. This poet grouped every two lines together so each stanza is two lines long.* Point out the spaces that indicate breaks between stanzas.
- *A poem usually has a rhythm that helps express the poet's ideas. Rhythm is the beat of the words in a poem like the beat of a drum in a song. Each syllable or word part in a poem is either stressed or unstressed.*

To demonstrate, write the first line of the poem and add stress marks to the stressed syllables. (*Trees, kind, things, know*) Read the line aloud, clapping for each stressed syllable. Have students choral read the first stanza with you several times as you guide them to clap for each stressed syllable.

- *Poets use colorful language to help readers understand their ideas.* Reread the third and fourth lines and say: *In "Trees", the poet wants to show how he feels about a tree's shade. Instead of saying a tree's leaves and branches make shade, he writes spread a shade for sleepy cows. These words help me imagine a cow sleeping on a warm day in cool shade under the many leaves and branches of a large tree.*

Have students point out and label the lines, stanzas, rhymes, and rhythmic pattern throughout the poem. Then have them explain how examples of colorful language helped them understand the poet's ideas. Then have students choral-read the entire poem, emphasizing its rhythm.

See **Differentiate**

Check & Reteach

OBJECTIVE: Identify Elements of a Poem ☑

As students discuss the poem, note whether they can identify elements of poetry. If students have difficulty, reteach line, stanza, rhythm and colorful language with a short, familiar poem, such as "Mary Had a Little Lamb" or "Jack and Jill Went Up a Hill."

Writing

⑤ Write a Poem

Tell students they will write poems about people they admire. Model the process.

Think Aloud	Write
I admire my Aunt Helen. She helps at the animal shelter. I'll use rhyme and rhythm in my poem.	Helen is a happy animal helper for homeless dogs and cats. They jump and lick and rub, and leave their hair all over her hats!

*For **Writing Routine 2**, see page BP48.*

Ask students to think about people they admire who are not students and select elements of poetry to include in their writing. Have students add their poems to their Weekly Writing folders.

WRAP-UP Have students share what they have learned about rhyme, rhythm, lines, stanzas, and colorful language in poetry.

Daily Language Arts

Daily Spelling and Word Work ☑
Pretest page T27m

Daily Grammar ☑
Read aloud the first two verses in the **Read Aloud**. Point to the word *They* and explain: *The word* they *takes the place of the noun* trees. Use page T27o to teach pronouns.

Daily Writing Skills ☑
Point to the verse *And when a moon floats on the sky* in the **Read Aloud**. Explain that the verb *floats* is a colorful, descriptive word. Then use page T27q to teach using colorful details.

Differentiate

EL English Learners

ISSUE Students lack sufficient English vocabulary to understand the poem.

STRATEGY Encourage students to consult dictionaries to understand any unfamiliar words.

SN Special Needs

ISSUE Students have trouble focusing on the various elements of the poem.

STRATEGY Assign each pair of students one element of poetry to focus on during the discussion. Allow them time to find one example of their assigned poetic element. Then have pairs share what they find.

OBJECTIVES
Thematic Connection: Heroic Deeds

☑ **Consult References: Dictionary**

☑ **Preview and Predict to Comprehend Text**

☑ **Identify Elements of a Poem**

PROGRAM RESOURCES
TECHNOLOGY ONLY

Word Scale: eVisual 1.16

MATERIALS
timer, dictionaries

Power Writing
Have students write as much as they can as well as they can for one minute about the word *alone*.

For **Writing Routine 1**, *see page BP47*.

COMMON CORE STANDARDS
Reading

Describe Characters and Explain Characters' Actions	CC.3.Rlit.3
Refer to Parts of Poems	CC.3.Rlit.5
Read with Fluency to Support Comprehension	CC.3.Rfou.4
Read Orally with Accuracy and Appropriate Rate on Successive Readings	CC.3.Rfou.4.b

Writing

Write Over Shorter Time for Specific Purposes	CC.3.W.10

Speaking and Listening

Discuss Texts, Building on Others' Ideas and Expressing Ideas Clearly	CC.3.SL.1

T28c Unit 1

WARM-UP
Have students write and display their names. Then invite groups of students to arrange themselves alphabetically by first name as quickly as possible.

Academic Talk

❶ Preview and Predict
Remind students: *Before you read, study the title and illustrations to* **preview** *and then predict what a text is about.* Project **Student eEdition** pages 29–31. Have students predict what the poem will be about. Remind students to build on one another's ideas and to express their own ideas clearly.

Vocabulary Strategy

❷ Alphabetical Order ☑
To review alphabetizing to the second letter, display the words *when* and *wanting* and ask: *Are the first letters the same or different?* (same) *Are the second letters the same or different?* (different) *Which letter comes first in the alphabet,* h or a? (a) *In a dictionary, which word comes first?* (wanting)

Use **Anthology** page 28 to review alphabetizing to the third letter. Display *sad, all, guardian, give, classroom, alone,* and *cry* and have partners alphabetize them.

Model how to find a word in a dictionary. Say: *To find the word* alone *in the dictionary, I turn to the section that begins with* a. *Then, I look for the words that begin with* al *and* come before words beginning with am. *When I find the words beginning in* al, *I narrow down the search by looking for the words beginning with* alo.

Have students use dictionaries to find and share the definition of *guardian*.

Check & Reteach
OBJECTIVE: Consult References: Dictionary ☑

Listen as partners use alphabetizing to consult dictionaries.

If students have difficulty finding *guardian* in the dictionary, ask: *What letter section will you look in?* (g) After students turn to the *g* section in the dictionary, have each student put a sticky note beside the first word in the dictionary that begins with *gu*, and another sticky note beside the last word that begins with *gu*. Tell students to search for words beginning with *gua* between the two points marked by the sticky notes. Then have them read aloud each word that begins with *gua* until they find *guardian*.

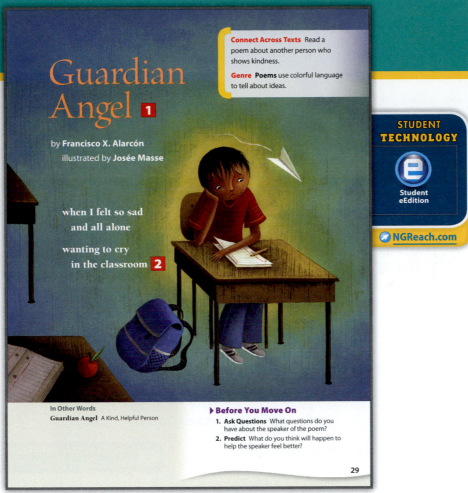

Anthology page 29

Reading

❸ Read a Poem

CONNECT ACROSS TEXTS Project **Student eEdition** page 29. Ask students to recall how Jeremy shows kindness to Antonio in "Those Shoes." Then have a volunteer read aloud **Connect Across Texts**.

GENRE Read aloud the explanation of the genre. Clarify: *The writer of "Trees" uses line lengths, stanzas, rhyme, rhythm, and colorful language to express his feelings about trees. The writer of "Guardian Angel" also uses line lengths, stanzas, and colorful language to express his ideas about* **kindness**.

SOCIAL STUDIES BACKGROUND Explain that the characteristics of poetry vary, depending on the culture and the time. One form of Japanese poetry, called *haiku,* consists of a certain number of syllables in each line. Rhyme was rarely used in ancient Greek and Roman poetry. In the 1500s English sonnets always had fourteen lines per stanza.

Read and Build Comprehension

❶ Preview and Predict ☑ *Who or what do you think the poem is about?* (The poem is about someone who does something nice.) *What part of your* **preview** *helped you predict?* The title is "Guardian Angel," so I know the poem is about someone who is nice.)

❷ Identify Elements of a Poem ☑ *How many stanzas do you see on this page?* (2) *How many lines are there in each of the first two stanzas?* (2) *Do words at the ends of lines rhyme?* (no)

Fluency

Practice Phrasing, Accuracy, Rate As students read, monitor their phrasing, accuracy, and rate.

Answers Before You Move On

1. **Ask Questions** Possible response: Why is he sad? Is he a new student? Did something else happen to make him sad?
2. **Predict** ☑ Possible response: I see that the boy is in a classroom, so maybe a teacher or another student will make him feel better.

Daily Language Arts

Daily Spelling and Word Work ☑
Practice page T27m

Daily Grammar ☑
Write the sentence "You're not alone" and explain that it expresses a complete thought. Then use page T27o to teach complete sentences.

Daily Writing Skills ☑
Point out the phrase "and with the darkest/ most tender eyes" in the poem on **Anthology** page 31. Then use page T27q to practice writing descriptions.

Mini Lesson

Analyze Characters
Writers use vivid words to express exactly what they mean and make their writing interesting. In stories, writers use vivid words to express how a character feels. Project **Student eEdition** page 29 and read aloud the second stanza. Say: *The poet tells us that the boy is* wanting to cry.

Display and read aloud **eVisual 1.16**.

The Good Writer's Guide

Unclear ◄――――――――► Vivid

unhappy   *very sad*   *wanting to cry*

NGReach.com   Word Scale: eVisual 1.16   **INTERACTIVE WHITEBOARD TIP:** Highlight the most intense phrase, *wanting to cry.*

Explain: *The writer could have said* when I felt very sad. *That would be unclear because it doesn't show how sad the character is.* Wanting to cry *tells exactly how sad the character feels.* Have students find vivid words that show exactly how kind the girl in the poem looks. (*most tender eyes*)

Read and Build Comprehension
1 **Analyze Character** *How do you think the girl feels?* (calm; caring) *How do you know?* (Without words, she tells the speaker not to worry, he's not alone.)
2 **Identify Elements of a Poem** ☑ *How do the lines on pages 30 and 31 differ?* (some lines are longer than others) *Point out examples.* (Students should point to the first two stanzas on page 31)

Check & Reteach
OBJECTIVE: Preview and Predict to Comprehend Literature ☑

Listen to students' responses to the previewing and predicting question.

If students do not understand how to preview and make predictions, prompt them with questions: *How does the boy look in the picture on page 30?* (happy) *What do you think will happen to make him look happy?* (Possible response: Another student will be nice to him.)

OBJECTIVE: Identify Elements of a Poem ☑

Listen to students' responses to the questions about the elements of a poem.

If students have trouble describing elements of poetry, model how to measure spaces between lines and stanzas using a finger. Ask: *Which space is bigger, the space between lines or the space between stanzas?* (space between stanzas) Have students read the last word in each line of each stanza and ask: *Do these words have the same ending sounds?* (no) *Does this poet use rhyme in this poem?* (no)

Answers Before You Move On

1. **Confirm Prediction** ☑ Possible response: Another student let him know that he was not alone.
2. **Character** The girl is kind, friendly, and helpful. When she holds his hand, and tells him not to worry, the speaker feels better.

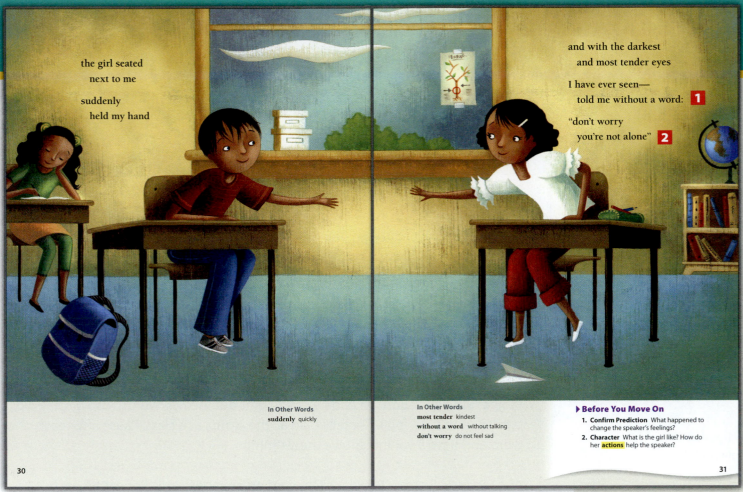

the girl seated
next to me

suddenly
held my hand

and with the darkest
and most tender eyes

I have ever seen—
told me without a word: **1**

"don't worry
you're not alone" **2**

In Other Words
suddenly quickly

In Other Words
most tender kindest
without a word without talking
don't worry do not feel sad

▶ **Before You Move On**
1. **Confirm Prediction** What happened to change the speaker's feelings?
2. **Character** What is the girl like? How do her **actions** help the speaker?

30

31

Anthology
pages 30–31

Writing

❹ Write a Response

Remind students that one way to respond to something they have read is to tell what they like or dislike about the text and why. Model a response to the poem: *I enjoyed the poem because it reminded me of what it is like to feel lonely. The way the girl reached out to the boy gave me a warm feeling.*

Have individuals write what they like or dislike about the poem, and tell why. Then have students add their responses to their Weekly Writing folders.

See **Differentiate**

WRAP-UP Have groups brainstorm three acts of kindness that each student can do in the next three days at home or at school.

Differentiate

BL **Below Level**

ISSUE Students have difficulty generating words that describe how the poem made them feel.

STRATEGY Provide a word bank of feeling words such as: *sad, concerned, carefree, afraid, brave, gloomy, joyful.*

AL **Above Level**

ISSUE Students are ready to be challenged more.

STRATEGY Encourage them use *rhythm* and *colorful language* in their responses.

OBJECTIVES

Thematic Connection: Heroic Deeds

☑ **Identify Elements of a Poem**

☑ **Grammar: Use Complete Sentences**

PROGRAM RESOURCES

PRINT & TECHNOLOGY

Compare Genres: Practice Master PM1.11

Complete Sentences: Practice Master PM1.12

TECHNOLOGY ONLY

Grammar Passage: eVisual 1.18

MATERIALS

timer • index cards

Power Writing

Have students write as much as they can as well as they can in one minute about poetry.

*For **Writing Routine 1**, see page BP47.*

Fluency

Practice Phrasing As partners reread the poem aloud, circulate and listen for correct phrasing.

COMMON CORE STANDARDS

Reading

Refer to Parts of Stories and Parts of Poems	CC.3.Rlit.5
Read and Comprehend Literature	CC.3.Rlit.10
Read with Fluency to Support Comprehension	CC.3.Rfou.4
Read Orally with Accuracy and Appropriate Rate on Successive Readings	CC.3.Rfou.4.b

Speaking and listening

Discuss Topics and Texts, Building on Others' Ideas and Expressing Ideas Clearly	CC.3.SL.1

Language and Vocabulary

Demonstrate Command of Grammar	CC.3.L.1
Use Knowledge of Language and Conventions	CC.3.L.3
Acquire and Use Domain-Specific Words	CC.3.L.6

WARM-UP

Have partners review "Those Shoes" and "Guardian Angel," using the illustrations. Have partners take turns retelling what is happening in an illustration, following the order in which they appear.

Vocabulary Review

① Review Social Studies and Academic Vocabulary

Project **Student eEdition** page 32 and point out the Key Words. Also display *plot, preview,* and *prediction*. Chorally read all the words as a class. Pause after each word and have a volunteer give the definition.

Ask each small group to write each word on an index card. Repeat for each definition. Have students shuffle the cards and spread them face up. Have students in each group take turns matching a word with its definition, reading both cards aloud, and then saying a sentence with the word.

Review and Integrate Ideas

② Compare Genres Anthology page 32

Read aloud the introduction on **Student eEdition** page 32. Have partners reread the poem aloud and review the story. Review: *Both poets and short story writers use colorful language, but they arrange lines in different ways.* As students answer the questions, have them cite examples of colorful language and line arrangements in both the poem and the story.

Display **Practice Master PM1.11**. Read aloud the first row of the Checklist Chart and model how to fill out the first row: *In the story, I see that the sentences are arranged in paragraphs in which the ideas flow from one sentence to another. In the poem, I see short lines, each of which expresses a different idea. I'll check* Poem.

Have partners work together to complete the chart. Encourage them to refer to specific elements of the story and poem as they discuss their answers.

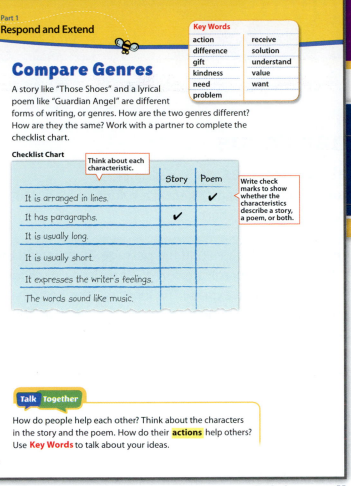

Key Words

action	receive
difference	solution
gift	understand
kindness	value
need	want
problem	

Compare Genres

A story like "Those Shoes" and a lyrical poem like "Guardian Angel" are different forms of writing, or genres. How are the two genres different? How are they the same? Work with a partner to complete the checklist chart.

Checklist Chart

Think about each characteristic.

Write check marks to show whether the characteristics describe a story, a poem, or both.

	Story	Poem
It is arranged in lines.		✔
It has paragraphs.	✔	
It is usually long.		
It is usually short.		
It expresses the writer's feelings.		
The words sound like music.		

Talk Together

How do people help each other? Think about the characters in the story and the poem. How do their **actions** help others? Use **Key Words** to talk about your ideas.

32

Anthology page 32

STUDENT TECHNOLOGY

e

Student eEdition

NGReach.com

Best Practices

Group Strategically Assess students' strengths and needs periodically and rearrange groupings so that students may grow at their own rates and find themselves continually challenged.

Check & Reteach

OBJECTIVE: Identify Elements of a Poem ✅

As partners compare genres, determine whether they can accurately identify the elements of a poem.. If students have difficulty, guide the discussion with prompts, such as:

- *Point to a paragraph in the story and a line in the poem. Do both texts have paragraphs?* (no)
- *Which is shorter, the story or the poem?* (poem)
- *Do writers of both texts express their feelings?* (yes) *Point out examples.*

Academic Talk

3 Talk Together Anthology page 32

Read aloud the **Talk Together** prompt. Review which characters help someone else in "Those Shoes" and "Guardian Angel." (Grandma, Mr. Alfrey, Jeremy; the girl in class) Use a **Three-Step Interview** and have students discuss how the characters helped someone else.

- Have students work in pairs.
- Have student A interview student B about "Those Shoes" and the questions.
- Have partners reverse roles with student B interviewing student A about "Guardian Angel."
- Have student A report student B's answers to the class and student B report student A's answers.

*For **Three-Step Interview**, see page BP46.*

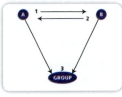

Three-Step Interview

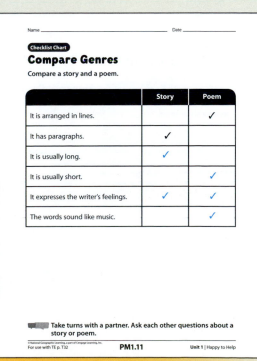

Name _____ Date _____

Checklist Chart
Compare Genres

Compare a story and a poem.

	Story	Poem
It is arranged in lines.		✓
It has paragraphs.	✓	
It is usually long.	✓	
It is usually short.		✓
It expresses the writer's feelings.	✓	✓
The words sound like music.		✓

Take turns with a partner. Ask each other questions about a story or poem.

© National Geographic Learning, a part of Cengage Learning, Inc.
For use with TE p. T32   **PM1.11**   Unit 1 | Happy to Help

NGReach.com **Practice Master PM1.11**

Differentiate

BL Below Level

ISSUE Students have difficulty identifying the parts of a complete sentence.

STRATEGY Break down the concept for students. For each sentence, guide with questions, such as: *Who or what is the subject of the sentence? Which words tell what the subject is, has or does? Does the group of words have both a subject and a predicate? Is the group of words a complete sentence?*

AL Above Level

ISSUE Students are ready to be challenged more.

STRATEGY Have students read the last paragraph on **Anthology** page 18 and find a complete sentence. ("We ride the bus to the second thrift shop.") Then have students explain how they know it is complete. (It has a subject and a predicate.)

Have students explain why "Not a pair of those shoes in sight." is incomplete. (There is no subject or verb.)

Name _____ Date _____

Grammar: Complete Sentences
Where's the Kitten?

Grammar Rules Complete Sentences

A complete sentence expresses a complete thought. It has a subject and a predicate.

Example: A young girl has a small kitten.
                         subject   predicate

Circle the complete sentence in each pair. Then copy correct sentences on the lines below to make a story.

1. My friend Maria.	My friend Maria has a kitten.
2. The kitten ran away.	Ran away.
3. Looked everywhere.	Maria looked everywhere.
4. Her sister Lisa helped her.	Her sister Lisa.
5. The girls found the kitten!	Found the kitten!

My friend Maria has a kitten. The kitten ran away. Maria looked
everywhere. Her sister Lisa helped her. The girls found the kitten!

_____

_____

_____

Tell a partner about how you know each sentence is complete.

© National Geographic Learning, a part of Cengage Learning, Inc.
For use with TE p. T32a   **PM1.12**   Unit 1 | Happy to Help

NGReach.com Practice Master PM1.12

Grammar Focus

4 Complete Sentences ✓ Anthology page 33

Project **Student eEdition** page 33. Have a volunteer read aloud the introduction. Then teach each rule in the chart.

Display **eVisual 1.18** and read aloud the passage. Then reread the first sentence to identify its subject and predicate. (*Greg; is a new boy in school*) Reread aloud the second group of words and explain: *The subject is missing from this group of words. The group of words does not say who sits slumped at his desk. This group of words is not a complete sentence.*

Have students identify each group of words that fails to express a complete thought and explain which part is missing.

Grammar Passage

Greg is a new boy in school. Sits slumped at his desk. Greg feels alone. On the first day, Clara. Sits next to him in class. Clara notices his sad face. Clara wants him to feel better. Then Greg glances up at Clara. Clara doesn't say anything. Just smiles at him. The new boy. Greg feels better now.

NGReach.com Grammar Passage: eVisual 1.18   **INTERACTIVE WHITEBOARD TIP:** Circle each subject. Underline each predicate.

5 Read Sentences Anthology page 33

Read aloud the directions and the excerpt from "Those Shoes." After students identify the complete sentence ("I have dreams about those shoes."), have them explain why the other two groups of words are not complete. (Neither has a predicate.)

See **Differentiate**

6 Write Sentences Anthology page 33

Read aloud the directions and have students work independently. Provide support as necessary. Assign **Practice Master PM1.12**.

Check & Reteach
OBJECTIVE: Use Complete Sentences ✓

As students write sentences, check for subjects and predicates.
If students have difficulty using complete sentences, prompt with:
- *Who or what is your sentence about? That is the subject of the sentence.*
- *What is the subject like or what does the subject have or do? That is the predicate of the sentence.*

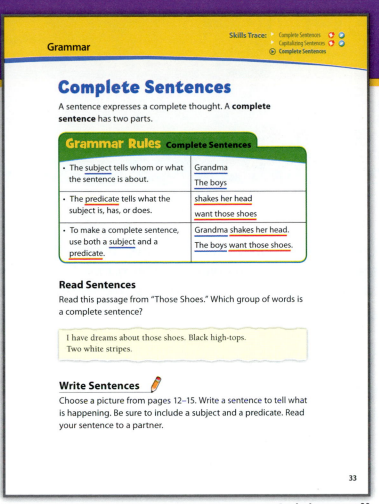

Complete Sentences

A sentence expresses a complete thought. A **complete sentence** has two parts.

Grammar Rules Complete Sentences

• The <u>subject</u> tells whom or what the sentence is about.	<u>Grandma</u> <u>The boys</u>
• The <u>predicate</u> tells what the subject is, has, or does.	<u>shakes her head</u> <u>want those shoes</u>
• To make a complete sentence, use both a <u>subject</u> and a <u>predicate</u>.	<u>Grandma</u> <u>shakes her head</u>. <u>The boys</u> <u>want those shoes</u>.

Read Sentences

Read this passage from "Those Shoes." Which group of words is a complete sentence?

> I have dreams about those shoes. Black high-tops. Two white stripes.

Write Sentences ✏️

Choose a picture from pages 12–15. Write a sentence to tell what is happening. Be sure to include a subject and a predicate. Read your sentence to a partner.

33

Anthology page 33

Writing

❼ Write to Reinforce Grammar

Have each student write a paragraph about a way to help others in their community, school, or family. Remind: *Each sentence should express a complete thought.* Have students look at the list of Key Words on page 32 and use as many as possible in their paragraphs.

Model writing something that you could do to help others, such as: *I want to organize a food drive for people who need help. Students and teachers bring canned and boxed food to school. We will give the food to a local food bank.*

After students write their paragraphs, have partners circle subjects and underline predicates in each other's writing. Allow time for students to revise their paragraphs for complete sentences. Then have them add their paragraphs to their Weekly Writing folders.

Daily Language Arts

Daily Spelling and Word Work ☑️
Practice page T27n

Daily Grammar ☑️
Write the sentence *The boy sits in the classroom.* and point out that *the boy* is what the sentence is about, and *sits in the classroom* tells what the boy does. Then use page T27p to review complete sentences.

Daily Writing Skills ☑️
Point out the phrase *slumped at his desk* in the Grammar Passage. Then use page T27r to practice using colorful details.

WRAP-UP Have students think about why characters in "Those Shoes" and "Guardian Angel" needed help. Have them discuss how else people could help Jeremy, Antonio, and the boy in the poem.

OBJECTIVES

Thematic Connection: Heroic Deeds

☑ **Identify Elements of a Poem**

☑ **Consult References: Dictionary**

PROGRAM RESOURCES

PRINT & TECHNOLOGY

Mark-Up Reading: Practice Masters PM1.13–PM1.14

TECHNOLOGY ONLY

Mark-Up Model 1.1 or Model 1.1 PDF

Vocabulary Strategy Practice: eVisual 1.19

MATERIALS

dictionaries

Ⓝ **NGReach.com** **Practice Master PM1.13–PM1.14**

COMMON CORE STANDARDS

Reading

Refer to Parts of Poems CC.3.Rlit.5

Read with Fluency to Support CC.3.Rfou.4
    Comprehension

Read Orally with Accuracy, CC.3.Rfou.4.b
    Appropriate Rate, and Expression
    on Successive Readings

Writing

Write Over Shorter Time for CC.3.W.10
    Specific Tasks

Language and Vocabulary

Choose Words for Effect CC.3.L.3.a

Determine Meaning of Words CC.3.L.4
    and Phrases

WARM-UP

Recite these lines to stress the rhymes: *"One, two / buckle my shoe, / three, four / close the door."* Ask: *Which words rhyme?* (*two, shoe; four, door*) Have students recite other familiar songs and poems, stressing the end rhymes.

Comprehension

➊ Elements of a Poem ☑

Explain that students will learn how to identify elements of poetry.

SCREEN 1

1 Read aloud the definition of *rhyme* on **Mark-Up Model 1.1**. Then read aloud the first stanza of the poem, stressing the rhymes. Have students follow along using **Practice Master PM1.13**. Read aloud the definition of *stanza*, if necessary. Ask: *What are some words that rhyme with* today? (Possible responses: *play, stay, away*) Have volunteers underline the rhyming words and click the Rhyme button to confirm. Have students mark up **Practice Master PM1.13** accordingly. Click on the arrow.

SCREEN 2

2 Read aloud the definition of *rhyme scheme*. Explain: *We name rhyme scheme in each line with the letters a, b, c, and so on. The first line of a poem is always labeled* a. *If the next line rhymes with the first one, it is also* a. Ask: *Do the first two lines rhyme?* (No.) *Then the second line is labeled* b. Have volunteers drag the corresponding letters for the first two lines. Ask: *Does the third line rhyme with any other?* (No.) *Then how do we label it?* (with the letter *c*) *Does the fourth line rhyme with any other?* (Yes, the second.) *Which letter should it be given?* (*b*) Have a volunteer drag the corresponding letters to the last two lines. Ask: *What is the rhyme scheme for this stanza?* (*abcb*) Remind students to mark up **Practice Master PM1.13** accordingly. Click on the arrow.

SCREEN 3

3 Read aloud the definition of *rhythm*. Reread the first two lines, stressing the rhythm. Explain: *When I read these lines, I hear a rhythm*. Tap out two soft beats, a loud beat and a soft beat as you say "I sat FROW ning." Then tap out soft, soft, loud, soft, for "by my WIN dow." Have students join you as you tap and say the words again. Work with students to tap out line 3. Ask: *How are these taps like the rhythm in line 1?* (the same) Note how the rhythm, or pattern of beats, repeats.

4 Play the recording and have students tap along to the rhythm they hear.

Have students mark up **Practice Masters PM1.13–PM1.14** by underlining rhyming words and marking the rhyme scheme. Have partners share their mark-ups.

INTERACTIVE WHITEBOARD Lesson
Don't have an interactive whiteboard? Print or display the PDF file of Mark-Up Model 1.1.

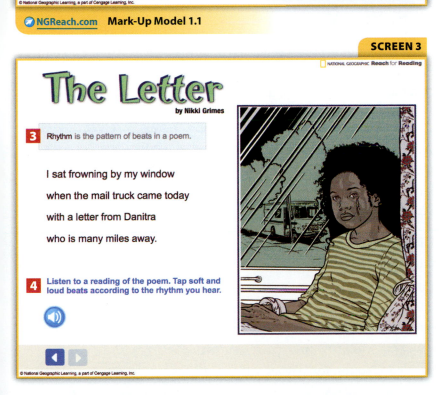

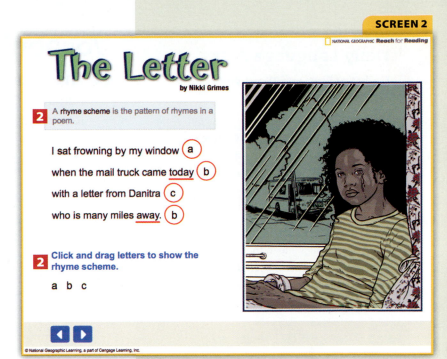

Check & Reteach

OBJECTIVE: Identify Elements of a Poem ✓

Review students' marked-up **Practice Masters PM1.13–PM1.14** to check their understanding of rhyme scheme.

If students have difficulty, model with the first stanza of "The Lunchroom": *To mark rhyme scheme, we give the first line a. Does miles rhyme with boulder?* (No.) *What letter do we give it?* (b) *Does right rhyme with miles?* (No.) *Which letter do we give right?* (c) *Does smiles rhyme with any ending word?* (Yes, miles.) *Then what letter do we give it?* (b)

Fluency ✓

Model and Practice Phrasing Explain: *Fluent readers recognize that some words should be said together, such as the phrase by my window. Fluent readers also know that the end of a line of poetry tells you that you should pause briefly before reading the next line.* Model phrasing by reading aloud the first two lines from **Practice Master PM1.13**. Then have students put slash marks in the text to indicate where to pause. Have the class read the poem chorally several times, reminding students to pause according to their marks.

Daily Language Arts

Daily Spelling and Word Work ☑
Practice page T27n

Daily Grammar ☑
Point out the line "are meant for someone else" on **Practice Master 1.14**. Ask students to identify the missing sentence part (subject). Then use page T27p to review complete sentences.

Daily Writing Skills ☑
Point out the first line in the last stanza on **Practice Master 1.13**. Then use page T27r to practice using colorful details to elaborate.

Power Writing

Have students write as much as they can as well as they can in one minute about a time they helped a friend.

*For **Writing Routine 1**, see page BP47.*

Vocabulary Practice

❷ Alphabetical Order ☑

Remind students that they have learned how to use alphabetical order when looking up words in the dictionary. Then display **eVisual 1.19**.

Vocabulary Strategy Practice

1. k̲indness, s̲olution, i̲ntroduce _introduce, kindness, solution_
2. f̲ear, b̲reak, d̲ifference _break, difference, fear_
3. sm̲ile, so̲meone, sh̲are _share, smile, someone_
4. mi̲les, ma̲d, ma̲ny _mad, many, miles_
5. lun̲ch, lug̲ged, luc̲k _luck, lugged, lunch_
6. fro̲st, fra̲gile, fri̲end, _fragile, friend, frost_

◉ NGReach.com **Vocabulary Strategy: eVisual 1.19** **INTERACTIVE WHITEBOARD TIP:** Underline the letter used to alphabetize in each row.

Explain that partners will write each set of words in alphabetical order. Explain that they'll need to use the first, second, or third letter in each word to arrange the words correctly. Model with *fear, fun,* and *fit*: *The first letter of each word is the same—f. The second letter of each word is different. So, I will use the second letter to alphabetize the words. The letter* e *comes before* u *and* i*, so* fear *is the first word. The letter* i *comes before* u*, so* fit *is the second word. The correct alphabetical order is* fear, fit, *and* fun. Then have partners rewrite the words on the **eVisual** in the correct order. Have students consult a dictionary to check their answers.

Check & Reteach

OBJECTIVE: Consult References: Dictionary ☑

Review students' lists to check whether they alphabetize words correctly and to make sure that they consult a dictionary to confirm their answers.

If students have difficulty, support the process by asking the following questions:

- *In item 3, is the first letter of each word the same?* (Yes.) *Is the second letter of each word the same?* (No.) *Which letter should you use to alphabetize the words?* (the second letter)

- *In item 5, is the first letter of each word the same?* (Yes.) *Is the second letter of each word the same?* (Yes.) *Is the third letter of each word the same?* (No.) *Which letter should you use to alphabetize the words?* (the third letter)

Have students alphabetize the words. Then have them use a dictionary to look up the words in the same order and confirm whether they are correct.

Writing

❸ Write a Poem

Introduce the activity: *Now the class will work together to write a poem about how friends help each other. The poem will be divided into two four-line stanzas. It will use rhyme and rhythm.* Use prompts and questions to guide the process.

- **Topic:** Ask: *What should the poem say about how a friend might help us?* Give some examples: *A friend is someone who cheers us up when we're sad. A friend is someone who shares with us. A friend is someone who listens.*
- **Title:** Explain that the poem's title should reflect the topic. Give some examples: *"When We Need a Friend" or "Funny Friends Bring Smiles."*
- **First Line:** Help students create the first line. Give some examples: *"A friend can help when you're sad." "A funny friend makes us giggle."*
- **Rhythm:** When students have created the first line, have them repeat it to hear the rhythm, or pattern of beats. Ask: *How do you tap that out?*
- **Rhyme and Rhyme Scheme:** *Using the first line, help students find rhymes for succeeding lines. Ask: Which words rhyme with _____? When the first stanza is completed, help students determine the rhyme scheme. Then explain: Use the same rhyme scheme to create the second stanza.*

Guide the class to generate the poem. Then have the class do a choral reading of the poem. Remind students to add the poem to their Weekly Writing folders.

See **Differentiate**

Academic Talk

❹ Read Poetry Aloud

Explain: *Now you will take turns reading the poem aloud with expression.* Briefly review the fluency skill: *To read with expression means to change your voice to reflect the feeling of the text.* Model by reading a passage from "The Letter" or "The Lunchroom," such as "My lunch tray's like a boulder/I've lugged around for miles." Have partners take turns reading the poems with expression.

WRAP-UP   Form small groups. Explain: *An acrostic is a poem that uses the first letter of each line to name its topic.* Model by displaying the word *FRIEND* vertically, one letter per row, and using each letter to initiate a line: *F* becomes *Funny*; *R* becomes *Ready to help*; *I* becomes *Is always there for you*; and so on. Invite volunteers to suggest lines. Then have each group create and share a simple acrostic using the word *HELP*.

Differentiate

EL **English Learners**

ISSUE Students lack vocabulary necessary to generate rhyming words.

STRATEGY Provide sample rhyming pairs for students to consider, or have students work with an English speaker to brainstorm word pairs.

AL **Above Level**

ISSUE Students satisfy the minimum requirement for the assignment.

STRATEGY Encourage students to take a leading part in the process of composing the class poem. For example, when the class has created the first line, have above-level students provide a variety of rhyming words for students to choose from in creating the succeeding lines.

OBJECTIVES
Thematic Connection: Heroic Deeds

☑ **Consult References: Dictionary**

Analyze and Compare Characters

PROGRAM RESOURCES
PRINT & TECHNOLOGY

Unit Concept Map: Practice Master PM1.1

Mark-Up Reading: Practice Masters PM1.13–PM1.14

TECHNOLOGY ONLY

Vocabulary Strategy Practice: eVisual 1.20

Comparison Chart: eVisual 1.21

Power Writing
Have students write as much as they can as well as they can in one minute about being the new kid.

*For **Writing Routine 1**, see page BP47.*

WARM-UP
Have students line up in alphabetical order by first name, then by last name.

Vocabulary Practice

❶ Alphabetical Order ☑
Briefly review alphabetical order with students. Then display **eVisual 1.20**.

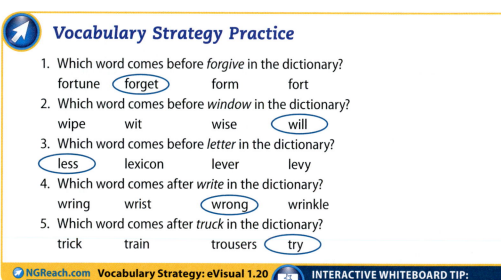

Vocabulary Strategy Practice

1. Which word comes before *forgive* in the dictionary?
   fortune · (forget) · form · fort
2. Which word comes before *window* in the dictionary?
   wipe · wit · wise · (will)
3. Which word comes before *letter* in the dictionary?
   (less) · lexicon · lever · levy
4. Which word comes after *write* in the dictionary?
   wring · wrist · (wrong) · wrinkle
5. Which word comes after *truck* in the dictionary?
   trick · train · trousers · (try)

◉ NGReach.com Vocabulary Strategy: eVisual 1.20   **INTERACTIVE WHITEBOARD TIP:** Have students circle the correct answer.

Model using the fourth letter in the words to answer the question for item 1. Then have students work in pairs. One partner writes the answer to the next question, and the second partner checks it. Students reverse roles and complete all five.

Check & Reteach
OBJECTIVE: Consult References: Dictionary ☑

Review students' lists to check if they can answer the questions correctly.

If students have difficulty, have them follow the alphabetizing process that they already know, then use their results to answer questions. Model: *In item 2, what do you want to find out?* (the word that comes before *window* in the dictionary) *Which letter should you use to alphabetize the word choices?* (the third letter) *What are the third letters in each of the word choices?* (*p, t, s, l*) *Which of the letters comes before letter* n *in the dictionary?* (*l*) *What is the correct answer?* (will)

After students alphabetize the words, have them use a dictionary to look up the words in the same order and confirm whether they are correct.

COMMON CORE STANDARDS
Reading

Describe Characters — CC.3.Rlit.3

Writing

Write Over Shorter Time for Specific Purposes — CC.3.W.10

Speaking and Listening

Discuss Texts, Building on Others' Ideas and Expressing Ideas Clearly — CC.3.SL.1

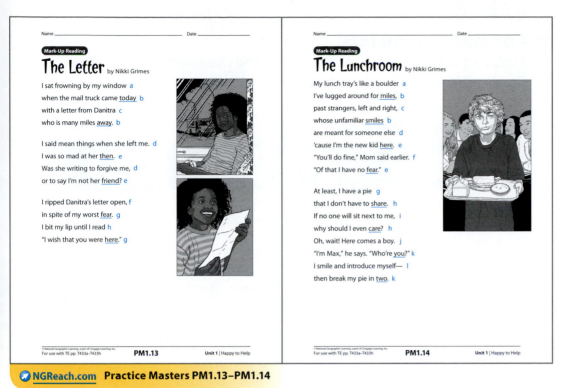

Review and Integrate Ideas

❷ Analyze Characters

Explain that students will describe and analyze the characters in the poems in **Practice Masters PM1.13–PM1.14**. Create a chart to identify the characters, what they do, and what these actions show about them.

Model: *I read that the speaker is frowning, so I ask myself why. Frowning tells me she is unhappy or worried. The fact that she is sitting by a window tells me she is waiting for something.* Ask: *After the mail truck comes, what action do we learn about?* (The speaker said mean things to her friend.) Have students ask themselves what this shows about the speaker. Ask them to copy and complete the chart.

Character	Action	What Action Shows
Speaker ("The Letter")	• frowns and sits by the window • said mean things • rips open letter and bites lip	• is worried or waiting • could not accept that her friend would move • worries that Danitra won't still be her friend
Danitra	• Writes, "I wish that you were here."	• wants to stay friends
Speaker ("The Lunchroom")	• lugs his lunch past strangers • sits by himself • pretends not to care • smiles and shares his pie	• is a new student • feels unhappy and lonely • covers up real feelings • is glad to see Max
Mom	• Says, "You'll do fine."	• believes in speaker
Max	• introduces himself	• is friendly

Daily Language Arts

Daily Spelling and Word Work ☑
Test page T27m

Daily Grammar ☑
Have students find the first complete sentence in the second stanza on **Practice Master 1.14**. ("At least I have a pie that I don't have to share.") Then use page T27p to review complete sentences.

Daily Writing Skills ☑
Point out the first line in the first stanza on **Practice Master 1.14**. Then use page T27r to practice using colorful details to elaborate.

3 Compare Characters

Explain to students that they will compare the characters in the poems in **Practice Masters PM1.13–PM1.14**. Display **eVisual 1.21**.

Comparison Chart

Characters	"The Letter"	"The Lunchroom"	"Guardian Angel"
Speaker	The speaker sits alone and frowns. She is worried because she said mean things to her friend. Now she's afraid Danitra won't stay her friend.	The speaker is a new student. He is alone, but he pretends not to care. He is glad to meet Max and shares his pie with him.	The speaker feels sad and alone. He wants to cry.
Other Characters	Danitra writes that she misses her, so she still wants to be friends.	Max is friendly to the speaker. He wants him to feel welcome.	A girl next to him takes his hand and comforts him.

NGReach.com Comparison Chart: eVisual 1.21   **INTERACTIVE WHITEBOARD TIP:** Have students add details from the poems to the chart.

Have partners copy and complete the chart. Model: *To compare, I ask myself first which actions or feelings are the same. I think the speakers in all three poems are alike because they feel alone and unhappy.* Ask: *How are Danitra and Max alike?* (They both do things to make the speakers feel better.)

Differentiate

 BL **Below Level**

ISSUE Students have trouble identifying details and what they show about characters.

STRATEGY Have students use one of the character charts they made to help them write their paragraphs. Have them describe a character's action and what it tells about the character's feelings.

 SN **Special Needs**

ISSUE Students have difficulty recognizing characters' feelings.

STRATEGY Help students to relate a character's actions to words in the poem that describe feelings. Suggest that they focus on one action at time. Provide an example: *The speaker in "The Letter" said mean things to her friend Danitra. Which feeling word in the poem explains how she felt?* (mad) *Why do you think she was mad?* (It says her friend left her.)

Check & Reteach

OBJECTIVE: Analyze and Compare Characters

Review students' charts to check if they are able to analyze characters.

If students have difficulty, use the following questions to guide them:

• *What does the first stanza in "The Lunchroom" tell us about the speaker?* (He walks around with his lunch tray feeling heavy; he's a new kid at school.)

• *What do his actions show about him?* (He's unhappy and alone.)

• *How is that like sitting by a window and frowning?* (It shows unhappiness.)

Writing

❹ Write About Characters

Introduce the activity: *Now you'll write a paragraph to describe a character you read about this week.* Remind students to include specific details. Have volunteers share descriptions. Have students add their paragraphs to their Weekly Writing folders.

See **Differentiate**

Academic Talk

❺ Relate Readings to the Big Question

Have students recall the unit's Big Question: How do people help each other? Say: *Think about "Those Shoes," "Guardian Angel," "The Letter," "The Lunchroom," and a **Small Group Reading** book you have read. What do these selections show about how people help each other?*

Model a response to the question for the story "Those Shoes": *In "Those Shoes," the author shows how people help each other even when they don't want to do so. For example, right up to the point where he decides to give Antonio his shoes, Jeremy still tells himself, "I'm not going to do it!"*

Use a **Think, Pair, Share** to have students continue discussion about how the readings relate to the Big Question. Remind students to build on the ideas of others in the discussion and to express themselves using clear language.

- Have students individually share information with the class.
- Have partners discuss how the readings relate to the Big Question. Use additional questions to prompt discussion:
  - *In "Those Shoes," how does Grandmother help Jeremy?*
  - *In "Guardian Angel," how does the girl help the speaker?*
  - *How do people show understanding in each of the selections?*
- Have students individually share information with the class.

For **Think, Pair, Share**, see page BP46.

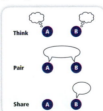

Think, Pair, Share

Best Practices

Link to Experience As students talk, link selection topics to students' personal experiences: *The boy in "Those Shoes" gave up something he really wanted in order to make someone else happy. Have you ever done something like that?*

WRAP-UP Ask: *What are some of the best ways people can help one another?* (Possible responses: comforting others, showing affection, sharing things, or teaching new things)

OBJECTIVES

Thematic Connection: Heroic Deeds

☑ Write a Poem: Word Choice

PROGRAM RESOURCES

PRINT & TECHNOLOGY

Writing Rubric: Assessment Master A1.41

TECHNOLOGY ONLY

Sample Poem: eVisual 1.14

Writing Trait: Word Choice: eVisual 1.15

Magazine Maker

SUGGESTED PACING

DAY 1	Study a Model
DAY 2	Prewrite
DAY 3	Draft
DAY 4	Revise/Edit and Proofread
DAY 5	Publish and Present

COMMON CORE STANDARDS

Reading

| Read Orally with Accuracy and Appropriate Rate on Successive Readings | CC.3.Rfou.4b |

Writing

Use Description	CC.3.W.3.b
Use Appropriate Development and Organization	CC.3.W.4
Plan, Revise, and Edit Writing	CC.3.W.5
Write Over Extended Time Frames for Specific Tasks	CC.3.W.10

Speaking and Listening

| Create Audio Recordings | CC.3.SL.5 |

Language and Vocabulary

Demonstrate Command of Grammar	CC.3.L.1
Explain the Function of Nouns and Pronouns	CC.3.L.1.a
Use Knowledge of Language and Conventions	CC.3.L.3

Write a Poem

Display and read aloud the prompt.

> Write a poem to describe the experience of helping someone. You will make an audio recording of your poem to share with other students.

Study a Model
Read a Poem

Explain: *Let's read one student's poem.* Display and read aloud **eVisual 1.14**.

 Sample Poem

Autumn Afternoon

Dad smiles
as we rake
the leaves
   crackle and crunch
and stuff them
into the bag
   for a few dollars

I follow Dad's example
   as I wash off the thick dirt
     like smudges of black ink
under my fingernails
Dad ruffles my hair
   warm and happy
this autumn afternoon

NGReach.com Sample Poem: eVisual 1.14   **INTERACTIVE WHITEBOARD TIP:** Underline the descriptive words as you read them.

Teach the Trait: Word Choice

Introduce the concept: *Writers of poetry, or poets, use very few words, so they have to choose their words carefully. They choose words to describe people, places, objects, or feelings. If they choose the right words, poets can paint a picture that helps readers see what they see and understand how they feel.* Display and read aloud **eVisual 1.15**.

 Writing Trait: Word Choice

Poetry with strong word choice
- includes colorful language
- uses descriptive words that connect with the reader

NGReach.com Trait: Word Choice: eVisual 1.15   **INTERACTIVE WHITEBOARD TIP:** Place a check next to each point as you explain it.

Reread the second stanza of the poem in **eVisual 1.14**. Point out how the poet describes dirty hands. Explain that the writer chose the words *smudges of black ink* to describe dirty hands. Ask: *How would you describe dirty hands?* Then reread **eVisual 1.14** and point out all of the descriptive words the poet uses.

Prewrite

Choose a Topic

Reread the first sentence of the prompt. Ask: *What is your role?* (myself) Continue with the remainder of the prompt in order to determine the Role, Audience, and Form for the RAFT.

> **Role:** Myself
> **Audience:** Other students
> **Form:** Poem

Have students brainstorm ways that they can help someone. Suggest that they think of friends, family members, or neighbors who might need their help doing something. Then have them think of how they and the other person might feel before, during, and after the event. Have students individually complete their RAFTs, choosing the experience that they feel they can best describe.

Get Organized

Review the sample: *In "Autumn Afternoon," the writer uses descriptive words to describe helping his dad rake leaves.* Display a word web and explain: *Fill in a word web as you brainstorm descriptive words and phrases about your idea.* Model completing the word web with words and phrases from "Autumn Afternoon."

Have students create their own word webs to help them plan their poems. Have them write the topic in the center, and then brainstorm descriptive words to tell about the experience. Remind them to include words about feelings.

Word Web

Draft

Write Ideas

Have students choose appropriate layouts from **Magazine Maker** for their poems. Then have them write their drafts based on their word webs. Remind them to use descriptive words and colorful language.

See **Differentiate**

NGReach.com **Magazine Maker**

Differentiate

AL Above Level

ISSUE Students struggle to choose just the right descriptive words to use in their poems and want to add more than necessary.

STRATEGY Have partners exchange their word webs and discuss the descriptive words and phrases they used to describe their topics. Have partners suggest details that could be added to or deleted from their poems.

Revise

Read, Retell, Respond

Have students read their poems to partners. Have listeners restate what they think the poem is about and offer ideas to improve the word choice. Display language frames to guide the discussion.

Language Frames	
Retell	**Make Suggestions**
• The poem is about _____. • The word or phrase _____ describes _____.	• I really liked the words _____ you used to describe _____. • Can you use better words to describe _____?

Make Changes

Have students revise their poems. Remind them to use colorful language and descriptive words to connect with the reader. Then review the point of view in the poem "Guardian Angel" with students. Point out how the writer uses specific words such as *so sad* and *all alone* to show the main character's feelings. Encourage students to describe the feelings of characters in their own poems

Students may need assistance cutting and pasting text in **Magazine Maker**. Model the process: *Highlight the text you wish to move; click the Cut button; place the cursor where you wish to paste the text; and click the Paste button.*

See **Differentiate**

Student Sample: Revise **Sample Analysis**

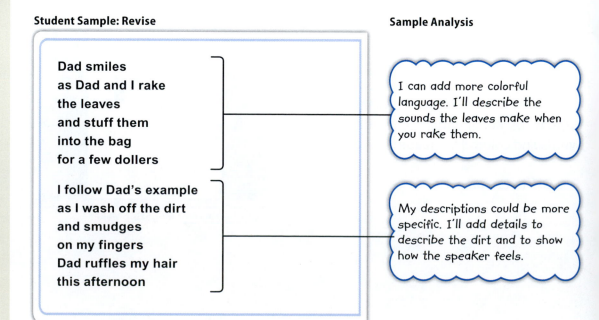

Edit and Proofread

Check the Poems

Have students check their grammar and spelling, focusing on the Week 2 spelling words and the proper use of nouns and pronouns.

Student Sample: Edit and Proofread

Sample Analysis

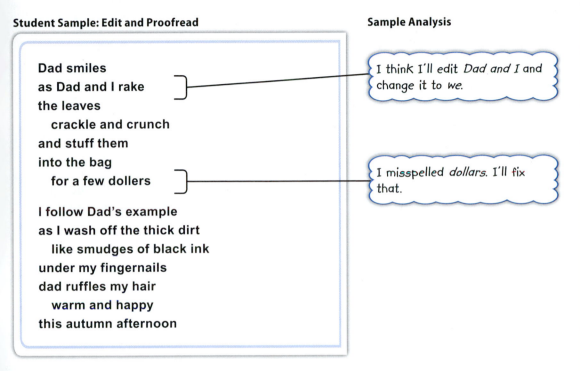

Dad smiles
as Dad and I rake
the leaves
  crackle and crunch
and stuff them
into the bag
  for a few dollers

I follow Dad's example
as I wash off the thick dirt
  like smudges of black ink
under my fingernails
dad ruffles my hair
  warm and happy
this autumn afternoon

I think I'll edit Dad and I *and change it to* we.

I misspelled dollars. *I'll fix that.*

Publish and Present

Make a Final Copy

Remind students that they can change the font in **Magazine Maker**. Have students try different fonts and choose one that fits the poem and is readable. Remind students to add a title and their name to their poem.

Share with Others

Have students practice reading aloud their poem several times. Remind students to read clearly, accurately, and at an appropriate pace. Then have them record their final reading. Share the recording with other classes.

Have students make additional copies of their poems and add them to their Weekly Writing folders. Use the **Writing Rubric** to assess each student's poem.

Student Sample: Publish

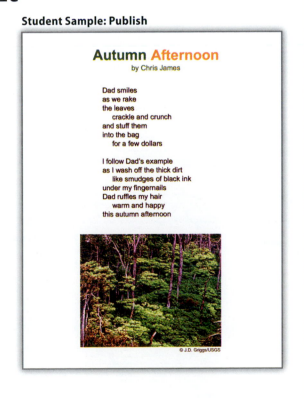

Autumn Afternoon
by Chris James

Dad smiles
as we rake
the leaves
  crackle and crunch
and stuff them
into the bag
  for a few dollers

I follow Dad's example
as I wash off the thick dirt
  like smudges of black ink
under my fingernails
Dad ruffles my hair
  warm and happy
this autumn afternoon

© J.D. Griggs/USGS

Best Practices

Focus on the Trait When reviewing students' poems, focus on the Word Choice column in the **Writing Rubric**.

Writing Rubric

☑ = TESTED

Assess

OBJECTIVES | **ASSESSMENTS**

Reading

☑ Preview and Predict to Comprehend Literature

☑ Identify Elements of a Poem

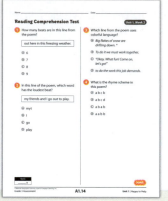
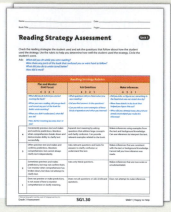

Reading Comprehension Test
A1.13–A1.14

Reading Strategy Assessment
SG1.30–SG1.31

Fluency

☑ Phrasing

☑ Accuracy and Rate

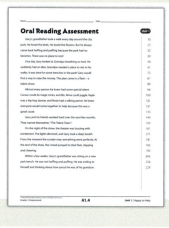

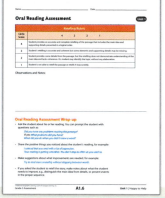

Oral Reading Assessment
A1.4–A1.6

Use these passages throughout Unit 1. Work with Below Level students this week.

Vocabulary and Spelling

☑ Consult References: Dictionary

☑ Spell Words with Short *a* and Short *o*

☑ Use Commonly Misspelled Words Correctly

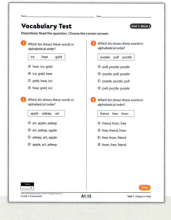

Vocabulary Test
A1.15

Spelling Pretest/ Spelling Test
T27m

Grammar and Writing

☑ Use Pronouns

☑ Use Sentences

☑ Use colorful Details to Elaborate

Writing, Revising, and Editing Test
A1.16–A1.17

Writing Rubric
A1.41

T33m Unit 1

ExamView®

Reteach and Practice

RESOURCES AND ROUTINES

Reading

RETEACH

Elements of a Poem: Reteaching Master RT1.4

Plan and Monitor: Reteaching Master RT1.5

ADDITIONAL PRACTICE

Comprehension Coach **NGReach.com**

PRINT & ONLINE
Report Forms

Student Profile: Weekly and Unit Assessments	A1.37–A1.38
Class Profile: Weekly and Unit Assessments	A1.39
Student Profile: Strengths and Needs Summary	A1.40
Student Profile: Oral Reading Assessment Progress Tracker	A1.3

Fluency

RETEACH

Fluency Routines, page BP33

ADDITIONAL PRACTICE

Comprehension Coach **NGReach.com**

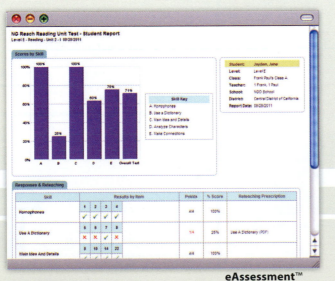

eAssessment™

ONLINE ONLY
Automated Reports

Student Profile: Weekly and Unit Tests

Class Profile: Weekly and Unit Tests

Standards Summary Report

Vocabulary and Spelling

RETEACH

Vocabulary Routine 6, page BP40

Spelling and Word Work Routine, page BP52

ADDITIONAL PRACTICE

Vocabulary Games **NGReach.com**

Daily Spelling Practice, pages T27m–T27n

Grammar and Writing

RETEACH

Pronouns: Anthology Handbook, page 588

Sentences: Anthology Handbook, page 581

Writing: Reteaching Writing Routine, page BP51

Writing Trait: Word Choice: Reteaching Master RT1.6

ADDITIONAL PRACTICE

More Grammar Practice PM1.16

Daily Writing Skills Practice, pages T27q–T27r

☑ = TESTED

	Day 1	**Day 2**
WHOLE GROUP TIME	**Listen and Comprehend**	**Read and Comprehend**

Anthology

Speaking and Listening
🕐 5–10 minutes

Day 1 — Listen and Comprehend
Academic Talk — CC.3.SL.4
Make Comparisons T34

Day 2 — Read and Comprehend
Academic Talk — CC.3.SL.1, CC.3.SL.1.b; CC.3.SL.2
Discuss Photographs T36a

Language and Vocabulary
🕐 15–25 minutes

Day 1
Daily Spelling and Word Work — CC.3.Rfou.3; CC.3.L.2
☑ Short *i* and *u* and Commonly Misspelled Words T33u
Daily Grammar — CC.3.L.1
☑ Complete Subjects and Predicates T33w
Social Studies Vocabulary — CC.3.L.4, 6
☑ Learn Key Words T34
   improve individual neighborhood offer volunteer

Day 2
Daily Spelling and Word Work — CC.3.Rfou.3; CC.3.L.2; CC.3.L.2.f
☑ Practice T33u
Daily Grammar — CC.3.L.1; CC.3.L.1.a
☑ Simple Subjects and Predicates T33w
Academic Vocabulary — CC.3.L.4, 6
☑ Learn More Key Words T36a
   benefit clarify comparison duty identify impact learn

Reading
🕐 20–40 minutes

Day 1
Reading
Read Aloud: Realistic Fiction T35a
Comprehension
☑ Make Comparisons T35a
Fluency — CC.3.Rfou.4
☑ Model Intonation T35a

Day 2
Reading — CC.3.Rinf.10
Read a Letter T39
Comprehension — CC.3.Rinf.10
☑ Learn to Plan and Monitor T38

Fluency — CC.3.Rfou.4
☑ Practice Intonation T38

Writing
🕐 15–45 minutes

Day 1
Power Writing T34 — CC.3.W.10
Daily Writing Skills — CC.3.W.7; CC.3.W.8
☑ Narrow a Topic, Plan an Interview T33y
Writing — CC.3.W.10
Write About Comparisons T36
Research Project: Biographical Sketch — CC.3.W.3.a
☑ Plan T55a

Day 2
Power Writing T36a
Daily Writing Skills — CC.3.W.7, 8
☑ Narrow a Topic T33y
Writing — CC.3.W.10
Write About Monitoring and Clarifying T38
Research Project: Biographical Sketch — CC.3.W.3.a; CC.3.W.3.b; CC.3.W.3.c; CC.3.W.7; CC.3.W.8
☑ Research T55a

Nonfiction

SMALL GROUP READING TIME	**Read Social Studies Articles**	**Read Nonfiction Books**

🕐 20 minutes

Day 1 — Read Social Studies Articles
Vocabulary — CC.3.L.6
Learn Social Studies Vocabulary SG17
Reading — CC.3.Rinf.9; CC.3.Rinf.10
Compare Points and Details SG16
Build Comprehension SG17

Day 2 — Read Nonfiction Books
Vocabulary — CC.3.L.6
Learn Story Words SG18–SG19
Reading — CC.3.Rinf.8; CC.3.Rinf.10
Introduce SG18–SG19
Read and Integrate Ideas SG20–SG21
☑ Plan and Monitor SG20–SG21
☑ Make Comparisons SG20–SG21

LEARNING STATION TIME/DAILY PHONICS INTERVENTION

🕐 20 minutes

Speaking and Listening T33q — CC.3.SL.3; CC.3.SL.4
Language and Vocabulary T33q — CC.3.L.6
Writing T33q — CC.3.W.7; CC.3.W.8; CC.3.W.10
Cross-Curricular T33r — CC.3.Rinf.10; CC.3.SL.1
Reading and Intervention T33r; SG68 — CC.3.Rlit.3; CC.3.Rlit.10; CC.3.Rinf.10; CC.3.Rfou.3; CC.3.Rfou.4.b
Daily Phonics Intervention T33s–T33t — CC.3.Rfou.3.d; CC.3.L.2.e; CC.3.L.2.f

BIG Question **How do people help each other?**

Day **3**	Day **4**	Day **5**
Read and Comprehend	**Read and Comprehend**	**Review and Apply**

Day 3 — Read and Comprehend

Academic Talk   CC.3.SL.1.d
Preview and Predict T40

Daily Spelling and Word Work   CC.3.Rfou.3;
✔ Practice T33v   CC.3.L.2.e, f; CC.2.L.4.d

Daily Grammar   CC.3.L.1; CC.3.L.1.a
✔ Phrases and Clauses T33x
Vocabulary Practice   CC.3.L.6
✔ Expand Word Knowledge T40

Reading   CC.3.Rinf.10
Read an Autobiography
T41–T43
Comprehension   CC.3.Rinf.6, 8
✔ Make Comparisons   CC.3.Rinf.10
T42–T43
✔ Monitor and Clarify
T42–43, T44–45

Fluency   CC.3.Rfou.4; CC.3.Rfou.4.a, b
✔ Practice Intonation, Accuracy,
and Rate T42–43

Power Writing T40   CC.3.W.10
Daily Writing Skills   CC.3.W.8; CC.3.SL.1.c; CC.3.SL.3
✔ Plan an Interview T33z
Writing   CC.3.W.10
Write a Prediction T44–45

Research Project: Biographical Sketch   CC.3.W.3.a;
✔ Research T55a   CC.3.W.3.b; CC.3.W.3.c;
   CC.3.W.7; CC.3.W.8

Read Nonfiction Books (Day 3)

Vocabulary   CC.3.L.6
Expand Vocabulary Through
Wide Reading SG18–SG21
Reading   CC.3.Rinf.8;
Read and Integrate   CC.3.Rinf.10
Ideas SG20–SG21
✔ Plan and Monitor SG20–SG21
✔ Make Comparisons SG20–SG21

Day 4 — Read and Comprehend

Academic Talk   CC.3.SL.1
Summarize Reading T46

Daily Spelling and Word Work   CC.3.Rfou.3; CC.3.L.2.e;
✔ Practice T33v   CC.3.L.2.g

Daily Grammar   CC.3.W.5; CC.3.L.1; CC.3.L.1.a
✔ Grammar and Writing T33x
Vocabulary Practice   CC.3.L.6
✔ Share Word Knowledge T48
point of view   **narrator**

Reading   CC.3.Rinf.10
Read an Autobiography
T47–T53
Comprehension   CC.3.Rinf.10
✔ Make Comparisons   CC.3.Rinf.8
T47, T50–51   CC.3.Rinf.6
✔ Monitor and Clarify
T47, T49, T52
Identify Point of View T48

Fluency   CC.3.Rfou.4.a, b
✔ Practice Intonation, Accuracy, Rate T47

Power Writing T46   CC.3.W.10
Daily Writing Skills   CC.3.W.7; CC.3.W.8
✔ Narrow a Topic, Plan an Interview T33z
Writing   CC.3.W.10
Writer's Craft T53a

Research Project: Biographical Sketch   CC.3.W.3.a;
✔ Organize T55b   CC.3.W.3.b; CC.3.W.3.c;
   CC.3.W.8; CC.3.SL.3

Read Nonfiction Books (Day 4)

Vocabulary   CC.3.L.6
Expand Vocabulary Through
Wide Reading SG18–SG21
Reading   CC.3.Rinf.8;
Read and Integrate   CC.3.Rinf.10
Ideas SG20–SG21
✔ Plan and Monitor SG20–SG21
✔ Make Comparisons SG20–SG21

Day 5 — Review and Apply

Academic Talk   CC.3.SL.1.d
Talk About "The World's Greatest
Underachiever" T54

Daily Grammar   CC.3.L.1; CC.3.L.1.a
✔ Review T33x

Vocabulary Review   CC.3.L.6
✔ Apply Word Knowledge T53b

Reading   CC.3.Rlit.10
Reread an Autobiography T41–T53
Comprehension   CC.3.Rinf.8
✔ Make Comparisons T54a

Fluency   CC.3.Rfou.4.b
✔ Check Intonation, Accuracy, and Rate T55

Power Writing T53b   CC.3.W.10
Daily Writing Skills   CC.3.W.7; CC.3.W.8
✔ Narrow a Topic. Plan an Interview T33z
Writing   CC.3.W.10
Write About "The World's Greatest
Underachiever" T54

Research Project: Biographical Sketch   CC.3.SL.4;
✔ Present T55b   CC.3.SL.5

Read Nonfiction Books (Day 5)

Vocabulary   CC.3.L.6
Expand Vocabulary Through
Wide Reading SG18–SG21
Reading   CC.3.Rinf.8;
Connect Across Texts CC.3.Rinf.10;
SG21   CC.3.SL.1.a
Writing   CC.3.W.10
Choose a Writing Option
SG20–SG21

ASSESSMENT & RETEACHING

Assessment and Reteaching T55c–T55d

✔ Reading Comprehension Test A1.18–A1.19   CC.3.Rinf.8
✔ Reading Strategy Assessment   CC.3.Rinf.10
SG1.30–SG1.31
✔ Oral Reading Assessment A1.4–A1.6   CC.3.Rfou.4
✔ Vocabulary Test A1.20–A1.21   CC.3.L.6

✔ Spelling: Short *i* and *u* and   CC.3.L.2;
Commonly Misspelled Words T33u   CC.3.L.2.e-g
✔ Writing, Revising, and Editing Test   CC.3.W.10;
A1.22–A1.23   CC.3.L.1; CC.3.L.1.a
Reteaching Masters RT1.7–RT1.8

Week **3** Learning Stations

Speaking and Listening

Option 1: People in the Community

PROGRAM RESOURCES

Cross-Curricular Teamwork Activities: Card 9

Language Builder Picture Cards D1–D10

Teacher's Guide on

| Tell a Story | CC.3.SL.4 |

Option 2: Interview

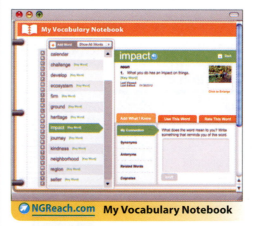

"What did you do next?"

Have one student interview another about a time when he or she helped at home, at school, or in the community.

Remind students to ask questions about important details of the event. Both students should speak in complete sentences.

When the first interview is finished, have students switch roles.

| Ask and Answer Questions and Elaborate | CC.3.SL.3 |
| Recount an Experience | CC.3.SL.4 |

Language and Vocabulary

Key Words

benefit · clarify · comparison · duty · identify
impact · improve · individual · learn · narrator
neighborhood · offer · point of view · volunteer

Option 1: Vocabulary Games

NGReach.com **Online Vocabulary Games**

| Acquire and Use Conversational, General Academic, and Domain-Specific Words | CC.3.L.6 |

Option 2: My Vocabulary Notebook

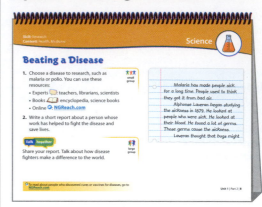

NGReach.com **My Vocabulary Notebook**

Have students expand their word knowledge.

Under: Add More Information > Use This Word > Power Writing Routine, have students write as much as they can as well as they can about the word in one minute.

| Acquire and Use Conversational, General Academic, and Domain-Specific Words | CC.3.L.6 |

Writing

Option 1: Beating a Disease

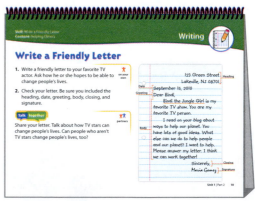

PROGRAM RESOURCES & MATERIALS

Cross-Curricular Teamwork Activities: Card 8

Teacher's Guide on NGReach.com

Student Resources Directory

encyclopedia · science books

| Conduct Research | CC.3.W.7 |
| Gather Information and Take Notes | CC.3.W.8 |

Option 2: Write a Friendly Letter

PROGRAM RESOURCES

Language and Literacy Teamwork Activities: Card 10

Teacher's Guide on NGReach.com

| Write Over Shorter Time for Specific Audiences | CC.3.W.10 |

✶ = one student   ✶✶ = two students   ✶✶✶ = three or more students

Cross-Curricular

Option 1: Heroic Athletes

NGReach.com Student Resources

Have students read an online article about Scout's heroic efforts to overcome obstacles. Go to: Resources > Unit 1 > Learning Stations > Week 3 > Succeeding in Life

Have partners discuss the courage Scout needed to become a competitive runner.

Read and Comprehend Informational Texts	CC.3.Rinf.10
Discuss Topics, Expressing Ideas Clearly and Building on Others' Ideas	CC.3.SL.1

Option 2: Dyslexia

NGReach.com Student Resources

Have students read an online article about dyslexia. Go to: Resources > Unit 1 > Learning Stations > Week 3 > Dyslexia

• Have students create fact sheets with the information they learned and share them with the class.

Read and Comprehend Informational Texts CC.3.Rinf.10

Reading

Option 1: Comprehension Coach

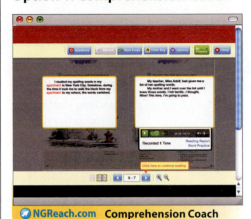

NGReach.com Comprehension Coach

Read and Comprehend Informational Text	CC.3.Rinf.10
Read Orally with Accuracy and Appropriate Rate on Successive Readings	CC.3.Rfou.4.b

Option 2: Author Study
Henry Winkler

	Character:	Character:
Detail:		
Detail:		
Detail:		

MATERIALS

books by Henry Winkler such as Help! Somebody Get Me Out of Fourth Grade!, I Got a "D" in Salami, *and* Niagara Falls, Or Does It?

Have students select and read a book. Ask them to pick two characters and create a chart listing the two characters and three or four descriptive details for each.

Students can also choose other books. See **Independent Reading** on page SG68.

Describe Characters	CC.3.Rlit.3
Read and Comprehend Literature	CC.3.Rlit.10

Intervention

Phonics Games

NGReach.com Online Phonics Games

Apply Phonics and Word Analysis Skills	CC.3.Rfou.3

For Reteaching Masters, see pages RT1.7–RT1.8

Additional Resources

ESL Kit

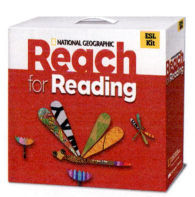

ESL Teacher's Edition pages T34–T55

OBJECTIVES

Thematic Connection: Heroes Then and Now

Recognize High Frequency Words

Develop Phonological Awareness: Isolate Sounds

Associate Sounds and Spellings /ĭ/i, /ŭ/u

Blend Sounds to Decode Words

Teach	**Day 1**

PROGRAM RESOURCES

High Frequency Words:
  Teaching Master 3

Sound/Spelling Card 11

Word Builder: Transparency 16

Decodable Passage: *Dip Tips*
  Practice Book, page 95

Reach into Phonics

Lesson 8, page T14

Lesson 10, pages T16–T17

High Frequency Words

Follow Lesson 8 to present High Frequency Words:

something	make	long	large	move

Short Vowel /ĭ/i

Follow Lesson 10. Use **Reading Routine 1** and **Sound/Spelling Card 11** to teach sound and spelling /ĭ/i. Guide students through **Transparency 16**. Use **Reading Routine 3** to guide students as they read Decodable text.

*For **Reading Routine 1**, see Reach into Phonics, page vi.*

*For **Reading Routine 3**, see Reach into Phonics, page ix*

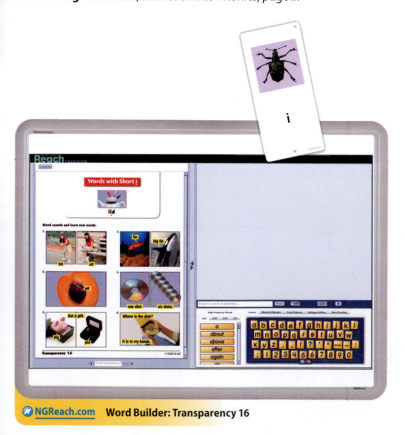

NGReach.com **Word Builder: Transparency 16**

Teach	**Day 2**

PROGRAM RESOURCES

High Frequency Words:
  Teaching Master 4

Sound/Spelling Card 24

Word Builder: Transparency 17

Decodable Passage: *Jim and Big Gus*
  Practice Book, page 96

Decodable Passage: *Dig into a Bun*
  Practice Book, page 97

Reach into Phonics

Lesson 9, page T15

Lesson 11, pages T18–T19

High Frequency Words

Follow Lesson 9 to present High Frequency Words:

different	small	open	same	eat

Short Vowel /ŭ/u

Follow Lesson 11. Use **Reading Routine 1** and **Sound/Spelling Card 24** to teach sound and spelling /ŭ/u. Guide students through **Transparency 17**. Use **Reading Routine 3** to guide students as they read Decodable text.

*For **Reading Routine 1**, see Reach into Phonics, page vi.*

*For **Reading Routine 3**, see Reach into Phonics, page ix.*

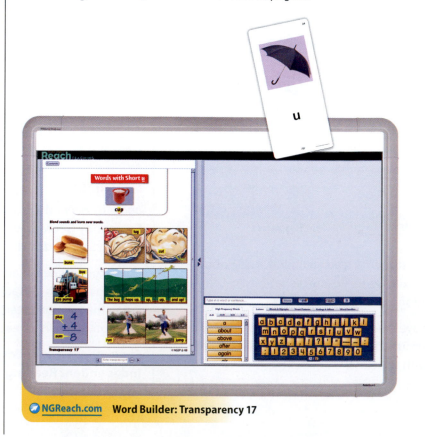

NGReach.com **Word Builder: Transparency 17**

✗ = one student ✗✗ = two students ✗✗✗ = three or more students

Words with Short *i, u*

COMMON CORE STANDARDS

Use Conventional Spelling	CC.3.L.2.e
Use Spelling Patterns and Generalizations	CC.3.L.2.f
Read Grade-Appropriate Irregularly Spelled Words	CC.3.Rfou.3.d

Crack the Code! Day 3   Option 1

MATERIALS

computer

Prepare

- Have partners use a computer to type the alphabet on one line. Tell them to paste that line onto the next line, and then change the second line to a symbol font.
- Next, have partners type all the words from the word bank below in random order, and then change their typing of the words into the same symbol font.
- Tell partners to type a blank line next to each word.

long	move	limp	spin	plum	sprint	stump

Play a Game

- Have pairs use the symbol alphabet to decode the letters used in each word, and then write the word.
- Remind students that they might be able to figure out the word after decoding only a few of its letters.

Pick It Up! Day 3  Option 2

MATERIALS

index cards, 10 per group

Prepare

- Arrange students in groups of three to six. Have students collaborate to print the vowels *i* and *u*, and then print the consonants *b, c, d, g, n, p, r, t* separately on index cards.
- Have students set the vowel cards together and arrange the consonant cards together on a desk.

Play a Game

- A Caller calls out a word from the word bank below.

big	bit	rid	grid	grit	rid	bid
bug	bud	rub	grub	gut	rut	tug
pig	pit	tin	grip	grin	crib	pin
cup	nut	bun	cub	cut	punt	drug

- A Reader picks up the letters needed to spell the word. The Reader places the cards down in order and reads the word.
- Group members listen and watch as the Reader reads the word. If a student notices an error, he or she takes the Reader's place.
- Students take turns as the Caller and Reader.

Missing Vowels Day 4

MATERIALS

index cards, 15 per pair of students

Prepare

- Have partners collaborate to write 15 words with short *i* or short *u*, each on a separate card. Tell students to underline the short vowel.
- Explain that students will write a short phrase or short sentence containing the word on the back of each card, leaving a blank in place of the vowel. Display examples: *a ticket st_b; take the b_s home; a squealing p_g; the baby's cr_b.* Have partners collaborate to complete one card in this way.
- Then have partners complete the remaining cards individually, with each partner completing seven cards.

Play a Game

- Partners exchange cards and add the missing vowels.
- When both partners are finished, students take turns holding up cards and reading phrases to each other.

Hop and Read Day 5

MATERIALS

masking tape • large index cards, 10 per pair of students • markers

Prepare

- Have partners work together to write each High Frequency Word from the word bank on separate cards.
- Have partners use tape to make a hopscotch grid on the classroom floor. Tell students to tape a word card in each box of the hopscotch grid.

something	make	long	large	move
different	small	open	same	eat

Play a Game

- Have Player 1 toss a marker inside the first box and then hop through the boxes reading each word, skipping the box the marker is on. Player 1 turns around, hops back, and picks up the marker. Have Player 2 repeat the process.
- The first player to complete the hopscotch grid with the marker on each box wins the game.

OBJECTIVES

Thematic Connection: Heroes Then and Now

☑ Spell Words with Short *i* and Short *u*

☑ Use Commonly Misspelled Words Correctly

SUGGESTED PACING

DAY 1	Spelling Pretest
DAY 2–4	Daily Practice Options
DAY 5	Spelling Test

| **Spelling Pretest** | **Day 1** | |
| **Spelling Test** | **Day 5** | |

Spelling Words

Use these words and sentences for the weekly Spelling Pretest and Spelling Test.

Words with Short *i* and Short *u*	
1. awful	The people did something about the **awful** working conditions in the factories.
2. citizen	If you are born in a country, you are a **citizen** of it.
3. conduct	His heroic **conduct** made others act bravely, too.
4. decision	We need a **decision,** so please make up your mind.
5. disagree	A hero may **disagree** with others if she knows something is unfair.
6. establish	To **establish** something often means working hard to set up something new.
7. hectic	We rushed to finish our shopping like everyone else in the **hectic** crowd.
8. inquire	I'll **inquire** at the office, and maybe they can answer my question about this difficult task.
9. interrupt	He will **interrupt** his game to help me with homework.
10. opinion	I hope you agree with my **opinion** that laws need to be changed to help the disabled.
11. results	Tia read her test **results** and saw that she passed!
12. submit	I will **submit** my best recipe and maybe I'll win.
13. success	We won the game, and our **success** made us happy.
14. suggestion	We'll think about your **suggestion** for the class play.
15. witness	As a **witness** to her heroic deed, I saw her save a life.
Watch-Out Words	
16. could have	We **could have** seen a movie, but we went to the zoo.
17. should have	We **should have** changed our minds when we saw dark clouds.
18. would have	We **would have** stayed dry if we had gone to the movies!
19. might have	It **might have** been a bad day, but it didn't rain too hard.

| **Short *i* and *u* Syllables** | **Day 2** | | **Option 1** |

MATERIALS

index cards, 15 per pair of students

Teach

Display the words *hectic* and *submit* with a line between the syllables: *hec/tic, sub/mit.* Say each word, emphasizing the short vowel sounds. Point to the second syllable in *hectic* and review the rule: *When a syllable ends with a consonant, the vowel is usually short.* Review the rule for short *u* in the first syllable in *sub/mit.*

Prepare

Have partners check a dictionary and collaborate to write each of the first 15 spelling words on a separate index card, displaying the syllable breaks. Then, have partners stack the cards face down.

Play a Game

- Have Player 1 pick and display a card. Player 2 points to the syllable with *i* or *u* followed by a consonant, names the consonant, pronounces the word, and spells it aloud.
- Player 1 decides if Player 2 has pronounced and spelled the word correctly. If so, Player 2 keeps the card. If not, the card goes to the bottom of the stack.
- Players switch roles and take turns playing until they have displayed all of the cards and spelled all of the words correctly. The player with more cards wins.

| Apply Phonics Skills | CC.3.Rfou.3 |
| Use Spelling Patterns and Generalizations | CC.3.L.2.f |

| **Should Have!** | **Day 2** | | **Option 2** |

MATERIALS

large index cards, 4 per group

Prepare

Have groups of four students collaborate to create word cards for the Watch-Out Words, including the definitions.

could have: shows a choice that was possible

should have: expresses a feeling of duty

would have: expresses something that was likely

might have: says that something was possible

Play

- Have each player pick one card. Explain that players will have a turn to make a gesture, such as pointing, smiling, walking, sitting, turning, or bending.
- Have each student use his or her card to comment on the gesture in a complete sentence: *You should have pointed to me.*
- The student gets a point if everyone agrees that he or she used the term correctly. Play until each player has had a turn to gesture twice.

| Demonstrate Command of Spelling | CC.3.L.2 |

Daily Language Arts

Short *i*, Short *u* — Day 3 — Option 1

MATERIALS
index cards, 15 per pair of students • highlighter, one per pair

Prepare
Have partners collaborate to write each of the first 15 spelling words on a separate index card.

Play a Game
- Have partners softly read each word in unison, tapping a finger lightly as they pronounce each syllable. Tell them to put the two-syllable words in one stack and three-syllable words in another stack.

- Have partners say each two-syllable word aloud, highlight the short *i* or *u*, and organize cards according to whether the short *i* or *u* is in syllable one or two.
- Have partners follow the same steps for three-syllable words and organize cards according to whether short *i* or *u* is in syllable one, two, or three.

| Apply Word Analysis Skills | CC.3.Rfou.3 |
| Use Spelling Patterns and Generalizations | CC.3.L.2.f |

Classify Words — Day 3 — Option 2

MATERIALS
dictionary, one per student • index cards, as needed per student

Practice

Words I Know	Words I Think I Know	Words I Don't Know
awful	conduct	citizen
decision	hectic	establish
could have	success	witness

- Have students create a chart and write the spelling words they know in the first column, the words they might know in the middle column, and unfamiliar words in the third column.
- Have students write words from columns two and three on index cards, look them up in a dictionary, and write their meanings in their own words.

| Use Conventional Spelling | CC.3.L.2.e |
| Use Glossaries and Dictionaries | CC.3.L.4.d |

It Looks Like... — Day 4 — Option 1

Use Spelling Pronunciations
- Have students write the spelling words that are causing them difficulty. Tell them to write a special spelling pronunciation for each. For example, they might write four syllables for *de-ci-si-on* and pronounce every letter.

decision
de-ci-si-on

- Have students say the word aloud several times using the spelling pronunciation. Tell them to close their eyes, visualize the letters, and repeat the pronunciation.
- Finally, have students say it aloud as they write the word several times, still using the spelling pronunciation. Tell students to visualize the spelling pronunciation each time they read or hear the word. Explain that eventually the correct spelling will come to mind automatically.

| Use Conventional Spelling | CC.3.L.2.e |

Word Scramble — Day 4 — Option 2

MATERIALS
scissors, one per student • timer • index cards, 5–7 per student

Prepare
- Arrange students in small groups. Assign five to seven different spelling words to each student in the group. Have students print their words on a separate index card with spaces between the letters for cutting.
- Tell students to cut the first 15 words into syllables and the Watch-Out Words into two words. If needed, have them check a dictionary to see where syllable breaks appear.

Play a Game
- Have students mix up their words and syllables and give them to another person in the group. Give students five minutes to unscramble and put together as many spelling words as possible.
- Students receive one point for each word they complete. The player with the most points wins.

| Apply Word Analysis Skills | CC.3.Rfou.3 |

OBJECTIVES

Thematic Connection: Heroes Then and Now

✓ **Grammar:** Use Complete Subjects and Predicates
✓ **Grammar:** Use Simple Subjects and Predicates

COMMON CORE STANDARDS

Edit Writing	CC.3.W.5
Demonstrate Command of Grammar	CC.3.L.1
Explain the Function of Nouns, Pronouns, and Verbs	CC.3.L.1.a

---

Day 1

PROGRAM RESOURCES
Complete Subjects and Predicates: eVisual 1.23

MATERIALS
blue and pink highlighters

Teach the Rules

Use the suggestion on page T36 to introduce complete subjects and predicates. Explain: *A subject tells whom or what a sentence is about. A predicate tells what a subject is, has, or does.* Use **eVisual 1.23** to teach complete subjects and predicates.

> #### Complete Subjects and Predicates
>
> - The **complete subject** includes all of the words that tell about the subject.
> - The **complete predicate** includes all of the words in the predicate.
>
> <u>My aunt's heroism inspired many people.</u>
>
> <u>Today I follow her brave example.</u>

🌐 **NGReach.com** Subjects and Predicates: eVisual 1.23

Play a Game 👫

Have partners collaborate to write each sentence below on a separate strip of paper. Explain:

- *Player 1 reads a sentence. Player 2 underlines the complete subject once and the complete predicate twice. Players switch roles for the next sentence and play until all four sentences are used.*
- *Each partner chooses two sentences and rewrites one with a new complete subject and the other with a new complete predicate.*
- *Players get two points for identifying each complete subject and predicate and one point for each new correct sentence.*

My brother Scott started a swim club.	He invited his friend Emma to join.
Emma likes swimming a lot.	She volunteers as a lifeguard.

Differentiate

EL English Learners

ISSUE In some languages, word order differs from English.

STRATEGY Before playing, help students highlight the subject of each sentence in blue and the predicate in pink.

Day 2

PROGRAM RESOURCES
Simple Subjects and Predicates: eVisual 1.26

Game: Practice Master PM1.18

MATERIALS
index cards, 6 per student • scissors

Teach the Rules

Use the suggestion on page T38 to introduce simple subjects and predicates. Then use **eVisual 1.26** to help students identify simple subjects and simple predicates.

> #### Simple Subjects and Predicates
>
> - The **simple subject** is the most important word in a complete subject. It may be a **noun** or a **pronoun**.
>
>   My <u>grandpa</u> <u>volunteers</u> every week.
>
> - The **simple predicate** is the most important word in a complete predicate. It is the **verb**.
>
>   Even as a boy, <u>he</u> <u>found</u> volunteering to be rewarding.

🌐 **NGReach.com** Subjects and Predicates: eVisual 1.26

Play a Game 👫

Distribute **Practice Master PM1.18** and have students follow the directions to play the game.

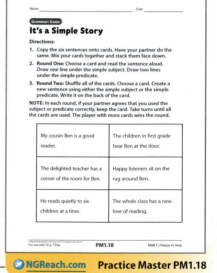

🌐 **NGReach.com** Practice Master PM1.18

Differentiate

SN Special Needs

ISSUE Students have difficulty thinking in the abstract.

STRATEGY After Round One, cut the simple subjects and simple predicates from the cards and place them face up. Students choose a card and use it as the simple subject or predicate in a new, written sentence.

 👤 = one student 👫 = two students 👪 = three or more students

Day 3

PROGRAM RESOURCES
Phrases and Clauses: eVisual 1.27

MATERIALS
index cards, 6 per pair of students

Teach the Rules

Use the suggestion on page T44–45 to introduce phrases and clauses. Explain: *Sometimes words work together but are not complete sentences.* Display **eVisual 1.27**.

> **Phrases and Clauses**
>
> - **Phrases** and **dependent clauses** are groups of words that work together but are not sentences.
> ---
> - A **phrase** is a group of words that does not have a subject and a predicate.
>
>   **in the park**
>
>   **with a smile**
>
> - A **dependent clause** has a <u>subject</u> and a <u>verb</u> but does not express a complete thought.
>
>   **after <u>they</u> <u>won</u> the race**
>
>   **because <u>we</u> <u>tried</u>**
>
> NGReach.com   Phrases and Clauses: eVisual 1.27

Play a Game 👫

Have partners collaborate to copy the sentences, phrases, and dependent clauses below onto cards. Explain:

- *Choose a card. Tell if it is a complete sentence, a phrase, or a clause. If it is a phrase or a clause, use it in a complete sentence.*
- *Keep the card if your partner agrees you are right. When all cards have been used, play again. The player with more cards wins.*

at the school	when it was tired	as we got near
because she needed help	Ms. Hu's dog ran past the gate	after a game

Differentiate

AL Above Level

ISSUE Students have a firm understanding of what makes a complete sentence and what is a phrase or a clause.

STRATEGY Have students identify the word group and correctly explain why it is a phrase, clause, or complete sentence.

Day 4

PROGRAM RESOURCES
Grammar and Writing: Practice Master PM1.19

Grammar and Writing 👤

Distribute **Practice Master PM1.19**. Have students use editing and proofreading marks to correct errors with sentences.

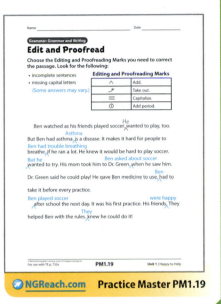

NGReach.com   **Practice Master PM1.19**

Day 5

PROGRAM RESOURCES
Writing, Revising, and Editing Test: Assessment Masters A1.22–A1.23

MATERIALS
timer

Review and Assess 👥👥👥

Allow two minutes for small groups to write a mix of complete sentences, phrases, and dependent clauses. Have groups trade papers and label phrases, dependent clauses, and complete sentences. Then have groups underline the simple subjects and simple predicates in the complete sentences.

dependent clauses	phrases	complete sentences
while we waited	after the race	<u>We</u> joined the volunteer group.

☑ Administer the **Writing, Revising, and Editing Test**.

OBJECTIVES
Thematic Connection: Heroes Then and Now
- ☑ Choose and Narrow a Topic
- ☑ Develop Interview Questions

COMMON CORE STANDARDS

Conduct Research	CC.3.W.7
Recall Relevant Information and Take Notes	CC.3.W.8
Ask Questions to Check Understanding	CC.3.SL.1.c
Ask and Answer Questions	CC.3.SL.3

Introduce — Day 1

PROGRAM RESOURCES
Narrow a Topic: eVisual 1.24
Plan an Interview: eVisual 1.25

Teach the Skill

Display **eVisual 1.24.** Explain: *The first step in writing a report is to choose a topic. The next step is to narrow it down, or focus it.*

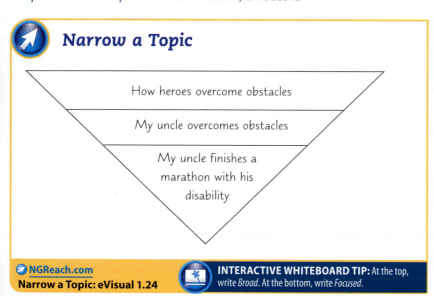

Narrow a Topic

- How heroes overcome obstacles
- My uncle overcomes obstacles
- My uncle finishes a marathon with his disability

◎ NGReach.com
Narrow a Topic: eVisual 1.24

INTERACTIVE WHITEBOARD TIP: At the top, write *Broad*. At the bottom, write *Focused*.

Read the topics inside the diagram. Explain: *Raina decided "How heroes overcome obstacles" was too big to cover in one report. She narrowed down her topic for a brief report. She asked research questions and decided how to find answers to them. You might find answers in books, magazines, or on the Internet. Raina decided to interview her uncle. She began with one main question, then wrote others beginning with words like who, what, where, when, why, and how.* Display **eVisual 1.25.**

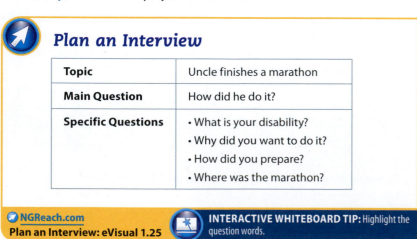

Plan an Interview

Topic	Uncle finishes a marathon
Main Question	How did he do it?
Specific Questions	• What is your disability? • Why did you want to do it? • How did you prepare? • Where was the marathon?

◎ NGReach.com
Plan an Interview: eVisual 1.25

INTERACTIVE WHITEBOARD TIP: Highlight the question words.

Narrow a Topic — Day 2 Option 1

Introduce

Copy and display the following phrases:

> My dad in the military
> The military
> The day my dad won a medal for heroism

Create and display a blank Narrow a Topic diagram like the one in **eVisual 1.24,** labeling the top triangle "Broad" and the bottom triangle "Focused." Have students copy the diagram.

Practice

Have partners write the phrases in the diagram from broad to focused. Encourage partners to talk about how they decided to arrange the topics.

Next, have partners fill out two more Narrow a Topic diagrams. This time, have them begin with the broad topic: *Firefighting.* Tell them to fill out the diagram each time showing a different way to narrow down, or focus, the topic.

Narrow a Topic — Day 2 Option 2

Introduce

Tell partners that they are going to narrow down the broad topic of overcoming obstacles. Copy and display the following diagram:

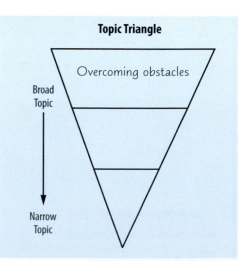

Topic Triangle
Broad Topic — Overcoming obstacles — Narrow Topic

Practice

Have students fill out the diagrams twice, narrowing "overcoming obstacles" differently in each.

When the diagrams are complete, tell partners to compare both of their diagrams with another pair of students. Have each pair choose one focused topic for which they could conduct an interview as part of their research.

 = one student   = two students   = three or more students

Daily Language Arts

SUGGESTED PACING

DAY 1   Teach the Skill
DAY 2–4   Daily Practice Options
DAY 5   Review and Assess

Conduct an Interview   Day 3 ✶✶✶ Option 1

PROGRAM RESOURCES

Digital Library: Language Builder Picture Card D5

MATERIALS

timer

Introduce

Arrange students in small groups. Display **Language Builder Picture Card D5** and explain: *Imagine that you are about to interview a firefighter. What questions will you ask?* Have groups discuss the image and what they know about some of the obstacles that firefighters face.

Practice

Set a timer for 10 minutes. Have each group write four questions. Tell them one question should be a main question, and three questions should be more specific. If students need help, remind them to begin their questions with words such as *who, what, where, when, why,* and *how.*

When students are finished, set the timer for 10 minutes again. This time, have one person from the group pretend to be the firefighter. Have the remainder of the group interview the student playing the firefighter and take notes.

Conduct an Interview   Day 3 ✶✶ Option 2

MATERIALS

timer

Introduce

Have students work with the same partners with whom they worked on Day 2. Explain: *Yesterday you narrowed the topic about overcoming obstacles. Today, you will write and ask interview questions.*

Practice

Set a timer for 10 minutes and have partners write questions as in Option 1, above. Remind students to write one main question and then generate questions that begin with words like *who, what, where, how, when,* and *why.*

When time is up, set the timer for 10 minutes again. Have one partner pretend to be the person being interviewed and the other partner be the interviewer. Encourage students to ask follow-up questions to clarify the interviewee's answers and to obtain more information.

Tell the interviewer to take notes as he or she listens to the interviewee's answers.

Focus Topic/Write Questions   Day 4 ✶✶

MATERIALS

computers with Internet access, one per pair of students

Practice

Have partners search the **Digital Library** for images of a person they would like to interview. Tell them to discuss why they find the person interesting, and then have them generate a narrow topic to research about the person.

Once they have narrowed a topic, have partners generate one main question and two or three specific questions they could ask during an interview.

If time allows, have partners share and discuss their topic and questions with another pair of students.

Review and Assess   Day 5 ✶✶✶

PROGRAM RESOURCES

Writing, Revising, and Editing Test:
    Assessment Masters A1.22–A1.23

MATERIALS

timer

Review the Skill

Have students quickly review "The World's Greatest Underachiever" on **Anthology** pages 41–52. Tell them to pretend that they will interview the author Henry Winkler about how he faced challenges in his life.

Copy and display the following chart:

> General Topic: _____
> Narrow Topic: _____
> Main Question: _____
> Specific Question: _____
> Specific Question: _____

Arrange students in small groups. Have each group generate a general topic about which they could interview Henry (for example: acting), and then narrow it down (for example: how he got started in television).

Set the timer for 10 minutes and have groups complete the chart as if they were going to interview Henry Winkler for a research report.

☑ Administer the **Writing, Revising, and Editing Test**

OBJECTIVES

Thematic Connection: Heroes Then and Now

☑ **Use Domain-Specific Words**

☑ **Explain Text Structure: Comparison**

PROGRAM RESOURCES

PRINT & TECHNOLOGY

Family Newsletter 1

Thinking Map: Practice Master PM1.17

TECHNOLOGY ONLY

Sing with Me MP3

Digital Library: Key Word Images

My Vocabulary Notebook

Read Aloud: eVisual 1.22

MATERIALS

timer

Power Writing

Have students write as much as they can as well as they can in one minute about the word *volunteer*.

For **Writing Routine 1**, see page BP47.

COMMON CORE STANDARDS

Reading

Read with Fluency to Support   CC.3.Rfou.4
   Comprehension

Writing

Write Over Shorter Time for Specific   CC.3.W.10
   Purposes

Speaking and Listening

Recount an Experience   CC.3.SL.4

Language and Vocabulary

Determine Meaning of Words   CC.3.L.4
   and Phrases

Acquire and Use General Academic   CC.3.L.6
   and Domain-Specific Words,
   and Use Words that Signal
   Spatial and Temporal Relationships

WARM-UP

Ask: *Do you think one person can make a difference in the lives of many people? Why or why not?* Invite volunteers to share their responses.

Academic Talk

1 Make Comparisons   Anthology   page 34

Explain: *When you make a comparison, you show how two or more things are alike and different. You also can compare how something changes over time.* Read aloud the instructions and play the **Sing With Me Language Song**: "I Am Feeling Good." Explain that Kemal makes comparisons to show how he made a difference in his neighborhood.

Use the song to model the steps for how to make comparisons:

- First, name the topic: *Kemal helped clean the street.*
- Then, tell the way it was before: *Before Kemal's hard work, the street was a mess.*
- Finally, tell how it is different now: *Now, his street is clean and safe.*

Explain that you used the words *before* and *now* to signal comparisons.

Ask: *When have you made a difference in your school or community? Tell what things were like before and after your work.* Encourage students to make clear comparisons as they recount their experiences.

Social Studies Vocabulary

2 Key Words ☑   Anthology   page 35

Explain and model using **Vocabulary Routine 1** and the graphic organizer on **Student eEdition** page 35 to teach the Key Words.

> **Key Words**
> improve · individual · neighborhood
> offer · volunteer

- ***Pronounce the word*** *and point to the image:* **volunteer**.
- ***Rate the word.*** *Hold up your fingers to show how well you know the word (1=very well; 2=a little; 3=not at all). Tell what you know about this word.*
- ***Define the word:*** *A* **volunteer** *is someone who works or helps without pay.*
- ***Elaborate:*** *Relate words to knowledge and experience: A* **volunteer** *comes to the cafeteria every day to help kids open their milk.*

For **Vocabulary Routine 1**, see page BP34.

For more images of the Key Words, use the **Digital Library**.

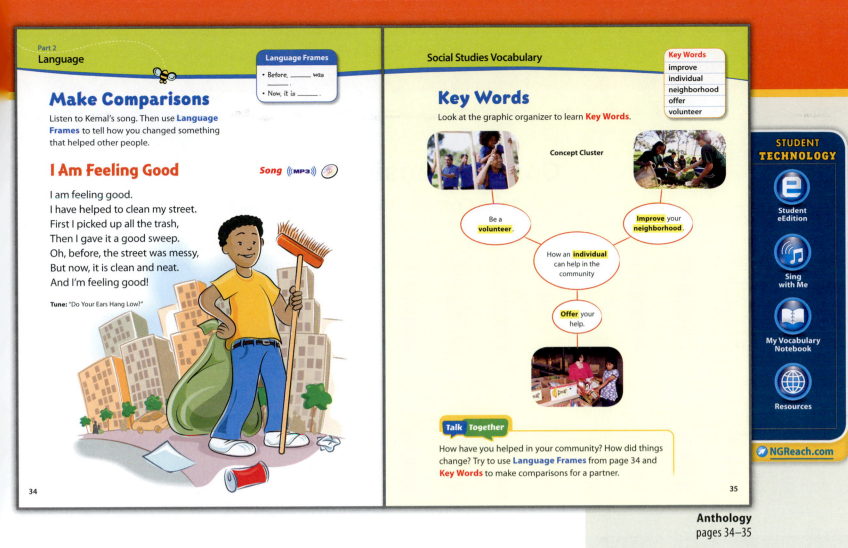

Anthology
pages 34–35

Have partners take turns repeating the routine for each word using page 35. Have each student add the words to **My Vocabulary Notebook**.

See **Differentiate**

3 Talk Together Anthology page 35
Read aloud the directions. Clarify that a community could be a street, neighborhood, or school. Provide an example: *Last summer, I was a* **volunteer** *in my* **neighborhood**. *My family joined a group that planted trees in our local park. Before, the park had no shade and was too hot during the summer for kids to play. Now, the park is shady and beautiful. I see kids playing there all of the time.*

NGReach.com My Vocabulary Notebook

Check & Reteach

OBJECTIVE: Use Domain-Specific Words ✓

As students make comparisons, listen for correct usage of the Key Words.
If students use words incorrectly, provide sentences for them to complete orally, such as:

- *We should _____ to help our neighbor walk her dog because she has a broken foot.* (**offer**)
- *If every* **individual** *picked up trash in the halls, it would _____ our school.* (**improve**)
- *A* **volunteer** *weeds the flower beds in our _____ every Saturday.* (**neighborhood**)

Weekly Writing

Gather students' writing throughout the week:

- ✓ Daily Writing Skills Practice (T33y–T33z)
- ✓ Power Writing (T34, T36a, T40, T46, T53b)
- ✓ Writing (T36, T38–T39, T44–T45, T53a)
- ✓ Research Project (T55a–T55b)

Differentiate

EL English Learners

ISSUE Students do not understand definitions.

STRATEGY Provide translations of the Key Words. Access **Family Newsletter 1** for translations in seven languages. Use cognates for Spanish speakers:

individual/individuo   offer/ofrecer
volunteer/voluntario

BL Below Level

ISSUE Students have difficulty relating the Key Words to their own experience.

STRATEGY Pair each student with a more proficient partner. The pair can work together to brainstorm ideas for each word. For example, have them brainstorm a list of people who volunteer in their school.

Word Map

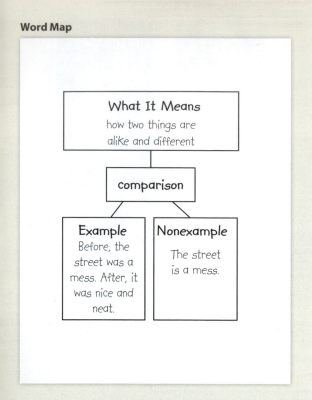

Fluency

Model Intonation Explain the concept: *Fluent readers read with intonation. They change their voices to match what they read. For example, drop your voice at the end of a statement. Raise your voice at the end of a question or exclamation.* Model reading with intonation as you read aloud sentences from "Mia's Project." Have students practice intonation by reading aloud the song lyrics from **Anthology** page 34.

Comprehension

4 Make Comparisons  **Anthology** page 36

Read aloud the first paragraph on page 36. Use a Word Map to review the word **comparison**. Then display **eVisual 1.22** and read aloud "Mia's Project." Ask students to listen for comparisons as you read.

> ### Read Aloud   Realistic Fiction
>
> #### Mia's Project
>
> I frowned as I walked home from school. Paper, aluminum cans, and plastic bottles were scattered across the sidewalk. Ugly weeds surrounded all of the trees. The whole street was filthy and unsafe. I had to do something to make our **neighborhood** safe and beautiful again. But what could one **individual** do?
>
> The next day I asked my teacher Mrs. Shogan if I could talk to the class about a service project. She agreed. I asked my classmates if they liked walking home along dirty sidewalks. All of them responded with a definite "No!" I suggested that we choose one day a month to pick up the trash. Everyone **offered** to help with the cleanup.
>
> On Saturday, my class, Mrs. Shogan, and several parents met in front of our school. We wore thick gloves, grabbed enormous trash bags, and got to work. By lunch we had cleared away all of the litter. Then, Eva's mom showed us how to plant bright red flowers around the trees. By the end of the day, the area had **improved** a lot! Before it was dirty, unsafe, and ugly. Now, thanks to many dedicated **volunteers**, it was clean, beautiful, and, most importantly, safe!

NGReach.com **Read Aloud: eVisual 1.22**   **INTERACTIVE WHITEBOARD TIP:** Underline details about the sidewalk before and after the project.

5 Map and Talk **Anthology** page 36

After students read how to make a comparison chart, ask: *What did the tree look like before?* (There were weeds and trash around it.) *What does it look like now?* (It's clean and surrounded by pretty flowers.) Ask students to find other comparisons from the **Read Aloud** that they can add to the comparison chart.

6 Talk Together **Anthology** page 36

Have students use **Practice Master PM1.17** to make a comparison chart about something that has improved.

> ### Check & Reteach
> **OBJECTIVE:** Explain Text Structure: Comparison
>
> As partners discuss the topic, monitor that students are able to make clear comparisons. If students have difficulty making comparisons, ask: *What was it like before? How is it like now?* Provide sentence frames to help students remember the steps to make comparisons:
>
> Before, _____ was _____. Now, it is _____.

Make Comparisons

You **make comparisons** to show how two things are alike and different, or to show how something has changed. When you talk about something that has changed over time, use:

- *before* and *then* to tell about the past
- *now* and *after* to tell about the present

Compare the pictures. How has the area near the tree changed?

Map and Talk

You can make a comparison chart to show how something has changed.

Comparison Chart

Before	Now
There were weeds and trash around the tree.	There are flowers around the tree.

Tell a partner about something that has **improved**. Tell what it was like before and what it is like now. Your partner makes a comparison chart.

36

Anthology page 36

Writing

7 Write About Comparisons

Introduce: *Now you will write a paragraph about the comparisons you discussed with your partner.* Model the process with "Mia's Project."

Think Aloud	Write
First, I write what the sidewalk was like before the cleanup.	Before, the sidewalk was not safe because it was covered in trash.
Then, I write what the sidewalk was like after.	Now, the sidewalk is clean and safe because Mia and her friends picked up the trash.

For **Writing Routine 2,** see page BP48.

Have students use the comparison chart they prepared in **Talk Together** to help them write paragraphs about something that has improved. Then have partners share their paragraphs and add them to their Weekly Writing folders.

WRAP-UP Have students review how Kemal and Mia made a difference in their communities.

Daily Language Arts

Daily Spelling and Word Work ✓
Pretest page T33u

Daily Grammar ✓
Point out the verse *I am feeling good.* on **Anthology** page 34 and explain that it contains a subject (I) and a predicate (am feeling good). Then use page T33w to teach complete subjects and predicates.

Daily Writing Skills ✓
Remind students that writers have to focus their topics when they are writing reports. Then use page T33y to teach how to narrow a topic.

Name _____ Date _____

Making Comparisons

Something That Has Improved

Make a comparison chart about something that has improved.

Before	Now
Possible Response: The bookshelf was a mess! Some books were upside down. Some books were on the floor.	Possible Response: The bookshelf is neat. The books are all rightside up. There are no books on the floor.

Tell how you improved something. Tell how it was before and how it is now. Use the words *before, then, now,* and *after* to compare.

© National Geographic Learning, a part of Cengage Learning, Inc.
For use with TE p. T35a   PM1.17   Unit 1 | Happy to Help

NGReach.com **Practice Master PM1.17**

OBJECTIVES
Thematic Connection: Heroes Then and Now
☑ Use Academic Words
☑ Monitor and Clarify to Comprehend Literature

PROGRAM RESOURCES
PRINT & TECHNOLOGY
Family Newsletter 1
TECHNOLOGY ONLY
Digital Library: Key Word Images
My Vocabulary Notebook

MATERIALS
timer

Power Writing
Have students write as much as they can as well as they can in one minute about the word *duty*.
*For **Writing Routine 1**, see page BP47.*

COMMON CORE STANDARDS
Reading
Read and Comprehend Informational Text   CC.3.Rinf.10
Read with Fluency to Support Comprehension   CC.3.Rfou.4
Writing
Write Over Shorter Time for Specific Audiences   CC.3.W.10
Speaking and Listening
Discuss Topics, Building on Others' Ideas and Expressing Ideas Clearly   CC.3.SL.1
Follow Rules for Discussions   CC.3.SL.1.b
Determine the Main Ideas and Supporting Details of Information Presented Visually in Diverse Media   CC.3.SL.2
Language and Vocabulary
Determine Meaning of Words and Phrases   CC.3.L.4
Acquire and Use General Academic Words, and Use Words that Signal Spatial and Temporal Relationships   CC.3.L.6

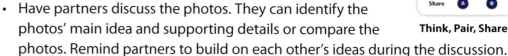

WARM-UP

Ask: *How can young* **volunteers** *make a difference in the world?* Brainstorm a list of ideas with the group.

Academic Talk
① Discuss Photographs
Introduce options for how to discuss photographs:
- *You can discuss a photo by saying what it is mostly about. Then you can point out details in the photo that support that main idea.*
- *You can also compare two or more photos to tell how they are alike and different.*

Project **Student eEdition** page 37. Point to a photo and ask: *What is this photo mostly about?* Build on the student's idea by providing supporting details. Then model how to compare the photo to another.

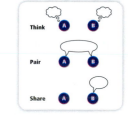

Review classroom rules for discussion, including speaking clearly, taking turns, and listening respectfully. Then have partners use a **Think, Pair, Share** to discuss the photos of community helpers on page 35.
- Have students study two photos on their own.
- Have partners discuss the photos. They can identify the photos' main idea and supporting details or compare the photos. Remind partners to build on each other's ideas during the discussion.

Think, Pair, Share

- Have students individually share their observations with the class.

*For **Think, Pair, Share**, see page BP46.*

Academic Vocabulary
② More Key Words ☑   Anthology   page 37

Key Words
benefit · duty · identify
impact · learn

Say: *Let's learn some more words to help us talk about how* **individuals** *can make a difference.* Explain and model using **Vocabulary Routine 1** and the images in the **Student eEdition** to teach Key Words.
- **Pronounce the word** *and point to the image:* **benefit**.
- **Rate the word**. *Hold up your fingers to show how well you know the word (1 = very well; 2 = a little; 3 = not at all). Tell what you know about this word.*
- **Define the word**: *A* **benefit** *is something that is helpful.*
- **Elaborate**. *Relate the words to your experience: One* **benefit** *of a computer is that it helps me find information quickly.*

*For **Vocabulary Routine 1**, see page BP34.*
*For more images of the Key Words, use the **Digital Library**.*

Anthology page 37

Have partners use page 37 to take turns repeating the routine for each word. Have students add the words to **My Vocabulary Notebook**

See **Differentiate**

3 **Talk Together** Anthology page 37
Read aloud the instructions. Have partners make a Study Card for each Key Word and then compare their cards. Explain: *When you compare your cards,* **identify** *what is the same and what is different in the definition, example, and nonexample.* Ask volunteers to share their Study Cards with the class.

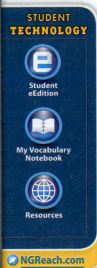

NGReach.com **My Vocabulary Notebook**

Check & Reteach
OBJECTIVE: **Use Academic Words** ✓

As partners make and compare their Study Cards, listen for correct usage of the Key Words. If students have difficulty, have them match each Key Word on page 37 with a photo on page 35. Then have them use the Key Word to tell about the picture.

Best Practices

Encourage Participation To involve shy or nonparticipatory students in the Warm Up or the Academic Talk activity, have them develop and discuss ideas in pairs before sharing with the class.

Differentiate

EL **English Learners**

ISSUE Students do not understand definitions.

STRATEGY Provide translations of the Key Words. Access **Family Newsletter 1**. Use cognates for Spanish speakers:

benefit/beneficio, identify/identificar, impact/impacto

BL **Below Level**

ISSUE Students have difficulty relating to the Key Words.

STRATEGY Provide sentence frames to help students connect to the Key Words:

- One **duty** you have in the classroom is _____.
- When you look outside a window at home, you can **identify** _____.
- You have an **impact** on someone if you help him or her _____.

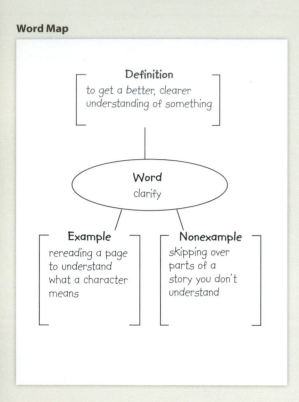

Daily Language Arts

Daily Spelling and Word Work ☑
Practice page T33u

Daily Grammar ☑
Point out the simple subject *I* and the simple predicate *learned* in the first paragraph of the letter on **Anthology** page 39. Then use page T33w to teach simple subjects and predicates.

Daily Writing Skills ☑
Point out how Kemal wrote about a narrow topic in his letter on **Anthology** page 39. Then use page T33y to practice narrowing a topic.

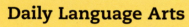

Fluency

Practice Intonation As partners read aloud Kemal's letter, circulate and listen for correct intonation.

Comprehension

❹ Learn to Plan and Monitor ☑ Anthology pages 38–39

Use a Word Map to teach the term **clarify**. Then project **Student eEdition** page 38 and read aloud the instructions. Point to details in the illustration as you model monitoring and clarifying:

- *I see Kemal and other people building a wall.*
- *I ask myself, "What are they using to build the wall?"*
- *The round picture shows a close-up. When I look closely, I find out that the people are using sandbags to build the wall.*

❺ Talk Together Anthology page 39

Read aloud the instructions on page 39. Have partners chorally read the first two paragraphs of the letter and the sample clarification. Have students identify details that help them clarify.

Ask: *How does monitoring and clarifying help you check your understanding as you read?* (Possible response: They help me better understand what I may have missed or not understood the first time I read the paragraphs.)

Have partners read the rest of the letter and monitor and clarify to check their understanding of the text. Circulate and monitor their conversations.

Check & Reteach

OBJECTIVE: Monitor and Clarify to Comprehend Literature ☑

Ask: *What is something you didn't understand the first time you read Kemal's letter? What helped you clarify what the text meant?*

If students have difficulty, ask: *What can you do if you don't understand the problem Kemal describes?* (reread the paragraph or read on to find out more information)

Writing

❻ Write About Monitoring and Clarifying

Introduce: *You are going to write a paragraph about how you clarified something you didn't understand in Kemal's letter.* Model the process.

Think Aloud	Write
First, I write about something I didn't understand.	I read that Kemal wrote, "My help made an impact."
Then, I write a question I asked myself about the text.	I asked myself, "What does Kemal mean when he says that he made an impact?"
Next, I will write about how I clarified the answer.	I reread the letter and found out that Kemal helped stop the flooding. That's how he made an impact.

*For **Writing Routine 2**, see page BP48.*

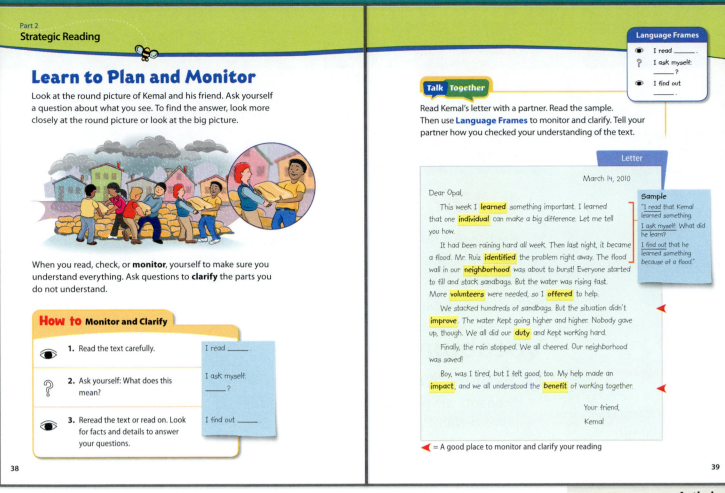

Learn to Plan and Monitor

Look at the round picture of Kemal and his friend. Ask yourself a question about what you see. To find the answer, look more closely at the round picture or look at the big picture.

When you read, check, or **monitor**, yourself to make sure you understand everything. Ask questions to **clarify** the parts you do not understand.

How to Monitor and Clarify

👁	1. Read the text carefully.	I read _____ .
❓	2. Ask yourself: What does this mean?	I ask myself: _____ ?
👁	3. Reread the text or read on. Look for facts and details to answer your questions.	I find out _____ .

38

Language Frames

- 👁 I read _____ .
- ❓ I ask myself: _____ ?
- 👁 I find out _____ .

Talk Together

Read Kemal's letter with a partner. Read the sample. Then use **Language Frames** to monitor and clarify. Tell your partner how you checked your understanding of the text.

Letter

March 14, 2010

Dear Opal,

   This week I **learned** something important. I learned that one **individual** can make a big difference. Let me tell you how.

   It had been raining hard all week. Then last night, it became a flood. Mr. Ruiz **identified** the problem right away. The flood wall in our **neighborhood** was about to burst! Everyone started to fill and stack sandbags. But the water was rising fast. More **volunteers** were needed, so I **offered** to help.

   We stacked hundreds of sandbags. But the situation didn't **improve**. The water kept going higher and higher. Nobody gave up, though. We all did our **duty** and kept working hard.

   Finally, the rain stopped. We all cheered. Our neighborhood was saved!

   Boy, was I tired, but I felt good, too. My help made an **impact**, and we all understood the **benefit** of working together.

Your friend,
Kemal

Sample
"I read that Kemal learned something.
I ask myself: What did he learn?
I find out that he learned something because of a flood."

◄ = A good place to monitor and clarify your reading

39

Anthology
pages 38–39

Have students write a paragraph about how monitoring and clarifying ideas helped them understand Kemal's letter. Remind them to think about the questions they asked themselves while reading and review how they found the answers. Have students add their writing to their Weekly Writing folders.

See **Differentiate**

WRAP-UP Have one partner pose a yes-or-no question that incorporates two Key Words. The other partner restates the question and responds with a complete sentence. Then have partners trade roles to ask and answer new questions.

Differentiate

SN Special Needs

ISSUE Students have difficulty writing about how they monitored and clarified during reading.

STRATEGY Have students point to something in Kemal's letter that they didn't understand. Provide a sentence frame to help them form a question: What does _____ mean? Then have students point to where they found the answer in the text. Provide a sentence frame for the answer: I reread/read on and found out that _____ .

OBJECTIVES

Thematic Connection: Heroes Then and Now

☑ **Explain Text Structure: Comparison**

☑ **Monitor and Clarify to Comprehend Text**

PROGRAM RESOURCES

TECHNOLOGY ONLY

My Vocabulary Notebook

Read with Me: Selection Recordings: MP3 or CD1
   Track 4

MATERIALS

timer

Power Writing

Have students write as much as they can as well as they can in one minute about the word *impact*.

*For **Writing Routine 1,** see page BP47.*

COMMON CORE STANDARDS

Reading

Distinguish Points of View	CC.3.Rinf.6
Describe Text Structure	CC.3.Rinf.8
Read and Comprehend Informational Text	CC.3.Rinf.10
Read with Fluency to Support Comprehension	CC.3.Rfou.4
Read with Purpose and Understanding	CC.3.Rfou.4.a
Read Orally With Expression on Successive Readings	CC.3.Rfou.4.b

Writing

Write Over Shorter Time for Specific Tasks	CC.3.W.10

Speaking and Listening

Explain Ideas and Understanding	CC.3.SL.1.d

Language and Vocabulary

Acquire and Use General Academic and Domain-Specific Words, and Use Words that Signal Spatial and Temporal Relationships	CC.3.L.6

WARM-UP

Explain that throughout history, heroes have faced challenges. Ask: *How can facing a personal challenge be heroic?* Tell students that today, they will read a true story about someone who faced a big challenge.

Vocabulary Practice

❶ Expand Word Knowledge ☑

Students will practice Key Words by creating a Word Web. Use **Vocabulary Routine 2** to model how to make a Word Web for the word **impact**.

- Write the word.
- Add a picture.
- Add a definition.
- Add a context sentence.

*For **Vocabulary Routine 2,** see page BP35.*

Key Words

benefit · clarify · comparison · duty identify · impact · improve · individual learn · neighborhood · offer · volunteer

Assign a Key Word to each set of partners. After they complete their Word Webs, have them add the context sentences to **My Vocabulary Notebook**. Display the Word Webs in the classroom.

Academic Talk

❷ Preview and Predict

REVIEW   Remind students: *One way to preview a text is to look at the photographs, captions, and illustrations, and predict what the story will be about.*

Display these Key Words: *identify, neighborhood.* Use **Numbered Heads Together** to have students share their predictions about "The World's Greatest Underachiever."

- Have students preview the photographs, captions, and illustrations on **Anthology** pages 41–52 independently.
- Arrange students into groups of four. Have students in each group number off from one to four.
- Groups discuss their predictions so that any member can report for the group.
- Call a number and have the student from each group with that number report for the group. Encourage students to use Key Words in their predictions.

*For **Numbered Heads Together,** see page BP46.*

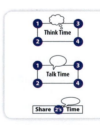

Numbered Heads Together

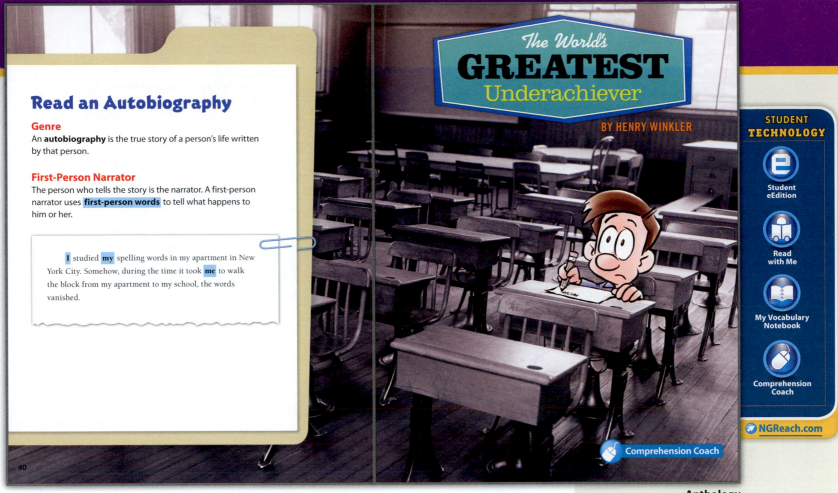

Read an Autobiography

Genre

An **autobiography** is the true story of a person's life written by that person.

First-Person Narrator

The person who tells the story is the narrator. A first-person narrator uses **first-person words** to tell what happens to him or her.

> **I** studied **my** spelling words in my apartment in New York City. Somehow, during the time it took **me** to walk the block from my apartment to my school, the words vanished.

The World's
GREATEST
Underachiever

BY HENRY WINKLER

Comprehension Coach

Anthology
pages 40–41

Reading

❸ Read a Story Anthology pages 40–41

GENRE Have a volunteer read aloud the definition of an autobiography. Elaborate: *Autobiographies are nonfiction and often include visual information, such as photographs, illustrations, and captions.*

FIRST-PERSON NARRATOR Ask a volunteer to read aloud the definition of first-person narrator. Reinforce the concept: *The writer uses words like* I, me, *and* my *to tell about his or her life.*

SOCIAL STUDIES BACKGROUND Explain that *grade school* is another name for elementary school. Grade school usually includes kindergarten through fifth grade.

Have students read pages 42–45. See **Differentiate**

Differentiate

BL Below Level

TEXT-TALK READ ALOUD
As you read the story aloud to students, pause to provide a short explanation of each Key Word as you come to it.

OL On Level

READ TOGETHER Have partners read the selection together. Use the questions to build comprehension.

AL Above Level

READ INDEPENDENTLY
As students read silently, have them make comparisons. Use the questions to build comprehension.

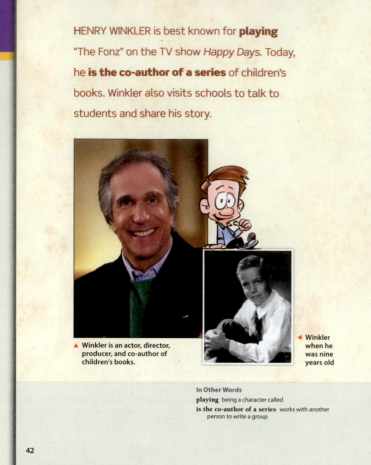

HENRY WINKLER is best known for **playing** "The Fonz" on the TV show *Happy Days*. Today, he **is the co-author of a series** of children's books. Winkler also visits schools to talk to students and share his story.

▲ Winkler is an actor, director, producer, and co-author of children's books.

◄ Winkler when he was nine years old

In Other Words
playing being a character called
is the co-author of a series works with another person to write a group

42

1 ▶ Set a Purpose
Henry has trouble in school.
Find out what the problem is.

All through grade school, I **was tutored**. If I got a D, I was **in heaven**. If I got a C-minus, I had **achieved greatness**. A's and B's were a **kingdom I could never enter**. **2**

▲ Winkler with his classmates at school

In Other Words
was tutored got extra help with schoolwork
in heaven very happy
achieved greatness done a great job
kingdom I could never enter goal I could never reach

43

Anthology
pages 42–43

Fluency

Practice Intonation, Accuracy, and Rate As students read, monitor their intonation, accuracy, and rate.

Best Practices

Encourage Elaboration As students respond to the Read and Build Comprehension questions, use general prompts.

- *What do you mean by that?*
- *Can you give some examples from the text to explain what you mean?*
- *Can you make a connection to what someone else said?*

Read and Build Comprehension   Anthology pages 42–45

1 Set a Purpose Have a student read aloud the purpose statement. Discuss what kind of problem Henry might have at school.

2 Monitor and Clarify ☑ *What idea or detail from page 43 do you need to clarify?* (Possible response: I read that Henry was in heaven if he got a D. I asked myself why he was pleased with a low grade. I kept reading and found out that Henry's best grades were C's. He means that he learned to be happy with C's and D's.)

3 Make Comparisons ☑ *How well did Henry know his spelling words before and after he was at school?* (Possible response: Before, when Henry was home, he studied hard and knew all the words. Later at school, the words vanished and he forgot how to spell them on the test.)

Check & Reteach

OBJECTIVE: Explain Text Structure: Comparison ☑

As students respond to question 3, listen to make sure that they can make comparisons. If students are unable to make comparisons, provide sentence frames: At home, Henry _____. Later at school, Henry _____.

OBJECTIVE: Monitor and Clarify to Comprehend Text ☑

Monitor students' responses to monitor and clarify question 3, above.

If students are unable to monitor and clarify, ask: *What did you read? What questions did you ask based on what you read? What did you find out as you reread or read on?*

I studied my spelling words in my apartment in New York City. Somehow, during the time it took me to walk the block from my apartment to my school, the words **vanished**.

In Other Words
vanished disappeared

44

My teacher, Miss Adolf, had given me a list of ten spelling words.

My mother and I **went over** the list until I *knew* those words. I felt **terrific**. I thought, *Wow! This time, I'm going to* **pass**.

In Other Words
went over studied
terrific great
pass get a good grade

▶ **Before You Move On**
1. **Clarify** What does Henry mean when he says "the words vanished"? How is this a problem at school?
2. **Point of View** Who is telling the story? How do you know?

45

Anthology
pages 44–45

Writing

④ Write a Prediction

GENRE Ask: *What is a prediction?* (what you guess will happen next) Explain: *You will summarize what you have read so far and then predict what will happen next.*

Think Aloud	Write
First, I write a summary of the most important events.	When Henry was young, he got very low grades. One day, he studied hard for a spelling test.
Next, I write a prediction based on what I have read.	I predict that Henry will do well on the spelling test because he feels terrific about how much he studied.

For **Writing Routine 2**, see page BP48.

Explain that the summary should include the most important events. Remind students to give reasons and cite evidence from the text to support their predictions. Have students add their paragraphs to their Weekly Writing folders.

WRAP-UP Have partners think about the challenges Henry faces. Ask partners to discuss past challenges they have faced.

Daily Language Arts

Daily Spelling and Word Work ☑
Practice page T33v

Daily Grammar ☑
Show students the phrase *in my apartment* and the dependent clause *until I knew those words* on **Anthology** pages 44–45. Then use page T33x to teach phrases and clauses.

Daily Writing Skills ☑
Model asking a question about the narrator, such as: *Why did Henry have a hard time learning in school?* Then use page T33z to practice writing research questions.

Answers Before You Move On

1. **Clarify** ☑ I read that Henry says "the words vanished." I asked myself how this is a problem for him at school. I read on and found out that Henry needs to know the words to pass the spelling test.
2. **Point of View** ☑ Henry tells the story. I know this because he is the author and he uses the words *I, me, my,* and *I'm* to tell about his own life.

OBJECTIVES

Thematic Connection: Heroes Then and Now

☑ Explain Text Structure: Comparison

☑ Monitor and Clarify to Comprehend Text

PROGRAM RESOURCES

PRINT & TECHNOLOGY

Family Newsletter 1

Read with Me: Selection Recordings: MP3 or CD1
Tracks 5–6

My Vocabulary Notebook

MATERIALS

timer

Power Writing

Have students write as much as they can as well as they can in one minute about the word *neighborhood*.

*For **Writing Routine 1**, see page BP47.*

COMMON CORE STANDARDS

Reading

Distinguish Points of View	CC.3.Rinf.6
Describe Text Structure	CC.3.Rinf.8
Read and Comprehend Informational Text	CC.3.Rinf.10
Read with Purpose and Understanding	CC.3.Rfou.4.a
Read Orally with Expression on Successive Readings	CC.3.Rfou.4.b

Writing

Write Over Shorter Time for Specific Purposes	CC.3.W.10

Speaking and Listening

Discuss Texts, Building on Others' Ideas and Expressing Ideas Clearly	CC.3.SL.1

Language and Vocabulary

Acquire and Use General Academic and Domain-Specific Words, and Use Words that Signal Spatial and Temporal Relationships	CC.3.L.6

WARM-UP

Have students share what they learned when talking to their families about ways they could help the community from **Family Newsletter 1**.

Vocabulary Practice

❶ Share Word Knowledge ☑

REVIEW Have students use the Word Webs they made on Day 3. Review what the Word Webs show.

Key Words

benefit · clarify · comparison
duty · identify · impact · improve
individual · learn · neighborhood
offer · volunteer

Group each student with a partner who studied a different Key Word. Have partners follow **Vocabulary Routine 3**.

- Have partners take turns reading their Word Webs.
- Encourage partners to talk about how the pictures show the meanings of the Key Words.
- Have partners create sentences using both Key Words.
- Have each student add the sentences to **My Vocabulary Notebook**.

*For **Vocabulary Routine 3**, see page BP36.*

Academic Talk

❷ Summarize Reading

REVIEW Remind students: *When you summarize something you have read, you briefly tell the most important events.* Explain that students will use Key Words to summarize what they have read from "The World's Greatest Underachiever."

Write these Key Words: *improve, learn*. Use a **Fishbowl** to help students summarize what they have read so far.

- Have students on the inside summarize pages 42–43.
- Have students on the outside listen for Key Words and the most important events.
- Have groups change positions. The new inside group summarizes pages 44–45.

*For **Fishbowl**, see page BP45.*

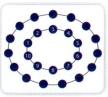

Fishbowl

Anthology
pages 46–47

Reading

3 Read and Build Comprehension   Anthology pages 46–48

1 Predict Read aloud the predict question. Have students give reasons to support their predictions.

2 Monitor and Clarify ☑ *What idea from page 46 or 47 would you like to clarify?* (Possible response: I read that Henry's heart sinks. I ask myself, "What makes Henry feel so upset?" I reread/read on and I find out that Henry thinks he's failed his test.)

3 Make Comparisons ☑ *How does Henry feel before his spelling test and how does he feel after?* (Before he hears the word **neighbor**, Henry feels confident. After three more words, he feels upset because he can't remember how to spell them.)

Differentiate

EL English Learners

ISSUE Students do not have the language to express predictions.

STRATEGY Have students draw pictures of their predictions. Then have students repeat as you describe what you see in the drawings.

AL Above Level

ISSUE Students do not remember to connect unit concepts.

STRATEGY Prompt students to connect unit concepts while reading: *What challenges does Henry face? What can he do to overcome these challenges?*

Fluency

Practice Intonation, Accuracy, and Rate As students read, monitor their intonation, accuracy, and rate.

Word Map

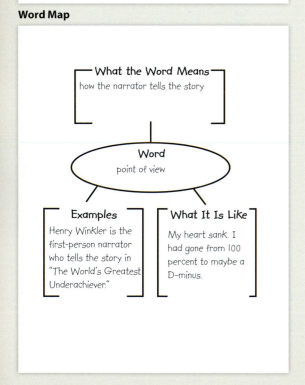

┌─ What the Word Means ─┐
the person who tells the story

Word
narrator

┌─ Examples ─┐
Henry Winkler tells the story about his life as a student.

┌─ What It Is Like ─┐
The next day, I went into the classroom and took out a sheet of paper.

Word Map

┌─ What the Word Means ─┐
how the narrator tells the story

Word
point of view

┌─ Examples ─┐
Henry Winkler is the first-person narrator who tells the story in "The World's Greatest Underachiever."

┌─ What It Is Like ─┐
My heart sank. I had gone from 100 percent to maybe a D-minus.

1 Some people talk about **information sliding off the blackboard of your brain.** That was my life. I was called "stupid," "lazy." **My self-image was down around my ankles.**

In Other Words
information sliding off the blackboard of your brain forgetting things you know
My self-image was down around my ankles. I did not feel good about myself.

48

Anthology page 48

Mini Lesson

Identify Point of View

Use Word Maps to teach the terms **narrator** and **point of view**. Elaborate:
- *The **narrator** is the person who tells the story. This can be a character in the story or a **narrator** who is not a character.*
- ***Point of view** describes how the **narrator** tells the story. In some **points of view**, the **narrator** knows everything. In others, the **narrator** only knows what the character knows.*

Explain: *If a **narrator** uses words like I, me, my, and mine to tell what happens in the story, the **narrator** is a character. This is called first-person **point of view**.*

Display **Student eEdition** page 48 and point out the text "That was my life." Model identifying point of view: *The **narrator** uses the word my to tell about something that belongs to him. The **narrator** is a character, and he is telling something about his life.*

Have students reread the introduction on page 42. Ask: *What clues show that Henry Winkler didn't write this introduction about his own life?* (Possible response: the words *Henry Winkler, he,* and *his*)

To check understanding, use **Student eEdition** page 43 to display the text "All through grade school, I was tutored. If I got a D, I was in heaven." Have students identify the narrator's point of view and explain their answer. (Possible response: The sentence is told by a first-person **narrator**. I know this because he uses the word *I*, and he is part of the story.)

The one thing **I had going for me** was my **sense of humor**. It sure didn't get me any A's, though. It got me a trip to the principal's office.

No matter what I did, it didn't seem to **make a difference**. **2** **BL**

In Other Words
I had going for me that helped
sense of humor way of making people laugh
make a difference help

▶ **Before You Move On**
1. **Confirm Prediction** Did Henry's spelling **improve** on the test? Explain.
2. **Goal/Outcome** What does Henry want?

49

Anthology page 49

Read and Build Comprehension   Anthology page 49

1 **Monitor and Clarify** ☑ *What idea from page 49 would you like to clarify?* (Possible response: I read that Henry got a "trip to the principal's office." I ask myself, "Why did Henry have to go to the office?" I reread and find out that Henry got into trouble because he was always making people laugh.)

2 **Summarize** *Summarize the most important idea on page 49.* (Possible response: Henry had a good sense of humor, but it got him into trouble.)

Differentiate

BL Below Level

ISSUE Students are unable to summarize a text.

STRATEGY Identify the main idea for partners. Have them write down all of the details and then take turns reading the main idea aloud and crossing out details that aren't needed. Have students use the remaining details to summarize.

AL Above Level

ISSUE Students are ready to analyze the narrator's point of view.

STRATEGY Have students reread page 49 and identify the idioms. Remind them that they can refer to **In Other Words** for restatements of unfamiliar phrases. Have partners work together to paraphrase the text into simpler language. Then ask: *How would the story be different if another* **narrator** *told it?*

Answers Before You Move On

1. **Confirm Prediction** Possible response: No, Henry's spelling did not **improve** on the test. He remembered only one word and the beginning letters of the other words.
2. **Goal/Outcome** Based on the text, Henry wants to get good grades and **improve** his self-image.

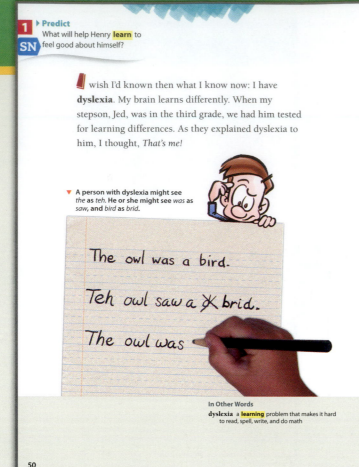

1 ▸ Predict

SN What will help Henry **learn** to feel good about himself?

▌ wish I'd known then what I know now: I have **dyslexia**. My brain learns differently. When my stepson, Jed, was in the third grade, we had him tested for learning differences. As they explained dyslexia to him, I thought, *That's me!*

▼ A person with dyslexia might see *the* as *teh*. He or she might see *was* as *saw*, and *bird* as *brid*.

The owl was a bird.

Teh owl saw a brid.

The owl was

In Other Words
dyslexia a **learning** problem that makes it hard to read, spell, write, and do math

50

2 A learning disability can really **affect** the way you feel about yourself. Now I know that even if a person learns differently, he or she can still **be filled with greatness**. **3** **BL**

▼ Winkler became famous when he grew up. Here he is as "The Fonz."

In Other Words
affect change
be filled with greatness do wonderful things

51

Anthology
pages 50–51

Read and Build Comprehension

1 Predict Read aloud the predict question. Remind students to support their predictions with evidence from the text, photos, or illustrations.

2 Make Comparisons ☑ *How are Henry and his stepson Jed similar?* (Both Henry and Jed have a learning difference called dyslexia. Their brains learn differently than most people.)

2 Identify Author's Viewpoint *What impact does Henry think learning differences can have on a person?* (Learning differences can affect the way you feel about yourself.)

Differentiate

SN Special Needs

ISSUE Students lack conceptual structure to make predictions.

STRATEGY Facilitate a discussion of what students know about Henry based on what they read on the previous pages. Remind students that Henry felt bad about school before they predict what will change his attitude.

BL Below Level

ISSUE Students have difficulty making comparisons.

STRATEGY Have partners reread pages 48 and 51. Ask: *How did Henry feel when he wasn't doing well in school? How does he feel now? Are those feelings the same or different? Why or why not?*

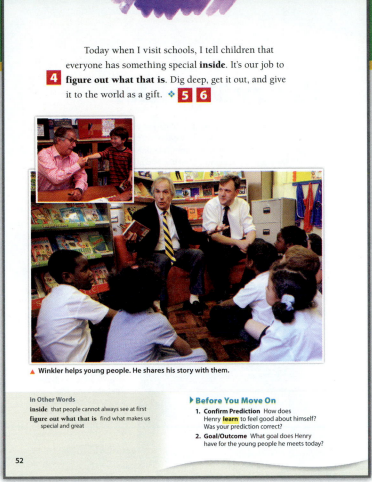

Today when I visit schools, I tell children that everyone has something special **inside**. It's our job to
4 **figure out what that is**. Dig deep, get it out, and give it to the world as a gift. ❖ **5** **6**

▲ Winkler helps young people. He shares his story with them.

In Other Words
inside that people cannot always see at first
figure out what that is find what makes us special and great

▶ **Before You Move On**
1. **Confirm Prediction** How does Henry **learn** to feel good about himself? Was your prediction correct?
2. **Goal/Outcome** What goal does Henry have for the young people he meets today?

52

Anthology page 52

4 **Monitor and Clarify** ☑ *What idea on page 52 is unclear?* (Possible response: I read that Henry says we have a job. I ask myself, "What job is Henry talking about?" I reread and I find out that Henry thinks that each person should work hard to figure out what is special about him or her.)

5 **Clarify Meaning** ☑ *What do you think Henry means when he says "give it to the world as a gift"?* (Possible response: When you find out what you can do well, your talent will be a ==benefit== to others as well as to yourself.)

6 **Express Opinions** *Do you think Henry's efforts will have a positive ==impact== on students? Why or why not?* (Possible response: Yes, because he is visiting schools and teaching students that everyone is special.)

Check & Reteach

OBJECTIVE: Explain Text Structure: Comparison ☑

Check for accurate responses to the comparison questions.
If students have difficulty, help them identify similarities and differences about Henry. Ask:
What was Henry like when he was a boy? What is he like today?

OBJECTIVE: Monitor and Clarify to Comprehend Text ☑

Check for accurate responses to the monitor and clarify questions.
If students have difficulty clarifying the text, remind them to ask themselves, "What does, this mean?" Tell them to reread, read on, or look at visuals to help them figure out what the text means.

Answers Before You Move On

1. **Confirm Prediction** Possible response: Henry learns to feel good about himself when he finds out his brain works in a special way. My prediction was correct because he found out the reason for why he had difficulty learning.
2. **Goal/Outcome** The goal Henry sets for young people is to find out what they have that is special and give it to the world.

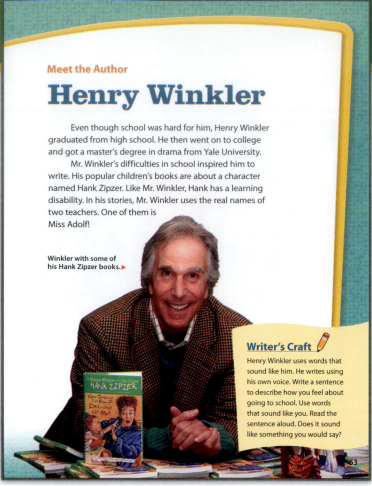

Meet the Author

Henry Winkler

Even though school was hard for him, Henry Winkler graduated from high school. He then went on to college and got a master's degree in drama from Yale University.

Mr. Winkler's difficulties in school inspired him to write. His popular children's books are about a character named Hank Zipzer. Like Mr. Winkler, Hank has a learning disability. In his stories, Mr. Winkler uses the real names of two teachers. One of them is Miss Adolf!

Winkler with some of his Hank Zipzer books.▶

Writer's Craft 🖉
Henry Winkler uses words that sound like him. He writes using his own voice. Write a sentence to describe how you feel about going to school. Use words that sound like you. Read the sentence aloud. Does it sound like something you would say?

53

Anthology page 53

❹ Meet the Author Anthology page 53

Have students silently read the biography on page 53. Point out that the character in Mr. Winkler's book, Hank Zipzer, has a problem that Mr. Winkler understands well: a learning difference. Like most writers, Mr. Winkler uses what he knows to write stories. After students read the biography, build comprehension:

- **Monitor and Clarify** ☑️ *What idea in the biography would you like to clarify about Mr. Winkler's life?* (Possible response: I read that Mr. Winkler writes about a character called Hank Zipzer. I ask myself, "What inspired him to write about Hank Zipzer?" I reread and find out that Mr. Winkler's difficulties in school inspired him to write children's books.)
- **Relate to Personal Experience** *What challenges have you faced in school? How can you use Mr. Winkler's experience in your own life?* (Possible response: I have a hard time with math. Mr. Winkler let his difficulties give him a bad self-image. I shouldn't let my difficulties in math give me a bad self image.)
- **Make Inferences** *Why do you think Mr. Winkler uses the real names of the two teachers?* (Possible response: I read that one of the names is Miss Adolf. I know Miss Adolf was his teacher in the story. I also know that I remember the names of important teachers in my life. And so, I think he uses their real names because those teachers were important to him.)

Best Practices

Encourage Respect Encourage students to validate each others' points of view. Provide examples:

- *Good point.*
- *That makes sense.*
- *I can tell you've thought about this a lot.*

Writing

5 Writer's Craft Anthology page 53

Explain: *One thing that makes Henry's books fun to read is the way he uses words. His words, or voice, sound like the way he might talk to a friend.* Point out some examples in "The World's Greatest Underachiever."

- "If I got a D, I was in heaven." (page 43)
- "My self-image was down around my ankles." (page 48)
- "...I thought, *That's me!*" (page 50)

Have students identify more lines from the autobiography that emphasize the author's voice.

Read aloud the instructions for the Writer's Craft feature on page 53. Clarify that each student will write a sentence about how he or she feels about going to school using words that sound like his or her own voice.

Clarify: *You will write sentences that sound like the way you talk. Start by thinking of how you feel about a subject. Then imagine you are talking to your friends. Write sentences you might say to them.*

Model writing sentences about students' feelings about school.

Think Aloud	Write
I will write how I sometimes feel when I wake up on a Monday morning.	Sometimes when I hear my alarm clock, I moan and groan like a monster. I growl, "No! No! Let me sleep!"

For **Writing Routine 2**, see page BP48.

Have partners brainstorm ideas for their sentences. Then have them work independently to write sentences that describe their feelings about going to school.

Have students add their sentences to their Weekly Writing folders.

See **Differentiate**

WRAP-UP Have students work in groups of three to write sentences about the impact Mr. Winkler might have on students who read his Hank Zipzer books. Have students use at least one Key Word in each sentence.

Daily Language Arts

Daily Spelling and Word Work ☑
Practice page T33v

Daily Grammar ☑
Point out the dependent clause *Even though school was hard for him* in the first sentence on **Anthology** page 53. Then use page T33x to practice writing sentences correctly.

Daily Writing Skills ☑
Model writing a question you would ask Henry Winkler if you were interviewing him, such as: *What was your favorite subject in school?* Then use page T33z to practice focusing a topic and writing questions.

Differentiate

EL English Learners

ISSUE Students lack English language proficiency necessary to express ideas.

STRATEGY Pair students with more proficient partners to brainstorm ideas for their sentences. Provide sentence frames based on their brainstorming, for example: When I think about going to school, I _____.

BL Below Level

ISSUE Students have difficulty expressing their feelings about going to school.

STRATEGY Invite students to make a Mind Map with the word *school* in the middle. Have them write words that come to mind when they hear the word *school* and attach feeling words to the words they listed. Then have them use the ideas from the Mind Map to create their sentences.

OBJECTIVES

Thematic Connection: Heroes Then and Now

☑ **Explain Text Structure: Comparison**

☑ **Read with Fluency**

PROGRAM RESOURCES

PRINT & TECHNOLOGY

Test-Taking Strategy Practice: Practice Master PM1.20

Comparison Chart: Practice Master PM1.21

Fluency Practice: Practice Master PM1.22

TECHNOLOGY ONLY

Online Vocabulary Games

Comprehension Coach

Read with Me: Fluency Models: MP3 or CD 1 Track 2

MATERIALS

timer

Power Writing

Have students write as much as they can as well as they can in one minute about the word *benefit*.

*For **Writing Routine 1**, see page BP47.*

COMMON CORE STANDARDS

Reading

Describe Text Structure	CC.3.Rinf.8
Read Informational Text	CC.3.Rinf.10
Read Orally with Expression on Successive Readings	CC.3.Rfou.4.b

Writing

Write Over Shorter Time for Specific Purposes	CC.3.W.10

Speaking and Listening

Explain Ideas and Understanding	CC.3.SL.1.d

Language and Vocabulary

Acquire and Use General Academic and Domain-Specific Words, and Use Words that Signal Spatial and Temporal Relationships	CC.3.L.6

WARM-UP

How is Henry a hero to others in "The World's Greatest Underachiever"? Explain that today students will talk and write about the autobiography.

Vocabulary Review

❶ Apply Word Knowledge ☑

Write: ***clarify***, ***comparison***, ***narrator***, ***point of view***. Call students' attention to the other Key Words on **Student eEdition** page 54. Then have students apply their knowledge of the Key Words to play a game called Around the World. Share these instructions:

- *I will choose a Traveler. The Traveler will stand near the desk of the closest student. That student will be the Challenger.*
- *I will say a Key Word definition or ask a question that should be answered by a Key Word.*
- *If the Traveler is the first to correctly call out the Key Word, the Traveler will move to the next desk. If the Challenger identifies the word first, the Challenger will become the new Traveler and travel to the next desk.*

> **Key Words**
>
> benefit · clarify · comparison · duty
> identify · impact · improve · individual
> learn · narrator · neighborhood
> offer · point of view · volunteer

Have students play the game.

- Choose the first Traveler and have him or her stand beside the nearest desk, the desk of the Challenger.
- State the definition of a Key Word, or ask a question that can be answered by a Key Word. For the word **benefit**, for example, the clue might be "something that is helpful."
- If the Traveler identifies the Key Word first, allow the Traveler to travel to the next desk. There you will ask about another Key Word.
- If the Traveler does not identify the Key Word first, the Traveler must return to his or her desk. Allow the Challenger to become the Traveler and travel to the next desk.
- Continue play for ten minutes or until one player makes it all the way through the classroom.

*For **More Vocabulary Routines**, see pages BP41–BP43.*

For additional practice, have students play the **Online Vocabulary Games** in pairs or individually.

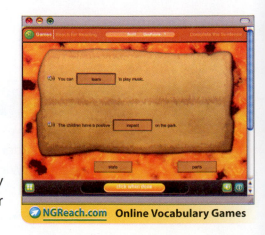

NGReach.com **Online Vocabulary Games**

Part 2
Think and Respond

Talk About It

Key Words
benefit	individual
duty	learn
identify	neighborhood
impact	offer
improve	volunteer

1. How do you know that "The World's Greatest Underachiever" is an **autobiography**?

   I know that it is an autobiography because _____ .

2. **Compare** how the author felt about himself when he was young to how he feels now.

   Before, Henry felt _____ .

   Now, he feels _____ because _____ .

3. Why do you think Henry calls himself an underachiever in school?

   Henry calls himself an underachiever because _____ .

Learn test-taking strategies.
NGReach.com

Write About It

Henry helps children. Write a letter thanking him. Tell him what you **learned** from his story. Then share how you can have a positive **impact** on people's lives. Use **Key Words**.

_____, 20_____

Dear Mr. Winkler,

Thank you _____ . I learned _____ .

Your friend,

_____

54

Anthology page 54

Academic Talk

② Talk About It Anthology page 54

Have partners use Key Words as they discuss the questions. Prompt students to cite specific details from the text, particularly for question 2. Remind students to use words such as *before* and *now* to express comparisons.

Then use the test-taking strategy lesson from **NGReach.com** and **Practice Master PM1.20** to ask more questions about the selection.

Writing

③ Write About It Anthology page 54

Read aloud the directions. Point out the sentence frames and explain: *You can use these sentence frames to write your letter.*

Remind students to focus their letter on three ideas:
- thanking Henry Winkler
- something the student learned from the story
- what the student can do to have a positive impact on people's lives.

Model using Key Words as you write to the author: Thank you for telling us about learning disabilities. I **learned** that I can have a positive **impact** on other **individuals**. I can look for ways to help students in my class and school.

Have students add their letters to their Weekly Writing folders.

Daily Language Arts

Daily Spelling and Word Work ☑
Test page T33u

Daily Grammar ☑
Point out the phrase *on people's lives* on **Anthology** page 54. Then use page T33x to review and assess students' understanding of complete sentences.

Daily Writing Skills ☑
Remind students that writing research questions can help them narrow a topic. Then use page T33z to review and assess students' understanding of how to narrow a topic.

Answers Talk About It

1. **Autobiography** Possible response: I know that it is an autobiography because it is a story that Henry wrote about his own life. He uses first-person words like *I, me,* and *my* to tell his story.
2. **Make Comparisons** Possible response: Before, Henry felt like he was stupid because he didn't do well in school. Now, he feels proud because he has achieved things like graduating from Yale University and writing a popular series of books.
3. **Make Inferences** Possible response: Henry calls himself an underachiever because he got low grades in school no matter how hard he tried.

Name _____ Date _____

Test-Taking Strategy Practice
Know the Test Format
Directions: Read each question and choose the best answer.

Sample

❶ In the sentence "It got me a trip to the principal's office," what does the word trip mean?
  Ⓐ a fall
  Ⓑ a map
  Ⓒ a seat
  ● a journey

❷ In the sentence "My mother and I went over the list until I knew those words," what do the words went over mean?
  Ⓐ walked over
  Ⓑ threw away
  ● studied
  Ⓓ forgot

Directions: Read the question. Then write a short answer below.

❸ How does Henry find out he has dyslexia?
  Henry's stepson, Jed, was tested for dyslexia. It was then that he learned about it.

  _____

  How did you use the test test-taking strategy to answer the question?

© National Geographic Learning, a part of Cengage Learning, Inc.
For use with TE p. T54   PM1.20   Unit 1 | Happy to Help

NGReach.com **Practice Master PM1.20**

Differentiate

SN Special Needs

ISSUE Students have difficulty seeing differences.

STRATEGY Read and point to a detail about Mr. Winkler as a child. Ask students to give a thumbs-up if Henry is the same today. If not, have students point to something in the text that shows how he is different as an adult. Help students record these details in the chart.

BL Below Level

ISSUE Students are unfamiliar with the process of making comparisons.

STRATEGY Have partners ask and answer questions such as:

- What does Mr. Winkler try to do as a child?
- What problems does he have?
- How does he feel about himself?

AL Above Level

ISSUE Students do not use newly acquired vocabulary in comparing and contrasting Henry as a child and Henry as an adult.

STRATEGY Prompt students to use Key Words in making comparisons with questions such as:

- How can you restate that using one or more Key Words?
- What Key Word can you use to say the two ideas are different?

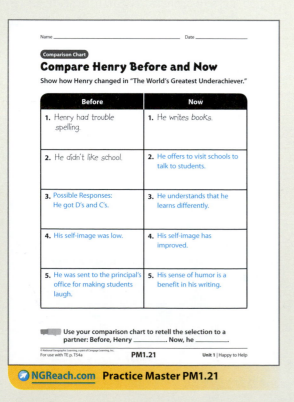

NGReach.com Practice Master PM1.21

Comprehension

④ Make Comparisons ✔ Anthology page 55

REVIEW Remind students: *We can make comparisons by telling how things change.* Display **Student eEdition** page 55. Read aloud the instructions and the sample comparison chart. Explain that Henry changed in some ways as he got older. The entries under *Before* tell how he was when he was young. The entries under *Now* tell how he is as an adult.

Reread the first paragraph on page 53. Then model how to add an entry to the chart. Point to the second row of the Before column. Explain: *Before, when Henry was younger, he didn't like school.* Point to the second row of the Now column. Explain: *He worked hard and overcame his difficulties. Now he has a master's degree.*

Have partners work together to complete **Practice Master PM1.21**. Circulate and use the questions below to guide students in making comparisons:

- *Look at page 48. How did Henry feel about himself?*
- *Reread page 51. How does Henry feel about himself now?*

See **Differentiate**

Check & Reteach

OBJECTIVE: Explain Text Structure: Comparison ✔

Monitor comprehension as partners share their comparisons.

If students have difficulty identifying differences between Henry as a child and Henry as an adult, have them reread page 49. Say: *I read that when Henry was a student, he was sent to the principal's office for making students laugh. This is how Henry was before.*

Then have students reread **Writer's Craft** on page 53. Ask: *How does Henry's sense of humor help him with writing now?* (Possible response: He is funny and he shows his humor in his writing.)

⑤ Fluency ✔ Anthology page 55

Have students read aloud the passage on **Practice Master PM1.22** or use the **Comprehension Coach** to practice fluency.

Check & Reteach

OBJECTIVE: Read with Fluency ✔

Monitor students' oral reading.

If students need additional fluency practice, have them read along with the **Fluency Models**.

Make Comparisons

Create a comparison chart to show how Henry changed in "The World's Greatest Underachiever."

Comparison Chart

Before	Now
1. Henry had trouble spelling.	1. He writes books.
2. He didn't like school.	2.

Use your comparison chart to compare things about Henry's story for a partner. Use the sentence frames and **Key Words**. Record your discussion.

> Before, Henry _____.
> Now, he _____.

Fluency  Comprehension Coach

Use the Comprehension Coach to practice reading with intonation. Rate your reading.

Talk Together

How do adults help students in school? With a partner, brainstorm a list of ways. Use **Key Words**. Share your list with the class.

55

Anthology page 55

6 Talk Together Anthology page 55

Read aloud the instructions. Have partners discuss the question. Post the Key Words so that students can refer to them as they brainstorm ways adults can help students in school. Ask partners to share their list.

WRAP-UP Ask students to make comparisons between the **Small Group Reading** books they read and "The World's Greatest Underachiever." Ask: *How are the topics similar? How are they different? How do the stories show everyday heroes in action?*

Name _____ Date _____

Fluency: Practice

"The World's Greatest Underachiever"

Use this passage to practice reading with proper intonation.

The next day, I went into the classroom and took out a sheet of paper.	15
Then Miss Adolf gave us the words. The first word was *carpet*.	27
I wrote that one down: *c-a-r-p-e-t*. I was feeling pretty confident.	38
Then came *neighbor*—I wrote down the letter *n*.	47
Then *rhythm*—I knew there was an *r*. *Suburban*—I wrote *s-u-b*.	59
My heart sank. I had gone from 100 percent to maybe a D-minus.	72
Where did the words go?	77

From "The World's Greatest Underachiever," pages 46–47

Intonation

1 ☐ Does not change pitch.   3 ☐ Changes pitch to match some of the content.
2 ☐ Changes pitch, but does not match content.   4 ☐ Changes pitch to match all of the content.

Accuracy and Rate Formula
Use the formula to measure a reader's accuracy and rate while reading aloud.

_____ – _____ = _____
words attempted   number of errors   words correct per minute
in one minute   (wcpm)

For use with TE p. T54a   **PM1.22**   Unit 1 | Happy to Help

OBJECTIVES

Thematic Connection: Heroes Then and Now

☑ Write a Biographical Sketch

☑ Choose and Narrow Topic; Develop Interview Questions

☑ Choose Appropriate Language

PROGRAM RESOURCES

PRINT & TECHNOLOGY

Research Rubric: Assessment Master A1.42

TECHNOLOGY ONLY

Project Checklist: eVisual 1.28

MATERIALS

index cards

SUGGESTED PACING

DAY 1	Plan
DAY 2	Research
DAY 3	Research
DAY 4	Organize
DAY 5	Present

Daily Language Arts

Daily Spelling and Word Work ☑
Practice pages T33u–T33v

Daily Grammar ☑
Use pages T33w–T33x to teach and to provide practice with subjects and predicates, clauses and phrases.

Daily Writing Skills ☑
Use pages T33y–T33z to teach and to provide practice with focusing a topic and creating research questions.

COMMON CORE STANDARDS

Writing

Organize Events in a Sequence	CC.3.W.3.a
Use Description	CC.3.W.3.b
Use Temporal Words and Phrases	CC.3.W.3.c
Conduct Research	CC.3.W.7
Gather Information, Take Notes, and Categorize Evidence	CC.3.W.8

Speaking and Listening

Ask and Answer Questions	CC.3.SL.3
Report on a Topic	CC.3.SL.4
Add Visual Displays	CC.3.SL.5

Write a Biographical Sketch

Display and read the prompt aloud.

> Who do you know who is your personal hero? Interview this person to find out more about him or her. You will share your information in an oral report, with visuals, that you present to a small group of classmates.

Plan

Choose a Topic

Guide discussion to unpack the prompt and determine the Role, Audience, and Form for the RAFT:

Role: Interviewer
Audience: Small group of classmates
Form: Oral report

REVIEW Review the Daily Writing Skills lesson (pages T33y–T33z). Model narrowing the topic for this project: *The prompt says I need to interview someone who is my personal hero. My uncle, who is a firefighter, is my hero. That's a pretty broad topic, so I need to narrow it. I could focus on asking him about a day he acted heroically.* Have students narrow their topics and complete the RAFT.

Develop Research Questions

Have students choose a topic and write three interview questions using separate index cards. The cards should include questions asking for personal details, such as how the person felt before, during, or after the event. Encourage students to write questions that will get more than just a "yes" or "no" response from the interviewee.

> What did you do on the day that you acted heroically?

Research

Gather Information

Provide students with ideas for how to structure their interviews. First, they should explain the purpose of the interview to the interviewee. Next, they should ask the questions they have prepared. Explain to students that they should quote the person accurately. Point out that the answers they receive might lead them to ask different follow-up questions. They should have extra index cards on which they can record these questions and answers.

See **Differentiate**

Organize

Arrange Information

REVIEW Suggest that students begin the report by introducing the topic and the person they interviewed. Remind students that they should include a visual display as part of the report. Students should end the report with a conclusion that summarizes the topic. Display and read **eVisual 1.28**.

Project Checklist

- Begin by introducing the person and the heroic deed.
- Present the details in a logical order.
- Make sure you quote the person's words accurately. If you use your own words, make sure the interviewee's meaning is clear.
- End the report with a conclusion that summarizes what you learned.
- Include a visual display.

NGReach.com **Project Checklist: eVisual 1.28**   **INTERACTIVE WHITEBOARD TIP:** As you read each item, place a check mark next to it.

Draft Ideas

Have students prepare their oral reports and a visual element. For example, they might display a labeled photograph or drawing of their person on a small poster board, along with an interesting quote. Explain that students can use their note cards as a guide while presenting to the group. They can make new cards for their introductions and conclusions.

This is my uncle. He is a firefighter. "I'll never forget that family with five kids. It was a miracle."

Present

Practice Speaking Skills

Remind students that they should use appropriate language when giving their oral reports. In this case, it is acceptable to use friendly, informal language. Model the following for students: *My uncle will never forget the day he rescued a family with five children from a raging house fire.*

Have students practice their oral reports with a partner, using their visual displays. Tell them to speak slowly and clearly, and to make eye contact with the audience.

Share with Others

Have students take turns presenting their oral reports in small groups. Once each student finishes presenting, allow time for the audience to ask questions. Use the **Research Rubric** to evaluate students' oral reports.

Differentiate

EL English Learner

ISSUE Students are unsure about interviewing someone in English.

STRATEGY Allow students to interview a person who speaks their native language. Have them write the person's answers in English for their presentations.

BL Below Level

ISSUE Students have difficulty generating research questions.

STRATEGY Provide students with the following prompts as they work on their research questions. Have them change the prompts into questions they would ask this person:

What did this person do? (What did you do?)

How did the person do this? (How did you do this?)

Why did the person do this? (Why did you do this?)

Research Rubric   Unit 1, Week 3

Scale	Content	Speaking/Listening
4	• Oral report contains plenty of information about a person's accomplishment. • Information was presented in a logical order.	• Speaker speaks clearly and at an appropriate pace during the entire oral report. • Speaker presents a visual display that enhances the presentation.
3	• Oral report contains enough information about a person's accomplishment. • Information was presented in a mostly logical order.	• Speaker speaks clearly and at an appropriate pace most of the time during the oral report. • Speaker presents a visual display that mostly enhances the presentation.
2	• Oral report contains some information about a person's accomplishment. • Information was presented in a somewhat logical order.	• Speaker speaks clearly and at an appropriate pace during some of the oral report. • Speaker presents a visual display that somewhat enhances the presentation.
1	• Oral report does not contain information about a person's accomplishment. • Information was not presented in a logical order.	• Speaker does not speak clearly or at an appropriate pace during the oral report. • Speaker does not present a visual display.

© National Geographic Learning, a part of Cengage
Grade 3 Assessment   A1.42   Unit 1 | Happy to Help

NGReach.com **Assessment Master A1.42**

☑ = TESTED

Assess

OBJECTIVES   **ASSESSMENTS**

Reading

☑ Explain Text Structure: Comparison

☑ Monitor and Clarify to Comprehend Text

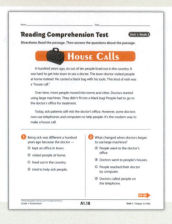

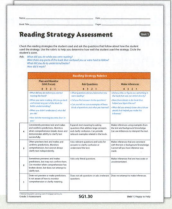

Reading Comprehension Test
A1.18–A1.19

Reading Strategy Assessment
SG1.30–SG1.31

Fluency

☑ Intonation

☑ Accuracy and Rate

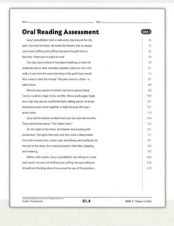

Oral Reading Assessment
A1.4–A1.6

Use these passages throughout Unit 1. Work with Below Level students this week.

Vocabulary and Spelling

☑ Use Domain-Specific Words

☑ Use Academic Words

☑ Spell Words with Short *i, u*

☑ Use Commonly Misspelled Words Correctly

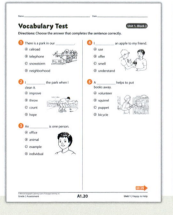

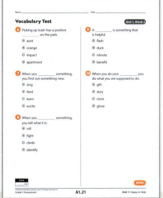

Vocabulary Test
A1.20–A1.21

Spelling Pretest/ Spelling Test
T33u

Grammar and Writing

☑ Use Complete Sentences and Predicates

☑ Use Simple Subjects and Predicates

☑ Choose and Narrow a Topic

☑ Develop Interview Questions

Writing, Revising, and Editing Test
A1.22–A1.23

Research Rubric
A1.42

ExamView®

Reteach and Practice

REPORTS

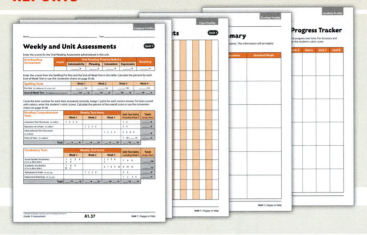

A1.37

PRINT & ONLINE
Report Forms

Student Profile: Weekly and Unit Assessments   A1.37–A1.38

Class Profile: Weekly and Unit Assessments   A1.39

Student Profile: Strengths and Needs Summary   A1.40

Student Profile: Oral Reading Assessment   A1.3
    Progress Tracker

eAssessment™

ONLINE ONLY
Automated Reports

Student Profile: Weekly and Unit Tests

Class Profile: Weekly and Unit Tests

Standards Summary Report

Reading

RETEACH

Make Comparisons: Reteaching Master RT1.7

Plan and Monitor: Reteaching Master RT1.8

ADDITIONAL PRACTICE

Comprehension Coach   NGReach.com

Fluency

RETEACH

Fluency Routines, page BP33

ADDITIONAL PRACTICE

Comprehension Coach   NGReach.com

Vocabulary and Spelling

RETEACH

Vocabulary Routine 6, page BP40

Spelling and Word Work Routine, page BP52

ADDITIONAL PRACTICE

Vocabulary Games   NGReach.com

Daily Spelling Practice, pages T33u–T33v

Grammar and Writing

RETEACH

Sentences: Anthology Handbook, page 581

Writing: Reteaching Writing Routine, page BP51

ADDITIONAL PRACTICE

More Grammar Practice PM1.23

Daily Writing Skills Practice, pages T33y–T33z

Week 4 Planner

Online Lesson Planner
NGReach.com

☑ = TESTED

	Day 1	**Day 2**
WHOLE GROUP TIME	**Listen and Comprehend**	**Read and Comprehend**

Anthology

Speaking and Listening
🕐 5–10 minutes

Day 1 — Listen and Comprehend

Academic Talk CC.3.SL.1; CC.3.SL.1.b
Discuss the Big Question T55q

Day 2 — Read and Comprehend

Academic Talk CC.3.SL.1
Preview and Predict T56c

Language and Vocabulary
🕐 15–25 minutes

Day 1

Daily Spelling and Word Work CC.3.Rfou.3; CC.3.L.2;
☑ Pretest: Words with Digraphs *ch, tch* CC.3.L.2.e
and Commonly Misspelled Words T55k
Daily Grammar CC.3.L.1; CC.3.L.1.f
☑ Subject-Verb Agreement T55m
Vocabulary Strategy CC.3.L.4, CC.3.L.4.d;
☑ Determine Meanings T55q CC.3.L.6

Day 2

Daily Spelling and Word Work CC.3.Rfou.3; CC.3.L.2
☑ Practice T55k
Daily Grammar CC.3.L.1; CC.3.L.1.f; CC.3.L.1.h
☑ Compound Subjects T55m
Vocabulary Strategy CC.3.L.4, CC.3.L.4.d;
☑ Determine Meanings T56c CC.3.L.6

Reading
🕐 20–40 minutes

Day 1

Reading CC.3.Rinf.10
Read Aloud: Autobiography T56a

Comprehension CC.3.Rinf.6, 10
☑ Identify Point of View T56a

Fluency CC.3.Rfou.4
☑ Model Expression T56a

Day 2

Reading CC.3.Rinf.10
Read a Biography T57–T61

Comprehension CC.3.Rinf.2, 5, 6, 10
☑ Determine Point of View T57
☑ Monitor and Clarify T58–T59

Fluency CC.3.Rfou.4
☑ Practice Expression, Accuracy, and Rate T57

Writing
🕐 15–45 minutes

Day 1

Power Writing T55q CC.3.W.10
Daily Writing Skills CC.3.L.1; CC.3.L.3.b
☑ Use Formal and Informal Language T55o
Writing CC.3.W.10
Write with Third-Person Point of View T56b

Writing Project: Personal Narrative CC.3.W.3
☑ Study a Model T64

Day 2

Power Writing T56c CC.3.W.10
Daily Writing Skills CC.3.L.1; CC.3.L.3.b
☑ Use Formal and Informal Language T55o
Writing CC.3.W.10
Write a Response T60–61

Writing Project: Personal Narrative CC.3.W.3
☑ Prewrite T64

Fiction & Nonfiction

SMALL GROUP READING TIME	**Read Social Studies Articles**	**Read Nonfiction Books**

🕐 20 minutes

Day 1 — Read Social Studies Articles

Vocabulary CC.3.L.6
Learn Social Studies
Vocabulary SG22–SG23
Reading CC.3.Rinf.8, 10
Explain Text Structure:
Sequence SG22
Build Comprehension SG23

Day 2 — Read Nonfiction Books

Vocabulary CC.3.L.6
Learn Story Words
SG24–SG25
Reading CC.3.Rinf.10
Introduce SG24–SG25 CC.3.Rinf.8
Read SG26–SG27
☑ Monitor and Clarify SG26–SG27
☑ Make Comparisons SG26–SG27

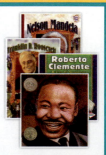

LEARNING STATION TIME/DAILY PHONICS INTERVENTION

🕐 20 minutes

Speaking and Listening T55g CC.3.SL.1; CC.3.SL.3; CC.3.SL.4
Language and Vocabulary T55g CC.3.L.6
Writing T55g CC.3.W.2; CC.3.W.10
Cross-Curricular T55h CC.3.Rinf.5; CC.3.Rinf.10;
  CC.3.W.8
Reading and Intervention T55h CC.3.Rinf.10; CC.3.Rfou.3
Daily Phonics Intervention T55i–T55j CC.3.Rfou.3.d;
  CC.3.L.2.e; CC.3.L.2.f

BIG Question **How do people help each other?**

Day 3	Day 4	Day 5
Read and Compare	**Read and Comprehend**	**Review and Compare**

Day 3 — Read and Compare

Academic Talk CC.3.SL.1
Talk Together T62

Daily Spelling and Word Work CC.3.Rfou.3; CC.3.L.2.e;
☑ Practice T55l CC.3.L.2.f

Daily Grammar CC.3.L.1; CC.3.L.1.f;
☑ More Subjects and Predicates T55n, T62a CC.3.L.3
Vocabulary Review CC.3.L.6
Review Social Studies and
Academic Vocabulary T61a

Reading CC.3.Rinf.10
Reread a Biography
T61a
Comprehension CC.3.Rinf.9
☑ Compare Points
of View T61a

Fluency CC.3.Rfou.4
☑ Practice Expression T62

Power Writing T61a CC.3.W.10
Daily Writing Skills CC.3.L.1; CC.3.L.3.b
☑ Use Formal and Informal Language T55p
Writing CC.3.L.1; CC.3.L.1.f; CC.3.L.3
Write to Reinforce Grammar T63

Writing Project: Personal Narrative CC.3.W.3;
☑ Draft T65 CC.3.W.3.a; CC.3.W.3.b;
  CC.3.W.3.d; CC.3.W.10

Read Nonfiction Books

Vocabulary CC.3.L.6
Expand Vocabulary Through
Wide Reading SG24–SG27
Reading CC.3.Rinf.10
Read and Integrate CC.3.Rinf.8
Ideas SG26–SG27
☑ Monitor and Clarify SG26–SG27
☑ Make Comparisons SG26–SG27

Day 4 — Read and Comprehend

Academic Talk CC.3.SL.1.a
Discuss Points of View T63d

Daily Spelling and Word Work CC.3.Rfou.3; CC.3.L.4.d
☑ Practice T55l

Daily Grammar CC.3.W.5; CC.3.L.1;
☑ Grammar and Writing T55n CC.3.L.1.f
Vocabulary Practice CC.3.L.4; CC.3.L.4.d; CC.3.L.6
☑ Determine Meanings T63c

Reading CC.3.Rinf.10
Read a Biography and an
Autobiography T63a–T63b
Comprehension CC.3.Rinf.10
☑ Distinguish Point
of View T63a–T63b

Fluency CC.3.Rfou.4
☑ Model and Practice Expression T63b

Power Writing T63c CC.3.W.10
Daily Writing Skills CC.3.L.1; CC.3.L.3.b
☑ Use Formal and Informal Language T55p
Writing CC.3.W.10
Write a First-Person Account T63d

Writing Project: Personal Narrative C.3.W.5; CC.3.L.1;
☑ Revise; Edit, and Proofread T66 CC.3.L.1.f; CC.3.L.3;
  CC.3.W.10

Read Nonfiction Books

Vocabulary CC.3.L.6
Expand Vocabulary Through
Wide Reading SG24–SG27
Reading CC.3.Rinf.10
Introduce SG26–SG27 CC.3.Rinf.8
Read and Integrate
Ideas SG26–SG27
☑ Monitor and Clarify SG26–SG27
☑ Make Comparisons SG26–SG27

Day 5 — Review and Compare

Academic Talk CC.3.SL.1
Relate Readings to the Big Question T63h

Daily Grammar CC.3.L.1; CC.3.L.1.f
☑ Review T55n

Vocabulary Practice CC.3.L.4; CC.3.L.4.d; CC.3.L.6
☑ Determine Meanings T63e

Reading CC.3.Rinf.10
Reread a Biography and
an Autobiography T63f
Comprehension CC.3.Rinf.9
Identify Events T63f
Compare Events T63g

Power Writing T63e CC.3.W.10
Daily Writing Skills CC.3.L.1; CC.3.L.3.b
☑ Use Formal and Informal Language T55p
Writing CC.3.W.10
Write to Compare Events T63g

Writing Project: Personal Narrative CC.3.W.3
☑ Publish T67

Read Nonfiction Books

Vocabulary CC.3.L.6
Expand Vocabulary Through
Wide Reading SG24–SG27
Reading CC.3.Rinf.8;
Connect Across Texts CC.3.Rinf.10;
SG27 CC.3.SL.1.a
Writing CC.3.W.10
Choose a Writing Option
SG26–SG27

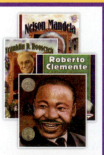

ASSESSMENT & RETEACHING

Assessment and Reteaching T67a–T67b
☑ Reading Comprehension Unit Test CC.3.Rinf.10
A1.24–A1.29
☑ Reading Strategy Assessment CC.3.Rinf.2; CC.3.Rinf.5
SG1.30–SG1.31
☑ Oral Reading Assessment A1.4–A1.6 CC.3.Rfou.4
☑ Vocabulary Unit Test A1.30–A1.32 CC.3.L.6

☑ Words with Digraphs *ch, tch* and CC.3.L.2
Commonly Misspelled Words T55k
☑ Writing, Revising, and Editing CC.3.W.10
Unit Test A1.33–A1.36
Reteaching Masters RT1.9–RT1.11

Speaking and Listening

Option 1: Making a Difference

PROGRAM RESOURCES

Language and Literacy Teamwork Activities: Card 9

Digital Library: Language Builder Picture Cards D1–D10

Teacher's Guide on NGReach.com

Tell a Story	CC.3.SL.4

Option 2: Holiday Helping

NGReach.com **Student Resources**

Have students read and discuss an online article about helping during the holidays. Go to: Resources > Unit 1 > Learning Stations > Week 4 > Holiday Helping

Have small groups brainstorm other ways to help during the holidays.

Discuss Topics, Building on Others' Ideas and Expressing Ideas Clearly	CC.3.SL.1
Ask and Answer Questions and Elaborate	CC.3.SL.3

Language and Vocabulary

Key Words

benefit · comparison · clarify · duty · identify
impact · improve · individual · learn · narrator
neighborhood · offer · point of view · volunteer

Option 1: Vocabulary Games

NGReach.com **Online Vocabulary Games**

Acquire and Use Academic and Domain-Specific Words	CC.3.L.6

Option 2: My Vocabulary Notebook

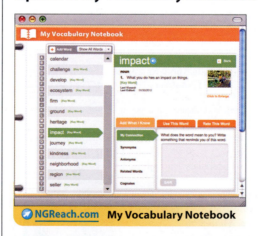

NGReach.com **My Vocabulary Notebook**

Have students expand word knowledge.

- Under: Add More Information > Use This Word > Restate the Definition, have, students write a definition of the word.
- Under: Add More Information > Use This Word > Write More, have students use the, word to write a short first-person narrative.

Acquire and Use Academic, Conversational, and Domain-Specific Words	CC.3.L.6

Writing

Option 1: Discover the Difference

PROGRAM RESOURCES & MATERIALS

Language and Literacy Teamwork Activities: Card 8

Teacher's Guide on NGReach.com

A biography and an autobiography that students have read

Write Informative/Explanatory Text to Convey Information	CC.3.W.2
Write Over Shorter Time for Specific Tasks	CC.3.W.10

Option 2: Write a Letter

Dear Mr. Lekuton,
I read about you in my Language Arts class.

Have students write a letter to Joseph Lekuton. Display the following writing prompt:

What questions would you like to ask Joseph Lekuton about his life in Kenya? Write a letter to Mr. Lekuton to ask your questions. Remember to use formal language when you write.

Write Over Shorter Time for Specific Audiences	CC.3.W.10

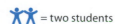 = one student   = two students   = three or more students

Cross-Curricular

Option 1: The Long Road Home

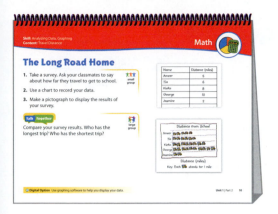

PROGRAM RESOURCES & MATERIALS

Cross-Curricular Teamwork Activities: Card 10

Teacher's Guide on NGReach.com

colored markers or crayons

Gather Information	CC.3.W.8

Option 2: Research Kenya

MATERIALS

library books • encyclopedia • online resources

Have students use a variety of resources to research Kenya. Go to: Resources > Unit 1 > Learning Stations > Week 4 > Kenya

- Have students use different resources to gather information about Kenya.
- Have students create a fact sheet with the information they have gathered.
- Have students share their fact sheets.

Use Search Tools	CC.3.Rinf.5
Read and Comprehend Informational Text	CC.3.Rinf.10

Reading

Option 1: Kakenya's School

NGReach.com **Student Resources**

Have students read an online article about a school for girls in Kenya. Go to: Resources > Unit 1 > Learning Stations > Week 4 > Kakenya's School

Have students read the article and write one or two sentences about something new they learned about Kakenya and her school.

Read and Comprehend Informational Text	CC.3.Rinf.10

Option 2: Additional Reading

PROGRAM RESOURCES

Week 4 Small Group Reading Titles, page SG1

Independent Reading Recommended Books, page SG68

Leveled Book Finder

Have students choose a book they haven't read before from the Week 4 **Small Group Reading** titles, the Independent Reading Recommended Books list, or the Leveled Book Finder.

After reading, have students write a sentence about something new they learned. Students may also wish to take books home for additional reading.

Read and Comprehend Informational Text	CC.3.Rinf.10

Intervention

Phonics Games

NGReach.com **Online Phonics Games**

Apply Phonics and Word Analysis Skills	CC.3.Rfou.3

For Reteaching Masters, see pages RT1.9–RT1.11.

Additional Resources

ESL Instruction

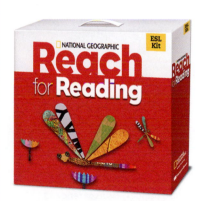

ESL Teacher's Edition pages T56a–T69

OBJECTIVES

Thematic Connection: Heroes Then and Now

Develop Phonological Awareness: Rhyming, Blend Onset-Rime, Isolate Sounds

Associate Sounds and Symbols: Short *i, u*; Phonograms *-ig, -it, -in, -ug, -up*

Concepts of Print (title; directionality)

Associate Sounds and Spellings /ch/*ch, tch*

Teach — Day 1 🧍🧍🧍

PROGRAM RESOURCES

Word Builder: Transparency 18

Sound/Spelling Card 27

Word Builder: Transparency 19

Decodable Passage: *Chad Can Chop*
  Practice Book, page 98

Reach into Phonics

Lesson 12, pages T20–T21

Lesson 13, pages T22–T23

Words with Short *i* and Short *u*

Follow Lesson 12 to review words with short *i* and short *u*. Guide students through **Transparency 18**.

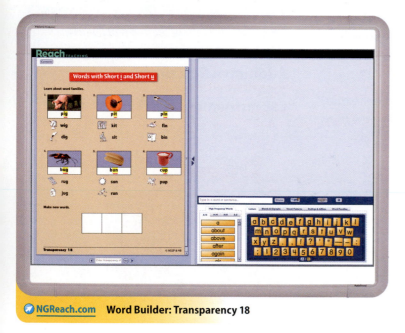

🌐 NGReach.com   **Word Builder: Transparency 18**

Words with Digraph /ch/*ch, tch*

Follow Lesson 13. Use **Reading Routine 1** and **Sound/Spelling Card 27** to teach sound and spellings /ch/*ch, tch*. Guide students through **Transparency 19**. Use **Reading Routine 3** to guide students as they read Decodable text.

*For **Reading Routine 1**, see Reach into Phonics page vi.*

*For **Reading Routine 3**, see Reach into Phonics page ix.*

Practice — Day 2 🧍🧍🧍

PROGRAM RESOURCES

Decodable Reader: *Pop!*
  Practice Book, page 135

Reach into Phonics

Lesson 14, pages T24–T26

Build Reading Fluency

Use **Reading Routine 3** to guide students as they read Decodable text. Provide students with the **Decodable Reader**, *Pop!* Then follow Lesson 14.

*For **Reading Routine 3**, see Reach into Phonics page ix.*

🧍 = one student   🧍🧍 = two students   🧍🧍🧍 = three or more students

COMMON CORE STANDARDS

Use Conventional Spelling	CC.3.L.2.e
Use Spelling Patterns and Generalizations	CC.3.L.2.f
Read Grade-Appropriate Irregularly-Spelled Words	CC.3.Rfou.3.d

Bingo!   Day 3   Option 1

MATERIALS

32 squares of colored paper, each about 2 inches square

Prepare

Have students play in groups of three with one student as the game host. Each student makes a bingo card by folding a sheet of paper in half twice horizontally and twice vertically to create 16 squares. Hosts cut their cards into individual squares. As hosts read words from the word bank below and write each word on a square of paper, the players print the words in any empty square on their bingo cards.

open	then	there	different	bunch	patch	chops	catch
pump	club	crust	swim	pinch	print	chin	stretch

Play a Game

- Tell the host to read each word in a different order than before.
- The first player to find the word on his or her card identifies the word by spelling it. The host listens for accuracy. The player places a square over the word if he or she spells it correctly. If the word is not identified correctly, the player leaves the space uncovered.
- When a player has four squares in a row, the player calls out, "Bingo!"
- The student reads aloud the words to verify the win.

Name the /ch/ Spelling   Day 3   Option 2

MATERIALS

index cards, 12 per pair of students

Prepare

Have pairs of students collaborate to write each word from the word bank below on a separate card. Then have them place the cards face down in a pile.

chimp	stitch	pitch	punch	chin	chill
chug	switch	clutch	crutch	chip	crunch

Play a Game

- Player 1 picks and displays a card. Then, Player 1 identifies the vowel sound and the /ch/ spelling and pronounces the word.
- Player 2 decides if Player 1 has identified the vowel sound and /ch/ spelling correctly. If so, Player 1 keeps the card. If not, the card goes back in the pile.
- Play ends after all of the words have been identified correctly. The partner with the most cards wins.

Concentration   Day 4

MATERIALS

index cards, 5 per student • scissors

Prepare

- Arrange students in pairs. Have each partner write five words with short *i*, short *u*, or /ch/ spelled *ch, tch*. Students should fold their cards in half, writing the word on the left side.
- Then, have students draw a picture of the word on the right side.
- Have students cut their cards in half, and then have partners shuffle both sets of cards together.

Play a Game

- Have partners place all the cards face down on a table in a five by four grid. Tell students to take turns turning over two cards.
- If the word matches the picture, the student says the word aloud and identifies the short *i*, short *u*, or /ch/ spelling and keeps the cards.
- If the cards do not match, if the player does not say the word correctly, or if the player does not identify the spelling correctly, the player returns the cards face down to the table.
- Students play until all the cards have been matched and identified correctly. The student with more cards wins.

Review and Assess   Day 5

PROGRAM RESOURCES

Word Builder: Transparency 20

Reach into Phonics

Lesson 15, page T27
Progress Check 1, page T283

Review and Assess

Follow Lesson 20 to review words with short *i*, short *u*, and digraph /ch/*ch, tch*. Guide students through **Transparency 20**. Administer Progress Check 1 to measure learning.

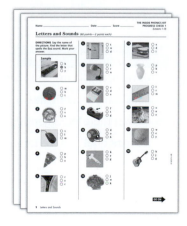

OBJECTIVES

Thematic Connection: Heroes Then and Now

☑ Spell Words with Digraphs ch, tch
☑ Use Commonly Misspelled Words Correctly

SUGGESTED PACING

DAY 1	Spelling Pretest
DAY 2–4	Daily Practice Options
DAY 5	Spelling Test

Spelling Pretest Day 1

Spelling Test Day 5

Spelling Words

Use these words and sentences for the weekly Spelling Pretest and Spelling Test.

Words with Digraphs ch, tch

1. approach	My little brother walks behind me as I **approach** the dark cave.
2. catch	Watch how I **catch** the football with both hands.
3. change	Heroes can **change** the world from unfair to fair.
4. charming	A **charming** person laughs and makes others laugh.
5. chosen	He has **chosen** to help others instead of doing nothing.
6. coach	The **coach** is a hero to her baseball team because she is a great teacher and plays fair.
7. ditch	If you use the right shovel, it won't take long to dig a **ditch** for the water.
8. itching	My hands feel dry because of the **itching** of wool gloves against my skin.
9. latch	Jerry fixed the **latch** on the gate so it would open.
10. pitched	I **pitched** balls to players who needed batting practice.
11. pouches	Postal workers carry letters in **pouches**.
12. reach	A tall person could **reach** the jars on the top shelf.
13. riches	Having friends adds **riches** to my life like joy and laughter.
14. searching	Dad has been **searching** for books about heroes and found some at the bookstore.
15. watchful	That **watchful** bird stares at the water, looking for a fish to eat.

Watch-Out Words

16. this	I'll put **this** magazine in my book bag.
17. these	**These** books in my arms are heavy.
18. that	**That** book over there looks good, too.
19. those	In fact, all **those** books on the far shelf look good.

Digraphs ch, tch   Day 2   Option 1

MATERIALS

white self-stick notes, 15 per pair of students • highlighters, 2 colors per pair

Teach

Display and pronounce *catch* and *change*. Have students listen for /ch/ as you pronounce the words again. Underline the digraphs *tch* and *ch*. Explain: *The single sound /ch/ is spelled with the two letters c-h or the three letters t-c-h.*

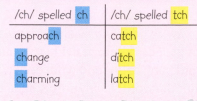

Prepare

- Have partners collaborate to write each of the first 15 spelling words on a separate self-stick note.
- Tell students to create a T-chart with headings /ch/ spelled *ch* and /ch/ spelled *tch*.

Word Sort

- Have partners take turns choosing a word and highlighting the spelling of /ch/, using a different color marker for each different spelling. Direct them to place each word under the correct heading.
- After they have sorted all 15 words, have partners alternate reading and spelling the words to each other.
- Tell students to keep their words for another activity.

Apply Phonics Skills   CC.3.Rfou.3

Find Hidden Words   Day 2   Option 2

Create Sentences

- Have students write eight of the spelling words that have smaller words within them and then circle the smaller words.

> *Those charming people over there would not harm a fly.*

- Tell students to write sentences that include three things:
  1. the small word
  2. the whole word
  3. one of the Watch-Out Words
- Tell students to use each Watch-Out Word at least once and underline the spelling words and smaller words.

Demonstrate Command of Spelling   CC.3.L.2

 = one student   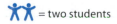 = two students   = three or more students

Word Sort — Day 3 ✕✕ — Option 1

MATERIALS
highlighted self-stick notes from Day 2 activity

Prepare

Tell students to create a three-column chart with the headings Beginning, Middle, and End.

Beginning	Middle	End
change	pouches	approach
charming	riches	coach
chosen	searching	reach
	itching	catch
	pitched	ditch
	watchful	latch

- Have students sort the spelling words into two stacks, one for /ch/ spelled _ch_ and the other for /ch/ spelled _tch_.
- Tell them to place all of the _ch_ spellings in the correct columns of the chart and then place the _tch_ spellings.
- Tell students to note where the spellings come in the words, then take turns reading and spelling the words.

Use Spelling Patterns and Generalizations   CC.3.L.2.f

Bingo! — Day 3 ✕✕✕ — Option 2

MATERIALS
32 squares of colored paper, each about 2 inches square

Prepare

- Have students play in groups of three. One student serves as game host and the other two each make a 16-square bingo card by folding a sheet of paper in half twice horizontally and twice vertically.
- Have the host call out the first 15 spelling words. Players write them in random order, adding a Watch-Out Word for the extra square.

Play a Game

- The host reads each word in random order. The first player who finds the word on his or her card spells it with eyes closed.
- If spelled correctly, the player places a square over the word.
- When a player has four colored squares in a row, he or she calls out "Bingo!" and spells the words to verify.

Use Conventional Spelling   CC.3.L.2.e

Pick It Up! — Day 4 ✕✕✕ — Option 1

MATERIALS
index cards, 23 per group • poster board, one per group • scissors, one per group

Prepare

- Arrange students in small groups and have them print every consonant of the alphabet on a separate index card. Tell them to print digraphs _ch_ and _tch_ on each of the two remaining cards.
- Tell two students to cut five, 6-inch x 6-inch squares from the poster board and write one vowel on each square.
- Students line up the vowel cards on the floor _a_ to _u_ and arrange the consonant cards on a table in a grid _b_ to _z_ next to the two digraph cards.

Play the Game

- A Caller calls out a spelling word.
- A Speller picks up the initial consonant or the _ch_ card and then stands beside the first vowel in the word. If the word begins with a vowel, he or she stands beside it.
- The Speller continues picking up consonants or digraphs and standing beside vowels to spell the word, saying each letter as he or she picks up or stands beside the letter.
- Group members listen and watch as the Speller spells the word. If a student notices an error, he or she takes the Speller's place and spells the rest of the word.
- Students take turns as Caller and Speller until all of the words are spelled correctly.

Apply Phonics Skills   CC.3.Rfou.3

Use a Dictionary — Day 4 ✕✕✕ — Option 2

MATERIALS
index cards, 10 per team • dictionaries, 2 per team

Prepare

Divide the spelling words between two teams. Have teams write each of their spelling words on a separate card, look up their words in a dictionary, and write the definition on the back of each card.

Play a Game

- Have both teams place all 20 cards on a table with the definitions visible. Teams take turns picking up a card, reading the definition, and stating and spelling the spelling word without looking at the spelling. If a student names and spells a word correctly, his or her team keeps the card.
- Play continues until all words have been spelled correctly. The team with more cards at the end wins.

Consult References   CC.3.L.4.d

Week 4 Daily Grammar

OBJECTIVES

Thematic Connection: Heroes Then and Now

☑ **Grammar: Use Subject-Verb Agreement**

☑ **Grammar: Use Compound Subjects**

☑ **Grammar: Use Subjects and Predicates**

Day 1

PROGRAM RESOURCES

Subject-Verb Agreement:
eVisual 1.30

Game: Practice Master PM1.24

MATERIALS

coin, one per group • paper clip or other small object, one per student

Teach the Rules

Use the suggestion on page T56b to introduce subject-verb agreement. Use **eVisual 1.30** to teach more about agreement.

Subject-Verb Agreement

The verb, which is the most important word in the predicate, must agree with the simple subject.

When the subject is **one** person or thing (or singular) the verb ends in **-s**.	Joseph **wants** to go to school. He **wants** to go.
When the subject is **more than one** person or thing (or plural) the verb does **not** end in **-s**.	Many children **want** to go to school. They **want** to go.
The verbs **to have** and **to be** have special forms: **has/have am/is/are**	Joseph **has** brothers. They **are** cattle farmers.

NGReach.com   Subject-Verb Agreement: eVisual 1.30

Play a Game 🏃🏃🏃

Distribute **Practice Master PM1.24** and have small groups follow the directions to play the game.

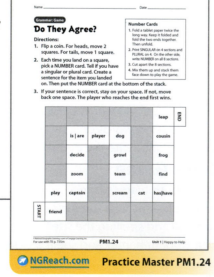

NGReach.com   Practice Master PM1.24

Differentiate

SN Special Needs

ISSUE Students have difficulty using the number cards.

STRATEGY Have students write "one" on the singular cards and "more than one" on the plural cards.

Day 2

PROGRAM RESOURCES

Compound Subjects: eVisual 1.34

Game: Practice Master PM1.25

MATERIALS

index cards, 12 per pair of students

Teach the Rules

Use the suggestion on page T57 to introduce compound subjects. Use **eVisual 1.34** to teach subject-verb agreement.

Compound Subjects

When <u>subjects are joined by</u> **and**, the <u>verb</u> must be plural.	Joseph **and** his <u>brother</u> <u>watch</u> the cattle.
If the subjects are joined by **or** and the <u>last subject is singular</u>, the <u>verb</u> must be singular.	The girls **or** their <u>brother</u> <u>attends</u> the school.
If the subjects are joined by **or** and the <u>last subject is plural</u>, the <u>verb</u> must be plural.	Joseph or his <u>brothers</u> <u>attend</u> the school.

NGReach.com   Compound Subjects: eVisual 1.34

Play a Game 🏃🏃

Distribute **Practice Master PM1.25** and have students follow the directions to play the game.

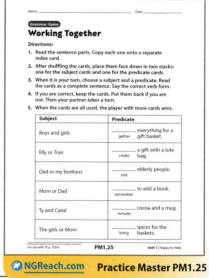

NGReach.com   Practice Master PM1.25

Differentiate

BL Below Level

ISSUE Students have difficulty using the correct verb form.

STRATEGY Have students circle the last subject in each subject card they choose and tell if it is singular or plural.

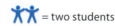  = one student   🏃🏃 = two students   🏃🏃🏃 = three or more students

COMMON CORE STANDARDS

Edit Writing	CC.3.W.5	Use Coordinating Conjunctions	CC.3.L.1.h
Demonstrate Command of Grammar	CC.3.L.1		
Ensure Subject-Verb Agreement	CC.3.L.1.f		

Day 3

PROGRAM RESOURCES

More Subjects and Predicates:
  eVisual 1.36

MATERIALS

scissors

Teach the Rules

Use **Anthology** page 63 to teach more about subject-verb agreement. Explain: *A verb must agree with the simple subject of a sentence.* Extend with **eVisual 1.36**.

More Subjects and Predicates

For a sentence that tells what is happening now:

If a subject is singular, add **-s** to an action verb unless it ends with **x, ch, sh, ss,** or **z.** Then add **-es**.	Joseph like**s** school. He teach**es** now. Joseph wish**es** for more books.
The verb **to be** does not show action. It links words in the predicate to the <u>subject</u>. It has special forms for subject-verb agreement.	I **am** smart. <u>Joseph</u> **is** a hero to others. They **are** from Africa. You **are** a student.

NGReach.com   Subjects and Predicates: eVisual 1.36

Play a Game 👥

Have partners draw the grid shown below and write the *-s* or *-es* form below each verb to make it singular. Have them cut the words apart, mix them up, and put them face down. Explain:

• *Player 1 picks a card and uses the verb in a sentence. If Player 2 agrees, he or she says "I Agree," and Player 1 keeps the card. If not, Player 2 offers a correction and puts the card back down.*
• *Take turns until all cards are used.*

visit	send	wish	pay	drive	catch

Differentiate

EL English Learners

ISSUE Students lack the vocabulary to form sentences.

STRATEGY Provide students with a list of possible singular subjects, such as *I, Joseph, he,* and *the student.*

Day 4

PROGRAM RESOURCES

Grammar and Writing: Practice
  Master PM1.30

Grammar and Writing 🧍

Distribute **Practice Master PM1.30**. Have students use editing and proofreading marks to correct errors with subject-verb agreement.

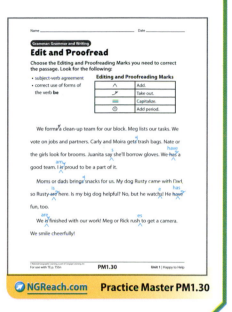

NGReach.com   **Practice Master PM1.30**

Day 5

PROGRAM RESOURCES

Writing, Revising, and Editing Unit
  Test: Assessment Masters
  A1.33–A1.36

Review and Assess 🧍🧍🧍

Have students work in small groups to write rules for subject-verb agreement. Have groups give examples for each rule. Tell them to include both singular and plural subjects, compound subjects with *and* and *or,* and verb forms *to be* and *to have.*

Rule	Example
When the subject is singular, the verb ends in -s.	He builds a school.
Add -es if the verb ends with x, ch, sh, ss, or z.	She watches him.

☑ Administer the **Writing, Revising, and Editing Unit Test.**

OBJECTIVES

Thematic Connection: Heroes Then and Now

 Use Formal and Informal Language

COMMON CORE STANDARDS

Demonstrate Command of Usage
Recognize Conventions of Spoken and Written English

CC.3.L.1
CC.3.L.3.b

Introduce Formal Language — Day 1

PROGRAM RESOURCES
Formal vs. Informal: eVisual 1.31

Teach the Skill

Ask students to compare how they speak to a team member on the playground and how they speak to an adult, such as the principal. Then clarify: *When you speak to a teammate during a soccer match, you use informal language. When you speak to the principal, you use formal language.*

Explain that writers also use formal and informal language in writing. Sum up: *The type of language writers use depends on both their topic and their audience.*

Provide an example: *If I am writing an email to a friend, I might use informal language by asking, "How's it going?" If I'm writing a letter to an important person, I might use more formal language and say, "I hope you had a nice summer."*

Display **eVisual 1.31**. Have volunteers read each passage aloud. Explain: *In an email or personal narrative in which you use the words "I" and "me" to tell about an event, you will probably write using informal language. However, if you are writing a biography or a school report, formal language is more appropriate.*

Informal Language

I squeezed my eyes shut and swung the bat as hard as I could. Crack! LOL! I hit a home run! I started running around the bases as my teammates did a crazy jig in the dugout. BTW, it was pretty funny.

Formal Language

Baseball is one of the most popular sports in the United States. Two teams of nine players each play on a field shaped like a diamond. They take turns batting and fielding.

NGReach.com Formal vs. Informal: eVisual 1.31

INTERACTIVE WHITEBOARD TIP: Underline examples of formal and informal language.

Review the first passage. Point out the abbreviations and discuss their meanings (LOL – Laugh out loud; BTW – By the way) Ask: *Why is the first passage more informal?* (It sounds friendly and personal and includes contractions, abbreviations, and slang.) Ask: *Why is the second passage more formal?* (It sounds serious and does not use contractions or slang.) Explain that both passages are respectful and that each uses language appropriate for its audience.

Adjust Your Language — Day 2 Option 1

Introduce

Copy each type of writing assignment below on a separate strip of paper. Post the strips around the room and arrange students in pairs.

> Email to a friend
> Newspaper article about a crossing guard
> Journal entry about helping someone
> Report about ants

Practice

Have partners discuss whether formal or informal language should be used in each type of writing assignment and why.

Have each pair of students collaborate to write at least one sentence that is appropriate for each type of writing assignment. Tell partners to post each sentence under the appropriate strip of paper.

Have students conduct a gallery walk. Have partners take turns reading the sentences beneath each strip and discussing whether or not each uses the appropriate style of language.

Formal vs. Informal — Day 2 Option 2

Introduce

Arrange students in two groups. Give the groups two minutes to brainstorm people they know who have performed heroic deeds such as saving a life, overcoming a personal challenge, and volunteering in the community. Have each group choose one person to write about. Assign formal language to one group and informal language to the other.

Practice

Allow a few minutes for each group to discuss its person. Tell the group using formal language to write a newspaper article about its person. Tell the group using informal language to write a short personal narrative as if they were the chosen person.

Remind students to keep their type of language in mind as they write.

Combine the two groups and have each one read its passage aloud. Tell the combined group to discuss how each passage exemplifies formal or informal language.

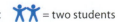 = one student    = two students   = three or more students

SUGGESTED PACING

DAY 1   Teach the Skill
DAY 2–4   Daily Practice Options
DAY 5   Write on Demand

Formal vs. Informal   Day 3   Option 1

Introduce

Arrange students in pairs. Tell partners to choose a person they know who acts heroically by helping others. Tell partners that they will each write for a different audience. One partner will use formal language and the other partner will use informal language.

Practice

Have partners decide who will write using formal language and who will write using informal language. Then have them write a paragraph about their person. Remind them to include how this person behaves heroically.

Have partners read their paragraphs to their partners. Tell students to point out and discuss examples of formal or informal language in the paragraphs.

Switch Paragraphs   Day 3   Option 2

Introduce

Have students work in pairs. Tell each partner to choose a person he or she knows or has read about who has performed a heroic deed.

Tell students that they will write a short paragraph about this person. If students have difficulty thinking of someone, have them review "Joseph Lekuton: Making a Difference" on **Anthology** pages 57–61.

Tell students that they may use formal or informal language in their paragraphs, but that they should have a specific audience in mind (such as a friend, teacher, or book editor) and use language that is appropriate for that audience.

Practice

Have each partner write his or her paragraph.

When both students are finished writing, have them exchange papers and rewrite the other person's paragraph using the opposite style of language.

Display the paired paragraphs side by side in the classroom.

Rewrite for Language   Day 4

Practice

Have each student select a piece of writing from his or her Weekly Writing folder and identify the language of the piece as formal or informal.

Then have each student rewrite the piece, or a portion of a long piece, using the opposite style of language. Before students begin, have them imagine an audience for the revision. Have students write the intended audience at the top of the page.

Invite volunteers to read and compare their paragraphs in small groups.

Review and Assess   Day 5

PROGRAM RESOURCES
Writing, Revising, and Editing Unit Test: Assessment Masters A1.33–A1.36

Review the Skill

Arrange students in four groups. Have each group create a chart showing the differences between formal and informal language.

Tell students to include characteristics in the left column and examples in the right column. For example, they might write "slang" for informal language in the left column and write "way cool!" in the right column.

☑ Administer the **Writing, Revising, and Editing Unit Test**

OBJECTIVES
Thematic Connection: Heroes Then and Now
☑ **Consult References: Dictionary and Glossary**
☑ **Distinguish Point of View**

PROGRAM RESOURCES
TECHNOLOGY ONLY
My Vocabulary Notebook
Read Aloud: eVisual 1.29

MATERIALS
timer

Power Writing
Have students write as much as they can as well as they can in one minute about the word *individual*.
*For **Writing Routine 1**, see page BP47.*

COMMON CORE STANDARDS
Reading
Distinguish Points of View — CC.3.Rinf.6
Read and Comprehend Informational Text — CC.3.Rinf.10
Read with Fluency to Support Comprehension — CC.3.Rfou.4
Writing
Write Over Shorter Time for Specific Purposes — CC.3.W.10
Speaking and Listening
Discuss Topics, Building on Others' Ideas and Expressing Ideas Clearly — CC.3.SL.1
Follow Rules for Discussions — CC.3.SL.1.b
Language and Vocabulary
Determine Meaning of Words and Phrases — CC.3.L.4
Use Glossaries and Dictionaries — CC.3.L.4.d
Acquire and Use General Academic Words — CC.3.L.6

WARM-UP
Have students review the readings from Week 3, including "The World's Greatest Underachiever" and the **Small Group Reading** books. Lead students to discuss how people in each selection overcame challenges.

Academic Talk

❶ Discuss the Big Question
Tell students that they will discuss the question: How do people help each other? Explain that students can use photographs and illustrations to answer it.

Display **Student eEdition** page 52 and model the process: *In the large photo, I see Henry Winkler in a classroom. By sharing some of the challenges he overcame when he was younger, he helps students realize that they can overcome challenges, too.*

Use a **Roundtable** to have students use photos and illustrations from selections in this unit to discuss the Big Question.
- Have students form groups of four.
- Have students in each group use a different visual to answer the question.
- Ask a member from each group to share one example with the class.

*For **Roundtable**, see page BP45.*

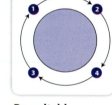

Roundtable

Vocabulary Strategy

❷ Determine Meanings ☑ Anthology page 56
Have students think about the last time they saw words they didn't know. Ask: *What was the word? How did you find out its meaning?* Project **Student eEdition** page 605 and explain: *This is a glossary. It gives information about all the Key Words taught in this book. A dictionary gives information about different kinds of words.*

Project **Student eEdition** page 56 and read aloud the introduction. Point to each part of the entry, read aloud each callout, and explain each kind of information an entry provides. Remind students that they have learned that each syllable has one vowel sound and that words have at least one stressed syllable. Then project **Student eEdition** page 604 and model using the Pronunciation Key to pronounce each sound in *benefit* and the whole word.

Model finding *benefit* in **My Vocabulary Notebook**. Compare the information there with the information found in **Picture Dictionary** page 604.

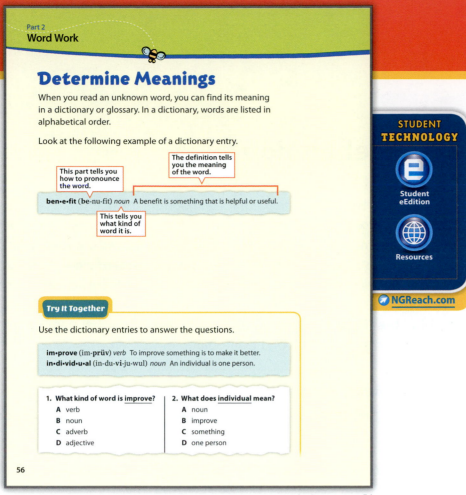

Determine Meanings

When you read an unknown word, you can find its meaning in a dictionary or glossary. In a dictionary, words are listed in alphabetical order.

Look at the following example of a dictionary entry.

This part tells you how to pronounce the word.

The definition tells you the meaning of the word.

ben•e•fit (be-nu-fit) *noun* A benefit is something that is helpful or useful.

This tells you what kind of word it is.

Try It Together

Use the dictionary entries to answer the questions.

im•prove (im-prüv) *verb* To improve something is to make it better.
in•di•vid•u•al (in-du-vi-ju-wul) *noun* An individual is one person.

1. What kind of word is **improve**?
   A verb
   B noun
   C adverb
   D adjective

2. What does **individual** mean?
   A noun
   B improve
   C something
   D one person

56

Anthology page 56

STUDENT TECHNOLOGY

Student eEdition

Resources

NGReach.com

---

③ Try It Together Anthology page 56

Read the directions aloud and have partners work together to answer the questions. (question 1: A; question 2: D)

After students complete the activity, remind them of the unfamiliar words they mentioned at the beginning of the lesson. Demonstrate how to add the words and information about them to **My Vocabulary Notebook**.

See **Differentiate**

Check & Reteach

OBJECTIVE: Consult References: Dictionary and Glossary ✓

As students consult the dictionary entries to answer the questions, determine whether they use the different parts of the entries effectively.

If students cannot use the entries effectively, review each part of the entry for *improve* on page 56: new word, how to pronounce it, the kind of word it is, what the word means. Guide students to create similar labels for the entry for *individual*.

Weekly Writing

Gather students' writing throughout the week:

✓ Daily Writing Skills Practice (T55o–T55p)
✓ Power Writing (T55q, T56c, T61a, T63c, T63e)
✓ Writing (T56b, T60–T61, T63, T63d, T63g)
✓ Writing Project (T64–T67)

Differentiate

SN Special Needs

ISSUE Students have difficulty using the parts of entries.

STRATEGY Have students use sticky notes to mark page 604 in their books to remind them that they have learned about each entry.

AL Above Level

ISSUE Students are ready for more complex word work.

STRATEGY Have students compete to see who can add the most information about the most new words to **My Vocabulary Notebook**.

Fluency

Model Expression As you read the **Read Aloud**, model how to read informational text that includes details about someone's life. Explain: *When you read with expression, change your voice to support the meaning of the text.*

Comprehension

④ Point of View

Introduce: *When you read a story, it is important to understand the ==narrator's== ==point of view==. ==Point of view== describes who tells the story. In first-person ==point of view==, the ==narrator== uses clue words like* I, me, my, we, us, *and* our *to tell what the ==narrator== experiences as part of the story. In third-person ==point of view==, a ==narrator== outside the story tells the story. This ==narrator== uses clue words like* he, him, *and* his.

Display **eVisual 1.29** and read aloud the title, the author name, the introduction, and the first paragraph of the autobiography excerpt.

 Read Aloud

Autobiography

Facing the Lion: Growing Up Maasai on the African Savanna

by Joseph Lemasolai Lekuton

Joseph Lekuton grew up in Kenya, a country in Africa. His family took care of cattle. This part of his story tells a little about his life as a child.

I spent two days in the village with (my) mom, then (my) brother Ngoliong came home to have his hair braided and asked (me) to go to the cattle camp along with an elder who was on his way there. (I'd) say the cattle camp was 18 to 24 miles away, depending on the route, through some rocky areas and a lot of shrubs. (My) spear was broken, so (I) left it at home. (I) carried a small stick and a small club. (I) wore (my) *nanga*, which is a red cloth, tied around (my) waist.

It took (us) all day to get there, but at sunset (we) were walking through the gap in the acacia-branch fence that surrounded (our) camp. There were several cattle camps scattered over a five-mile radius. At night (we) could see fires in the distance, so (we) knew that (we) were not alone. As soon as (we) got there (my) brother Lmatarion told (us) that two lions had been terrorizing the camps. But lions are smart. Like thieves, they go somewhere, they look, they take, but they don't go back to the same place again.

NGReach.com **Read Aloud: eVisual 1.29**   **INTERACTIVE WHITEBOARD TIP:** Circle each first-person clue word.

Display and explain a chart of clue words for first- and third-person narration:

	First-Person Clue Words	**Third-Person Clue Words**
Clue words for one person	*I, me, my*	*he, him, his*
Clue words for more than one person	*we, us, our*	*they, them, their*

Model how to distinguish the point of view: *I see the clue word* I *in many of the sentences.* Circle each *I* and continue: *These clue words tell me that the person telling the story is part of the story. So, the ==point of view== is first-person.* Have partners read on and identify all the clue words that reflect first-person point of view.

Explain that students will change one sentence from the first-person point of view to the third-person point of view. Reread the last sentence of the first paragraph and explain how to use the chart to change the first sentence of the second paragraph. Then have students write the sentence in the third-person.

See **Differentiate**

Check & Reteach

OBJECTIVE: Distinguish Point of View ✅

As partners discuss the passage, note whether they can distinguish the narrator's point of view. If students have difficulty, ask: *What is the* ==point of view== *of a story?* (the person telling the story) *Which words tell you that a story is told in first-person* ==point of view==*?* (I, me, my, we, our) *Which words tell you that a character outside the story is telling it?* (he, she, his, her, hers, they)

Writing

5 Write with Third-Person Point of View

Explain: *When you write about your own life, you usually use first-person* ==point of view==*. Now imagine someone else is writing about you.* Model writing a sentence with first-person point of view, then change it to third-person point of view.

Think Aloud	Write
I will use first-person clue words like I, me *and* my *to write about my life.*	When I was a child, my grandmother taught me how to make my favorite cookies.
Now I'll use third-person clue words like he, she, her, *and* him *to write about my life.*	When s/he was a child, her/his grandmother taught her/him how to make her/his favorite cookies.

*For **Writing Routine 2**, see page BP48.*

Have students use the first-person point of view to write two sentences about themselves. Then have pairs exchange sentences and use the third-person point of view to rewrite their partner's sentences. Have them add their sentences to their Weekly Writing folders.

WRAP-UP
Have students review the texts they read today and discuss examples of clue words that indicate the narrators' points of view.

Daily Language Arts
Daily Spelling and Word Work ✅
Pretest page T55k

Daily Grammar ✅
Point to the second to last sentence in the **Read Aloud**. Say: *This sentence has a plural subject,* lions, *that takes the verb form* are. Use page T55m to teach subject-verb agreement.

Daily Writing Skills ✅
Remind students that they write in different ways for different audiences. Then use page T55o to teach using formal and informal language.

Differentiate

EL English Learners

ISSUE Students lack English language proficiency to write third-person sentences.

STRATEGY Offer limited choices for students to use to replace each first-person clue word with a third-person clue word. For example, have students use the chart on page T56a to choose between *him* and *them* to change this sentence to the third-person point of view: It took us all day to get there.

BL Below Level

ISSUE Students have difficulty distinguishing narrator's point of view.

STRATEGY Have students write a sentence from the **Read Aloud** and circle each first-person clue word. Then have them use the chart to find clue words that change the sentence to the third-person point of view.

OBJECTIVES

Thematic Connection: Heroes Then and Now

☑ Consult References: Dictionary and Glossary
☑ Monitor and Clarify to Comprehend Text
☑ Distinguish Point of View

PROGRAM RESOURCES

TECHNOLOGY ONLY
Vocabulary Strategy: eVisual 1.33

MATERIALS

timer

Power Writing

Have students write as much as they can as well as they can for one minute about the word *dictionary*.

*For **Writing Routine 1**, see page BP47.*

COMMON CORE STANDARDS

Reading
Determine the Main Idea of Text   CC.3.Rinf.2
  and Explain How Details
  Support the Main Idea
Use Text Features   CC.3.Rinf.5
Distinguish Points of View   CC.3.Rinf.6
Read Informational Text   CC.3.Rinf.10
Read with Fluency to Support   CC.3.Rfou.4
  Comprehension
Writing
Write Over Shorter Time for   CC.3.W.10
  Specific Tasks
Speaking and Listening
Discuss Texts, Building on Others'   CC.3.SL.1
  Ideas and Expressing
  Ideas Clearly
Language and Vocabulary
Determine Meaning of Words   CC.3.L.4
  and Phrases
Use Glossaries and Dictionaries   CC.3.L.4.d
Acquire and Use General   CC.3.L.6
  Academic Words

WARM-UP

Have a dictionary race with small groups. Write several Key Words on the board in random order. Have members of each group take turns looking up each word and writing definitions as quickly as possible.

Vocabulary Strategy

❶ Determine Meanings ☑

Tell students that today they will use what they learned about dictionary or glossary entries to determine the meanings of more words. Review the parts of a dictionary or glossary entry. Display **eVisual 1.33**.

 Vocabulary Strategy

• ra • di • us (**rā**-di-us) *noun* the distance from the center of a circle to its edge
• sur • round (sur-**ound**) *verb* to close in on all sides
• ter • ror • ize (**tair**-ur-īz) *verb* to fill with fear; to cause to be afraid

 **NGReach.com**   **Vocabulary Strategy: eVisual 1.33**   **INTERACTIVE WHITEBOARD TIP:** Underline pronunciations and circle definitions.

Use the entry for *radius* to model determining a word's meaning: *The last part of the entry tells the meaning, or definition. I can see that radius means "the distance from the center of a circle to its edge."* Then have partners work together to determine the meanings of *surround* and *terrorize*.

Check & Reteach

OBJECTIVE: Consult References: Dictionary and Glossary ☑

Observe as partners work together to determine the meanings of the words.
If students have difficulty determining the meanings of the words, repeat modeling with *surround*.

Academic Talk

❷ Preview and Predict

Remind: *Before you begin reading a selection, it is important to preview it and think about what it will be about.* Project **Student eEdition** pages 57–61. Point out and have students read the titles, section headings, and photo captions and then predict what they think the biography will tell about Lekuton's life.

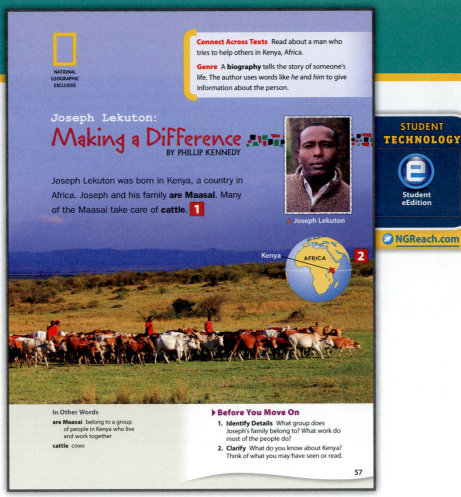

Connect Across Texts Read about a man who tries to help others in Kenya, Africa.

Genre A **biography** tells the story of someone's life. The author uses words like *he* and *him* to give information about the person.

NATIONAL GEOGRAPHIC EXCLUSIVE

Joseph Lekuton:
Making a Difference
BY PHILLIP KENNEDY

Joseph Lekuton was born in Kenya, a country in Africa. Joseph and his family **are Maasai**. Many of the Maasai take care of **cattle**. **1**

▲ Joseph Lekuton

STUDENT TECHNOLOGY

e

Student
eEdition

NGReach.com

Kenya   AFRICA   **2**

In Other Words

are Maasai belong to a group of people in Kenya who live and work together

cattle cows

▶ **Before You Move On**

1. **Identify Details** What group does Joseph's family belong to? What work do most of the people do?

2. **Clarify** What do you know about Kenya? Think of what you may have seen or read.

57

Anthology page 57

Reading

❸ Read a Biography

CONNECT ACROSS TEXTS Project **Student eEdition** page 57. Have students recall the problems the author of "The World's Greatest Underachiever" had in school, and how, as an adult, he helps others. Then have a volunteer read aloud **Connect Across Texts**.

GENRE Have students recall what they have learned about a narrator's point of view. Read aloud the explanation of the genre and ask: *What is the **narrator's point of view** in a biography?*

SOCIAL STUDIES BACKGROUND Maasai families live in kraals, groups of huts made of grass and branches. A fence of thorn bushes surrounds each kraal to keep out dangerous animals. Many family members, as well as the family's cattle, live within the kraal's fence.

Read and Build Comprehension

1 **Determine Point of View** ☑ *Is the story told from the first-person or third-person **point of view**? How do you know?* (The story is told from the third-person **point of view**. I know because the **narrator** uses the third-person clue word *his* and tells about the life of someone else.)

2 **Use Text Features** *What can you learn about Kenya from the picture of the globe?* (The map shows me that Kenya is in Africa.)

Daily Language Arts

Daily Spelling and Word Work ☑
Practice page T55k

Daily Grammar ☑
Point out the subject of the sentence: *Joseph and his family are Maasai* on **Anthology** page 57. Then use page T55m to review the rules for compound subjects.

Daily Writing Skills ☑
Read aloud **Anthology** page 60, and point out that the biography uses formal language. Use page T55o to teach more about formal and informal language.

Fluency

Practice Expression, Accuracy, and Rate As students read the biography, monitor their expression, accuracy, and rate.

Answers   Before You Move On

1. **Identify Details** Joseph and his family belong to a group called the Maasai. Most of the Maasai people take care of cattle.

2. **Clarify** Answers will vary. Possible answers: I've read that Kenya has many animal reserves. A map I saw showed that the capital of Kenya is Nairobi.

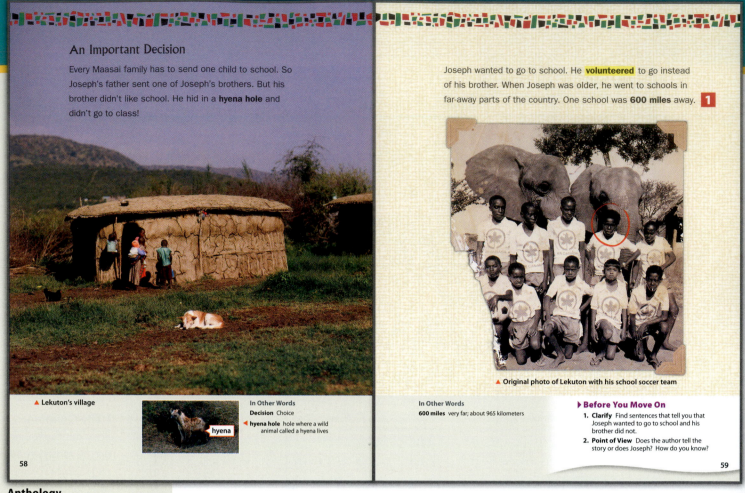

An Important Decision

Every Maasai family has to send one child to school. So Joseph's father sent one of Joseph's brothers. But his brother didn't like school. He hid in a **hyena hole** and didn't go to class!

Joseph wanted to go to school. He **volunteered** to go instead of his brother. When Joseph was older, he went to schools in far-away parts of the country. One school was **600 miles** away. **1**

▲ Lekuton's village

hyena

In Other Words
Decision Choice
◄ **hyena hole** hole where a wild animal called a hyena lives

In Other Words
600 miles very far; about 965 kilometers

▲ Original photo of Lekuton with his school soccer team

▶ **Before You Move On**
1. **Clarify** Find sentences that tell you that Joseph wanted to go to school and his brother did not.
2. **Point of View** Does the author tell the story or does Joseph? How do you know?

58

59

Anthology
pages 58–59

Answers Before You Move On

1. **Clarify** ☑ Students should point out "But his brother didn't like school," "Joseph wanted to go to school," and "He volunteered to go instead of his brother."
2. **Point of View** ☑ The author tells the story. I know because the author uses the first-person clue words *he* and *his*.

Answers Before You Move On

1. **Make Comparisons** Before Joseph went to school, he lived with his family and helped them take care of their cattle. After he started school, he went far away and couldn't help his family anymore.
2. **Details** Joseph became a teacher, helped build schools, and created scholarships to help students pay for school.

Read and Build Comprehension

1 **Monitor and Clarify** ☑ *What idea on pages 58–59 can you clarify?* (Possible response: I read that every Maasai family has to send one child to school. I ask myself, "How will the family decide who goes to school?" I read on and find out that one of Joseph's brothers did not want to go, so Joseph went instead.)

2 **Understand Main Ideas and Details** *How does Joseph Lekuton make a difference in other people's lives?* (The schools he built and the scholarships he created made it easier for other Maasai children to get an education.)

Check & Reteach

OBJECTIVE: Monitor and Clarify to Comprehend Text ☑

Listen to students' responses to the comprehension question about monitoring and clarifying. If students do not understand how to monitor and clarify, model using the sentence frames on **Student eEdition** page 38 to monitor and clarify the sentence: "But his brother didn't like school." Use this question: *How did Joseph know his brother didn't like school?*

OBJECTIVE: Distinguish Point of View ☑

Listen to students' responses to the comprehension question about point of view. If students have difficulty, ask: Who is the story about? (Joseph Lekuton) Have students read the top of page 59. Ask: *What point-of-view clue words does the author use?* (*he, his*) *What do these clue words tell you about the narrator's point of view?* (The narrator has a third-person point of view.)

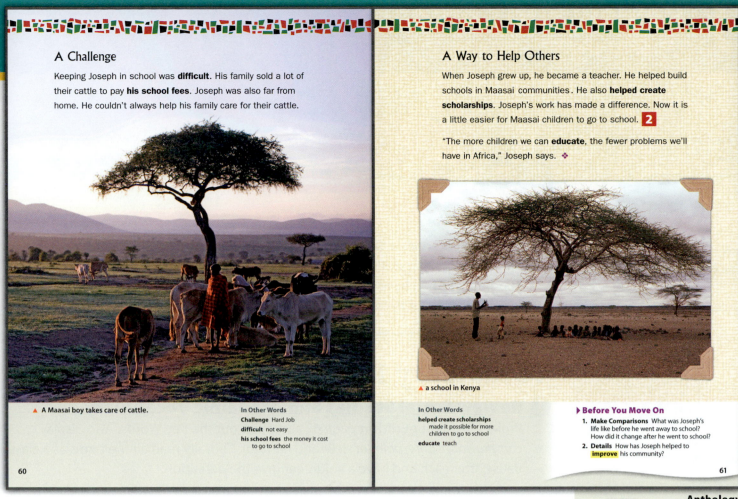

A Challenge

Keeping Joseph in school was **difficult**. His family sold a lot of their cattle to pay **his school fees**. Joseph was also far from home. He couldn't always help his family care for their cattle.

▲ A Maasai boy takes care of cattle.

In Other Words
Challenge Hard Job
difficult not easy
his school fees the money it cost to go to school

60

A Way to Help Others

When Joseph grew up, he became a teacher. He helped build schools in Maasai communities. He also **helped create scholarships**. Joseph's work has made a difference. Now it is a little easier for Maasai children to go to school. **2**

"The more children we can **educate**, the fewer problems we'll have in Africa," Joseph says. ❖

▲ a school in Kenya

In Other Words
helped create scholarships made it possible for more children to go to school
educate teach

▶ **Before You Move On**
1. **Make Comparisons** What was Joseph's life like before he went away to school? How did it change after he went to school?
2. **Details** How has Joseph helped to **improve** his community?

61

Anthology
pages 60–61

Writing

❹ Write a Response

Remind students that one way to respond to something they have read is to say how it relates to their own lives. Model a response to the biography. For example:
The way Joseph helped other students reminds me of my second-grade teacher, Mrs. Bell. She would always give students extra help whenever they had trouble with a lesson.

Have individuals write responses to the biography. Then have students add their responses to their Weekly Writing folders.

See **Differentiate**

WRAP-UP Have partners think of other details they would like to know about Joseph Lekuton's life and work. Have pairs share their ideas with the class.

Differentiate

EL **English Learners**

ISSUE Students are uncomfortable expressing personal experiences.

STRATEGY Adjust the prompt so they can write about imaginary connections.

BL **Below Level**

ISSUE Students have trouble generating responses.

STRATEGY Prompt with questions, such as:
What teacher/family member/friend does Lekuton remind you of? How did that person help others?

OBJECTIVES

Thematic Connection: Heroes Then and Now

☑ **Distinguish Point of View**

☑ **Grammar: Use Subjects and Predicates**

PROGRAM RESOURCES

PRINT & TECHNOLOGY

Comparison Chart: Practice Master PM1.26

Grammar Practice: Practice Master PM1.27

TECHNOLOGY ONLY

Grammar Passage: eVisual 1.35

MATERIALS

timer · index cards

Power Writing

Have students write as much as they can as well as they can in one minute about biographies.

*For **Writing Routine 1**, see page BP47.*

COMMON CORE STANDARDS

Reading

Compare Important Points and Details in Two Texts	CC.3.Rinf.9
Read Informational Text	CC.3.Rinf.10
Read with Fluency to Support Comprehension	CC.3.Rfou.4

Writing

Write over Shorter Time for Specific Purposes and Audiences	CC.3.W.10

Speaking and Listening

Discuss Texts, Building on Others' Ideas and Expressing Ideas Clearly	CC.3.SL.1

Language and Vocabulary

Demonstrate Command of Grammar	CC.3.L.1
Ensure Subject-Verb Agreement	CC.3.L.1.f
Use Knowledge of Language and Conventions	CC.3.L.3
Acquire and Use General Academic and Domain-Specific Words	CC.3.L.6

WARM-UP

Have students review "Joseph Lekuton: Making a Difference." Ask a volunteer to identify the narrator's point of view (third-person) and the genre of text (biography). Then have small groups or pairs look at the reading and find as many examples of third-person clue words as they can within a time limit.

Vocabulary Review

❶ Review Social Studies and Academic Vocabulary

Project **Student eEdition** page 62 and point out the Key Words. Also display *comparison, clarify, point of view,* and *narrator*. Chorally read all the terms as a class. Pause after each and have a volunteer give the definition.

Have small groups write each term on a separate index card and place the cards face down in a pile. Let students in each group take turns drawing cards, reading the terms aloud, and sharing their definitions or other information about them.

narrator

Review and Integrate Ideas

❷ Compare Points of View ☑ Anthology page 62

Project **Student eEdition** page 62 and read aloud the first paragraph. Remind students that they have learned how to identify narrators' points of view. Guide students in answering the questions. Read aloud the rest of the instructions and have partners review the selections and agree on how to fill in the blanks. Then have students identify the point of view of the narrator in each selection.

Distribute and display **Practice Master PM1.26** and explain the structure of the comparison chart. Then read aloud and model how to complete the first cell below "The World's Greatest Underachiever." Have partners work together to complete the chart and discuss their comparisons.

Check & Reteach

OBJECTIVE: Distinguish Point of View ☑

Monitor students as they complete **Practice Master PM1.26** to make sure they can differentiate first- and third-person points of view. If students have difficulty, have them use the clue words *I, me,* or *my* to say something about themselves. Explain: *You used the first-person* **point of view** *to tell about yourself.*

Then have students use *he, she, his,* or *her* to tell about a friend or classmate. Say: *You used the third-person* **point of view** *to tell about someone else.*

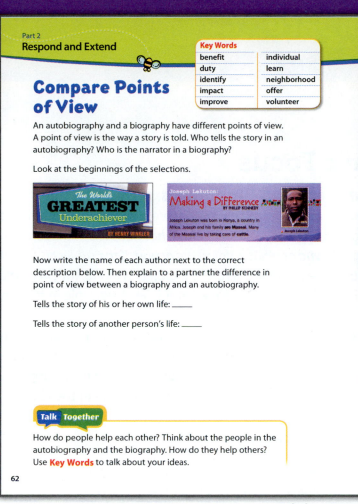

Key Words

benefit	individual
duty	learn
identify	neighborhood
impact	offer
improve	volunteer

Compare Points of View

An autobiography and a biography have different points of view. A point of view is the way a story is told. Who tells the story in an autobiography? Who is the narrator in a biography?

Look at the beginnings of the selections.

Now write the name of each author next to the correct description below. Then explain to a partner the difference in point of view between a biography and an autobiography.

Tells the story of his or her own life: _____

Tells the story of another person's life: _____

Talk Together

How do people help each other? Think about the people in the autobiography and the biography. How do they help others? Use **Key Words** to talk about your ideas.

62

Anthology page 62

STUDENT TECHNOLOGY

Student eEdition

Resources

NGReach.com

Academic Talk

3 Talk Together Anthology page 62

Read aloud the **Talk Together** questions. Use a **Think, Pair, Share** to have partners discuss answers to the questions.

- Have each partner think individually about the questions.
- Have partners share their answers to the questions.
- Have partners share their ideas with the class.

For **Think, Pair, Share**, see page BP46.

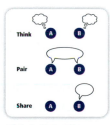

Think, Pair, Share

Fluency

Practice Expression As partners reread the biography aloud, circulate and listen for correct expression.

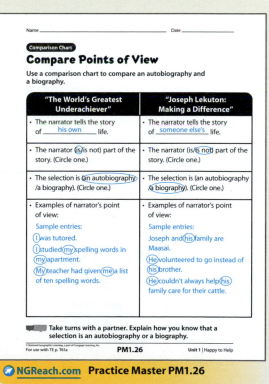

NGReach.com **Practice Master PM1.26**

Best Practices

Encourage Elaboration As students talk, use general prompts:

- *What do you mean by that?*
- *Can you give more details about what you think the author wanted us to know?*
- *Can you connect that to something your partner said?*

Differentiate

EL **English Learners**

ISSUE Verb conjugations in English can be confusing to students whose first language is Spanish.

STRATEGY Display conjugation charts of common verbs in both languages.

AL **Above Level**

ISSUE Students are ready to be challenged further.

STRATEGY Challenge students to add additional examples that fit each rule in the chart on page 63.

Grammar Focus

4 **More Subjects and Predicates** ✔ Anthology page 63

Project **Student eEdition** page 63 and have a volunteer read the introduction aloud. Elaborate: *The verb is the action or what happens in the sentence. The subject of the sentence is who or what is doing the action. If the subject is singular, the predicate must have a singular verb. If the subject is plural, the predicate must have a plural verb.* Read aloud and explain each rule and example in the chart.

Display **eVisual 1.35**. Read aloud the passage, pausing to identify the first subject and predicate. (*I am*) Explain how the sentence illustrates the third rule on **Anthology** page 63. Have students identify the remaining subject and verb pairs in the passage and explain how each illustrates a rule in the chart.

> *Grammar Passage*
>
> I am a boy in Kenya. My parents and brother and sister live with me. My parents raise cattle. My brother is on a soccer team. He plays soccer every day. My sister draws beautiful pictures. She wants to be an artist.
>
> I walk to school every day with my brother and sister. The school is far away. We like our teacher very much.

 **NGReach.com** **Grammar Passage: eVisual 1.35** **INTERACTIVE WHITEBOARD TIP:** Circle each subject. Draw an arrow to the verb that agrees with it.

5 **Read Sentences** Anthology page 63

Read aloud the directions and the excerpt from "The World's Greatest Underachiever." After students find the subjects and the verbs in the excerpt, have them refer to the Grammar Rules chart as they explain how each verb agrees with its corresponding subject.

See **Differentiate**

6 **Write Sentences** Anthology page 63

Write and read aloud this sentence: *They are heroes to their grandchildren.* Have volunteers identify the rule in the chart that the sentence illustrates. Repeat with examples to illustrate other rules. Read aloud the directions and tell students to write two sentences that illustrate two different rules in the chart. Then have students read their sentences to partners and explain the rule each illustrates. Assign **Practice Master PM1.27**.

> ## Check & Reteach
>
> **OBJECTIVE:** Use Subjects and Predicates ✔
>
> As students write sentences, check for agreement of subjects and predicates. If students have trouble, use students' sentences to reteach the rules in the chart on page 63.

Name _____ Date _____

Grammar: Practice
We Like to Read

Grammar Rules Adding -s to Action Verbs

• Use -s at the end of an action verb if the subject is *he, she,* or *it.*	Danny reads a story. He looks at the pictures.
• Do not use -s for *I, you, we,* or *they.*	I read to my friends. They look at the pictures.

Read each sentence. Write the correct form of the verb for each subject.

1. We ___read___ many stories.
   read / reads
2. I ___like___ autobiographies.
   like / likes
3. They ___tell___ about real people.
   tell / tells
4. Henry Winkler ___tells___ his own story.
   tell /tells
5. He ___remembers___ his problems in school.
   remember / remembers
6. His brain ___learns___ differently.
   learn / learns
7. You ___like___ autobiographies, too.
   like / likes

Tell a partner about a story you have read. Use complete sentences. Make sure the subject and the predicate in your sentences agree.

© National Geographic Learning, a part of Cengage Learning, Inc.
For use with TE p. T62a   **PM1.27**   Unit 1 | Happy to Help

NGReach.com **Practice Master PM1.27**

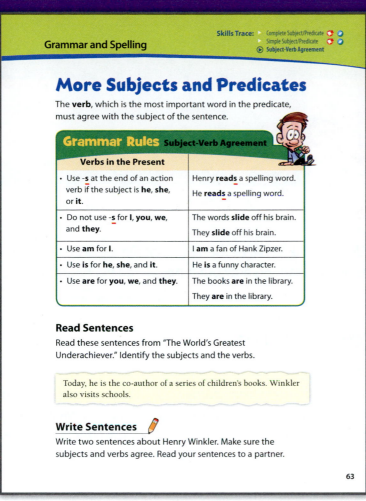

More Subjects and Predicates

The **verb**, which is the most important word in the predicate, must agree with the subject of the sentence.

Grammar Rules Subject-Verb Agreement

Verbs in the Present	
• Use **-s** at the end of an action verb if the subject is **he**, **she**, or **it**.	Henry **reads** a spelling word.
	He **reads** a spelling word.
• Do not use **-s** for **I**, **you**, **we**, and **they**.	The words **slide** off his brain.
	They **slide** off his brain.
• Use **am** for **I**.	I **am** a fan of Hank Zipzer.
• Use **is** for **he**, **she**, and **it**.	He **is** a funny character.
• Use **are** for **you**, **we**, and **they**.	The books **are** in the library.
	They **are** in the library.

Read Sentences

Read these sentences from "The World's Greatest Underachiever." Identify the subjects and the verbs.

> Today, he is the co-author of a series of children's books. Winkler also visits schools.

Write Sentences

Write two sentences about Henry Winkler. Make sure the subjects and verbs agree. Read your sentences to a partner.

63

Anthology page 63

Writing

❼ Write to Reinforce Grammar

Tell students that they will write paragraphs about personal heroes. Remind them to make sure that the verb in each sentence agrees with the subject. Model writing about a personal hero. For example: *My grandmother is my personal hero.* *She is a* **volunteer** *at the local community center. She helps people* **learn** *to read.*

After students write their paragraphs, have each student circle each subject and draw an arrow to the verb it agrees with. Encourage students to use the Grammar Rules chart on page 63 to check for subject-verb agreement. Then have them add their paragraphs to their Weekly Writing folders.

WRAP-UP Have students discuss what they learned from the week's readings about people who are heroes to others. Ask questions to guide the discussion: *What did you learn about that person? What else would you like to learn about that person?*

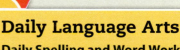

Daily Language Arts

Daily Spelling and Word Work ✓
Practice page T55l

Daily Grammar ✓
Point out the phrase *She wants* in the **Grammar Passage** on page T62a. Explain that *She* is the subject, and *wants* is the verb. Then use page T55n to teach more about subject-verb agreement.

Daily Writing Skills ✓
Remind students that they should use formal language when they are writing biographies or school reports. Then use page T55p to teach more about using formal and informal language.

OBJECTIVES

Thematic Connection: Heroes Then and Now
☑ **Consult References: Dictionary and Glossary**
☑ **Distinguish Point of View**

PROGRAM RESOURCES

PRINT & TECHNOLOGY
Mark-Up Reading: Practice Masters PM1.28–PM1.29
TECHNOLOGY ONLY
Mark-Up Model 1.2 or Model 1.2 PDF
Vocabulary Strategy Practice: eVisual 1.37
My Vocabulary Notebook

MATERIALS

timer, highlighters

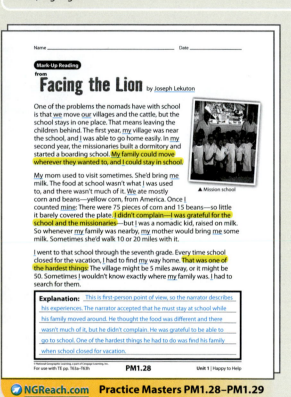

Name _____ Date _____

Mark-Up Reading
from
Facing the Lion by Joseph Lekuton

One of the problems the nomads have with school is that we move our villages and the cattle, but the school stays in one place. That means leaving the children behind. The first year, my village was near the school, and I was able to go home easily. In my second year, the missionaries built a dormitory and started a boarding school. My family could move wherever they wanted to, and I could stay in school.

My mom used to visit sometimes. She'd bring me milk. The food at school wasn't what I was used to, and there wasn't much of it. We ate mostly corn and beans—yellow corn, from America. Once I counted mine: There were 75 pieces of corn and 15 beans—so little it barely covered the plate. I didn't complain—I was grateful for the school and the missionaries—but I was a nomadic kid, raised on milk. So whenever my family was nearby, my mother would bring me some milk. Sometimes she'd walk 10 or 20 miles with it.

I went to that school through the seventh grade. Every time school closed for the vacation, I had to find my way home. That was one of the hardest things: The village might be 5 miles away, or it might be 50. Sometimes I wouldn't know exactly where my family was. I had to search for them.

▲ Mission school

Explanation: This is first-person point of view, so the narrator describes his experiences. The narrator accepted that he must stay at school while his family moved around. He thought the food was different and there wasn't much of it, but he didn't complain. He was grateful to be able to go to school. One of the hardest things he had to do was find his family when school closed for vacation.

© National Geographic Learning, a part of Cengage Learning, Inc.
For use with TE pp. T63a–T63h
PM1.28
Unit 1 | Happy to Help

🌐 **NGReach.com** **Practice Masters PM1.28–PM1.29**

COMMON CORE STANDARDS

Reading
Read with Fluency to Support Comprehension — CC.3.Rfou.4
Read and Comprehend Informational Texts — CC.3.Rinf.10
Writing
Write Over Shorter Time for Specific Purposes — CC.3.W.10
Speaking and Listening
Draw on Information to Explore Ideas — CC.3.SL.1.a
Language and Vocabulary
Determine Meaning of Words and Phrases — CC.3.L.4
Use Glossaries and Dictionaries — CC.3.L.4.d
Acquire and Use General Academic Words — CC.3.L.6

WARM-UP

Ask: *What do you think would be the biggest challenge of living in a new culture?* (Possible response: learning how other people do everyday tasks)

Comprehension

❶ Point of View ☑

Remind students that they have learned about first-person and third-person point of view. Explain that they will identify the point of view in an autobiography and a biography and discuss how the point of view affects how events are described.

SCREEN 1

1 Display and read aloud the first paragraph on **Mark-Up Model 1.2**. Have students follow along using **Practice Master PM1.28** as you model the thinking. Read aloud the definition of point of view and review the definition of *subject*, if necessary. Ask: *Is this text a biography or an autobiography?* (autobiography) *What is the point of view?* (first-person) *How do you know?* (The subject is Joseph Lekuton. He is writing about himself.) Have volunteers underline the clues and click the Point of View button. Click the arrow to go to the next screen.

SCREEN 2

2 Display and read aloud the next paragraph on **Mark-Up Model 1.2**. Explain: *This biography has the same subject and describes the same event.* Have volunteers underline clue words that show the point of view (third person) and click the Point of View button. Click the arrow to go to the next screen.

SCREEN 3

3 Explain: *A narrator's point of view can influence how an event is told.* Ask: *What did it mean for Joseph when the boarding school was built?* (It meant he could stay in school while his family moved around.) Have a volunteer highlight this text in the first passage. Ask: *How does Olivia Hodgson view this same event?* (She thinks Joseph was brave to stay behind. She thinks his life must have been very different from his life as a nomad.) Have a volunteer highlight the text that shows this narrator's point of view, and click the Events button.

Have partners mark up **Practice Masters PM1.28–PM1.29**, underlining clue words that show each narrator's point of view. Have students write explanations of how each narrator's point of view affects how the narrator describes similar events. Finally, have partners review **Practice Masters PM1.28–PM1.29** and compare their mark-ups.

SCREEN 1

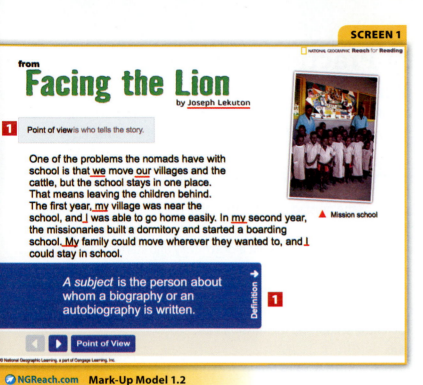

NATIONAL GEOGRAPHIC **Reach** for **Reading**

from
Facing the Lion
by Joseph Lekuton

1 Point of view is who tells the story.

One of the problems the nomads have with school is that we move our villages and the cattle, but the school stays in one place. That means leaving the children behind. The first year, my village was near the school, and I was able to go home easily. In my second year, the missionaries built a dormitory and started a boarding school. My family could move wherever they wanted to, and I could stay in school.

▲ Mission school

A subject is the person about whom a biography or an autobiography is written.

Definition → **1**

◀ ▶ Point of View

© National Geographic Learning, a part of Cengage Learning, Inc.

 **NGReach.com** **Mark-Up Model 1.2**

SCREEN 2

NATIONAL GEOGRAPHIC **Reach** for **Reading**

Boy Between Two Cultures
by Olivia Hodgson

2 Because the Lekutons were nomads, their children faced special problems attending school. Nomads move around, but schools remain in the same place. During most of his school years, Joseph lived in a boarding school that missionaries had built. What a different life he had there! He bravely stayed behind at school when his family left.

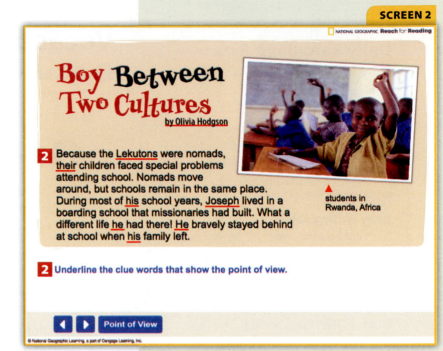

▲ students in Rwanda, Africa

2 Underline the clue words that show the point of view.

◀ ▶ Point of View

© National Geographic Learning, a part of Cengage Learning, Inc.

SCREEN 3

NATIONAL GEOGRAPHIC **Reach** for **Reading**

from
Facing the Lion

Boy Between Two Cultures

3 One of the problems the nomads have with school is that we move our villages and the cattle, but the school stays in one place. That means leaving the children behind. The first year, my village was near the school, and I was able to go home easily. In my second year, the missionaries built a dormitory and started a boarding school. My family could move wherever they wanted to, and I could stay in school.

Because the Lekutons were nomads, their children faced special problems attending school. Nomads move around, but schools remain in the same place. During most of his school years, Joseph lived in a boarding school that missionaries had built. What a different life he had there! He bravely stayed behind at school when his family left.

3 Highlight how each narrator views the same events.

◀ ▶ Events

© National Geographic Learning, a part of Cengage Learning, Inc.

Check & Reteach

OBJECTIVE: Distinguish Point of View ✓

Review students' marked-up **Practice Masters PM1.28–PM1.29**.

If students have difficulty, reteach using examples from **Practice Master PM1.28**:

1. Start with the subject. Ask: *Whom is this passage about?* (a boy from a nomadic family)

2. Now ask about the author: *Who wrote this?* (Joseph Lekuton) Remind students: *When a person writes about himself or herself, the* point of view *is first-person.*

Fluency ✓

Model and Practice Expression Explain: *When you read aloud, change your voice to match the meaning of the ideas conveyed by the text.*

Model reading the last paragraph of **Practice Master PM1.28**. Stress the phrases *hardest things* and *search*. Have students practice expression by reading this sentence aloud: How can one person live in such different worlds?

Power Writing

Have students write as much as they can as well as they can in one minute about facing challenges.

For **Writing Routine 1**, see page BP47.

Vocabulary Practice

❷ Determine Meanings ☑

Remind students that they have learned to use a dictionary to determine the pronunciations and meanings of unfamiliar words. Display **eVisual 1.37**.

 Vocabulary Strategy Practice

1. "One of the problems the <u>nomads</u> have with school is that we move our villages and the cattle."
2. "In my second year, the missionaries built a <u>dormitory</u> and started a boarding school."
3. "Also, the individual <u>portions</u> were small."
4. "By going home, he kept his ties to both <u>cultures</u>."
5. "I was <u>grateful</u> for the school and the missionaries."

Dictionary Entries

cul • ture (**kul**-chur) *noun* the way a group of people lives

dor • mi • to • ry (**dawr**-mu-tawr-ē) *noun* a building with many rooms for sleeping

grate • ful (**grāt**-ful) *adjective* thankful

no • mad (**nō**-mad) *noun* a group of people who move from place to place instead of living in one place

por • tion (**pawr**-shun) *noun* a part or share of something

🔵 NGReach.com **Vocabulary Strategy: eVisual 1.37**   **INTERACTIVE WHITEBOARD TIP:** Have students circle the stressed syllable in each word.

Read aloud the fourth sentence. Ask: *What is the meaning of the word* culture? (the way a group of people lives) *How do you know?* (The definition appears in the dictionary entry.) *What kind of word is* culture? (noun) Have a student circle the part of speech. *Which syllable is stressed in the word* culture? (the first) *How do you know?* (It appears in bold.)

Have partners work together to match the underlined word in each sentence with its dictionary entry. Have them take turns explaining what each word means.

Explain: *Now we will add these words to the glossary we are creating in **My Vocabulary Notebook**.* Model for students how to add each new entry to **My Vocabulary Notebook** on NGReach.com. Students may wish to add additional information, such as sentences, via the "Add More Information" link.

Check & Reteach

OBJECTIVE: Consult References: Dictionary and Glossary ☑

As students look up words in the dictionary entries, determine if they understand the definition of each word. If students have difficulty with the definitions, they should substitute them for the word in each sentence and read the sentence again.

Academic Talk

❸ Discuss Points of View

Explain that students will use evidence from "Joseph Lekuton: Making a Difference" on **Anthology** pages 57–61 and "Facing the Lion" and "Boy Between Two Cultures" in **Practice Masters PM1.28–PM1.29** to discuss the following:

- how Joseph Lekuton feels about what he does
- how the author feels about Lekuton and how he faced challenges
- what students as readers feel about Lekuton

Form small groups. Give groups time for their discussions. Then reassemble students to discuss the differences between the points of view of Lekuton, the author, and the readers.

Writing

❹ Write a First-Person Account

Remind students that in a first-person account, the writer tells the story. Model:

Think Aloud	Write
I'm going to write about how I met my best friend.	On the first day of school last year, I met the person who has become my best friend.
I'll describe where and how we met.	He was a new student, and my locker was next to his. I wanted to be helpful, so I started talking to him.
Then I'll tell what happened next.	At first he was quiet, and I wasn't sure if I would like him. But later I found out he was nervous about being in a new school. He's actually really funny!

Introduce the activity: *Now write a paragraph giving a first-person account of an experience you had in school, such as meeting a new person, or* ==learning== *something exciting. Use first-person pronouns, such as* I, me, my, *and* mine, *in your account.*

Have students add their accounts to their Weekly Writing folders.
*For **Writing Routine 2**, see page BP48.*

See **Differentiate**

WRAP-UP   Form small groups and brainstorm questions to ask Henry Winkler and Joseph Lekuton. Reassemble and have students discuss their questions and why they would like to know that information.

Differentiate

EL English Learners

ISSUE Students lack the language skills to express their ideas vividly in words.

STRATEGY Provide first-person sentence frames such as these:

- On the first day of school, I _____ .
- One thing I like about school is _____ .
- This year, I hope that _____ happens again in my school.

SN Special Needs

ISSUE Students have trouble choosing something to write about.

STRATEGY Have students narrow their focus. Ask them to think about an experience they had today in school. Prompt with questions:

- What was the most interesting thing you learned today?
- How did you spend your recess or lunch time?

OBJECTIVES

Thematic Connection: Heroes Then and Now

☑ **Consult References: Dictionary and Glossary**

Identify and Compare Events

PROGRAM RESOURCES

PRINT & TECHNOLOGY

Unit Concept Map: Practice Master PM1.1

Mark-Up Reading: Practice Masters PM1.28–PM1.29

TECHNOLOGY ONLY

Vocabulary Strategy Practice: eVisual 1.38

Venn Diagram: eVisual 1.39

Power Writing

Have students write as much as they can as well as they can in one minute about why school is important.

For **Writing Routine 1**, *see page BP47.*

COMMON CORE STANDARDS

Reading

Compare Two Texts	CC.3.Rinf.9
Read Informational Text	CC.3.Rinf.10

Writing

Write Over Shorter Time for Specific Purposes	CC.3.W.10

Speaking and Listening

Discuss Topics, Building on Others' Ideas and Expressing Ideas Clearly	CC.3.SL.1

Language and Vocabulary

Determine Meaning of Words and Phrases	CC.3.L.4
Use Glossaries and Dictionaries	CC.3.L.4.d
Acquire and Use General Academic Words	CC.3.L.6

WARM-UP

Give students a word and challenge them to give as many examples and nonexamples of the word as they can.

Vocabulary Practice

❶ Determine Meanings ☑

Remind students that they have learned to use a dictionary to determine the pronunciations and meanings of unfamiliar words. Then display **eVisual 1.38**.

Vocabulary Strategy Practice

1. "He <u>bravely</u> stayed behind at school when his family left."
2. "Yet, Joseph saw it as his duty not to <u>complain</u>."
3. "There were 75 pieces of corn and 15 beans—so little it <u>barely</u> covered the plate."
4. "By going home, he kept his <u>ties</u> to both cultures."

Dictionary Entries

bare • ly (**bair**-lē) *adverb* hardly, almost did not

brave • ly (**brāv**- lē) *adverb* in a courageous or fearless way

com • plain (cum-**plān**) *verb* to say that you do not like something

tie (**tī**) *noun* connection

NGReach.com Vocabulary Strategy: eVisual 1.38 | **INTERACTIVE WHITEBOARD TIP:** Draw lines between the sentence words and their definitions.

Remind students that they can use the dictionary to help them determine the meanings of words when they read. Read aloud the first sentence. Ask: *What is the meaning of the word* bravely? (in a courageous or fearless way) *How do you know?* (The definition appears in the dictionary entry.) *What kind of word is* bravely? (adverb) Have a student circle the part of speech. *Which syllable is stressed in the word* bravely? (the first) *How do you know?* (It appears in bold.)

Check & Reteach

OBJECTIVE: Consult References: Dictionary and Glossary ☑

Check if students are able to consult the dictionary entries to determine the meanings of the words. If students have difficulty, support the process using the following questions:

- *Which is a characteristic of* complain—*joy or discontent?* (discontent)
- *Which would be an example of* complain—*to compliment or to nag?* (to nag)
- *Which would be a nonexample—cheering or moaning?* (cheering)

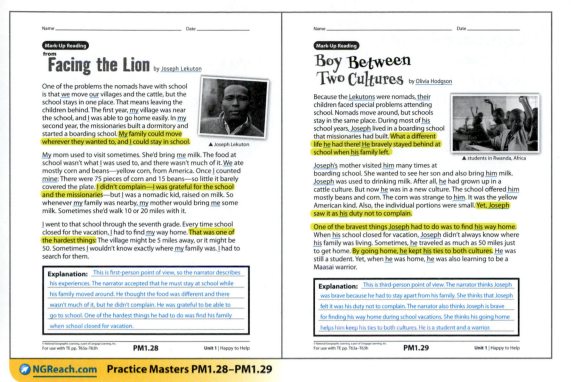

The images above show two worksheet pages:

Mark-Up Reading
from
Facing the Lion by Joseph Lekuton

One of the problems the nomads have with school is that we move our villages and the cattle, but the school stays in one place. That means leaving the children behind. The first year, my village was near the school, and I was able to go home easily. In my second year, the missionaries built a dormitory and started a boarding school. My family could move wherever they wanted to, and I could stay in school.

My mom used to visit sometimes. She'd bring me milk. The food at school wasn't what I was used to, and there wasn't much of it. We ate mostly corn and beans—yellow corn, from America. Once I counted mine: There were 75 pieces of corn and 15 beans—so little it barely covered the plate. I didn't complain—I was grateful for the school and the missionaries—but I was a nomadic kid, raised on milk. So whenever my family was nearby, my mother would bring me some milk. Sometimes she'd walk 10 or 20 miles with it.

I went to that school through the seventh grade. Every time school closed for the vacation, I had to find my way home. That was one of the hardest things: The village might be 5 miles away, or it might be 50. Sometimes I wouldn't know exactly where my family was. I had to search for them.

Explanation: This is first-person point of view, so the narrator describes his experiences. The narrator accepted that he must stay at school while his family moved around. He thought the food was different and there wasn't much of it, but he didn't complain. He was grateful to be able to go to school. One of the hardest things he had to do was find his family when school closed for vacation.

▲ Joseph Lekuton

PM1.28   Unit 1 | Happy to Help

Mark-Up Reading
Boy Between Two Cultures by Olivia Hodgson

Because the Lekutons were nomads, their children faced special problems attending school. Nomads move around, but schools stay in the same place. During most of his school years, Joseph lived in a boarding school that missionaries had built. What a different life he had there! He bravely stayed behind at school when his family left.

Joseph's mother visited him many times at boarding school. She wanted to see her son and also bring him milk. Joseph was used to drinking milk. After all, he had grown up in a cattle culture. But now he was in a new culture. The school offered him mostly beans and corn. The corn was strange to him. It was the yellow American kind. Also, the individual portions were small. Yet, Joseph saw it as his duty not to complain.

One of the bravest things Joseph had to do was to find his way home. When his school closed for vacation, Joseph didn't always know where his family was living. Sometimes, he traveled as much as 50 miles just to get home. By going home, he kept his ties to both cultures. He was still a student. Yet, when he was home, he was also learning to be a Maasai warrior.

Explanation: This is third-person point of view. The narrator thinks Joseph was brave because he had to stay apart from his family. She thinks that Joseph felt it was his duty not to complain. The narrator also thinks Joseph is brave for finding his way home during school vacations. She thinks his going home helps him keep his ties to both cultures. He is a student and a warrior.

▲ students in Rwanda, Africa

PM1.29   Unit 1 | Happy to Help

Review and Integrate Ideas

② Identify Events

Explain that students will identify the events in **Practice Masters PM1.28–1.29**. Explain: *An event is something that happens.* Model the process of identifying the event that occurs in the first paragraph of "Boy Between Two Cultures": *In this paragraph, I learn that Joseph stayed at boarding school even though his family moved away.*

Have partners list all the major events in "Boy Between Two Cultures" and "Facing the Lion." Explain that the events in the biography and the autobiography are almost the same.

"Facing the Lion" and "Boy Between Two Cultures"
• Joseph stayed at boarding school when his family moved away.
• His mother visited and brought milk.
• He ate food that was strange to him.
• During school vacations, he had to find his way home.
• At home, he was learning to be a Maasai warrior.

Differentiate

BL **Below level**

ISSUE Students have difficulty comparing and contrasting events.

STRATEGY Have partners ask and answer questions such as these:

- What events happen in "Joseph Lekuton: Making a Difference"? What events happen in "Boy Between Two Cultures"?
- How are the events the same?
- How are the events different?

AL **Above Level**

ISSUE Students do not use newly acquired vocabulary.

STRATEGY Prompt students to use Key Words in comparing and contrasting:

- *In "Joseph Lekuton: Making a Difference," what events take place when Joseph grows up?* (He helps others.) *What Key Word can you use to describe that?* (**benefit**)
- *What is the main event in all three selections?* (Joseph going to school) *Use two Key Words to describe why it's important.* (Joseph's family wants to **improve** Joseph's life and they want him to **learn** .)

❸ Compare Events

Have students review "Joseph Lekuton: Making a Difference" on **Anthology** pages 57–61. Explain that they will compare the events in this selection with the events from **Practice Master PM1.28**, "Facing the Lion." Display **eVisual 1.39**.

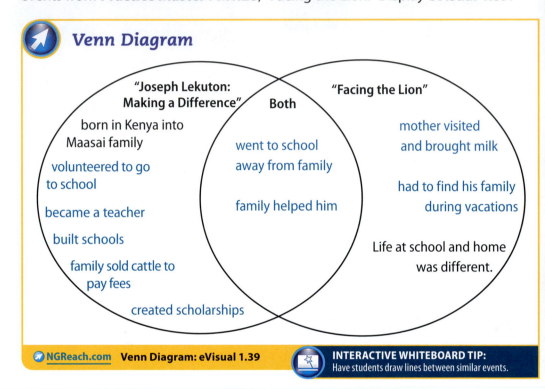

Venn Diagram

"Joseph Lekuton: Making a Difference"
- born in Kenya into Maasai family
- volunteered to go to school
- became a teacher
- built schools
- family sold cattle to pay fees
- created scholarships

Both
- went to school away from family
- family helped him

"Facing the Lion"
- mother visited and brought milk
- had to find his family during vacations
- Life at school and home was different.

🌐 NGReach.com **Venn Diagram: eVisual 1.39**

INTERACTIVE WHITEBOARD TIP: Have students draw lines between similar events.

Explain that students will recreate and complete the diagram. Model comparing events: *Events in "Facing the Lion" are about Lekuton's life as a schoolboy. "Joseph Lekuton: Making a Difference" includes events about Lekuton's whole life, from birth to adulthood.* Have partners complete the chart and discuss their comparisons.

Check & Reteach

OBJECTIVE: Identify and Compare Events

Review students' diagrams to check if they are able to identify and compare events. If students have difficulty, ask: *Which event in "Joseph Lekuton: Making a Difference" shows how Joseph's family helped him?* (They sold cattle to pay his school fees.) *Which event from "Facing the Lion" shows family help?* (His mother brought him milk.)

Writing

❹ Write to Compare Events

Introduce the activity: *Now you will write a paragraph that compares the events in "Joseph Lekuton: Making a Difference" and "Facing the Lion."* Have students share their comparisons and add them to their Weekly Writing folders.

See **Differentiate**

Academic Talk

⑤ Relate Readings to the Big Question

Have students recall the unit's Big Question: How do people help each other? Ask: *Think about "The World's Greatest Underachiever," "Joseph Lekuton: Making a Difference," "Facing the Lion," "Boy Between Two Cultures," and a* **Small Group Reading** *book you have read. How did those selections show different ways people help one another?*

Model a response to the question for "Joseph Lekuton: Making a Difference": *One way people help each other is by giving up something important. For example, Joseph's family was willing to sell their cattle to pay his school fees. Cattle are very important to the Maasai people.*

Use an **Inside-Outside Circle** to have students continue discussion about how the readings relate to the Big Question.

- Have students stand in concentric circles facing each other.
- Direct students in the outside to ask questions. Those on the inside answer. Offer questions to get students started:
  - *In what ways did Joseph help his family?*
  - *How does Joseph help people today?*
  - *How did Joseph's teacher help him?*
  - *How did Joseph's mother help him?*
- On a signal, have students rotate to create new partnerships.
- On another signal, have students trade inside/outside roles.

For **Inside-Outside Circle**, *see page BP45.*

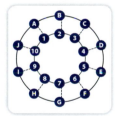

Inside-Outside Circle

Have students add their ideas to their unit concept maps.

WRAP-UP Have students decide individually which event in Joseph Lekuton's life was the most interesting to them. Then form small groups. Have students explain the events they chose and why they chose them. Then have each group decide on one event to share with the class.

Best Practices

Encourage Respect Encourage students to validate each others' points of view. Provide examples:

- *Good point.*
- *That makes sense.*
- *I can tell you've thought about this a lot.*

OBJECTIVES

Thematic Connection: Heroes Then and Now

☑ **Write a Personal Narrative: Voice**

PROGRAM RESOURCES

PRINT & TECHNOLOGY

Writing Rubric: Assessment Master A1.41

TECHNOLOGY ONLY

Writing Trait: Voice: eVisual 1.32

SUGGESTED PACING

DAY 1	Study a Model
DAY 2	Prewrite/Gather Information
DAY 3	Get Organized/Draft
DAY 4	Revise/Edit and Proofread
DAY 5	Publish and Present

COMMON CORE STANDARDS

Writing

Write Narratives	CC.3.W.3
Introduce Narrator and/or Characters	CC.3.W.3.a
Use Dialogue and Description	CC.3.W.3.b
Provide Closure	CC.3.W.3.d
Plan, Revise, and Edit Writing	CC.3.W.5
Write Over Extended Time Frames for Specific Tasks, Purposes, and Audiences	CC.3.W.10

Language and Vocabulary

Demonstrate Command of Grammar and Usage	CC.3.L.1
Ensure Subject-Verb Agreement	CC.3.L.1.f
Use Knowledge of Language and Conventions	CC.3.L.3

T64 Unit 1

Study a Model

Read the Personal Narrative Anthology page 67

Read aloud the prompt on **Student eEdition** page 64. Have students read the model silently or in pairs. Then have volunteers read aloud the notes next to the student sample and ask them to identify the features of the model personal narrative (uses words like *I*, *me*, and *my*; has a beginning, middle, and end).

Teach the Trait: Voice

Display and read aloud **eVisual 1.32**. Tell students that when they write, they should use a voice that is appropriate for the situation. In a personal narrative, they should be especially sure to let their own voice shine through. Point out the words *I*, *me*, and *my* in the model, as well as the underlined sentences in the second paragraph. Tell students that when writing a personal narrative, they can use informal language that sounds natural and includes words they would actually say.

Writing Trait: Voice

The voice of a personal narrative:

- sounds real and includes words the writer would actually say.
- uses informal language.

NGReach.com   Trait: Voice: eVisual 1.32   **INTERACTIVE WHITEBOARD TIP:** Place a check mark next to each point as you explain it.

Prewrite

Choose a Topic Anthology page 65

Have students reread the prompt. Then ask questions such as *Who is the audience?* to unpack the prompt and begin completing a RAFT.

> **Role**: Yourself
> **Audience**: Classmates
> **Form**: Story for a class book

Have students read step 1 on page 65. Then have each student choose an event from his or her life that demonstrates witnessing or performing a heroic deed, to complete a RAFT.

Gather Information Anthology page 65

Have a volunteer read Step 2. As students think about their events, have them ask themselves: *What happened first? Next? Last?* Explain that they will add their answers to a story map.

Get Organized Anthology page 65

Draw students' attention to the story map on page 65. Explain that a story map can help them put their events in order. Have students add their own events.

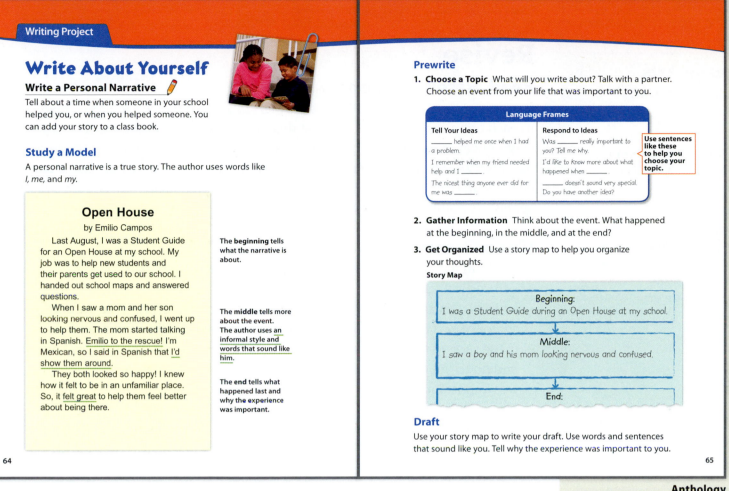

Writing Project

Write About Yourself

Write a Personal Narrative 🖉

Tell about a time when someone in your school helped you, or when you helped someone. You can add your story to a class book.

Study a Model

A personal narrative is a true story. The author uses words like *I, me,* and *my.*

Open House
by Emilio Campos

Last August, I was a Student Guide for an Open House at my school. My job was to help new students and their parents get used to our school. I handed out school maps and answered questions.

When I saw a mom and her son looking nervous and confused, I went up to help them. The mom started talking in Spanish. Emilio to the rescue! I'm Mexican, so I said in Spanish that I'd show them around.

They both looked so happy! I knew how it felt to be in an unfamiliar place. So, it felt great to help them feel better about being there.

> The **beginning** tells what the narrative is about.

> The **middle** tells more about the event. The author uses an informal style and words that sound like him.

> The **end** tells what happened last and why the experience was important.

64

Prewrite

1. **Choose a Topic** What will you write about? Talk with a partner. Choose an event from your life that was important to you.

Language Frames	
Tell Your Ideas	**Respond to Ideas**
_____ helped me once when I had a problem.	Was _____ really important to you? Tell me why.
I remember when my friend needed help and I _____ .	I'd like to know more about what happened when _____ .
The nicest thing anyone ever did for me was _____ .	_____ doesn't sound very special. Do you have another idea?

> Use sentences like these to help you choose your topic.

2. **Gather Information** Think about the event. What happened at the beginning, in the middle, and at the end?

3. **Get Organized** Use a story map to help you organize your thoughts.

Story Map

> **Beginning:**
> I was a Student Guide during an Open House at my school.

> **Middle:**
> I saw a boy and his mom looking nervous and confused.

> **End:**

Draft

Use your story map to write your draft. Use words and sentences that sound like you. Tell why the experience was important to you.

65

Anthology
pages 64–65

Draft

Write Ideas Anthology page 65

Invite a volunteer to read the instructions aloud.

Explain how to turn a story map into a personal narrative: *You begin your personal narrative by telling what it is about. In the middle of your narrative, you add details by telling more about the event. At the end, you tell what happened last and why this event was important to you.*

Remind students that they are telling events from their own lives, so they should include the words *I, me,* and *my.* Point out that they should also use words that sound like their own voice, such as: *I was really scared. I had no clue what to do.* Say: *Your writing should be clear and easy to understand, but it should also sound like your own personal way of speaking.*

Then have students use their story maps to write their personal narratives.

See **Differentiate**

Differentiate

EL English Learners

ISSUE Students struggle with pronoun usage.

STRATEGY Review usage of the first-person pronouns *I, me,* and *my.* Give several examples, such as *I like juice. Play with me. My bicycle is red.* Then write other examples on the board, but have students supply the pronouns.

BL Below Level

ISSUE Students have trouble understanding the concept of a personal narrative.

STRATEGY Ask students to think of a story about themselves they would like to share. As they tell their story, make sure that students use pronouns such as *I, me,* and *my.* Tell them to use the same exercise to write their personal narratives.

Daily Language Arts

Daily Spelling and Word Work ☑
Practice Pages T55k–T55l

Daily Grammar ☑
Use pages T55m–T55n to have students practice using compound subjects and subject-verb agreement.

Daily Writing Skills ☑
Point out the sentence *Emilio to the rescue!* in the student model on **Anthology** page 66. Then use pages T55o–T55p to have students practice using informal language.

Differentiate

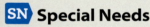 **Special Needs**

ISSUE Students struggle with revising their personal narratives.

STRATEGY Work individually with students. Read a sentence aloud and work together to revise the sentence for informal language. Also, work with the student to be sure the personal narrative has a beginning, middle, and end. When you are finished, read aloud the revised personal narratives, noting the improvements you made.

AL Above Level

ISSUE Students are not challenged by writing a personal narrative.

STRATEGY Challenge students to reread their personal narratives and add as many specific and vivid details to their sentences as they can. They can also include dialogue, practicing using others' voices in this way.

Revise

Read, Retell, Respond Anthology page 66

Read aloud step 1 on page 66. Have partners take turns reading their narratives to each other and then retelling what they have heard. Then have them hold peer conferences to aid in revising. Model how to offer feedback using the sample personal narrative: *The language sounds a little like how Emilio would speak, but I would add more details to the experience. I would also add more natural language, maybe even a phrase in Spanish, to point out that Emilio knows the language.*

Make Changes Anthology page 66

Read aloud the instructions and the sample changes in step 2 on page 66. Check understanding:

- *In the first revision, why did the writer revise the second sentence?* (The second sentence was too formal and did not sound like how Emilio would talk.)
- *In the second revision, why did the writer add a sentence?* (The sentence adds an ending to the narrative that tells the audience why the experience was important.)

Have students use Revising Marks to edit their own drafts. Remind students to focus on retaining their own personal voice and style. They can do this by using an informal style in their writing.

See **Differentiate**

Edit and Proofread

Check the Personal Narrative Anthology page 67

Have students work with a partner to edit and proofread their personal narratives. Have them check to make sure they have used complete sentences, and that their writing uses subject-verb agreement. Then have students edit and proofread their drafts, focusing on the Week 4 spelling words.

Writing Project, continued

Revise

1. **Read, Retell, Respond** Read your draft aloud to a partner. Your partner listens and then retells the story. Next, talk about ways to improve your writing.

Language Frames	
Retell	**Make Suggestions**
You told me about the time when ____.	I'm not sure why ____ was special to you. Can you explain why you chose this topic?
I think this experience was important to you because ____.	The language is too formal/informal. Maybe you could change ____.

Use sentences like these to respond to your partner's writing.

2. **Make Changes** Think about your draft and your partner's suggestions. Then use the Revising Marks on page 573 to mark your changes.
   - Do your words and sentences sound like you? If not, change some.

     The mom started talking in Spanish. ~~I knew I could help them.~~ Emilio to the rescue!

   - Make sure your narrative has an ending. Did you tell why the experience was important?

     I knew how it felt to be in an unfamiliar place. So, it felt great to help them feel better about being there.

66

Edit and Proofread

Work with a partner to edit and proofread your personal narrative. Be sure the subject and verb agree in each sentence. Use the marks on page 578 to show your changes.

Spelling Tip

When you use the present tense, put **-s** at the end of an action verb if the subject is **he**, **she**, or **it**.

Publish

1. **On Your Own** Make a final copy of your personal narrative. Choose a way to share it with your classmates. You might read one another's narratives or sit in a circle and take turns telling your experiences.

Presentation Tips

If you are the speaker...	If you are the listener...
Make eye contact with your listeners. Look up even if you are reading your story.	Nod or smile to show the reader that you are listening attentively.
Keep your expression friendly as you tell about your experience.	Think about why the event was important to the speaker.

2. **In a Group** Collect all the personal narratives. Bind them into a book called "Helping Others." Tell your family and friends about the book. They might want a copy!

67

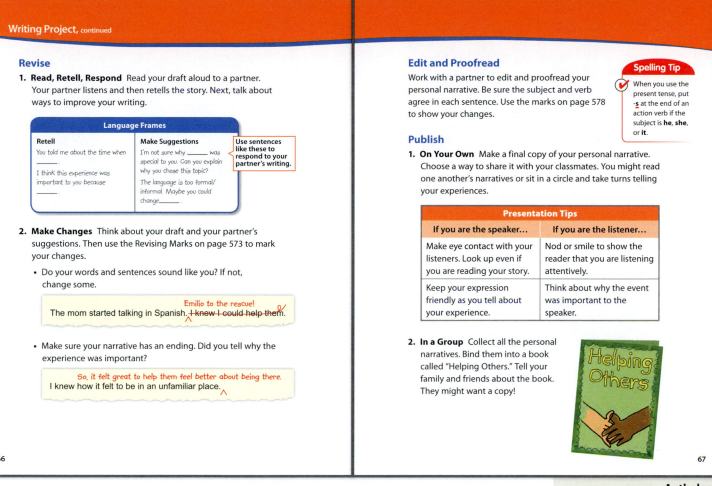

Anthology
pages 66–67

Publish

On Your Own **Anthology** page 67

Have students write final drafts of their personal narratives. Give students the option of typing their personal narratives in a word processing program before reading them aloud to the class. Demonstrate how to read the personal narrative using the model and Presentation Tips. Explain and model how students should look at the audience to show confidence and to emphasize certain points. Tell students it is also important to use gestures and expressions that look natural and match what they are saying. Encourage them to look friendly as they tell about their personal experiences.

In a Group **Anthology** page 67

Combine all of the personal narratives into a class book called "Helping Others." Display the book in the classroom or in the school library so that students from other classes can read it.

Writing Rubric

Score Point	Ideas	Organization	Voice	Word Choice	Fluency	Conventions	Presentation
4	• The writing has a clear, focused message that keeps readers interested. • Details are accurate and relevant, showing in-depth knowledge of the topic.	• The writing has a clear structure throughout that suits the writer's audience and purpose. • All content flows smoothly and logically.	• The writing sounds genuine and unique. • The writer's tone is appropriate to the purpose and audience.	• Appropriate words were chosen to clearly convey the writer's message. • Language used throughout is appropriate for the audience and grabs readers' attention.	• All sentences are varied and effective and have appropriate transitions. • When read aloud, the writing sounds natural and rhythmic.	• The writing has only a few minor errors in spelling, punctuation, capitalization, grammar, usage, and paragraphing. • All the sentences are complete.	• The text is presented in an orderly way, significantly helping to convey the message. • Visuals are appropriate for the purpose and audience, and effectively support meaning.
3	• Most of the writing has a clear, focused message that keeps readers interested. • Most details are accurate and relevant, showing reasonable knowledge of the topic.	• Most of the writing has a clear structure that suits the writer's audience and purpose. • Most of the content flows smoothly and logically.	• Most of the writing sounds genuine and unique. • The writer's tone is mostly appropriate for the purpose and audience.	• Many appropriate words were chosen to clearly convey the writer's message. • Most language is appropriate for the audience and grabs readers' attention.	• Most sentences are varied and effective and have appropriate transitions. • When read aloud, most of the writing sounds natural and rhythmic.	• The writing has some errors in spelling, punctuation, capitalization, grammar, usage, and paragraphing. • Most of the sentences are complete.	• Most of the text is presented in an orderly way, generally helping to convey the message. • Most visuals are appropriate for the purpose and audience, and effectively support meaning.
2	• The writing has a fairly unclear and unfocused message, causing readers some confusion. • Some details are relevant and accurate, showing minimum knowledge of the topic.	• The writing does not have a structure that suits the writer's audience and purpose. • Some content flows smoothly and logically.	• Some of the writing sounds genuine and unique. • The writer's tone is somewhat inappropriate for the purpose and audience.	• Some appropriate words were chosen to clearly convey the writer's message. • Some language is appropriate for the audience and grabs readers' attention.	• Some sentences are varied and effective and have appropriate transitions. • When read aloud, some of the writing sounds natural and rhythmic.	• The writing has several errors in spelling, punctuation, capitalization, grammar, usage, and paragraphing. • Some of the sentences are complete.	• Some of the text is presented in an orderly way, but it is a little difficult to track and comprehend the message. • Some visuals are appropriate for the purpose and audience and support meaning.
1	• The writing does not have a clear, focused message, causing readers confusion. • Many details are irrelevant and inaccurate, indicating a lack of knowledge of the topic.	• The writing does not have a structure. • The content does not flow smoothly or logically.	• The writing does not sound genuine or unique. • The writer's tone is not appropriate for the purpose or audience.	• Few appropriate words were chosen to clearly convey the writer's message. • Language is dull, vague, and inappropriate for the audience, losing the readers' attention.	• Few or none of the sentences are varied or effective or have appropriate transitions. • When read aloud, the writing sounds unnatural.	• The writing has many errors in spelling, punctuation, capitalization, grammar, usage, and paragraphing. • Few sentences are complete.	• The text is not presented in an orderly way, making it very difficult to track and comprehend the message. • None of the visuals are appropriate for the purpose or audience, and do not support meaning.

Grade 3 Assessment A1.41 Unit 1 | Happy to Help

NGReach.com **Assessment Master A1.41**

☑ = TESTED

Assess

OBJECTIVES

ASSESSMENTS

Reading
☑ Distinguish Point of View
☑ Comprehend Plot
☑ Identify Elements of a Poem
☑ Explain Text Structure: Comparison
☑ Preview, Predict, Monitor, and Clarify to Comprehend Text

  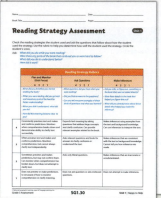

Reading Comprehension Unit Test
A1.24–A1.29

Reading Strategy Assessment
SG1.30–SG1.31

Fluency
☑ Expression
☑ Accuracy and Rate

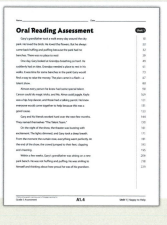  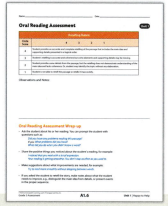

Oral Reading Assessment
A1.4–A1.6

Use these passages throughout Unit 1. Work with Below Level students this week.

Vocabulary and Spelling
☑ Use Domain-Specific Words
☑ Use Academic Words
☑ Consult References: Dictionary and Glossary
☑ Spell Words with the Digraphs *ch, tch*
☑ Use Commonly Misspelled Words Correctly

 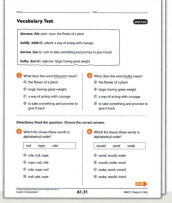 

Vocabulary Unit Test
A1.30–A1.32

Spelling Pretest/ Spelling Test
T55k

Grammar and Writing
☑ Use Concrete, Abstract, Common, and Proper Nouns
☑ Use Pronouns
☑ Use Complete Sentences and Predicates
☑ Use Simple and Compound Subjects
☑ Use Subject-Verb Agreement

 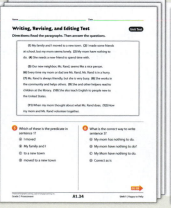 

Writing, Revising, and Editing Unit Test
A1.33–A1.36

Writing Rubric
A1.41

ExamView®

Reteach and Practice

RESOURCES AND ROUTINES

A1.37

Reading

RETEACH

Point of View: Reteaching Master RT1.9

Plan and Monitor: Reteaching Master RT1.10

ADDITIONAL PRACTICE

Comprehension Coach NGReach.com

PRINT & ONLINE
Report Forms

Student Profile: Weekly and Unit Assessments	A1.37–A1.38
Class Profile: Weekly and Unit Assessments	A1.39
Student Profile: Strengths and Needs Summary	A1.40
Student Profile: Oral Reading Assessment Progress Tracker	A1.3

Fluency

RETEACH

Fluency Routines, page BP33

ADDITIONAL PRACTICE

Comprehension Coach NGReach.com

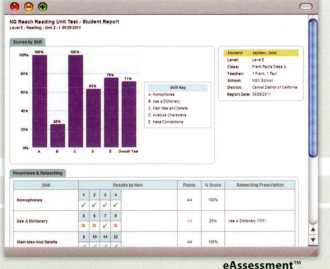

eAssessment™

ONLINE ONLY
Automated Reports

Student Profile: Weekly and Unit Tests

Class Profile: Weekly and Unit Tests

Standards Summary Report

Vocabulary and Spelling

RETEACH

Vocabulary Routine 6, page BP40

Spelling and Word Work Routine, page BP52

ADDITIONAL PRACTICE

Vocabulary Games NGReach.com

Daily Spelling Practice, pages T55k–T55l

Grammar and Writing

RETEACH

Subject-Verb Agreement: Anthology Handbook, page 594

Compound Subjects: Anthology Handbook, page 581

Writing: Reteaching Writing Routine, page BP51

Writing Trait: Voice: Reteaching Master RT1.11

ADDITIONAL PRACTICE

More Grammar Practice PM1.31

Daily Writing Skills Practice, pages T55o–T55p

Anthology
pages 68–69

OBJECTIVES
Thematic Connection: Helping Others
Review Content

PROGRAM RESOURCES
PRINT & TECHNOLOGY
Unit Concept Map: Practice Master PM1.1

COMMON CORE STANDARDS
Writing
Write Informative/Explanatory Text   CC.3.W.2
   to Examine a Topic
Speaking and Listening
Ask and Answer Questions   CC.3.SL.3
Report on a Topic   CC.3.SL.4
Language and Vocabulary
Use Knowledge of Language   CC.3.L.3
Choose Words for Effect   CC.3.L.3.a

Academic Talk

❶ Talk Together   Anthology   page 68

Display the Big Question. Read aloud the first paragraph on page 68. Have students revisit **Practice Master PM1.1** to remind them of their answers to the Big Question. Encourage them to think about their class discussions, the selections in the unit, and the books they read during **Small Group Reading**. Ask: *What did you learn about how different people help each other?*

Writing

❷ Write a Plan   Anthology   page 68

Read aloud the instructions. Remind students that when you write a plan, you should put the steps of the plan in the order that you will do them. To show the order of the steps, they should use sequence words. Provide language frames: *First, _____. Next, _____. Then, _____. Finally, _____.*

On the board, model a plan for helping others: *I want to clean up the park in my neighborhood. First, I will get garbage bags. Next, I will ask my friends to help. Then, we will go to the park and pick up trash. Finally, we'll tell people to come to a neighborhood picnic so they can see that the park is a nice place to visit.*

Unit Projects

③ Share Your Ideas Anthology page 69

Read aloud the project options. Have students who have chosen projects that require a partner or small group gather in designated areas. Have the other students work independently at their desks.

Do It!

MATERIALS

paper, colored pencils or markers

Plan

Have students think about a time when they did something nice for someone. Then have them think about words or phrases that describe how they felt about their good deed. Provide words and phrases to get them started, such as *proud, helpful, satisfied, happy to help, cheerful,* etc.

Suggest that before students begin to draw, they act out the feeling and look at themselves in a mirror.

Draw a Self-Portrait

Allow students time to draw their self-portraits. Have students post their self-portraits in the classroom.

Choose Words for Effect   CC.3.L.3.a

Talk About It!

Plan

Have three students think about ways to be a hero at school by helping teachers or other students. Tell students to make a list of ways, and for each way, write why it would be helpful.

Form a Panel

Have the three students form a panel by putting their chairs in front of the class and taking turns presenting their ideas. After they have presented, they should ask the other students if they have any questions. The class can then vote on which idea they like best.

Ask and Answer Questions   CC.3.SL.3
Report on a Topic   CC.3.SL.4

Write It!

Plan

Have pairs think of everyday heroes or people in their community who help others and choose one to write about. Suggest that, before they write, they should make a list of details about how the person helps others. Tell students that their mini-biographies should answer the questions: *Who is the person? What does he or she do to help others? How are other people's lives changed?*

Write a Mini-Biography

As students work together to write their mini-biographies, have them refer to their list of details. Tell them that when they finish, they should make sure they answered the three questions.

Write Informative/Explanatory
    Text to Examine a Topic   CC.3.W.2

Do It!

Plan

Have each student in the group think of one worker in the community, but not tell anyone else who they are thinking of. Then they should think about how to act out that person doing his or her job. Encourage students to use props that they can find in the classroom to help them role-play.

Role-Play Workers

Have students take turns role-playing their worker as the rest of the group guesses what job they are acting out. After someone guesses correctly, the group discusses how that worker helps others.

Use Knowledge of Language   CC.3.L.3

 = one student   = two students   = three or more students

Unit 1 Reflection

Successful Teaching Moments	Adjustments for Next Year

Additional Notes or Resources

Click links in the Teacher eEdition

Access all resources using the Lesson Planner

Browse the Resource Directory

Display Practice Masters using the Presentation Tool

More Practice

Phonics Games and Vocabulary Games

Comprehension Coach

My Vocabulary Notebook

Read With Me MP3s

Sing With Me MP3s

 Go to **NGReach.com** for practice resources.

Contents at a Glance

Dear Family Member,

"How do people help each other?" That is the big question we are exploring in this unit. To answer it, we are reading, writing, and talking about the ways people reach out to one another, and how small actions can make a big difference. Be a part of our exploration! With your student, read the New Words on the next page. Then follow these directions.

Directions:

1. Talk together about the ways your family can help in your community. Try to use some of the New Words in your discussion.

2. Work together to make notes. On the lines below, write words, phrases, or sentences that tell your ideas about ways to help in your community. Use the New Words when you can.

3. Remind your student to bring the completed notes to class.

What We're Reading

"Those Shoes"
by Maribeth Boelts
In this story, a pair of popular shoes teach a lesson in generosity.

"Guardian Angel"
by Francisco X. Alarcón
In this poem, a girl reaches out to a lonely classmate.

"The World's Greatest Underachiever"
by Henry Winkler
In this autobiography, actor Henry Winkler describes his childhood struggle with dyslexia and his success in spite of it.

"Making a Difference"
by Phillip Kennedy
In this biography, the author highlights the important role education has played in the life of explorer Joseph Lekuton.

And more!

_____

_____

_____

_____

_____

_____

Family Newsletter 1 | English

New Words

Weeks 1 and 2

action	need	understand
difference	problem	value
gift	receive	want
kindness	solution	

Weeks 3 and 4

benefit	improve	offer
duty	individual	volunteer
identify	learn	
impact	neighborhood	

Learn and play with words. **NGReach.com**

New Words | English

COPY READY

COPY READY

Estimado miembro de la familia,

"¿Cómo se ayudan las personas entre sí?" Esa es la gran pregunta que estamos explorando en esta unidad. Para responderla, estamos leyendo, escribiendo y hablando acerca de las diferentes maneras en que las personas se ayudan entre sí y cómo las pequeñas acciones pueden lograr la gran diferencia. ¡Sea parte de nuestra exploración! Con su estudiante, lea las Nuevas Palabras en la siguiente página. Luego siga estas instrucciones.

Instrucciones:

1. Juntos, hablen acerca de algunas de las maneras en que su familia puede ayudar en su comunidad. Intenten usar algunas de las Nuevas Palabras en su conversación.

2. Juntos, tomen notas. En las líneas siguientes, escriban palabras, frases u oraciones que expresen ideas acerca de las maneras de ayudar en su comunidad. Usen las Nuevas Palabras cada vez que puedan.

3. Recuerde a su estudiante traer las notas completas a clase.

Qué estamos leyendo

"Those Shoes"
por Maribeth Boelts
En esta historia, un par de zapatos populares enseña una lección sobre generosidad.

"Guardian Angel"
por Francisco X. Alarcón
En este poema, una niña ayuda a un solitario compañero de clase.

"The World's Greatest Underachiever"
por Henry Winkler
En esta autobiografía, el actor Henry Winkler describe las dificultades que tuvo en su niñez a causa de la dislexia y como logró ser exitoso a pesar de ello.

"Making a Difference"
por Phillip Kennedy
En esta biografía, el autor resalta el importante papel de la educación en la vida del explorador Joseph Lekuton.

¡Y más!

Family Newsletter 1 | Spanish

Nuevas Palabras

Semanas 1 y 2

action	need	understand
acción	necesitar	entender

difference	problem	value
diferencia	problema	valorar

gift	receive	want
regalo	recibir	querer

kindness	solution	
amabilidad	solución	

Semanas 3 y 4

benefit	improve	offer
beneficio	mejorar	ofrecer

duty	individual	volunteer
deber	individual	voluntario

identify	learn	
identificar	aprender	

impact	neighborhood	
impacto	vecindario	

Aprenda y juegue con palabras. **NGReach.com**

New Words | Spanish

How people
help each
other

Unit Concept Map

Happy to Help

Make a concept map with the
answers to the Big Question:
How do people help each other?

For use with TE p. T3

PM1.1

Unit 1 | Happy to Help

Name _____ Date _____

Story Map

Someone Who Needs Help

Make a story map about someone you know who needs help.

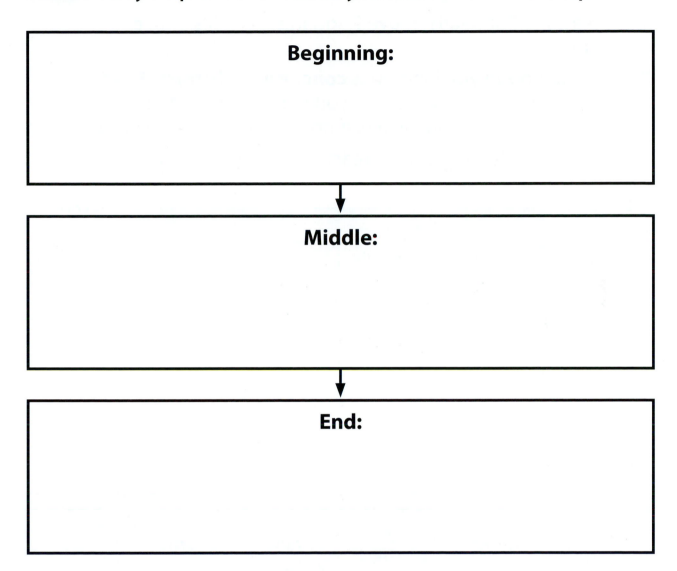

Beginning:

Middle:

End:

Name _____ Date _____

Grammar: Game

What's the Big Idea?

Directions:

1. Flip a coin. For heads, move 2 squares. For tails, move 1 square.

2. Tell if the noun you land on is **concrete** or **abstract**. Then use the noun in a sentence. If you name and use the word correctly, stay on your space. If not, move back one space.

3. Take turns. The player who reaches the end first wins.

START					END
sneaker		Is it a concrete noun?	Can you see it?		hot cocoa
fun	snow	Can you hear it?	Can you smell it?	kindness	fear
	backpack	Can you touch it?	Can you taste it?	cookie	
	health	Is it abstract?	Can you only think about it?	drums	
	love	stars	anger	friendship	

© National Geographic Learning, a part of Cengage Learning, Inc.
For use with TE p. T1o

PM1.3

Unit 1 | Happy to Help

Name _____ Date _____

Edit and Proofread

Choose the Editing and Proofreading Marks you need to correct the passage. Look for the following:

- correct use of common and proper nouns
- correct use of capitalization

Editing and Proofreading Marks

Mark	Meaning
∧	Add.
๙	Take out.
≡	Capitalize.
⊙	Add period.
/	Make lower case.

Today I walked into my new class. It was my first day at my new

school on lincoln Street. Mom said I would get over my fear. I didn't

feel any courage at first. I missed emily. She was my best Friend at

my old school.

My new Teacher is mr. lang, and he asked rita to be my buddy

today. Rita smiled and said she would show me how to do things.

Pretty soon, I was feeling much better. Maybe Change isn't so bad

after all!

© National Geographic Learning, a part of Cengage Learning, Inc.
For use with TE p. T1o

PM1.4

Unit 1 | Happy to Help

Name _____ Date _____

Know the Test Format

Directions: Read each question about "Those Shoes." Choose the best answer.

Sample

1 What does Jeremy buy with his own money?

Ⓐ snow boots

Ⓑ shoes for Antonio

● black-and-white shoes

Ⓓ blue shoes with cartoons

2 Why does Jeremy give his shoes to Antonio?

Ⓐ Jeremy does not like them.

Ⓑ Antonio needs new shoes.

Ⓒ Antonio asked Jeremy for his shoes.

Ⓓ Jeremy wants Antonio to be his friend.

Directions: Read the statement. Then write your answer in the space provided.

3 Explain why the new snow boots are better for Jeremy than the black-and-white shoes.

_____

_____

_____

 How did you use the test-taking strategy?

_____

Name _____ Date _____

"Those Shoes"

Make a story map.

```
┌─────────────────────────────────────────┐
│              Beginning:                   │
│  First, Jeremy wants new shoes,           │
│  but they cost too much.                  │
└─────────────────────────────────────────┘
                    ↓
┌─────────────────────────────────────────┐
│               Middle:                     │
│  Next, Jeremy buys shoes that are         │
│  too small.                               │
└─────────────────────────────────────────┘
                    ↓
┌─────────────────────────────────────────┐
│                                           │
│  Then, _____    │
│                                           │
│  _____    │
│                                           │
│  _____    │
└─────────────────────────────────────────┘
                    ↓
┌─────────────────────────────────────────┐
│                 End:                      │
│  Finally, _____   │
│                                           │
│  _____    │
│                                           │
│  _____    │
└─────────────────────────────────────────┘
```

 Use your story map to summarize the story's plot for a partner.

Name _____ Date _____

"Those Shoes"

Use this passage to practice reading with the proper expression.

I have dreams about those shoes. Black high-tops.	8
Two white stripes.	11
"Grandma, I want them."	15
"There's no room for 'want' around here," Grandma says.	24
"What you *need* are new boots for winter."	32

From "Those Shoes," page 12

Fluency: Expression

1 ☐ Does not read with feeling.

2 ☐ Reads with some feeling, but does not match content.

3 ☐ Reads with appropriate feeling with most content.

4 ☐ Reads with appropriate feeling for all content.

Accuracy and Rate Formula
Use the formula to measure a reader's accuracy and rate while reading aloud.

_____ − _____ = _____
words attempted in one minute — number of errors — words correct per minute (wcpm)

Grammar: Reteach

Helping Hands

Grammar Rules: Nouns

A **common noun** names any **person**, **animal**, **place**, or **thing**.	My friend Berto wants to come along.
A **proper noun** names a particular **person**, **animal**, **place**, or **thing**. All important words in a proper noun start with a capital letter.	The soup kitchen is on Main Street.
A **concrete noun** names something you can see, hear, smell, touch, **or** taste.	table *(see)* cheers *(hear)*
An **abstract noun** names something you can **think about** but can't see, hear, smell, touch, or taste	goodness health joy

Write the noun with a capital or a small letter to complete each sentence correctly. Then find and underline the abstract noun.

1. Berto and I met the _____ at the soup kitchen.
   cook

2. Then _____ gave us things to do to help.
   mrs. chang

3. Many people came to the kitchen from _____.
   columbus street

4. Everyone said, "Thanks for your kindness, _____."
   dr. juarez

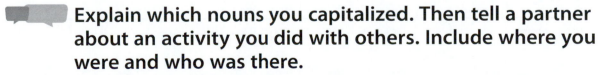 Explain which nouns you capitalized. Then tell a partner about an activity you did with others. Include where you were and who was there.

_____

Game: Grammar

Tails for Reading

1. Copy the eight sets of sentences onto index cards. Have your partner do the same to make 16 cards.

2. Mix your cards with your partner's. Stack them face down.

3. Take turns turning over a card. Read the text and decide which **pronoun** best fits the blank. Read the sentence aloud. If your pronoun is correct, keep the card.

4. At the end of the game, the player with more cards wins.

Tucker is a cheerful dog. _____ likes kids.	Zoe is Tucker's sister. _____ is a tail-wagger.
The dogs visit schools. _____ listen as the children read.	Mrs. Mullaly likes dogs at her school. _____ says the program helps classes.
Kids who like the dogs say, "_____ love the visits!"	Mr. Chou volunteers in the program. "_____ set up visits," he says.
The school is careful. _____ has rules for safety.	Check out the program. _____ will like it!

Name _____ Date _____

Game: Grammar

Putting It Together

Rules for Playing "Putting It Together"

1. Take turns spinning the spinner.

2. Read the sentence part you land on. Add a subject or a predicate to make a complete sentence.

3. Write your sentence on paper.

4. Take five turns each.

5. Choose your three favorite sentences. Read them to another pair of students.

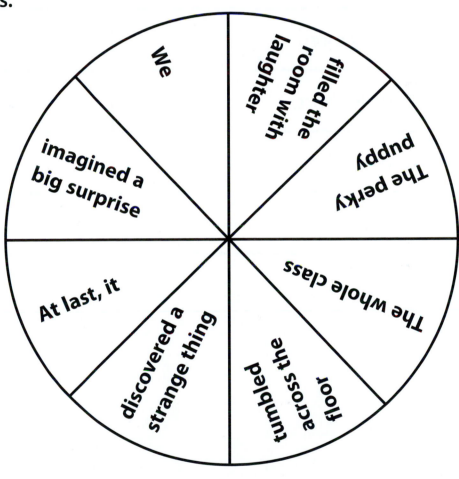

Make a Spinner

1. Put a paper clip over the center of the spinner.
2. Touch the point of a pencil on the middle of the wheel and through the loop of the paper clip.
3. Spin the paper clip to make a spinner.

© National Geographic Learning, a part of Cengage Learning, Inc.
For use with TE p. T27o

PM1.10

Unit 1 | Happy to Help

Name _____ Date _____

Checklist Chart

Compare Genres

Compare a story and a poem.

	Story	Poem
It is arranged in lines.		✓
It has paragraphs.	✓	
It is usually long.		
It is usually short.		
It expresses the writer's feelings.		
The words sound like music.		

Take turns with a partner. Ask each other questions about a story or poem.

For use with TE p. T32   **PM1.11**   Unit 1 | Happy to Help

Grammar: Complete Sentences

Where's the Kitten?

Grammar Rules Complete Sentences

A complete sentence expresses a complete thought. It has a subject and a predicate.

Example: <u>A young girl</u> <u>has a small kitten.</u>
                  ↑   ↑
           subject   predicate

Circle the complete sentence in each pair. Then copy correct sentences on the lines below to make a story.

1. My friend Maria.	My friend Maria has a kitten.
2. The kitten ran away.	Ran away.
3. Looked everywhere.	Maria looked everywhere.
4. Her sister Lisa helped her.	Her sister Lisa.
5. The girls found the kitten!	Found the kitten!

_____

_____

_____

_____

_____

 Tell a partner about how you know each sentence is complete.

COPY READY

Mark-Up Reading

The Letter by Nikki Grimes

I sat frowning by my window

when the mail truck came today

with a letter from Danitra

who is many miles away.

I said mean things when she left me.

I was so mad at her then.

Was she writing to forgive me,

or to say I'm not her friend?

I ripped Danitra's letter open,

in spite of my worst fear.

I bit my lip until I read

"I wish that you were here."

For use with TE pp. T33a–T33h   **PM1.13**   **Unit 1** | Happy to Help

Name _____   Date _____

Mark-Up Reading

The Lunchroom by Nikki Grimes

My lunch tray's like a boulder

I've lugged around for miles,

past strangers, left and right,

whose unfamiliar smiles

are meant for someone else

'cause I'm the new kid here.

"You'll do fine," Mom said earlier.

"Of that I have no fear."

At least, I have a pie

that I don't have to share.

If no one will sit next to me,

why should I even care?

Oh, wait! Here comes a boy.

"I'm Max," he says. "Who're you?"

I smile and introduce myself—

then break my pie in two.

Grammar: Grammar and Writing

Edit and Proofread

Choose the Editing and Proofreading Marks you need to correct the passage. Look for the following:

- incomplete sentences
- missing capital letters

Editing and Proofreading Marks

∧	Add.
ℐ	Take out.
≡	Capitalize.
⊙	Add period.

M̲y̲ friend Janet went out of town. One night, I. It was Janet's

neighbor. she said my friend's house was on fire! ran to her house.

The firefighters. They were battling the blaze. was worried about

Janet's dog. was still in the house! the firefighters did not know. I

told them. asked for the dog's name, so I told him. He smashed a

window. then he yelled, Buddy!" After a few minutes, Buddy! He

was safe.

was upset about her house. but she was happy, too. We had

saved her dog.

Name _____ Date _____

Grammar: Reteach

Ouch, That Hurt!

Grammar Rules: Pronouns and Complete Sentences	
A **pronoun** takes the place of a <u>noun</u>.	The <u>nurse</u> visits our school. **She** helps sick students.
Use a <u>subject</u> and a <u>predicate</u> to make a **complete sentence**. • A <u>subject</u> tells whom or what a sentence is about. It is usually a noun or a pronoun. • A <u>predicate</u> tells what the subject is, has, or does.	<u>Emily</u> <u>has</u> a cut. <u>She</u> <u>goes</u> to the nurse. The <u>nurse</u> <u>cleans</u> the cut. <u>Emily</u> <u>is</u> better.

Add words to make each of the following a complete sentence. Use capital letters correctly.

1. were playing soccer at school

_____

2. one of the players

_____

3. scraped his knees

_____

4. his best friends

_____

 With a partner, discuss why your sentences are complete.

Making Comparisons

Something That Has Improved

Make a comparison chart about something that has improved.

Before	Now

 Tell how you improved something. Tell how it was before and how it is now. Use the words *before, then, now,* **and** *after* **to compare.**

For use with TE p. T35a

PM1.17

Unit 1 | Happy to Help

Grammar: Game

It's a Simple Story

Directions:

1. Copy the six sentences onto cards. Have your partner do the same. Mix your cards together and stack them face down.

2. **Round One:** Choose a card and read the sentence aloud. Draw one line under the simple subject. Draw two lines under the simple predicate.

3. **Round Two:** Shuffle all of the cards. Choose a card. Create a new sentence using either the simple subject or the simple predicate. Write it on the back of the card.

NOTE: In each round, if your partner agrees that you used the subject or predicate correctly, keep the card. Take turns until all the cards are used. The player with more cards wins the round.

My cousin Ben is a good reader.	The children in first grade hear Ben at the door.
The delighted teacher has a corner of the room for Ben.	Happy listeners sit on the rug around Ben.
He reads quietly to six children at a time.	The whole class has a new love of reading.

Grammar: Grammar and Writing

Edit and Proofread

Choose the Editing and Proofreading Marks you need to correct the passage. Look for the following:

- incomplete sentences
- missing capital letters

Editing and Proofreading Marks

∧	Add.
‿	Take out.
≡	Capitalize.
⊙	Add period.

Ben watched as his friends played soccer. ^He^ wanted to play, too.

But Ben had asthma. is a disease. It makes it hard for people to

breathe. if he ran a lot. He knew it would be hard to play soccer.

wanted to try. His mom took him to Dr. Green. when he saw him.

Dr. Green said he could play! He gave Ben medicine to use. had to

take it before every practice.

after school the next day. It was his first practice. His friends. They

helped Ben with the rules. knew he could do it!

Name _____   Date _____

Test-Taking Strategy Practice

Know the Test Format

Directions: Read each question and choose the best answer.

Sample

> **1** In the sentence "It got me a <u>trip</u> to the principal's office," what does the word <u>trip</u> mean?
>
> Ⓐ a fall
>
> Ⓑ a map
>
> Ⓒ a seat
>
> ● a journey

2 In the sentence "My mother and I <u>went over</u> the list until I knew those words," what do the words <u>went over</u> mean?

Ⓐ walked over

Ⓑ threw away

Ⓒ studied

Ⓓ forgot

Directions: Read the question. Then write a short answer below.

3 How does Henry find out he has dyslexia?

_____

_____

_____

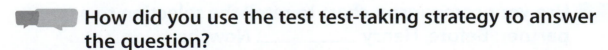 **How did you use the test test-taking strategy to answer the question?**

_____

For use with TE p. T54   **PM1.20**   Unit 1 | Happy to Help

Comparison Chart

Compare Henry Before and Now

Show how Henry changed in "The World's Greatest Underachiever."

Before	Now
1. Henry had trouble spelling.	**1.** He writes books.
2. He didn't like school.	**2.**
3.	**3.**
4.	**4.**
5.	**5.**

Use your comparison chart to retell the selection to a partner: Before, Henry _____. Now, he _____.

PM1.21

Unit 1 | Happy to Help

COPY READY

Name _____ Date _____

Fluency: Practice

"The World's Greatest Underachiever"

Use this passage to practice reading with proper intonation.

The next day, I went into the classroom and took out a sheet of paper.   15

Then Miss Adolf gave us the words. The first word was *carpet*.   27

I wrote that one down: *c-a-r-p-e-t*. I was feeling pretty confident.   38

Then came *neighbor*—I wrote down the letter *n*.   47

Then *rhythm*—I knew there was an *r*. *Suburban*—I wrote *s-u-b*.   59

My heart sank. I had gone from 100 percent to maybe a D-minus.   72

Where did the words go?   77

From "The World's Greatest Underachiever," pages 46–47

Intonation

1 ☐ Does not change pitch.   3 ☐ Changes pitch to match some of the content.

2 ☐ Changes pitch, but does not match content.   4 ☐ Changes pitch to match all of the content.

Accuracy and Rate Formula
Use the formula to measure a reader's accuracy and rate while reading aloud.

	−		=	
_____		_____		_____
words attempted in one minute		number of errors		words correct per minute (wcpm)

Grammar: Reteach

The Lion and the Mouse

Grammar Rules Sentences, Phrases, and Clauses

A **complete subject** is all of the words that tell about the subject.

A (simple subject) is the main word. It may be a **noun** or a **pronoun**.

> A big, strong (lion) trapped a tiny gray mouse.

A **complete predicate** is all of the words in the predicate.

A **simple predicate** is the main word, which is the **verb**. (trapped)

A **phrase** is a group of words that does not have a subject and predicate.

> within his big paws

A **dependent clause** has a subject and a verb but does not express a complete thought.

> if you will let me go

Directions: Draw a line under a <u>complete subject</u> and <u>two lines</u> under a <u>complete predicate</u>. Circle a (simple subject) and (simple predicate.)

1. The golden lion released the mouse from his grasp.

2. The happy mouse promised the lion a favor in return.

Add words to make complete sentences. Capitalize correctly.

3. because the lion was tangled in a net

_____

4. with sharp little teeth

_____

PM1.23

COPY READY

Name _____ Date _____

Do They Agree?

Directions:

1. Flip a coin. For heads, move 2 squares. For tails, move 1 square.

2. Each time you land on a square, pick a NUMBER card. Tell if you have a singular or plural card. Create a sentence for the item you landed on. Then put the NUMBER card at the bottom of the stack.

3. If your sentence is correct, stay on your space. If not, move back one space. The player who reaches the end first wins.

Number Cards

1. Fold a tablet paper twice the long way. Keep it folded and fold the two ends together. Then unfold.

2. Print SINGULAR on 4 sections and PLURAL on 4. On the other side, write NUMBER on all 8 sections.

3. Cut apart the 8 sections.

4. Mix them up and stack them face down to play the game.

					leap	END
	is | are	player	dog		cousin	
	decide		growl		frog	
	zoom		team		find	
play	captain		scream	cat	has|have	
START	friend					

Grammar: Game

Working Together

Directions:

1. Read the sentence parts. Copy each one onto a separate index card.

2. After shuffling the cards, place them face down in two stacks: one for the subject cards and one for the predicate cards.

3. When it is your turn, choose a subject and a predicate. Read the cards as a complete sentence. Say the correct verb form.

4. If you are correct, keep the cards. Put them back if you are not. Then your partner takes a turn.

5. When the cards are all used, the player with more cards wins.

Subject	Predicate
Boys and girls	_____ everything for a gather gift basket.
Elly or Tran	_____ a gift with a tote create bag.
Dad or my brothers	_____ elderly people. visit
Mom or Dad	_____ to add a book. remember
Ty and Carol	_____ cocoa and a mug. include
The girls or Mom	_____ spices for the bring baskets.

Name _____   Date _____

Comparison Chart

Compare Points of View

Use a comparison chart to compare an autobiography and a biography.

"The World's Greatest Underachiever"	"Joseph Lekuton: Making a Difference"
• The narrator tells the story of _____ life.	• The narrator tells the story of _____ life.
• The narrator (is/is not) part of the story. (Circle one.)	• The narrator (is/is not) part of the story. (Circle one.)
• The selection is (an autobiography /a biography). (Circle one.)	• The selection is (an autobiography /a biography). (Circle one.)
• Examples of narrator's point of view:	• Examples of narrator's point of view:

 Take turns with a partner. Explain how you know that a selection is an autobiography or a biography.

Name _____ Date _____

Grammar: Practice

We Like to Read

Grammar Rules Adding -s to Action Verbs

• Use -s at the end of an action verb if the subject is *he, she,* or *it*.	Danny <u>reads</u> a story. He <u>looks</u> at the pictures.
• Do not use -s for *I, you, we,* or *they*.	I <u>read</u> to my friends. They <u>look</u> at the pictures.

Read each sentence. Write the correct form of the verb for each subject.

1. We _____ many stories.

    read / reads

2. I _____ autobiographies.

   like / likes

3. They _____ about real people.

   tell / tells

4. Henry Winkler _____ his own story.

   tell /tells

5. He _____ his problems in school.

   remember / remembers

6. His brain _____ differently.

   learn / learns

7. You _____ autobiographies, too.

   like / likes

 Tell a partner about a story you have read. Use complete sentences. Make sure the subject and the predicate in your sentences agree.

For use with TE p. T62a   **PM1.27**   Unit 1 | Happy to Help

Name _____   Date _____

Mark-Up Reading

from

Facing the Lion by Joseph Lekuton

One of the problems the nomads have with school is that we move our villages and the cattle, but the school stays in one place. That means leaving the children behind. The first year, my village was near the school, and I was able to go home easily. In my second year, the missionaries built a dormitory and started a boarding school. My family could move wherever they wanted to, and I could stay in school.

▲ Mission school

My mom used to visit sometimes. She'd bring me milk. The food at school wasn't what I was used to, and there wasn't much of it. We ate mostly corn and beans—yellow corn, from America. Once I counted mine: There were 75 pieces of corn and 15 beans—so little it barely covered the plate. I didn't complain—I was grateful for the school and the missionaries—but I was a nomadic kid, raised on milk. So whenever my family was nearby, my mother would bring me some milk. Sometimes she'd walk 10 or 20 miles with it.

I went to that school through the seventh grade. Every time school closed for the vacation, I had to find my way home. That was one of the hardest things: The village might be 5 miles away, or it might be 50. Sometimes I wouldn't know exactly where my family was. I had to search for them.

Explanation: _____

_____

_____

_____

_____

For use with TE pp. T63a–T63h   **PM1.28**   Unit 1 | Happy to Help

Mark-Up Reading

Boy Between Two Cultures by Olivia Hodgson

Because the Lekutons were nomads, their children faced special problems attending school. Nomads move around, but schools stay in the same place. During most of his school years, Joseph lived in a boarding school that missionaries had built. What a different life he had there! He bravely stayed behind at school when his family left.

▲ students in Rwanda, Africa

Joseph's mother visited him many times at boarding school. She wanted to see her son and also bring him milk. Joseph was used to drinking milk. After all, he had grown up in a cattle culture. But now he was in a new culture. The school offered him mostly beans and corn. The corn was strange to him. It was the yellow American kind. Also, the individual portions were small. Yet, Joseph saw it as his duty not to complain.

One of the bravest things Joseph had to do was to find his way home. When his school closed for vacation, Joseph didn't always know where his family was living. Sometimes, he traveled as much as 50 miles just to get home. By going home, he kept his ties to both cultures. He was still a student. Yet, when he was home, he was also learning to be a Maasai warrior.

Explanation: _____

_____

_____

_____

_____

Grammar: Grammar and Writing

Edit and Proofread

Choose the Editing and Proofreading Marks you need to correct the passage. Look for the following:

- subject-verb agreement
- correct use of forms of the verb **be**

Editing and Proofreading Marks

∧	Add.
✐	Take out.
≡	Capitalize.
⊙	Add period.

We forms a clean-up team for our block. Meg lists our tasks. We

vote on jobs and partners. Carly and Moira gets trash bags. Nate or

the girls look for brooms. Juanita say she'll borrow gloves. We has a

good team. I is proud to be a part of it.

Moms or dads brings snacks for us. My dog Rusty came with Dad,

so Rusty are here. Is my big dog helpful? No, but he watchs! He have

fun, too.

We is finished with our work! Meg or Rick rush to get a camera.

We smile cheerfully!

Grammar: Reteach

Ants at Work!

Grammar Rules Subject-Verb Agreement

When a subject is **one** person or thing, the verb ends in **-s**.
An <u>ant</u> live<u>s</u> in a colony.

If the verb ends with **x, ch, sh, x,** or **z**, then the singular ends in **-es**.
It <u>fix**es**</u> up several rooms.

When a subject is **more than one**, the verb does <u>not</u> end in **-s**.
Many <u>ants</u> live together in one colony.

<u>Compound subjects</u> joined by **and** take a plural verb.
Workers **and** soldiers live in a colony.

<u>Singular compound subjects</u> joined by **or** take a singular verb.
A black ant **or** a red ant live<u>s</u> in a colony.

<u>Plural compound subjects</u> joined by **or** take a plural verb.
Sometimes black ants **or** red ants live in colonies of thousands!

Some verbs have special forms:	Each ant **has** a job to do.
has have am is are	Ants **are** very organized.

Read each sentence. Circle the correct verb.

1. An ant nest (has | have) rooms for different purposes.

2. A nursery and a resting place (is | are) two kinds of rooms.

3. Tunnels and rooms (keeps | keep) ants safe underground.

4. Worker ants (digs | dig) the tunnels in the ant nest.

Answer Keys

Also available in Resource Directory ⊚ NGReach.com

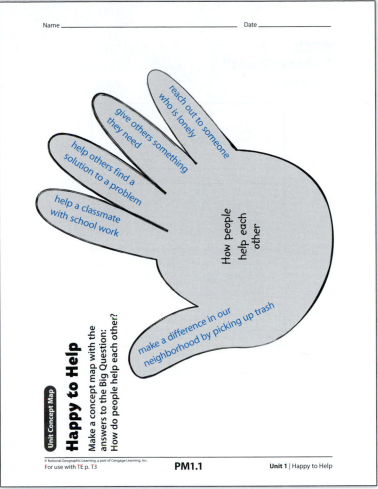

Name _____ Date _____

Story Map

Someone Who Needs Help

Make a story map about someone you know who needs help.

Beginning:
Answers will vary, depending on the stories chosen.

↓

Middle:

↓

End:

© National Geographic Learning, a part of Cengage Learning, Inc.
For use with TE p. T6   **PM1.2**   Unit 1 | Happy to Help

Name _____ Date _____

Grammar: Game

What's the Big Idea?

Directions:

1. Flip a coin. For heads, move 2 squares. For tails, move 1 square.
2. Tell if the noun you land on is **concrete** or **abstract**. Then use the noun in a sentence. If you name and use the word correctly, stay on your space. If not, move back one space.
3. Take turns. The player who reaches the end first wins.

START					END
sneaker		Is it a concrete noun?	Can you see it?		hot cocoa
fun	snow	Can you hear it?	Can you smell it?	kindness	fear
	backpack	Can you touch it?	Can you taste it?	cookie	
	health	Is it abstract?	Can you only think about it?	drums	
	love	stars	anger	friendship	

© National Geographic Learning, a part of Cengage Learning, Inc.
For use with TE p. T1o   **PM1.3**   Unit 1 | Happy to Help

Name _____ Date _____

Grammar: Grammar and Writing

Edit and Proofread

Choose the Editing and Proofreading Marks you need to correct the passage. Look for the following:

- correct use of common and proper nouns
- correct use of capitalization

Editing and Proofreading Marks

∧	Add.
﹍	Take out.
≡	Capitalize.
⊙	Add period.

Today I walked into my new class. It was my first day at my new
school on lincoln Street. Mom said I would get over my fear. I didn't
feel any courage at first. I missed emily. She was my best Friend at
my old school.

My new Teacher is mr. lang, and he asked rita to be my buddy
today. Rita smiled and said she would show me how to do things.
Pretty soon, I was feeling much better. Maybe Change isn't so bad
after all!

© National Geographic Learning, a part of Cengage Learning, Inc.
For use with TE p. T1o   **PM1.4**   Unit 1 | Happy to Help

Answer Keys, continued

Answer Keys

Page PM1.5

Name _____   Date _____

Test-Taking Strategy Practice

Know the Test Format

Directions: Read each question about "Those Shoes." Choose the best answer.

Sample

1 What does Jeremy buy with his own money?
- Ⓐ snow boots
- Ⓑ shoes for Antonio
- ● black-and-white shoes
- Ⓓ blue shoes with cartoons

2 Why does Jeremy give his shoes to Antonio?
- Ⓐ Jeremy does not like them.
- ● Antonio needs new shoes.
- Ⓒ Antonio asked Jeremy for his shoes.
- Ⓓ Jeremy wants Antonio to be his friend.

Directions: Read the statement. Then write your answer in the space provided.

3 Explain why the new snow boots are better for Jeremy than the black-and-white shoes.

The snow boots are better because they fit and they will keep

Jeremy's feet warm and dry in the snow.

_____

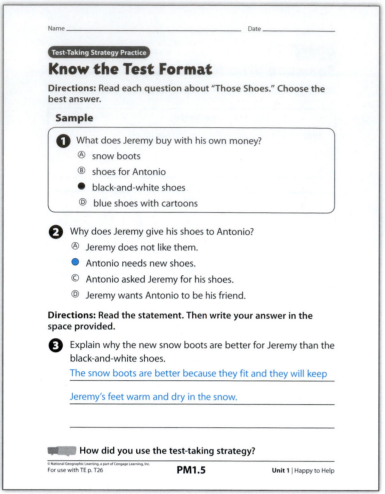 How did you use the test-taking strategy?

© National Geographic Learning, a part of Cengage Learning, Inc.
For use with TE p. T26   **PM1.5**   Unit 1 | Happy to Help

Page PM1.5

Page PM1.6

Name _____   Date _____

Story Map

"Those Shoes"

Make a story map.

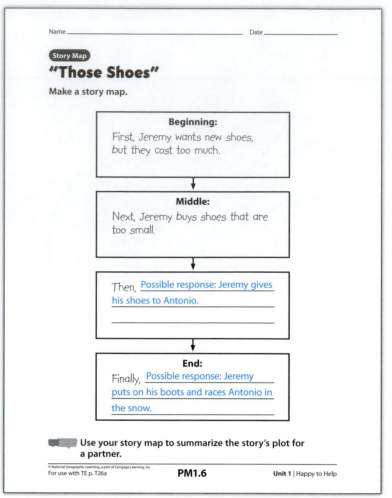

Beginning:
First, Jeremy wants new shoes, but they cost too much.

↓

Middle:
Next, Jeremy buys shoes that are too small.

↓

Then, Possible response: Jeremy gives his shoes to Antonio.

↓

End:
Finally, Possible response: Jeremy puts on his boots and races Antonio in the snow.

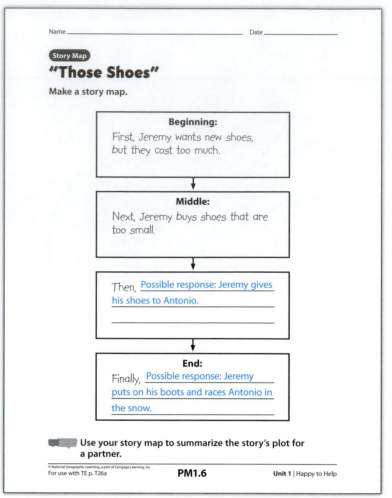 Use your story map to summarize the story's plot for a partner.

© National Geographic Learning, a part of Cengage Learning, Inc.
For use with TE p. T26a   **PM1.6**   Unit 1 | Happy to Help

Page PM1.6

Page PM1.7

Name _____   Date _____

Fluency Practice

"Those Shoes"

Use this passage to practice reading with the proper expression.

I have dreams about those shoes. Black high-tops.	8
Two white stripes.	11
"Grandma, I want them."	15
"There's no room for 'want' around here," Grandma says.	24
"What you *need* are new boots for winter."	32

From "Those Shoes," page 12

Fluency: Expression
- 1 ☐ Does not read with feeling.
- 2 ☐ Reads with some feeling, but does not match content.
- 3 ☐ Reads with appropriate feeling with most content.
- 4 ☐ Reads with appropriate feeling for all content.

Accuracy and Rate Formula
Use the formula to measure a reader's accuracy and rate while reading aloud.

words attempted in one minute	–	number of errors	=	words correct per minute (wcpm)

© National Geographic Learning, a part of Cengage Learning, Inc.
For use with TE p. T27   **PM1.7**   Unit 1 | Happy to Help

Page PM1.7

Page PM1.8

Name _____   Date _____

Grammar: Reteach

Helping Hands

Grammar Rules: Nouns

A **common noun** names any **person, animal, place,** or **thing.**	My friend Ⓑerto wants to come along.
A **proper noun** names a particular **person, animal, place,** or **thing.** All important words in a proper noun start with a capital letter.	The soup kitchen is on Ⓜain Ⓢtreet.
A **concrete noun** names something you can see, hear, smell, touch, **or** taste.	table (see) cheers (hear)
An **abstract noun** names something you can **think about** but can't see, hear, smell, touch, or taste	goodness health joy

Write the noun with a capital or a small letter to complete each sentence correctly. Then find and underline the two abstract nouns.

1. Berto and I met the ___cook___ at the soup kitchen.
   cook

2. Then ___Mrs. Chang___ gave us things to do to help.
   mrs. chang

3. Many people came to the kitchen from ___Columbus Street___.
   columbus street

4. Everyone said, "Thanks for your underline{kindness}, ___Dr. Juarez___."
   dr. juarez

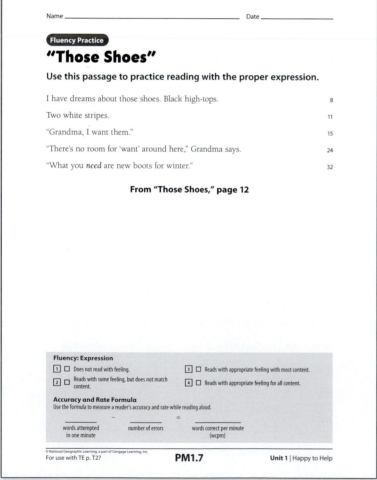 Tell a partner about an activity you did with others. Include where you were and who was there. Explain which nouns you capitalized.

© National Geographic Learning, a part of Cengage Learning, Inc.
For use with TE p. T10   **PM1.8**   Unit 1 | Happy to Help

Page PM1.8

Page PM1.9

Game: Grammar

Tails for Reading

1. Copy the eight sets of sentences onto index cards. Have your partner do the same to make 16 cards.
2. Mix your cards with your partner's. Stack them face down.
3. Take turns turning over a card. Read the text and decide which **pronoun** best fits the blank. Read the sentence aloud. If your pronoun is correct, keep the card.
4. At the end of the game, the player with more cards wins.

Tucker is a cheerful dog. _____ likes kids.	Zoe is Tucker's sister. _____ is a tail-wagger.
The dogs visit schools. _____ listen as the children read.	Mrs. Mullaly likes dogs at her school. _____ says the program helps classes.
Kids who like the dogs say, "_____ love the visits!"	Mr. Chou volunteers in the program. "_____ set up visits," he says.
The school is careful. _____ has rules for safety.	Check out the program. _____ will like it!

PM1.9   Unit 1 | Happy to Help

Page PM1.9

Page PM1.10

Game: Grammar

Putting It Together

Rules for Playing "Putting It Together"
1. Take turns spinning the spinner.
2. Read the sentence part you land on. Add a subject or a predicate to make a complete sentence.
3. Write your sentence on paper.
4. Take five turns each.
5. Choose your three favorite sentences. Read them to another pair of students.

Make a Spinner
1. Put a paper clip over the center of the spinner.
2. Touch the point of a pencil on the middle of the wheel and through the loop of the paper clip.
3. Spin the paper clip to make a spinner.

Spinner sections: We / filled the room with laughter / The perky puppy / The whole class / tumbled across the floor / discovered a strange thing / At last, it / imagined a big surprise

PM1.10   Unit 1 | Happy to Help

Page PM1.10

Page PM1.11

Checklist Chart

Compare Genres

Compare a story and a poem.

	Story	Poem
It is arranged in lines.		✓
It has paragraphs.	✓	
It is usually long.	✓	
It is usually short.		✓
It expresses the writer's feelings.	✓	✓
The words sound like music.		✓

🗨 Take turns with a partner. Ask each other questions about a story or poem.

PM1.11   Unit 1 | Happy to Help

Page PM1.11

Page PM1.12

Grammar: Complete Sentences

Where's the Kitten?

Grammar Rules Complete Sentences

A complete sentence expresses a complete thought. It has a subject and a predicate.

Example: A young girl has a small kitten.
            ↑   ↑
          subject   predicate

Circle the complete sentence in each pair. Then copy correct sentences on the lines below to make a story.

1.	My friend Maria.	My friend Maria has a kitten.
2.	The kitten ran away.	Ran away.
3.	Looked everywhere.	Maria looked everywhere.
4.	Her sister Lisa helped her.	Her sister Lisa.
5.	The girls found the kitten!	Found the kitten!

My friend Maria has a kitten. The kitten ran away. Maria looked everywhere. Her sister Lisa helped her. The girls found the kitten!

_____

_____

_____

🗨 Tell a partner about how you know each sentence is complete.

PM1.12   Unit 1 | Happy to Help

Page PM1.12

Practice Masters | Answer Key   **PM1.34**

Answer Keys, continued

Mark-Up Reading

The Letter by Nikki Grimes

I sat frowning by my window a
when the mail truck came <u>today</u> b
with a letter from Danitra c
who is many miles <u>away</u>. b

I said mean things when she left me. d
I was so mad at her <u>then</u>. e
Was she writing to forgive me, d
or to say I'm not her <u>friend</u>? e

I ripped Danitra's letter open, f
in spite of my worst <u>fear</u>. g
I bit my lip until I read h
"I wish that you were <u>here</u>." g

Page PM1.13

Mark-Up Reading

The Lunchroom by Nikki Grimes

My lunch tray's like a boulder a
I've lugged around for <u>miles</u>, b
past strangers, left and right, c
whose unfamiliar <u>smiles</u> b
are meant for someone else d
'cause I'm the new kid <u>here</u>. e
"You'll do fine," Mom said earlier. f
"Of that I have no <u>fear</u>." e

At least, I have a pie g
that I don't have to <u>share</u>. h
If no one will sit next to me, i
why should I even <u>care</u>? h
Oh, wait! Here comes a boy. j
"I'm Max," he says. "Who're <u>you</u>?" k
I smile and introduce myself— l
then break my pie in <u>two</u>. k

Page PM1.14

Grammar: Grammar and Writing

Edit and Proofread

Choose the Editing and Proofreading Marks you need to correct the passage. Look for the following:

- incomplete sentences
- missing capital letters
- *Some answers may vary.*

Editing and Proofreading Marks

∧	Add.
℘	Take out.
≡	Capitalize.
⊙	Add period.

M̲y friend Janet went out of town. One night, I̲ *got a phone call* It was Janet's neighbor. s̲he said my friend's house was on fire! *We* ran to her house. The firefighters. They were battling the blaze. *were already there* *I* was worried about Janet's dog. *He* was still in the house! the firefighters did not know. I *One firefighter* told them. asked for the dog's name, so I told him. He smashed a window. t̲hen he yelled, Buddy!" After a few minutes, Buddy! He *jumped out the window* was safe.

J̲anet was upset about her house. b̲ut she was happy, too. We had saved her dog.

Page PM1.15

Grammar: Reteach

Ouch, That Hurt!

Grammar Rules: Pronouns and Complete Sentences

A **pronoun** takes the place of a <u>noun</u>.	<u>nurse</u> visits our school. **She** helps sick students.
Use a <u>subject</u> and a <u>predicate</u> to make a **complete sentence**.	<u>Emily</u> <u>has</u> a cut.
• A <u>subject</u> tells whom or what a sentence is about. It is usually a noun or a pronoun.	<u>She</u> <u>goes</u> to the nurse.
	The <u>nurse</u> <u>cleans</u> the cut.
• A <u>predicate</u> tells what the subject is, has, or does.	<u>Emily</u> <u>is</u> better.

Add words to make each of the following a complete sentence. Use capital letters correctly. *Answers will vary.*

1. were playing soccer at school
   Children were playing soccer at school.

2. one of the players
   One of the players fell on the ground.

3. scraped his knees
   He scraped his knees.

4. his best friends
   His best friends helped him.

🗨 **With a partner, discuss why your sentences are complete.**

Page PM1.16

Something That Has Improved

Make a comparison chart about something that has improved.

Before	Now
Possible Response: The bookshelf was a mess! Some books were upside down. Some books were on the floor.	Possible Response: The bookshelf is neat. The books are all rightside up. There are no books on the floor.

Tell how you improved something. Tell how it was before and how it is now. Use the words *before*, *then*, *now*, and *after* to compare.

It's a Simple Story

Directions:

1. Copy the six sentences onto cards. Have your partner do the same. Mix your cards together and stack them face down.

2. **Round One:** Choose a card and read the sentence aloud. Draw one line under the simple subject. Draw two lines under the simple predicate.

3. **Round Two:** Shuffle all of the cards. Choose a card. Create a new sentence using either the simple subject or the simple predicate. Write it on the back of the card.

NOTE: In each round, if your partner agrees that you used the subject or predicate correctly, keep the card. Take turns until all the cards are used. The player with more cards wins the round.

My cousin Ben is a good reader.	The children in first grade hear Ben at the door.
The delighted teacher has a corner of the room for Ben.	Happy listeners sit on the rug around Ben.
He reads quietly to six children at a time.	The whole class has a new love of reading.

Edit and Proofread

Choose the Editing and Proofreading Marks you need to correct the passage. Look for the following:

- incomplete sentences
- missing capital letters

(Some answers may vary.)

Editing and Proofreading Marks

∧	Add.
✎	Take out.
≡	Capitalize.
⊙	Add period.

Ben watched as his friends played soccer. *He* wanted to play, too.

Asthma
But Ben had asthma. is a disease. It makes it hard for people to

Ben had trouble breathing
breathe. if he ran a lot. He knew it would be hard to play soccer.

But he   *Ben asked about soccer*
wanted to try. His mom took him to Dr. Green. when he saw him.

Ben
Dr. Green said he could play! He gave Ben medicine to use. had to

take it before every practice.

Ben played soccer   *were happy*
after school the next day. It was his first practice. His friends. They

They
helped Ben with the rules. knew he could do it!

Know the Test Format

Directions: Read each question and choose the best answer.

Sample

❶ In the sentence "It got me a trip to the principal's office," what does the word trip mean?
   Ⓐ a fall
   Ⓑ a map
   Ⓒ a seat
   ● a journey

❷ In the sentence "My mother and I went over the list until I knew those words," what do the words went over mean?
   Ⓐ walked over
   Ⓑ threw away
   ● studied
   Ⓓ forgot

Directions: Read the question. Then write a short answer below.

❸ How does Henry find out he has dyslexia?
Henry's stepson, Jed, was tested for dyslexia. It was then that he learned about it.

How did you use the test test-taking strategy to answer the question?

Answer Keys, continued

Comparison Chart

Compare Henry Before and Now

Show how Henry changed in "The World's Greatest Underachiever."

Before	Now
1. Henry had trouble spelling.	1. He writes books.
2. He didn't like school.	2. He offers to visit schools to talk to students.
3. Possible Responses: He got D's and C's.	3. He understands that he learns differently.
4. His self-image was low.	4. His self-image has improved.
5. He was sent to the principal's office for making students laugh.	5. His sense of humor is a benefit in his writing.

Use your comparison chart to retell the selection to a partner: Before, Henry _____. Now, he _____.

© National Geographic Learning, a part of Cengage Learning, Inc.
For use with TE p. T54a

PM1.21

Unit 1 | Happy to Help

Page PM1.21

Fluency: Practice

"The World's Greatest Underachiever"

Use this passage to practice reading with proper intonation.

The next day, I went into the classroom and took out a sheet of paper.	15
Then Miss Adolf gave us the words. The first word was *carpet*.	27
I wrote that one down: *c-a-r-p-e-t*. I was feeling pretty confident.	38
Then came *neighbor*—I wrote down the letter *n*.	47
Then *rhythm*—I knew there was an *r*. Suburban—I wrote *s-u-b*.	59
My heart sank. I had gone from 100 percent to maybe a D-minus.	72
Where did the words go?	77

From "The World's Greatest Underachiever," pages 46–47

Intonation

1 ☐ Does not change pitch.	3 ☐ Changes pitch to match some of the content.
2 ☐ Changes pitch, but does not match content.	4 ☐ Changes pitch to match all of the content.

Accuracy and Rate Formula
Use the formula to measure a reader's accuracy and rate while reading aloud.

_____	–	_____	=	_____
words attempted in one minute		number of errors		words correct per minute (wcpm)

© National Geographic Learning, a part of Cengage Learning, Inc.
For use with TE p. T54a

PM1.22

Unit 1 | Happy to Help

Page PM1.22

Grammar: Reteach

The Lion and the Mouse

Grammar Rules Sentences, Phrases, and Clauses

A **complete subject** is all of the words that tell about the subject.

A **simple subject** is the main word. It may be a **noun** or a **pronoun**.

A **complete predicate** is all of the words in the predicate.

A **simple predicate** is the main word, which is the **verb**. (trapped)

A **phrase** is a group of words that does not have a subject and predicate.
  within his big paws

A **dependent clause** has a subject and a verb but does not express a complete thought.
  if you will let me go

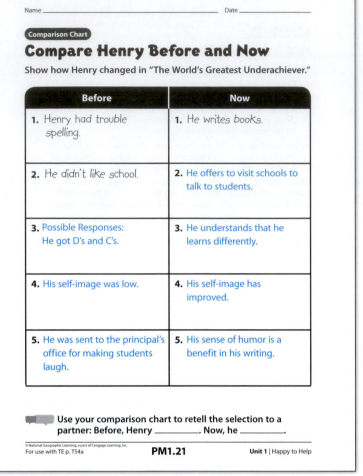

A big, strong lion trapped a tiny gray mouse.

Directions: Draw a line under a complete subject and two lines under a complete predicate. Circle a simple subject and simple predicate.

1. The golden lion released the mouse from his grasp.

2. The happy mouse promised the lion a favor in return.

Add words to make complete sentences. Capitalize correctly.

3. because the lion was tangled in a net
   Because the lion was tangled in a net, he roared and roared.

4. with sharp little teeth
   The mouse chewed through the net with sharp little teeth.

© National Geographic Learning, a part of Cengage Learning, Inc.
For use with TE p. T33x

PM1.23

Unit 1 | Happy to Help

Page PM1.23

Grammar: Game

Do They Agree?

Directions:

1. Flip a coin. For heads, move 2 squares. For tails, move 1 square.

2. Each time you land on a square, pick a NUMBER card. Tell if you have a singular or plural card. Create a sentence for the item you landed on. Then put the NUMBER card at the bottom of the stack.

3. If your sentence is correct, stay on your space. If not, move back one space. The player who reaches the end first wins.

Number Cards

1. Fold a tablet paper twice the long way. Keep it folded and fold the two ends together. Then unfold.

2. Print SINGULAR on 4 sections and PLURAL on 4. On the other side, write NUMBER on all 8 sections.

3. Cut apart the 8 sections.

4. Mix them up and stack them face down to play the game.

				leap	END
	is | are	player	dog	cousin	
	decide		growl	frog	
	zoom		team	find	
play	captain		scream	cat	has|have
START	friend				

© National Geographic Learning, a part of Cengage Learning, Inc.
For use with TE p. T55m

PM1.24

Unit 1 | Happy to Help

Page PM1.24

Panel 1 (Page PM1.25)

Name _____ Date _____

Working Together

Directions:

1. Read the sentence parts. Copy each one onto a separate index card.
2. After shuffling the cards, place them face down in two stacks: one for the subject cards and one for the predicate cards.
3. When it is your turn, choose a subject and a predicate. Read the cards as a complete sentence. Say the correct verb form.
4. If you are correct, keep the cards. Put them back if you are not. Then your partner takes a turn.
5. When the cards are all used, the player with more cards wins.

Subject	Predicate
Boys and girls	_____ everything for a gift basket. gather
Elly or Tran	_____ a gift with a tote bag. create
Dad or my brothers	_____ elderly people. visit
Mom or Dad	_____ to add a book. remember
Ty and Carol	_____ cocoa and a mug. include
The girls or Mom	_____ spices for the baskets. bring

PM1.25   Unit 1 | Happy to Help

Panel 2 (Page PM1.26)

Name _____ Date _____

Compare Points of View

Use a comparison chart to compare an autobiography and a biography.

"The World's Greatest Underachiever"	"Joseph Lekuton: Making a Difference"
• The narrator tells the story of ___*his own*___ life.	• The narrator tells the story of ___*someone else's*___ life.
• The narrator (is/is not) part of the story. (Circle one.) [is circled]	• The narrator (is/is not) part of the story. (Circle one.) [is not circled]
• The selection is (an autobiography /a biography). (Circle one.) [an autobiography circled]	• The selection is (an autobiography /a biography). (Circle one.) [a biography circled]
• Examples of narrator's point of view: Sample entries: (I) was tutored. (I) studied (my) spelling words in (my) apartment. (My) teacher had given (me) a list of ten spelling words.	• Examples of narrator's point of view: Sample entries: Joseph and (his) family are Maasai. (He) volunteered to go instead of (his) brother. (He) couldn't always help (his) family care for their cattle.

🗨 Take turns with a partner. Explain how you know that a selection is an autobiography or a biography.

PM1.26   Unit 1 | Happy to Help

Panel 3 (Page PM1.27)

Name _____ Date _____

We Like to Read

Grammar Rules Adding *-s* to Action Verbs	
• Use *-s* at the end of an action verb if the subject is *he, she,* or *it*.	Danny reads a story. He looks at the pictures.
• Do not use *-s* for *I, you, we,* or *they*.	I read to my friends. They look at the pictures.

Read each sentence. Write the correct form of the verb for each subject.

1. We ___*read*___ many stories.
 read / reads
2. I ___*like*___ autobiographies.
 like / likes
3. They ___*tell*___ about real people.
 tell / tells
4. Henry Winkler ___*tells*___ his own story.
 tell / tells
5. He ___*remembers*___ his problems in school.
 remember / remembers
6. His brain ___*learns*___ differently.
 learn / learns
7. You ___*like*___ autobiographies, too.
 like / likes

🗨 Tell a partner about a story you have read. Use complete sentences. Make sure the subject and the predicate in your sentences agree.

PM1.27   Unit 1 | Happy to Help

Panel 4 (Page PM1.28)

Name _____ Date _____

from

Facing the Lion by Joseph Lekuton

One of the problems the nomads have with school is that we move our villages and the cattle, but the school stays in one place. That means leaving the children behind. The first year, my village was near the school, and I was able to go home easily. In my second year, the missionaries built a dormitory and started a boarding school. My family could move wherever they wanted to, and I could stay in school.

▲ Mission school

My mom used to visit sometimes. She'd bring me milk. The food at school wasn't what I was used to, and there wasn't much of it. We ate mostly corn and beans—yellow corn, from America. Once I counted mine: There were 75 pieces of corn and 15 beans—so little it barely covered the plate. I didn't complain—I was grateful for the school and the missionaries—but I was a nomadic kid, raised on milk. So whenever my family was nearby, my mother would bring me some milk. Sometimes she'd walk 10 or 20 miles with it.

I went to that school through the seventh grade. Every time school closed for the vacation, I had to find my way home. That was one of the hardest things: The village might be 5 miles away, or it might be 50. Sometimes I wouldn't know exactly where my family was. I had to search for them.

> **Explanation:** This is first-person point of view, so the narrator describes his experiences. The narrator accepted that he must stay at school while his family moved around. He thought the food was different and there wasn't much of it, but he didn't complain. He was grateful to be able to go to school. One of the hardest things he had to do was find his family when school closed for vacation.

PM1.28   Unit 1 | Happy to Help

Answer Keys, continued

Name _____   Date _____

Mark-Up Reading

Boy Between Two Cultures by Olivia Hodgson

▲ students in Rwanda, Africa

Because the Lekutons were nomads, their children faced special problems attending school. Nomads move around, but schools stay in the same place. During most of his school years, Joseph lived in a boarding school that missionaries had built. ==What a different life he had there! He bravely stayed behind at school when his family left.==

Joseph's mother visited him many times at boarding school. She wanted to see her son and also bring him milk. Joseph was used to drinking milk. After all, he had grown up in a cattle culture. But now he was in a new culture. The school offered him mostly beans and corn. The corn was strange to him. It was the yellow American kind. Also, the individual portions were small. ==Yet, Joseph saw it as his duty not to complain.==

==One of the bravest things Joseph had to do was to find his way home.== When his school closed for vacation, Joseph didn't always know where his family was living. Sometimes, he traveled as much as 50 miles just to get home. ==By going home, he kept his ties to both cultures.== He was still a student. Yet, when he was home, he was also learning to be a Maasai warrior.

Explanation: This is third-person point of view. The narrator thinks Joseph was brave because he had to stay apart from his family. She thinks that Joseph felt it was his duty not to complain. The narrator also thinks Joseph is brave for finding his way home during school vacations. She thinks his going home helps him keep his ties to both cultures. He is a student and a warrior.

For use with TE pp. T63a–T63h   **PM1.29**   Unit 1 | Happy to Help

Page PM1.29

Name _____   Date _____

Grammar: Grammar and Writing

Edit and Proofread

Choose the Editing and Proofreading Marks you need to correct the passage. Look for the following:

- subject-verb agreement
- correct use of forms of the verb **be**

Editing and Proofreading Marks

Mark	Meaning
∧	Add.
ﻻ	Take out.
≡	Capitalize.
⊙	Add period.

We form a clean-up team for our block. Meg lists our tasks. We vote on jobs and partners. Carly and Moira gets trash bags. Nate or the girls look for brooms. Juanita say she'll borrow gloves. We has a good team. I is proud to be a part of it.

Moms or dads brings snacks for us. My dog Rusty came with Dad, so Rusty are here. Is my big dog helpful? No, but he watchs! He have fun, too.

We is finished with our work! Meg or Rick rush to get a camera.

We smile cheerfully!

For use with TE p. T55n   **PM1.30**   Unit 1 | Happy to Help

Page PM1.30

Name _____   Date _____

Grammar: Reteach

Ants at Work!

Grammar Rules — Subject-Verb Agreement

When a subject is **one** person or thing, the verb ends in **-s**.
An <u>ant</u> live<u>s</u> in a colony.

If the verb ends with **x**, **ch**, **sh**, **x**, or **z**, then the singular ends in **-es**.
It fix<u>es</u> up several rooms.

When a subject is **more than one**, the verb does **not** end in **-s**.
Many <u>ants</u> live together in one colony.

Compound subjects joined by **and** take a plural verb.
<u>Workers</u> **and** soldiers live in a colony.

<u>Singular compound subjects</u> joined by **or** take a singular verb.
A black ant **or** a red ant live<u>s</u> in a colony.

<u>Plural compound subjects</u> joined by **or** take a plural verb.
Sometimes black ants **or** red ants live in colonies of thousands!

Some verbs have special forms:	Each ant **has** a job to do.
has have am is are	Ants **are** very organized.

Read each sentence. Circle the correct verb.

1. An ant nest ((has) | have) rooms for different purposes.

2. A nursery and a resting place (is | (are)) two kinds of rooms.

3. Tunnels and rooms (keeps | (keep)) ants safe underground.

4. Worker ants (digs | (dig)) the tunnels in the ant nest.

For use with TE p. T55n   **PM1.31**   Unit 1 | Happy to Help

Page PM1.31

Small Group Reading Time

TEACHER

- Introduce Books
- Conduct Mini Lessons
- Monitor Small Group Reading
- Guide Discussion
- Assess Progress

STUDENTS

- Read and Discuss Books
- Extend Content Knowledge
- Apply Reading Skills
- Connect and Compare Texts
- Demonstrate Comprehension

Contents

 Go to **NGReach.com** for the Leveled Book Finder.

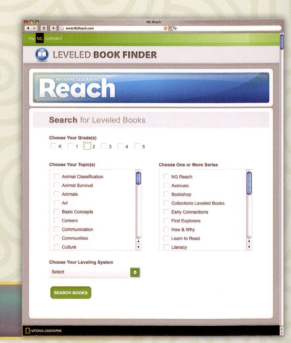

Books at a Glance

LEXILE KEY

| BL | Below Level = 250L–400L | OL | On Level = 550L–700L |
| BL | Below Level = 400L–550L | AL | Above Level = 700L–850L |

			Level* & Title	Author	Content Connection	Pages
Week 1 **Individual Responsibility**	DAY 1	☐	Explorer Books, *The Children's Forest* BL Pioneer Edition OL Pathfinder Edition	Peter Winkler	Educators	SG4–SG5
	DAYS 2–5	BL	*A Chance to Shine*	Steve Seskin	Business Owners	SG6, SG8
		BL	*Tomás and the Library Lady*	Pat Mora	Educators	SG6, SG8
		OL	*The Quiltmaker's Gift*	Jeff Brumbeau	Rulers	SG7, SG9
		AL	*The Quiltmaker's Journey*	Jeff Brumbeau	Artists	SG7, SG9
Week 2 **Heroic Deeds**	DAY 1	☐	Explorer Books, *To the Rescue* BL Pioneer Edition OL Pathfinder Edition	Leslie Hall and Marissa Moss	Saving Lives	SG10–SG11
	DAYS 2–5	BL	*New York's Bravest*	Mary Pope Osborne	Fighting Fires	SG12, SG14
		BL	*The Snow Walker*	Margaret K. and Charles M. Wetterer	Saving Lives	SG12, SG14
		OL	*Passage to Freedom*	Ken Mochizuki	Saving Lives	SG13, SG15
		AL	*Mercedes and the Chocolate Pilot*	Margo Theis Raven	Providing Food	SG13, SG15
Week 3 **Heroes Then and Now**	DAY 1	☐	Explorer Books, *Freedom Readers* BL Pioneer Edition OL Pathfinder Edition	Fran Downey	Activists	SG16–SG17
	DAYS 2–5	BL	*Harriet Tubman*	Wil Mara	Abolitionists	SG18, SG20
		BL	*Helen Keller: Courage in the Dark*	Johanna Hurwitz	Activists	SG18, SG20
		OL	*Louis Braille*	Madeline Donaldson	Activists	SG19, SG21
		AL	*Mary McLeod Bethune*	Eloise Greenfield	Educators	SG19, SG21
Week 4 **Heroes Then and Now**	DAY 1	☐	Explorer Books, *Kids Connect* BL Pioneer Edition OL Pathfinder Edition	Kent Page, Terrell Smith, and Peter Winkler	Leaders	SG22–SG23
	DAYS 2–5	BL	*Martin's Big Words*	Doreen Rappaport	Activists	SG24, SG26
		BL	*Roberto Clemente: A Life of Generosity*	Sheila Anderson	Athletes	SG24, SG26
		OL	*Franklin D. Roosevelt*	Laura Hamilton Waxman	World Leaders	SG25, SG27
		AL	*Nelson Mandela*	Judith Pinkerton Josephson	World Leaders	SG25, SG27

*See page R2 for Guided Reading (GR) and other leveling translation information.

Unit 1 Reading Routines
Fiction & Nonfiction

PROGRAM RESOURCES

PRINT ONLY

Fiction and Nonfiction Books

PRINT & TECHNOLOGY

Unit 1 Practice Masters: SG1.1–SG1.28

Unit 1 Assessment Masters:
SG1.29–SG1.32

TECHNOLOGY

My Vocabulary Notebook

WEEK 1 Fiction

WEEK 2 Fiction and Nonfiction

WEEK 3 Nonfiction

WEEK 4 Nonfiction

Introduce

Assign books. Use the summaries of the books in the Teaching Resources for an overview of content. Assign books according to students' interests and reading levels.

Introduce books. Activate prior knowledge and build background for the books, using the Teaching Resources. Remind students that all of the books connect to the Big Question: *How do people help each other?*

Introduce vocabulary. Use **Vocabulary Routine 1** to teach the story words for each book.

1. **Display** the words for each book.
2. **Pronounce** each word.
3. Have students **rate** each word, holding up their fingers to show how well they know the word (1 = very well; 2 = a little; 3 = not at all). Ask: *What do you know about this word?*
4. Have students **define** each word, using the Story Words **Practice Masters**, for example: *If you recognize someone, you know and remember the person.*
5. Relate each word to students' knowledge and experience. *I recognize George Washington from the one-dollar bill.* Have students work in pairs to **elaborate**.
6. Have students **record** each word in **My Vocabulary Notebook**.

*For **Vocabulary Routine 1**, see page BP46.*

Read and Integrate Ideas

Have students read independently. Circulate to observe students as they read. Ask individuals to read sections aloud. Note any miscues as they read, and encourage students to self-correct. Model by asking questions like: *Did that make sense in the sentence? You said _____. Does that sound right?*

Monitor students' understanding. As students read, have them complete the Graphic Organizer **Practice Master** for their books. Prompt them to show you where in the books they gathered the information to complete their organizers.

Form homogeneous discussion groups. Group students who have read the same book. Distribute the Discussion Guide **Practice Master** for that book to each group member.

Monitor group discussions. Have students discuss the book they read, using the questions on the Discussion Guide. Use the build comprehension questions in the Teaching Resources to develop higher-order thinking skills. See the Discussion Guide Answer Keys on pages SG60–SG67.

Provide writing options. Have each student complete one of the writing options from the Teaching Resources. Encourage students to share their writing with their group.

BEFORE READING

NGReach.com
NGReach.com **Practice Masters**
SG1.1, SG1.8, SG1.15, SG1.22

AFTER READING

Speaking and Listening Observation Log

SG3.29 — Unit 3 | Nature's Network

NGReach.com
Assessment Master SG1.29

DURING CONFERENCES

Reading Strategy Assessment — Unit 3

	Reading Strategy Rubrics	
Plan and Monitor 4 3 2 1	**Ask Questions** 4 3 2 1	**Determine Importance** (Unit Focus) 4 3 2 1

SG3.30 — Unit 3 | Nature's Network

NGReach.com
Assessment Masters SG1.30– SG1.32

Connect Across Texts 👤👤👤👤

Form heterogeneous groups. Group students who have read different books. Include at least one representative for each book read that week.

Introduce the activity. Distribute the Connect Across Texts **Practice Master** for the week. Explain to each group that they will share the books they read, talk about their themes, and discuss what the books say about helping others.

Have students summarize. Ask students to summarize the books they just read, including new story words that helped them understand the themes and content. Have them refer to their graphic organizers as they share their books with the group.

Have students connect across texts. Have groups use the questions provided on the Connect Across Texts **Practice Masters** to guide discussions. See the Discussion Guide Answer Keys for possible responses.

Monitor groups. Use Unit 1 Speaking and Listening Observation Log **Assessment Master SG1.29** to assess students' participation in discussions.

Conduct Conferences 👤

Assess reading. Have each student select and read aloud from a section of the book that connects to the Big Question. Listen for fluency. Ask: *Which strategies did you use to help you understand this section?* Use the reading strategy rubrics on **Assessment Masters SG1.30–SG1.31** to assess how well the student uses the reading strategies. Then have the student complete Reader Reflection **Assessment Master SG1.32**.

Assess writing. Have the student share a completed writing option. Say: *Tell me about what you wrote.* Monitor responses to gauge how well the writing relates to the book. Ask: *How did your writing help you understand the book?*

Plan intervention or acceleration. Ask the student to summarize what he or she has learned. Plan for further instruction:
- If the student needs additional support with planning and monitoring, analyzing the plot, or making comparisons, use the Assessment and Reteaching resources provided on pages RT1.1–RT1.13.
- If the student successfully applies the focus skills, use the Recommended Books on page SG68 to guide the student in choosing books for independent reading.

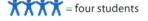

OBJECTIVES
Thematic Connection: Individual Responsibility
Read and Comprehend Informational Text
Determine Main Idea

The Children's Forest by Peter Winkler

Summary The *Children's Forest* describes how children in Peru protect the rain forest. It also discusses South America's geography and habitats, including two types of rain forests. In "Children in Charge," Peter Winkler tells how Joaquin Leguía, a conservationist, convinced people in Peru to give children a part of the rain forest. This is called the Children's Forest. The children work to protect their forest by making trails and learning about its plants and animals. In "Explore South America," students discover the varied environments of that continent. A map shows physical features, such as the Andes, and habitats, such as the rain forests. "Rain Forests of the World" explains that tropical rain forests are near the Equator and stay warm all year. They may get as much as 400 inches of rain each year. Temperate rain forests are farther from the Equator. They have cool winters and get about 100 inches of rain.

Activate Prior Knowledge Display the front cover and read the title aloud. Ask: *What things in this picture might come from a forest?* (leaves; beads)

Build Background Explain that about half of the Earth's plants and animal species live in rain forests. Tell students that rain forests get between 80 and 400 inches of rain per year. Use the locator globe and map on page 7 to point out South America and its rain forests. Have volunteers name the countries and use the map key to identify their physical features.

PROGRAM RESOURCES

PRINT ONLY
The Children's Forest, **Pioneer Edition**
The Children's Forest, **Pathfinder Edition**

TECHNOLOGY ONLY
My Vocabulary Notebook

COMMON CORE STANDARDS

Reading
Determine the Main Idea of Text   CC.3.Rinf.2
Read and Comprehend Informational Text   CC.3.Rinf.10

Language
Acquire and Use Domain-Specific Words   CC.3.L.6

Mini Lesson

Determine Main Idea

Explain: *A main idea is the most important idea. It is what a piece of writing is mostly about. Texts such as articles have several main ideas.* Point out that good readers know how to identify the main ideas in a text.

Read aloud the following text from page 5 of the Pioneer Edition of *The Children's Forest* as students listen.

Kids at Work

Caring for a rain forest is a big job. How do the kids do it? They hold meetings to come up with some ideas. They also ask teachers and park rangers for help. Then they get down to work.

The kids have made many trails and signs. This lets them explore the forest without getting lost.

Text from Pioneer Edition

Then, think aloud to model how to determine the main idea of a text: *To determine the main idea of the first paragraph, I ask myself, "What is this text mostly about? What is the most important idea?" This paragraph is mostly about:*
- *taking care of a rain forest*

The most important idea is:
- *Caring for a rain forest is a big job.*

Point out that in this paragraph, the main idea is stated in the first sentence, but that is not always the case. The sentences that follow the first sentence tell more about the main idea.

Have students determine the main idea of the second paragraph. Then have them restate it in their own words. (Possible response for restatement: The kids make trails and signs so they can explore the forest.)

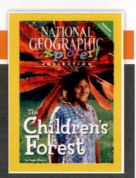

BL ▶ BELOW LEVEL

PIONEER EDITION
GR: P

Content Connection: Educators

Social Studies Vocabulary

Use Wordwise on page 5 to introduce new words:

conservation   *pollution*   *rain forest*

Have students add new words to **My Vocabulary Notebook**.

Build Comprehension

After reading, use the Concept Check on page 12. Remind students to use details and examples to support each answer.

1. **Determine Main Idea** What is conservation? (Conservation is the protection of places, plants, and animals on Earth.)
2. **Explain** Why does Leguía think children should own land? (He thinks that if children own land, they can learn how to take care of it and find ways to protect the Earth.)
3. **Define** What is the Children's Forest? (It is a piece of the rain forest in Peru that people have given to children to take care of.)
4. **Details** What did kids learn from the Children's Forest? (They learned about plants and animals and how to take care of the land. They also learned how to make money by selling crafts made from the forest's nuts and leaves.)
5. **Compare/Contrast** How are the two kinds of rain forests alike? (They both get a lot of rain and have many plants and animals. They both need to be protected.) How are they different? (Temperate rain forests are farther from the Equator than tropical forests, so they are cool in winter. Temperate rain forests get less rain and have fewer kinds of plants and animals.)

OL ▶ ON LEVEL 660L

PATHFINDER EDITION
Lexile: 660L | GR: Q

Content Connection: Educators

Social Studies Vocabulary

Use Wordwise on page 5 to introduce new words:

conservation   *pollution*   *rain forest*

Have students add new words to **My Vocabulary Notebook**.

Build Comprehension

After reading, use the Concept Check on page 12. Remind students to use details and examples to support each answer.

1. **Determine Main Idea** What is conservation? (Conservation is the protection of wild places, plants, and animals on Earth.) Why is conservation sometimes hard? (People often have to change how they live. Such changes can cost time and money.)
2. **Explain** Why are rain forests important? (They make oxygen that people need to breathe, and they take harmful gases out of the air. Half of all plant and animal species on Earth live there.)
3. **Describe** Where is the Children's Forest? (It is in the southeastern part of Peru.) What is unusual about it? (Children explore it and take care of it.)
4. **Details** Where are most rain forests found? (They are near the Equator.) Why? (It is warm there all year round. The plants and animals thrive in this climate.)
5. **Compare/Contrast** How are tropical rain forests like temperate rain forests? (Both get a lot of rain, have many plants and animals, and need protection.) How are they different? (Temperate rain forests are farther from the Equator, so they are cool in winter. Temperate rain forests get less rain and have fewer kinds of plants and animals.)

Check & Reteach

OBJECTIVE: Determine Main Idea

Have partners determine the main idea for the first paragraph of "The Future of Forests" on page 10. (Rain forests are in danger)
For students who cannot determine the main idea, reteach with the fourth paragraph of "Tropical Rain Forests" on page 8. Say: *The main idea is the most important idea. It is what the text is mostly about. Which sentence in this paragraph tells the main idea?* Have students skim the text, looking for the sentence that contains the most important idea. Record the sentence(s) they identify. (Correct response–Pioneer: "Tropical rain forests are full of life"; Pathfinder: "Tropical rain forests provide homes for many kinds of animals.") Have groups discuss how they selected a sentence as a statement of the main idea.

BL BELOW LEVEL

A Chance to Shine
by Steve Seskin

Content Connection:
Business Owners

Realistic Fiction | Pages: 22

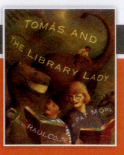

BL BELOW LEVEL 440L

Tomás and the Library Lady
by Pat Mora

Content Connection:
Educators

Biographical Fiction | Pages: 32 | Lexile: 440L | GR: L

OBJECTIVES

Thematic Connection: Individual Responsibility

Read and Comprehend Literature

☑ **Plan and Monitor: Preview and Predict**

☑ **Plot**

PROGRAM RESOURCES

PRINT & TECHNOLOGY

Practice Master SG1.1, page SG28

Practice Master SG1.2, page SG29

Practice Master SG1.3, page SG30

Practice Master SG1.7, page SG34

SUGGESTED PACING

DAY 2   Introduce and read pages 2–11

DAY 3   Read pages 12–22 and discuss

DAY 4   Reteach or conduct intervention

DAY 5   Connect across texts

Summary   A boy notices a homeless man outside of his father's store. The boy's father gives the man, Joe, a job sweeping the sidewalk in front of the store in exchange for food. Joe works hard and, in time, becomes store manager. He finds an apartment and a better way of life. The boy learns that everyone deserves a chance and begins treating students at school differently.

Activate Prior Knowledge   Ask: *When has someone given you a chance or been kind to you when no one else would? How did it make you feel?*

Build Background   Ask students to think about what it would be like to not have a place to live. Explain that more than six hundred thousand people in America are homeless on any given night. This includes men, women, and children. Many people become homeless because they can't find affordable housing or jobs that pay enough money.

Story Words   Use **Practice Master SG1.1** to extend vocabulary.

boss, page 13   *chance*, page 7   *deal*, page 5

recognize, page 8   *rent*, page 15

PROGRAM RESOURCES

PRINT & TECHNOLOGY

Practice Master SG1.1, page SG28

Practice Master SG1.2, page SG29

Practice Master SG1.4, page SG31

Practice Master SG1.7, page SG34

TECHNOLOGY ONLY

Digital Library: Migrant Workers

SUGGESTED PACING

DAY 2   Introduce and read pages 4–19

DAY 3   Read pages 20–32 and discuss

DAY 4   Reteach or conduct intervention

DAY 5   Connect across texts

Summary   Tomás's family travels to Iowa to do farm work for the season. Tomás visits the library, where the librarian introduces him to books and stories that spark his imagination. When his family returns to Texas, Tomás takes his love of reading with him.

Activate Prior Knowledge   Ask: *What is your favorite book? Why is it your favorite?*

Build Background   Display the photo of migrant workers from the **Digital Library**. Explain that about 1.3 million migrant workers go from state to state to work on farms. Because they move around so often, and because their parents need them to work in order for the family to have enough money, many of the children don't have the same chances to go to school as other children.

Story Words   Use **Practice Master SG1.1** to extend vocabulary.

borrow, page 19   *ceiling*, page 14   *eager*, page 19

howl, page 11   *press*, page 12

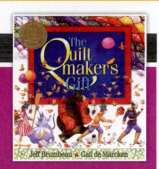

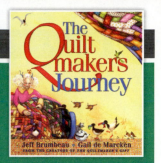

OL ON LEVEL **630L**

The Quiltmaker's Gift
by Jeff Brumbeau

Content Connection:
Rulers

Fable | Pages: 48 | Lexile: 630L | GR: O

AL ABOVE LEVEL **AD840L**

The Quiltmaker's Journey
by Jeff Brumbeau

Content Connection:
Artists

Fable | Pages: 48 | Lexile: AD840L | GR: S

COMMON CORE STANDARDS

Reading

Read and Comprehend Literature	CC.3.Rlit.10
Refer to Parts of Stories	CC.3.Rlit.5
Describe How Successive Parts Build	CC.3.Rlit.5
Recount Stories	CC.3.Rlit.2

Writing

Write Over Shorter Time for Specific Tasks	CC.3.W.10

Speaking and Listening

Draw on Preparation to Explore Ideas	CC.3.SL.1.a

Language and Vocabulary

Acquire and Use Academic Words	CC.3.L.6

PROGRAM RESOURCES

PRINT & TECHNOLOGY

Practice Master SG1.1, page SG28
Practice Master SG1.2, page SG29
Practice Master SG1.5, page SG32
Practice Master SG1.7, page SG34

TECHNOLOGY ONLY

Digital Library: Quilts

PROGRAM RESOURCES

PRINT & TECHNOLOGY

Practice Master SG1.1, page SG28
Practice Master SG1.2, page SG29
Practice Master SG1.6, page SG33
Practice Master SG1.7, page SG34

TECHNOLOGY ONLY

Digital Library: Quilts

SUGGESTED PACING, PART 1

DAY 2   Introduce and read pages 4–25
DAY 3   Read pages 26–48
DAY 4   Reread and discuss
DAY 5   Connect across texts

SUGGESTED PACING, PART 1

DAY 2   Introduce and read pages 4–25
DAY 3   Read pages 26–48
DAY 4   Reread and discuss
DAY 5   Connect across texts

Summary   A greedy king orders a quiltmaker, who makes quilts only for the poor, to make him a quilt. She refuses unless he gives all his possessions away. The act of giving makes the king poor—but rich in spirit—and he is rewarded with a beautiful quilt.

Activate Prior Knowledge   Ask: *How does it feel to give to others? Tell about a time you felt good about giving.*

Build Background   Display photos of quilts from the **Digital Library**. Explain that quilts are made by first sewing scraps of fabric together to make a pattern, called piecing. The quilt top is then sewn to a large piece of fabric with a layer of stuffing, or batting, between. This sewing together of the three layers is called quilting.

Story Words   Use **Practice Master SG1.1** to extend vocabulary.

arrive, page 26   *grateful*, page 25   *recall*, page 4

seize, page 16   *wander*, page 8

Summary   A girl lives in a walled village of wealthy people, but feels unfulfilled. She ventures out to seek the true meaning of happiness and is shocked to see the poverty that exists. She wants desperately to help, but thinks she has nothing to give, until she comes across a freezing mother and child huddled in a doorway. Then she realizes she can do something to help, and so she dedicates her life to making quilts for the poor.

Activate Prior Knowledge   Ask: *What does it mean to be kind?* (Possible response: to be nice and helpful) *How do you show kindness?* (Possible response: I share my toys.)

Build Background   Display the photos of quilts from the **Digital Library**. Explain that quilts were used as early as 3400 BC. In the 11th century, knights wore quilted clothes under their armor. American settlers brought their quilting skills with them, beginning a rich tradition of quilting in America.

Story Words   Use **Practice Master SG1.1** to extend vocabulary.

awkward, page 38   *creature*, page 7   *deed*, page 4

furious, page 14   *toil*, page 4

BL ▶ BELOW LEVEL

A Chance to Shine
by Steve Seskin

Build Comprehension

- **Character's Motivation** *Why does the boy's father give Joe a job sweeping the sidewalk before making him the store manager?* (Possible response: He wants Joe to prove that he can work hard and that he wants to improve his life.)
- **Evaluate** *How do the boy's feelings toward others change because of Joe?* (Possible response: He realizes that everyone should be given a chance because people are not always what they seem.)

Writing Options

- **Interview Questions** Have students write three interview questions they would ask Joe if they were going to give him a job. Then have them share their questions with a partner.
- **Thank You Note** Have students write a thank you note from Joe to the boy's father, thanking him for giving Joe a chance.
- **Journal Entry** Invite students to write about a time when someone turned out to be different from how they expected him or her to be.

BL ▶ BELOW LEVEL   440L

Tomás and the Library Lady
by Pat Mora

Build Comprehension

- **Make Inferences** *Why does Tomás like visiting the library?* (Possible responses: He can read books that take him to other worlds. He can drink cool water there. He can learn stories to share with his family.)
- **Explain** *How does the library lady change Tomás's life?* (Possible response: She helps him learn to love books and reading.)

Writing Options

- **Friendly Letter** Have students write a letter from Tomás to the library lady telling her about his life when he returns to Texas.
- **Dialogue** Have students write a dialogue between Tomás and the library lady in which they discuss a book they both like.
- **Journal Entry** Invite students to write about their favorite book and tell why it is their favorite.

Check & Reteach

Ask students to describe the plot of each book.
If students have difficulty identifying the plot, refer them to their story maps. Ask: *What happens in the beginning, middle, and end of the story?*

DURING READING

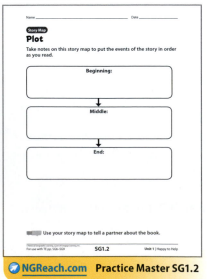

AFTER READING

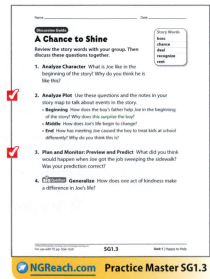

AFTER READING

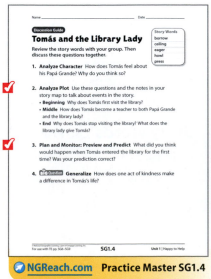

OL ON LEVEL 630L

The Quiltmaker's Gift
by Jeff Brumbeau

Build Comprehension

- **Form Generalizations** *Why won't the quiltmaker make a quilt for the king?* (Possible response: She will only make quilts for people who are poor and who really need the quilts.)
- **Draw Conclusions** *Why is the king happier at the end of the story?* (Possible response: He has learned that sharing is better than keeping everything for himself.)

Writing Options

- **Sequel** Have students write a paragraph telling what happens after the story ends. For instance, they might tell how life in the kingdom changes because the king has changed, or they might write about what happens to the king and the quiltmaker.
- **Character Sketch** Have students write a character sketch that outlines the changes the king went through from the beginning to the end of the story.
- **Journal Entry** Invite students to write about an important lesson they have learned about how to treat other people.

AL ABOVE LEVEL AD840L

The Quiltmaker's Journey
by Jeff Brumbeau

Build Comprehension

- **Goal and Outcome** *What was the girl's goal?* (Possible response: She wanted to help the poor.) *How did she reach her goal?* (Possible response: She made quilts for them.)
- **Make Comparisons** *What makes the girl different from the other people in her town?* (Possible responses: She wants to do something important and is brave enough to leave the town and see the world. She wants to help other people.)

Writing Options

- **News Report** Have students write a news report telling about the good deeds of the quiltmaker. Remind students to answer the questions *who, what, when, where,* and *why*.
- **Book Review** Have students write a book review in which they tell what happens in the book and what they thought about it.
- **Journal Entry** Invite students to write about a time someone was kind to them.

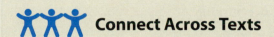 **Connect Across Texts** **AFTER READING** Form heterogeneous groups, and have each member of the group summarize his or her book. Then have groups use **Practice Master SG1.7** to guide discussion.

AFTER READING

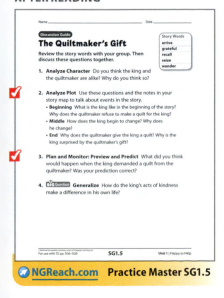

NGReach.com Practice Master SG1.5

AFTER READING

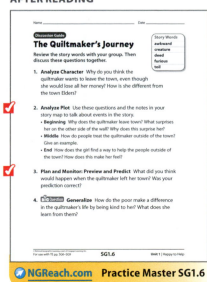

NGReach.com Practice Master SG1.6

AFTER READING

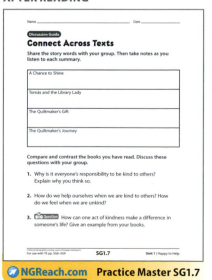

NGReach.com Practice Master SG1.7

OBJECTIVES

Thematic Connection: Heroic Deeds

Read and Comprehend Informational Text

Identify Supporting Details

To the Rescue by Leslie Hall and Marissa Moss

Summary *To the Rescue* introduces students to two kinds of rescue workers, firefighters and lighthouse keepers, and it looks at the tough jobs these everyday heroes do. In "Firestorm!" Leslie Hall explains that the U.S. has thousands of wildfires each year. Although wildfires destroy, they also clean out dead plants and allow new growth. Wildfires are growing more dangerous, though. More people live near potential fire areas. And forests are drier because of higher temperatures and less snow. Brave firefighters attack fires by digging fire lines and starting backfires to cut off a fire's fuel supply. "Lighthouse Lives" by Marissa Moss explores how lighthouse keepers kept sailors safe. Before electricity, they made sure the light always burned. Moss describes several heroic keepers who risked their lives to guide sailors and to rescue people from deep, cold waters.

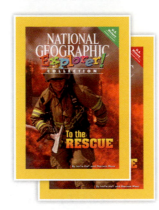

Activate Prior Knowledge Display the front cover and ask: *Why are firefighters brave?* (Possible responses: Putting out fires is dangerous work; they risk their lives to save people, animals, and houses.)

Build Background Explain that each year in the U.S., about 100,000 wildfires destroy land and injure or kill people. Scientists and firefighters work to protect people from such disasters. Use the photos on pages 6–7 to discuss those who risk their lives during blazes and one way to fight them. Have volunteers point to each photo and describe what it shows.

PROGRAM RESOURCES

PRINT ONLY

To the Rescue, **Pioneer Edition**

To the Rescue, **Pathfinder Edition**

TECHNOLOGY ONLY

My Vocabulary Notebook

COMMON CORE STANDARDS

Reading

Explain How Key Details Support the Main Idea	CC.3.Rinf.2
Read and Comprehend Informational Text	CC.3.Rinf.10

Language

Acquire and Use Domain-Specific Words	CC.3.L.6

Mini Lesson

Identify Supporting Details

Explain: *Authors provide details, such as facts and examples, to support main ideas, or show that they are true.* Point out that good readers can explain how key details support a main idea in a text.

Read aloud the following text from page 4 of the Pioneer Edition of *To the Rescue* as students listen.

Fire Facts

A fire needs heat, fuel, and oxygen to burn.

Heat starts a fire. It can come from lightning. Fuel makes a fire burn. Fuel can be anything from dead trees to dry grass. Oxygen is a gas in the air. It helps to start a fire. It also helps keep a fire burning.

Text from Pioneer Edition

Then, think aloud to model how to identify key details and explain how they support the main idea of the text: *The main idea is stated in the first paragraph:*
- *A fire needs heat, fuel, and oxygen to burn.*

The second paragraph gives details that support this main idea by explaining why a fire needs these things. The key details are:
- *Heat starts a fire. It can come from lightning.*
- *Fuel makes a fire burn. It can be dead trees or dry grass.*

Point out that these details include both facts and examples.

Have students identify details about oxygen in the text above. Then have them explain how all the details support the main idea in the text. (Details: Oxygen is a gas in the air. It helps start a fire and keeps it going. Possible response: The details explain why a fire needs each of these three things to burn. The details also give specific examples for heat, fuel, and oxygen.)

NATIONAL GEOGRAPHIC Explorer! COLLECTION

BL BELOW LEVEL 420L

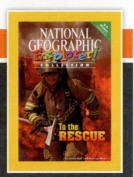

PIONEER EDITION
Lexile: 420L

Content Connection: Saving Lives

Social Studies Vocabulary

Use Wordwise on page 6 to introduce new words:

brave   *courage*   *danger*   *firefighter*   *risk*

Have students add new words to **My Vocabulary Notebook**.

Build Comprehension

After reading, use the Concept Check on page 12. Remind students to use details and examples to support each answer.

1. **Explain** Name the three parts of a fire triangle. (The three parts are heat, fuel, and oxygen.) Why is the fire triangle important? (Without these three things, wildfires cannot burn. Knowing this helps people understand wildfires.)

2. **Identify Supporting Details** What details support the idea that wildfires help forests? (Small fires help prevent larger ones. When trees burn, more light reaches the ground. This lets new plants grow. Burned plants make the soil richer. Some trees need heat to release seeds.)

3. **Details** Give examples of two ways that firefighters stop fires. (They dig fire lines and they start backfires.)

4. **Describe** How did lighthouse keepers help sailors? (Lights warned about sharp rocks so sailors could sail to safer waters. Patterns of flashing lights told sailors where they were at night. Sometimes they risked their lives to rescue people from water.)

5. **Compare** How are the jobs of firefighters and lighthouse keepers alike? (Both work hard and have dangerous jobs. Both need to be brave. Both help rescue people from danger.)

OL ON LEVEL 720L

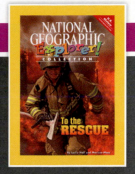

PATHFINDER EDITION
Lexile: 720L

Content Connection: Saving Lives

Social Studies Vocabulary

Use Wordwise on page 6 to introduce new words:

brave   *courage*   *danger*   *firefighter*   *risk*

Have students add new words to **My Vocabulary Notebook**.

Build Comprehension

After reading, use the Concept Check on page 12. Remind students to use details and examples to support each answer.

1. **Explain** What three things make up a fire triangle? (heat, fuel, oxygen) How do they keep wildfires burning? (Heat starts the fire. Fuel feeds the fire. Oxygen helps start the fire and keep it burning.)

2. **Identify Supporting Details** What details support the main idea that wildfires help forests? (Small fires remove fuel and help prevent larger ones. Fires allow more light to reach the ground. This lets new plants grow. Fires add nutrients to the soil. Some trees need heat to drop seeds.)

3. **Details** Give examples of three ways that firefighters stop fires. (dig fire lines, drop water and chemicals on fires, start backfires)

4. **Describe** How did lighthouse keepers help sailors? (Lights warned sailors about dangerous rocks. Patterns of flashing lights at night and painted patterns on the towers during the day helped sailors know where they were. Keepers risked their lives to rescue people from the water.)

5. **Compare** What is similar about firefighters and lighthouse keepers? (Both work hard at dangerous jobs. Both need to be brave. And both help rescue people from danger.)

Check & Reteach

OBJECTIVE: Identify Supporting Details

Have partners identify key details in "A Growing Danger" on page 4 and explain how the details support the main idea that wildfires are a bigger danger to people than they were in the past. (Details: More people live closer to forests; less snow and warmer temperatures mean forests are drier; drier forests burn more easily. These details explain why wildfires are a bigger danger to people now.)

For students who cannot identify key details, reteach with "Hard Living" on page 10. Say: *The main idea is that a lighthouse keeper's job was tough. What details support, or explain, this idea?* Have students skim text. Make a class list. (went up tower each night to light lamp; checked light during the night; went up in morning to put out light) Have students explain how details support the main idea. (Details explain why the job was tough.)

BL ▸ BELOW LEVEL AD350L

New York's Bravest
by Mary Pope Osborne

Content Connection:
Fighting Fires

Historical Fiction | Pages: 32 | Lexile: AD350L | GR: K

BL ▸ BELOW LEVEL 520L

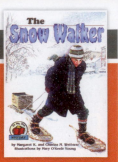

The Snow Walker
by Margaret K. and Charles M. Wetterer

Content Connection:
Saving Lives

Historical Fiction | Pages: 48 | Lexile: 520L | GR: N

OBJECTIVES

Thematic Connection: Heroic Deeds

> **Read and Comprehend Literature and Informational Text**
>
> **Plan and Monitor: Preview and Predict**
>
> **Analyze Character**

PROGRAM RESOURCES

PRINT & TECHNOLOGY

Practice Master SG1.8, page SG35
Practice Master SG1.9, page SG36
Practice Master SG1.10, page SG37
Practice Master SG1.14, page SG41

TECHNOLOGY ONLY

Digital Library: New York Firefighter Photos

SUGGESTED PACING

DAY 2   Introduce and read pages 4–16
DAY 3   Read pages 20–32 and discuss
DAY 4   Reteach or conduct intervention
DAY 5   Connect across texts

Summary   Standing eight feet tall, Mose Humphreys is the most famous fireman in New York City. Because of his bravery and strength, there is no fire he can't put out and no person he can't save. After a terrible fire at a hotel, Mose is lost. Legends begin about where he has gone, until the other firefighters decide he is with them in their hearts and memories.

Activate Prior Knowledge   Ask: *What does it mean to be brave?* (Possible response: to do something scary without thinking about it) *When have you been brave?*

Build Background   Display photos of New York firefighters from the **Digital Library** and explain that today, the New York City Fire Department is made up of over 14,000 people, which includes uniformed firefighters, paramedics, fire inspectors, fire marshals, dispatchers, and administrative support people.

Story Words   Use **Practice Master SG1.8** to extend vocabulary.

danger, page 7	*famous*, page 5	*ragged*, page 13
rumor, page 26	*wedge*, page 13	

PROGRAM RESOURCES

PRINT & TECHNOLOGY

Practice Master SG1.8, page SG35
Practice Master SG1.9, page SG36
Practice Master SG1.11, page SG38
Practice Master SG1.14, page SG41

TECHNOLOGY ONLY

Digital Library: Blizzard Photos

SUGGESTED PACING

DAY 2   Introduce and read pages 3–25
DAY 3   Read pages 26–48 and discuss
DAY 4   Reteach or conduct intervention
DAY 5   Connect across texts

Summary   In March of 1888, a blizzard rages in the northeastern United States. Twelve-year-old Milton Daub and his father make snowshoes so Milton can go to the store for milk. He braves snowdrifts that are two stories high and helps deliver groceries and medicine to many neighbors. As his snowshoes begin to break, Milton fears he will be lost in the storm, but he safely returns to his waiting family.

Activate Prior Knowledge   Ask: *What do you know about blizzards?* (Possible responses: There is a lot of snow and wind. It is hard to see.) *Have you ever been outside during a blizzard? What was it like?*

Build Background   Display the photos of blizzards from the **Digital Library**. Explain that blizzards are winter storms that occur when strong winds and cold temperatures combine with falling snow or blowing snow, making it extremely difficult to see for three hours or more.

Story Words   Use **Practice Master SG1.8** to extend vocabulary.

frantic, page 26	*imagine*, page 23	*ledge*, page 16
lonely, page 30	*medicine*, page 32	

OL ON LEVEL AD670L

Passage to Freedom
by Ken Mochizuki

Content Connection:
Saving Lives

Biography | Pages: 32 | Lexile: AD670L | GR: P

AL ABOVE LEVEL 850L

Mercedes and the Chocolate Pilot
by Margo Theis Raven

Content Connection:
Providing Food

Historical Fiction | Pages: 48 | Lexile: 850L | GR: T

COMMON CORE STANDARDS

Reading
Read and Comprehend Literature	CC.3.Rlit.10
Describe Characters	CC.3.Rlit.3

Writing
Write Over Shorter Time for Specific Tasks	CC.3.W.10

Speaking and Listening
Draw on Preparation to Explore Ideas	CC.3.SL.1.a

Language and Vocabulary
Acquire and Use Academic Words	CC.3.L.6

PROGRAM RESOURCES
PRINT & TECHNOLOGY
Practice Master SG1.8, page SG35
Practice Master SG1.9, page SG36
Practice Master SG1.12, page SG39
Practice Master SG1.14, page SG41

SUGGESTED PACING
DAY 2	Introduce and read pages 3–19
DAY 3	Read pages 20–32
DAY 4	Reread and discuss
DAY 5	Connect across texts

Summary Chiune Sugihara is a Japanese diplomat in Lithuania during World War II. One night, hundreds of Jews crowd outside the family's home in hopes that Sugihara will grant them visas to Japan. Japan's government refuses, but Sugihara signs a visa for every person, even as a train takes him out of Lithuania to Germany. He is remembered as someone who saved thousands of people from the Nazis.

Activate Prior Knowledge Ask: *Have you ever helped someone when they were in trouble? What happened?*

Build Background Explain that during World War II, the Nazis believed Jews were their enemies. During this period, called the Holocaust, over six million Jews died.

Story Words Use **Practice Master SG1.8** to extend vocabulary.

approach, page 28	*celebration*, page 3	*encourage*, page 26
permission, page 12	*reply*, page 14	

PROGRAM RESOURCES
PRINT & TECHNOLOGY
Practice Master SG1.8, page SG35
Practice Master SG1.9, page SG36
Practice Master SG1.13, page SG40
Practice Master SG1.14, page SG41

SUGGESTED PACING
DAY 2	Introduce and read pages 4–25
DAY 3	Read pages 26–47
DAY 4	Reread and discuss
DAY 5	Connect across texts

Summary In Berlin, after World War II, Mercedes's family has little food. She hears a story about a pilot who drops candy to children from a plane that airlifts food into Berlin. Mercedes visits the airfield, hoping to catch some chocolate, but she is unlucky. She writes to the pilot, asking him to drop candy in her yard. The pilot sends her a package of candy. Years later, Mercedes meets the pilot and is able to express her gratitude.

Activate Prior Knowledge Ask: *When has someone surprised you with a treat you did not expect? How did it make you feel?*

Build Background Explain that during an airlift, supplies are delivered to people in need, who live in areas that are hard to reach on the ground. There have been a number of humanitarian airlifts throughout history. They have happened during wartime or after natural disasters, such as Hurricane Katrina.

Story Words Use **Practice Master SG1.8** to extend vocabulary.

capture, page 24	*personal*, page 30	*promise*, page 20
scold, page 8	*shelter*, page 27	

BL > BELOW LEVEL AD350L

New York's Bravest
by Mary Pope Osborne

Build Comprehension
- **Character's Actions** *What does Mose Humphreys do that shows he is brave and kind?* (Possible response: He shows his bravery by saving many people from fires and giving his life to help others.)
- **Draw Conclusions** *Why do you think people make up stories about Mose's whereabouts?* (Possible responses: They do not want to believe that someone so brave and strong could be gone.)

Writing Options
- **Thank You Note** Have students write a thank you note to Mose from someone he saved from a fire.
- **Interview Questions** Have students write five questions they would like to ask Mose and then share their questions with a partner.
- **Journal Entry** Invite students to write about a time when someone made a sacrifice for them.

BL > BELOW LEVEL 520L

The Snow Walker
by Margaret K. and Charles M. Wetterer

Build Comprehension
- **Form Opinions** *What do you think about what Milton did for his neighbors? Would you have done the same? Why or why not?* (Possible response: What he did was brave. I would have done the same thing because it is good to help others.)
- **Goal and Outcome** *What is Milton's goal for using the snowshoes?* (Possible response: He wants to go to the grocery store for milk and return home right away.) *What really happens?* (Possible response: He helps many other people in his neighborhood get groceries and medicine because they cannot leave their homes.)

Writing Options
- **Description** Have students write a description that explains Milton's actions in the story.
- **Dialogue** Have students write a dialogue between Milton and one of his neighbors who needs his help.
- **Journal Entry** Invite students to write about a time when they helped someone.

Check & Reteach

Ask students to describe the main characters of each book.
If students have difficulty describing characters, refer them to their character description chart. Ask: *What does the character do? What does this say about the character?*

DURING READING

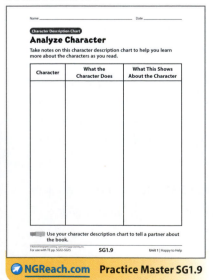

NGReach.com **Practice Master SG1.9**

AFTER READING

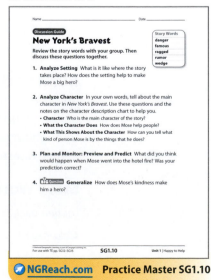

NGReach.com **Practice Master SG1.10**

AFTER READING

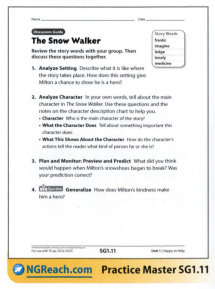

NGReach.com **Practice Master SG1.11**

OL ON LEVEL AD670L

Passage to Freedom
by Ken Mochizuki

Build Comprehension

- **Identify Problem and Solution** *What is the problem the Jewish people have? How does Sugihara help to solve this problem?* (Possible response: The Jewish people need to escape from Lithuania, where their lives are in danger. Sugihara gets them visas, so they can get out of the country.)
- **Explain** *Why does Sugihara decide to go against the wishes of the Japanese government?* (Possible response: He knows that giving the people visas will save their lives.)

Writing Options

- **Book Review** Have students write a book review in which they explain why someone should or should not read the book.
- **Blog Post** Have students write a blog post in which they tell about the heroic actions of Chiume Sugihara.
- **Journal Entry** Invite students to write about someone they consider to be a hero.

AL ABOVE LEVEL 850L

Mercedes and the Chocolate Pilot
by Margo Theis Raven

Build Comprehension

- **Form Generalizations** *Why do you think it is so important to Mercedes to visit the airfield?* (Possible response: She wants to see for herself that candy can fall from the sky, and she wants to have a treat after being hungry for so long.)
- **Evaluate** *How does the pilot's act of kindness affect Mercedes? How do you know?* (Possible responses: His kindness gave her joy in a difficult time. I know because she felt tears of "love and gratitude" when she met him years later.)

Writing Options

- **Thank You Note** Have students write a thank you note to the pilot from Mercedes, telling him what his kindness meant to her.
- **News Report** Ask students to write a news report telling about the first reunion between Mercedes and the Chocolate Pilot.
- **Journal Entry** Invite students to write about a time when someone was generous to them and tell how it made them feel.

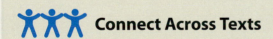 **Connect Across Texts**

AFTER READING Form heterogeneous groups, and have each member of the group summarize his or her book. Then have groups use **Practice Master SG1.14** to guide discussion.

AFTER READING

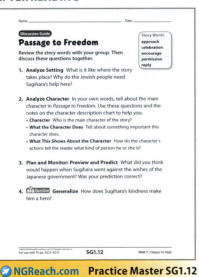

NGReach.com **Practice Master SG1.12**

AFTER READING

NGReach.com **Practice Master SG1.13**

AFTER READING

NGReach.com **Practice Master SG1.14**

OBJECTIVES
Thematic Connection: Heroes Then and Now
Read and Comprehend Informational Text
Compare Points and Details

Freedom Readers *by Fran Downey*

Summary *Freedom Readers* describes how some slaves learned to read, an important step toward gaining freedom. It also discusses the struggles former slaves faced after the Civil War. In "Freedom Readers," Fran Downey introduces famous former slaves Olaudah Equiano, Phillis Wheatley, and Frederick Douglass. As children, each found a way to learn to read. Each later spoke out against slavery. Equiano wrote his life story. Wheatley wrote poems about freedom. Douglass escaped to freedom and started a newspaper to fight for the abolition of slavery. Many other slaves risked their lives to learn to read. They knew that reading was a step to freedom. "From Slavery to Freedom" explains the difficulties freed slaves faced. They had no money to buy their own land or homes. Some children had to work instead of going to school. Some people still treated African Americans unfairly. Until the 1960s, they did not have equal rights.

Activate Prior Knowledge Display the front cover and read the title aloud. Ask: *How does learning to read help people?* (Possible responses: Learning to read helps people get an education; learn things on their own; know about the world.)

Build Background Explain that slavery existed in the U.S. until 1865, and many slaves could not read. Use the portraits on pages 4–6 to introduce students to people who learned to read as slaves and then spoke out against slavery. Have volunteers identify the person in each portrait.

PROGRAM RESOURCES

PRINT ONLY
Freedom Readers, **Pioneer Edition**
Freedom Readers, **Pathfinder Edition**

TECHNOLOGY ONLY
My Vocabulary Notebook

COMMON CORE STANDARDS

Reading
Compare Important Points and Details in Two Texts   CC.3.Rinf.9
Read and Comprehend Informational Text   CC.3.Rinf.10

Language
Acquire and Use Domain-Specific Words   CC.3.L.6

Mini Lesson

Compare Points and Details
Explain: *When two texts discuss the same topic, some important points and key details may be similar. However, some may be different.* Point out that good readers know how to compare and contrast points and details from two texts on the same topic.

Read aloud the following text from pages 7 and 10 of the Pioneer Edition of *Freedom Readers* as students listen.

> ### More Freedom Readers
> (page 7)
> Slavery ended in 1865. Then many former slaves went to school. They needed to learn to read. Reading would help them live as free people.
>
> ### Finding Freedom (page 10)
> Reading and writing were steps to freedom. These skills could help freed slaves get better jobs.

Text from Pioneer Edition

Think aloud to model how to identify similarities and differences in two texts on the same topic: *Both paragraphs discuss former slaves and their education. Some points are the same:*

- *The text on page 7 says that many former slaves went to school to learn how to read. This helped them live as free people.*
- *The text on page 10 says that reading and writing led to freedom.*

However, some points are different, or give additional information:

- *The text from page 10 also says that education helped freed slaves get better jobs.*

Have students compare and contrast important points in the texts above. (Possible response: Both texts make the point that reading helped former slaves. The second makes the point that reading also helped them get better jobs. So, the texts make a similar point, but the second text states an additional point.)

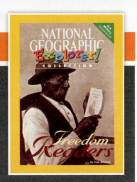

PIONEER EDITION
Lexile: 300L | GR: Q

Content Connection: Activists

Social Studies Vocabulary
Use Wordwise on page 7 to introduce new words:

illegal   *kidnap*   *master*   *syllable*

Have students add new words to **My Vocabulary Notebook**.

Build Comprehension
After reading, use the Concept Check on page 12. Remind students to use details and examples to support each answer.

1. **Main Idea** Why did slaves want to read? (They knew that learning to read would help them gain freedom.)
2. **Details** Who was Frederick Douglass? (He was a freedom fighter who grew up as a slave in Maryland.) Why is he famous? (As an adult, he fought against slavery and helped to end it. He wrote books and made speeches. He ran a newspaper, too.)
3. **Compare Points and Details** How did slaves learn to read? ("Freedom Readers" says they learned from members of their masters' families, from children, from other slaves, or they taught themselves. "From Slavery to Freedom" says they went to school, or learned in church or from friends.)
4. **Explain** What rights did slaves get after they were freed? (They could go to school, own land, and vote. They could get married, too.)
5. **Evaluate** Why was life still hard for freed slaves? (Many could not get an education. They did not have money to buy their own land or homes. Some people still treated them as slaves. So they did not always have the same rights as other Americans.)

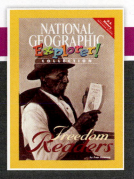

PATHFINDER EDITION
GR: R

Content Connection: Activists

Social Studies Vocabulary
Use Wordwise on page 7 to introduce new words:

abolish   *kidnap*   *plantation*   *syllable*

Have students add new words to **My Vocabulary Notebook**.

Build Comprehension
After reading, use the Concept Check on page 12. Remind students to use details and examples to support each answer.

1. **Main Idea** Why did slaves want to learn to read? (They knew reading was important. It would help them gain freedom.)
2. **Details** Who was Frederick Douglass? (a freedom fighter who was born into slavery in Maryland) Why is he famous? (He helped end slavery. He wrote books and ran a newspaper, too.)
3. **Compare Points and Details** What are some ways African Americans learned to read? ("Freedom Readers" says they learned from their masters' families, from children, from other slaves, or they taught themselves. "From Slavery to Freedom" says they learned in schools, in churches, or from friends.)
4. **Contrast** After slavery ended, how was life different for African Americans? (They could go to school, own land, and get married. In 1870, they got the right to vote.)
5. **Explain** Why did African Americans still have many hardships after the Civil War? (Many could not get an education. They did not have money to buy land or homes. Also, some people still treated them unfairly, and they did not always have the same rights as other Americans.)

Check & Reteach
OBJECTIVE: Compare Points and Details

Have partners compare points and details from "A Chief's Son" on page 4 and "The Poet" on page 5. (Possible response: Both people were kidnapped, sold as slaves, and spoke out about slavery; a friend taught Equiano to read; her master's child taught Wheatley.)
For students who cannot compare points and details, reteach using "Freedom Fighter" on page 6 and "Farm Work" on page 9. Have students scan the text. Say: *Both texts discuss the end of slavery. Page 5 tells how Douglass helped end slavery. Page 9 explains that after slavery ended, former slaves still did not have true freedom.* List information from each text, and help students compare and contrast the important points and key details. (Possible response: The first text describes how Douglass worked hard to help end slavery. The second text gives details about the problems freed slaves faced, such as no money to buy land.)

BL › BELOW LEVEL 350L

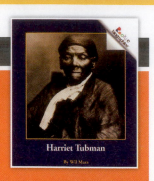

Harriet Tubman
by Wil Mara

Content Connection:
Abolitionists

Biography | Pages: 32 | Lexile: 350L | GR: K

BL › BELOW LEVEL 520L

Helen Keller: Courage in the Dark
by Johanna Hurwitz

Content Connection: **Activists**

Biography | Pages: 48 | Lexile: 520L | GR: N

OBJECTIVES

Thematic Connection: Heroes Then and Now

Read and Comprehend Informational Text

☑ **Plan and Monitor: Monitor and Clarify**

☑ **Make Comparisons**

PROGRAM RESOURCES

PRINT & TECHNOLOGY

Practice Master SG1.15, page SG42
Practice Master SG1.16, page SG43
Practice Master SG1.17, page SG44
Practice Master SG1.21, page SG48

SUGGESTED PACING

DAY 2 Introduce and read pages 3–15
DAY 3 Read pages 16–29 and discuss
DAY 4 Reteach or conduct intervention
DAY 5 Connect across texts

Summary
Harriet Tubman was born into slavery around 1820 in Maryland. In 1849, she escaped to freedom in Pennsylvania. Tubman joined the Underground Railroad and helped over 300 slaves escape. During the Civil War, Tubman worked as a nurse and a spy for the North. After the war, she married, bought property, and continued to help African Americans for the rest of her life.

Activate Prior Knowledge
Ask: *What does freedom mean to you? What do you think it would be like if you were not free?*

Build Background
Explain that for about 250 years in the United States, it was legal to own African Americans. Slavery was a way of life in the southern United States and continued until 1865, when the Thirteenth Amendment was added to the Constitution, freeing the nation's four million slaves.

Story Words
Use **Practice Master SG1.15** to extend vocabulary.

dangerous, page 15   *escape*, page 15   *owner*, page 19

smart, page 8   *swamp*, page 19

PROGRAM RESOURCES

PRINT & TECHNOLOGY

Practice Master SG1.15, page SG42
Practice Master SG1.16, page SG43
Practice Master SG1.18, page SG45
Practice Master SG1.21, page SG48

SUGGESTED PACING

DAY 2 Introduce and read pages 4–23
DAY 3 Read pages 24–48 and discuss
DAY 4 Reteach or conduct intervention
DAY 5 Connect across texts

Summary
Helen Keller was born in 1880. By the time she was a year and a half old, an illness had left her deaf and blind. Her inability to communicate made life difficult for her family. Her parents wanted a better life for her. A teacher named Annie Sullivan taught Helen to use sign language. She also learned to read lips by touch, read braille, and even speak. Helen Keller's determination continues to inspire people today.

Activate Prior Knowledge
Ask: *What do you think life would be like if you could not see or hear? What would be some of the hardest things to do?*

Build Background
Explain that American Sign Language (ASL) is its own language and is not based on a spoken language. People use hand gestures, rather than spoken words, to speak to one another. Sign language allows many hearing impaired, or deaf, people to communicate with each other and the world.

Story Words
Use **Practice Master SG1.15** to extend vocabulary.

behave, page 6   *fever*, page 4   *progress*, page 22

silence, page 13   *stubborn*, page 14

OL ON LEVEL 680L

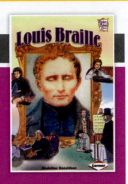

Louis Braille
by Madeline Donaldson

Content Connection:
Activists

Biography | Pages: 48 | Lexile: 680L | GR: P

AL ABOVE LEVEL 750L

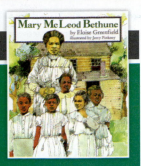

Mary McLeod Bethune
by Eloise Greenfield

Content Connection:
Educators

Biography | Pages: 32 | Lexile: 750L | GR: R

COMMON CORE STANDARDS

Reading
Read and Comprehend Text	CC.3.Rinf.10
Describe Text Structure	CC.3.Rinf.8

Writing
Write Over Shorter Time for Specific Tasks	CC.3.W.10

Speaking and Listening
Draw on Preparation to Explore Ideas	CC.3.SL.1.a

Language and Vocabulary
Acquire and Use Academic Words	CC.3.L.6

PROGRAM RESOURCES

PRINT & TECHNOLOGY
Practice Master SG1.15, page SG42
Practice Master SG1.16, page SG43
Practice Master SG1.19, page SG46
Practice Master SG1.21, page SG48

PROGRAM RESOURCES

PRINT & TECHNOLOGY
Practice Master SG1.15, page SG42
Practice Master SG1.16, page SG43
Practice Master SG1.20, page SG47
Practice Master SG1.21, page SG48

SUGGESTED PACING

DAY 2   Introduce and read pages 5–25
DAY 3   Read pages 26–45
DAY 4   Reread and discuss
DAY 5   Connect across texts

SUGGESTED PACING

DAY 2   Introduce and read pages 1–17
DAY 3   Read pages 18–32
DAY 4   Reread and discuss
DAY 5   Connect across texts

Summary   Louis Braille, born in 1809, became blind at the age of three. He attended a blind school, where he invented a system of reading and writing for the blind. Today, the braille system is used in many languages, and modern technology has allowed braille users to communicate through email and other means.

Activate Prior Knowledge   Ask: *What would life be like if you could not see? What would be hard to do without sight?*

Build Background   It was not until the 18th century when schools were developed where the blind could be educated. Before that time, it was common to send the blind to live in asylums where they were not educated.

Story Words   Use **Practice Master SG1.15** to extend vocabulary.

avoid, page 10	*curious*, page 8	*describe*, page 14
earn, page 12	*quite*, page 6	

Summary   Mary McLeod Bethune was the daughter of freed slaves. At that time, there were few schools for black children. Mary was the only one of the seventeen McLeod children to attend school. She became a teacher and dedicated her life to improving life for African Americans. She opened a school and a hospital, helped many people find jobs, and lived as an example that belief in one's self can lead to a better world.

Activate Prior Knowledge   Ask: *What do you want to be when you grow up? How would your goals be different if you were not allowed to go to school or learn to read?*

Build Background   Explain that for a period of time after slavery ended in the United States, freed slaves found it difficult to exercise their new freedoms. Few became landowners, and many continued to work on white-owned plantations.

Story Words   Use **Practice Master SG1.15** to extend vocabulary.

decision, page 16	*favorite*, page 22	*nervous*, page 9
struggle, page 26	*unpleasant*, page 15	

BL BELOW LEVEL 350L

Harriet Tubman
by Wil Mara

Build Comprehension

- **Explain** *What kind of person was Harriet Tubman?* (Possible responses: She was brave, smart, and hardworking. She helped many slaves escape, which showed her kindness.)
- **Form Generalizations** *What did freedom mean to Harriet Tubman? Why do you think so?* (Possible responses: Freedom was important to her. She took risks to escape from slavery, and she spent her life helping others to become free.)

Writing Options

- **Speech** Have students write a speech in which Harriet Tubman explains why every person should be free.
- **Interview Questions** Have students write five questions they would like to ask Harriet Tubman. Then have them share their questions with a partner.
- **Journal Entry** Invite students to write about what freedom means to them.

BL BELOW LEVEL 520L

Helen Keller: Courage in the Dark
by Johanna Hurwitz

Build Comprehension

- **Goal and Outcome** *What did Annie Sullivan want Helen to learn? Did she succeed? Explain.* (Possible response: She wanted Helen to learn to communicate with others. Helen not only learned to communicate, she learned many languages, went to college, and was a writer and speaker.)
- **Evaluate** *How did Helen's deafness and blindness affect her life?* (Possible response: She spent her life having to face many challenges, and she needed a lot of help from others, but she also might not have been such a famous and inspiring person without these challenges.)

Writing Options

- **Letter** Have students write a letter to Helen Keller telling her what they think of her life's story.
- **Thank You Note** Have students write a thank you note from Helen to Annie Sullivan, thanking her for all she did for Helen.
- **Journal Entry** Invite students to write about a challenge they had to work hard to overcome.

Check & Reteach

Ask students to make comparisons between what life was like before and after the person from each book existed. If students have difficulty making comparisons, refer them to their comparison chart. Ask: *What was life like before? What was life like after?*

DURING READING

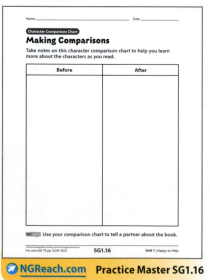

NGReach.com **Practice Master SG1.16**

AFTER READING

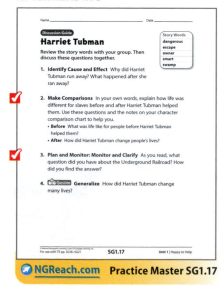

NGReach.com **Practice Master SG1.17**

AFTER READING

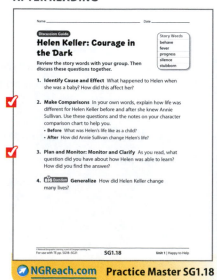

NGReach.com **Practice Master SG1.18**

OL ON LEVEL 680L

Louis Braille
by Madeline Donaldson

Build Comprehension

- **Make Comparisons** *How was Louis Braille's system of writing better than the system that already existed?* (Possible response: The old system had large print that took up many pages, and the books were hard to make. Braille's system was smaller and easier to read.)
- **Identify Problem and Solution** *What were some of the problems with Braille's first writing system?* (Possible response: The system only included French letters and sounds. It did not include letters, such as *w*, that were from other languages.)

Writing Options

- **Time Line** Invite students to write a time line of Louis Braille's life. It should include at least five important events from his life.
- **Interview** Have students write five questions they would like to ask Louis Braille. Then have them share their questions with a partner.
- **Journal Entry** Invite students to write about a challenge they have overcome.

AL ABOVE LEVEL 750L

Mary McLeod Bethune
by Eloise Greenfield

Build Comprehension

- **Goal and Outcome** *What did Mary McLeod Bethune want to do in Africa? Why did her goal change? What did she do instead?* (Possible responses: She wanted to become a missionary, but there were no jobs for black missionaries. So, Mary dedicated her life to educating African Americans.)
- **Draw Conclusions** *How did Mary McLeod Bethune help African Americans?* (Possible response: She dedicated her life to making sure African Americans received a good education. By getting a good education, she knew her students would be able to make better lives for themselves.)

Writing Options

- **Description** Have students write a list of words that describe Mary McLeod Bethune. Then have them write a paragraph about what she was like, using the words from their lists and facts from their books.
- **Speech** Have students write a speech they would give to former slaves, explaining why it is important for everyone to get a good education.
- **Journal Entry** Invite students to write about why going to school is important to them.

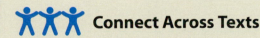 **Connect Across Texts**   **AFTER READING** Form heterogeneous groups, and have each member of the group summarize his or her book. Then have groups use **Practice Master SG1.21** to guide discussion.

AFTER READING

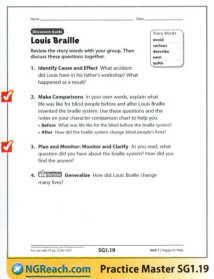

Practice Master SG1.19

AFTER READING

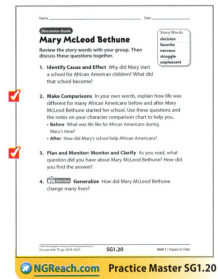

Practice Master SG1.20

AFTER READING

Practice Master SG1.21

OBJECTIVES

Thematic Connection: Heroes Then and Now

Read and Comprehend Informational Text

Explain Text Structure: Sequence

Kids Connect by Kent Page, Terrell Smith, and Peter Winkler

Summary *Kids Connect* describes the life of a young Afghan refugee in Pakistan, the reopening of schools in Afghanistan, and the creation of a school in Jerusalem for Jewish and Palestinian students. In "Garana's Story," author Kent Page introduces Garana, a ten-year-old refugee living in Pakistan. Her family's life is difficult, but Garana attends school and learns English. She hopes to return home once peace is restored to her country. "Back to School" by Terrell Smith explains how U.S. students donated money for supplies after schools reopened in Afghanistan. In "Making Friends," author Peter Winkler describes the Hand in Hand School in Jerusalem, a school for both Jewish and Palestinian students. This unique school works to bridge differences between the two communities in Israel.

Activate Prior Knowledge Display the front cover and read the title aloud. Ask: *What is a community?* (a place where people live and work) *How can young people connect with their community?* (help out; do chores; go to school)

Build Background Explain that there has been war in Afghanistan for 30 years. Many people have left for Pakistan to find peace. Also explain that in Israel, Jews and Palestinians live in separate communities. In both places, people are helping each other survive and get along. Use the maps and locator globes to point out Pakistan and Afghanistan (page 4) and Israel and Jerusalem (page 10). Have volunteers point to each location.

PROGRAM RESOURCES

PRINT ONLY

Kids Connect, **Pioneer Edition**

Kids Connect, **Pathfinder Edition**

TECHNOLOGY ONLY

My Vocabulary Notebook

COMMON CORE STANDARDS

Reading

Describe Text Structure	CC.3.Rinf.8
Read and Comprehend Informational Text	CC.3.Rinf.10

Language

Acquire and Use Domain-Specific Words	CC.3.L.6

Mini Lesson

Explain Text Structure: Sequence

Explain: *Authors use connections in a text to organize information. Often, authors describe events in sequence, or in the order they happen. Authors may include time order words such as* then, next, *and* after. Point out that good readers know how to explain the sequence connections in a text.

Read aloud the following text from page 4 of the Pioneer Edition of *Kids Connect* as students listen.

Early Morning

Garana begins her morning chores after prayers. She walks to the water pump. She fills two bottles. Then she goes home. She eats bread with hot tea for breakfast. Then she goes to the backyard. Next she sweeps the floor.

Text from Pioneer Edition

Then, think aloud to model how to identify sequence connections in a text: *In this text, the author explains what Garana does each morning. I see the heading "Early Morning." Then I see the time order words* after, then, *and* next. *These are clues that the events are being described in the order they happen:*

- *After prayers, Garana walks to the water pump and fill bottles.*
- *Then she goes home and eats breakfast.*

The author is using sequence to make connections between events.

Have students identify two more events that take place after Garana eats breakfast. Then have them explain how the events are connected in a sequence. (Events: Garana goes to the backyard. She sweeps the floor. Possible response: The author uses the time order words *then* and *next* to tell what Garana does after breakfast. The events take place in sequence. The author describes the events in the order they happen.)

BL ❭ BELOW LEVEL 400L

PIONEER EDITION
Lexile: 400L

Content Connection: Leaders

Social Studies Vocabulary

Use Wordwise on pages 6 and 11 to introduce new words:

attend　*bilingual*　*bridge*　*donate*　*organization*
peace　*refugee*

Have students add new words to **My Vocabulary Notebook**.

Build Comprehension

After reading, use the Concept Check on page 12. Remind students to use details and examples to support each answer.

1. **Details**　What does Garana do around the house to help her family? (She carries water, washes dishes, sweeps the floor, and gets bread from the bakery. She also cleans the yard, feeds the chickens, and shops for food at the store.)
2. **Evaluate**　Why does Garana like learning English? (She can understand what people are saying. Also, speaking another language makes it easier to get things done.)
3. **Explain**　How have students in the U.S. helped students in Afghanistan? (They have donated money for school supplies, such as pencils, chalk, notebooks, jump ropes, and soccer balls.)
4. **Describe**　How do teachers in the Hand in Hand School work together? (Each class has two teachers. One speaks in Arabic; one speaks in Hebrew. They plan and teach lessons together.)
5. **Explain Text Structure: Sequence**　What do Hand in Hand School students do after classes? (They have lunch and take part in activities.) How does the author present the events that take place at school? (The author uses time order to tell the events in the order they happen.)

OL ❭ ON LEVEL 640L

PATHFINDER EDITION
Lexile: 640L

Content Connection: Leaders

Social Studies Vocabulary

Use Wordwise on pages 6 and 11 to introduce new words:

attend　*bilingual*　*bridge*　*donate*　*mission*　*organization*
peace　*refugee*

Have students add new words to **My Vocabulary Notebook**.

Build Comprehension

After reading, use the Concept Check on page 12. Remind students to use details and examples to support each answer.

1. **Details**　What household tasks does Garana do to help her family? (She carries water, washes dishes, sweeps the floor, and gets bread from the bakery. She also cleans the yard, feeds the chickens, and shops for food at the store.)
2. **Evaluate**　What is Garana's favorite subject in school? (English) Why does she like it? (She can understand what people are saying. She says that this makes it easier to get things done.)
3. **Explain**　How have students in the U.S. helped students in Afghanistan? (They have donated money for school supplies, such as pencils, chalk, notebooks, jump ropes, and soccer balls.)
4. **Describe**　How do Hand in Hand School students use activities to bridge differences? (By spending time together with sports and music, they see each other as ordinary people and form friendships that bridge differences.)
5. **Explain Text Structure: Sequence**　What do Hand in Hand School students do after classes? (have lunch, do activities) How does the author organize events that take place at school? (The author uses time order to tell events in order.)

Check & Reteach

OBJECTIVE: Explain Text Structure: Sequence

Have partners explain how the events in "Lunch Break" on page 5 are connected in a sequence. (The author uses time order to make connections between events. Time order words and phrases include "before lunch," "soon," "then," and "when she returns.")
For students who cannot explain sequence connections in a text, reteach using the first paragraph of "Afternoon and Evening" on page 5. Say: *This section describes more of Garana's day. How does the author present the events?* Have students skim the text, focusing on the events. Then have groups discuss the connections and identify the order of events. (Garana goes to the pump. She sweeps, cleans the yard, and feeds chickens. She may buy food. She does homework. The author uses sequence to connect events.)

BL   BELOW LEVEL   AD410L

BL   BELOW LEVEL   AD410L

Martin's Big Words
by Doreen Rappaport

Content Connection: **Activists**

Picture Book Biography | Pages: 40 | Lexile: AD410L | GR: L

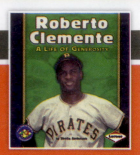

BL   BELOW LEVEL   550L

Roberto Clemente: A Life of Generosity
by Sheila Anderson

Content Connection: **Athletes**

Biography | Pages: 32 | Lexile: 550L | GR: N

OBJECTIVES

Thematic Connection: Heroes Then and Now

    Read and Comprehend Informational Text

    Plan and Monitor: Monitor and Clarify

    Make Comparisons

PROGRAM RESOURCES

PRINT & TECHNOLOGY

Practice Master SG1.22, page SG49

Practice Master SG1.23, page SG50

Practice Master SG1.24, page SG51

Practice Master SG1.28, page SG55

TECHNOLOGY ONLY

Digital Library: Segregation Signs

SUGGESTED PACING

DAY 2   Introduce and read pages 1–19

DAY 3   Read pages 8–36 and discuss

DAY 4   Reteach or conduct intervention

DAY 5   Connect across texts

Summary   Dr. Martin Luther King, Jr., grew up in the South when black people and white people were segregated. The son of a minister, Martin grew up believing that love and peace would lead the way to change. He worked with others to stand up for equal rights until he was killed in April of 1968. But his words live on.

Activate Prior Knowledge   Ask: *How does it make you feel when someone does not treat you fairly? What do you do?*

Build Background   Use photos of "Whites Only" signs from the **Digital Library** to discuss segregation in the 1960s. Explain that after the Civil War, new laws said that African Americans were not allowed to use the same water fountains, schools, hotels, restaurants, trains, or buses as white people. These laws were in effect until 1964, when the Civil Rights Act made them illegal.

Story Words   Use **Practice Master SG1.22** to extend vocabulary.

admire, page 31   *continue,* page 28   *convince,* page 24

courage, page 21   *separate,* page 16

PROGRAM RESOURCES

PRINT & TECHNOLOGY

Practice Master SG1.22, page SG49

Practice Master SG1.23, page SG50

Practice Master SG1.25, page SG52

Practice Master SG1.28, page SG55

SUGGESTED PACING

DAY 2   Introduce and read pages 4–18

DAY 3   Read pages 19–30 and discuss

DAY 4   Reteach or conduct intervention

DAY 5   Connect across texts

Summary   Roberto Clemente, born in Puerto Rico in 1934, played baseball with the Pittsburgh Pirates. He often returned to Puerto Rico, where he taught children to play baseball, visited sick children, and planned to build a free sports center for children. He was killed in a plane crash on his way to help after an earthquake in Nicaragua. His family built the sports center and named it after him.

Activate Prior Knowledge   Ask: *What does it mean to be generous? When have you been generous with others?*

Build Background   Explain that in the early 1900s, Major League Baseball was segregated. But, in 1911, two Latino players from Cuba joined. Over time, more Latino players joined, mostly from Cuba. In the 1940s, Latinos from other countries, including Puerto Rico, joined in greater numbers.

Story Words   Use **Practice Master SG1.22** to extend vocabulary.

decide, page 24   *load,* page 23   *selfish,* page 15

special, page 19   *travel,* page 17

OL ▶ ON LEVEL

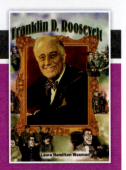

Franklin D. Roosevelt
by Laura Hamilton Waxman

Content Connection:
World Leaders

Biography | Pages: 48

AL ▶ ABOVE LEVEL 770L

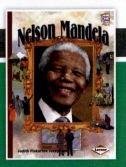

Nelson Mandela
by Judith Pinkerton Josephson

Content Connection:
World Leaders

Biography | Pages: 48 | Lexile: 770L | GR: R

COMMON CORE STANDARDS

Reading
Read and Comprehend Text	CC.3.Rinf.10
Describe Text Structure	CC.3.Rinf.8

Writing
Write Over Shorter Time for Specific Tasks	CC.3.W.10

Speaking and Listening
Draw on Preparation to Explore Ideas	CC.3.SL.1.a

Language and Vocabulary
Acquire and Use Academic Words	CC.3.L.6

PROGRAM RESOURCES

PRINT & TECHNOLOGY
Practice Master SG1.22, page SG49
Practice Master SG1.23, page SG50
Practice Master SG1.26, page SG53
Practice Master SG1.28, page SG55

PROGRAM RESOURCES

PRINT & TECHNOLOGY   **TECHNOLOGY ONLY**
Practice Master SG1.22, page SG49   **Map of the World**
Practice Master SG1.23, page SG50
Practice Master SG1.27, page SG54
Practice Master SG1.28, page SG55

SUGGESTED PACING

DAY 2	Introduce and read pages 4–26
DAY 3	Read pages 27–45
DAY 4	Reread and discuss
DAY 5	Connect across texts

SUGGESTED PACING

DAY 2	Introduce and read pages 4–25
DAY 3	Read pages 26–45
DAY 4	Reread and discuss
DAY 5	Connect across texts

Summary Franklin D. Roosevelt, born in 1882, dreamed of being President of the United States. He did not let his disability—he used a cane and a wheel chair—stop him. During his three terms as president, he started many new programs that provided jobs and help to the unemployed during the Great Depression.

Activate Prior Knowledge Ask: *What do you think the President does?*

Build Background Explain that the Great Depression began in 1929 and lasted until the start of World War II in the early 1940s. During this time, many people in the United States did not have jobs and were very poor.

Story Words Use **Practice Master SG1.22** to extend vocabulary.

citizen, page 13	*collection*, page 7	*comfort*, page 27
confident, page 23	*private*, page 7	

Summary Nelson Mandela was born in 1918, in a small South African village. When Nelson left the village, he learned about the inequality between black and white South Africans, and he joined protests against apartheid. He was arrested and sentenced to life in prison. After ten thousand days, he was set free and, in 1994, he became the president of South Africa.

Activate Prior Knowledge Ask: *Do you know someone who has stood up for something he or she believes in? Tell about him or her. What do you think of that person?*

Build Background Display the world map from the **Digital Library** and point to South Africa. Explain that between 1948 and 1994, the government in South Africa did not give black South Africans the same rights as white South Africans. This system of laws was called *apartheid*, which means "apartness," because black people and white people were kept apart.

Story Words Use **Practice Master SG1.22** to extend vocabulary.

haul, page 8	*limit*, page 5	*stern*, page 12
urge, page 36	*wealth*, page 23	

BL BELOW LEVEL AD410L

Martin's Big Words
by Doreen Rappaport

Build Comprehension
- **Explain** *Why did Martin Luther King, Jr., win the Nobel Peace Prize?* (He taught people to fight with words, not fists.)
- **Identify Problem and Solution** *What happened when a white man told Rosa Parks to give up her seat on a bus? How did the black citizens of Montgomery react?* (She refused to get up and was arrested. Black citizens were so angry that they decided not to ride the bus anymore, until the law was changed.)

Writing Options
- **Interview Questions** Have students write five questions they would like to ask Dr. Martin Luther King, Jr. Then have them share their questions with a partner.
- **Opinion Statement** Rosa Parks broke the law when she refused to give up her seat on the bus. Invite students to tell whether or not they think she did the right thing and why they think so.
- **Journal Entry** Invite students to write about how they can handle a difficult situation in a peaceful way.

BL BELOW LEVEL 550L

Roberto Clemente: A Life of Generosity
by Sheila Anderson

Build Comprehension
- **Explain** *How did Roberto Clemente show generosity?* (Possible response: He always helped children, taught children baseball, and visited hospitals. He wanted to build a sports center that would be free for children.)
- **Draw Conclusions** *Why do you think Roberto Clemente's family built the sports center after he died?* (Possible response: They knew it was very important to him, and they wanted people to remember him.)

Writing Options
- **List** Have children write a list of words that describe Roberto Clemente. Then have them write a few sentences about him using those words.
- **Building Plan** Have students draw a design for their own sports center for kids. Then have them write a few sentences describing the center.
- **Journal Entry** Invite students to write about a time someone was generous toward them or they were generous toward someone else and tell how it felt.

Check & Reteach
Ask students to make comparisons between what life was like before and after the person from each book existed. If students have difficulty making comparisons, refer them to their Venn diagram. Ask: *What was life like before this person changed things? What was life like after? What stayed the same?*

DURING READING

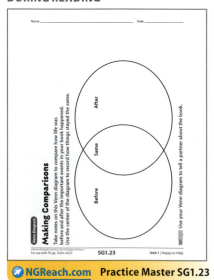

AFTER READING

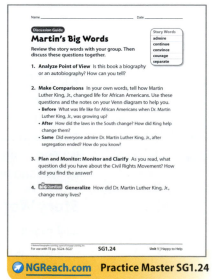

AFTER READING

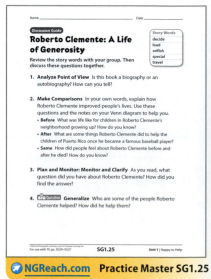

OL ▸ ON LEVEL

Franklin D. Roosevelt
by Laura Hamilton Waxman

Build Comprehension

- **Identify Problem and Solution** *Why did Franklin D. Roosevelt think his disability might be a problem?* (He thought people might not want to vote for someone in a wheelchair.) *How did he solve this problem?* (He taught himself how to stand without a wheelchair, and he wore braces under his pants. No one noticed his disability.)
- **Explain** *What was life like during the Great Depression?* (Possible response: Many people lost their jobs and their homes. People could not afford to buy the things they needed. Many businesses shut down.)

Writing Options

- **Speech** Have students write a speech in which Franklin D. Roosevelt tells Americans not to give up hope and tells why.
- **News Brief** Have students write a news brief in which they announce Franklin D. Roosevelt's death and give details that tell about his life.
- **Journal Entry** Invite students to write about what they would do for the country if they were the president.

AL ▸ ABOVE LEVEL 770L

Nelson Mandela
by Judith Pinkerton Josephson

Build Comprehension

- **Explain** *What is apartheid? Give an example from the book.* (Possible responses: Apartheid was a set of laws in South Africa to keep white people and black people apart. For example, black people in South Africa could not walk on the sidewalk in white neighborhoods.)
- **Form Opinions** *Nelson Mandela's given name meant "troublemaker." Do you think this fits his life's story? Explain.* (Possible response: Yes, it fits because Nelson was not happy with how life was in South Africa, and he got into trouble when he tried to change things.)

Writing Options

- **Book Review** Have students write a book review telling about the book, whether or not they liked it, and why.
- **Friendly Letter** Have students write a letter from Nelson Mandela, while he was in prison, to his wife, telling her about what he is doing to improve conditions for the prisoners.
- **Journal Entry** Invite students to write about something they do not think is fair that they think should change.

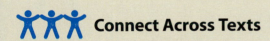 **Connect Across Texts**

AFTER READING Form heterogeneous groups, and have each member of the group summarize his or her book. Then have groups use **Practice Master SG1.28** to guide discussion.

AFTER READING

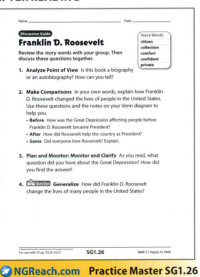

NGReach.com **Practice Master SG1.26**

AFTER READING

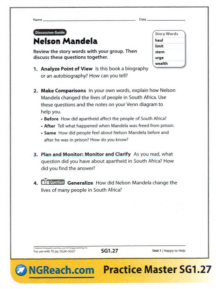

NGReach.com **Practice Master SG1.27**

AFTER READING

NGReach.com **Practice Master SG1.28**

Academic Vocabulary

Story Words

A Chance to Shine

boss (baws) *noun*
The **boss** is the person who is in charge. *I have to call my boss if I am going to be late for work.*

chance (chans) *noun*
A **chance** is an opportunity for something. *He knew he could hit a home run if the coach would give him a chance to play.*

deal (dēl) *noun*
A **deal** is an agreement two people make. *My mom and I have a deal that if I eat all my dinner, I'll get dessert.*

recognize (rek-ig-nīz) *verb*
If you **recognize** someone, you know and remember the person. *They recognize the movie star from the poster.*

rent (rent) *verb*
To **rent** something means to pay money to use it. *We should rent some bikes to tour the city.*

Tomás and the Library Lady

borrow (bä-rō) *verb*
If you **borrow** something, you take it and use it for a while and then return it. *You can borrow my books, but I'll need them back next week.*

ceiling (sē-ling) *noun*
A **ceiling** is the space at the top of all the walls around a room. *We will paint the walls blue and the ceiling white.*

eager (ē-gur) *adjective*
If you are **eager**, you are excited or interested about something. *After a long summer, he is eager to start school.*

howl (howl) *verb*
A **howl** is a long, loud cry. *We listened for the howl of wolves when we were camping under the full moon.*

press (pres) *verb*
If you **press** something, you push it against something else. *Press the button in the elevator to close the doors.*

The Quiltmaker's Gift

arrive (u-rīv) *verb*
When you **arrive** somewhere, you get there. *We will arrive home in time for dinner.*

grateful (grāt-ful) *adjective*
To be **grateful** means to feel thanks. *I am grateful for the gift you gave me.*

recall (rē-cal) *verb*
To **recall** something means to remember it. *I can't recall what my math homework is.*

seize (sēz) *verb*
To **seize** something means to take it by force. *If you are not careful, the other team will seize the ball.*

wander (wan-dur) *verb*
To **wander** means to move around without a reason. *Because it is a beautiful day, we should wander around outside.*

The Quiltmaker's Journey

awkward (aw-kwurd) *adjective*
When something is **awkward**, it is not graceful. *I look awkward when I dance.*

creature (crē-chur) *noun*
A **creature** is a made-up being. *We heard many stories about a scary creature in the woods.*

deed (dēd) *noun*
A **deed** is something you do. *Helping your neighbor shovel snow is a good deed.*

furious (fyur-ē-us) *adjective*
If you are **furious**, you are very angry. *I was furious when my sister put gum in my hair.*

toil (toil) *verb*
To **toil** means to work very hard. *If we toil in the garden today, we'll have many vegetables in a few weeks.*

Name _____ Date _____

Story Map

Plot

Take notes on this story map to put the events of the story in order as you read.

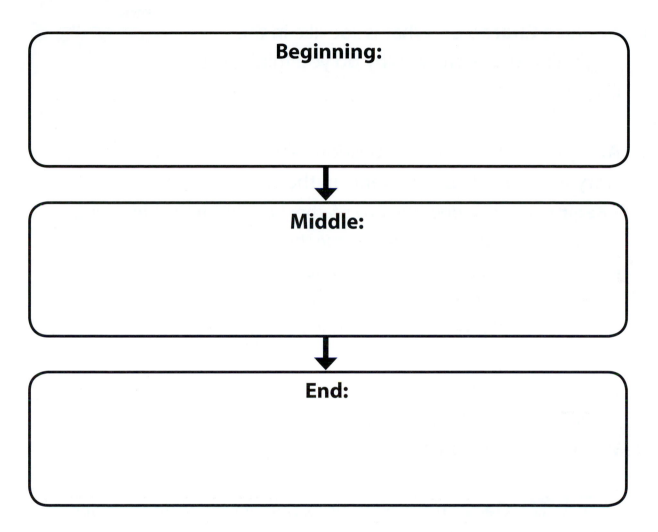

Beginning:

Middle:

End:

Use your story map to tell a partner about the book.

© National Geographic Learning, a part of Cengage Learning, Inc.
For use with TE pp. SG6–SG9 **SG1.2** **Unit 1** | Happy to Help

Name _____ Date _____

Discussion Guide

A Chance to Shine

Review the story words with your group. Then discuss these questions together.

Story Words
- boss
- chance
- deal
- recognize
- rent

1. **Analyze Character** What is Joe like in the beginning of the story? Why do you think he is like this?

2. **Analyze Plot** Use these questions and the notes in your story map to talk about events in the story.
   - **Beginning** How does the boy's father help Joe in the beginning of the story? Why does this surprise the boy?
   - **Middle** How does Joe's life begin to change?
   - **End** How has meeting Joe caused the boy to treat kids at school differently? Why do you think this is?

3. **Plan and Monitor: Preview and Predict** What did you think would happen when Joe got the job sweeping the sidewalk? Was your prediction correct?

4. **BIG Question** **Generalize** How does one act of kindness make a difference in Joe's life?

SG1.3

Name _____ Date _____

Discussion Guide

Tomás and the Library Lady

Review the story words with your group. Then discuss these questions together.

Story Words

borrow
ceiling
eager
howl
press

1. **Analyze Character** How does Tomás feel about his Papá Grande? Why do you think so?

2. **Analyze Plot** Use these questions and the notes in your story map to talk about events in the story.
   - **Beginning** Why does Tomás first visit the library?
   - **Middle** How does Tomás become a teacher to both Papá Grande and the library lady?
   - **End** Why does Tomás stop visiting the library? What does the library lady give Tomás?

3. **Plan and Monitor: Preview and Predict** What did you think would happen when Tomás entered the library for the first time? Was your prediction correct?

4. **BIG Question Generalize** How does one act of kindness make a difference in Tomás's life?

Discussion Guide

The Quiltmaker's Gift

Review the story words with your group. Then discuss these questions together.

Story Words
- arrive
- grateful
- recall
- seize
- wander

1. **Analyze Character** Do you think the king and the quiltmaker are alike? Why do you think so?

2. **Analyze Plot** Use these questions and the notes in your story map to talk about events in the story.
   - **Beginning** What is the king like in the beginning of the story? Why does the quiltmaker refuse to make a quilt for the king?
   - **Middle** How does the king begin to change? Why does he change?
   - **End** Why does the quiltmaker give the king a quilt? Why is the king surprised by the quiltmaker's gift?

3. **Plan and Monitor: Preview and Predict** What did you think would happen when the king demanded a quilt from the quiltmaker? Was your prediction correct?

4. **BIG Question** **Generalize** How do the king's acts of kindness make a difference in his own life?

COPY READY

Discussion Guide

The Quiltmaker's Journey

Review the story words with your group. Then discuss these questions together.

Story Words
awkward
creature
deed
furious
toil

1. **Analyze Character** Why do you think the quiltmaker wants to leave the town, even though she would lose all her money? How is she different from the town Elders?

2. **Analyze Plot** Use these questions and the notes in your story map to talk about events in the story.
   - **Beginning** Why does the quiltmaker leave town? What surprises her on the other side of the wall? Why does this surprise her?
   - **Middle** How do people treat the quiltmaker outside of the town? Give an example.
   - **End** How does the girl find a way to help the people outside of the town? How does this make her feel?

3. **Plan and Monitor: Preview and Predict** What did you think would happen when the quiltmaker left her town? Was your prediction correct?

4. **Big Question** **Generalize** How do the poor make a difference in the quiltmaker's life by being kind to her? What does she learn from them?

Discussion Guide

Connect Across Texts

Share the story words with your group. Then take notes as you listen to each summary.

A Chance to Shine
Tomás and the Library Lady
The Quiltmaker's Gift
The Quiltmaker's Journey

Compare and contrast the books you have read. Discuss these questions with your group.

1. Why is it everyone's responsibility to be kind to others? Explain why you think so.

2. How do we help ourselves when we are kind to others? How do we feel when we are unkind?

3. **BIG Question** How can one act of kindness make a difference in someone's life? Give an example from your books.

Name _____ Date _____

Story Words

New York's Bravest

danger (dān-jur) *noun*
Danger is something that can harm you. *If you don't wear a seatbelt, you are in **danger** of getting hurt in a crash.*

famous (fā-mus) *adjective*
Someone who is **famous** is known by many people. *The actor is **famous** because she has been in many movies.*

ragged (rag-ud) *adjective*
Something that is **ragged** is worn out. *I'll save this **ragged** shirt to wear when we paint the house.*

rumor (rü-mur) *noun*
A **rumor** is a bit of information that might or might not be true. *We heard a **rumor** that they are going to open a grocery store in our town.*

wedge (wej) *verb*
To **wedge** something means to press something into a narrow space. *Please **wedge** the doorstop under the door to hold it open.*

The Snow Walker

frantic (fran-tik) *adjective*
If you are **frantic**, you are wildly excited or upset. *I felt **frantic** when I couldn't find my grandfather's watch.*

imagine (im-aj-un) *verb*
When you **imagine** something, you see a picture of it in your mind. *When I am cold, I like to **imagine** I am in front of a warm fire.*

ledge (lej) *noun*
A **ledge** is flat shelf that sticks out of a wall. *She is growing flowers in a pot on the window **ledge**.*

lonely (lōn-lē) *adjective*
When you are **lonely**, you feel sad because no one else is around. *I felt **lonely** after my friend moved away.*

medicine (me-du-sun) *noun*
Medicine is something you take when you are sick to help you feel better. *I took some **medicine** to make my fever go away.*

Passage to Freedom

approach (u-prōch) *verb*
When you **approach** something, you get closer to it. *It is not a good idea to **approach** a wild animal.*

celebration (sel-u-brā-shun) *noun*
A **celebration** is a special event in honor of someone or something. *We will have cake at my birthday **celebration**.*

encourage (in-kur-ij) *verb*
When you **encourage** someone, you tell that person they should try something. *I will **encourage** him to try out for the play because he is talented.*

permission (pur-mi-shun) *noun*
If you give someone **permission**, you allow the person to do something. *Mom and Dad gave me **permission** to go on the field trip.*

reply (rē-plī) *noun*
When you **reply** to someone, you give the person an answer. *When the teacher asks a question, I think before I **reply**.*

Mercedes and the Chocolate Pilot

capture (kap-chur) *verb*
To **capture** something means to take it by force. *We will call animal control to **capture** the raccoon in the attic.*

personal (pur-su-nul) *adjective*
If something is **personal**, it is done directly from one person to another. *The manager promised to give the matter her **personal** attention.*

promise (prä-mus) *verb*
If you give someone a **promise**, you give the person your word that you will do something. *I **promise** to keep your secret.*

scold (skold) *verb*
If you **scold** someone, you tell the person he or she did something wrong. *If we don't clean up the mess, Mom will **scold** us.*

shelter (shel-tur) *noun*
A **shelter** is a covering that gives protection. *During the rainstorm, we found **shelter** in the barn.*

For use with TE pp. SG12–SG15   **SG1.8**   Unit 1 | Happy to Help

Name _____ Date _____

Analyze Character

Take notes on this character description chart to help you learn more about the characters as you read.

Character	What the Character Does	What This Shows About the Character

 Use your character description chart to tell a partner about the book.

For use with TE pp. SG12–SG15   **SG1.9**   **Unit 1** | Happy to Help

COPY READY

Discussion Guide

New York's Bravest

Review the story words with your group. Then discuss these questions together.

Story Words
- danger
- famous
- ragged
- rumor
- wedge

1. **Analyze Setting** What is it like where the story takes place? How does the setting help to make Mose a big hero?

2. **Analyze Character** In your own words, tell about the main character in *New York's Bravest*. Use these questions and the notes on the character description chart to help you.
   - **Character** Who is the main character of the story?
   - **What the Character Does** How does Mose help people?
   - **What This Shows About the Character** How can you tell what kind of person Mose is by the things that he does?

3. **Plan and Monitor: Preview and Predict** What did you think would happen when Mose went into the hotel fire? Was your prediction correct?

4. **BIG Question** **Generalize** How does Mose's kindness make him a hero?

Discussion Guide

The Snow Walker

Review the story words with your group. Then discuss these questions together.

Story Words
frantic
imagine
ledge
lonely
medicine

1. **Analyze Setting** Describe what it is like where the story takes place. How does this setting give Milton a chance to show he is a hero?

2. **Analyze Character** In your own words, tell about the main character in *The Snow Walker*. Use these questions and the notes on the character description chart to help you.
   - **Character** Who is the main character of the story?
   - **What the Character Does** Tell about something important this character does.
   - **What This Shows About the Character** How do the character's actions tell the reader what kind of person he or she is?

3. **Plan and Monitor: Preview and Predict** What did you think would happen when Milton's snowshoes began to break? Was your prediction correct?

4. **BIG Question** **Generalize** How does Milton's kindness make him a hero?

Name _____ Date _____

Discussion Guide

Passage to Freedom

Review the story words with your group. Then discuss these questions together.

Story Words
approach
celebration
encourage
permission
reply

1. **Analyze Setting** What is it like where the story takes place? Why do the Jewish people need Sugihara's help here?

2. **Analyze Character** In your own words, tell about the main character in *Passage to Freedom*. Use these questions and the notes on the character description chart to help you.
   - **Character** Who is the main character of the story?
   - **What the Character Does** Tell about something important this character does.
   - **What This Shows About the Character** How do the character's actions tell the reader what kind of person he or she is?

3. **Plan and Monitor: Preview and Predict** What did you think would happen when Sugihara went against the wishes of the Japanese government? Was your prediction correct?

4.  **Generalize** How does Sugihara's kindness make him a hero?

Discussion Guide

Mercedes and the Chocolate Pilot

Review the story words with your group. Then discuss these questions together.

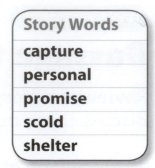

Story Words

capture

personal

promise

scold

shelter

1. **Analyze Setting** Where does the story take place? What is life like here for many families?

2. **Analyze Character** In your own words, tell about the main characters in *Mercedes and the Chocolate Pilot*. Use these questions and the notes on the character description chart to help you.
   - **Character** Who are the main characters of the story?
   - **What the Character Does** Tell about something important each of these characters does.
   - **What This Shows About the Character** How do each character's actions tell the reader what kind of person he or she is?

3. **Plan and Monitor: Preview and Predict** What did you think would happen when Mercedes did not catch any candy that was dropped by the pilot? Was your prediction correct?

4. **BIG Question** **Generalize** How does the pilot's kindness make him a hero?

SG1.13

COPY READY

Name _____ Date _____

Discussion Guide

Connect Across Texts

Share the story words with your group. Then take notes as you listen to each summary.

New York's Bravest
The Snow Walker
Passage to Freedom
Mercedes and the Chocolate Pilot

Compare and contrast the books you have read. Discuss these questions with your group.

1. What do the characters in each of the books do that is heroic?

2. Why do you think the characters in these books took risks for others?

3. **BIG Question** How do each of these books show us how kindness can make you a hero?

Academic Vocabulary
Story Words

Harriet Tubman

dangerous (**dān**-jur-us) *adjective*
Something that is **dangerous** can harm you. *It is too **dangerous** to walk that close to the edge of the cliff.*

escape (i-**skāp**) *verb*
When you **escape** from something, you get away from it. *If you leave the gate open, the dog will **escape** from the yard.*

owner (**ō**-nur) *noun*
An **owner** is the person something belongs to. *We returned the lost keys to their **owner**.*

smart (**smärt**) *adjective*
When you are **smart**, you learn and understand things easily. *My sister gets good grades because she is **smart** and studies hard.*

swamp (**swamp**) *noun*
A **swamp** is a wetland area. *Many alligators live in this **swamp**.*

Helen Keller: Courage in the Dark

behave (bē-**hāv**) *verb*
The way you **behave** is the way you act. *You must **behave** differently in class than you do on the playground.*

fever (**fē**-vur) *noun*
You have a **fever** when your body temperature is higher than normal. *I feel hot when I have a **fever**.*

progress (**prä**-grus) *noun*
Progress happens when something is getting better. *My B+ on the test shows I am making **progress** in math.*

silence (**sī**-luns) *noun*
Silence means complete quiet. *There was **silence** in the audience when she spoke because everyone wanted to hear.*

stubborn (**stu**-burn) *adjective*
Someone **stubborn** is not willing to change their mind. *The **stubborn** mule would not move an inch.*

Louis Braille

avoid (u-**void**) *verb*
When you **avoid** something, you try to stay away from it. ***Avoid** the bee's nest while you are playing outside so that you are not stung.*

curious (**kyur**-ē-us) *adjective*
If you are **curious**, you want to know about something. *I was **curious** to learn more about the Civil War, so I looked online.*

describe (dis-**krīb**) *verb*
When you **describe** something, you give details about it. *When you **describe** your vacation, I feel like I was there.*

earn (**urn**) *verb*
When you **earn** something, you deserve it because you worked hard for it. *Our teacher said that to get an A, you have to work hard to **earn** it.*

quite (**kwīt**) *adjective*
Quite means very much. *We were **quite** happy with how well our choir did in the concert.*

Mary McLeod Bethune

decision (di-**si**-shun) *noun*
To make a **decision** means to choose one option and stick with it. *We finally made a **decision** about which movie to see.*

favorite (**fā**-vu-rut) *adjective*
If something is your **favorite**, it is the one you like best. *Chocolate is my **favorite** ice cream flavor.*

nervous (**nur**-vus) *adjective*
If you are **nervous**, you are worried and uncomfortable. *She was **nervous** to perform in the piano recital.*

struggle (**stru**-gul) *verb*
If you **struggle**, you work hard to overcome obstacles. *We had to **struggle** to get the boat into the water.*

unpleasant (un-**ple**-zent) *adjective*
If something is **unpleasant**, you don't enjoy it. *There was an **unpleasant** smell in the house after I burned the toast.*

Name _____ Date _____

Character Comparison Chart

Making Comparisons

Take notes on this character comparison chart to help you learn more about the characters as you read.

Before	After

 Use your comparison chart to tell a partner about the book.

Discussion Guide

Harriet Tubman

Review the story words with your group. Then discuss these questions together.

Story Words
- dangerous
- escape
- owner
- smart
- swamp

1. **Identify Cause and Effect** Why did Harriet Tubman run away? What happened after she ran away?

2. **Make Comparisons** In your own words, explain how life was different for slaves before and after Harriet Tubman helped them. Use these questions and the notes on your character comparison chart to help you.
   - **Before** What was life like for people before Harriet Tubman helped them?
   - **After** How did Harriet Tubman change people's lives?

3. **Plan and Monitor: Monitor and Clarify** As you read, what question did you have about the Underground Railroad? How did you find the answer?

4. **BIG Question** **Generalize** How did Harriet Tubman change many lives?

Discussion Guide

Helen Keller: Courage in the Dark

Review the story words with your group. Then discuss these questions together.

Story Words
- behave
- fever
- progress
- silence
- stubborn

1. **Identify Cause and Effect** What happened to Helen when she was a baby? How did this affect her?

2. **Make Comparisons** In your own words, explain how life was different for Helen Keller before and after she knew Annie Sullivan. Use these questions and the notes on your character comparison chart to help you.
   - **Before** What was Helen's life like as a child?
   - **After** How did Annie Sullivan change Helen's life?

3. **Plan and Monitor: Monitor and Clarify** As you read, what question did you have about how Helen was able to learn? How did you find the answer?

4. **BIG Question** **Generalize** How did Helen Keller change many lives?

Discussion Guide

Louis Braille

Review the story words with your group. Then discuss these questions together.

Story Words

avoid

curious

describe

earn

quite

1. **Identify Cause and Effect** What accident did Louis have in his father's workshop? What happened as a result?

2. **Make Comparisons** In your own words, explain what life was like for blind people before and after Louis Braille invented the braille system. Use these questions and the notes on your character comparison chart to help you.
   - **Before** What was life like for the blind before the braille system?
   - **After** How did the braille system change blind people's lives?

3. **Plan and Monitor: Monitor and Clarify** As you read, what question did you have about the braille system? How did you find the answer?

4. **BIG Question** **Generalize** How did Louis Braille change many lives?

Discussion Guide

Mary McLeod Bethune

Review the story words with your group. Then discuss these questions together.

Story Words

decision

favorite

nervous

struggle

unpleasant

1. **Identify Cause and Effect** Why did Mary start a school for African American children? What did that school become?

2. **Make Comparisons** In your own words, explain how life was different for many African Americans before and after Mary McLeod Bethune started her school. Use these questions and the notes on your character comparison chart to help you.
   - **Before** What was life like for African Americans during Mary's time?
   - **After** How did Mary's school help African Americans?

3. **Plan and Monitor: Monitor and Clarify** As you read, what question did you have about Mary McLeod Bethune? How did you find the answer?

4. **BIG Question Generalize** How did Mary McLeod Bethune change many lives?

Discussion Guide

Connect Across Texts

Share the story words with your group. Then take notes as you listen to each summary.

Harriet Tubman
Helen Keller: Courage in the Dark
Louis Braille
Mary McLeod Bethune

Compare and contrast the books you have read. Discuss these questions with your group.

1. What makes the people from your book heroes?

2. What was something you wanted to know as you read your book? What is something you learned?

3. **BIG Question** How do the books show us that one person can change many lives?

Academic Vocabulary

Story Words

Martin's Big Words

admire (ad-**mīr**) *verb*
When you **admire** someone, you think highly of that person. *I **admire** her because she is kind and helpful.*

continue (kun-**tin**-yü) *verb*
When you **continue**, you keep going. *We are enjoying this nice weather, and we hope it will **continue**.*

convince (kun-**vints**) *verb*
When you **convince** someone, you get that person to agree to something. *What will it take to **convince** you to eat your vegetables?*

courage (**kur**-ij) *noun*
If you have **courage**, you are not afraid. *I will have to show **courage** when I give my speech.*

separate (**sep**-rut) *adjective*
If two things are **separate**, they are kept apart. *My brother and I have **separate** rooms.*

Roberto Clemente: A Life of Generosity

decide (di-**sīd**) *verb*
When you **decide** something, you make a choice. *Let's **decide** which movie to see.*

load (**lōd**) *verb*
To **load** something means to fill a container with something heavy. *We will **load** the rocks into the wheelbarrow to move them out of the garden.*

selfish (**sel**-fish) *adjective*
If you are **selfish**, you want everything for yourself. *It would be **selfish** of you to not share your toys.*

special (**spe**-shul) *adjective*
Something that is **special** is unusual or important. *The watch was a **special** gift from his grandfather.*

travel (**tra**-vul) *verb*
When you **travel**, you go on a trip. *This summer, we will **travel** to Florida for vacation.*

Franklin D. Roosevelt

citizen (**si**-tu-zun) *noun*
A **citizen** of a place is a person who lives there. *I am a **citizen** of the United States of America.*

collection (ku-**lek**-shun) *noun*
A **collection** is a group of related things. *She is proud of her stamp **collection**.*

comfort (**kum**-furt) *verb*
When you **comfort** someone, you make the person feel better. *I know my friends will **comfort** me when I am sad.*

confident (**kän**-fi-dunt) *adjective*
When you are **confident** about something, you feel good about it. *I am **confident** I will get a good grade because I studied hard.*

private (**prī**-vut) *adjective*
Something that is **private** is not meant for everyone. *The museum was closed to the public because of a **private** party.*

Nelson Mandela

haul (**hawl**) *verb*
To **haul** means to carry something heavy over a distance. *We had to **haul** our suitcases up two flights of stairs.*

limit (**lim**-ut) *verb*
If you **limit** something, you set an amount for it. *My parents **limit** me to two hours of television a night.*

stern (**sturn**) *adjective*
If you are **stern**, you are very serious. *My mother gave me a **stern** look that told me I should stop talking.*

urge (**urj**) *verb*
If you **urge** someone to do something, you try to get that person to do it. *I want to **urge** you to change your mind about what color to paint the room.*

wealth (**welth**) *noun*
Wealth is a large amount of money. *If you have great **wealth**, you should give to the poor.*

For use with TE pp. SG24–SG27   **SG1.22**   **Unit 1** | Happy to Help

Name _____   Date _____

Venn Diagram

Making Comparisons

Take notes on this Venn diagram to compare how life was before and after the important events in your book happened. Use the center of the diagram to record how things stayed the same.

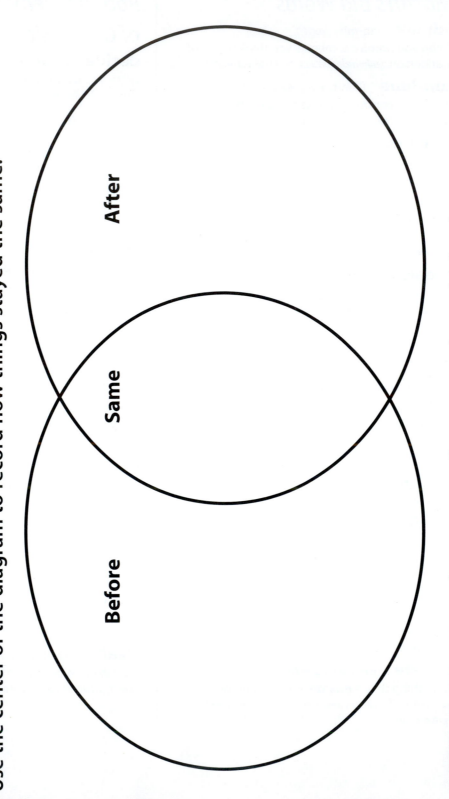

Before

Same

After

Use your Venn diagram to tell a partner about the book.

© National Geographic Learning, a part of Cengage Learning, Inc.
For use with TE pp. SG24–SG27

SG1.23

Unit 1 | Happy to Help

Discussion Guide

Martin's Big Words

Review the story words with your group. Then discuss these questions together.

Story Words

admire

continue

convince

courage

separate

1. **Analyze Point of View** Is this book a biography or an autobiography? How can you tell?

2. **Make Comparisons** In your own words, tell how Martin Luther King, Jr., changed life for African Americans. Use these questions and the notes on your Venn diagram to help you.
   - **Before** What was life like for African Americans when Dr. Martin Luther King, Jr., was growing up?
   - **After** How did the laws in the South change? How did King help change them?
   - **Same** Did everyone admire Dr. Martin Luther King, Jr., after segregation ended? How do you know?

3. **Plan and Monitor: Monitor and Clarify** As you read, what question did you have about the Civil Rights Movement? How did you find the answer?

4. **BIG Question** **Generalize** How did Dr. Martin Luther King, Jr., change many lives?

For use with TE pp. SG24–SG27   **SG1.24**   Unit 1 | Happy to Help

Discussion Guide

Roberto Clemente: A Life of Generosity

Review the story words with your group. Then discuss these questions together.

Story Words
decide
load
selfish
special
travel

1. **Analyze Point of View** Is this book a biography or an autobiography? How can you tell?

2. **Make Comparisons** In your own words, explain how Roberto Clemente improved people's lives. Use these questions and the notes on your Venn diagram to help you.
   - **Before** What was life like for children in Roberto Clemente's neighborhood growing up? How do you know?
   - **After** What are some things Roberto Clemente did to help the children of Puerto Rico once he became a famous baseball player?
   - **Same** How did people feel about Roberto Clemente before and after he died? How do you know?

3. **Plan and Monitor: Monitor and Clarify** As you read, what question did you have about Roberto Clemente? How did you find the answer?

4. **BIG Question Generalize** Who are some of the people Roberto Clemente helped? How did he help them?

Discussion Guide

Franklin D. Roosevelt

Review the story words with your group. Then discuss these questions together.

Story Words

citizen

collection

comfort

confident

private

1. **Analyze Point of View** Is this book a biography or an autobiography? How can you tell?

2. **Make Comparisons** In your own words, explain how Franklin D. Roosevelt changed the lives of people in the United States. Use these questions and the notes on your Venn diagram to help you.

   • **Before** How was the Great Depression affecting people before Franklin D. Roosevelt became President?

   • **After** How did Roosevelt help the country as President?

   • **Same** Did everyone love Roosevelt? Explain.

3. **Plan and Monitor: Monitor and Clarify** As you read, what question did you have about the Great Depression? How did you find the answer?

4. **BIG Question Generalize** How did Franklin D. Roosevelt change the lives of many people in the United States?

Discussion Guide

Nelson Mandela

Review the story words with your group. Then discuss these questions together.

Story Words
haul
limit
stern
urge
wealth

1. **Analyze Point of View** Is this book a biography or an autobiography? How can you tell?

2. **Make Comparisons** In your own words, explain how Nelson Mandela changed the lives of people in South Africa. Use these questions and the notes on your Venn diagram to help you.
   - **Before** How did apartheid affect the people of South Africa?
   - **After** Tell what happened when Mandela was freed from prison.
   - **Same** How did people feel about Nelson Mandela before and after he was in prison? How do you know?

3. **Plan and Monitor: Monitor and Clarify** As you read, what question did you have about apartheid in South Africa? How did you find the answer?

4. **BIG Question** **Generalize** How did Nelson Mandela change the lives of many people in South Africa?

Name _____ Date _____

Discussion Guide

Connect Across Texts

Share the story words with your group. Then take notes as you listen to each summary.

Martin's Big Words
Roberto Clemente: A Life of Generosity
Franklin D. Roosevelt
Nelson Mandela

Compare and contrast the books you have read. Discuss these questions with your group.

1. Why are the people from your books thought of as heroes?

2. How did life change for others because of the actions of the people from your books?

3. **BIG Question** How do the books show us that one person can change many lives? What do all the people in these books have in common?

Speaking and Listening Observation Log

As you monitor students in their small groups, put a check mark beside each behavior that you observe. Use conferences to coach students in developing speaking and listening skills.

Student Name

Speaking and Listening Standards

Comprehension and Collaboration

1. Engage effectively in a range of collaborative discussions (one-on-one, in groups, and teacher-led) with diverse partners on *grade 3 topics and texts*, building on others' ideas and expressing their own clearly. CC.3.SL.1

  a. Come to discussions prepared, having read or studied required material; explicitly draw on that preparation and other information known about the topic to explore ideas under discussion. CC.3.SL.1.a

  b. Follow agreed upon rules for discussions (e.g., gaining the floor in respectful ways, listening to others with care, speaking one at a time about the topics and text under discussion). CC.3.SL.1.b

  c. Ask questions to check understanding of information presented, stay on topic, and link their comments to the remarks of others. CC.3.SL.1.c

  d. Explain their own ideas and understanding in light of the discussion. CC.3.SL.1.d

2. Determine the main ideas and supporting details of a text read aloud or information presented in diverse media and formats, including visually, quantitatively, and orally. CC.3.SL.2

3. Ask and answer questions about information from a speaker, offering appropriate elaboration and detail. CC.3.SL.3

Grade 3 Assessment

SG1.29

Unit 1 | Happy to Help

Name _____ Date _____

Book Title _____ Pages _____

Reading Strategy Assessment

 Unit 1

Check the reading strategies the student used and ask the questions that follow about how the student used the strategy. Use the rubric to help you determine how well the student used the strategy. Circle the student's score.

Ask: *What did you do while you were reading?*
Were there any parts of the book that confused you or were hard to follow?
What did you do to understand better?
How did it work?

Reading Strategy Rubrics		
Plan and Monitor (Unit Focus) 4 3 2 1	**Ask Questions** 4 3 2 1	**Make Inferences** 4 3 2 1
• *What did you do before you started reading the book?* • *When you were reading, did you go back and reread any part of the book for better understanding?* • *When you didn't understand, what did you do?* • *How did the meaning become clear to you?*	• *What questions did you have when you were reading?* • *Did you find answers to the questions?* • *Can you tell me some examples of these kinds of questions and what you learned?*	• *Did you infer, or figure out, something in the book that was not stated directly?* • *Were there details in the book that helped you figure this out?* • *What did you already know about those details that helped you make this inference?*

	Plan and Monitor	Ask Questions	Make Inferences
4	Consistently previews text and makes and confirms predictions. Monitors when comprehension breaks down and demonstrates ability to clarify text successfully.	Expands text meaning by asking questions that address large concepts and clarify confusion. Can provide relevant examples related to the book.	Makes inferences using examples from the text and background knowledge. Can use inferences to interpret the text.
3	Often previews text and makes and confirms predictions. Monitors comprehension, but cannot always clarify text independently.	Asks relevant questions and looks for answers to clarify confusion or understand the text.	Makes inferences that are consistent with the text or background knowledge. Cannot tell you how inference was made.
2	Sometimes previews and makes predictions, but may not confirm them. Can monitor when comprehension has broken down, but does not attempt to clarify text.	Asks only literal questions.	Makes inferences that are inaccurate or unsubstantiated.
1	Does not preview or make predictions. Is not aware of how to monitor comprehension or clarify meaning.	Does not ask questions or asks irrelevant questions.	Does not attempt to make inferences.

Grade 3 Assessment

SG1.30

Unit 1 | Happy to Help

COPY READY

Reading Strategy Assessment

 Unit 1

Reading Strategy Rubrics			
Determine Importance 4 3 2 1	**Make Connections** 4 3 2 1	**Visualize** 4 3 2 1	**Synthesize** 4 3 2 1
• *What is an important idea in the book you chose?* • *Why do you think that is important?* • *How would you summarize this book for someone who has not read it?*	• *Did you read anything in the book that connects to your life? What was that, and how does it connect?* • *Did you read anything that reminded you of something else you read? What was that, and how does it connect?* • *Did you read anything you already knew about in the world around you? What was that, and how does it connect?*	• *Was there a part of the book that made you visualize (see pictures in your mind)?* • *How did this help you understand what you were reading?* • *Are there particular words that helped you visualize?*	• *Tell me about the book you read. What about the book can you generalize, or say is true most of the time?* • *What can you conclude from these parts?* • *Based on this book and what you know about (topic), what do you think is probably true about (topic)?*
4 Uses many parts of the text (pictures, title, words) to accurately identify an important idea, and summarizes the important ideas in the book.	Makes text-to-self, text-to-text, and/or text-to-world connections to enhance comprehension. Can explain how connections enrich understanding.	Describes multi-sensory mental images that go beyond the literal text. Explains how this helped understanding.	Synthesizes text accurately to draw conclusions and/or make generalizations. Can explain how synthesis helps comprehension.
3 Identifies and summarizes some important ideas from the text using a few parts of the text. Cannot explain importance.	Makes some type of relevant connection, but does not elaborate on how the connection helped understanding.	Describes multi-sensory mental images and goes beyond the literal text.	Combines some information from the text to draw basic conclusions or make limited generalizations.
2 Attempts to identify and summarize important ideas, but is inaccurate.	Attempts to make connections, but the connections are not relevant to understanding the text.	Describes few mental images directly related to text descriptions or pictures.	Attempts to synthesize, but synthesis is limited or leads to inaccurate conclusions or generalizations.
1 Cannot identify an important idea.	Does not make connections with the text.	Does not describe mental images related to the text.	Does not draw a conclusion or make a generalization about the text.

Name _____   Date _____

Reader Reflection

Date	Title of Book	Author

Check all that apply.

1. Before I read this book, I:

   ☐ read the title.

   ☐ looked at the pictures.

   ☐ predicted what I would read about.
   I predicted: _____

   _____

   _____

2. If I didn't understand what I was reading, I:

   ☐ stopped to think about what I had
   just read.

   ☐ read it again.

   ☐ other (describe): _____

   _____

   _____

3. If I didn't understand a word while reading, I:

   ☐ stopped to think about its meaning.

   ☐ looked for clues to its meaning.

   ☐ checked in a dictionary or asked
   someone about the meaning of the word.

   ☐ other (describe): _____

   _____

   _____

4. This book reminded me of something I know
   or read already. It reminded me of:

   _____

   _____

   _____

   _____

This book was: ☐ easy   ☐ about right   ☐ hard

Rate this book!   ☆

I would like to read other books: ☐ about this topic   ☐ by this author

Grade 3 Assessment   **SG1.32**   **Unit 1** | Happy to Help!

Practice Master SG1.2

Story Map   Practice Master SG1.2

BL | A Chance to Shine

Beginning:

The boy sees the homeless man, Joe, and thinks he's weird and smells funny.

The boy's father gives him a job.

↓

Middle:

Joe does a good job and ends up working as the store manager.

↓

End:

The boy begins to think differently about people he used to think of as weird. He thinks everyone deserves a chance.

BL | Tomás and the Library Lady

Beginning:

Tomás and his family travel from Texas to Iowa to work.

Tomás enjoys listening to his grandfather's stories.

↓

Middle:

Tomás visits the library, where he meets a lady who introduces him to a love for books and reading. Soon, Tomás becomes the storyteller in his family.

↓

End:

Tomás must say goodbye to the library lady and return to Texas, but he takes his love for books with him.

OL | The Quiltmaker's Gift

Beginning:

A quiltmaker makes quilts for the poor. An unhappy and greedy king wants one of her quilts, but she says she will not give him one until he gives away his possessions. So the king punishes the quiltmaker.

↓

Middle:

The king begins to give his possessions away. He becomes happier. After the king gives away all his possessions, he is poor, but happy.

↓

End:

The quiltmaker makes the king a quilt. The king begins helping her give quilts away.

AL | The Quiltmaker's Journey

Beginning:

A girl lives in a walled town where everyone has everything they need. She leaves town to explore the world outside the walls and learns that many people are poor.

↓

Middle:

The girl wanders with nothing, but finds that people are kind to her and help her. She wants do something to help others in need.

↓

End:

The girl begins making quilts for people, to keep them warm. In making others happy, she makes herself happy.

Discussion Guides

✖✖✖ Analyze Books

BL ▶ A Chance to Shine **Practice Master SG1.3**

1. **Analyze Character** Joe seems a little weird. He smells funny and dresses funny. He also talks to pigeons. I think he is like this because he is homeless and people do not give him a chance.
2. **Analyze Plot**
   - **Beginning** The boy's father gives Joe a job sweeping the sidewalk. This surprises the boy because he thinks that Joe is weird and smells funny.
   - **Middle** Joe does a good job and ends up as the store manager.
   - **End** The boy begins to talk to kids that he used to think were weird. Meeting Joe has helped him to realize that you shouldn't judge people before you know them.
3. **Plan and Monitor: Preview and Predict** (Encourage students to tell in detail what they predicted would happen and to explain why their prediction was or was not correct.)
4. **Generalize** When the boy's father gives Joe a job, he is able to show that he wants to work and that he can do a good job. He is then able to earn money and find a place to live.

BL ▶ Tomás and the Library Lady **Practice Master SG1.4**

1. **Analyze Character** Tomás loves his grandfather because he tells Tomás stories. Tomás loves listening to his grandfather's stories because he is the best storyteller in the family.
2. **Analyze Plot**
   - **Beginning** Tomás visits the library so that he can learn new stories. He has already heard all of his grandfather's stories.
   - **Middle** Tomás teaches his grandfather English by reading the library books to him in English. While he is at the library, he teaches the library lady Spanish.
   - **End** Tomás stops visiting the library because he has to return to Texas. But the library lady gives him a book.
3. **Plan and Monitor: Preview and Predict** (Encourage students to tell in detail what they predicted would happen and to explain why their prediction was or was not correct.)
4. **Generalize** When the library lady shares books with Tomás, he wants to read all the time and share the stories with his family. Reading helps him escape from real life.

OL ▶ The Quiltmaker's Gift **Practice Master SG1.5**

1. **Analyze Character** They are not alike at first because he is greedy and she is kind. After the king learns to give and becomes poor, he also is kind.
2. **Analyze Plot**
   - **Beginning** The king is greedy. The quiltmaker only gives her quilts to people who really need them. The king does not need one.
   - **Middle** The king becomes nice when he begins to give his things away. He enjoys giving. It makes him happy.
   - **End** She gives him a quilt because he gave all his things away and became poor. But he does not feel poor.
3. **Plan and Monitor: Preview and Predict** (Encourage students to tell in detail what they predicted would happen and to explain why their prediction was or was not correct.)
4. **Generalize** By giving all of his things away, the king learns that giving makes him happy. He learns that having many things is not the key to happiness.

AL ▶ The Quiltmaker's Journey **Practice Master SG1.6**

1. **Analyze Character** Money does not make her happy. She wants to help the poor. The town Elders want to pretend the poor do not exist.
2. **Analyze Plot**
   - **Beginning** She wants to see what the rest of the world is like. She is surprised to find people in need. She is surprised because there is no poverty in her town.
   - **Middle** People are nice to her and help her. They give her the little they have, like shoes and a flower.
   - **End** She makes them quilts, and she learns that happiness comes from giving.
3. **Plan and Monitor: Preview and Predict** (Encourage students to tell in detail what they predicted would happen and to explain why their prediction was or was not correct.)
4. **Generalize** When the poor are kind and helpful to the quiltmaker, she realizes that a person does not need to have many possessions to be happy and good.

✖✖✖✖ Connect Across Texts Practice Master SG1.7

---

1. Possible responses: When you are kind to others, it makes the world a better place. If you are kind to people, they will want to be kind, too. Then there will be more kind people in the world.
2. Possible responses: When you are kind to others, it makes you feel happy. When you are unkind, you don't feel very good about yourself.

3. One act of kindness can change a person's life. Joe's life is changed because he gets a job and a place to live. Tomás makes a friend and learns to love reading. By being kind to others, the king learns that giving makes him happier than getting. He learns that you can be poor and still feel rich.

Practice Master SG1.9

Character Description Chart Practice Master SG1.9

BL *New York's Bravest*

Character	What the Character Does	What This Shows About the Character
Mose	He saves people from fires. He risks his life for others.	He is brave and heroic.

BL *The Snow Walker*

Character	What the Character Does	What This Shows About the Character
Milton	He uses his snowshoes to help people get food and medicine during a blizzard.	He is kind. He likes helping people.

OL *Passage to Freedom*

Character	What the Character Does	What This Shows About the Character
Sugihara	He goes against the Japanese government and gives visas to help save people's lives.	He is a caring person who is not afraid to get in trouble to do the right thing.

AL *Mercedes and the Chocolate Pilot*

Character	What the Character Does	What This Shows About the Character
Mercedes; the pilot	Mercedes: She tries to catch the candy falling from the sky; she writes a letter to the pilot. Pilot: He drops candy from his plane; he sends candy to children to give them hope.	Mercedes: She is determined. Pilot: He is kind and generous.

Discussion Guides

👤👤👤 Analyze Books

BL **New York's Bravest**
Practice Master SG1.10

1. **Analyze Setting** The setting is the busy city of New York. This is important because it means there are a lot of people that Mose helped.
2. **Analyze Character** Mose is courageous in the face of danger and will do anything to help others—even give his own life. This shows that he has a strong and good character.
   - **Character** Mose
   - **What the Character Does** He risks his life to save people from fires. He dies while saving people from a hotel fire.
   - **What This Shows About the Character** He is brave and caring because he risks his life for others.
3. **Plan and Monitor: Preview and Predict** (Encourage students to tell in detail what they predicted would happen and to explain why their prediction was or was not correct.)
4. **Generalize** Mose shows kindness by risking his life for others to save them from fires. Other people look at his kindness and bravery as an example. This makes him a hero.

BL **The Snow Walker**
Practice Master SG1.11

1. **Analyze Setting** The setting is the Bronx in 1888, during a terrible blizzard. Milton goes out in the storm and ends up helping many of his neighbors who could not leave home.
2. **Analyze Character** Milton is a boy who goes into a blizzard to help others. This shows that he is brave and helpful.
   - **Character** Milton
   - **What the Character Does** He builds snowshoes and goes into a blizzard to get milk for his family. He risks his safety to get food and medicine for many of his neighbors.
   - **What This Shows About the Character** He is brave and knows that helping others is the right thing to do.
3. **Plan and Monitor: Preview and Predict** (Encourage students to tell in detail what they predicted would happen and to explain why their prediction was or was not correct.)
4. **Generalize** Milton showed kindness by risking his safety to help his neighbors in need. He continued to go back and forth to the store, even though his snowshoe was breaking. His willingness to help others, even while risking his own safety, makes him a hero.

OL **Passage to Freedom**
Practice Master SG1.12

1. **Analyze Setting** The setting is Lithuania during World War II. The Jewish people need Sugihara's help because they are being killed.
2. **Analyze Character** Sugihara is worried about the safety of the people who ask for his help. This shows that he is a brave and caring person.
   - **Character** Sugihara
   - **What the Character Does** He risks his safety and his family's safety to sign visas for many Jews whose lives were in danger.
   - **What This Shows About the Character** He is brave and caring. He believes that he should help others as much as he can.
3. **Plan and Monitor: Preview and Predict** (Encourage students to tell in detail what they predicted would happen and to explain why their prediction was or was not correct.)
4. **Generalize** Sugihara saved many people's lives, even though it was difficult for him to do so. He did something for others that not everyone would have done. So he is a hero.

AL **Mercedes and the Chocolate Pilot**
Practice Master SG1.13

1. **Analyze Setting** The setting is Berlin after World War II, when people did not have enough food to live and other countries were airlifting food and supplies into the city.
2. **Analyze Character** Mercedes is determined to find hope by writing to the pilot. The pilot wants to give the children hope.
   - **Character** Mercedes and the pilot
   - **What the Character Does** The pilot drops candy from his plane to hungry children. Mercedes writes to the pilot to ask for candy, and she always remembers his kindness.
   - **What This Shows About the Character** The pilot is kind. He cares about the children. Mercedes is determined to find hope. Kindness is important to both characters.
3. **Plan and Monitor: Preview and Predict** (Encourage students to tell in detail what they predicted would happen and to explain why their prediction was or was not correct.)
4. **Generalize** The pilot breaks the rules to bring joy to children. This shows great kindness and makes him a hero in the eyes of the children.

👤👤👤👤 Connect Across Texts   Practice Master SG1.14

1. Mose saves people from fires; Milton risks getting lost in a blizzard to help people get food; Sugihara gives visas to many Jews who are in danger during World War II; the Chocolate Pilot, Gail Halvorsen, provides candy and hope to hungry children in Berlin during the Berlin airlift.
2. In all the books, the characters take risks to save people's lives, help them, or give them hope. They take these risks because they are heroes.

3. Each book gives an example of a person who took risks to help others in need. They helped people, even though it was difficult for them to do so. Sometimes they even had to break rules to help. Whenever people take risks to do what is right, they are heroes.

Practice Master SG1.16

Character Comparison Chart Practice Master SG1.16

BL Harriet Tubman

Before	After
Before Harriet Tubman, there were many slaves who wanted to be free.	After Harriet Tubman, many slaves had found their way to freedom along the Underground Railroad.

BL Helen Keller: Courage in the Dark

Before	After
Before Helen Keller, people did not think that people with disabilities could live fulfilling lives.	After Helen Keller, people realized that if someone who was deaf and blind could accomplish so much, then others could, too.

OL Louis Braille

Before	After
Before Louis Braille, the blind were kept in institutions. They could not read or write, and they had to depend on others for everything.	After Louis Braille, the blind were able to read and write in many languages. People saw that blind people could accomplish great things.

AL Mary McLeod Bethune

Before	After
Before Mary McLeod Bethune, African Americans had few chances to get an education or good jobs.	After Mary McLeod Bethune, African Americans had a good school to go to and other opportunities.

Discussion Guides

✦✦✦ Analyze Books

BL ❯ *Harriet Tubman* — Practice Master SG1.17

1. **Identify Cause and Effect** She ran away to escape slavery. After she ran away, she joined the Underground Railroad and helped other slaves run away.
2. **Make Comparisons** Before Harriet Tubman and the Underground Railroad, slaves were not free. After Harriet helped many slaves escape, they were free.
   - **Before** People were slaves before Harriet Tubman helped them. They were owned by other people. Children could not play or go to school.
   - **After** Harriet Tubman helped many slaves escape to freedom on the Underground Railroad.
3. **Plan and Monitor: Monitor and Clarify** (Encourage students to tell in detail what they wanted to know and explain whether they found their answer and, if so, where in the book.)
4. **Generalize** Harriet Tubman helped many slaves escape to freedom on the Underground Railroad.

BL ❯ *Helen Keller: Courage in the Dark* — Practice Master SG1.18

1. **Identify Cause and Effect** Helen was very sick when she was a baby and had a high fever. She became deaf and blind as a result.
2. **Make Comparisons** Before Helen knew Annie, she was frustrated and unable to communicate. After she met Annie, she learned to communicate. Her life improved, and she became an inspiring person.
   - **Before** As a child, Helen was wild. Her parents couldn't control her. No one could understand her.
   - **After** After she met Annie, she learned sign language and how to speak. She went to college and had an interesting and fulfilling life.
3. **Plan and Monitor: Monitor and Clarify** (Encourage students to tell in detail what they wanted to know and explain whether they found their answer and, if so, where in the book.)
4. **Generalize** Helen Keller was an example to all disabled people that you can accomplish more than you dreamed, if you work hard enough.

OL ❯ *Louis Braille* — Practice Master SG1.19

1. **Identify Cause and Effect** Louis poked his eye with a leather tool. This caused an infection in his eye that spread to his good eye. Soon, he was blind.
2. **Make Comparisons** Before the braille system, blind people were dependent on others. The braille system gave them the chance to learn on their own and be independent.
   - **Before** Before the braille system, blind people had to depend on others to help them learn. They were not able to read and write easily. Many were kept in institutions.
   - **After** After the braille system, blind people could read and write and were able to learn on their own.
3. **Plan and Monitor: Monitor and Clarify** (Encourage students to tell in detail what they wanted to know and explain whether they found their answer and, if so, where in the book.)
4. **Generalize** Louis Braille changed many lives by inventing the braille system as a way for blind people to read and write easily. This changed many lives because the blind were able to be more self-reliant.

AL ❯ *Mary McLeod Bethune* — Practice Master SG1.20

1. **Identify Cause and Effect** Mary started a school for African American children because no good schools existed. This school became a college.
2. **Make Comparisons** Before Mary started a school, most African Americans did not go to school. After she started her school, African Americans had a place to go to learn. They could get better jobs and improve their lives.
   - **Before** There were no schools for African Americans.
   - **After** Mary's school helped African Americans get an education. She also helped them get better jobs.
3. **Plan and Monitor: Monitor and Clarify** (Encourage students to tell in detail what they wanted to know and explain whether they found their answer and, if so, where in the book.)
4. **Generalize** Mary McLeod Bethune changed many lives by making sure that African Americans were given the chance to get a good education.

✦✦✦✦ Connect Across Texts — Practice Master SG1.21

1. Harriet Tubman was a hero because she helped many slaves escape to freedom; Helen Keller was a hero because she was an example that disabled people are capable of great things; Louis Braille was a hero because he created a system of reading and writing that helped the blind find independence; Mary McLeod Bethune was a hero because she dedicated her life to providing a good education for African American children.
2. (Students will have a variety of responses. Encourage them to share their questions and explain what they did to find the answers to their questions.)
3. Each book describes a heroic person who dedicated his or her life to making their own lives better, as well as the lives of other people. Each is about one person who overcame challenges and was an example to many others.

Venn Diagram   Practice Master SG1.23

BL Martin's Big Words

Before

African Americans did not have civil rights.

Same

People admired Martin Luther King, Jr.

People felt hatred toward King.

After

Segregation ended.

BL Roberto Clemente: A Life of Generosity

Before

There was no sports center in Puerto Rico that was free for children.

Same

People admired Roberto Clemente's generosity.

After

A sports center was built in memory of Roberto Clemente, and stadiums, schools, and bridges were named after him.

OL Franklin D. Roosevelt

Before

The country was suffering from the Great Depression.

People were poor and without jobs.

Same

Many people admired Franklin D. Roosevelt. Some did not.

After

People had a new hope for the future.

AL Nelson Mandela

Before

Black South Africans did not have the same rights as white South Africans because of apartheid.

Same

People admired Nelson Mandela.

After

Nelson Mandela became President, and apartheid ended.

Discussion Guides

👤👤👤 Analyze Books

BL *Martin's Big Words* **Practice Master SG1.24**

1. **Analyze Point of View** It is a biography because it is told in third person and uses words like *he* and *his,* instead of *I* and *my.*
2. **Make Comparisons** African Americans did not have civil rights before Dr. Martin Luther King, Jr., spoke out for change. His movement helped end segregation.
   - **Before** African Americans did not have civil rights. There was segregation. African Americans were not treated with respect.
   - **After** Segregation ended. King helped by marching in protests, giving speeches, and telling people to fight with words and not violence.
   - **Same** Not everyone admired King. Someone shot him when he was helping garbage collectors on strike.
3. **Plan and Monitor: Monitor and Clarify** (Encourage students to tell in detail what they wanted to know and explain whether they found their answer and where in the book they found it.)
4. **Generalize** Dr. Martin Luther King, Jr., used peace and love to fight laws that were not fair. He helped end segregation and make life better for African Americans.

BL *Roberto Clemente: A Life of Generosity* **Practice Master SG1.25**

1. **Analyze Point of View** It is a biography because it is told in third person and uses words like *he* and *his,* instead of *I* and *my.*
2. **Make Comparisons** Roberto Clemente always wanted children in Puerto Rico to have a place to learn about and enjoy sports. His family built it in his memory. People admired his generosity and still do.
   - **Before** Many children were poor. They did not have toys to play with.
   - **After** He taught children about baseball. He visited the sick and the poor. He planned to build a sports center.
   - **Same** People admired Clemente's generosity. After he died, his parents built the sports center in his name. People named bridges, schools, and stadiums after him.
3. **Plan and Monitor: Monitor and Clarify** (Encourage students to tell in detail what they wanted to know and explain whether they found their answer and where in the book they found it.)
4. **Generalize** Roberto Clemente helped many people. He built a house for his parents; helped children by planning to build a sports center for them; and collected money for people after an earthquake in Nicaragua.

OL *Franklin D. Roosevelt* **Practice Master SG1.26**

1. **Analyze Point of View** It is a biography because it is told in third person and uses words like *he* and *his,* instead of *I* and *my.*
2. **Make Comparisons** The United States was facing the Great Depression. Roosevelt helped create jobs and improve life in the United States. He told people not to lose hope.
   - **Before** Many lost their homes and jobs and did not have money to buy what they needed. Businesses closed. People had given up hope.
   - **After** Roosevelt gave people hope. He started programs that created jobs and helped the economy improve.
   - **Same** Many people admired Roosevelt. But some thought he spent too much money and did not do enough to end the Depression.
3. **Plan and Monitor: Monitor and Clarify** (Encourage students to tell in detail what they wanted to know and explain whether they found their answer and where in the book they found it.)
4. **Generalize** Franklin D. Roosevelt changed many lives by giving the American people hope for the future. He also began programs that provided jobs and help to those in need.

AL *Nelson Mandela* **Practice Master SG1.27**

1. **Analyze Point of View** It is a biography because it is told in third person and not by the subject of the book.
2. **Make Comparisons** South Africa was a segregated country where black people were not treated fairly. Mandela inspired people and helped to end apartheid. He was elected President of South Africa.
   - **Before** Apartheid divided the country between blacks and whites. Black South Africans were treated badly. There was violence.
   - **After** Mandela became president and helped to end apartheid.
   - **Same** People admired Mandela for being a peaceful leader. They elected him President, even after he was in prison.
3. **Plan and Monitor: Monitor and Clarify** (Encourage students to tell in detail what they wanted to know and explain whether they found their answer and where in the book they found it.)
4. **Generalize** Nelson Mandela changed many lives by helping to end apartheid. This meant that black South Africans had more rights than they had before.

👤👤👤👤 Connect Across Texts **Practice Master SG1.28**

---

1. Dr. Martin Luther King, Jr., helped African Americans have rights in this country; Roberto Clemente gave back to the people in his country; Franklin D. Roosevelt was a leader who gave hope to the American people during the Great Depression; Nelson Mandela stood up for what he believed in and helped to end apartheid in South Africa.

2. In all the books, the people worked to make life better for others. People either gained rights or were helped when they needed it.
3. Each book describes a person who worked to make life better for others. The people changed the lives of others by acting with love and kindness, rather than anger and hate.

Recommended Books

Fiction About Helping Others	Nonfiction About Helping Others
Cohen, Miriam. **Down in the Subway.** Star Bright Books, 2003.	Kottke, Jan. **A Day with Firefighters.** Scholastic Library Publishing, 2000.
Cosby, Bill. **The Meanest Thing to Say.** Scholastic Trade Books, 1997.	Miller, Heather. **Doctor.** Heinemann-Raintree, 2002.
Galdone, Paul. **The Elves and the Shoemaker.** Houghton Mifflin Harcourt, 1986.	Owen, Ann. **Delivering Your Mail.** Picture Window Books, 2003.
Padma, T.V. **Growing Gold.** National Book Network, 2008.	Ring, Susan. **Helping Hands.** Capstone Press, 2005.
Munson, Derek. **Enemy Pie.** Chronicle Books, 2000.	Lawrence, Jacob. **Harriet and the Promised Land.** Simon & Schuster Children's Publishing, 1997.
Reynolds, Peter. **The Dot.** Candlewick Press, 2003.	Moor, Eva. **Buddy, the First Seeing Eye Dog.** Scholastic Trade Books, 1996.
Soto, Gary. **Too Many Tamales.** Penguin Young Readers Group, 1996.	Raatma, Lucia. **Responsibility.** Capstone Press, 2001.
Zolotow, Charlotte. **I Know a Lady.** HarperCollins Publishers, 1992.	Redmond, Shirley Raye. **The Dog That Dug for Dinosaurs.** Simon & Schuster Children's Publishing, 2004.
Polacco, Patricia. **Chicken Sunday.** Penguin Young Readers Group, 1998.	Houston, Gloria. **My Great-Aunt Arizona.** HarperColllins Publishers, 2000.
Polacco, Patricia. **Thunder Cake.** Penguin Young Readers Group, 1997.	Lakin, Patricia. **Clara Barton: Spirit of the American Red Cross.** Simon & Schuster Children's Publishing, 2004.
Williams, Mary. **Brothers in Hope: The Story of the Lost Boys of Sudan.** Lee & Low Publishers, 2005. 🏅 **CORETTA SCOTT KING ILLUSTRATOR HONOR BOOK**	Polette, Nancy. **Pocahontas.** Scholastic Library Publishing, 2003.
Williams, Vera B. **A Chair for My Mother.** HarperCollins Publishers, 1984. 🏅 **CALDECOTT HONOR BOOK**	Raatma, Lucia. **Respect.** Capstone Press, 2001.
Carlson, Natalie Savage. **The Family Under the Bridge.** HarperCollins Publishers, 2000. 🏅 **CALDECOTT HONOR BOOK**	Ferris, Jeri. **What Are You Figuring Now? A Story about Benjamin Banneker.** Lerner Publishing Group, 1990.
Hesse, Karen. **Just Juice.** Scholastic Trade Books, 1999.	Fritz, Jean. **And Then What Happened, Paul Revere?** Penguin Young Readers Group, 1996.
Peet, Bill. **The Ant and the Elephant.** Houghton Mifflin Harcourt, 1980.	Marzollo, Jean. **Happy Birthday, Martin Luther King.** Scholastic Trade Books, 2006.
Van Leeuwen, Jean. **Hanna of Fairfield.** Penguin Young Readers Group, 2000.	Millender, Dharathula. **Crispus Attucks: Black Leader of Colonial Patriots.** Simon & Schuster Children's Publishing, 1986.

Author Study: Francisco X. Alarcón

Animal Poems of the Iguazú. Children's Book Press, 2008.

From the Bellybutton of the Moon and Other Summer Poems. Children's Book Press, 2005.

Poems to Dream Together. Lee and Low Books, 2005.

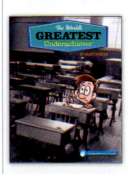

Author Study: Henry Winkler

Help! Somebody Get Me Out of Fourth Grade! Grosset & Dunlap, 2004.

I Got a "D" in Salami. Grosset & Dunlap, 2003.

Niagara Falls, or Does It? Grosset & Dunlap, 2003.

Assessment Overview

		Printed Components	Online PDFs NGReach.com	eAssessment™ NGReach.com	ExamView®
Oral Reading Assessments	Oral Reading Assessments	✔	✔		
Progress Monitoring Assessments	**Weekly Tests** Reading Comprehension Vocabulary Writing, Revising, and Editing	✔	✔	✔	✔
	Spelling	✔			
	Phonics*	✔	✔		
	Unit Tests Reading Comprehension Vocabulary Writing, Revising, and Editing	✔	✔	✔	✔
	Reading Strategy Assessments	✔	✔		
Benchmark Assessments	**Benchmark Assessments***	✔	✔	✔	
Scoring and Reporting Tools	**Rubrics**	✔	✔		
	Student Profiles	✔	✔		
	Strengths and Needs Summary	✔	✔		
	Oral Reading Progress Tracker	✔	✔		
	Class Profiles	✔	✔	✔	
	School and District Reports			✔	
Additional Assessment Tools	**Speaking and Listening Observation Log**	✔	✔		
	Reader Reflections	✔	✔		
	Unit Self-Assessments	✔	✔		
	Affective and Metacognitive Measures		✔		
	Test-Taking Strategies		✔		
Reteaching	**Reteaching Masters**	✔	✔		

* Available in separate books.

Contents at a Glance

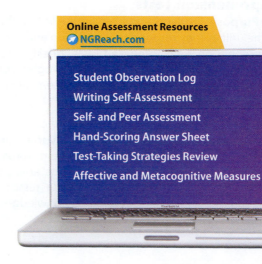

Online Assessment Resources
NGReach.com

Student Observation Log
Writing Self-Assessment
Self- and Peer Assessment
Hand-Scoring Answer Sheet
Test-Taking Strategies Review
Affective and Metacognitive Measures

Assessment Overview

ExamView®

Multiple Measures to Assess Student Learning

National Geographic Reach for Reading offers a comprehensive array of assessments and tools to

- monitor student progress and inform instruction throughout the year
- encourage students to actively participate in their learning
- document student progress on Common Core Standards.

In each unit, there is a variety of assessments and tools you can use to monitor student progress on a weekly and unit level.

Weekly Tests	Unit Tests
Reading Comprehension	Reading Comprehension
Vocabulary	Vocabulary
Writing, Revising, and Editing	Writing, Revising, and Editing
Spelling	Oral Reading
Reading Strategies	

Additional assessments and tools can be used periodically throughout the program:

- Reteaching Masters for Weekly and Unit Tests
- Speaking and Listening Observation Log
- Test-Taking Strategies
- Comprehension Coach
- Benchmark Assessments
- Affective and Metacognitive Measures

Weekly and Unit Tests

National Geographic Reach for Reading offers weekly and unit tests to monitor your students' progress on skills taught in each unit of instruction. Weekly Tests provide immediate feedback about students' performance on the skills they learned that week.

Unit Tests provide a comprehensive view of student performance on all the tested skills in the unit, including Week 4 skills. Unit assessments help you determine which students are making gains on Common Core Standards and which students may benefit from reteaching before moving on to the next unit.

Reading Comprehension Tests

Description and Purpose: Students apply reading skills that they have learned each week and throughout the unit as they respond to new fiction and nonfiction reading passages in the Reading Comprehension Weekly and Unit Tests. Weekly Tests, which consist of multiple-choice items, provide a quick tool to check students' progress. Unit Tests, which also include a constructed-response item, provide a more comprehensive view of what the students have learned during the unit.

Vocabulary Tests

Description and Purpose: In the Week 1 and Week 3 Vocabulary Tests, students demonstrate their understanding of social studies and science content words and academic vocabulary definitions they have learned. You can monitor students' ability to apply unit vocabulary strategies in the Week 2 Vocabulary Test. The Unit Test assesses all vocabulary strategies taught in the unit and encourages students to stretch their knowledge of the unit's vocabulary by answering questions using the unit's key words in context.

Reading Comprehension Weekly Test

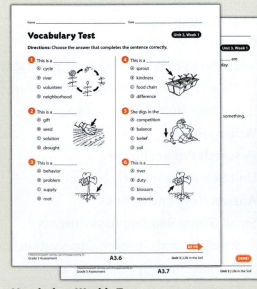

Vocabulary Weekly Test

Writing, Revising, and Editing Tests

Description and Purpose: Multiple-choice items and a writing prompt in the Writing, Revising, and Editing Weekly Tests present an opportunity for students to demonstrate their command of the language conventions and writing skills they have learned each week. The Unit Test assesses language and writing skills from the unit with

- discrete grammar items
- a selection with editing and revising items
- an editing task
- a writing prompt based on the skills students learned in the unit Writing Project.

Administration and Scoring for Weekly Tests and Unit Tests: Administer the Weekly Tests at the end of each week of instruction for Weeks 1 through 3. Unit tests are administered at the end of Week 4. Use the following suggested administration times to schedule test-taking.

	Weekly Test		Unit Test	
Reading Comprehension	10-15 minutes		30-35 minutes	
Vocabulary	5-10 minutes		10-15 minutes	
Writing, Revising, and Editing	10-15 minutes		25-30 minutes	

Times are approximate

Answer Keys and Rubrics provide keys to score multiple-choice items and easy-to-use rubrics for all constructed-response items, editing tasks, and skill-based writing prompts. The Unit Test writing prompt can be scored by using the skill-based writing rubric or the trait-based Writing Rubric, which is included in each unit.

After tests are scored, you can compile a student's results for all assessments in the Student Profile for the unit. By analyzing a student's scores from the Student Profile, you can determine where a student is making progress toward program goals and where additional reteaching or intervention might be needed. This information can be recorded for each student on the Strengths and Needs Summary. The Class Profile provides an overall view of student performance so that you can easily group students for reteaching.

Reading Strategy Assessments

Description and Purpose: Assess reading strategies while you conduct student reading conferences during Small Group Reading time. Although the strategy covered in the instruction is noted for each unit, all strategies are provided in every assessment to give you the flexibility to assess the strategies students actually use.

Administration and Scoring: Make a copy of the assessment to use during each student's individual reading conference. During the conference, ask the student which strategies he or she used. Use the Reading Strategy Assessment rubrics to evaluate how well the student used the reading strategies. After circling the student's score for each strategy assessed, you can transfer the scores to the Student Profile for that unit. See the Reading Routines in the Small Group section for specific instructions about conducting reading conferences.

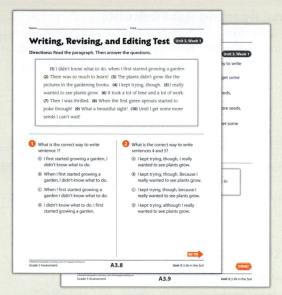

Writing, Revising, and Editing Weekly Test

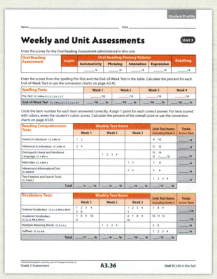

Student Profile

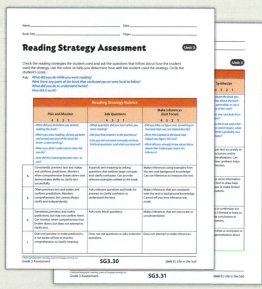

Reading Strategy Assessment

Oral Reading Assessments

Description and Purpose: Oral reading fluency is strongly correlated to reading comprehension. These individualized assessments enable you to measure oral reading fluency at least once during each unit. The timed readings and corresponding teacher pages incorporate

- features of a running record
- a Words Correct Per Minute score (wcpm)
- rubrics to assess the oral reading fluency focus for the unit
- a retelling rubric to check student comprehension.

Administration and Scoring: Refer to the Oral Reading Assessment Routine on page A1.1 for administration and scoring instructions. Use the Oral Reading Assessment Progress Tracker on page A1.3 to monitor each student's progress in fluency as he or she moves through the units in the program.

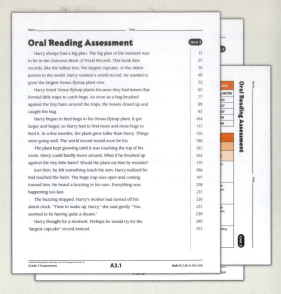

Oral Reading Assessment Passage and Rubrics

Other Assessments and Tools

Reteaching Masters

After using the results of the Weekly and Unit Tests to determine your students' needs, use the Reteaching Masters to support students who need additional help in learning key skills. A Reteaching Master is provided for key tested skills in each unit.

Speaking and Listening Observation Log

Description and Purpose: Use the Speaking and Listening Observation Log to guide and record your observations about students' speaking and listening behaviors. The behaviors included align with the Common Core Standards. The log is located in the Small Group Reading section of the Teacher's Edition for each unit.

Administration and Scoring: Make one copy of the Speaking and Listening Observation Log for your class. As you observe individual student behaviors, record your observations on the log.

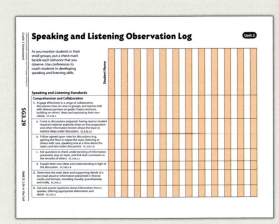

Speaking and Listening Observation Log

Test-Taking Strategies

Becoming more familiar with test-taking strategies can help students be more comfortable and confident when taking any test. Short, structured lessons reinforce each strategy while the students apply these test-taking tips and strategies to practice material.

These materials are available as online PDFs and can be printed or projected easily on interactive whiteboards or other display devices. Additional test-taking strategy practice can be found in the Practice Masters.

Comprehension Coach

The **Comprehension Coach** provides students with a suite of tools for the Student Book eEditions that help students build comprehension skills and oral reading fluency. Students can choose a reading selection, answer comprehension questions while they read, and record and listen to themselves reading a selection out loud to practice oral fluency. Progress reports, reading reports, and individualized word practice lists help you and your students monitor their progress and engage in their learning.

Comprehension Coach

Benchmark Tests

Description and Purpose: Measure student progress against grade-level Common Core Standards to inform instruction and help ensure student success. Three forms of the Benchmark Tests are available in a separate Benchmark Tests Masters booklet.

Administration and Scoring: Benchmark tests should be administered periodically throughout the year, such as at the beginning, middle, and end of the school year. Select one form to administer and make a copy for each student. Use the Answer Key, Student Profile, and Class Profile in the Benchmark Test Masters to score and evaluate student progress on the Common Core Standards.

Affective and Metacognitive Measures

Description and Purpose: Personal interests and attitudes affect motivation, and motivation is an important factor in reading and writing performance. You can help students make personal connections and think about their own learning through reflection and metacognition with the personal surveys and inventories available in *National Geographic Reach for Reading*. These materials are available as online PDFs and can be printed or projected easily on interactive whiteboards or other display devices.

- Affective Measures help you and your students pursue their interests in and examine their attitudes toward reading and writing.
- Metacognitive Measures, such as the Unit Self-Assessment, help you and your students think about and monitor their learning. The metacognitive ability to monitor, evaluate, and adjust the processes one uses while reading and writing is essential to becoming an effective reader and writer.

Administration and Scoring: Administer Unit Self-Assessments at the end of each unit of instruction, just prior to administering the Unit Test. Administer the Reader Reflection during Small Group Reading time. Other Affective and Metacognitive Measures may be administered at your discretion. We recommend that you administer them at the beginning of the program as a survey of students' interests and attitudes toward reading and writing. You may also choose to administer them multiple times to compare changes in interests and attitudes over time.

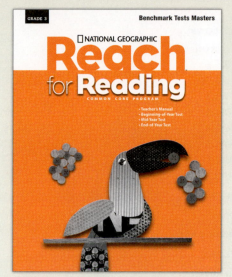

Benchmark Tests Masters

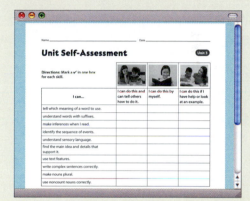

Affective and Metacognitive Measures

MATERIALS

timer • audio recording device

Administering the Assessment

Oral Reading Fluency Routine

1. Choose a reasonably quiet area that is free from distractions where you can conduct the one-on-one assessment. Sit directly across from the student.

2. Place a copy of the passage in front of the student. To get an objective measure, do not show the passage to the student in advance. The passage should be new for the student. Shield your version so the student cannot see what is marked. (A clipboard that can rest on your lap is effective.) Keep the timer or stopwatch out of sight to prevent the student from focusing on speed.

3. Provide instructions:
   - *Please read this passage out loud as well as you can.*
   - *If you have trouble with a word, I will tell you the word so you can keep reading.*
   - *I will tell you when it is time to stop.*

4. Point to the first word in the passage. Say: *Start here. Begin now.*

5. Start your stopwatch when the student reads the first word. If the student does not read the first word after three seconds, say the word and mark it incorrect.

6. As the student reads, mark the passage as shown below.

7. At the end of one minute, put a bracket after the last word read, but allow the student to finish the sentence before you say stop.

Sample of Scored Oral Reading Fluency Passage

Miscues

Slashes indicate words that the student skips or mispronounces.

Self-Corrects

If a student self-corrects, annotate the word with *sc*.

Stopping Point

After one minute, use a bracket to indicate the last word read.

Name __Sam Park__   Date __Nov. 10__

Oral Reading Assessment   Unit 1

Gary's grandfather took a walk every day around the city	10
park. He loved the birds. He loved the flowers. But he always	22
came back huffing and puffing because the park had no	32
benches. There was no place to rest!	39
One day, Gary looked at Grandpa breathing so hard. He	49
suddenly had an idea. Grandpa needed a place to rest in his	61
walks. It was time for some benches in the park! Gary would	73
find a way to raise the money. The plan came in a flash—a	87
talent show.	89
Almost every person he knew had some special talent.	98
Carson could do magic tricks, and Ms. Alma could juggle. Kayla	109
was a hip-hop dancer, and Rosie had a talking parrot. He knew	121
everyone would come together to help beca... th...	

Oral Reading Comprehension Routine (Optional)

For students who read with automaticity, assess comprehension by asking them to retell the passage. To begin the retelling, say: *Please read this passage out loud again. This time I will not stop you. When you finish, I will ask you to tell me about what you read. Try to tell me everything you can.*

Scoring the Assessment and Tracking Scores

1. For Accuracy and Rate, calculate the number of words correct per minute (wcpm). Words marked with *sc* should be counted as correct. The Hasbrouck and Tindal grade-level norms are provided if you want to compare a student's wcpm to a national sample.

Accuracy and Rate

_____ - _____ = _____
words attempted in   number of errors   words correct per
one minute   minute (wcpm)

2. Use the Oral Reading Fluency Rubrics to rate the student's Automaticity and the oral reading fluency focus for the week (Phrasing, Intonation, or Expression).

3. Use the Retelling Rubric to rate the student's retelling of the passage.

4. To view a student's performance over time, enter scores on the Student Profile: Oral Reading Fluency Progress Tracker.

Reteaching and Practice

Use Learning Station Time to differentiate instruction and provide practice for every learner.

Score	Issue	Strategy
4	• Students are ready for more challenging texts • Students can model fluency for lower-level readers	• Assign an OL or AL Small Group Reading book. Invite students to select a portion of the book and rehearse and record a dramatic oral reading of that section. Save recordings and pages at a listening station for other students. • Encourage students to monitor wcpm for longer readings using the **Comprehension Coach**. • For oral reading fluency, group higher-level readers with lower-level readers for paired reading. *Use the Paired Reading Routine, page BP31.*
3	• Students need repeated practice to develop automaticity • Students can build fluency with leveled texts	• **For students who can improve accuracy and rate:** • Have students practice rereading the Oral Reading Assessment passage to improve rate and improve automaticity. • Have students select a portion of their Small Group Reading book. Have them rehearse and record a dramatic oral reading of that section. • Encourage students to monitor wcpm for longer readings using the **Comprehension Coach**. • **For students who can improve comprehension:** • Encourage students to underline key ideas and take notes as they silently reread the passage. Then have students retell the passage again.
2	• Students need targeted phonics intervention • Students can build fluency with leveled texts and reading routines	• Evaluate miscues to identify gaps in decoding proficiency. Use **Reach into Phonics** for intervention. • *Use Additional Reading Routines on pages BP30–BP31 for fluency practice.*
1	• Students need intensive phonics intervention • Students can build fluency with leveled texts and reading routines	• Evaluate miscues to identify common errors. Use the **Reach into Phonics** Placement Test to place students for intensive phonics intervention. See **Reach into Phonics**, pages T257–T282. • *Use Additional Reading Routines on pages BP30–BP31 for fluency practice.*

Name _____

Oral Reading Assessment Progress Tracker

Record the student's scores from the Oral Reading Assessment to track progress over time. For Accuracy and Rate, enter words correct per minute (wcpm). For the other rows, enter the student's rubric score.

	Unit 1	Unit 2	Unit 3	Unit 4	Unit 5	Unit 6	Unit 7	Unit 8
Accuracy and Rate (wcpm)								
Automaticity and Pace								
Phrasing								
Intonation								
Expression								
Retelling (optional)								

Grade 3 Assessment

A1.3

Oral Reading Assessment

Gary's grandfather took a walk every day around the city	10
park. He loved the birds. He loved the flowers. But he always	22
came back huffing and puffing because the park had no	32
benches. There was no place to rest!	39
One day, Gary looked at Grandpa breathing so hard. He	49
suddenly had an idea. Grandpa needed a place to rest in his	61
walks. It was time for some benches in the park! Gary would	73
find a way to raise the money. The plan came in a flash—a	87
talent show.	89
Almost every person he knew had some special talent.	98
Carson could do magic tricks, and Ms. Alma could juggle. Kayla	109
was a hip-hop dancer, and Rosie had a talking parrot. He knew	121
everyone would come together to help because this was a	131
good cause.	133
Gary and his friends worked hard over the next few months.	144
They named themselves "The Talent Team."	150
On the night of the show, the theater was buzzing with	161
excitement. The lights dimmed, and Gary took a deep breath.	171
From the moment the curtain rose, everything went perfectly. At	181
the end of the show, the crowd jumped to their feet, clapping	193
and cheering.	195
Within a few weeks, Gary's grandfather was sitting on a new	206
park bench. He was not huffing and puffing. He was smiling to	218
himself and thinking about how proud he was of his grandson.	229

Oral Reading Assessment

2006 Hasbrouck & Tindal Oral Reading Fluency Data

Grade	Percentile	Fall WCPM	Winter WCPM	Spring WCPM
3	90	128	146	162
	75	99	120	137
	50	71	92	107
	25	44	62	78
	10	21	36	48

Accuracy and Rate

words attempted in one minute	−	number of errors	=	words correct per minute (wcpm)

Oral Reading Fluency Rubrics

Circle Score	Automaticity 4 3 2 1	Phrasing 4 3 2 1	Intonation 4 3 2 1	Expression 4 3 2 1
4	Reads smoothly and automatically. Pace is consistent.	Consistently pauses at all appropriate places in the text.	Changes pitch to match all of the content.	Reads with appropriate feeling for all content.
3	Reads most words automatically but still pauses to decode some words. Pace varies but is mostly consistent.	Frequently pauses at all appropriate places in the text.	Changes pitch to match some of the content.	Reads with appropriate feeling for most content.
2	Pauses to decode many words. Pace is slow with occasional stops and starts.	Occasionally pauses while reading the text.	Changes pitch, but does not match the content.	Reads with appropriate feeling for some content.
1	Can only read some high frequency words automatically. Pauses to decode all others or skips words. Pace is very slow and irregular with many stops and starts.	Rarely pauses while reading the text.	Does not change pitch.	Does not read with feeling.

© National Geographic Learning, a part of Cengage Learning, Inc.

Grade 3 Assessment

A1.5

Unit 1 | Happy to Help

Name _____   Date _____

Oral Reading Assessment

Retelling Rubric	
Circle Score	4 3 2 1
4	Student provides an accurate and complete retelling of the passage that includes the main idea and supporting details presented in a logical order.
3	Student's retelling is accurate and coherent but some elements and supporting details may be missing.
2	Student provides some details from the passage, but the retelling does not demonstrate understanding of the main idea and lacks coherence. Or, student may identify the topic without any elaboration.
1	Student is not able to retell the passage or retells it inaccurately.

Observations and Notes:

_____

Oral Reading Assessment Wrap-up

• Ask the student about his or her reading. You can prompt the student with questions such as:

> *Did you have any problems reading this passage?*
> If yes: *What problems did you have?*
> *What did you do when you didn't know a word?*

• Share the positive things you noticed about the student's reading, for example:

> *I noticed that you read with a lot of expression.*
> *Your reading is getting smoother. You don't stop as often as you used to.*

• Make suggestions about what improvements are needed, for example:

> *Try to read more smoothly without stopping between words.*

• If you asked the student to retell the story, make notes about what the student needs to improve, e.g., distinguish the main idea from details, or present events in the proper sequence.

Reading Comprehension Test   Unit 1, Week 1

Directions: Read the story. Then answer the questions about the story.

A Beautiful Park

Everyone knew Mr. Rubin. He worked in a special garden in the park. He arrived at the first light of day and stayed until the sun set. He took care of the flowers, cut the grass, and raked the leaves. He was very proud of the garden. He knew that many people came to the park just to see it.

One morning, as Mr. Rubin was leaving his house, he got an exciting telephone call from his daughter. She lived in another state. His daughter invited Mr. Rubin to visit her. She wanted to show her father all the interesting places to visit near her town. Mr. Rubin wanted to see her. He was worried, though. He would be away for an entire week. Who would take care of the garden while he was gone?

The other gardeners at the park told Mr. Rubin he should go. He worked very hard and never took a vacation. They told him not to worry. They would take care of everything while he was away. Mr. Rubin decided to leave the next week.

GO ON →

Reading Comprehension Test

Mr. Rubin had a wonderful vacation with his daughter. When he returned, Mr. Rubin was happy to see how good the garden looked. The flowers were watered. The leaves were raked. He knew his friends had worked hard while he was away.

1 The first part of the story tells about —

Ⓐ Mr. Rubin's job.

Ⓑ Mr. Rubin's friends.

Ⓒ Mr. Rubin's vacation.

Ⓓ Mr. Rubin's daughter.

2 Mr. Rubin's daughter calls him. What happens next?

Ⓐ He worries about the garden.

Ⓑ He tells his friends he is going away.

Ⓒ He goes to the park to cut the grass.

Ⓓ He feels proud about how good the garden looks.

3 The other gardeners learn about Mr. Rubin's trip. What happens next?

Ⓐ They ask where Mr. Rubin is going.

Ⓑ They help Mr. Rubin plan his vacation.

Ⓒ They tell Mr. Rubin that he works too hard.

Ⓓ They tell Mr. Rubin he should go.

4 What happens at the end of the story?

Ⓐ Mr. Rubin tells his daughter about the garden.

Ⓑ Mr. Rubin sees that the garden still looks nice.

Ⓒ Mr. Rubin waters the flowers and rakes the leaves.

Ⓓ Mr. Rubin thinks the gardeners have worked too hard.

Score
_____/4

COPY READY

ANSWER KEY: 1. A 2. A 3. D 4. B

Name _____ Date _____

Vocabulary Test

Directions: Choose the answer that completes the sentence correctly.

1 The broken toy is a _____.

Ⓐ minute

Ⓑ country

Ⓒ problem

Ⓓ birthday

2 She _____ a package in the mail.

Ⓐ baked

Ⓑ looked

Ⓒ learned

Ⓓ received

3 This is a _____.

Ⓐ gift

Ⓑ lion

Ⓒ nose

Ⓓ clown

4 She is making a _____. She is fixing the house.

Ⓐ foot

Ⓑ color

Ⓒ number

Ⓓ difference

5 I picked more apples than I can carry! The _____ is for my big sister to help carry them.

Ⓐ splash

Ⓑ trouble

Ⓒ solution

Ⓓ mountain

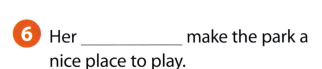

6 Her _____ make the park a nice place to play.

Ⓐ stairs

Ⓑ actions

Ⓒ world

Ⓓ clothes

GO ON →

Grade 3 Assessment   **A1.9**   Unit 1 | Happy to Help

ANSWER KEY: 1. C   2. D   3. A   4. D   5. C   6. B

COPY READY

Name ______________________ Date ______________________

Vocabulary Test

Unit 1, Week 1

7 When you __________ something, you cannot live without it.

Ⓐ need

Ⓑ lock

Ⓒ drop

Ⓓ answer

8 You show __________ when you are nice to someone.

Ⓐ kindness

Ⓑ evening

Ⓒ feather

Ⓓ secret

9 When you hope or wish for something, you __________ it.

Ⓐ ride

Ⓑ send

Ⓒ want

Ⓓ bring

10 When you __________ a story, you know what it means.

Ⓐ hide

Ⓑ dress

Ⓒ return

Ⓓ understand

11 When you __________ something, you care about it.

Ⓐ guess

Ⓑ value

Ⓒ leave

Ⓓ drive

Score ______/11

DONE!

ANSWER KEY: 7. A 8. A 9. C 10. D 11. B

Writing, Revising, and Editing Test   Unit 1, Week 1

Directions: Read the paragraph. Then answer the questions.

> My grandma lives in the country. She lives on ___1___ . She used to check her mailbox every day for letters from her grandchildren. We don't send letters anymore. Instead, we use e-mail! Grandma wanted to learn how to use e-mail, too. Her friend, ___2___ , helped her buy a computer from a store over in ___3___ . Our cousin also helped. She taught Grandma how to use e-mail. Grandma has the ___4___ to learn something new. I think it is because of the ___5___ she feels for her family.

1 Choose the answer that goes in Blank 1.

Ⓐ rose lane

Ⓑ rose Lane

Ⓒ Rose Lane

Ⓓ Rose lane

2 Choose the answer that goes in Blank 2.

Ⓐ Mrs. benton

Ⓑ mrs. benton

Ⓒ mrs. Benton

Ⓓ Mrs. Benton

3 Choose the answer that goes in Blank 3.

Ⓐ Ridge City

Ⓑ ridge City

Ⓒ Ridge city

Ⓓ ridge city

4 Choose the answer that goes in Blank 4.

Ⓐ courage

Ⓑ mailbox

Ⓒ children

Ⓓ neighbors

GO ON

Writing, Revising, and Editing Test

Unit 1, Week 1

5 Choose the answer that goes in Blank 5.

Ⓐ friends

Ⓑ water

Ⓒ pets

Ⓓ love

6 Read this sentence from the paragraph. Choose the noun.

> My grandma lives in the country.

Ⓐ My

Ⓑ grandma

Ⓒ lives

Ⓓ in

7 Read this sentence from the paragraph. Choose the noun.

> We don't send letters anymore.

Ⓐ don't

Ⓑ send

Ⓒ letters

Ⓓ anymore

8 Read this sentence from the paragraph. Choose the noun.

> Our cousin also helped.

Ⓐ Our

Ⓑ cousin

Ⓒ also

Ⓓ helped

9 Write a short story for your classmates about someone who helped someone else. Tell what happened in order. Underline words and phrases that help show the order.

Score	
_____ /8	multiple-choice
_____ /4	writing

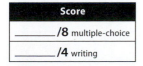

© National Geographic Learning, a part of Cengage Learning, Inc.

Grade 3 Assessment   **A1.12**   Unit 1 | Happy to Help

ANSWER KEY: 5. **D**   6. **B**   7. **C**   8. **B**   9. **See Rubric**

COPY READY

Reading Comprehension Test

Directions: Read the poem. Then answer the questions about the poem.

It's snowing hard in our small town.
Big flakes of snow are drifting down.
But since this is a weekend day,
my friends and I go out to play.

"Let's build a person out of snow."
"Okay. What fun! Come on, let's go!"
To do it we must work together,
out here in this freezing weather.

Inside our mittens are strong hands
to do the work this job demands.
We start with little balls of snow.
We roll them far and watch them grow!

We push, we lift, our faces gleam
while helping each other, like a team.
We add a hat, and now we're done.
Working together was lots of fun.

GO ON ➡

Name _____ Date _____

Reading Comprehension Test

1 How many beats are in this line from the poem?

> out here in this freezing weather.

Ⓐ 6

Ⓑ 7

Ⓒ 8

Ⓓ 9

2 In this line of the poem, which word has the loudest beat?

> my friends and I go out to play.

Ⓐ my

Ⓑ I

Ⓒ go

Ⓓ play

3 Which line from the poem uses colorful language?

Ⓐ *Big flakes of snow are drifting down.* *

Ⓑ *To do it we must work together,*

Ⓒ *"Okay. What fun! Come on, let's go!"*

Ⓓ *to do the work this job demands.*

4 What is the rhyme scheme in this poem?

Ⓐ a b c b

Ⓑ a b c d

Ⓒ a b a b

Ⓓ a a b b

Score

_____ /4

DONE!

ANSWER KEY: 1. C   2. D   3. A   4. D

COPY READY

Vocabulary Test

Directions: Read the question. Choose the correct answer.

1 Which list shows these words in alphabetical order?

| ice   hear   gold |

Ⓐ hear, ice, gold

Ⓑ ice, gold, hear

Ⓒ gold, hear, ice

Ⓓ hear, gold, ice

2 Which list shows these words in alphabetical order?

| apple   asleep   art |

Ⓐ art, apple, asleep

Ⓑ art, asleep, apple

Ⓒ asleep, art, apple

Ⓓ apple, art, asleep

3 Which list shows these words in alphabetical order?

| purple   pull   puzzle |

Ⓐ pull, purple, puzzle

Ⓑ puzzle, pull, purple

Ⓒ purple, puzzle, pull

Ⓓ pull, puzzle, purple

4 Which list shows these words in alphabetical order?

| friend   free   from |

Ⓐ friend, from, free

Ⓑ free, friend, from

Ⓒ free, from, friend

Ⓓ from, free, friend

Score

_____/4

DONE!

Grade 3 Assessment

A1.15

Unit 1 | Happy to Help

ANSWER KEY: 1. C 2. D 3. A 4. B

Name _____ Date _____

Writing, Revising, and Editing Test Unit 1, Week 2

Directions: Read the paragraph. Then answer the questions.

> A man named Mr. Smitt lives across the street. __**1**__ lives alone. His children live far away, so __**2**__ can't visit often. One day, my mother received a letter addressed to Mr. Smitt. __**3**__ both took it to him. Mr. Smitt __**4**__. We sat and talked on his front porch. __**5**__ was pretty tall. We offered to mow the lawn. Now we visit his house every week to help him around the house. __**6**__ are easy, and we keep Mr. Smitt company.

1 Choose the answer that goes in Blank 1.

Ⓐ It

Ⓑ He

Ⓒ We

Ⓓ She

2 Choose the answer that goes in Blank 2.

Ⓐ I

Ⓑ we

Ⓒ you

Ⓓ they

3 Choose the answer that goes in Blank 3.

Ⓐ We

Ⓑ She

Ⓒ You

Ⓓ They

4 Choose the answer that goes in Blank 4.

Ⓐ with the letter

Ⓑ across the street

Ⓒ glad to have visitors

Ⓓ was happy to see us

GO ON ➡

ANSWER KEY:　1. B　2. D　3. A　4. D

Writing, Revising, and Editing Test

5 Choose the answer that goes in Blank 5.

- Ⓐ Growing fast
- Ⓑ needing to be cut
- Ⓒ The grass in his yard
- Ⓓ the lawn was green and

6 Choose the answer that goes in Blank 6.

- Ⓐ So far
- Ⓑ The chores
- Ⓒ most of the jobs
- Ⓓ take me an hour

7 Read this sentence from the paragraph. Choose the predicate.

> A man named Mr. Smitt lives across the street.

- Ⓐ A man
- Ⓑ Mr. Smitt lives across
- Ⓒ lives across the street
- Ⓓ A man named Mr. Smitt

8 Read this sentence from the paragraph. Choose the subject.

> One day, my mother received a letter addressed to Mr. Smitt.

- Ⓐ One day
- Ⓑ Mr. Smitt
- Ⓒ my mother
- Ⓓ received a letter

9

> Think of a time when teamwork solved a problem. It could be something that happened in real life, on television, or in the movies. Write a paragraph with colorful details to describe what happened. Underline the colorful details in your paragraph.

Score	
_____ /8	multiple-choice
_____ /4	writing

DONE!

ANSWER KEY: 5. C   6. B   7. C   8. C   9. See Rubric

COPY READY

Reading Comprehension Test

Unit 1, Week 3

Directions: Read the passage. Then answer the questions about the passage.

HOUSE CALLS

A hundred years ago, six out of ten people lived out in the country. It was hard to get into town to see a doctor. The town doctor visited people at home instead. He carried a black bag with his tools. This kind of visit was a "house call."

Over time, more people moved into towns and cities. Doctors started using large machines. They didn't fit into a black bag! People had to go to the doctor's office for treatment.

Today, sick patients still visit the doctor's office. However, some doctors now use telephones and computers to help people. It's the modern way to make a house call.

---

1 Being sick was different a hundred years ago because the doctor —

Ⓐ kept an office in town.

Ⓑ visited people at home.

Ⓒ lived out in the country.

Ⓓ tried to help sick people.

2 What changed when doctors began to use large machines?

Ⓐ People went to the doctor's office.

Ⓑ Doctors went to people's houses.

Ⓒ People reached their doctor by computer.

Ⓓ Doctors called people on the telephone.

GO ON ➡

Grade 3 Assessment

A1.18

Unit 1 | Happy to Help

Reading Comprehension Test

Directions: Read the passage. Then answer the questions about the passage.

Long ago, most people lived on farms. Farmers sold their harvest to people they knew.

Over time, trains and trucks were invented. They could carry large loads over long distances. Farmers could sell to more people. Some farms became huge. When planes were invented, farm harvests could go all over the world. Most of the time, farmers didn't know the people they were feeding.

Today, some people want to get fresh food from small farms near their home. They give money to the farm. In return, they get a weekly basket of vegetables or fruit. This is called Community Supported Agriculture. People often visit the farms. Once again, the farmers know who is eating their harvest!

---

3 How did farming change after trains, trucks, and planes were invented?

Ⓐ More people moved to farms.

Ⓑ Farmers grew different kinds of crops.

Ⓒ Harvests could be sold to people far away.

Ⓓ Farmers could spend more time with their neighbors.

4 How is Community Supported Agriculture like farms in the past?

Ⓐ The farmers grow food on very large farms.

Ⓑ The farmers ship their food around the world.

Ⓒ The farmers give out weekly baskets of food.

Ⓓ The farmers know the people they are feeding.

Score

_____/4

DONE!

ANSWER KEY: 3. C   4. D

Vocabulary Test

Directions: Choose the answer that completes the sentence correctly.

1 There is a park in our _____.

Ⓐ railroad

Ⓑ telephone

Ⓒ snowstorm

Ⓓ neighborhood

2 I _____ the park when I clean it.

Ⓐ improve

Ⓑ throw

Ⓒ count

Ⓓ hope

3 An _____ is one person.

Ⓐ office

Ⓑ animal

Ⓒ example

Ⓓ individual

4 I _____ an apple to my friend.

Ⓐ use

Ⓑ offer

Ⓒ smell

Ⓓ understand

5 A _____ helps to put books away.

Ⓐ volunteer

Ⓑ squirrel

Ⓒ puppet

Ⓓ bicycle

GO ON ➡

ANSWER KEY: **1. D   2. A   3. D   4. B   5. A**

Vocabulary Test

6 Picking up trash has a positive _____ on the park.

Ⓐ aunt

Ⓑ orange

Ⓒ impact

Ⓓ apartment

7 When you _____ something, you find out something new.

Ⓐ sing

Ⓑ feed

Ⓒ learn

Ⓓ excite

8 When you _____ something, you tell what it is.

Ⓐ roll

Ⓑ fight

Ⓒ climb

Ⓓ identify

9 A _____ is something that is helpful.

Ⓐ flash

Ⓑ duck

Ⓒ minute

Ⓓ benefit

10 When you do your _____, you do what you are supposed to do.

Ⓐ gift

Ⓑ duty

Ⓒ clock

Ⓓ glove

Score

_____/10

DONE!

Grade 3 Assessment

A1.21

Unit 1 | Happy to Help

ANSWER KEY: 6. C   7. C   8. D   9. D   10. B

COPY READY

Name _____ Date _____

Writing, Revising, and Editing Test Unit 1, Week 3

Directions: Read the paragraph. Then answer the questions.

> Amy was a good student. ___**1**___ was fun for her. Then in second grade, she ___**2**___. Her teacher, Mr. Fritz, asked her to stay after class. He gave her a note to take home. It said, "Amy ___**3**___ glasses." The next day, ___**4**___ went to the eye doctor. They chose a new pair of glasses. Soon, Amy was reading everything in sight!

1 Choose the answer that goes in Blank 1.

Ⓐ School

Ⓑ Always

Ⓒ Study hard

Ⓓ In the classroom

2 Choose the answer that goes in Blank 2.

Ⓐ when she studied

Ⓑ and her classmates

Ⓒ had trouble reading

Ⓓ who wanted to do well

3 Choose the answer that goes in Blank 3.

Ⓐ reading

Ⓑ needs

Ⓒ with

Ⓓ now

4 Choose the answer that goes in Blank 4.

Ⓐ Mr. Fritz said

Ⓑ with the teacher

Ⓒ when school was out

Ⓓ Amy and her mother

GO ON ➡

Grade 3 Assessment

A1.22

Unit 1 | Happy to Help

ANSWER KEY: 1. A   2. C   3. B   4. D

Writing, Revising, and Editing Test

Unit 1, Week 3

5 Which of these is a sentence that could be added to the paragraph?

Ⓐ After they returned from the eye doctor.

Ⓑ The glasses made everything look clear.

Ⓒ Many kinds of glasses to choose from.

Ⓓ In the eye doctor's exam room.

6 Which of these is a sentence that could be added to the paragraph?

Ⓐ After school that day.

Ⓑ Because Amy likes books.

Ⓒ Mr. Fritz was happy for Amy.

Ⓓ Helping Amy with her schoolwork.

7 You are planning to interview someone for a research report about solving problems. First, narrow your topic and write it down. Then write one main question and two specific questions to ask in the interview. Use a question word in each question: *who, what, when, where, which, why,* or *how.* Underline the question words.

General Topic: _solving problems_ _____

Narrow Topic: _____

Main Question: _____

Specific Question: _____

Specific Question: _____

Score
_____ /6 multiple-choice
_____ /4 writing

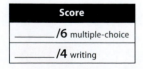

DONE!

ANSWER KEY: 5. B   6. C   7. See Rubric

Name _____ Date _____

Reading Comprehension Test

Directions: Read the poem. Then answer the questions about the poem.

Sun	Mon	Tue	Wed	Thu	Fri	Sat
						★

Saturday Helpers

My sis and I keep busy.

We lend a helping hand.

When there's a job, we do it.

Our parents think it's grand!

On Saturdays, we all wake up.

We have a bite to eat.

Then after that, we start the list

Of chores we must complete!

We make our beds with clean sheets,

Then put our toys away.

We hardly ever take a break

And do not stop to play!

We need to dust the tabletops.

The floors need sweeping, too.

If something sticky spilled on them,

They're mopped till they look new!

When at last we've done it all,

It's noon and time for lunch.

Everyone is hungry now

For something good to munch!

GO ON ▶

Name ____________________ Date ____________________

Reading Comprehension Test

Unit Test

1 In the middle of the poem, the children —

Ⓐ wake up.

Ⓑ eat breakfast.

Ⓒ mop the floor.

Ⓓ put away their toys.

2 At the end of the poem, the children —

Ⓐ stop to play.

Ⓑ make the beds.

Ⓒ are ready for lunch.

Ⓓ look at a list of chores.

3 Which is the rhyme scheme in this poem?

Ⓐ a b c b

Ⓑ a b a b

Ⓒ a a b b

Ⓓ a b b c

4 Which line from the poem uses colorful words?

Ⓐ Our parents think it's grand!

Ⓑ We hardly ever take a break

Ⓒ They're mopped till they look new!

Ⓓ It's noon and time for lunch.

GO ON

COPY READY

ANSWER KEY: **1.** D **2.** C **3.** A **4.** C

Name _____   Date _____

Reading Comprehension Test

Directions: Read the passage. Then answer the questions about the passage.

Many people know the story of Johnny Appleseed. It might surprise them to learn that Johnny Appleseed was a real person. His name was John Chapman. He lived more than 200 years ago. Johnny loved apples, apple trees, and apple blossoms. He wanted to see apple trees planted all over the country.

Johnny decided to make his dream come true. He walked miles through the open land. He carried a bag of apple seeds with him. When Johnny found a place he liked, he stopped. He checked the soil. If the soil was good, he dug holes and planted his seeds. He cared for the seeds until they grew into small trees.

One day, Johnny came to a small farm. A man and a woman waved at Johnny. They asked him to stay for dinner. After dinner, they brought out a bowl of big, red apples. Johnny smiled. Their apples were from a tree Johnny had planted many years before!

Soon apple trees were everywhere. People began to call John Chapman Johnny Appleseed. Now, when you bite into your next apple, you can think of Johnny Appleseed's dream. You can thank him for making it come true.

GO ON ➡

Reading Comprehension Test

5 Before Johnny's travels, the open land was without —

Ⓐ farms.

Ⓑ good soil.

Ⓒ apple trees.

Ⓓ kind neighbors.

6 How was Johnny's life different after his dream came true?

Ⓐ He moved to a small farm.

Ⓑ He could see apple trees everywhere.

Ⓒ He started a business selling apple seeds.

Ⓓ He didn't like the taste of apples anymore.

7 Think about the point of view for "Johnny Appleseed." What clue words help you know the point of view?

Ⓐ "he" and "him"

Ⓑ "you" and "your"

Ⓒ "they" and "their"

GO ON ➡

Reading Comprehension Test

Directions: Read the passage. Then answer the questions about the passage.

Homework Pals

My name is Marc Molino. My family moved a lot when I was young. Each time we moved, everything was new. I lived in a different home and went to a different school. I was part of a new city. It was hard to feel comfortable.

When we moved to Centerville, things were new again. This time, though, I felt at home right away. I made friends quickly and liked my teacher. Changing schools for so many years was hard sometimes, but I got good grades anyway. I knew that school was not easy for everyone. Some students had trouble with reading and math. I started to wonder what I could do to help.

One day, I saw a poster at school. It read, "Homework Pals Wanted. Students helping students. Come to the library." This was my chance to help!

After school, I told the librarian that I was a pretty good student, and I wanted to be a homework pal. Right away she took me to a younger boy sitting at a table. I saw that he had a book and a notebook open, but he was frowning and pushing his pencil around on the table. The book was one I had read last year. When the librarian introduced me, the boy smiled up at me. I smiled back.

Being a homework pal was yet another reason to like my new home.

GO ON ➡

Reading Comprehension Test

8 What was Marc's life like before he lived in Centerville?

Ⓐ He made friends easily.

Ⓑ He had a favorite teacher.

Ⓒ He spent time helping others.

Ⓓ He was often in a new place.

9 How did Marc's life change after he moved to Centerville?

Ⓐ He had more spare time.

Ⓑ He felt like he belonged.

Ⓒ He wanted to get better grades.

Ⓓ He started a new club at the library.

10 What is the author's point of view in "Homework Pals"? First write the point of view. Then write two sentences that tell the author's view about changing schools.

Score

_____ /12

DONE!

Name _____   Date _____

Vocabulary Test

Directions: Read the question. Use the dictionary entry to choose the correct answer.

> **dark** (**dark**) *adjective* having little or no light
>
> **daughter** (**daw**-ter) *noun* a parent's girl child
>
> **differently** (**dif**-er-unt-lē) *adverb* not in the same way
>
> **discover** (dis-**ku**-ver) *verb* to see, find out, or learn about

1 What does the word <u>differently</u> mean?

Ⓐ a parent's girl child

Ⓑ not in the same way

Ⓒ having little or no light

Ⓓ to see, find out, or learn about

2 What does the word <u>discover</u> mean?

Ⓐ a parent's girl child

Ⓑ not in the same way

Ⓒ having little or no light

Ⓓ to see, find out, or learn about

GO ON

Grade 3 Assessment   **A1.30**   **Unit 1** | Happy to Help

COPY READY

Vocabulary Test

---

blossom (**blo**-sum) *noun* the flower of a plant

boldly (**bōld**-lē) *adverb* a way of acting with courage

borrow (**bar**-ō) *verb* to take something and promise to give it back

bulky (**bul**-kē) *adjective* large; having great weight

---

3 What does the word <u>blossom</u> mean?

Ⓐ the flower of a plant

Ⓑ large; having great weight

Ⓒ a way of acting with courage

Ⓓ to take something and promise to give it back

4 What does the word <u>bulky</u> mean?

Ⓐ the flower of a plant

Ⓑ large; having great weight

Ⓒ a way of acting with courage

Ⓓ to take something and promise to give it back

Directions: Read the question. Choose the correct answer.

5 Which list shows these words in alphabetical order?

rod   rope   role

Ⓐ role, rod, rope

Ⓑ rope, rod, role

Ⓒ role, rope, rod

Ⓓ rod, role, rope

6 Which list shows these words in alphabetical order?

would   word   woke

Ⓐ word, would, woke

Ⓑ would, woke, word

Ⓒ woke, word, would

Ⓓ woke, would, word

GO ON →

ANSWER KEY: 3. A   4. B   5. D   6. C

COPY READY

Name ______________________ Date ______________________

Vocabulary Test

Unit Test

Directions: Choose the answer that completes the sentence correctly.

7 Ben __________ a good grade on his test.

Ⓐ served

Ⓑ survived

Ⓒ received

Ⓓ provided

8 One __________ of books is to learn about new places.

Ⓐ action

Ⓑ benefit

Ⓒ problem

Ⓓ kindness

9 The new park will __________ our town.

Ⓐ want

Ⓑ require

Ⓒ measure

Ⓓ improve

10 The principal's speech made a big __________ on the students.

Ⓐ impact

Ⓑ variety

Ⓒ character

Ⓓ individual

11 My aunt is a __________ at the animal shelter.

Ⓐ gift

Ⓑ duty

Ⓒ volunteer

Ⓓ neighborhood

12 We __________ to collect food for our town's food bank every year.

Ⓐ offer

Ⓑ value

Ⓒ identify

Ⓓ understand

Score
_____/12

DONE!

ANSWER KEY: 7. C 8. B 9. D 10. A 11. C 12. A

Writing, Revising, and Editing Test   **Unit Test**

Directions: Read the paragraph. Then answer the questions.

> My uncle is so nice. I try to be like him. He is full of ____**1**____. He would never show ____**2**____ toward anyone. For example, ____**3**____ went to the repair shop to pick up his truck last week. When he got there, the truck was not ready. Instead of getting upset, my uncle smiled at the shop owner. He told her he would pick it up later.

---

1 Choose the answer that goes in Blank 1.

- Ⓐ family
- Ⓑ friends
- Ⓒ kindness
- Ⓓ presents

2 Choose the answer that goes in Blank 2.

- Ⓐ cars
- Ⓑ anger
- Ⓒ gasoline
- Ⓓ nephews

3 Choose the answer that goes in Blank 3.

- Ⓐ my uncle
- Ⓑ walked very far
- Ⓒ with my cousins
- Ⓓ when it broke down

4 Read this sentence from the paragraph. Choose the noun.

> My uncle is so nice.

- Ⓐ My
- Ⓑ uncle
- Ⓒ is
- Ⓓ nice

GO ON ➡

ANSWER KEY: 1. C   2. B   3. A   4. B

Name _____   Date _____

Writing, Revising, and Editing Test

Directions: Read the paragraphs. Then answer the questions.

(1) My family and I moved to a new town. (2) I made some friends at school, but my mom seems lonely. (3) My mom have nothing to do. (4) She needs a new friend to spend time with.

(5) Our new neighbor, Ms. Rand, seems like a nice person. (6) Every time my mom or dad see Ms. Rand, Ms. Rand is in a hurry. (7) Ms. Rand is always friendly, but she is very busy. (8) She works in the community and helps others. (9) She and other helpers read to children at the library. (10) She also teach English to people new to the United States.

(11) When my mom thought about what Ms. Rand does. (12) Now my mom and Ms. Rand volunteer together.

---

5 Which of these is the predicate in sentence 1?

Ⓐ I moved

Ⓑ My family and I

Ⓒ to a new town

Ⓓ moved to a new town

6 What is the correct way to write sentence 3?

Ⓐ My mom has nothing to do.

Ⓑ My mom have nothing to do?

Ⓒ My Mom have nothing to do.

Ⓓ Correct as is

GO ON

Writing, Revising, and Editing Test

7 What is the correct way to write sentence 6?

(A) Every time my mom or dad see Ms. Rand, she are in a hurry.

(B) Every time my mom or dad see Ms. Rand, who is in a hurry.

(C) Every time my mom or dad sees Ms. Rand, she is in a hurry.

(D) Correct as is

8 What is the correct way to write sentence 9?

(A) She and other helpers who read to children at the library.

(B) She and other helpers reads to children at the library.

(C) She and other helpers read to childrens at the library.

(D) Correct as is

9 What is the correct way to write sentence 10?

(A) She also teach english to people new to the United States.

(B) She also teaches English to people new to the United States.

(C) She also teach English to people new to the united states.

(D) Correct as is

10 What is the correct way to write sentence 11?

(A) When my mom thought about what Ms. Rand does, who lives next door to us.

(B) When my mom thought about what Ms. Rand does to help others.

(C) When my mom thought about what Ms. Rand does, she decided to help others, too.

(D) Correct as is

GO ON →

ANSWER KEY: 7. C   8. D   9. B   10. C

Writing, Revising, and Editing Test

11 Read the paragraph. There are six mistakes in grammar and usage, punctuation, capitalization, or spelling. Use the Editing and Proofreading Marks to correct each mistake.

(1) My dad and I takes my new baby sister to the doctor. (2) It needs to see dr. Kaplan. (3) The doctor are a tall man with a big smile. (4) He says that the baby very healthy. (5) Then he tell me to set a good example for my new sister. (6) I smile and promise that I will be a good big brother.

Editing and Proofreading Marks

∧	Add.
ℰ	Take out.
⌒⌒	Move to here.
∧	Add comma.
⊙	Add period.

12 Your class is writing personal narratives to share with classmates. Write about a time you set a good example for someone else. Your narrative should have at least three paragraphs.

Score	
_____ /10	multiple-choice
_____ /6	editing task
_____ /4	weekly writing skill
_____ /24	writing traits

DONE!

COPY READY

ANSWER KEY: **11. See Rubric** **12. See Rubric**

Name _____   Date _____

Weekly and Unit Assessments   Unit 1

Enter the scores for the Oral Reading Assessment administered in this unit.

Oral Reading Assessment	wcpm	Oral Reading Fluency Rubrics				Retelling
		Automaticity	Phrasing	Intonation	Expression	
		_____/4	_____/4	_____/4	_____/4	_____/4

Enter the scores from the Spelling Pre-Test and the End-of-Week Test in the table. Calculate the percent for each End-of-Week Test or use the conversion charts on page A1.46.

Spelling Tests	Week 1	Week 2	Week 3	Week 4
Pre-Test CC.3.Rfou.3, L.2, L.2.e, L.2.f	_____/19	_____/19	_____/19	_____/19
End-of-Week Test CC.3.Rfou.3, L.2, L.2.e, L.2.f	____/19 ____%	____/19 ____%	____/19 ____%	____/19 ____%

Circle the item number for each item answered correctly. Assign 1 point for each correct answer. For tests scored with rubrics, enter the student's rubric scores. Calculate the percent of the overall score or use the conversion charts on page A1.46.

Reading Comprehension Tests	Weekly Test Items			Unit Test Items	Totals
	Week 1	Week 2	Week 3	Including Week 4	Across Tests
Literature Text Structures CC.3.Rlit.5	1 2 3 4			1 2	_____/6
Elements of a Poem CC.3.Rlit.5		1 2 3 4		3 4	_____/6
Informational Text Structures CC.3.Rinf.8			1 2 3 4	5 6 8 9	_____/8
Point of View CC.3.Rinf.10				7 10 (____/3)	_____/4
Total	____/4 ____%	____/4 ____%	____/4 ____%	____/12 ____%	

Vocabulary Tests	Weekly Test Items			Unit Test Items	Totals
	Week 1	Week 2	Week 3	Including Week 4	Across Tests
Social Studies Vocabulary CC.3.L.6, Rlit.4, Rinf.4	1 2 3 4 5 6		1 2 3 4 5	7 9 11	_____/14
Academic Vocabulary CC.3.L.6, Rlit.4, Rinf.4	7 8 9 10 11		6 7 8 9 10	8 10 12	_____/13
Alphabetical Order CC.3.L.2.g		1 2 3 4		5 6	_____/6
Determine Meanings CC.3.L.4.d				1 2 3 4	_____/4
Total	____/11 ____%	____/4 ____%	____/10 ____%	____/12 ____%	

Name _____   Date _____

Weekly and Unit Assessments

Unit 1

Writing, Revising, and Editing Tests		Weekly Test Items			Unit Test Items Including Week 4	Totals Across Tests
		Week 1	Week 2	Week 3		
Revising and Editing	Nouns CC.3.L.2, L.1.c, L.1.a, W.5	1 2 3 4 5 6 7 8			1 2 4 11c	_____/12
	Pronouns CC.3.L.1.a, W.5		1 2 3		11b	_____/4
	Sentence Structure CC.3.L.1, L.1.a, L.2, L.1.h, W.5		4 5 6 7 8	1 2 3 4 5 6	3 5 7 8 10 11a 11e	_____/18
	Subject-Verb Agreement CC.3.L.1.f, W.5				6 9 11d 11f	_____/4
	Subtotal	_____/8	_____/8	_____/6	_____/16	
Weekly Writing Skills (Writing Prompts)	Develop a Plot Sequence CC.3.W.3.a, W.3.c, W.3.d	_____/4				_____/4
	Use Colorful Details to Elaborate CC.3.W.3.b, L.3.a		_____/4			_____/4
	Choose and Narrow Topic, Develop Interview Questions CC.3.W.7, W.8			_____/4		_____/4
	Use Formal and Informal Language CC.3.L.3.b, W.3				_____/4	_____/4
	Subtotal	_____/4	_____/4	_____/4	_____/4	
	Total	____/12 ____%	____/12 ____%	____/10 ____%	____/20 ____%	

Unit Test Writing Prompt—Traits CC.3.L.3.b, W.3	Ideas	Organization	Voice	Word Choice	Fluency	Conventions	Total
	_____/4	_____/4	_____/4	_____/4	_____/4	_____/4	_____/24

Fill in the strategy or the strategies used each week and enter the score.

Reading Strategy Assessments	Week 1	Week 2	Week 3	Week 4
	_____/4	_____/4	_____/4	_____/4
	_____/4	_____/4	_____/4	_____/4
	_____/4	_____/4	_____/4	_____/4
	_____/4	_____/4	_____/4	_____/4

Enter the score for each Weekly Project.

Weekly Projects	Week 1	Week 2	Week 3	Week 4
Writing or Research Project	_____/24	_____/24	_____/24	_____/24

COPY READY

Weekly and Unit Assessments

Unit 1

The Class Profile will help you group students for review and reteaching. Use the Student Profiles to complete this summary information for your class. Write a minus sign (–) if the student would benefit from review and reteaching.

	Student Name										
Reading Comprehension — Literature Text Structures CC.3.Rlit.5											
Elements of a Poem CC.3.Rlit.5											
Informational Text Structures CC.3.Rinf.8											
Point of View CC.3.Rinf.10											
Writing, Revising, and Editing — Nouns CC.3.L.2, L.1.c, L.1.a, W.5											
Pronouns CC.3.L.1.a, W.5											
Sentence Structure CC.3.L.1, L.1.a, L.2, L.1.h, W.5											
Subject-Verb Agreement CC.3.L.1.f, W.5											
Writing in Response to Prompt CC.3.W.3, L.1.a, L.3.a, L.3.b, W.7, W.8											
Vocabulary — Social Studies Vocabulary CC.3.L.6, Rlit.4, Rinf.4,											
Academic Vocabulary CC.3.L.6, Rlit.4, Rinf.4											
Alphabetical Order CC.3.L.2.g											
Determine Meanings CC.3.L.4.d											

Name _____ Date _____

Strengths and Needs Summary

Use this chart to summarize the strengths and needs of individual students. This information will be helpful during student conferences and for instructional planning.

	Consistent Strengths	Some Successes	Greatest Needs
Reading Comprehension			
Oral Reading			
Vocabulary			
Spelling			
Grammar			
Written Composition			

Grade 3 Assessment

A1.40

Unit 1 | Happy to Help

Writing Rubric

Score Point	Ideas	Organization	Voice	Word Choice	Fluency	Conventions	Presentation
4	• The writing has a clear, focused message that keeps readers interested. • Details are accurate and relevant, showing in-depth knowledge of the topic.	• The writing has a clear structure throughout that suits the writer's audience and purpose. • All content flows smoothly and logically.	• The writing sounds genuine and unique. • The writer's tone is appropriate to the purpose and audience.	• Appropriate words were chosen to clearly convey the writer's message. • Language used throughout is appropriate for the audience and grabs readers' attention.	• All sentences are varied and effective and have appropriate transitions. • When read aloud, the writing sounds natural and rhythmic.	• The writing has only a few minor errors in spelling, punctuation, capitalization, grammar, usage, and paragraphing. • All the sentences are complete.	• The text is presented in an orderly way, significantly helping to convey the message. • Visuals are appropriate for the purpose and audience, and effectively support meaning.
3	• Most of the writing has a clear, focused message that keeps readers interested. • Most details are accurate and relevant, showing reasonable knowledge of the topic.	• Most of the writing has a clear structure that suits the writer's audience and purpose. • Most of the content flows smoothly and logically.	• Most of the writing sounds genuine and unique. • The writer's tone is mostly appropriate for the purpose and audience.	• Many appropriate words were chosen to clearly convey the writer's message. • Most language is appropriate for the audience and grabs readers' attention.	• Most sentences are varied and effective and have appropriate transitions. • When read aloud, most of the writing sounds natural and rhythmic.	• The writing has some errors in spelling, punctuation, capitalization, grammar, usage, and paragraphing. • Most of the sentences are complete.	• Most of the text is presented in an orderly way, generally helping to convey the message. • Most visuals are appropriate for the purpose and audience, and effectively support meaning.
2	• The writing is a fairly unclear and unfocused message, causing readers some confusion. • Some details are relevant and accurate, showing minimum knowledge of the topic.	• The writing does not have a structure that suits the writer's audience and purpose. • Some content flows smoothly and logically.	• Some of the writing sounds genuine and unique. • The writer's tone is somewhat inappropriate for the purpose and audience.	• Some appropriate words were chosen to clearly convey the writer's message. • Some language is appropriate for the audience and grabs readers' attention.	• Some sentences are varied and effective and have appropriate transitions. • When read aloud, some of the writing sounds natural and rhythmic.	• The writing has several errors in spelling, punctuation, capitalization, grammar, usage, and paragraphing. • Some of the sentences are complete.	• Some of the text is presented in an orderly way, but it is a little difficult to track and comprehend the message. • Some visuals are appropriate for the purpose and audience and support meaning.
1	• The writing does not have a clear, focused message, causing readers confusion. • Many details are irrelevant and inaccurate, indicating a lack of knowledge of the topic.	• The writing does not have a structure. • The content does not flow smoothly or logically.	• The writing does not sound genuine or unique. • The writer's tone is not appropriate for the purpose or audience.	• Few appropriate words were chosen to clearly convey the writer's message. • Language is dull, vague, and inappropriate for the audience, losing the readers' attention.	• Few or none of the sentences are varied or effective or have appropriate transitions. • When read aloud, the writing sounds unnatural.	• The writing has many errors in spelling, punctuation, capitalization, grammar, usage, and paragraphing. • Few sentences are complete.	• The text is not presented in an orderly way, making it very difficult to track and comprehend the message. • None of the visuals are appropriate for the purpose or audience, and do not support meaning.

Research Rubric

Scale	Content	Speaking/Listening
4	• Oral report contains plenty of information about a person's accomplishment. • Information was presented in a logical order.	• Speaker speaks clearly and at an appropriate pace during the entire oral report. • Speaker presents a visual display that enhances the presentation.
3	• Oral report contains enough information about a person's accomplishment. • Information was presented in a mostly logical order.	• Speaker speaks clearly and at an appropriate pace most of the time during the oral report. • Speaker presents a visual display that mostly enhances the presentation.
2	• Oral report contains some information about a person's accomplishment. • Information was presented in a somewhat logical order.	• Speaker speaks clearly and at an appropriate pace during some of the oral report. • Speaker presents a visual display that somewhat enhances the presentation.
1	• Oral report does not contain information about a person's accomplishment. • Information was not presented in a logical order.	• Speaker does not speak clearly or at an appropriate pace during the oral report. • Speaker does not present a visual display.

Name _____   Date _____

Unit Self-Assessment

Directions: Mark a ✔ in one box for each skill.

I can...	I can do this and can tell others how to do it.	I can do this by myself.	I can do this if I have help or look at an example.
put words in alphabetical order.			
use a dictionary to find the meanings of words.			
plan and monitor when I read.			
tell what happens in the beginning, middle, and end of a story.			
understand the parts of poems.			
make comparisons.			
identify an author's point of view.			
identify and use nouns and pronouns and understand when to capitalize them.			
use correct subject-verb agreement.			
identify the subject and predicate of a sentence.			
make complete and correct sentences.			

Of all the texts you read for Happy to Help, which one was your favorite? _____

_____

What did you like about it? _____

_____

_____

_____

Answer Keys and Rubrics

Reading Comprehension

Week 1

Item	Key	Item Descriptor	CCSS Code
1	A	Plot	CC.3.Rlit.5
2	A	Plot	CC.3.Rlit.5
3	D	Plot	CC.3.Rlit.5
4	B	Plot	CC.3.Rlit.5

Week 2

Item	Key	Item Descriptor	CCSS Code
1	C	Elements of a Poem	CC.3.Rlit.5
2	D	Elements of a Poem	CC.3.Rlit.5
3	A	Elements of a Poem	CC.3.Rlit.5
4	D	Elements of a Poem	CC.3.Rlit.5

Week 3

Item	Key	Item Descriptor	CCSS Code
1	B	Make Comparisons	CC.3.Rinf.8
2	A	Make Comparisons	CC.3.Rinf.8
3	C	Make Comparisons	CC.3.Rinf.8
4	D	Make Comparisons	CC.3.Rinf.8

Unit Test (including Week 4)

Item	Key	Item Descriptor	CCSS Code
1	D	Plot	CC.3.Rlit.5
2	C	Plot	CC.3.Rlit.5
3	A	Elements of a Poem	CC.3.Rlit.5
4	C	Elements of a Poem	CC.3.Rlit.5
5	C	Make Comparisons	CC.3.Rinf.8
6	B	Make Comparisons	CC.3.Rinf.8
7	A	Point of View	CC.3.Rinf.10
8	D	Make Comparisons	CC.3.Rinf.8
9	B	Make Comparisons	CC.3.Rinf.8
10	Skill Rubric	Point of View	CC.3.Rinf.10

Vocabulary

	Week 1 CC.3.L.6, Rlit.4, Rinf.4			Week 3 CC.3.L.6, Rlit.4, Rinf.4	
Item	Key	Word	Item	Key	Word
1	C	problem	1	D	neighborhood
2	D	received	2	A	improve
3	A	gift	3	D	individual
4	D	difference	4	B	offer
5	C	solution	5	A	volunteer
6	B	actions	6	C	impact
7	A	need	7	C	learn
8	A	kindness	8	D	identify
9	C	want	9	D	benefit
10	D	understand	10	B	duty
11	B	value			

Week 2

Item	Key	Item Descriptor	CCSS Code
1	C	Alphabetical Order	CC.3.L.2.g
2	D	Alphabetical Order	CC.3.L.2.g
3	A	Alphabetical Order	CC.3.L.2.g
4	B	Alphabetical Order	CC.3.L.2.g

Unit Test (including Week 4)

Item	Key	Item Descriptor	CCSS Code
1	B	Determine Meanings	CC.3.L.4.d
2	D	Determine Meanings	CC.3.L.4.d
3	A	Determine Meanings	CC.3.L.4.d
4	B	Determine Meanings	CC.3.L.4.d
5	D	Alphabetical Order	CC.3.L.2.g
6	C	Alphabetical Order	CC.3.L.2.g
7	C	Social Studies Vocabulary	CC.3.L.6, Rlit.4, Rinf.4
8	B	Academic Vocabulary	CC.3.L.6, Rlit.4, Rinf.4
9	D	Social Studies Vocabulary	CC.3.L.6, Rlit.4, Rinf.4
10	A	Academic Vocabulary	CC.3.L.6, Rlit.4, Rinf.4
11	C	Social Studies Vocabulary	CC.3.L.6, Rlit.4, Rinf.4
12	A	Academic Vocabulary	CC.3.L.6, Rlit.4, Rinf.4

COPY READY

Answer Keys and Rubrics

Writing, Revising, and Editing

Week 1

Item	Key	Item Descriptor	CCSS Code
1	C	Common and Proper Nouns	CC.3.L.2
2	D	Common and Proper Nouns	CC.3.L.2
3	A	Common and Proper Nouns	CC.3.L.2
4	A	Concrete and Abstract Nouns	CC.3.L.1.c
5	D	Concrete and Abstract Nouns	CC.3.L.1.c
6	B	Identify Nouns	CC.3.L.1.a
7	C	Identify Nouns	CC.3.L.1.a
8	B	Identify Nouns	CC.3.L.1.a
Prompt (9)	Skill Rubric	Develop a Plot Sequence	CC.3.W.3.a, W.3.c, W.3.d

Week 2

Item	Key	Item Descriptor	CCSS Code
1	B	Subject Pronouns	CC.3.L.1.a
2	D	Subject Pronouns	CC.3.L.1.a
3	A	Subject Pronouns	CC.3.L.1.a
4	D	Complete Sentences (formation)	CC.3.L.1, L.2
5	C	Complete Sentences (formation, capitalization)	CC.3.L.1, L.2
6	B	Complete Sentences (formation, capitalization)	CC.3.L.1, L.2
7	C	Parts of a Sentence	CC.3.L.1
8	C	Parts of a Sentence	CC.3.L.1
Prompt (9)	Skill Rubric	Use Colorful Details to Elaborate	CC.3.W.3.b, L.3.a

Week 3

Item	Key	Item Descriptor	CCSS Code
1	A	Simple Subject and Predicate	CC.3.L.1
2	C	Complete Subject and Predicate	CC.3.L.1
3	B	Simple Subject and Predicate	CC.3.L.1
4	D	Complete Subject and Predicate	CC.3.L.1
5	B	Phrases and Clauses	CC.3.L.1
6	C	Phrases and Clauses	CC.3.L.1
Prompt (7)	Skill Rubric	Choose and Narrow Topic, Develop Interview Questions	CC.3.W.7, W.8

Unit Test (including Week 4)

Item	Key	Item Descriptor	CCSS Code
1	C	Concrete and Abstract Nouns	CC.3.L.1.c
2	B	Concrete and Abstract Nouns	CC.3.L.1.c
3	A	Complete Subject and Predicate	CC.3.L.1
4	B	Identify Nouns	CC.3.L.1.a
5	D	Editing: Parts of a Sentence	CC.3.L.1, W.5
6	A	Editing: Subject-Verb Agreement	CC.3.L.1.f, W.5
7	C	Editing: Compound Subjects	CC.3.L.1.h, W.5
8	D	Editing: Compound Subjects	CC.3.L.1.h, W.5
9	B	Editing: Subject-Verb Agreement	CC.3.L.1.f, W.5
10	C	Editing: Phrases and Clauses	CC.3.L.1, W.5
11a	Editing Rubric	Editing Task: Compound Subjects	CC.3.L.1.h, W.5
11b	Editing Rubric	Editing Task: Subject Pronouns	CC.3.L.1.a, W.5
11c	Editing Rubric	Editing Task: Common and Proper Nouns	CC.3.L.2, L.1.a, W.5
11d	Editing Rubric	Editing Task: Subject-Verb Agreement	CC.3.L.1.f, W.5
11e	Editing Rubric	Editing Task: Simple Subject and Predicate	CC.3.L.1.a, W.5
11f	Editing Rubric	Editing Task: Subject-Verb Agreement	CC.3.L.1.f, W.5
Prompt (12)	Skill Rubric, Writing Rubric	Use Formal and Informal Language	CC.3.L.3.b, L.1.a, W.3

Answer Keys and Rubrics

 Unit 1

Conversion Charts: Points Earned to Percent Scored

4 points

Points	1	2	3	4
%	25	50	75	100

10 points

Points	1	2	3	4	5	6	7	8	9	10
%	10	20	30	40	50	60	70	80	90	100

11 points

Points	1	2	3	4	5	6	7	8	9	10	11
%	9	18	27	36	45	55	64	73	82	91	100

12 points

Points	1	2	3	4	5	6	7	8	9	10	11	12
%	8	17	25	33	42	50	58	67	75	83	92	100

19 points

Points	1	2	3	4	5	6	7	8	9	10	11	12	13	14	15	16	17	18	19
%	5	11	16	21	26	32	37	42	47	53	58	63	68	74	79	84	89	95	100

20 points

Points	1	2	3	4	5	6	7	8	9	10	11	12	13	14	15	16	17	18	19	20
%	5	10	15	20	25	30	35	40	45	50	55	60	65	70	75	80	85	90	95	100

Writing, Revising, and Editing

Week 1 Skill Rubric
Item 9 (Prompt) | Develop a Plot Sequence

Student writes a story with signal words that

4 points	clearly indicate the sequence of events.
3 points	adequately indicate the sequence of events.
2 points	occasionally indicate the sequence of events.
1 point	do not indicate the sequence of events.

Week 2 Skill Rubric
Item 9 (Prompt) | Use Colorful Details to Elaborate

Student describes people solving a problem using

4 points	vivid words and effective details.
3 points	adequate words and some details.
2 points	mediocre words and few details.
1 point	bland words and no details.

Week 3 Skill Rubric
Item 7 (Prompt) | Choose and Narrow Topic, Develop Interview Questions

Student writes interview questions that relate

4 points	closely to a clearly stated, narrow topic.
3 points	adequately to a broad stated topic.
2 points	somewhat to a vague topic.
1 point	minimally to a vague topic.

Scoring Note: Assign a score of zero for no response or an unscorable response.

Writing, Revising, and Editing

Unit Test Week 4 Skill Rubric
Item 12 (Prompt) | Use Formal and Informal Language

Student writes a personal narrative using formal and informal language

4 points	appropriately.
3 points	adequately.
2 points	haphazardly.
1 point	inappropriately.

Use the Writing Rubric on page A1.41 to assess the writing traits of student responses for the Unit Test Writing Prompt.

Unit Test Editing Task Rubric
Item 11 | 1 point correct per response

11a	In sentence 1, change "takes" to "take"
11b	In sentence 2, change "It" to "She"
11c	In sentence 2, change "dr." to "Dr."
11d	In sentence 3, change "are" to "is"
11e	In sentence 4, add "is," "looks," or "appears," after "baby"
11f	In sentence 5, change "tell" to "tells"

Reading Comprehension

Unit Test Rubric
Item 10 | Point of View

3 points	Correctly identifies the author's point of view, and provides details that tell about the author's viewpoint.
2 points	Correctly identifies the author's point of view, but does not provide details that tell about the author's viewpoint.
1 point	Does not correctly identify the author's point of view.

Name _____ Date _____

Plot

Review the Rules

The most important events in a story make up the plot.

- **The beginning tells what happens first.**
- **The middle tells what happens next.**
- **The end tells what happens last.**

Practice

Read "The Morning Rush" and complete the Story Map.

The Morning Rush

Kendall wakes up suddenly and looks at the clock. It's almost 8:00 a.m. She's late!

Kendall quickly dresses and eats a fast breakfast. She runs to the bus stop, but realizes she's forgotten her homework. She has to run back home!

Now Kendall has to take the later bus. That will make her late for school! Kendall is having a bad morning.

Story Map

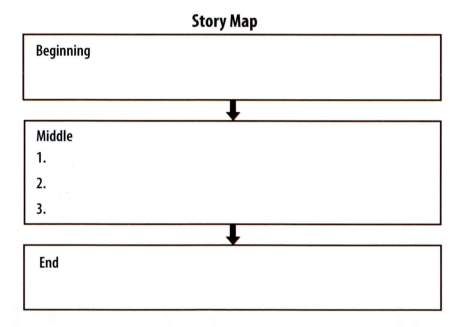

Beginning

Middle
1.
2.
3.

End

Apply

Share the plot of one of your Small Group Reading books with a partner. Tell about the events in the order they happened.

Plan and Monitor

Reteach

Review the Rules

Preview and predict to better understand what you read.

- **To preview, look ahead to see what you are about to read.**
- **As you read, make predictions about what will happen next. Read on to see if your prediction is correct.**

John Muir: Explorer

In 1879, Muir went to Alaska to search for glaciers. Glaciers are large pieces of ice that move slowly over the land. He climbed 1,460 feet to the top of a ridge and saw something amazing. It was a huge chunk of ice! He was the first white man to see Glacier Bay.

Muir wanted to remember the beautiful sight. He grabbed something from his pack. In his notebook, he drew pictures of the bay. He took a lot of notes. Muir came back many times to study the glaciers. He took notes on everything he saw.

Preview
The title says "John Muir," and I see a glacier. The text probably tells about Muir and glaciers.

Prediction
I predict that Muir found a glacier.

Check Prediction
My prediction was correct. Muir did see a glacier.

Practice

Read the first two sentences in the second paragraph. Finish the prediction.

1. I predict that Muir will get a _____ from his pack.

Now read the rest of the paragraph. Check your prediction. Complete one of the sentences:

2. My prediction was correct because _____.

   My prediction was not correct because _____.

Apply

Tell a partner about a prediction you made in one of your Small Group Reading books. How did you know it was correct or incorrect?

Writing Trait: Organization

Review the Rules

When you write, make sure that the order of events is clear. That way your readers can follow the events from beginning to end.

Practice

Revise the story. Use the Edit and Proofreading Marks.

- **Show sentences that are out of order.**
- **Add or change words to make the order clear.**

Edit and Proofreading Marks

∧	Add.
╱	Make lowercase.
⌒⌒∧	Move to here.

The Science Project

Lilah is excited about her science project. She proudly shows it to her friends and family. She builds a model of the solar system in her bedroom.

On the day of the science fair, Lilah starts to grab her model. It is gone! She is upset. Lilah hugs her mom.

Lilah's mom walks into the bedroom. "Your project already is at the school," her mom says. "I took it early this morning so that you didn't worry."

Apply

On a separate piece of paper, write an original story with events that follow a logical order. Let a partner read it to see if the order is clear.

Elements of a Poem

Review the Rules

A poem looks and sounds different from other kinds of writing.

- **A poet uses rhyme, rhythm, and colorful language to give the reader a special feeling.**
- **A poet uses a different number of lines or stanzas to tell about a topic.**

Practice

Read the poem. Then answer the questions.

> **Corn on the Cob**
>
> Corn on the cob is fun to eat.
>
> It's yellow and juicy and, oh, so sweet.
>
> With butter and salt it's hard to beat,
>
> So yummy and crunchy and fun to eat.

1. How many stanzas are in the poem? How many lines?

   _____

2. Draw a line under two words that tell how corn tastes.

3. Draw a box around three words that rhyme.

4. Tell how the poet feels about corn on the cob.

   _____

Apply

Read the poem.
- **Number the lines.**
- **Underline colorful language.**
- **Put a box around the words that rhyme.**

> The crunch of corn,
>
> The snap of peas,
>
> Give me more to eat, please!

Name _____ Date _____

Plan and Monitor

Reteach

Review the Rules

Preview and predict to better understand what you read.

- **To preview, look ahead to see what you are about to read.**
- **As you read, make predictions about what will happen next. Read on to see if your prediction is correct.**

Read the first paragraph of "Violet and Nadia." Look at the examples.

Violet and Nadia

Violet sat on her couch frowning. It was her birthday today. Violet and Nadia were together at school all day, but Nadia didn't say a word about it! How could that be? "I thought we were best friends," she thought sadly.

Suddenly, the doorbell rang. Violet dragged herself to the door to answer it.

"Surprise!" she said as she handed Violet a gift. "Your mom is taking us out for pizza."

"But I thought you forgot," Violet said.

"Of course not, Violet! You're my best friend!"

Preview
I read two girls' names in the title.

Predict
I predict that the girls are friends.

Check Prediction
My prediction is correct.

Practice

Read the second paragraph. Finish the prediction.

1. I predict that the person at the door is _____.

Now read the rest of the paragraph. Check your prediction. Complete one of the sentences:

2. My prediction was correct because _____.

My prediction was not correct because _____.

Apply

Tell a partner about a prediction you made in one of your Small Group Reading books. How did you know it was correct or incorrect?

COPY READY

Name _____   Date _____

Writing Trait: Word Choice

Review the Rules

When you write, choose words that

- **are colorful and descriptive**
- **paint a picture to help your readers "see" what things are like.**

Practice

Read each sentence. Circle the stronger word choice. Then read the sentences aloud.

1. The sleepy/exhausted kitten fell/tumbled off the bookshelf.

2. The room was jam-packed/filled with piles/towers of shoeboxes.

3. The velvety/soft kitten was terrified/scared.

4. The kind/nice girl gently/softly picked her up.

Apply

Write three sentences to continue the story above. Choose your words carefully to make the story interesting and help readers "see" what is the scene is like. Share your sentences with a partner.

_____

_____

_____

_____

_____

Make Comparisons

Reteach

Review the Rules

When you make comparisons, you tell how things are the same or how they are different. Sometimes you might compare how something has changed over time.

- Use *before* or *then* to tell what something was like in the past.
- Use *now* or *after* to tell what something is like in the present.

Practice

Read "A New Kind of Phone." Circle the words that show the past and the present.

A New Kind of Phone

Before 1973, mobile phones did not exist. The first mobile, or cellular, phones appeared in 1973. Back then, cell phones were shaped like bricks. They weighed almost two pounds! Cell phones then cost thousands of dollars.

After the 1980s, cell phones became smaller and smaller. Now, cell phones are shaped like a pack of cards. They only weigh a few ounces. Most are so small, they can fit right into your pocket! They don't cost nearly as much, either.

Use the words you circled to help you make comparisons. Complete the chart.

Cell phones

Before	After

Apply

Talk with a partner about one of your Small Group Reading books. Compare what something was like before with what it is like now.

Name _____   Date _____

Plan and Monitor

Review the Rules

When you read, check, or monitor, yourself to be sure you understand everything.

- **Ask questions to help you clarify the parts you don't understand.**
- **Reread or read on to find the answers to your questions.**

Read the first paragraph of "The Bald Eagle." Look at the example.

> ### The Bald Eagle
>
> Bald eagles are good hunters. They have amazing eyesight. They can see straight ahead and to the side at the same time. Their sharp talons help them capture prey. After grabbing food with their claws, eagles use their strong beaks to tear the food apart.
>
> Bald eagles really like fish. To capture fish, they fly down and grab them from the water. Sometimes an eagle will steal fish! The eagle waits for a hawk to bring a fish for its babies. The eagle bothers the hawk so much that it drops the fish. Then the eagle grabs it.

What are "talons"? I'll read on to see if I can find out.

Now I understand. "Talons" must be claws. Those are what eagles use to grab food.

Practice

Now read the second paragraph. What questions do you have? Write them on the lines below. How can you find the answers?

_____

_____

Apply

With a partner, review one of your Small Group Reading books. Share questions you had about the text and explain how you found the answers.

Point of View

Review the Rules

A narrator tells about topics using different points-of-view.

- **In the first-person point of view, the narrator tells about him- or herself. The narrator uses words such as** *I*, *me*, and *my*.
- **In the third-person point of view, the narrator tells about someone else. The narrator uses words such as** *she*, *her*, and *they*.

Practice

Read each selection. Circle the words in ( ) that describe it.

> ### Georgia O'Keefe
>
> Georgia O'Keefe is a famous American painter. Her close-ups of flowers changed the way people looked at nature. Georgia took her first art lessons at home, then learned more at college. Many people love Georgia's paintings. They study her paintings in museums around the world. After Georgia died, her house in New Mexico became a museum.

1. The selection uses the pronouns (*I*, *me*, *my*/*she*, *her*, *they*).

2. The narrator tells about (her own life/someone else's life).

3. The narrator (feels/does not feel) that art is important.

> ### My Favorite Subject
>
> I've always wanted to be a painter. As a girl, I drew pictures of my dog. As a teenager, I saw the ponies running in Assateague Island. That's what inspired me the most. In my art, I try to capture the beauty and grace of wild horses.

4. The selection uses the pronouns (*I*, *me*, *my*/*she*, *her*, *they*).

5. The narrator tells about (her own life/someone else's life).

6. The narrator (feels/does not feel) that animals are good art subjects.

Apply

Talk with a partner about one of your Small Group Reading books. Discuss the narrator's point of view.

RT1.9

Name _____ Date _____

Plan and Monitor

Review the Rules

When you read, check, or monitor, yourself to be sure you understand everything.

- Ask questions to help you clarify the parts you don't understand.
- Reread or read on to find the answers to your questions.

Read the first two paragraphs of "The Elephant and the Mouse." Look at the example.

The Elephant and the Mouse

One day, a tiny mouse bumped into an elephant. The elephant screamed and stood on a large tree trunk in fear. Mouse exclaimed, "Why would a big strong elephant be afraid of me?"

Elephant replied, "I may be a big strong elephant, but I'm afraid of things I don't understand. I don't understand how an animal can be so small!"

Mouse replied, "If you come down from there, I will be your friend. You can protect me, and I promise to help you with your fears." Mouse's idea made sense to Elephant, so he agreed and came down from the trunk.

> An elephant is huge. Why is it afraid of a mouse? As I read on, I see that Elephant tells Mouse why he is afraid.

Practice

Now read the third paragraph. What questions do you have? How can you find the answers?

_____

_____

Apply

With a partner, review one of your Small Group Reading books. Share questions you had about the text and explain how you found the answers.

Writing Trait: Voice

Review the Rules

Each writer has a unique voice, or way of using words. When you write, use your own voice. Use words that fit the situation and that sound like you.

Practice

Read Sarah's journal entry. Underline words or phrases that show her voice.

Thursday, January 28

   I'm so glad today's over! I had the worst day ever. This morning, I was late for the bus, so I forgot my lunch. Then, at lunch, Amy gave me half her sandwich. When I bit into it, I tasted pickles and peanut butter. Yuck! After that, I was working on my story when my pen started to leak. It dripped everywhere! I had to start over. What a pain! And on the way home I lost my notebook. Sure hope Mom doesn't get too upset with me!

Apply

Use your own voice to write about a day you had this week. Be sure that the writing sounds like you! Share your writing with a partner.

_____

_____

_____

_____

_____

_____

_____

_____

Reteaching Masters Answer Key

RT1.1 Plot

Story Map

Beginning
Kendall oversleeps.

↓

Middle
1. Kendall gets dressed and eats breakfast.
2. She runs for the bus, but forgets her homework.
3. She runs back home.

↓

End
Kendall takes the late bus, so she's late for school.

RT1.2 Plan and Monitor (Preview and Predict)

Answers will vary, but should reflect the content of the text.

1. I predict that Muir will get a camera/notebook from his pack.
2. My prediction was correct because Muir got a notebook from his pack to draw pictures in.
   My prediction was not correct because he used a notebook to help him remember everything, not a camera.

RT1.3 Writing Trait: Organization

The Science Project

Lilah is excited about her science project. She proudly shows it to her friends and family. She builds a model of the solar system in her bedroom.

On the day of the science fair, Lilah starts to grab her model. It is gone! She is upset. Lilah hugs her mom.
Then
∧ Lilah's mom walks into the bedroom. "Your project is already at the school," her mom says. "I took it early this morning so that you didn't worry."
∧

RT1.4 Elements of a Poem

Practice

1. There is one stanza and four lines.
2. Possible underlined words: *juicy, sweet, yummy*
3. Boxed rhyming words: *eat, sweet, beat*
4. The poet loves the taste of corn on the cob and thinks it's fun to eat.

Apply

The crunch of corn, 1

The snap of peas, 2

Give me more to eat, please! 3

RT1.5 Plan and Monitor (Preview and Predict)

Answers will vary, but should reflect the story's events.

1. I predict that the person at the door is the mail carrier/Nadia/Violet's neighbor.
2. My prediction was correct because it was Nadia at the door with a gift for Violet.
   My prediction was not correct because the person at the door was Nadia, not the mail carrier or the neighbor.

RT1.6 Writing Trait: Word Choice

1. The sleepy/exhausted kitten fell/tumbled off the bookshelf.
2. The room was jam-packed/filled with piles/towers of shoeboxes.
3. The velvety/soft kitten was terrified/scared.
4. The kind/nice girl gently/softly picked her up.

RT1.7 Make Comparisons

A New Kind of Phone

Before 1973, mobile phones did not exist. The first mobile, or cellular, phones appeared in 1973. Back then, cell phones were shaped like bricks. They weighed almost two pounds! Cell phones then cost thousands of dollars.

After the 1980s, cell phones became smaller and smaller. Now, cell phones are shaped like a pack of cards. They only weigh a few ounces. Most are so small, they can fit right into your pocket! They don't cost nearly as much either.

Cell Phones

Before	After
big, shaped like bricks	small, shaped like a pack of cards
heavy	light
expensive	not as expensive

RT1.8 Plan and Monitor (Monitor and Clarify)

Possible responses:

How does an eagle snatch fish? I can reread the first paragraph to find out. The claws, or talons, allow them to grab the fish from the water.

Does an eagle steal fish from a fisherman? I can read the next sentences to find out. It steals fish from a hawk as the hawk tries to feed its babies.

Reteaching Masters Answer Key, continued

RT1.9 Point of View

1. The selection uses the pronouns (*I, me, my*/she, her, they).

2 The narrator tells about (her own life/someone else's life).

3. The narrator (feels/does not feel) that art is important.

4. The selection uses the pronouns (*I, me, my*/she, her, they).

5. The narrator tells about (her own life/someone else's life).

6. The narrator (feels/does not feel) that animals are good art subjects.

RT1.10 Plan and Monitor (Monitor and Clarify)

Possible responses:

Why would Mouse want to be Elephant's friend? I can read on to find out. What did elephant agree to? I can reread the beginning of the paragraph to find out.

RT1.11 Writing Trait: Voice

Thursday, January 28

   I'm so glad today's over! I had the worst day ever. This morning, I was late for the bus, so I forgot my lunch. Then, at lunch, Amy gave me half her sandwich. When I bit into it, I tasted pickles and peanut butter. Yuck! After that, I was working on my story when my pen started to leak. It dripped everywhere! I had to start over. What a pain! And on the way home I lost my notebook. Sure hope Mom doesn't get too upset with me!

Contents

Reading Level Translation Key

	Guided Reading	DRA	Lexile®	Reading Recovery	
K	A	A–2		A–2	**K**
	B	3		3	
	C			4	
	D	4		5	
				6	
	E	6		7	
	F	8		8	
1			200L–400L	9	**1**
	G	10		10	
	H			11	
	I	12		12	
	J	14		14	
				15	
		16	200L–400L		
2	K				**2**
	L–M	18–28	300L–500L	18–20	
3	N–P	30–38	500L–700L	22–24	**3**
4	Q–R	40	650L–850L	26	**4**
5	S–U	44	750L–950L	28	**5**
6	V–W	50	850L–1000L		**6**

Reading levels are provided for each title in the *National Geographic Reach for Reading* Grade 1–2 Leveled Reading and Grades 3–5 Small Group Reading lessons. Please note that each leveling system is based on a different set of criteria. This may result in discrepancies when translating reading levels.

Grade 3 Unit 1 Cumulative Key Word List

accomplish (v)
achieve (v)
action (n)
advertisement (n)
agriculture (n)
alter (v)
alternative (n)
amount (n)
area (n)
artist (n)
balance (n)
behavior (n)
benefit (n)
blossom (n)
buyer (n)
carve (v)
category (n)
cause (n)
challenge (n)
character (n)
characteristic (n)
city (n)
clarify (v)
classify (v)
combine (v)
communicate (v)
compare (v)
comparison (n)
competition (n)
composition (n)
conclusion (n)
conditions (n)
connection (n)
conservation (n)
continent (n)
contrast (v)
control (v)
cooperation (n)
core (n)
create (v)
crop (n)
cycle (n)
decrease (v)
depend (v)
desert (n)
destination (n)
details (n)
determine (v)
develop (v)
difference (n)
direction (n)
discover (v)

distance (n)
diversity (n)
drought (n)
duty (n)
earthquake (n)
ecosystem (n)
effect (n)
endurance (n)
environment (n)
erupt (v)
estimate (v)
event (n)
evidence (n)
explore (v)
express (v)
farmer (n)
feelings (n)
feet (n)
field (n)
firm (adj)
flow (v)
food chain
force (n)
form (n)
freeze (v)
future (n)
generalization (n)
generation (n)
gift (n)
globe (n)
goal (n)
ground (n)
growth (n)
harvest (v)
heritage (n)
identify (v)
impact (n)
improve (v)
increase (v)
individual (n)
inference (n)
interact (v)
island (n)
journey (n)
kilometer (n)
kindness (n)
lava (n)
learn (v)
level (n)
liquid (n)
location (n)
magma (n)

main idea
market (n)
measurement (n)
melt (v)
meter (n)
method (n)
mixture (n)
money (n)
motive (n)
music (n)
narrator (n)
nature (n)
need (v)
negative (adj)
neighborhood (n)
occur (v)
ocean (n)
offer (v)
opinion (n)
order (n)
organism (n)
outcome (n)
paraphrase (v)
pay (v)
perform (v)
plate (n)
plenty (n)
plot (n)
plow (v)
point of view
popular (adj)
positive (adj)
power (n)
prediction (n)
prepare (v)
preservation (n)
pressure (n)
preview (v)
problem (n)
process (n)
produce (v)
protect (v)
purpose (n)
rainforest (n)
react (v)
receive (v)
region (n)
represent (v)
rescue (v)
resources (n)
reward (n)
rhythm (n)

river (n)
rock (n)
root (n)
sand (n)
scarce (adj)
scene (n)
seed (n)
seller (n)
sense (v)
sequence (n)
shore (n)
signal (n)
soil (n)
solid (n)
solution (n)
sprout (n)
stanza (n)
state (n)
storyteller (n)
strategy (n)
style (n)
substance (n)
summarize (v)
supply (n)
surface (n)
sustain (v)
tale (n)
temperature (n)
theme (n)
thermometer (n)
tradition (n)
trap (v)
tsunami (n)
understand (v)
unique (adj)
unit (n)
value (v)
vary (v)
vine (n)
visualize (v)
volcano (n)
volunteer (n)
want (v)
warn (v)
water (n)
wave (n)
weed (n)
wetland (n)
wood (n)

Words from Unit 1 appear in red type. For additional content words and story words, please see the Small Group Reading section.

Anthology Handbook

Handbook Contents

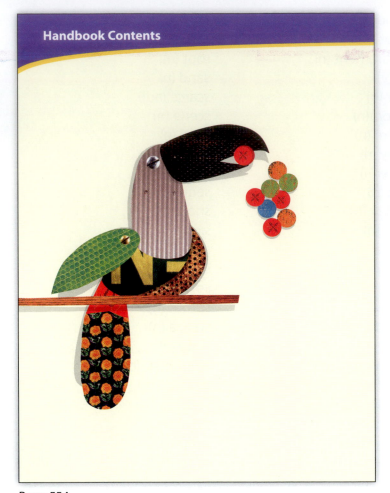

Page 554

555

Page 555

Strategies for Learning Language

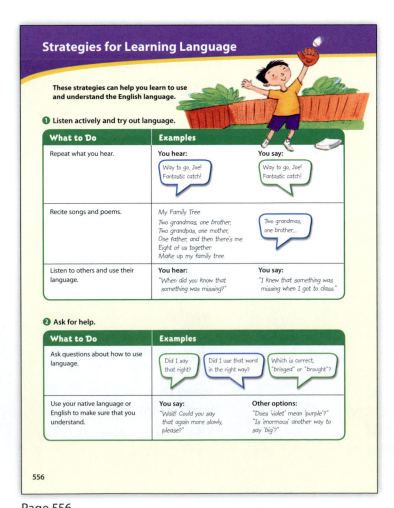

These strategies can help you learn to use and understand the English language.

1 Listen actively and try out language.

What to Do	Examples	
Repeat what you hear.	You hear: Way to go, Joe! Fantastic catch!	You say: Way to go, Joe! Fantastic catch!
Recite songs and poems.	My Family Tree Two grandmas, one brother; Two grandpas, one mother; One father; and then there's me. Eight of us together Make up my family tree.	Two grandmas, one brother,...
Listen to others and use their language.	You hear: "When did you know that something was missing?"	You say: "I knew that something was missing when I got to class."

2 Ask for help.

What to Do	Examples	
Ask questions about how to use language.	Did I say that right?	Did I use that word in the right way? Which is correct, "bringed" or "brought"?
Use your native language or English to make sure that you understand.	You say: "Wait! Could you say that again more slowly, please?"	Other options: "Does 'violet' mean 'purple'?" "Is 'enormous' another way to say 'big'?"

556

Page 556

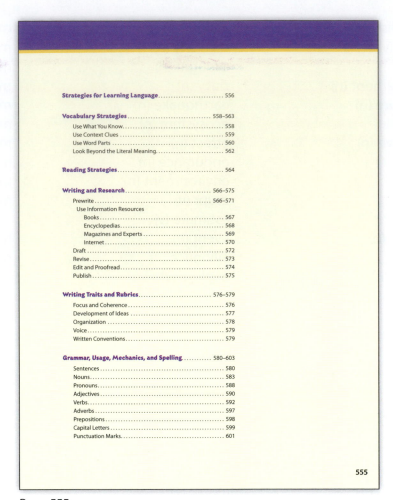

3 Use gestures and body language, and watch for them.

What to Do	Examples
Use gestures and movements to help others understand your ideas.	I will hold up five fingers to show that I need five more minutes.
Watch people as they speak. The way they look or move can help you understand the meaning of their words.	Let's give him a hand. Everyone is clapping. "Give him a hand" must mean to clap for him.

4 Think about what you are learning.

What to Do	Examples
Ask yourself: Are my language skills getting better? How can I improve?	Was it correct to use "they" when I talked about my grandparents? Did I add "'s" to show ownership?
Keep notes about what you've learned. Use your notes to practice using English.	How to Ask Questions • I can start a question with "is," "can," or "do": Do you have my math book? • I can start a question with "who," "what," "where," "when," "how," or "why" to get more information: Where did you put my math book?

557

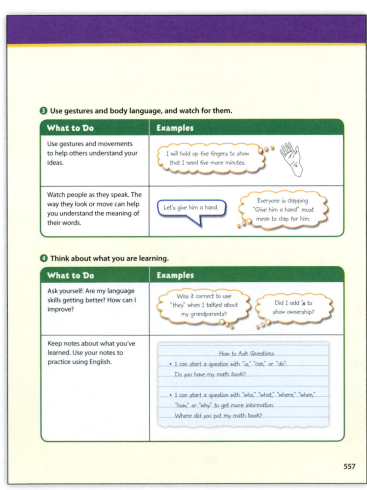

Page 557

Page 558

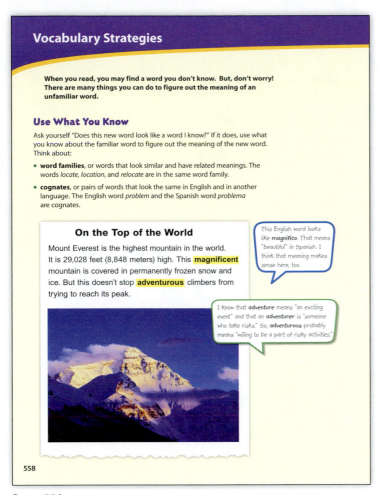

Vocabulary Strategies

When you read, you may find a word you don't know. But, don't worry! There are many things you can do to figure out the meaning of an unfamiliar word.

Use What You Know

Ask yourself "Does this new word look like a word I know?" If it does, use what you know about the familiar word to figure out the meaning of the new word. Think about:

- **word families**, or words that look similar and have related meanings. The words *locate*, *location*, and *relocate* are in the same word family.
- **cognates**, or pairs of words that look the same in English and in another language. The English word *problem* and the Spanish word *problema* are cognates.

> **On the Top of the World**
>
> Mount Everest is the highest mountain in the world. It is 29,028 feet (8,848 meters) high. This **magnificent** mountain is covered in permanently frozen snow and ice. But this doesn't stop **adventurous** climbers from trying to reach its peak.

This English word looks like magnifico. That means "beautiful" in Spanish. I think that meaning makes sense here, too.

I know that adventure means "an exciting event" and that an adventurer is "someone who take risks." So, adventurous probably means "willing to be a part of risky activities."

558

Page 559

Use Context Clues

Sometimes you can figure out a word's meaning by looking at other words and phrases near the word. Those words and phrases are called **context clues**.

There are different kinds of context clues. Look for signal words such as *means*, *like*, *but*, or *unlike* to help you find the clues.

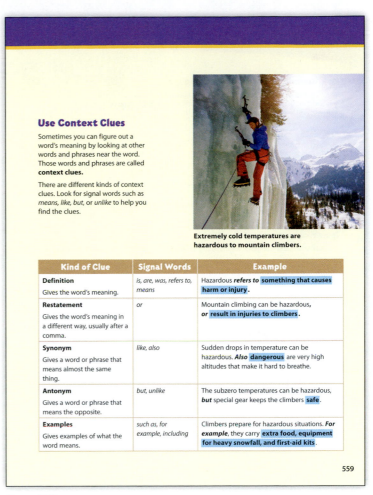

Extremely cold temperatures are hazardous to mountain climbers.

Kind of Clue	Signal Words	Example
Definition Gives the word's meaning.	*is, are, was, refers to, means*	Hazardous *refers to* something that causes harm or injury.
Restatement Gives the word's meaning in a different way, usually after a comma.	*or*	Mountain climbing can be hazardous, *or* result in injuries to climbers.
Synonym Gives a word or phrase that means almost the same thing.	*like, also*	Sudden drops in temperature can be hazardous. *Also* dangerous are very high altitudes that make it hard to breathe.
Antonym Gives a word or phrase that means the opposite.	*but, unlike*	The subzero temperatures can be hazardous, *but* special gear keeps the climbers safe.
Examples Gives examples of what the word means.	*such as, for example, including*	Climbers prepare for hazardous situations. *For example*, they carry extra food, equipment for heavy snowfall, and first-aid kits.

559

Page 560

Vocabulary Strategies, *continued*

Use Word Parts

Many English words are made up of parts. You can use these parts as clues to a word's meaning.

When you don't know a word, look to see if you know any of its parts. Put the meaning of the word parts together to figure out the meaning of the whole word.

Compound Words

A compound word is made up of two or more smaller words. To figure out the meaning of the whole word:

1. Break the long word into parts.
2. Put the meanings of the smaller words together to predict the meaning of the whole word.
3. If you can't predict the meaning from the parts, use what you know and the meaning of the other words to figure it out.

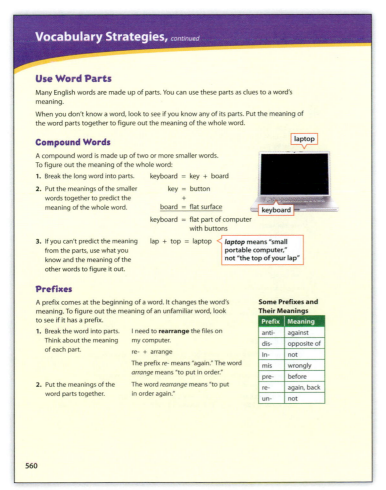

laptop

keyboard

keyboard = key + board

key = button
+
board = flat surface

keyboard = flat part of computer with buttons

lap + top = laptop

laptop means "small portable computer," not "the top of your lap"

Prefixes

A prefix comes at the beginning of a word. It changes the word's meaning. To figure out the meaning of an unfamiliar word, look to see if it has a prefix.

1. Break the word into parts. Think about the meaning of each part.

   I need to **rearrange** the files on my computer.

   re- + arrange

   The prefix *re-* means "again." The word *arrange* means "to put in order."

2. Put the meanings of the word parts together.

   The word *rearrange* means "to put in order again."

Some Prefixes and Their Meanings

Prefix	Meaning
anti-	against
dis-	opposite of
In-	not
mis-	wrongly
pre-	before
re-	again, back
un-	not

560

Page 561

Suffixes

A suffix comes at the end of a word. It changes the word's meaning and part of speech. To figure out the meaning of new word, look to see if it has a suffix.

1. Break the word into parts. Think about the meaning of each part.

   My **teacher** helps me find online articles.

   teach + -er

   verb

   The word *teach* means "to give lessons." The suffix *-er* means "one who."

2. Put the meanings of the word parts together.

   A *teacher* is "a person who gives lessons."

   noun

Some Suffixes and Their Meanings

Suffix	Meaning
-able	can be done
-al	having characteristics of
-ion	act, process
-er, -or	one who
-ful	full of
-less	without
-ly	in a certain way

Greek and Latin Roots

Many words in English have Greek and Latin roots. A root is a word part that has meaning, but it cannot stand on its own.

1. Break the unfamiliar word into parts.

   I won't be done in time if there's one more **interruption**!

   inter + rupt + ion

   prefix   root   suffix

2. Focus on the root. Do you know other words with the same root?

   "I've seen the root **rupt** in the words *erupt* and *rupture*. 'rupt' must have something to do with breaking or destroying something."

3. Put the meanings of all the word parts together.

   between   act or process

   inter + rupt + ion = interruption

   break   a break in activity

561

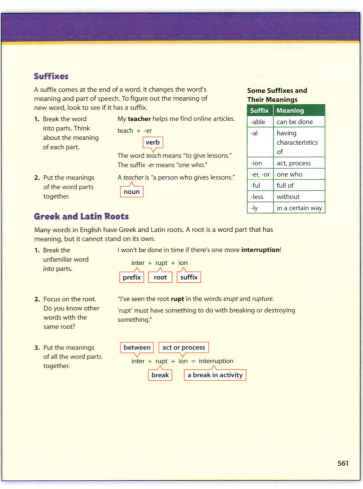

Handbook **R5**

Anthology Handbook, continued

Vocabulary Strategies, continued

Look Beyond the Literal Meaning

Writers use colorful language to keep their readers interested. They use words and phrases that mean something different from their usual definitions. Figurative language and idioms are kinds of colorful language.

Figurative Language: Similes

A simile compares two things that are alike in some way. It uses the words *like* or *as* to make the comparison.

Simile	Things Compared	How They're Alike
Cory hiked across the desert **as sluggishly as a snail**.	Cory and a snail	They both move very slowly.
His skin was **like sheets of sandpaper**.	skin and sandpaper	They are both rough and very dry.

Figurative Language: Metaphors

A metaphor compares two things without using the words *like* or *as*.

Metaphor	Things Compared	Meaning
The **sun's rays were a thousand bee stings** on his face.	sun's rays and bee stings	The sun's rays blistered his face.
His only **companion was thirst**.	friend and thirst	His thirst was always there with him.

Figurative Language: Personification

When writers use personification they give human qualities to nonhuman things.

Personification	Object	Human Quality
The **angry sun** kept punishing him.	sun	has feelings
A **cactus reached out to** him.	cactus	is able to be friendly

562

Idioms

An idiom is a special kind of phrase that means something different from what the words mean by themselves.

What you say:	What you mean:
If the topic is Mars, **I'm all ears**.	If the topic is Mars, **I'll listen very carefully**.
Break a leg!	**Good luck!**
Rachel had **to eat her words**.	Rachel had **to say she was wrong**.
Give me a break!	**That's ridiculous!**
Hang on.	**Wait**.
I'm **in a jam**.	I'm **in trouble**.
The joke was so funny, Lisa **laughed her head off**.	The joke was so funny, Lisa **laughed very hard**.
Juan was **steamed** when I lost his video game.	Juan was **very angry** when I lost his video game.
Let's **surf the Net** for ideas for report ideas.	Let's **look around the contents of the Internet** for report ideas.
I'm so tired, I just want to **veg out**.	I'm so tired, I just want to **relax and not think about anything**.
Rob and Zak are together **24-seven**.	Rob and Zak are together **all the time**.
You can say that again.	**I totally agree with you**.
Zip your lips!	**Be quiet!**

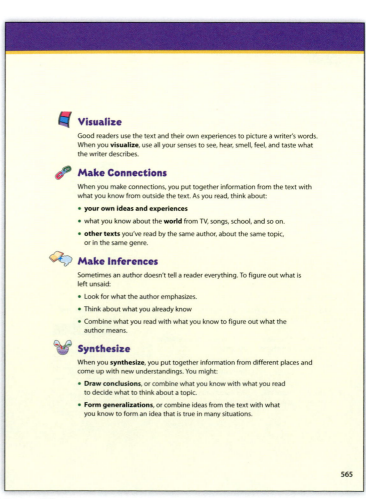

563

Reading Strategies

Good readers use a set of strategies before, during, and after reading. Knowing which strategy to use and when will help you understand and enjoy all kinds of text.

Plan and Monitor

Good readers have clear plans for reading. Remember to:

- **Set a purpose** for reading. Ask yourself: Why am I reading this? What do I hope to get from it?
- **Preview** what you are about to read. Look at the title. Scan the text, pictures, and other visuals.
- **Make predictions**, or thoughtful guesses, about what comes next. Check your predictions as you read. Change them as you learn new information.

Monitor, or keep track of, your reading. Remember to:

- **Clarify ideas and vocabulary** to make sure you understand what the words and passages mean. Stop and ask yourself: Does that make sense?
- **Reread, read on,** or **change your reading speed** if you are confused.

Determine Importance

How can you keep track of all the facts and details as you read? Do what good readers do and focus on the most important ideas.

- Identify the **main idea**. Connect details to the main idea.
- **Summarize** as you read and after you read.

Ask Questions

Asking yourself questions as you read keeps your mind active. You'll ask different types of questions, so you'll need to find the answers in different ways.

- Some questions are connected to answers **right there** in the text.
- Others cover more than one part of the text. So, you'll have to **think and search** to find the answers.

Not all answers are found in the book.

- **On your own** questions can focus on your experiences or on the big ideas of the text.
- **Author and you** questions may be about the author's purpose or point of view.

564

Visualize

Good readers use the text and their own experiences to picture a writer's words. When you **visualize**, use all your senses to see, hear, smell, feel, and taste what the writer describes.

Make Connections

When you make connections, you put together information from the text with what you know from outside the text. As you read, think about:

- **your own ideas and experiences**
- what you know about the **world** from TV, songs, school, and so on.
- **other texts** you've read by the same author, about the same topic, or in the same genre.

Make Inferences

Sometimes an author doesn't tell a reader everything. To figure out what is left unsaid:

- Look for what the author emphasizes.
- Think about what you already know
- Combine what you read with what you know to figure out what the author means.

Synthesize

When you **synthesize**, you put together information from different places and come up with new understandings. You might:

- **Draw conclusions**, or combine what you know with what you read to decide what to think about a topic.
- **Form generalizations**, or combine ideas from the text with what you know to form an idea that is true in many situations.

565

Page 566

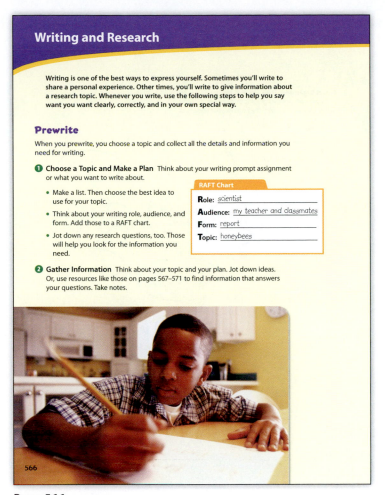

Writing and Research

Writing is one of the best ways to express yourself. Sometimes you'll write to share a personal experience. Other times, you'll write to give information about a research topic. Whenever you write, use the following steps to help you say want you want clearly, correctly, and in your own special way.

Prewrite

When you prewrite, you choose a topic and collect all the details and information you need for writing.

1 Choose a Topic and Make a Plan Think about your writing prompt assignment or what you want to write about.

- Make a list. Then choose the best idea to use for your topic.
- Think about your writing role, audience, and form. Add those to a RAFT chart.
- Jot down any research questions, too. Those will help you look for the information you need.

> **RAFT Chart**
>
> **Role:** scientist
> **Audience:** my teacher and classmates
> **Form:** report
> **Topic:** honeybees

2 Gather Information Think about your topic and your plan. Jot down ideas. Or, use resources like those on pages 567–571 to find information that answers your questions. Take notes.

566

Page 567

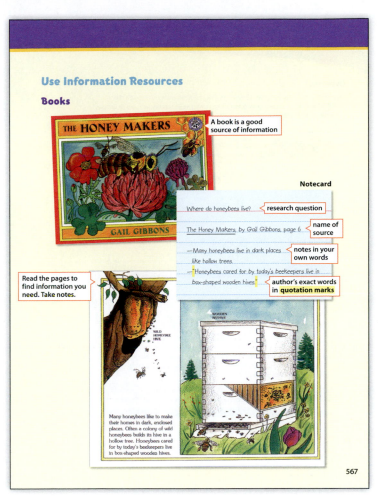

Use Information Resources

Books

THE HONEY MAKERS
GAIL GIBBONS

A book is a good source of information

Read the pages to find information you need. Take notes.

Many honeybees like to make their homes in dark, enclosed places. Often a colony of wild honeybees builds its hive in a hollow tree. Honeybees cared for by today's beekeepers live in box-shaped wooden hives.

Notecard

Where do honeybees live? — research question

The Honey Makers, by Gail Gibbons, page 6 — name of source

—Many honeybees live in dark places like hollow trees. — notes in your own words

"Honeybees cared for by today's beekeepers live in box-shaped wooden hives." — author's exact words in **quotation marks**

567

Page 568

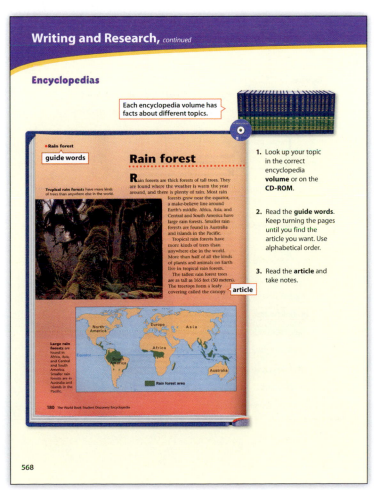

Writing and Research, continued

Encyclopedias

Each encyclopedia volume has facts about different topics.

guide words

Rain forest

Rain forests are thick forests of tall trees. They are found where the weather is warm the year around, and there is plenty of rain. Most rain forests grow near the equator, a make-believe line around Earth's middle. Africa, Asia, and Central and South America have large rain forests. Smaller rain forests are found in Australia and islands in the Pacific.

Tropical rain forests have more kinds of trees than anywhere else in the world. More than half of all the kinds of plants and animals on Earth live in tropical rain forests.

The tallest rain forest trees are as tall as 165 feet (50 meters). The treetop form a leafy covering called the canopy — article

Tropical rain forests have more kinds of trees than anywhere else in the world.

Large rain forests are found in Africa, Asia, and Central and South America. Smaller rain forests are in Australia and islands in the Pacific.

Rain forest area

180 The World Book Student Discovery Encyclopedia

1. Look up your topic in the correct encyclopedia **volume** or on the **CD-ROM**.

2. Read the **guide words**. Keep turning the pages until you find the article you want. Use alphabetical order.

3. Read the **article** and take notes.

568

Page 569

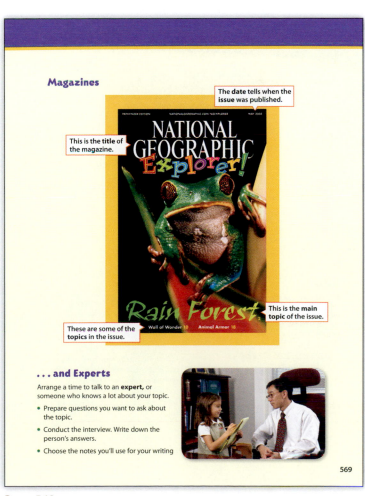

Magazines

The **date** tells when the issue was published.

This is the **title** of the magazine.

NATIONAL GEOGRAPHIC Explorer!

Rain Forest

This is the **main topic** of the issue.

These are some of the **topics** in the issue.

Wall of Wonder 10   Animal Armor 18

... and Experts

Arrange a time to talk to an **expert**, or someone who knows a lot about your topic.

- Prepare questions you want to ask about the topic.
- Conduct the interview. Write down the person's answers.
- Choose the notes you'll use for your writing

569

Anthology Handbook, continued

Writing and Research, *continued*

Internet

The Internet is a connection of computers that share information through the World Wide Web. It is like a giant library. Check with your teacher for how to access the Internet from your school.

1. **Go to a search page.** Type in your key words. Click Search.

2. **Read the list of Web sites, or pages, that have your key words.** The underlined words are links to the Web sites.

3. **Click on a link to go directly to the site, or Web page.** Read the article online. Or print it if it is helpful for your research. Later on, you can use the article to take notes.

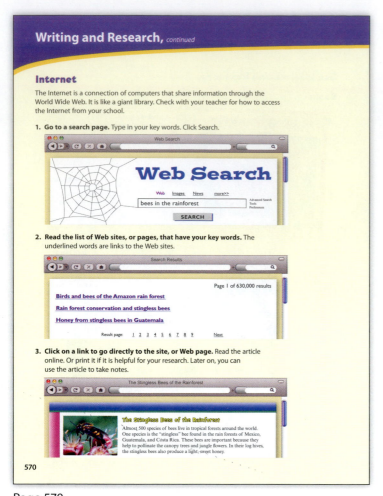

4. **Get Organized** Think about all the details you've gathered about your topic. Use a list, a chart, or other graphic organizer to show what you'll include in your writing. Use the organizer to show the order of your ideas, too.

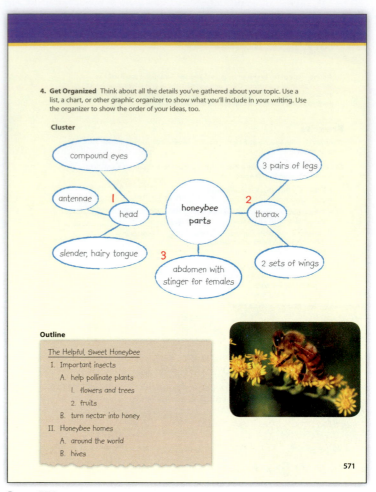

570

571

Writing and Research, *continued*

Draft

When you write your first draft, you turn all your ideas into sentences. You write quickly just to get all your ideas down. You can correct mistakes later.

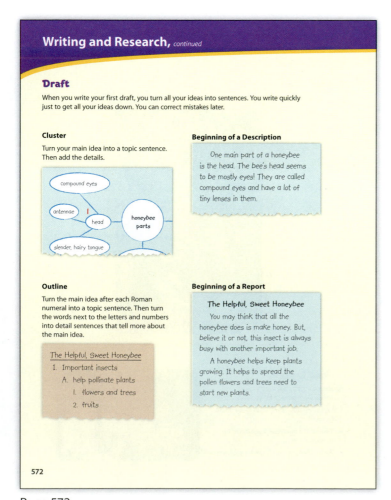

Revise

When you revise, you make changes to your writing to make it better and clearer.

❶ **Read, Retell, Respond** Read your draft aloud to a partner. Your partner listens and then retells your main points.

Your partner can help you discover what is unclear or what you need to add. Use your partner's suggestions to decide what you can do to make your writing better.

❷ **Make Changes** Think about your draft and what you and your partner discussed. What changes will you make? Use Revising Marks to mark your changes.

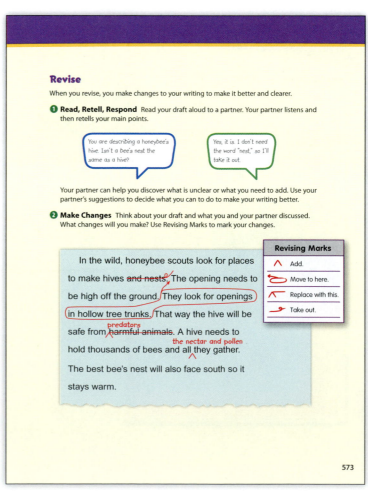

572

573

R8 Handbook

Page 574

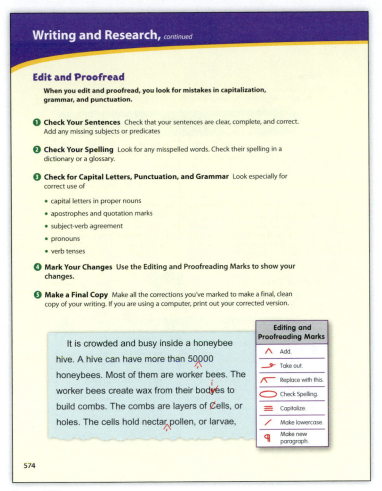

Writing and Research, *continued*

Edit and Proofread

When you edit and proofread, you look for mistakes in capitalization, grammar, and punctuation.

1 Check Your Sentences Check that your sentences are clear, complete, and correct. Add any missing subjects or predicates

2 Check Your Spelling Look for any misspelled words. Check their spelling in a dictionary or a glossary.

3 Check for Capital Letters, Punctuation, and Grammar Look especially for correct use of

- capital letters in proper nouns
- apostrophes and quotation marks
- subject-verb agreement
- pronouns
- verb tenses

4 Mark Your Changes Use the Editing and Proofreading Marks to show your changes.

5 Make a Final Copy Make all the corrections you've marked to make a final, clean copy of your writing. If you are using a computer, print out your corrected version.

It is crowded and busy inside a honeybee hive. A hive can have more than 50000 honeybees. Most of them are worker bees. The worker bees create wax from their bodies to build combs. The combs are layers of cells, or holes. The cells hold nectar pollen, or larvae,

Editing and Proofreading Marks	
∧	Add.
⤴	Take out.
⋏	Replace with this.
◯	Check Spelling.
≡	Capitalize.
/	Make lowercase.
¶	Make new paragraph.

574

Page 575

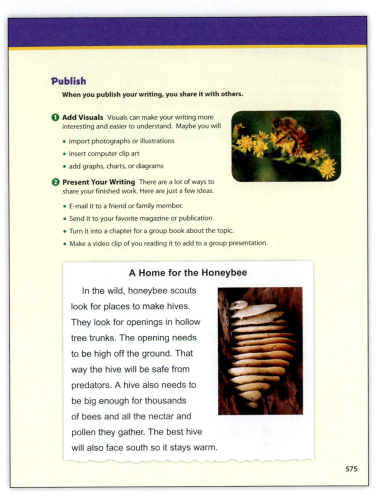

Publish

When you publish your writing, you share it with others.

1 Add Visuals Visuals can make your writing more interesting and easier to understand. Maybe you will

- import photographs or illustrations
- insert computer clip art
- add graphs, charts, or diagrams

2 Present Your Writing There are a lot of ways to share your finished work. Here are just a few ideas.

- E-mail it to a friend or family member.
- Send it to your favorite magazine or publication.
- Turn it into a chapter for a group book about the topic.
- Make a video clip of you reading it to add to a group presentation.

A Home for the Honeybee

In the wild, honeybee scouts look for places to make hives. They look for openings in hollow tree trunks. The opening needs to be high off the ground. That way the hive will be safe from predators. A hive also needs to be big enough for thousands of bees and all the nectar and pollen they gather. The best hive will also face south so it stays warm.

575

Page 576

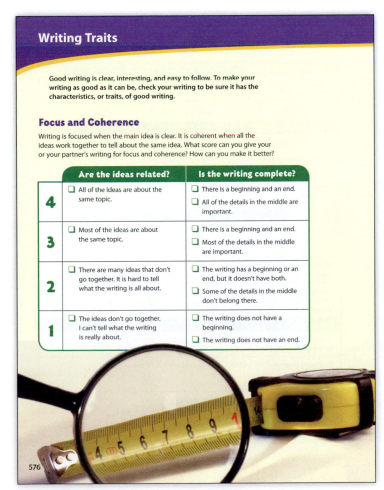

Writing Traits

Good writing is clear, interesting, and easy to follow. To make your writing as good as it can be, check your writing to be sure it has the characteristics, or traits, of good writing.

Focus and Coherence

Writing is focused when the main idea is clear. It is coherent when all the ideas work together to tell about the same idea. What score can you give your or your partner's writing for focus and coherence? How can you make it better?

	Are the ideas related?	Is the writing complete?
4	❏ All of the ideas are about the same topic.	❏ There is a beginning and an end. ❏ All of the details in the middle are important.
3	❏ Most of the ideas are about the same topic.	❏ There is a beginning and an end. ❏ Most of the details in the middle are important.
2	❏ There are many ideas that don't go together. It is hard to tell what the writing is all about.	❏ The writing has a beginning or an end, but it doesn't have both. ❏ Some of the details in the middle don't belong there.
1	❏ The ideas don't go together. I can't tell what the writing is really about.	❏ The writing does not have a beginning. ❏ The writing does not have an end.

576

Page 577

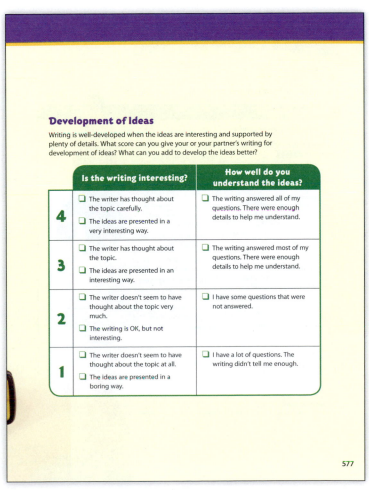

Development of Ideas

Writing is well-developed when the ideas are interesting and supported by plenty of details. What score can you give your or your partner's writing for development of ideas? What can you add to develop the ideas better?

	Is the writing interesting?	How well do you understand the ideas?
4	❏ The writer has thought about the topic carefully. ❏ The ideas are presented in a very interesting way.	❏ The writing answered all of my questions. There were enough details to help me understand.
3	❏ The writer has thought about the topic. ❏ The ideas are presented in an interesting way.	❏ The writing answered most of my questions. There were enough details to help me understand.
2	❏ The writer doesn't seem to have thought about the topic very much. ❏ The writing is OK, but not interesting.	❏ I have some questions that were not answered.
1	❏ The writer doesn't seem to have thought about the topic at all. ❏ The ideas are presented in a boring way.	❏ I have a lot of questions. The writing didn't tell me enough.

577

Anthology Handbook, continued

Page 578

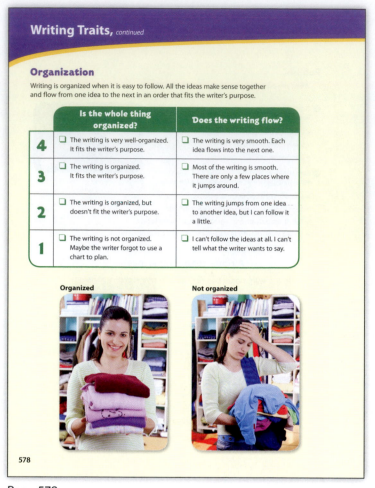

Writing Traits, continued

Organization

Writing is organized when it is easy to follow. All the ideas make sense together and flow from one idea to the next in an order that fits the writer's purpose.

	Is the whole thing organized?	Does the writing flow?
4	☐ The writing is very well-organized. It fits the writer's purpose.	☐ The writing is very smooth. Each idea flows into the next one.
3	☐ The writing is organized. It fits the writer's purpose.	☐ Most of the writing is smooth. There are only a few places where it jumps around.
2	☐ The writing is organized, but doesn't fit the writer's purpose.	☐ The writing jumps from one idea to another idea, but I can follow it a little.
1	☐ The writing is not organized. Maybe the writer forgot to use a chart to plan.	☐ I can't follow the ideas at all. I can't tell what the writer wants to say.

Organized

Not organized

578

Page 579

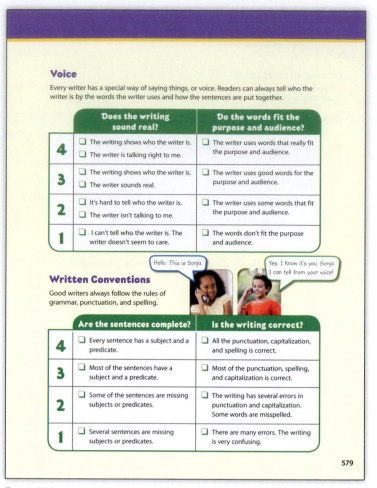

Voice

Every writer has a special way of saying things, or voice. Readers can always tell who the writer is by the words the writer uses and how the sentences are put together.

	Does the writing sound real?	Do the words fit the purpose and audience?
4	☐ The writing shows who the writer is. ☐ The writer is talking right to me.	☐ The writer uses words that really fit the purpose and audience.
3	☐ The writing shows who the writer is. ☐ The writer sounds real.	☐ The writer uses good words for the purpose and audience.
2	☐ It's hard to tell who the writer is. ☐ The writer isn't talking to me.	☐ The writer uses some words that fit the purpose and audience.
1	☐ I can't tell who the writer is. The writer doesn't seem to care.	☐ The words don't fit the purpose and audience.

Written Conventions

Good writers always follow the rules of grammar, punctuation, and spelling.

Hello. This is Sonja.

Yes. I know it's you, Sonja. I can tell from your voice!

	Are the sentences complete?	Is the writing correct?
4	☐ Every sentence has a subject and a predicate.	☐ All the punctuation, capitalization, and spelling is correct.
3	☐ Most of the sentences have a subject and a predicate.	☐ Most of the punctuation, spelling, and capitalization is correct.
2	☐ Some of the sentences are missing subjects or predicates.	☐ The writing has several errors in punctuation and capitalization. Some words are misspelled.
1	☐ Several sentences are missing subjects or predicates.	☐ There are many errors. The writing is very confusing.

579

Page 580

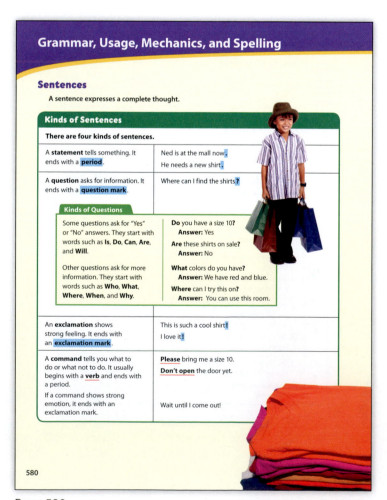

Grammar, Usage, Mechanics, and Spelling

Sentences

A sentence expresses a complete thought.

Kinds of Sentences	
There are four kinds of sentences.	
A **statement** tells something. It ends with a **period**.	Ned is at the mall now**.** He needs a new shirt**.**
A **question** asks for information. It ends with a **question mark**.	Where can I find the shirts**?**

Kinds of Questions	
Some questions ask for "Yes" or "No" answers. They start with words such as **Is, Do, Can, Are,** and **Will**.	**Do** you have a size 10**?** **Answer:** Yes
	Are these shirts on sale**?** **Answer:** No
Other questions ask for more information. They start with words such as **Who, What, Where, When,** and **Why**.	**What** colors do you have**?** **Answer:** We have red and blue.
	Where can I try this on**?** **Answer:** You can use this room.

An **exclamation** shows strong feeling. It ends with an **exclamation mark**.	This is such a cool shirt**!** I love it**!**
A **command** tells you what to do or what not to do. It usually begins with a **verb** and ends with a period. If a command shows strong emotion, it ends with an exclamation mark.	**Please** bring me a size 10. **Don't open** the door yet. Wait until I come out!

580

Page 581

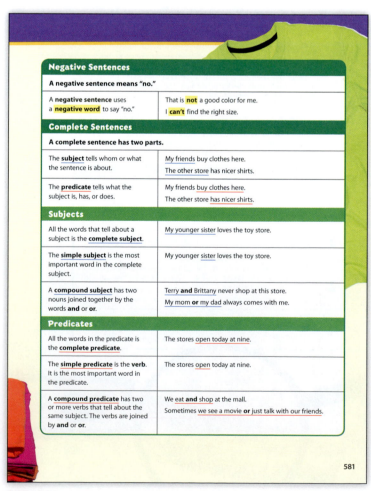

Negative Sentences	
A negative sentence means "no."	
A **negative sentence** uses a **negative word** to say "no."	That is **not** a good color for me. I **can't** find the right size.

Complete Sentences	
A complete sentence has two parts.	
The **subject** tells whom or what the sentence is about.	My friends buy clothes here. The other store has nicer shirts.
The **predicate** tells what the subject is, has, or does.	My friends buy clothes here. The other store has nicer shirts.

Subjects	
All the words that tell about a subject is the **complete subject**.	My younger sister loves the toy store.
The **simple subject** is the most important word in the complete subject.	My younger sister loves the toy store.
A **compound subject** has two nouns joined together by the words **and** or **or**.	Terry **and** Brittany never shop at this store. My mom **or** my dad always comes with me.

Predicates	
All the words in the predicate is the **complete predicate**.	The stores open today at nine.
The **simple predicate** is the verb. It is the most important word in the predicate.	The stores open today at nine.
A **compound predicate** has two or more verbs that tell about the same subject. The verbs are joined by **and** or **or**.	We eat **and** shop at the mall. Sometimes we see a movie **or** just talk with our friends.

581

Page 582

Sentences *(continued)*

Compound Sentences

When you join two sentences together you can make a compound sentence.

Use a comma and the conjunction **and** to combine two ideas that are alike.	My friends walk to the mall. I go with them. My friends walk to the mall**,** **and** I go with them.
Use a comma and the conjunction **but** to combine two ideas that show a difference.	My friends walk to the mall. I ride my bike. My friends walk to the mall**,** **but** I ride my bike.
Use a comma and the conjunction **or** to show a choice between two ideas.	You can walk to the mall with me. You can ride with Dad. You can walk to the mall with me**,** **or** you can ride with Dad.

Complex Sentences

When you join independent and dependent clauses, you can make a complex sentence.

An **independent clause** expresses a complete thought. It can stand alone as a sentence.	Mom and her friends walk around the mall for exercise.
A **dependent clause** does not express a complete thought. It is not a sentence.	before it gets busy
To make a **complex sentence**, join an **independent clause** with one or more **dependent clauses**. If the dependent clause comes first, put a **comma** after it.	Before it gets busy**,** Mom and her friends walk around the mall for exercise.

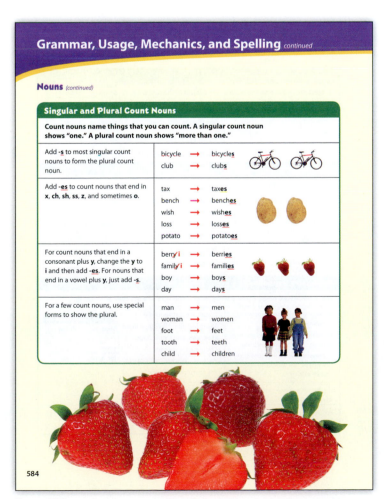

582

Page 583

Nouns

Nouns name people, animals, places, or things.

Common Nouns and Proper Nouns

There are two kinds of nouns.

A **common noun** names any person, animal, place, or thing of a certain type.	I know that **girl**. She rides a **horse**. I sometimes see her at the **park**. She walks her **dog** there.
A **proper noun** names a particular person, animal, place, or thing. • Start all the important words with a capital letter.	I know **Marissa**. I sometimes see her at **Hilltop Park**. She walks her dog **Chase** there.
• Start the names of streets, cities, and states with a capital letter.	Her family is from **Dallas, Texas**. They live on **Crockett Lane**.
• Also use capital letters when you abbreviate state names.	

Abbreviations for State Names in Mailing Addresses

Alabama	AL	Hawaii	HI	Massachusetts	MA	New Mexico	NM	South Dakota	SD
Alaska	AK	Idaho	ID	Michigan	MI	New York	NY	Tennessee	TN
Arizona	AZ	Illinois	IL	Minnesota	MN	North Carolina	NC	Texas	TX
Arkansas	AR	Indiana	IN	Mississippi	MS	North Dakota	ND	Utah	UT
California	CA	Iowa	IA	Missouri	MO	Ohio	OH	Vermont	VT
Colorado	CO	Kansas	KS	Montana	MT	Oklahoma	OK	Virginia	VA
Connecticut	CT	Kentucky	KY	Nebraska	NE	Oregon	OR	Washington	WA
Delaware	DE	Louisiana	LA	Nevada	NV	Pennsylvania	PA	West Virginia	WV
Florida	FL	Maine	ME	New Hampshire	NH	Rhode Island	RI	Wisconsin	WI
Georgea	GA	Maryland	MD	New Jersey	NJ	South Carolina	SC	Wyoming	WY

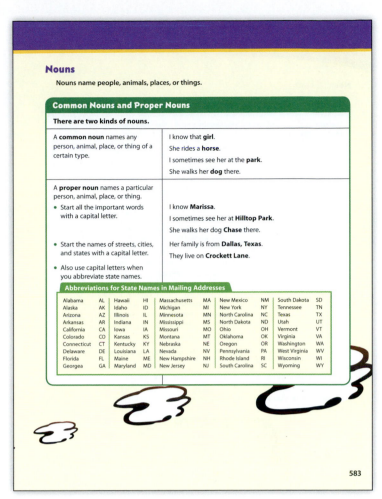

583

Page 584

Nouns *(continued)*

Singular and Plural Count Nouns

Count nouns name things that you can count. A singular count noun shows "one." A plural count noun shows "more than one."

Add **-s** to most singular count nouns to form the plural count noun.	bicycle → bicycle**s** club → club**s**	
Add **-es** to count nouns that end in **x, ch, sh, ss, z**, and sometimes **o**.	tax → tax**es** bench → bench**es** wish → wish**es** loss → loss**es** potato → potato**es**	
For count nouns that end in a consonant plus **y**, change the **y** to **i** and then add **-es**. For nouns that end in a vowel plus **y**, just add **-s**.	berr**y/i** → berri**es** famil**y/i** → famili**es** boy → boy**s** day → day**s**	
For a few count nouns, use special forms to show the plural.	man → men woman → women foot → feet tooth → teeth child → children	

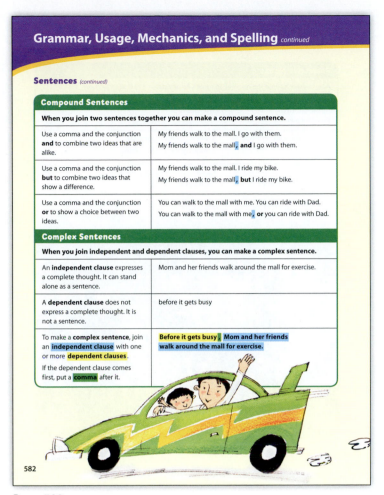

584

Page 585

Noncount Nouns

Noncount nouns name things that you cannot count.
Noncount nouns have one form for "one" and "more than one."

Weather Words	fog heat lightning thunder rain **YES:** **Thunder** and **lightning** scare my dog. **NO:** Thunders and lightnings scare my dog.
Food Words Some food items can be counted by using a measurement word such as **cup, slice, glass**, or **head** plus the word **of**. To show the plural form, make the measurement word plural.	bread corn milk rice soup **YES:** I'm thirsty for **milk**. I want **two glasses of milk**. **NO:** I'm thirsty for milks. I want milks.
Ideas and Feelings	fun help honesty luck work **YES:** I need **help** to finish my homework. **NO:** I need helps to finish my homework.
Category Nouns	clothing equipment mail money time **YES:** My football **equipment** is in the car. **NO:** My football equipments is in the car.
Materials	air gold paper water wood **YES:** Is the **water** in this river clean? **NO:** Is the waters in this river clean?
Activities and Sports	baseball dancing golf singing soccer **YES:** I played **soccer** three times this week. **NO:** I played soccers three times this week.

585

Anthology Handbook, continued

Page 586

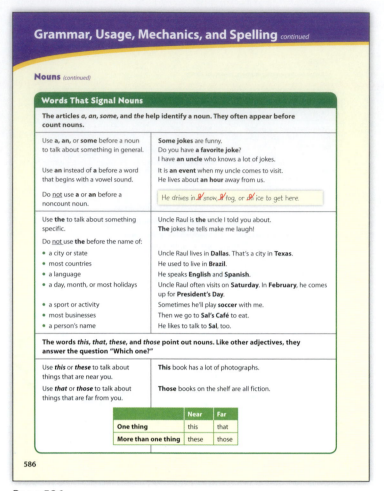

Grammar, Usage, Mechanics, and Spelling continued

Nouns (continued)

Words That Signal Nouns

The articles *a*, *an*, *some*, and *the* help identify a noun. They often appear before count nouns.

Use **a**, **an**, or **some** before a noun to talk about something in general.	**Some jokes** are funny. Do you have **a favorite joke**? I have **an uncle** who knows a lot of jokes.
Use **an** instead of **a** before a word that begins with a vowel sound.	It is **an event** when my uncle comes to visit. He lives about **an hour** away from us.
Do **not** use **a** or **an** before a noncount noun.	He drives in snow, fog, or ice to get here.
Use **the** to talk about something specific. Do **not** use **the** before the name of: • a city or state • most countries • a language • a day, month, or most holidays • a sport or activity • most businesses • a person's name	Uncle Raul is **the** uncle I told you about. **The** jokes he tells make me laugh! Uncle Raul lives in **Dallas**. That's a city in **Texas**. He used to live in **Brazil**. He speaks **English** and **Spanish**. Uncle Raul often visits on **Saturday**. In **February**, he comes up for **President's Day**. Sometimes he'll play **soccer** with me. Then we go to **Sal's Café** to eat. He likes to talk to **Sal**, too.

The words *this*, *that*, *these*, and *those* point out nouns. Like other adjectives, they answer the question "Which one?"

Use **this** or **these** to talk about things that are near you.	**This** book has a lot of photographs.
Use **that** or **those** to talk about things that are far from you.	**Those** books on the shelf are all fiction.

	Near	Far
One thing	this	that
More than one thing	these	those

586

Page 587

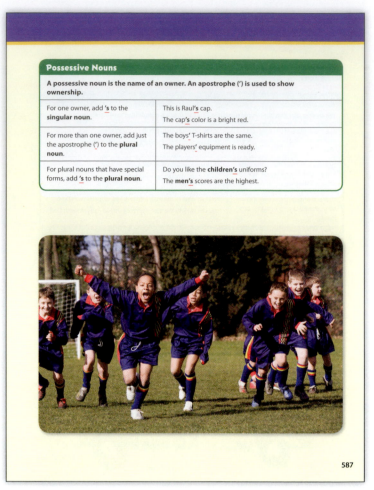

Possessive Nouns

A possessive noun is the name of an owner. An apostrophe (') is used to show ownership.

For one owner, add **'s** to the **singular noun**.	This is Raul**'s** cap. The cap**'s** color is a bright red.
For more than one owner, add just the apostrophe (') to the **plural noun**.	The boys**'** T-shirts are the same. The players**'** equipment is ready.
For plural nouns that have special forms, add **'s** to the **plural noun**.	Do you like the **children's** uniforms? The **men's** scores are the highest.

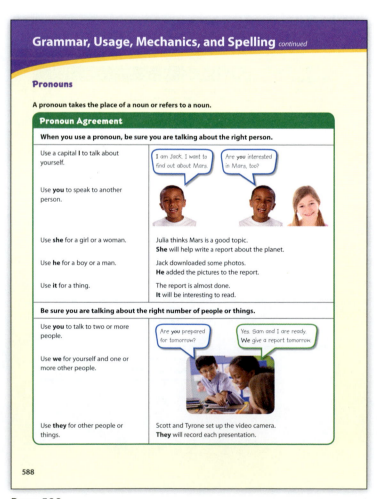

587

Page 588

Grammar, Usage, Mechanics, and Spelling continued

Pronouns

A pronoun takes the place of a noun or refers to a noun.

Pronoun Agreement

When you use a pronoun, be sure you are talking about the right person.

Use a capital **I** to talk about yourself.	I am Jack. I want to find out about Mars. Are you interested in Mars, too?
Use **you** to speak to another person.	
Use **she** for a girl or a woman.	Julia thinks Mars is a good topic. **She** will help write a report about the planet.
Use **he** for a boy or a man.	Jack downloaded some photos. **He** added the pictures to the report.
Use **it** for a thing.	The report is almost done. **It** will be interesting to read.

Be sure you are talking about the right number of people or things.

Use **you** to talk to two or more people.	Are **you** prepared for tomorrow? Yes. Sam and I are ready. **We** give a report tomorrow.
Use **we** for yourself and one or more other people.	
Use **they** for other people or things.	Scott and Tyrone set up the video camera. **They** will record each presentation.

588

Page 589

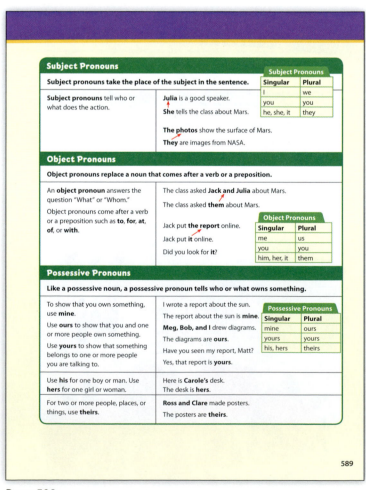

Subject Pronouns

Subject pronouns take the place of the subject in the sentence.

		Subject Pronouns	
		Singular	Plural
Subject pronouns tell who or what does the action.	**Julia** is a good speaker. **She** tells the class about Mars. **The photos** show the surface of Mars. **They** are images from NASA.	I you he, she, it	we you they

Object Pronouns

Object pronouns replace a noun that comes after a verb or a preposition.

		Object Pronouns	
		Singular	Plural
An **object pronoun** answers the question "What" or "Whom." Object pronouns come after a verb or a preposition such as **to**, **for**, **at**, **of**, or **with**.	The class asked **Jack and Julia** about Mars. The class asked **them** about Mars. Jack put **the report** online. Jack put **it** online. Did you look for **it**?	me you him, her, it	us you them

Possessive Pronouns

Like a possessive noun, a possessive pronoun tells who or what owns something.

		Possessive Pronouns	
		Singular	Plural
To show that you own something, use **mine**. Use **ours** to show that you and one or more people own something. Use **yours** to show that something belongs to one or more people you are talking to.	I wrote a report about the sun. The report about the sun is **mine**. **Meg, Bob, and I** drew diagrams. The diagrams are **ours**. Have you seen my report, Matt? Yes, that report is **yours**.	mine yours his, hers	ours yours theirs
Use **his** for one boy or man. Use **hers** for one girl or woman.	Here is **Carole's** desk. The desk is **hers**.		
For two or more people, places, or things, use **theirs**.	**Ross and Clare** made posters. The posters are **theirs**.		

589

Page 590

Adjectives

An adjective describes, or tells about, a noun.

How Adjectives Work

Usually, an **adjective** comes <u>before</u> the noun it tells about.	You can buy **delicious** fruits at the market.
But, an **adjective** can also appear <u>after</u> verbs such as *is, are, look, feel, smell,* and *taste.*	All the fruit looks **fresh**. The shoppers are **happy**.
Adjectives describe • what something is like	The market is a **busy** place.
• the size, color, and shape of something	The **round, brown** baskets are filled with fruits and vegetables.
• what something looks, feels, sounds, or smells like	The **shiny** peppers are in one basket. Another basket has **crunchy** cucumbers. The pineapples are **sweet** and **juicy**.
Some **adjectives** tell "how many" or "in what order."	The sellers have **two** baskets of beans. The **first** basket is near the limes.

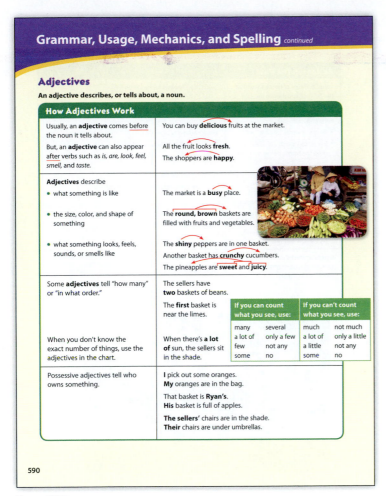

If you can count what you see, use:		If you can't count what you see, use:	
many	several	much	not much
a lot of	only a few	a lot of	only a little
few	not any	a little	not any
some	no	some	no

When you don't know the exact number of things, use the adjectives in the chart.	When there's **a lot of** sun, the sellers sit in the shade.
Possessive adjectives tell who owns something.	I pick out some oranges. **My** oranges are in the bag. That basket is **Ryan's**. **His** basket is full of apples. **The sellers'** chairs are in the shade. **Their** chairs are under umbrellas.

590

Page 591

Adjectives That Compare

Adjectives can help you make a comparison, or show how things are alike or different.

To compare two things, add **-er** to the adjective. You will often use the word **than** in your sentence, too.	This is a **small** pineapple. The guava is **smaller than** the pineapple.	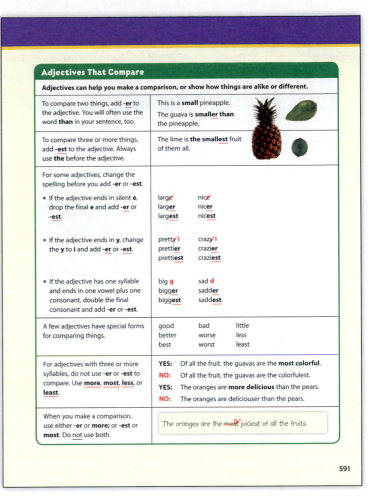
To compare three or more things, add **-est** to the adjective. Always use **the** before the adjective.	The lime is **the smallest** fruit of them all.	

For some adjectives, change the spelling before you add **-er** or **-est**.		
• If the adjective ends in silent **e**, drop the final **e** and add **-er** or **-est**.	large~~e~~	nic~~e~~
	larg**er**	nic**er**
	larg**est**	nic**est**
• If the adjective ends in **y**, change the **y** to **i** and add **-er** or **-est**.	pretty→i	crazy→i
	pretti**er**	crazi**er**
	pretti**est**	crazi**est**
• If the adjective has one syllable and ends in one vowel plus one consonant, double the final consonant and add **-er** or **-est**.	big **g**	sad **d**
	bigg**er**	sadd**er**
	bigg**est**	sadd**est**

A few adjectives have special forms for comparing things.	good	bad	little
	better	worse	less
	best	worst	least

For adjectives with three or more syllables, do not use **-er** or **-est** to compare. Use **more**, **most**, **less**, or **least**.	**YES:**	Of all the fruit, the guavas are the **most colorful**.
	NO:	Of all the fruit, the guavas are the colorfulest.
	YES:	The oranges are **more delicious** than the pears.
	NO:	The oranges are deliciouser than the pears.

When you make a comparison, use either **-er** or **more**; or **-est** or **most**. Do **not** use both.	The oranges are the ~~most~~ juiciest of all the fruits.

591

Page 592

Verbs

Verbs tell what the subject of a sentence is, has, or does. They show if something happened in the past, is happening now, or will happen in the future.

Action Verbs

An **action verb** tells what someone or something does.	The children **ride** bikes. They **wear** helmets for safety. They **pedal** as fast as they can.

The Verbs *Have* and *Be*

The verb **to have** tells what the subject of a sentence has.	I **have** a bicycle. It **has** twelve gears. My friend Pedro **has** a bicycle, too. Sometimes we **have** races.	**Forms of the Verb *have*** have has had
The verb **to be** does not show action. It tells what the subject of a sentence is (a noun) or what it is like (an adjective).	I **am** a fan of bicycle races. Pedro **is** excited about our next race.	**Forms of the Verb *be*** am was are were is

Linking Verbs

A few other verbs work like the verb **to be**. They do not show action. They just connect, or link, the subject to a word in the predicate. Some of these verbs are **look, seem, feel, smell,** and **taste**.	My bicycle **looks** fantastic! Pedro and I **feel** ready for the race.

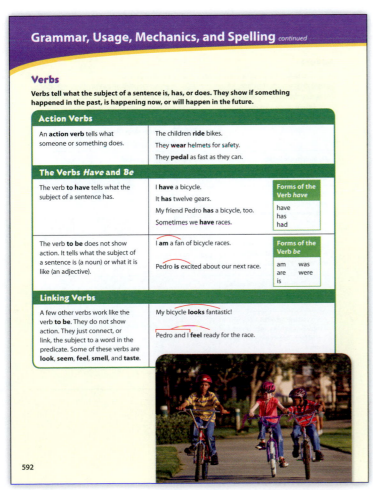

592

Page 593

Helping Verbs

A **helping verb** works together with an action verb. A helping verb comes before a **main verb**. Some helping verbs have special meanings. • Use **can** to tell that someone is able to do something. • Use **could, may,** or **might** to tell that something is possible. • Use **must** to tell that somebody has to do something. • Use **should** to give an opinion or advice.	Pedro and I **are racing** today. We **will do** our best. We **can work** as a team. We **may reach** the finish line first. We **must pedal** hard to win! You **should practice** more.

Contractions with Verbs

You can put a subject and verb together to make a **contraction**. In a contraction, an apostrophe (') shows where one or more letters have been left out.	**They are** riding fast. **They are** riding fast. **They're** riding fast.

You can make a contraction with the verbs **am**, **are**, and **is**.	**Contractions with *Be***	
	I + am = **I'm**	she + is = **she's**
	you + are = **you're**	where + is = **where's**
	we + are = **we're**	what + is = **what's**

You can make a contraction with the helping verbs **have**, **has**, and **will**.	**Contractions with *Have* and *Will***	
	I + have = **I've**	he + has = **he's**
	you + have = **you've**	I + will = **I'll**
	they + have = **they've**	it + will = **it'll**

In contractions with a verb and **not**, the word **not** is shortened to **n't**.	**Contractions with *Not***	
	do + not = **don't**	have + not = **haven't**
	did + not = **didn't**	has + not = **hasn't**
	are + not = **aren't**	could + not = **couldn't**
	was + not = **wasn't**	should + not = **shouldn't**

The contraction of the verb **can** plus **not** has a special spelling.	can + not = **can't**

593

Anthology Handbook, continued

Verbs, *(continued)*

Actions in the Present

All action verbs show when the action happens. Verbs in the **present tense** show	
• that the action happens now.	Pedro **eats** his breakfast. Then he **takes** his bike out of the garage.
• that the action happens often.	Pedro and I **love** to ride our bikes on weekends.
To show the present tense for the subjects **he, she,** or **it,** add **-s** to the end of most action verbs.	Pedro **checks** the tires on his bike. He **finds** a flat tire!
• For verbs that end in **x, ch, sh, ss,** or **z,** add **-es.**	Pedro **fixes** the tire. A pump **pushes** air into it.
• For verbs that end in a consonant plus **y,** change the **y** to **i** and then add **-es.** For verbs that end in a vowel plus **y,** just add **-s.**	"That should do it," he **says** to himself. He **carries** the pump back into the garage.
• For the subjects **I, you, we,** or **they,** do not add **-s** or **-es.**	I **arrive** at Pedro's house. We **coast** down the driveway on our bikes.
The **present progressive** form of a verb tells about an action as it is happening. It uses **am, is,** or **are** and a main verb. The main verb ends in **-ing**.	We **are pedaling** faster. I **am passing** Pedro! He **is following** right behind me.

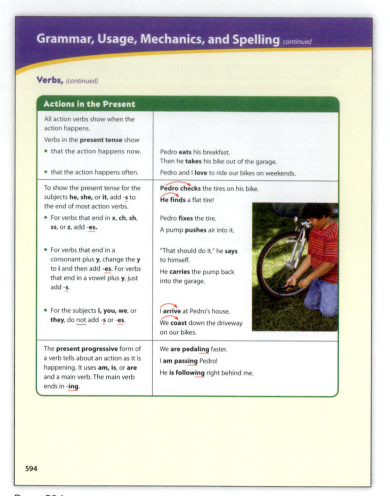

Page 594

Grammar, Usage, Mechanics, and Spelling *continued*

Actions in the Past

Verbs in the **past tense** show that the action happened in the past.	Yesterday, I **looked** for sports on TV.
The past tense form of a **regular verb** ends with **-ed.**	
• For most verbs, just add **-ed.**	I **watched** the race on TV.
• For verbs that end in silent **e,** drop the final **e** before you add **-ed.**	The bikers **arrived** from all different countries. They **raced** for several hours.
• For one-syllable verbs that end in one vowel plus one consonant, double the final consonant before you add **-ed.**	People **grabbed** their cameras. They **snapped** pictures of their favorite racer.
• For verbs that end in **y,** change the **y** to **i** before you add **-ed.** For verbs that end in a vowel plus **y,** just add **-ed.**	I **studied** the racer from Italy. I **stayed** close to the TV.
Irregular verbs do not add **-ed** to show the past tense. They have special forms.	The Italian racer **was** fast. He **broke** the speed record!

Some Irregular Verbs

Present Tense	Past Tense
begin	began
do	did
have	had
make	made
take	took
ride	rode
win	won

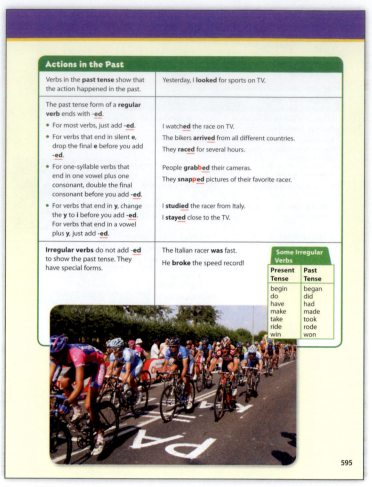

Page 595

Grammar, Usage, Mechanics, and Spelling *continued*

Verbs, *(continued)*

Actions in the Future

Verbs in the **future tense** tell what will happen later, or in the future.	Tomorrow, Shelley **will clean** her bike.
To show the future tense, you can	
• add the helping verb **will** before the **main verb**.	She **will remove** all the dirt.
• use **am going to, are going to,** or **is going to** before the **main verb**.	She **is going to remove** all the dirt. I **am going to help** her.
If the **main verb** is a form of the verb **to be,** use **be** to form the future tense.	The bike **will be** spotless. Shelley **is going to be** pleased!
To make negative sentences in the future tense, put the word **not** just after **will, am, is,** or **are.**	We are **not** going to stop until the bike shines. Pedro is **not** going to believe it. Her bike will **not** be a mess any longer.

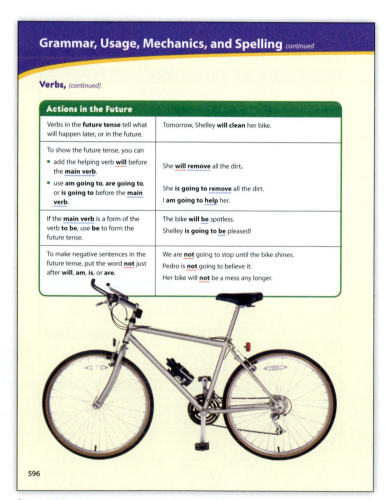

Page 596

Adverbs

An adverb tells more about a verb, an adjective, or another adverb.

How Adverbs Work

An **adverb** can come before or after a **verb** to tell "how," "where," "when," or "how often."	Josh **walks quickly** to the bus stop. (how) He **will travel downtown** on the bus. (where) He **will arrive** at school **soon**. (when) Josh **never misses** a day of school. (how often)
An **adverb** can make an **adjective** or another adverb stronger.	Josh is **really good** at baseball. He plays **very well**.
Some **adverbs** compare actions. Add **-er** to compare two actions. Add **-est** to compare three or more actions.	Josh **runs fast**. Josh runs **faster** than his best friend. Josh runs the **fastest** of all the players.
A few adverbs have special forms for comparing things.	well → better → best badly → worse → worst
If the adverb ends in **-ly,** use **more, most, less,** or **least** to compare the actions.	Josh drops a ball ~~frequently~~ *less* than the other players.
When you use **adverbs** to make a comparison with **-er, -est,** or with a special form, do not also use **more** or **most.**	Josh jumps ~~more~~ higher than I do. He is ~~more~~ *better* than I am at catching the ball.
Make sure to use an **adverb** (not an adjective) to tell about a verb.	I do not catch ~~good~~ *well* at all.

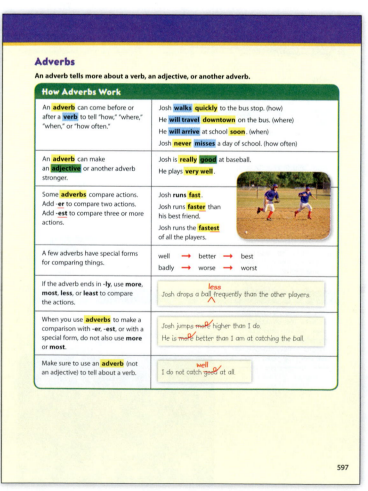

Page 597

Prepositions

A preposition links a noun or pronoun to other words in a sentence. A preposition is the first word in a prepositional phrase.

Prepositions	
Some prepositions tell **where** something is.	above over / under below beneath / beside next to by near / in front of / in back of behind / between in / out / inside / outside / on / off
Some prepositions show **direction**.	up / down / through / across / around / into
Some prepositions tell **when** something happens.	**before** lunch · **in** 2003 · **on** September 16 **during** lunch · **in** September · **at** four o'clock **after** lunch · **in** the afternoon · **from** noon **to** 3:30
Other prepositions have many uses.	about · among · for · to against · at · from · with along · except · of · without

Prepositional Phrases	
A **prepositional phrase** starts with a **preposition** and ends with a **noun** or a **pronoun**. Use prepositional phrases to add information or details to your writing.	**At our school**, we did many activities **for Earth Day**. We picked up the trash **along the fence**. Then we planted some flowers **next to it**.

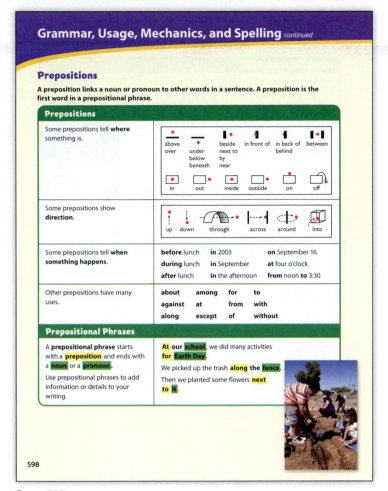

598

Page 598

Capital Letters

A word that begins with a capital letter is special in some way.

How to Use Capital Letters	
A word that begins with a capital letter is special in some way.	
Use a **capital letter** at the beginning of a sentence.	**O**ur class is taking an exciting field trip. **W**e are going to an airplane museum.
Always use a capital letter for the pronoun **I**.	My friends and **I** can't wait!
Use a capital letter for a person's • first and last name • initials • title	**M**att **J**. **K**elly and **M**att **R**oss will ride with **D**r. **B**ye. **M**agdalena and I are going with **M**rs. **L**iu.
Use a capital letter for the names of • the days of the week and their abbreviations • the twelve months of the year and their abbreviations	We're going the first **S**aturday in **J**anuary.
Use a capital letter for each important word in the names of special days and holidays.	That will be after **C**hristmas, **K**wanzaa, and **N**ew **Y**ear's **D**ay. **E**arth **D**ay **F**ourth of **J**uly **H**anukkah **T**hanksgiving

Days of the Week

Sunday	**S**un.
Monday	**M**on.
Tuesday	**T**ue.
Wednesday	**W**ed.
Thursday	**T**hurs.
Friday	**F**ri.
Saturday	**S**at.

Months of the Year

January	**J**an.
February	**F**eb.
March	**M**ar.
April	**A**pr.
May	
June	
July	
August	**A**ug.
September	**S**ep.
October	**O**ct.
November	**N**ov.
December	**D**ec.

These months are not abbreviated.

599

Page 599

Capital Letters, (continued)

More Ways to Use Capital Letters	
Use a capital letter for each important word in the names of • public places, buildings, and organizations	The **W**ilson **A**irplane **M**useum is in the **V**eterans **M**emorial **H**all. It's in the middle of **V**eterans **P**ark, right next to the **P**iney **W**oods **Z**oo.
• streets, cities, and states	The museum is on **F**light **A**venue. It is the biggest airplane museum in **F**lorida. It's the biggest in the whole **U**nited **S**tates!
• landforms and bodies of water, continents, and planets and stars	

Landforms and Bodies of Water	Continents	Planets and Stars
Rocky **M**ountains	**A**frica	**E**arth
Sahara **D**esert	**A**ntarctica	**M**ars
Grand **C**anyon	**A**sia	the **B**ig **D**ipper
Pacific **O**cean	**A**ustralia	the **M**ilky **W**ay
Colorado **R**iver	**E**urope	
Lake **E**rie	**N**orth **A**merica	
	South **A**merica	

Use a capital letter for the names of countries and adjectives formed from the names of countries.	My friend Magdalena is **C**hilean. She says they don't have a museum like that in **C**hile.
Use a capital letter for each important word in the title of a book, a story, a poem, or a movie.	We are reading *First Flight* about the Wright brothers. Magdalena wrote a poem about Amelia Earhart. She called it "**V**anished from the **S**ky." What a great title!

600

Page 600

Punctuation Marks

Punctuation marks make words and sentences easier to understand.

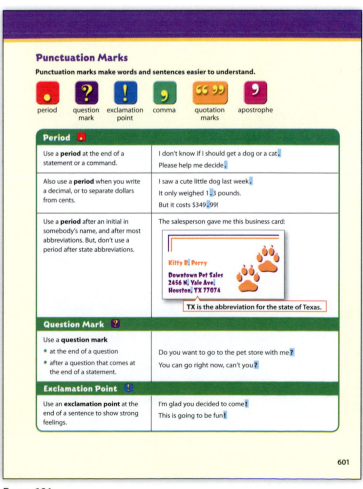

period · question mark · exclamation point · comma · quotation marks · apostrophe

Period ■	
Use a **period** at the end of a statement or a command.	I don't know if I should get a dog or a cat**.** Please help me decide**.**
Also use a **period** when you write a decimal, or to separate dollars from cents.	I saw a cute little dog last week**.** It only weighed 1**.**3 pounds. But it costs $349**.**99!
Use a **period** after an initial in somebody's name, and after most abbreviations. But, don't use a period after state abbreviations.	The salesperson gave me this business card: Kitty B**.** Perry Downtown Pet Sales 2456 N**.** Yale Ave**.** Houston, TX 77074 **TX is the abbreviation for the state of Texas.**

Question Mark ?	
Use a **question mark** • at the end of a question • after a question that comes at the end of a statement.	Do you want to go to the pet store with me**?** You can go right now, can't you**?**

Exclamation Point !	
Use an **exclamation point** at the end of a sentence to show strong feelings.	I'm glad you decided to come**!** This is going to be fun**!**

601

Page 601

Anthology Handbook, continued

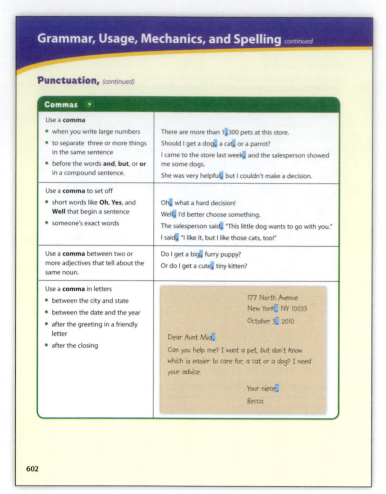

Grammar, Usage, Mechanics, and Spelling continued

Punctuation, *(continued)*

Commas

Use a **comma**	
• when you write large numbers	There are more than 1,300 pets at this store.
• to separate three or more things in the same sentence	Should I get a dog, a cat, or a parrot?
• before the words **and**, **but**, or **or** in a compound sentence.	I came to the store last week, and the salesperson showed me some dogs.
	She was very helpful, but I couldn't make a decision.
Use a **comma** to set off	
• short words like **Oh**, **Yes**, and **Well** that begin a sentence	Oh, what a hard decision!
	Well, I'd better choose something.
• someone's exact words	The salesperson said, "This little dog wants to go with you."
	I said, "I like it, but I like those cats, too!"
Use a **comma** between two or more adjectives that tell about the same noun.	Do I get a big, furry puppy?
	Or do I get a cute, tiny kitten?
Use a **comma** in letters	
• between the city and state	177 North Avenue
• between the date and the year	New York, NY 10033
• after the greeting in a friendly letter	October 3, 2010
• after the closing	Dear Aunt Mia,
	Can you help me? I want a pet, but don't know which is easier to care for, a cat or a dog? I need your advice.
	Your niece,
	Becca

602

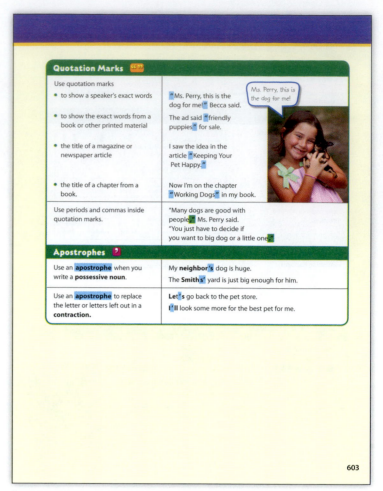

Quotation Marks

Use quotation marks		
• to show a speaker's exact words	"Ms. Perry, this is the dog for me!" Becca said.	*Ms. Perry, this is the dog for me!*
• to show the exact words from a book or other printed material	The ad said "friendly puppies" for sale.	
• the title of a magazine or newspaper article	I saw the idea in the article "Keeping Your Pet Happy."	
• the title of a chapter from a book.	Now I'm on the chapter "Working Dogs" in my book.	
Use periods and commas inside quotation marks.	"Many dogs are good with people," Ms. Perry said. "You just have to decide if you want to big dog or a little one."	

Apostrophes

Use an **apostrophe** when you write a **possessive noun**.	My **neighbor's** dog is huge.
	The **Smiths'** yard is just big enough for him.
Use an **apostrophe** to replace the letter or letters left out in a **contraction**.	**Let's** go back to the pet store.
	I'll look some more for the best pet for me.

603

R16 Handbook

Anthology Picture Dictionary

Page 604

Picture Dictionary

The definitions are for the words as they are introduced in the selections of this book.

Pronunciation Key

Say the sample word out loud to hear how to say, or pronounce, the symbol.

Symbols for Consonant Sounds		Symbols for Short Vowel Sounds	Symbols for R-controlled Sounds	Symbols for Variant Vowel Sounds
b box	p pan	a hat	ar barn	ah father
ch chick	r ring	e bell	air chair	aw ball
d dog	s bus	i chick	ear ear	oi boy
f fish	sh fish	o box	ir fire	oo book
g girl	t hat	u bus	or corn	ow cow
h hat	th Earth		ur girl	ü fruit
j jar	th father	**Symbols for Long Vowel Sounds**		
k cake	v vase	ā cake		**Miscellaneous Symbols**
ks box	w window	ē key		shun fraction ½
kw queen	hw whale	ī bike		chun question ?
l bell	y yarn	ō goat		zhun division
m mouse	z zipper	yū mule		
n pan	zh treasure			
ng ring				

Parts of an Entry

The **entry** shows how the word is spelled.

The **pronunciation** shows you how to say the word and how to break it into syllables.

The **picture** helps you understand more about the meaning of the word.

benefit
(be-nu-fit) *noun*
A **benefit** is something that is helpful.

part of speech

The **definition** gives the meaning of the word.

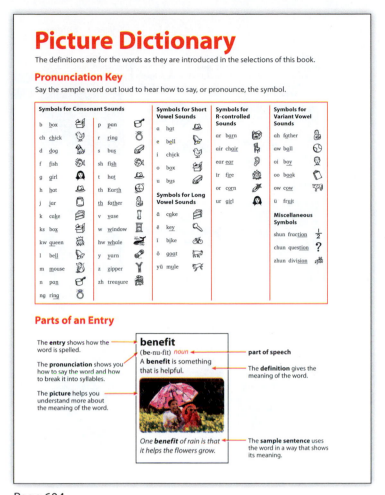

One **benefit** of rain is that it helps the flowers grow.

The **sample sentence** uses the word in a way that shows its meaning.

Page 605

a

accomplish
(u-kom-plish) *verb*
To **accomplish** means to finish something that you want to do.

What did she **accomplish**?

achieve
(u-chēv) *verb*
To **achieve** means to get something that you work for.

She worked hard to **achieve** her wish of winning first place.

action
(ak-shun) *noun*
An **action** is something that you do.

Their **actions** made the park a clean place to play.

advertisement
(ad-vur-tiz-munt) *noun*
Advertisements can be photos, pictures, or even short movies that give information and try to make people buy things.

The **advertisement** made my dad want to buy that new car.

agriculture
(a-gri-kul-chur) *noun*
The work of growing crops and raising animals for people to eat is called **agriculture**.

Many people who live outside of cities and towns work in **agriculture**.

alter
(awl-tur) *verb*
When you **alter** something, you change it.

She **alters** the dress to make it shorter.

alternative
(awl-tur-nu-tiv) *noun*
An **alternative** is another choice.

An apple is a healthy **alternative** to candy.

amount
(u-mownt) *noun*
The **amount** of something is how much of it there is.

Three hundred jelly beans is a large **amount** of candy.

605

Page 606

a
b

area
(air-ē-u) *noun*
An **area** is a part of a place.

A classroom can have an **area** for reading.

artist
(ar-tist) *noun*
An **artist** is someone who is skilled at drawing, painting, making things, or performing.

This **artist** paints what she sees outdoors.

balance
(ba-luns) *noun*
When things are in **balance**, they are even.

The two sides of the scale are in **balance**.

behavior
(bi-hā-vyur) *noun*
Behavior is what a person or animal does.

Squirrels store nuts for the winter. It's part of their **behavior**.

benefit
(be-nu-fit) *noun*
A **benefit** is something that is helpful.

One **benefit** of rain is that it helps the flowers grow.

blossom
(blah-sum) *noun*
A **blossom** is the flower of a seed plant.

This **blossom** comes from an apple tree.

buyer
(bi-ur) *noun*
A **buyer** is someone who gets something by paying money for it.

He wants a **buyer** for his flowers.

606

Page 607

a
c

carve
(karv) *verb*
To **carve** is to make something by cutting.

Dad **carves** the pumpkin while I watch.

challenge
(cha-lunj) *noun*
A **challenge** is something that is hard to do.

It is a **challenge** to climb up a rope.

characteristic
(kair-ik-tu-ris-tik) *noun*
A **characteristic** is how something looks or what something does.

A **characteristic** of this plant is white flowers.

city
(si-tē) *noun*
A **city** is a very large town.

San Francisco is a large **city** in California.

combine
(kum-bīn) *verb*
When you **combine** things, you mix them together.

What foods does she **combine**?

communicate
(ku-myū-ni-kāt) *verb*
When you **communicate**, you share words or feelings.

She **communicates** with a friend.

competition
(kom-pu-ti-shun) *noun*
A **competition** is a contest or struggle between two or more people or animals.

These pelicans are in **competition** for food.

composition
(kom-pu-zi-shun) *noun*
Composition is what things are made of.

The **composition** of mud is dirt and water.

607

Picture Dictionary **R17**

conditions
(kun-**di**-shunz) *noun*
When **conditions** are right, good things happen.

*Clear skies and wind are good **conditions** for sailing.*

conservation
(kon-sur-**vā**-shun) *noun*
Conservation means the opposite of waste.

***Conservation** of water is important.*

continent
(**kon**-tu-nunt) *noun*
A **continent** is one of the major divisions of land on Earth.

Africa

*Africa is one of seven **continents**.*

control
(kun-**trōl**) *verb*
To **control** means to make a person or thing do what you want.

*The boys **control** where the car goes.*

cooperation
(kō-ah-pu-**rā**-shun) *noun*
Cooperation is when people work together.

*It takes **cooperation** to row the boat quickly.*

core
(kor) *noun*
The **core** is the middle of something.

*An apple **core** is the center part of an apple.*

create
(krē-**āt**) *verb*
To **create** means to make something new.

*She **creates** a picture.*

crop
(krop) *noun*
A **crop** is a large amount of plants a farmer grows, usually for food.

*This farm had a very large orange **crop** this year.*

608

Page 608

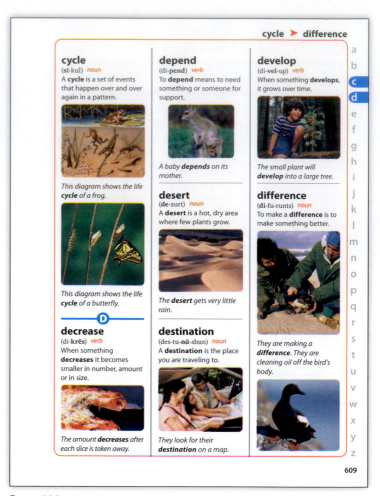

cycle
(**sī**-kul) *noun*
A **cycle** is a set of events that happen over and over again in a pattern.

*This diagram shows the life **cycle** of a frog.*

*This diagram shows the life **cycle** of a butterfly.*

D

decrease
(di-**krēs**) *verb*
When something **decreases** it becomes smaller in number, amount or in size.

*The amount **decreases** after each slice is taken away.*

depend
(di-**pend**) *verb*
To **depend** means to need something or someone for support.

*A baby **depends** on its mother.*

desert
(**de**-zurt) *noun*
A **desert** is a hot, dry area where few plants grow.

*The **desert** gets very little rain.*

destination
(des-tu-**nā**-shun) *noun*
A **destination** is the place you are traveling to.

*They look for their **destination** on a map.*

develop
(di-**vel**-up) *verb*
When something **develops**, it grows over time.

*The small plant will **develop** into a large tree.*

difference
(**di**-fu-runts) *noun*
To make a **difference** is to make something better.

*They are making a **difference**. They are cleaning oil off the bird's body.*

609

Page 609

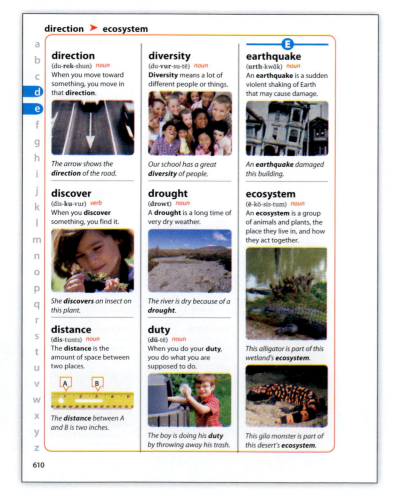

direction
(du-**rek**-shun) *noun*
When you move toward something, you move in that **direction**.

*The arrow shows the **direction** of the road.*

discover
(dis-**ku**-vur) *verb*
When you **discover** something, you find it.

*She **discovers** an insect on this plant.*

distance
(**dis**-tunts) *noun*
The **distance** is the amount of space between two places.

A   B

*The **distance** between A and B is two inches.*

diversity
(du-**vur**-su-tē) *noun*
Diversity means a lot of different people or things.

*Our school has a great **diversity** of people.*

drought
(drowt) *noun*
A **drought** is a long time of very dry weather.

*The river is dry because of a **drought**.*

duty
(**dū**-tē) *noun*
When you do your **duty**, you do what you are supposed to do.

*The boy is doing his **duty** by throwing away his trash.*

E

earthquake
(**urth**-kwāk) *noun*
An **earthquake** is a sudden violent shaking of Earth that may cause damage.

*An **earthquake** damaged this building.*

ecosystem
(**ē**-kō-sis-tum) *noun*
An **ecosystem** is a group of animals and plants, the place they live in, and how they act together.

*This alligator is part of this wetland's **ecosystem**.*

*This gila monster is part of this desert's **ecosystem**.*

610

Page 610

endurance
(in-**dur**-uns) *noun*
When you have **endurance**, you keep doing something.

*A long race takes **endurance**.*

environment
(in-**vī**-run-munt) *noun*
Your **environment** is the kind of place where you live.

*This is a hot, dry **environment**.*

erupt
(i-**rupt**) *verb*
When a volcano **erupts**, it throws out smoke, rocks, hot ashes, and lava.

*It is dangerous to be nearby when a volcano **erupts**!*

estimate
(**es**-tu-māt) *verb*
When you make a guess about something, you **estimate**.

*Can you **estimate** how many coins are in the jar?*

explore
(ik-**splor**) *verb*
To **explore** means to go somewhere to learn about people or things.

*He **explores** a new area.*

express
(ik-**spres**) *verb*
To **express** a thought or an emotion is to say or show it.

*She **expresses** her love for her dog.*

F

farmer
(**far**-mur) *noun*
A **farmer** is someone who grows crops or raises animals.

*The **farmer** picks carrots from the field.*

feelings
(**fē**-lingz) *noun*
Feelings are how you experience something.

*Happiness and surprise are kinds of **feelings**.*

feet
(fēt) *noun*
Feet are units of length. One foot is twelve inches long.

*He is almost four **feet** tall.*

611

Page 611

Page 612

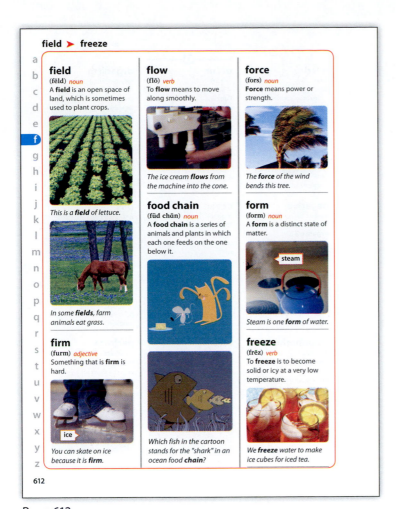

a b c d e **f** g h i j k l m n o p q r s t u v w x y z

field
(fēld) *noun*
A **field** is an open space of land, which is sometimes used to plant crops.

This is a field of lettuce.

In some fields, farm animals eat grass.

firm
(furm) *adjective*
Something that is **firm** is hard.

ice

You can skate on ice because it is firm.

flow
(flō) *verb*
To **flow** means to move along smoothly.

The ice cream flows from the machine into the cone.

food chain
(füd chān) *noun*
A **food chain** is a series of animals and plants in which each one feeds on the one below it.

Which fish in the cartoon stands for the "shark" in an ocean food chain?

force
(fors) *noun*
Force means power or strength.

The force of the wind bends this tree.

form
(form) *noun*
A **form** is a distinct state of matter.

steam

Steam is one form of water.

freeze
(frēz) *verb*
To **freeze** is to become solid or icy at a very low temperature.

We freeze water to make ice cubes for iced tea.

612

Page 613

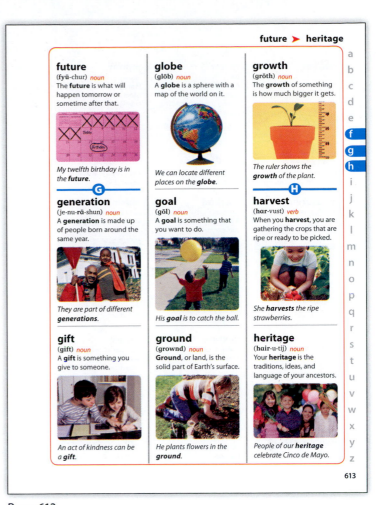

a b c d e **f g h** i j k l m n o p q r s t u v w x y z

future
(fyū-chur) *noun*
The **future** is what will happen tomorrow or sometime after that.

My twelfth birthday is in the future.

G

generation
(je-nu-rā-shun) *noun*
A **generation** is made up of people born around the same year.

They are part of different generations.

gift
(gift) *noun*
A **gift** is something you give to someone.

An act of kindness can be a gift.

globe
(glōb) *noun*
A **globe** is a sphere with a map of the world on it.

We can locate different places on the globe.

goal
(gōl) *noun*
A **goal** is something that you want to do.

His goal is to catch the ball.

ground
(grownd) *noun*
Ground, or land, is the solid part of Earth's surface.

He plants flowers in the ground.

growth
(grōth) *noun*
The **growth** of something is how much bigger it gets.

The ruler shows the growth of the plant.

H

harvest
(har-vust) *verb*
When you **harvest**, you are gathering the crops that are ripe or ready to be picked.

She harvests the ripe strawberries.

heritage
(hair-u-tij) *noun*
Your **heritage** is the traditions, ideas, and language of your ancestors.

People of our heritage celebrate Cinco de Mayo.

613

Page 614

a b c d e f g h **i j** k l m n o p q r s t u v w x y z

I

identify
(i-den-tu-fī) *verb*
When you **identify** something, you tell what it is.

She wants to identify a type of bird.

impact
(im-pakt) *noun*
What you do has an **impact** on things.

The children have a positive impact on the park.

improve
(im-prūv) *verb*
To **improve** something means to make it better.

They improve the beach when they clean it.

increase
(in-krēs) *verb*
To **increase** means to grow in size or in number.

When our dog eats too much food, its weight increases.

individual
(in-du-vi-ju-wul) *noun*
An **individual** is one person.

This individual is reading on her own.

interact
(in-tur-akt) *verb*
To **interact** means to act together.

The students interact with each other to do a science project.

island
(ī-lund) *noun*
An **island** is a piece of land completely surrounded by water.

This island is in the Caribbean Sea.

J

journey
(jur-nē) *noun*
A **journey** is a long trip.

Horses pulled covered wagons in the long, hard journey west.

614

Page 615

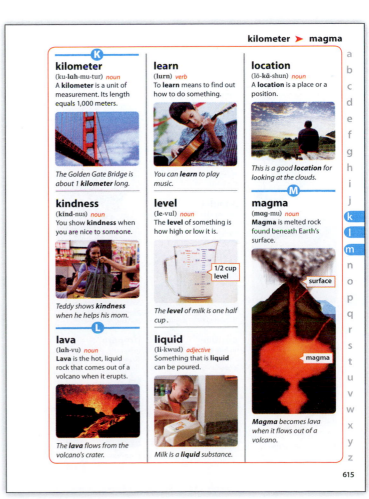

a b c d e f g h i j **k l m** n o p q r s t u v w x y z

K

kilometer
(ku-lah-mu-tur) *noun*
A **kilometer** is a unit of measurement. Its length equals 1,000 meters.

The Golden Gate Bridge is about 1 kilometer long.

kindness
(kīnd-nus) *noun*
You show **kindness** when you are nice to someone.

Teddy shows kindness when he helps his mom.

L

lava
(lah-vu) *noun*
Lava is the hot, liquid rock that comes out of a volcano when it erupts.

The lava flows from the volcano's crater.

learn
(lurn) *verb*
To **learn** means to find out how to do something.

You can learn to play music.

level
(le-vul) *noun*
The **level** of something is how high or low it is.

1/2 cup level

The level of milk is one half cup .

liquid
(li-kwud) *adjective*
Something that is **liquid** can be poured.

Milk is a liquid substance.

location
(lō-kā-shun) *noun*
A **location** is a place or a position.

This is a good location for looking at the clouds.

M

magma
(mag-mu) *noun*
Magma is melted rock found beneath Earth's surface.

surface

magma

Magma becomes lava when it flows out of a volcano.

615

Anthology Picture Dictionary, continued

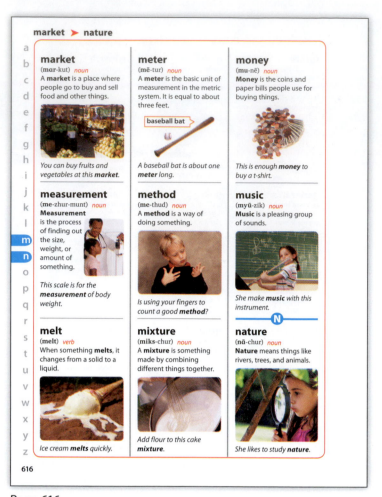

market
(mar-kut) *noun*
A **market** is a place where people go to buy and sell food and other things.

*You can buy fruits and vegetables at this **market**.*

meter
(mē-tur) *noun*
A **meter** is the basic unit of measurement in the metric system. It is equal to about three feet.

baseball bat

*A baseball bat is about one **meter** long.*

money
(mu-nē) *noun*
Money is the coins and paper bills people use for buying things.

*This is enough **money** to buy a t-shirt.*

measurement
(me-zhur-munt) *noun*
Measurement is the process of finding out the size, weight, or amount of something.

*This scale is for the **measurement** of body weight.*

method
(me-thud) *noun*
A **method** is a way of doing something.

*Is using your fingers to count a good **method**?*

music
(myū-zik) *noun*
Music is a pleasing group of sounds.

*She make **music** with this instrument.*

melt
(melt) *verb*
When something **melts**, it changes from a solid to a liquid.

*Ice cream **melts** quickly.*

mixture
(miks-chur) *noun*
A **mixture** is something made by combining different things together.

*Add flour to this cake **mixture**.*

nature
(nā-chur) *noun*
Nature means things like rivers, trees, and animals.

*She likes to study **nature**.*

616

Page 616

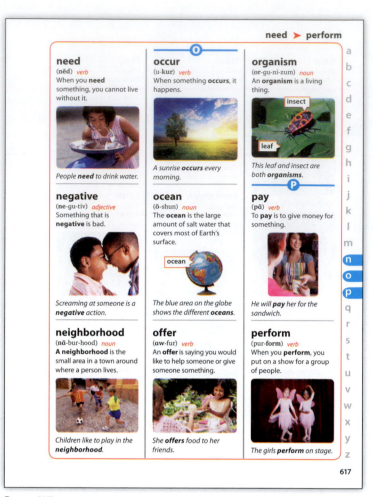

need
(nēd) *verb*
When you **need** something, you cannot live without it.

*People **need** to drink water.*

occur
(u-kur) *verb*
When something **occurs**, it happens.

*A sunrise **occurs** every morning.*

organism
(or-gu-ni-zum) *noun*
An **organism** is a living thing.

insect

leaf

*This leaf and insect are both **organisms**.*

negative
(ne-gu-tiv) *adjective*
Something that is **negative** is bad.

*Screaming at someone is a **negative** action.*

ocean
(ō-shun) *noun*
The **ocean** is the large amount of salt water that covers most of Earth's surface.

ocean

*The blue area on the globe shows the different **oceans**.*

pay
(pā) *verb*
To **pay** is to give money for something.

*He will **pay** her for the sandwich.*

neighborhood
(nā-bur-hood) *noun*
A **neighborhood** is the small area in a town around where a person lives.

*Children like to play in the **neighborhood**.*

offer
(aw-fur) *verb*
An **offer** is saying you would like to help someone or give someone something.

*She **offers** food to her friends.*

perform
(pur-form) *verb*
When you **perform**, you put on a show for a group of people.

*The girls **perform** on stage.*

617

Page 617

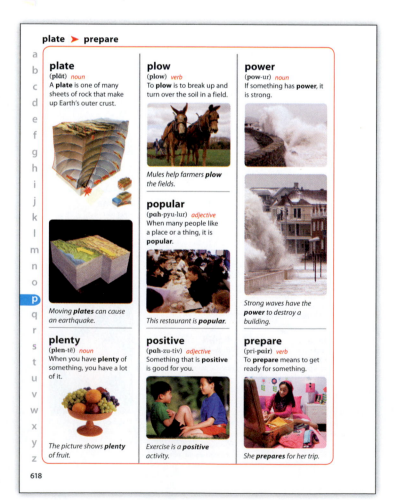

plate
(plāt) *noun*
A **plate** is one of many sheets of rock that make up Earth's outer crust.

*Moving **plates** can cause an earthquake.*

plow
(plow) *verb*
To **plow** is to break up and turn over the soil in a field.

*Mules help farmers **plow** the fields.*

popular
(pah-pyu-lur) *adjective*
When many people like a place or a thing, it is **popular**.

*This restaurant is **popular**.*

power
(pow-ur) *noun*
If something has **power**, it is strong.

*Strong waves have the **power** to destroy a building.*

plenty
(plen-tē) *noun*
When you have **plenty** of something, you have a lot of it.

*The picture shows **plenty** of fruit.*

positive
(pah-zu-tiv) *adjective*
Something that is **positive** is good for you.

*Exercise is a **positive** activity.*

prepare
(pri-pair) *verb*
To **prepare** means to get ready for something.

*She **prepares** for her trip.*

618

Page 618

preservation
(pre-zur-vā-shun) *noun*
Preservation is the act of keeping something safe for a long time.

*The **preservation** of old documents is important.*

process
(prah-ses) *noun*
When you follow a **process**, you do something step by step.

*He follows a **process** to put the model together.*

protect
(pru-tekt) *verb*
You **protect** something when you keep it safe.

spine

*Sharp spines **protect** the plant from animals.*

pressure
(pre-shur) *noun*
When one thing pushes against another, it makes **pressure**.

nutcracker

cracked nut

Pressure from the nutcracker causes the nuts to crack open.

problem
(prah-blum) *noun*
A **problem** is a difficult situation that needs to be figured out.

*A broken toy is a **problem**.*

produce
(pru-dūs) *verb*
To **produce** means to make something.

*This factory **produces** cars.*

purpose
(pur-pus) *noun*
A **purpose** is the reason for doing something.

*What is the **purpose** of studying for a test?*

619

Page 619

Page 620

rainforest
(rān-for-ust) *noun*
A **rainforest** is a thick, tropical forest where a lot of rain falls.

Rainforests are home to lots of interesting wildlife.

react
(rē-ăkt) *verb*
When things happen, you usually **react** to them.

*The child **reacts** to the snowball.*

receive
(ri-sēv) *verb*
To **receive** is to get something from someone.

*She **received** my package in the mail today.*

region
(rē-jun) *noun*
A **region** is an area.

*There are many **regions** in the United States.*

represent
(re-pri-zent) *verb*
To **represent** means to stand for.

*A heart **represents** love.*

rescue
(res-kyū) *verb*
When you **rescue** someone, you save the person.

*A dog helps to **rescue** a skier.*

*A fireman **rescues** a girl from a burning building.*

resources
(rē-sors-uz) *noun*
Resources are things that you can use.

*A library has many **resources**.*

620

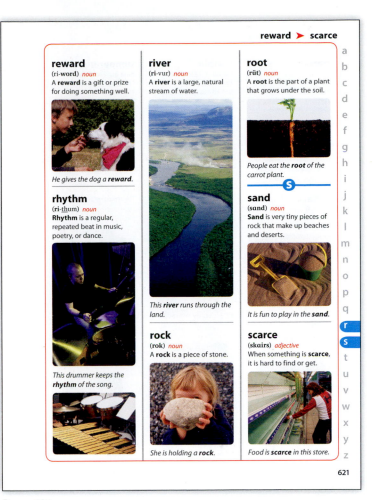

Page 621

reward
(ri-word) *noun*
A **reward** is a gift or prize for doing something well.

*He gives the dog a **reward**.*

rhythm
(ri-thum) *noun*
Rhythm is a regular, repeated beat in music, poetry, or dance.

*This drummer keeps the **rhythm** of the song.*

river
(ri-vur) *noun*
A **river** is a large, natural stream of water.

*This **river** runs through the land.*

rock
(rok) *noun*
A **rock** is a piece of stone.

*She is holding a **rock**.*

root
(rüt) *noun*
A **root** is the part of a plant that grows under the soil.

*People eat the **root** of the carrot plant.*

sand
(sand) *noun*
Sand is very tiny pieces of rock that make up beaches and deserts.

*It is fun to play in the **sand**.*

scarce
(skairs) *adjective*
When something is **scarce**, it is hard to find or get.

*Food is **scarce** in this store.*

621

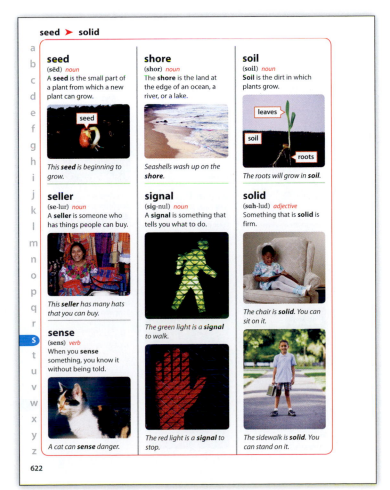

Page 622

seed
(sēd) *noun*
A **seed** is the small part of a plant from which a new plant can grow.

seed

*This **seed** is beginning to grow.*

seller
(se-lur) *noun*
A **seller** is someone who has things people can buy.

*This **seller** has many hats that you can buy.*

sense
(sens) *verb*
When you **sense** something, you know it without being told.

*A cat can **sense** danger.*

shore
(shor) *noun*
The **shore** is the land at the edge of an ocean, a river, or a lake.

*Seashells wash up on the **shore**.*

signal
(sig-nul) *noun*
A **signal** is something that tells you what to do.

*The green light is a **signal** to walk.*

*The red light is a **signal** to stop.*

soil
(soil) *noun*
Soil is the dirt in which plants grow.

leaves

soil

roots

*The roots will grow in **soil**.*

solid
(sah-lud) *adjective*
Something that is **solid** is firm.

*The chair is **solid**. You can sit on it.*

*The sidewalk is **solid**. You can stand on it.*

622

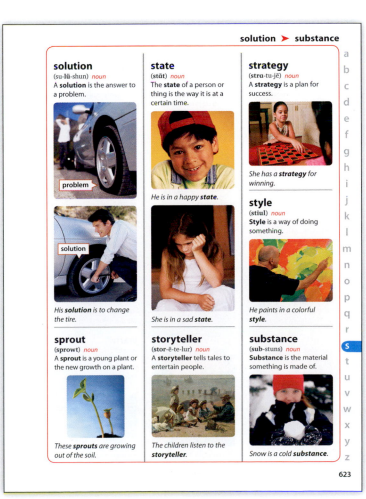

Page 623

solution
(su-lū-shun) *noun*
A **solution** is the answer to a problem.

problem

solution

*His **solution** is to change the tire.*

sprout
(sprowt) *noun*
A **sprout** is a young plant or the new growth on a plant.

*These **sprouts** are growing out of the soil.*

state
(stāt) *noun*
The **state** of a person or thing is the way it is at a certain time.

*He is in a happy **state**.*

*She is in a sad **state**.*

storyteller
(stor-ē-te-lur) *noun*
A **storyteller** tells tales to entertain people.

*The children listen to the **storyteller**.*

strategy
(strā-tu-jē) *noun*
A **strategy** is a plan for success.

*She has a **strategy** for winning.*

style
(stiul) *noun*
Style is a way of doing something.

*He paints in a colorful **style**.*

substance
(sub-stuns) *noun*
Substance is the material something is made of.

*Snow is a cold **substance**.*

623

Anthology Picture Dictionary, continued

supply
(su-plī) *noun*
A **supply** is the amount you have of something.

They have a large **supply** of canned peaches.

surface
(sur-fus) *noun*
The **surface** is the outside part of something.

The **surface** of this ball is bumpy.

The **surface** of this watermelon is smooth.

sustain
(su-stān) *verb*
To **sustain** means to keep something or someone alive or in existence.

A mother bird brings food to **sustain** her chicks.

T

tale
(tāl) *noun*
A **tale** is a story about things that are made up.

The Ant and the Grasshopper

TURTLE AND HIS FOUR COUSINS

Children enjoy reading folk **tales**.

temperature
(tem-pur-chur) *noun*
The **temperature** of something is how hot or cold it is.

hot

The **temperature** is hot.

The **temperature** outside is very cold.

thermometer
(thur-mah-mu-tur) *noun*
A **thermometer** is used to measure temperature.

The doctor uses a **thermometer** to check for a fever.

Page 624

tradition
(tru-di-shun) *noun*
A **tradition** is something that people have done for a long time and continue to do.

Traditions are important to many families.

trap
(trap) *verb*
To **trap** something means to catch it and not let it go.

Spiders **trap** insects with webs.

tsunami
(sü-nah-mē) *noun*
A **tsunami** is a huge, dangerous, ocean wave. Underwater earthquakes cause tsunamis.

The **tsunami** crashes into buildings and floods the city.

U

understand
(un-dur-stand) *verb*
When you **understand** something, you know what it means.

Now he **understands** his homework.

unique
(yü-nēk) *adjective*
Unique things are different from other things.

The yellow flower is **unique**.

What is **unique** about this?

unit
(yü-nut) *noun*
A **unit** is an amount used in measuring or counting.

one inch

An inch is a **unit** of length.

Page 625

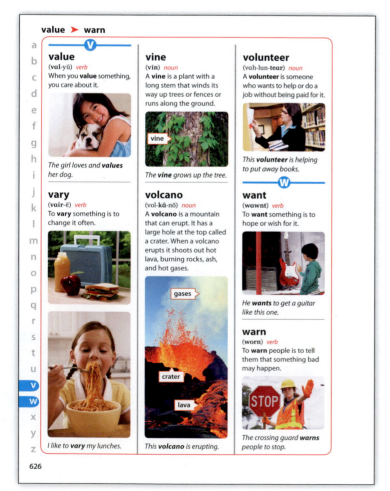

V

value
(val-yū) *verb*
When you **value** something, you care about it.

The girl loves and **values** her dog.

vary
(vair-ē) *verb*
To **vary** something is to change it often.

I like to **vary** my lunches.

vine
(vīn) *noun*
A **vine** is a plant with a long stem that winds its way up trees or fences or runs along the ground.

vine

The **vine** grows up the tree.

volcano
(vol-kā-nō) *noun*
A **volcano** is a mountain that can erupt. It has a large hole at the top called a crater. When a volcano erupts it shoots out hot lava, burning rocks, ash, and hot gases.

gases

crater

lava

This **volcano** is erupting.

volunteer
(vah-lun-tear) *noun*
A **volunteer** is someone who wants to help or do a job without being paid for it.

This **volunteer** is helping to put away books.

W

want
(wawnt) *verb*
To **want** something is to hope or wish for it.

He **wants** to get a guitar like this one.

warn
(worn) *verb*
To **warn** people is to tell them that something bad may happen.

STOP

The crossing guard **warns** people to stop.

Page 626

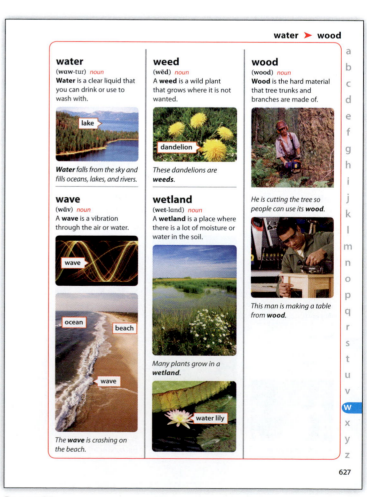

water
(waw-tur) *noun*
Water is a clear liquid that you can drink or use to wash with.

lake

Water falls from the sky and fills oceans, lakes, and rivers.

wave
(wāv) *noun*
A **wave** is a vibration through the air or water.

wave

ocean   beach

wave

The **wave** is crashing on the beach.

weed
(wēd) *noun*
A **weed** is a wild plant that grows where it is not wanted.

dandelion

These dandelions are **weeds**.

wetland
(wet-land) *noun*
A **wetland** is a place where there is a lot of moisture or water in the soil.

Many plants grow in a **wetland**.

water lily

wood
(wood) *noun*
Wood is the hard material that tree trunks and branches are made of.

He is cutting the tree so people can use its **wood**.

This man is making a table from **wood**.

Page 627

R22   Picture Dictionary

Anthology Index

Page 632

Page 633

Page 634

Page 635

Anthology Index, continued

Page 640

Page 641

Research Base and Bibliography

Language and Literacy

Asher, J., & Price, B. (1967). The learning strategy of total physical response: Some age differences. *Child Development*, 38, 1219–1227.

Asher, J. (1969). The total physical response approach to second language learning. The Modern Language Journal, 53, 1.

Au, K. (2006). *Multicultural issues and literacy achievement*. Mahwah, NJ: Lawrence Erlbaum.

August, D., & Hakuta, K. (1998). *Educating language-minority children*. Washington, DC: National Research Council.

August, D., & Shanahan, T. (Eds.). (2006). *Developing literacy in second-language learners: Report of the National Literacy Panel on Language-Minority Children and Youth*. Mahwah, NJ: Erlbaum.

August, D. L., & Shanahan, T. (2006). Synthesis: Instruction and professional development. In D. L. August & T. Shanahan (Eds.), *Developing literacy in a second language: Report of the National Literacy Panel*. Mahwah, NJ: Lawrence Erlbaum Associates.

Bailey, A. (Ed.). (2006). *The language demands of school: Putting academic English to the test*. New Haven, CT: Yale University Press.

Bauman, J. F., Russell, N.S., & Jones, L. A. (1992). Effects of think-aloud instruction on elementary students' comprehension abilities. *Journal of Reading Behavior*, 24 (2), 143–172.

Berg, C. (1999). The effects of trained peer response on esl students' revision types and writing quality. *Journal of Second Language Writing*, 8 (3), 215–241.

Bicais, J., & Correira, M. G. (2008). Peer-learning spaces: A staple in the English learner's tool kit for developing language and literacy. *Journal of Research in Childhood Education*, 22(4), 363–375.

Biemiller, A. (1999). *Language and reading success*. Newton Upper Falls, MA: Brookline Books.

Blum-Kulka, S., & Snow, C. E. (2004). Introduction: The potential of peer talk. *Discourse Studies*, 6(3), 291–306.

Brice, A., & Roseberry-McKibben, C. (1999). Turning frustration into success for English language learners. *Educational Leadership*, 56(7), 53–55.

Brown, A., Campoine, J., and Day, J. (1981). Learning to learn: On training students to learn from texts. *Educational Researcher*, 10, 14–24.

Bruner, J., Goodnow, J, & Austin, G. A. (1967). *A study of thinking*. New York: Science Editions.

Callow, J. (2008, May). Show me: principles for assessing students' visual literacy. *The Reading Teacher*, 61(8), 616–626.

Celce-Murcia, M., Brinton, D., & Goodwin, J. (1996). *Teaching pronunciation: A reference for teachers of English to speakers of other languages*. Cambridge: Cambridge University Press.

Chamot, A. U., & O'Malley, J. M. (1994) *The calla handbook: implementing the cognitive academic language learning approach*. White Plains, NY: Addison Wesley Longman.

Collier, V. P. (1995). *Promoting academic success for ESL students: Understanding second language acquisition for school*. Elizabeth, NJ: New Jersey Teachers of English to Speakers of Other Languages-Bilingual Educators.

Collier, V. P., & Thomas, W. P. (1989). How quickly can immigrants become proficient in school English? *Journal of Educational Issues of Language Minority Students*, 5, 26–38.

Crandall, J. (Ed.). 1987. *ESL through content area instruction: mathematics, science, social studies*. Englewood Cliffs, NJ: Prentice Hall.

Cummins, J. (2000). *Language, power and pedagogy: Bilingual children in the crossfire*. Buffalo, NY: Multilingual Matters.

Cunningham-Flores, M. (1998). *Improving adult esl learners' pronunciation skills*. National Center for ESL Literacy Education.

Day, J. P. (2002). We learn from each other: Collaboration and community in a bilingual classroom. In R. Allington & P. H. Johnston (Eds.), *Reading to learn: Lessons learned from exemplary fourth-grade classrooms* (pp. 99–122). New York: Guildford Press.

Diaz-Rico, L. T., & Weed, K. Z. (2002). *The crosscultural, language, and academic development handbook: A complete K–12 reference guide*. Boston, MA: Allyn & Bacon.

Dickinson, D. K., & Tabors, P. (Eds.). (2001). *Beginning literacy with language*. Baltimore: Brookes.

Dong, Y. R. (2006/2007). Learning to think in English. *Educational Leadership, Best of 2006–2007*, 9–13.

Dressler, C. (2006). First and second-language literacy. In D. L. August & T. Shanahan (Eds.), *Developing literacy in a second language: Report of the National Literacy Panel*. Mahwah, NJ: Lawrence Erlbaum Associates.

Droop, M., & Verhoeven, L. (2003). Language proficiency and reading ability in first- and second-language learners. *Reading Research Quarterly*, 38(1), 78–103.

Dutro, S., & Moran, C. (2002), Rethinking English language instruction: An architectural approach. In G. Garcia (Ed.), *English learners reading at the highest level of English literacy*. Newark, DE: International Reading Association.

Echevarria, J., Short, D., & Vogt, M. (2008). *Making content comprehensible. The sheltered instruction observation protocol*. Boston, MA: Pearson.

Echevarria, J., Vogt, M. A., & Short, D. J. (2004). *Making content comprehensible for English learners: The SIOP model* (2nd ed.). Boston, MA: Allyn & Bacon.

Feldman, K., & Kinsella, K. (2005). *Create an active participation classroom. The CORE Reading Expert*. Retrieved from www.corelearn.com/pdfs/Newsletters/CORE%202005%20Spring%20Newsletter.pdf.

Fillmore, L. W. (2004). *The role of language in academic development*. In Excerpts from a presentation by Lily Wong Fillmore at the Closing the Achievement Gap for EL Students conference. Santa Rosa: CA: Sonoma County Office of Education. Retrieved from www.scoe.k12.ca.us/aiming_high/docs/AH_language.pdf.

Fitzgerald, J. (1995). English-as-a-second-language learners' cognitive reading processes: A review of research in the United States. *Review of Educational Research, 65,* 145–190.

Fitzgerald, J. (1993). Literacy and students who are learning English as a second language. *The Reading Teacher, 46,* 638–647.

Francis, D., Lesaux, N., & August, D. (2006). Language instruction. In D. August & T. Shanahan (Eds.), *Developing literacy in second-language learners: Report of the National Literacy Panel on Language-Minority Children and Youth* (pp. 365–413). Mahwah, NJ: Erlbaum.

Francis, D. J., Rivera, M., Lesaux, N., Kieffer, M., & Rivera, H. (2006). *Practical guidelines for the education of English language learners: Research-based recommendations for instruction and academic interventions.* Retrieved from www.centeroninstruction.org/files/ELL1-Interventions.pdf.

Gambrell, L. B., Morrow, L. M., & Pressley, M. (Eds.). (2007) *Best Practices in Literacy Instruction.* New York: Guilford.

Garcia, G., & Beltran, D. (2005) Revisioning the blueprint: Building for the academic success of English learners. In G. Garcia (Ed.). *English learners: Reaching the highest levels of English literacy.* Newark: DE: International Reading Association.

Genesee, F., Lindholm-Leary, K., Saunders, W., & Christian, D. (2006). *Educating English language learners: A synthesis of research evidence.* New York: Cambridge University Press.

Genesee, F. & Geva, E. (2006). Cross-linguistic relationships in working memory, phonological processes, and oral language. In D. L. August & T. Shanahan (Eds.), *Developing literacy in a second language: Report of the National Literacy Panel.* Mahwah, NJ: Lawrence Erlbaum Associates.

Gersten, R., & Baker, S. (2000). What we know about effective instructional practices for English-language learners. *Exceptional Children, 66,* 454–470.

Gibbons, P. (2002). *Scaffolding language, scaffolding learning: Teaching second language learners in the mainstream classroom.* Portsmouth, NH: Heinemann.

Girard, V. (2005). English learners and the language arts. In V. Girard (Ed.), *Schools moving up: A WestEd initiative.* Retrieved November 8, 2006, from www.schoolsmovingup.net/cs/wested/view/e/140

Goldenberg, C. (2006). *Improving achievement for English learners: Conclusions from 2 research reviews.* Retrieved from www.colorincolorado.org/article/12918

Goldenberg, C. (2004). *Successful school change: Creating settings to improve teaching and learning.* New York: Teachers College Press.

Goldenberg, C. (1992–1993). Instructional conversations: promoting comprehension through discussion, *The Reading Teacher, 46* (4), 316–326.

Goldenberg, C., Rueda, R., & August, D. (2006). Sociocultural influences on the literacy attainment of language-minority children and youth. In D. August & T. Shanahan (Eds.), *Developing literacy in second-language learners: Report of the National Literacy Panel on Language-Minority Children and Youth* (pp. 269–318). Mahwah, NJ: Erlbaum.

High, J. (1993). *Second language learning through cooperative learning.* San Clemente, CA: Kagan Publishing.

Hill, J., & Flynn, K. (2006). *Classroom instruction that works with English language learners.* Alexandria, VA: Association for Supervision and Curriculum Development.

Johnson, D., & Johnson, R. (1995). *Creative controversy: Intellectual challenge in the classroom* (3rd ed.). Edina, MN: Interaction Book Company.

Kagan, S. (1990). Cooperative learning for students limited in language proficiency. In M. Brubacker, R. Payne & K. Rickett (Eds.), *Perspectives on small group learning.* Oakville, Ontario, Canada.

Kagan, S. (1992). *Cooperative learning.* San Juan Capistrano, CA: Kagan Cooperative Learning.

Kim, Y., & Turner, J. D. (2006). Creating literacy communities in multicultural and multilingual classrooms: Lessons learned from two European American elementary teachers. In R.T. Jimenez & V.O. Pang (Eds.), *Race, Ethnicity, and Education Volume 2: Language and Literacy in Schools* (pp.219–236). Westport, CT: Praeger Publishing Group.

Kirschner, P. A., Sweller, J., and Clark, R. E. (2006). Why minimal guidance during instruction does not work: An analysis of the failure of constructivist, discovery, problem-based, experiential, and inquiry-based teaching. *Educational Psychologist, 41,* 75–86.

Krashen, S. (1987). *Principles and practices in second language acquisition.* New York: Prentice-Hall.

Leeman, J. (2003). Recasts and second language development: Beyond negative evidence. *Studies in Second Language Acquisition, 25,* 37–63.

Lesaux, N. K. (2006). Development of literacy of language minority learners. In D. L. August & T. Shanahan (Eds.), *Developing literacy in a second language: Report of the National Literacy Panel.* Mahwah, NJ: Lawrence Erlbaum Associates.

Lesaux, N., & Siegel, L. (2003). The development of reading in children who speak English as a second language. *Developmental Psychology, 39,* 1005–1019.

Lesaux, N. K., Lipka, O., & Siegel, L.S. (2006). Investigating cognitive and linguistic abilities that influence the reading comprehension skills of children from diverse linguistic backgrounds. *Reading and Writing: An Interdisciplinary Journal, 19*(1), 99–131.

Lesaux, N. K. & Crosson, A.C. (2005). Addressing variability and vulnerability: Promoting the academic achievement of English learners in San Diego. In R. Hess (Ed.), *Urban reform: Lessons from San Diego* (pp. 263–281). Cambridge, MA: Harvard Education Press.

Lyman, F. T. (1981). The responsive classroom discussion: The inclusion of all students. In A. Anderson (Ed.), *Mainstreaming Digest* (pp. 109–113). College Park: University of Maryland Press.

Marzano, R. J., Pickering, D. J., & Pollock, J. E. (2001). *Classroom instruction that works: Research-based strategies for increasing student achievement.* Alexandria, VA: Association for Supervision and Curriculum Development.

Marzano, R. (2004). *Building academic background.* Alexandria, VA: MCREL, ASCD.

Mayer, R. (2003). *Learning and instruction.* New Jersey: Pearson Education, Inc.

Medina-Jerez, W., Clark, D.B., Medina, A., & Ramirez-Marin, F. (2007). Science for ELLs: Rethinking our approach. *The Science Teacher, 74*, 52–56.

Miller, J. F., Heilmann, J., Nockerts, A., Iglesias, A., Fabiano, L., & Francis, D. J. (2006). Oral language and reading in bilingual children. *Learning Disabilities Research & Practice, 21*, 30–43.

Morrison Institute for Public Policy. (2006). *Why some schools with Latino children beat the odds and others don't.* Tempe, AZ: Author.

National Research Council. (2000). *How people learn: Brain, mind, experience, and school.* Washington, DC: National Academies Press.

Novak, J. D. (1995). Concept mapping: a strategy for organizing knowledge. In S. M. Glynn & R. Duit (eds.), *Learning Science in the Schools: Research Reforming Practice.* Mahwah, NJ: Lawrence Erlbaum Associates.

Pearson, P. D., & Gallagher, G. (1983). The gradual release of responsibility model of instruction. *Contemporary Educational Psychology, 8*, 112–123.

Powell, M. (1996). *Presenting in English.* Hove: Language Teaching Publications.

Saenz, L. M., Fuchs, L. S., & Fuchs, D. (2005). Peer-assisted learning strategies for English language learners with learning disabilities. *Exceptional Children, 71*, 231–247.

Rousculp, E. E., & Maring, G. H. (1992). Portfolios for a community of learners. *Journal of Reading, 35*, 378–385.

Samway K., & McKeon, D. (2007). *Myths and realities: best practices for English language learners.* Portsmouth NH: Heineman.

Saunders, W. M., & Goldenberg, C. (1999). Effects of instructional conversations and literature logs on limited- and fluent-English proficient students' story comprehension and thematic understanding. *Elementary School Journal, 99*(4), 277–301.

Saunders, W. M., Foorman, B. P., & Carlson, C. D. (2006). Do we need a separate block of time for oral English language development in programs for English learners? *The Elementary School Journal, 107*, 181–198.

Scarcella, R. (2003). *Academic English: A conceptual framework.* Los Angeles: Language Minority Research Institute.

Scarcella, R. (2003). *Accelerating academic English: A focus on the English learner.* Oakland, CA: Regents of the University of California.

Schleppegrell, M. J. (2001). Linguistic features of the language of schooling. *Linguistics and Education, 12*, 431–459.

Schleppegrell, M. J. (2004). *The language of schooling: A functional linguistics perspective.* Mahwah, NJ: Erlbaum.

Seidlitz, J. (2008) *Navigating the ELPS: Using the new standards to improve instruction for English language learners.* San Antonio, TX: Canter Press.

Seidlitz, J. & Perryman, B., (2008) *Seven steps to building an interactive classroom: Engaging all students in academic conversation.* San Antonio TX: Canter Press.

Shanahan, T. & Beck, I.L. (2006). Effective literacy teaching for English-language learners. In D. L. August & T. Shanahan (Eds.), *Developing literacy in a second language: Report of the National Literacy Panel.* Mahwah, NJ: Lawrence Erlbaum Associates.

Snow, C. E., & Fillmore, L. W. (2000). *Clearinghouse on languages and linguistics.* Retrieved from www.cal.org/ericcll/teachers/teacher.pdf.

Tabors, P., Paez, M., & Lopez, L. (2003). Dual language abilities of bilingual four- year olds: Initial findings from the Early Childhood Study of language and literacy development of Spanish-speaking children. *NABE Journal of Research and Practice, 1*(1), 70–91.

Taba, H. (1962). *Curriculum development: Theory and practice.* New York: Harcourt Brace & World.

Thornburry, S. (2005). *How to teach speaking.* Essex, England: Pearson.

Turner, J. D., & Kim, Y. (2005). Learning about building literacy communities in multicultural and multilingual communities from effective elementary teachers. *Literacy Teaching and Learning, 10*, 21–42.

Turner, J. (2007). Beyond cultural awareness: Prospective teachers' visions of culturally responsive teaching. *Action in Teacher Education, 29*(3), 12–24.

Uchikoshi, Y. (2005). Narrative development in bilingual kindergarteners: Can Arthur help? Developmental Psychology, 41, 464–478.

Vail, N. J. and Papenfuss, J. (1993). *Daily oral language plus.* Evanston, IL: McDougal, Littell.

Vaughn, S., Cirino, P. T., Linan- Thompson, S., Mathes, P. G., Carlson, C. D., Cardenas-Hagan, E., et al. (2006). Effectiveness of a Spanish intervention and an English intervention for English language learners at risk for reading problems. *American Educational Research Journal, 43*, 449–487.

Weaver, C. (1996). *Teaching grammar in context.* Portsmouth, NH: Boynton, Cook Publishers.

Wennerstrom, A. (1993). Content-based pronunciation. *TESOL Journal, 1*(3), 15–18.

Wong-Fillmore, L. & Snow, C. (2000). *What teachers need to know about language.* Washington, DC: ERIC Clearinghouse on Languages and Linguistics.

Zwiers, J. (2008). *Building Academic Language.* Newark, DE: Jossey-Bass/International Reading Association.

Vocabulary

August, D., Carlo, M., Dressler, C., & Snow, C. (2005). The critical role of vocabulary development for English language learners. *Learning Disabilities Research and Practice, 20*, 50–57.

Bauman, J. F., & E. Kame'enui (Eds.). (2004). *Vocabulary Instruction: Research to Practice.* New York: Guilford.

Bear, D. R., Invernizzi, M., Templeton, S., & Johnson, F. (2004). *Words their way: Word study for phonics, vocabulary, and spelling instruction (2nd Ed.).* Upper Saddle River, NJ: Merrill Prentice Hall.

Beck, I. L., McKeown, M.G., & Kucan, L. (2002). *Bringing words to life.* New York: The Guilford Press.

Beck, I. L., & McKeown, M. G. (1991). Conditions of vocabulary acquisition. In R. Barr, M. L. Kamil, P. B. Mosenthal, & P. D. Pearson (Eds.), *Handbook of reading research* (Vol. 2, pp. 789–814). White Plains, NY: Longman.

Beck, I. L., McKeown, M. G., & Omanson, R. C. (1987). The effects and uses of diverse vocabulary instructional techniques. In M.G. McKeown & M.E. Curtis (Eds.), *The nature of vocabulary acquisition* (pp.147–163). Mahwah, NJ: Lawrence Erlbaum Associates.

Biemiller, A. (2004). Teaching vocabulary in the primary grades: Vocabulary instruction needed. In J.F. Baumann & E. Kame'enui (Eds.), *Vocabulary instruction: Bringing research to practice* (pp.209–242). Mahwah, NJ: Lawrence Erlbaum Associates.

Blachowicz, C. L. Z., & Fisher, P. J. L. (2000). Vocabulary instruction. In M. L. Kamil, P. B. Mosenthal, P. D. Pearson, & R. Barr (Eds.), *Handbook of reading research* (Vol. 3, pp. 503–523). White Plains, NY: Longman.

Blachowicz, C. L. Z., Fisher, P. J. L., Ogle D., & Watts-Taffe, S. (2006). Vocabulary: Questions from the classroom. *Reading Research Quarterly, 41*, 524–539.

Carlo, M. S., August, D., McLaughlin, B., Snow, C. E., Dressler, C., Lippman, D. N., Lively, T. J., & White, C. E. (2004). Closing the gap: Addressing the vocabulary needs of English-language learners in bilingual and mainstream classrooms. *Reading Research Quarterly, 39*, 188–215.

Carlo, M. S., August, D., & Snow, C. E. (2005). Sustained vocabulary-learning strategies for English language learners. In E. H. Hiebert & M. Kamil (Eds.), *Teaching and learning vocabulary: Bringing research to practice* (pp.137–153). Mahwah, NJ: Lawrence Erlbaum Associates.

Coxhead, A. (2000). A new Academic Word List. *TESOL Quarterly, 34*(2): 213–238.

Eyraud, K., Giles, G., Koenig, S., & Stoller, F. (2000). The word wall approach: Promoting L2 vocabulary learning. *English Teaching Forum, 38*, pp. 2–11.

Graves, M. F. (2006). *The vocabulary book: Learning and instruction.* New York: Teacher's College Press.

Harrington, M. J. (1996). Basic instruction in word analysis skills to improve spelling competence. *Education, 117*, 22. Available at: www.questia.com.

Kieffer, M. J., & Lesaux, N. K. (in press). Breaking down words to build meaning: Morphology, vocabulary, and reading comprehension in the urban classroom. *The Reading Teacher.*

Lehr, F., Osborn, J., & Hiebert, E. H. (2004). *A focus on vocabulary.* Honolulu, HI: Pacific Regional Educational Laboratory. Available at: www.prel.org/programs/rel/vocabularyforum.asp.

Nagy, W. E., & Scott, J. A. (2000). Vocabulary processes. In R. Barr, M. L. Kamil, P. Mosenthal, & P. D. Pearson (Eds.), *Handbook of reading research: Vol. 3* (pp. 269–284). New York: Longman.

Nagy, W. E., & Stahl, S. A. (2006). *Teaching word meanings.* Mahwah, NJ: Lawrence Erlbaum Associates.

Roser, N., & Juel, C. (1982). Effects of vocabulary instruction on reading comprehension. In J.A. Niles & L.A. Harris (Eds.), *Yearbook of the National Reading Conference: Vol. 31. New inquiries in reading research and Instruction* (pp. 110–118). Rochester, NY: National Reading Conference.

Ruddell, M. R., & Shearer, B. A. (2002). "Extraordinary," "tremendous," exhilarating," "magnificent": Middle school at-risk students become avid word learners with the vocabulary-self collection strategy (VSS). *Journal of Adolescent and Adult Literacy, 45*(4), 352–363.

Stahl, S. A. (1999). *Vocabulary development.* Cambridge, MA: Brookline Books.

Stahl, S. A., & Nagy, W. E. (2006). *Teaching word meanings.* Mahwah, NJ: Lawrence Erlbaum Associates.

White, T., Sowell, J., & Yanagihara, A. (1989). Teaching elementary students to use word-part clues. *The Reading Teacher, 42*, 302–308.

Wixson, K. K. (1986). Vocabulary instruction and children's comprehension of basal stories. *Reading Research Quarterly, 21*(3) 317–329.

Reading

Allington, R. L. (2001). *What really matters for struggling readers: Designing research-based programs.* New York, NY: Addison Wesley Educational Publishers Inc.

Baker, L. (2004). Reading comprehension and science inquiry: Metacognitive connections. In E.W. Saul (Ed.), *Crossing borders in literacy and science instruction: Perspectives on theory and practice.* Newark, DE: International Reading Association; Arlington, VA: National Science Teachers Association (NSTA) Press.

Beck, I. L. (2006). *Making sense of phonics: The hows and whys.* New York: Guilford Press.

Beck, I. L., & McKeown, M. G., (2001). Inviting students into the pursuit of meaning. *Educational Psychology Review, 13*(3), 225–241.

Beck, I. L., McKeown, M. G., Hamilton, R. L., and Kucan, L. (1997). *Questioning the Author: An approach for enhancing student engagement with text.* Delaware: International Reading Association.

Boulware, B. J., & Crow, M. (2008, March). Using the concept attainment strategy to enhance reading comprehension. *The Reading Teacher, 61*(6), 491–495.

Cain, K. & Oakhill, J. (1998). Comprehension skill and inference-making ability: Issues and causality. In C. Hulme and R.M. Joshi (Eds.), *Reading and spelling: Development and disorders.* London: Lawrence Erlbaum.

Cain, K. & Oakhill, J. (2000). Inference making ability and its relation to comprehension failure in young children. *Reading and Writing: An Interdisciplinary Journal, 11*, 489–503.

Calhoon, M. B., Al Otaiba, S., Cihak, D., King, A., & Avalos, A. C. (2006). *Effects of a peer-mediated program on reading skill acquisition for two-way bilingual first grade classrooms.* Manuscript submitted for publication.

Cirino, P. T., Vaughn, S., Linan-Thompson, S., Cardenas-Hagan, E., Fletcher, J. M., & Francis, D. J. (2007). *One year follow-up outcomes of Spanish and English interventions for English language learners at-risk for reading problems.* Manuscript submitted for publication.

Crawford, E. C., & Torgesen, J. K. (2006). *Teaching all students to read: Practices from Reading First schools with strong intervention outcomes.* Tallahassee, FL: Florida Center for Reading Research. Available at: www.fcrr.org.

Cunningham, A. E., & Stanovich, K. (1998). *What reading does to the mind*. American Educator, 22 (1), 8–15.

Denton, C. A., Anthony, J. L., Parker, R., & Hasbrouck, J. E. (2004). Effects of two tutoring programs on the English reading development of Spanish-English bilingual students. *The Elementary School Journal*, 104, 289–305.

Dole, J., Duffy, G., Roehler, L., & Pearson, P. (1991). Moving from the old to the new: Research in reading comprehension instruction. *Review of Educational Research*, 61, 239–264.

Duke, N. K., & Pearson, P. D. (2002). Effective practices for developing reading comprehension. In A. E. Farstrup & S. J. Samuels (Eds.), *What research has to say about reading instruction* (3rd ed.) (pp. 205–242). Newark, DE: International Reading Association.

Fielding, L., Kerr, N., & Rosier, P. (2007). *Annual growth for all students, catch-up growth for those who are behind*. Kennewick, WA: The New Foundation Press.

Garcia, G. E. (2000). Bilingual children's reading. In M. L. Kamil, P. B. Mosenthal, P. D. Pearson, & R. Barr (Eds.), *Handbook of reading research: Volume III* (pp. 813–834). Mahwah, NJ: Lawrence Erlbaum Associates.

Gerber, M., Jimenez, T., Leafstedt, J., Villaruz, J., Richards, C., & English, J. (2004). English reading effects of small-group intensive instruction in Spanish for K–1 English learners. *Learning Disabilities Research & Practice*, 19(4), 239–251.

Head, M., & Readence, J. (1986). Anticipation guides: Meaning through prediction. In E. Dishner, T. Bean, J. Readence, & D. Moore (Eds.), *Reading in the Content Areas*, Dubuque, IA: Kendall/Hunt.

Kosanovich, M., Ladinsky, K., Nelson, L., & Torgesen, J. (2006). *Differentiated reading instruction: Small group lesson structures for all students*. Tallahassee, FL: Florida Center for Reading Research. Available at: www.fcrr.org.

Lehr, F. & Osborne, J. (2006). *Focus on comprehension*. Honolulu, HI: Pacific Regional Educational Laboratory. Available at: www.prel.org/programs/rel/comprehensionforum.asp.

Lesaux, N. K., & Kieffer, M. J. (in press). Sources of reading comprehension difficulties for language minority learners and their classmates in early adolescence. *American Educational Research Journal*.

Lesaux, N. K., & Siegel, L. S. (2003). The development of reading in children who speak English as a second language. *Developmental Psychology*, 39(6), 1005–1019.

Lesaux, N. K., Lipka, O., & Siegel, L. S. (2006). Investigating cognitive and linguistic abilities that influence the reading comprehension skills of children from diverse linguistic backgrounds. *Reading and Writing: An Interdisciplinary Journal*, 19, 99–131.

Linan-Thompson, S., & Hickman-Davis, P. (2002). Supplemental reading instruction for students at risk for reading disabilities: Improve reading 30 minutes at a time. *Learning Disabilities Research and Practice*, 17(4), 242–251.

Linan-Thompson, S., Vaughn, S., Hickman-Davis, P., & Kouzekanani, K. (2003). Effectiveness of supplemental reading instruction for second-grade English language learners with reading difficulties. *The Elementary School Journal*, 103(3), 221–238.

McMaster, K. L., Kung, H., Han, I., & Cao, M. (in press). Peer-assisted learning strategies: A "tier 1" approach to promoting responsiveness to beginning reading instruction for English learners. *Exceptional Children*.

McKeown, M. G., Beck, I. L., & Worthy, M. J. (1993). Grappling with text ideas: Questioning the author. *Reading Teacher*, 46, 560–66.

National Reading Panel. (2000). *Report of the National Reading Panel: Teaching children to read*. Bethesda, MD: National Institute of Child Health and Human Development.

Ogle, D. S. (1986). K-W-L group instructional strategy. In A. S. Palincsar, D. S. Ogle, B. F. Jones, & E. G. Carr (Eds.), *Teaching reading as thinking*. Alexandria, VA: Association for Supervision and Curriculum Development.

Palincsar, A. S., & Brown, A. L. (1985). Reciprocal teaching: Activities to promote reading with your mind. In T. L. Harris & E. J. Cooper (Eds.), *Reading thinking and concept development: Strategies for the classroom*. New York: The College Board.

Pressley, M. (2000). What should comprehension instruction be the instruction of? In M. Kamil, P. B. Mosenthal, P. D. Pearson, & R. Barr (Eds.), *Handbook of Reading Research: Vol. 3* (pp. 545–561). Mahwah, NJ: Lawrence Erlbaum Associates.

Pressley, M., & Afflerbach, P. (1995). *Verbal protocols of reading: The nature of constructively responsive reading*. Hillsdale, NJ: Erlbaum.

Proctor, C. P., Carlo, M., August, D., & Snow, C. (2005). Native Spanish-speaking children reading in English: Toward a model of comprehension. *Journal of Educational Psychology*, 97, 246–256.

Quiroga, T., Lemos-Britton, Z., Mostafapour, E., Abbott, R. D., & Berninger, V. W. (2002). Phonological awareness and beginning reading in Spanish-speaking ESL first graders: Research into practice. *Journal of School Psychology*, 40, 85–111.

Riedel, B. W. (2007). The relation between DIBELS, reading comprehension, and vocabulary in urban, first grade students. *Reading Research Quarterly*, 42, 460–466.

Saunders, W. M., & Goldenberg, C. (1999). Effects of instructional conversations and literature logs on limited- and fluent- English-proficient students' story comprehension and thematic understanding. *Elementary School Journal*, 99, 277–301.

Schlick Noe, K., & Johnson, N. (1999). *Getting started with literature circles*. Norwood, MA: Christopher-Gordon Publishers, Inc.

Slavin, R., & Cheung, A. (2005). A synthesis of research on language of reading instruction for English language learners. *Review of Educational Research*, 75, 247–284.

Snow, C. E., Burns, M. S., & Griffin, P. (Eds.). (1998). *Preventing reading difficulties in young children*. Washington, DC: National Academy Press.

Swanson, H. L., Sáez, L., & Gerber, M. (2004). Do phonological and executive processes in English learners at risk for reading disabilities in grade 1 predict performance in grade 2? *Learning Disabilities Research & Practice*, 19, 225–238.

Taylor, W. (1953). Cloze procedure a new tool for measuring readability. *Journalism Quarterly*, 30, 415–433.

Torgesen, J. K. (2006). *A principal's guide to intensive reading interventions for struggling readers in early elementary school.* Portsmouth, NH: RMC Research Corporation, Center on Instruction. Available at: www.centeroninstruction.org.

Tumner, J., & Chapman, J. (1995). Context use in early reading development: Premature exclusion of a source or individual differences? *Issues in Education,*1, 97–100.

Vaughn, S., Cirino, P. T., Linan-Thompson, S., Mathes, P. G., Carlson, C. D., Cardenas-Hagan, E., et al. (2006). Effectiveness of a Spanish intervention and an English intervention for English language learners at risk for reading problems. *American Educational Research Journal, 43,* 449–487.

Vaughn, S., Mathes, P., Linan-Thompson, S., Cirino, P., Carlson, C., Pollard-Durodola, S., et al. (2006). Effectiveness of an English intervention for first-grade English language learners at risk for reading problems. *Elementary School Journal, 107,* 153–180.

Vaughn, S., Linan-Thompson, S., & Hickman-Davis, P. (2003). Response to treatment as a means for identifying students with reading/learning disabilities. *Exceptional Children, 69,* 391–410.

Vaughn, S., Mathes, P., Linan-Thompson, S., & Francis, D. (2005). Teaching English language learners at risk for reading disabilities to read: Putting research into practice. *Learning Disabilities Research and Practice,* 20(1), 58–67.

Verhoeven, L. (1990). Acquisition of reading in a second language. *Reading Research Quarterly,* 25, 90–114.

Verhoeven, L. T. (2000). Components in early second language reading and spelling. *Scientific Studies of Reading,* 4, 313–330.

Willhelm, J. (2002). *Action strategies for deepening comprehension.* New York: Scholastic.

Writing

Britton, J. (1983). Writing and the story of the world. In B. Kroll & E. Wells (Eds.), *Explorations in the development of writing theory, research, and practice* (p. 3–30). New York: Wiley.

Calderón, M., Hertz-Lazarowitz, R., & Slavin, R. (1998). Effects of bilingual cooperative integrated reading and composition on students transitioning from Spanish to English reading. *Elementary School Journal,* 99, 153–165.

Celce-Murcia, M. (2002). On the use of selected grammatical features in academic writing. In M. C. Colombi & M. J. Schleppegrell (Eds.), *Developing advanced literacy in first and second languages* (pp. 143–158). Mahwah, NJ: Erlbaum.

Cunningham, P., & Allington, R. (2003). *Classrooms that work.* New York: Pearson Education, Inc.

Dyson, A. H. (1989). *Multiple worlds of child writers: Friends learning to write.* New York: Teachers College Press.

Elbow, P. (1998). *Writing with power.* Oxford: Oxford University Press.

Fisher, D., & Frey, N. (2008). Releasing responsibility. *Educational Leadership,* 66(3), 32–37.

Fisher, D., & Frey, N. (2007). *Scaffolded writing instruction: Teaching with a gradual-release framework.* New York: Scholastic.

Fisher, D., Frey, N., & Rothenberg, C., (2008). *Content area conversations: How to plan discussion-based lessons for diverse language learners.* Alexandria, VA: Association for Supervision and Curriculum Development.

Fearn, L., & Farnan, N. (2001). *Interactions: Teaching writing and the language arts.* Boston: Houghton Mifflin.

Kirby, D., Kirby, D. L., & Liner, T. (2004). *Inside out: Strategies for teaching writing.* Portsmouth, NH: Heinemann.

McCarrier, A., Pinnell, G. S., & Fountas, I. C. (2000). *Interactive writing: How language and literacy come together, K–2.* Portsmouth, NH: Heinemann.

Samway, K. (2006). *When English language learners write: connecting research to practice.* Portsmouth: Heineman.

Schleppegrell, M. J., & Go, A. L. (2007). Analyzing the writing of English learners: A functional approach. *Language Arts, 84*(6), 529–538.

Strong, W. (2001). Coaching writing: *The power of guided practice.* Portsmouth, NH: Heinemann-Boynton/Cook.

Fluency

Breznitz, Z. (2006). *Fluency in reading.* Mahwah, NJ: Lawrence Erlbaum Associates.

Crosson, A. C., & Lesaux, N. K. (in press). Revisiting assumptions about the relationship of fluent reading to comprehension: Spanish-speakers' text-reading fluency in English. *Reading and Writing: An Interdisciplinary Journal.*

Dowhower, S. L. (1987). Effects of repeated reading on second grade transitional readers' fluency and comprehension. *Reading Research Quarterly,* 22(4), 389–406.

Geva, E., & Yaghoub-Zadeh, Z. (2006). Reading efficiency in native English-speaking and English-as-a-second-language children: The role of oral proficiency and underlying cognitive-linguistic processes. *Scientific Studies of Reading,* 10, 31–57.

Kuhn, M. R. (2005). Helping students become accurate, expressive readers: Fluency instruction for small groups. *The Reading Teacher,* 58, 338–344.

Kung, S. H. (2009). *Predicting the success on a state standards test for culturally and linguistically diverse students using curriculum-based oral reading measures.* Unpublished doctoral dissertation, University of Minnesota.

LaBerge, D., & Samuels, S. J. (1974). Toward a theory of automatic information processing in reading. *Cognitive Psychology,* 6, 293–323.

Maurice, K. (1983). The fluency workshop. *TESOL Newsletter,* 17, 4.

Osborn, J., Lehr, F., & Hiebert, E. H. (2003). *A Focus on Fluency.* Honolulu, HI: Pacific Resources for Education and Learning. Available at www.prel.org/programs/rel/rel.asp.

Pikulski, J., & Chard, D. (2005). Fluency: the bridge between decoding and reading comprehension. *The Reading Teacher,* 58, 510–521.

Samuels, S. J., & Farstrup, A. E. (2006). *What research has to say about fluency instruction.* Newark, DE: International Reading Association.

Schilling, S. G., Carlisle, J. F., Scott, S. E., & Zeng, J. (2007). Are fluency measures accurate predictors of reading achievement? *The Elementary School Journal, 107,* 429–448.

Vaughn, S., Chard, D. J., Bryant, D. P., Coleman, M., Tyler, B. J., Linan-Thompson, S., & Kouzekanani, K. (2000). Fluency and comprehension interventions for third-grade students. *Remedial and Special Education, 21*(6), 325–335.

Technology

Fisher, D., & Frey, N. (in press). *Literacy 2.0: Language, literacy and learning in a new century* [working title]. Bloomington, IN: Solution Tree.

Gee, J. P. (2007). *What video games have to teach us about learning and literacy.* New York: Palgrave Macmillan.

International Reading Association. (May 2009). *New literacies and 21st century technologies: A position statement of the International Reading Association.* Newark, DE: Author. Used with permission.

Leu, D. J., O'Byrne, W. I., Zawilinski, L., McVerry, J. G., & Everett-Cacopardo, H. (2009). Expanding the new literacies conversation. *Educational Researcher, 38*(4), 264–269.

Mayer, R. E. (2001). Multimedia learning. New York: Cambridge University Press. Partnership for 21st Century Skills. (2009). Framework for 21st century learning. Retrieved from www.21stcenturyskills.org/index.php?option=com_content&task=view&id=254&Itemid=120.

Ybarra, R. & Green, T. (2003). Using technology to teach ESL/EFL students to develop language skills. *The Internet TESL Journal, 9,* n.p.

Assessment

Afflerbach, P. (2007). *Understanding and using reading assessment K–12.* Newark, DE: International Reading Association.

Carpenter, S. K., Pashler, H., Cepeda, N. J., and Alvarez, D. (2007). Applying the principles of testing and spacing to classroom learning. In D. S. McNamara and J. G. Trafton (Eds.), *Proceedings of the 29th Annual Cognitive Science Society* (p. 19). Nashville, TN: Cognitive Science Society.

Carpenter, S. K., Pashler, H., Wixted, J. T., and Vul, E. (in press). The effects of tests on learning and forgetting. *Memory & Cognition.*

Dempster, F. N., & Perkins, P. G. (1993). Revitalizing classroom assessment: Using tests to promote learning. *Journal of Instructional Psychology, 20,* 197–203.

Dominguez de Ramirez, R., & Shapiro, E. S. (2006). Curriculum-based measurement and the evaluation of reading skills of Spanish-speaking English language learners in bilingual education classrooms. *School Psychology Review, 35,* 356–369.

Edwards, P., Turner, J. D., & Mokhtari, K. (2008). Balancing the assessment of and the assessment for learning in support of student literacy achievement. *Reading Teacher, 61,* 682–684.

Fisher, D., & Frey, N. (2007). *Checking for understanding: Formative assessment techniques for your classroom.* Alexandria, VA: Association for Supervision and Curriculum Development.

Frey, N., & Heibert, E. (2002). Teacher-based assessment of literacy learning. In J. Flood, D. Lapp, J. R. Squire, & J. M. Jensen (Eds.). *Handbook of Research on the Teaching of English Language Arts* (2nd ed.), pp.608–618. Mahwah, NJ: Lawrence Erlbaum.

Gersten, R., Dimino, J., & Jayanthi, M. (in press). Development of a classroom observational system. In B. Taylor & J. Ysseldyke (Eds.), *Reading instruction for English language learners: The Bond symposium.* New York: Teachers College.

Goodman, Y. (2002). Informal methods of evaluation. In J. Flood, D. Lapp, J. R. Squire, & J. M. Jensen (Eds.). *Handbook of Research on the Teaching of English Language Arts* (2nd ed.), pp. 600–607. Mahwah, NJ: Lawrence Erlbaum.

Johnston, P. (2005). Literacy assessment and the future. *The Reading Teacher, 58*(7), 684–686.

Limbos, M. (2006). Early identification of second language students at risk for reading disability. *Dissertation Abstracts International, 66* (10-A), 3566A.

Schumm, J. S. & Arguelles, M. E. (2006). No two learners are alike: The importance of assessment and differentiated instruction. In J. S. Schumm (Ed.), *Reading assessment and instruction for all learners.* New York: Guilford Press.

Torgesen, J. K. (2006). *A comprehensive K–3 reading assessment plan: Guidance for school leaders.* Portsmouth, NH: RMC Research Corporation, Center on Instruction. Available at: www.centeroninstruction.org.

Townsend, D., Lee, E., & Chiappe, P. (2006). *English or Spanish? The efficacy of assessing Latino/a children in Spanish for risk of reading disabilities.* Paper presented at the meeting of the Society for the Scientific Study of Reading, Vancouver, BC, Canada.

Wiley, H. I., & Deno, S. L. (2005). Oral reading and maze measures as predictors of success for English learners on a state standards assessment. *Remedial and Special Education, 26,* 207–214.

Scope and Sequence

Reading

	K	1	2	3	4	5
LITERATURE						
Key Ideas and Details						
Retell or Explain a Story	•	•	•	•	•	•
Analyze Story Elements	•	•	•	•	•	•
Plot	•	•	•	•	•	•
Characters	•	•	•	•	•	•
Setting	•	•	•	•	•	•
Theme, Lesson, or Moral		•	•	•	•	•
Use Reading Strategies	•	•	•	•	•	•
Preview and Make Predictions	•	•	•	•	•	•
Monitor Understanding	•	•	•	•	•	•
Ask and Answer Questions	•	•	•	•	•	•
Summarize Texts	•	•	•	•	•	•
Make Inferences	•	•	•	•	•	•
Visualize	•	•	•	•	•	•
Make Connections	•	•	•	•	•	•
Synthesize: Draw Conclusions			•	•	•	•
Synthesize: Draw Generalizations			•	•	•	•
Relate Ideas	•	•	•	•	•	•
Chronology	•	•	•	•	•	•
Comparison	•	•	•	•	•	•
Cause/Effect		•	•	•	•	•
Goal/Outcome				•	•	•
Problem/Solution					•	•
Craft and Structure						
Determine the Meaning of Words and Phrases in a Text	•	•	•	•	•	•
Identify Elements of Genre	•	•	•	•	•	•
Describe Structure of Stories, Dramas, and Poems			•	•	•	•
Identify Introduction and Conclusion			•	•	•	•
Identify Text Segments: Chapter, Scene, Stanza				•	•	•
Identify Elements of Poetry: Rhyme, Rhythm	•	•	•	•	•	•
Identify Elements of Poetry: Verse, Meter, Line Breaks					•	•
Identify Elements of Drama: List of Characters, Dialogue, Stage Directions					•	•
Compare Drama and Prose			•	•	•	•
Compare Poetry and Prose			•	•	•	•
Identify Author and Illustrator	•	•	•	•	•	•
Identify Narrator		•	•	•	•	•
Identify and Distinguish Points of View			•	•	•	•

Reading, continued

	K	1	2	3	4	5
Grade						

Integration of Knowledge and Ideas

	K	1	2	3	4	5
Analyze Text Elements	●	●	●	●	●	●
Use Information in Illustrations	●	●	●	●	●	●
Connect Text and Oral or Visual Presentation of Story or Versions of a Story	●	●	●	●	●	●
Analyze Visual or Multimedia Elements in a Text		●	●	●	●	●
Compare Ideas or Texts	●	●	●	●	●	●
Compare Fiction and Nonfiction	●	●	●	●	●	●
Compare Characters	●	●	●	●	●	●
Compare Settings	●	●	●	●	●	●
Compare Events	●	●	●	●	●	●
Compare Topics	●	●	●	●	●	●
Compare Themes				●	●	●

Range of Reading and Level of Text Complexity

	K	1	2	3	4	5
Read and Comprehend Literature at and Above Grade Level Complexity	●	●	●	●	●	●
Participate in Shared Reading	●	●	●	●	●	●
Read Independently	●	●	●	●	●	●

INFORMATIONAL TEXT

Key Ideas and Details

	K	1	2	3	4	5
Retell or Explain a Text	●	●	●	●	●	●
Use Reading Strategies	●	●	●	●	●	●
Preview and Make Predictions	●	●	●	●	●	●
Monitor Understanding	●	●	●	●	●	●
Ask and Answer Questions	●	●	●	●	●	●
Determine Importance: Identify the Topic, Main Idea, and Key Details	●	●	●	●	●	●
Determine Importance: Summarize		●	●	●	●	●
Make Inferences	●	●	●	●	●	●
Visualize	●	●	●	●	●	●
Make Connections	●	●	●	●	●	●
Synthesize: Draw Conclusions			●	●	●	●
Synthesize: Make Generalizations			●	●	●	●
Relate Ideas and Describe Text Structure	●	●	●	●	●	●
Logical Order	●	●	●	●	●	●
Chronology	●	●	●	●	●	●
Comparison		●	●	●	●	●
Cause/Effect		●	●	●	●	●
Problem/Solution, Goal/Outcome		●	●	●	●	●
Compare Text Structure					●	●

Reading, continued	Grade					
	K	1	2	3	4	5
Craft and Structure						
Determine the Meaning of Words and Phrases in a Text	●	●	●	●	●	●
Identify and Use Text Features	●	●	●	●	●	●
Covers and Title Page	●	●	●	●	●	●
Table of Contents or Electronic Menus	●	●	●		●	
Headings and Subheadings		●	●	●	●	●
Topic Sentence			●	●	●	●
Glossaries and Indexes		●	●	●	●	●
Captions, Labels, Icons, Hyperlinks and Callouts		●	●		●	●
Graphs, Diagrams, Tables, and Maps		●	●		●	●
Sidebars				●	●	●
Distinguish Between Information in Illustrations and Information in Text	●	●	●	●	●	●
Identify Author and Illustrator	●	●	●		●	●
Identify Author's Purpose		●	●		●	●
Distinguish Points of View or Accounts				●	●	●
Integration of Knowledge and Ideas						
Use Information in Illustrations and Media	●	●	●	●	●	●
Interpret Information Presented in Multiple Formats					●	●
Identify and Distinguish Facts and Opinions		●	●	●	●	●
Identify Author's Reasons and Evidence	●	●	●	●	●	●
Explain Connections Within a Text		●	●	●	●	●
Compare Texts	●	●	●	●	●	●
Range of Reading and Level of Text Complexity						
Read and Comprehend Text at and above Grade Level Complexity		●	●	●	●	●
Participate in Shared Reading	●	●	●	●	●	●
Read Independently	●	●	●	●	●	●

Reading, continued

	K	1	2	3	4	5

FOUNDATIONAL SKILLS

Print Concepts

	K	1	2	3	4	5
Understand Directionality of Text	●	●	●			
Recognize the Relationship of Letters and Words to Speech	●	●				
Recognize and Name Alphabet Letters	●	●				
Know the Order of the Alphabet	●	●				
Identify Letters	●	●	●			
Match Uppercase and Lowercase Letters	●	●	●			
Identify a Word	●	●	●			
Identify End Punctuation	●	●	●			
Identify Title	●	●	●			
Hold a Book and Turn the Pages	●	●	●			
Identify Sentence Capitalization	●	●	●			
Use Page Numbers	●	●	●			
Identify Dialogue			●			
Identify Indentions of Paragraphs			●			

Phonological Awareness

	K	1	2	3	4	5
Distinguish Long and Short Vowel Sounds	●	●	●			
Isolate Words in a Sentence	●	●	●			
Identify Syllables	●	●	●			
Blend Syllables to Form a Word	●	●	●			
Segment a Word into Syllables	●	●	●			
Identify Rhyming Words	●	●	●			
Generate Rhyming Words	●	●	●			
Match Initial, Medial, and Final Sounds	●	●	●			
Identify and Isolate Initial, Medial, and Final Sounds	●	●	●			
Blend Onset and Rime	●	●	●			
Blend Sounds to Form a Word	●	●	●			
Segment a Word into Sounds	●	●	●			
Manipulate Sounds in Words (Add, Delete, Substitute)	●	●	●			

Use **Reach into Phonics** to provide intervention for foundational reading skills in grades 3–5.

Reading, continued

Phonics and Word Recognition	K	1	2	3	4	5
Identify Letter/Sounds and Read Words	●	●	●			
Consonants	●	●	●			
Short Vowels	●	●	●			
Long Vowels	●	●	●			
Consonant Blends and Digraphs	●	●	●			
Vowel Digraphs: *ai, ay, ee, ea, ie, igh, oa, ow, oo, ou, ui*	●	●	●			
r-Controlled Vowels: *ar, or, -ore, er, ir, ur, air, -are, eer, ear*		●	●			
Sounds for -*y*: /ē/, /ī/	●	●	●			
Diphthongs: *oi, oy, ou, ow*	●	●	●			
Variant Vowels: *aw, au, al, all, oo, ew, ea*	●	●				
Vowel Patterns: *-igh, -old, -alk*	●	●	●			
Vowel Patterns: *o, i, -ight*			●			
Schwa			●			
Soft *c*	●	●	●			
Soft *g*	●	●	●			
Silent Consonants *kn, wr, gn, mb*	●	●	●			
Plurals -*s, -es, -ies*		●	●			
Read Words with Spelling Patterns		●	●			
CVC*e* Word Patterns with *a, i, o, u, e*	●	●	●			
CV Word Patterns with *o, e*	●	●	●			
Short and Long Vowels in CVC and CVC*e* Word Patterns	●	●	●			
CVVC Word Patterns		●	●			
Read Multisyllabic Words		●	●			
Compound Words		●	●			
VCCV Syllable Division (bas/ket, kit/ten)		●	●			
VCCCV Syllable Division (hun/dred)		●	●			
VCV Syllable Division (mu/sic, cab/in)		●	●			
Words with Consonant + *le*		●	●			
Suffixes		●	●			
Prefixes		●	●			
Inflected Forms		●	●			
Syllable Types: *r*-Controlled, Consonant + *le*, Vowel Team, Vowel + Silent *e*		●	●			
Final Syllables with -*tion, -ture, -ent, -ant*			●			

Use **Reach into Phonics** to provide intervention for foundational reading skills in grades 3–5.

Reading, continued

	K	1	2	3	4	5
Phonics and Word Recognition, continued						
Use Decoding Strategies	●	●	●			
Blend Sounds to Decode Words						
Recognize Word Families and Similarly-Spelled Words	●	●	●			
Use Structural Clues		●	●			
Identify Syllable Types		●	●			
Recognize High Frequency Words	●	●	●			
Distinguish Between Similarly-Spelled Words	●	●	●			
Read Irregularly-Spelled Words	●	●	●			
Fluency						
Read with Purpose and Understanding	●	●	●	●	●	●
Read with Accuracy and Appropriate Rate	●	●	●	●	●	●
Use Phrasing		●	●	●	●	●
Read with Expression		●	●	●	●	●
Read with Correct Intonation		●	●	●	●	●
Read Instructional Level Materials Fluently	●	●	●	●	●	●
Use Context to Support Decoding	●	●	●	●	●	●

Writing

	K	1	2	3	4	5
Text Types and Purposes						
Opinion Pieces	●	●	●	●	●	●
Informative/Explanatory Text	●	●	●	●	●	●
Interview			●	●	●	●
Letter or Email		●	●	●	●	●
Report			●	●	●	●
Persuasive Essay				●	●	●
Procedural Text		●	●	●	●	●
Explanatory Text		●	●	●	●	●
Narratives	●	●	●	●	●	●
Story or Account	●	●	●	●	●	●
Character Sketch				●	●	●
Poem		●	●	●	●	●
Tall Tale/Myth/Trickster Tale/Folk Tale			●	●	●	●
Science Fiction Story					●	●
Response Text	●	●	●	●	●	●
Write to Demonstrate Comprehension	●	●	●	●	●	●

Writing, continued

Writing Skills	Grade K	1	2	3	4	5
Organization and Purpose	•	•	•	•	•	•
Introduce a Topic	•	•	•	•	•	•
Write a Conclusion	•	•	•	•	•	•
Establish and Follow a Purpose	•	•	•	•		•
Identify Context for Formal and Informal English	•	•	•	•	•	•
State Main Ideas and Support with Details		•	•	•	•	•
Introduce and State an Opinion	•	•	•	•	•	•
Supply Reasons and Evidence		•	•	•	•	•
Write Facts, Definitions, and Details	•	•	•	•	•	•
Maintain Point of View					•	•
Use Persuasive Techniques or Language		•	•	•	•	•
Organize Writing	•	•	•	•	•	•
Sequence Events	•	•	•	•	•	•
Fiction			•	•	•	•
Include Dialogue					•	•
Tell About Events and Details	•	•	•	•	•	•
Introduce Characters or a Narrator				•	•	•
Word Choice	•	•	•	•	•	•
Use Signal Words		•	•	•	•	•
Use Concrete Words and Phrases		•	•	•	•	•
Use Sensory Words and Phrases		•	•	•	•	•
Use Figurative Language					•	•
Use Colorful Details to Elaborate				•	•	•
Use Linking Words		•	•	•	•	•
Use Quotations		•	•	•	•	•
Use Precise Language and Vocabulary				•	•	•
Use Your Own Words	•	•	•	•	•	•
Sentence Fluency	•	•	•	•	•	
Connect Ideas				•	•	•
Break Up Long Sentences				•	•	•
Combine Sentences				•	•	•
Vary Sentences		•	•	•	•	•
Production and Distribution of Writing						
Produce Writing for Specific Tasks, Purposes, and Audiences	•	•	•	•	•	•
Prewrite		•	•	•	•	•
Analyze a Model		•	•	•	•	•
Determine the Role, Audience, Form, and Topic		•	•	•	•	•
Organize Ideas		•	•	•	•	•

Writing, continued

	Grade					
	K	1	2	3	4	5
Production and Distribution of Writing, continued						
Draft	•	•	•	•	•	•
Use Appropriate Development and Organization		•	•	•	•	•
Use Technology to Produce Writing	•	•	•	•	•	•
Demonstrate Keyboarding Skills					•	•
Revise	•	•	•	•	•	•
Respond to Peer Suggestions	•	•	•	•	•	•
Add, Combine, or Delete Details	•	•	•	•	•	•
Edit and Proofread		•	•	•	•	•
Publish and Present	•	•	•	•	•	•
Use Visuals or Multimedia to Enhance Meaning		•	•	•	•	•
Keep a Portfolio	•	•	•	•	•	•
Writing Traits						
Ideas		•	•	•	•	•
Organization		•	•	•	•	•
Voice		•	•	•	•	•
Word Choice		•	•	•	•	•
Sentence Fluency		•	•	•	•	•
Conventions		•	•	•	•	•
Presentation		•	•	•	•	•
Research to Build and Present Knowledge						
Create Research and Writing Projects	•	•	•	•	•	•
Recall or Gather Information	•	•	•	•	•	•
Choose and Focus a Topic	•	•	•	•	•	•
Develop Research Questions					•	•
Locate Sources of Information		•	•	•	•	•
Evaluate Information					•	•
Find Information in Sources			•	•	•	•
Take and Sort Notes			•	•	•	•
Distinguish Plagiarism from Quoting or Paraphrasing					•	•
Distinguish Relevant from Irrelevant Information		•	•	•	•	•
Integrate Information from Multiple Sources				•	•	•
Provide a List of Sources				•	•	•
Draw Evidence from Text to Support Analysis, Reflection, and Research				•	•	•
Range of Writing						
Write Routinely for a Variety of Tasks, Purposes, and Audiences	•	•	•	•	•	•

Scope and Sequence, continued

Speaking and Listening

	Grade K	1	2	3	4	5
Comprehension and Collaboration						
Engage in Collaborative Discussions	●	●	●	●	●	●
Follow Agreed-Upon Rules	●	●	●	●	●	●
Build on and Connect Others' Ideas	●	●	●	●	●	●
Ask for Clarification	●	●	●	●	●	●
Come to Discussions Prepared	●	●	●	●	●	●
Explain and Review Ideas and Understanding	●	●	●	●	●	●
Restate Ideas	●	●	●	●	●	●
Elaborate	●	●	●	●	●	●
Evaluate Information Presented in Diverse Media and Formats	●	●	●	●	●	●
Analyze the Message			●	●	●	●
Identify or Describe Media Elements including Visual, Functional and Auditory Details		●	●	●	●	●
Ask and Answer Questions for Information, Clarification, or Understanding	●	●	●	●	●	●
Identify a Speaker's Reasons and Evidence					●	●
Presentation of Knowledge and Ideas						
Describe with Facts and Details	●	●	●	●	●	●
Tell a Story	●	●	●	●	●	●
Recount an Experience	●	●	●	●	●	●
Report on a Text or Topic	●	●	●	●	●	●
Present an Opinion					●	●
Speak Clearly, at an Appropriate Pace	●	●	●	●	●	●
Organize Ideas					●	●
Add Visual, Audio, or Multimedia Support	●	●	●	●	●	●
Produce Complete Sentences	●	●	●	●	●	●
Adapt Speech to the Context and Task	●	●	●	●	●	●

Language

	Grade K	1	2	3	4	5
Conventions of Standard English						
Print Upper and Lower Case Letters	●	●				
Sentences	●	●	●	●	●	●
Statements, Questions, Exclamations, and Commands	●	●	●	●	●	●
Negative Sentences	●	●	●	●	●	●
Compound Sentences		●	●	●	●	●
Complex Sentences				●	●	●
Complete Subject	●	●	●	●	●	●
Simple Subject	●	●	●	●	●	●
Compound Subject		●	●	●	●	●

	Grade					
	K	**1**	**2**	**3**	**4**	**5**
Conventions of Standard English, continued						
Complete Predicate	●	●	●	●	●	●
Simple Predicate	●	●	●	●	●	●
Compound Predicate		●	●	●	●	●
Complete Sentences	●	●	●	●	●	●
Fragment/Dependent Clause					●	●
Independent Clause			●	●	●	●
Participial Phrases						●
Run-On Sentences			●	●	●	●
Subject-Verb Agreement	●	●	●		●	●
Parts of Speech	●	●	●	●	●	●
Nouns	●	●	●	●	●	●
Common and Proper		●	●	●	●	●
Count and Noncount		●	●	●	●	●
Plurals	●	●	●	●		●
Possessive		●	●	●	●	●
Abstract				●		
Articles/Determiners		●	●	●	●	●
Pronouns		●	●	●	●	●
Subject	●	●	●	●	●	●
Object	●	●	●	●	●	●
Demonstrative			●	●	●	●
Indefinite		●	●	●	●	●
Reflexive			●	●	●	●
Relative					●	
Possessive		●	●	●	●	●
Pronoun Agreement	●	●	●	●	●	●
Adjectives	●	●	●	●	●	●
Comparative and Superlative			●	●	●	●
Relative					●	
Demonstrative	●	●	●	●	●	●
Predicate					●	●
Possessive		●	●	●	●	●
Indefinite		●	●	●	●	
Proper						●
Order within Sentences					●	●

Language, continued

	Grade K	1	2	3	4	5
Conventions of Standard English, continued						
Verbs	●	●	●	●	●	●
Action	●	●	●	●	●	●
Transitive/Intransitive	●	●	●	●	●	●
Linking			●	●	●	●
Modals			●	●	●	●
Helping			●	●	●	●
Present Tense	●	●	●	●	●	●
Past Tense (Regular and Irregular)		●	●	●	●	●
Future Tense		●	●	●	●	●
Present-Perfect Tense						●
Past-Perfect Tense						●
Future-Perfect Tense						●
Progressive Forms		●	●	●	●	●
Contractions		●	●	●	●	●
Adverbs		●	●	●	●	●
Comparative and Superlative			●	●	●	●
Relative					●	●
Adverbial Clauses					●	●
Prepositions	●	●	●	●	●	●
Prepositional Phrases			●	●	●	●
Conjunctions	●	●	●	●	●	●
Coordinating		●	●	●	●	●
Subordinating		●	●	●	●	●
Correlative						●
Interjections						●
Mechanics	●	●	●	●	●	●
Capitalization	●	●	●	●	●	●
End Punctuation	●	●	●	●	●	●
Abbreviations			●	●	●	●
Comma		●	●	●	●	●
Apostrophe			●	●	●	●
Quotation Marks				●	●	●
Underlining or Italics						●
Spelling	●	●	●	●	●	●
High Frequency Words	●	●	●	Use **Reach into Phonics** for		
Use Phonetic Knowledge to Spell	●	●	●	foundational spelling skills in G3–5		
Consult Reference Materials to Check Spelling		●	●	●	●	●
Use Spelling Patterns	●	●	●	●	●	●

Language, continued

Grade

	K	1	2	3	4	5
Knowledge of Language						
Compare Formal and Informal Uses of English	●	●	●		●	●
Recognize the Difference Between Spoken and Written English	●	●	●	●	●	
Choose Words and Phrases or Punctuation for Effect				●	●	●
Vary Sentences for Meaning, Interest, and Style		●	●	●	●	●
Vocabulary Acquisition and Use						
Determine Meanings of Unfamiliar and Multiple-Meaning Words	●	●	●	●	●	●
Acquire and Use Academic Vocabulary	●	●	●	●	●	●
Acquire and Use Domain-Specific Vocabulary	●	●	●	●	●	●
Use Inflections and Affixes	●	●	●	●	●	●
Use Context	●	●	●	●	●	●
Use Root Words		●	●	●	●	●
Use Prefixes and Suffixes		●	●	●	●	●
Use Individual Words Within Compound Words		●	●	●	●	●
Use a Glossary, Dictionary, and Thesaurus		●	●	●	●	●
Explore Word Relationships	●	●	●	●	●	●
Categorize Words	●	●	●	●	●	●
Identify Antonyms	●	●	●	●	●	●
Identify Synonyms	●	●	●	●	●	●
Identify Homographs					●	●
Identify Homophones					●	●
Connect Between Words and Their Uses	●	●	●	●	●	●
Distinguish Shades of Meaning	●	●	●	●	●	●
Identify Feeling Words and Sensory Words	●	●	●		●	●
Distinguish Literal from Nonliteral Meanings				●	●	●
Use Analogies					●	●
Figurative and Literary Language					●	●
Explain Similes and Metaphors					●	●
Identify Personification					●	●
Interpret Idioms, Expressions, Dialect, Adages, Proverbs, and Sayings					●	●

Grade 3 Common Core Standards

Reading

Strand	Code	Standards Text	Grade 3 Units 1–8 Standards Correlations
Literature			
Key Ideas and Details	CC.3.Rlit.1	(1) Ask and answer questions to demonstrate understanding of a text, referring explicitly to the text as the basis for the answers.	**Unit 2:** T76, T80–81, T82–83, T84–85, T89, T90–91, T94, T98, T100, SG8, SG9; **Unit 4:** T237a; **Unit 7:** T452–453, T457, T459, T460–461, T464
	CC.3.Rlit.2	(2) Recount stories, including fables, folktales, and myths from diverse cultures; determine the central message, lesson, or moral and explain how it is conveyed through key details in the text.	**Unit 1:** T12–13, T20, T22, SG8, SG9, SG15; **Unit 2:** SG8, SG9; **Unit 3:** T152–153, T154–155, T158, T162, T164a, SG9, SG15; **Unit 4:** T211a, T222, T227, T230, T232a, T236, T261, T262–263, T264–265, T267d, SG8; **Unit 6:** T396a, T396b, T402, T403a, T404, T405f, T405g, SG26, SG27; **Unit 7:** T430, T456, T462; **Unit 8:** T498, T506a, T508a, T517a, SG15
	CC.3.Rlit.3	(3) Describe characters in a story (e.g., their traits, motivations, or feelings) and explain how their actions contribute to the sequence of events.	**Unit 1:** T12–13, T14–15, T16–17, T18–19, T20, T23, T24, T25, T30, T33f, T33g, T33r; **Unit 2:** T94a; **Unit 3:** T141i, T154–155, T156, T162, SG10, SG11; Unit 4: T222, T223, T225, T227, T232a, T234a, T234b, T236, T237, T237a, T239a, T239b, T239d, T262–263, SG14, SG15; **Unit 5:** T277a, T286–287, T288–289, T293, T294–295, T296, T298, T298a; **Unit 8:** T496, T497, T502–503, T504, T506, T506a, T508a, T508a, T510–511, T512–513, T514–515, T519a, T519b, SG14
Craft and Structure	CC.3.Rlit.4	(4) Determine the meaning of words and phrases as they are used in a text, distinguishing literal from non-literal language.	**Unit 2:** T96a, T96b, T97, T98, T100, T101a, T103a, T103b, T103d; **Unit 3:** T160–161, T166a; **Unit 4:** T210, T211, T240, T241; **Unit 5:** T296; **Unit 6:** T359; **Unit 7:** T415a, T426–427, T432, T440; **Unit 8:** T494–495, T520, T521
	CC.3.Rlit.5	(5) Refer to parts of stories, dramas, and poems when writing or speaking about a text, using terms such as chapter, scene, and stanza; describe how each successive part builds on earlier sections.	**Unit 1:** T4, T5a, T20, T22, T24, T26, T26a, T28a, T28b, T29, T30, T31a, T32, T33a, T33b, SG8, SG9; **Unit 2:** T103f, T103g; **Unit 3:** T154–155, T156, T158, T159, T162, T164a, T166a, T166b, T167, T171a; **Unit 4:** T232a, T234a, T234b, T239a, T239b, SG14; **Unit 5:** T282, T284–285, T286–287, T292, T293, T298, T298a; **Unit 6:** T364, T364a, T400–401; **Unit 7:** T424–425, T426–427, T431, T432, T434a, T443o, T445a, T446, T464a; **Unit 8:** T506a, T517a, T519f, T519g
	CC.3.Rlit.6	(6) Distinguish their own point of view from that of the narrator or those of the characters.	**Unit 3:** T162; **Unit 4:** T217, T226, T228–229, T235, T267a, T267b, T267f, T267g; **Unit 7:** T464; **Unit 8:** T519a, T519b, T519d
Integration of Knowledge and Ideas	CC.3.Rlit.7	(7) Explain how specific aspects of a text's illustrations contribute to what is conveyed by the words in a story (e.g., create mood, emphasize aspects of a character or setting).	**Unit 2:** T97, T99; **Unit 6:** T354–355, T359, T392, T396c, T405a, T405b, T405d; **Unit 7:** T426–427, T450, T458, T463a; **Unit 8:** T500
	CC.3.Rlit.9	(9) Compare and contrast the themes, settings, and plots of stories written by the same author about the same or similar characters (e.g., in books from a series).	**Unit 2:** T69j; **Unit 4:** T233j, T239a, T239b, T239f, T239g, T267g; **Unit 5:** T273j; **Unit 7:** T411j; **Unit 8:** T507i
Range and Level of Complexity	CC.3.Rlit.10	(10) By the end of the year, read and comprehend literature, including stories, dramas, and poetry, at the high end of the grades 2–3 text complexity band independently and proficiently.	**Unit 1:** T1i, T8, T11, T12–13, T14–15, T16–17, T18–19, T20, T23, T24, T26a, T27j, T29, T31a, T32, T33a, T33f, T33r, SG8, SG9, SG14, SG15; **Unit 2:** T69j, T73a, T76, T79, T80–81, T82–83, T84–85, T89, T90–91, T94a, T95j, T96a, T96b, T97c, T98, T99, T100, T101, T101a, T103a, T103b, T103f, T103g, SG8, SG9; **Unit 3:** T141j, T145a, T146, T148, T149, T151, T152–153, T154–155, T156, T157, T158, T159, T160–161, T162, T163, T164, T164a, T166a, T166b, T167, T168–169, T170–171, T171a, T173r, SG8, SG9, SG14, SG15; **Unit 4:** T207j, T217, T218–219, T220–221, T222, T225, T226, T227, T228–229, T230, T231, T232a, T233j, T235, T236, T237a, T239a, T239b, T239f, T239r, T260a, T260b, T261, T262–263, T265a, T267a, T267b, T267f, T267g, SG8, SG9, SG14, SG15; **Unit 5:** T273j, T280, T281, SG8, SG9; **Unit 6:** T341j, T373r, T400–401, T402, SG8, SG9, SG20, SG26, SG27; **Unit 7:** T411j, T415a, T421, T422–423, T424–425, T426–427, T431, T432, T434a, T443p, T445a, T452–453, T454–455, T457, T458, T459, T460–461, T462, T463, T464a, T465, SG20, SG21; **Unit 8:** T481j, T485a, T491, T492–493, T494–495, T496, T499, T500, T501, T502–503, T504, T505, T507j, T509, T510–511, T512–513, T514–515, SG8, SG9, SG14, SG15

Search for activities that meet each
Common Core Standard. ◆NGReach.com

Strand	Code	Standards Text	Grade 3 Units 1–8 Standards Correlations
Informational Text			
Key Ideas and Details	CC.3.Rinf.1	(1) Ask and answer questions to demonstrate understanding of a text, referring explicitly to the text as the basis for the answers.	**Unit 2:** T108, T109, T112–113, T116–117, T122–123, T130–131, SG14, SG15, SG20, SG21, SG26, SG27; **Unit 6:** SG16, SG17; **Unit 7:** T437, T438, T439, T440, T467, T469, T470; **Unit 8:** SG10, SG11, SG16, SG17
	CC.3.Rinf.2	(2) Determine the main idea of a text; recount the key details and explain how they support the main idea.	**Unit 1:** T27j, T58–59, SG4, SG5, SG10, SG11; **Unit 2:** T128a, T128b, T129, T130–131, T135a, T135b, SG4, SG5, SG10, SG11, SG14, SG26; **Unit 3:** T175a, T176, T182–183, T184–185, T186, T188, T189, T191, T192, T193, T194a, T201f, T201g, SG4, SG5, SG20; **Unit 4:** T244, T248–249, T252, T255, T256, SG10, SG11; **Unit 5:** T307d, T324, SG14, SG16, SG17; **Unit 6:** T368, T390, SG10, SG11; **Unit 7:** T465j, T466a, T466b, T469, T470, SG26; **Unit 8:** T521a, T522, T530, T533, T534–535, T538a, T541, SG20
	CC.3.Rinf.3	(3) Describe the relationship between a series of historical events, scientific ideas or concepts, or steps in technical procedures in a text, using language that pertains to time, sequence, and cause/effect.	**Unit 2:** T105a, T112–113, T114–115, T116–117, T118–119, T121, T122–123, T126a, T133a, SG20, SG21, SG22, SG23; **Unit 3:** T173a, T173b, T173d, T173f, T173g, T173h, T190, T194, T194a, T198, SG10, SG11; **Unit 4:** SG22, SG23; **Unit 5:** T309a, T316–317, T321, T323, T324, T326a, T335a, T335b, SG4, SG5, SG20; **Unit 6:** T375a, T384–385, T386–387, T392, T394a, SG22, SG23; **Unit 7:** T435j, T436a, T436b, T438, T440, T443a, T443b, T443f; **Unit 8:** T521a, T532, T538a, T540a, T540b, T545a, T547a, T547b, SG4, SG5, SG20, SG26
Craft and Structure	CC.3.Rinf.4	(4) Determine the meaning of general academic and domain-specific words and phrases in a text relevant to a grade 3 topic or subject area.	**Unit 5:** SG22, SG23; **Unit 7:** T473c, T473e
	CC.3.Rinf.5	(5) Use text features and search tools (e.g., key words, sidebars, hyperlinks) to locate information relevant to a given topic efficiently.	**Unit 1:** T55h, T57; **Unit 2:** T103y, T103z, T114–115, T116–117, T121, T122–123, T127a, T129; **Unit 3:** T165i, T181, T182–183, T184–185, T189, T191, T196a, T196b, T197, T198, T199a, T201a, T201b, T201d, SG22, SG23, SG26; **Unit 4:** T246, T247, T250–251, T252; **Unit 5:** T303, T307a, T307b, T314, T315, T322, T328a, T328b, T330, T331, T332, T333a, T335f, T335g, SG10, SG11, SG26; **Unit 6:** T380, T381, T382–383, T384–385, T386–387, T388–389; **Unit 7:** T443p, T467, T468; **Unit 8:** T526, T527, T528, T531
	CC.3.Rinf.6	(6) Distinguish their own point of view from that of the author of a text.	**Unit 1:** T41, T48, T53a, T56a, T56b, T57, T58–59; **Unit 2:** T135f, T135g; **Unit 4:** T250–251, T257, SG16, SG17; **Unit 5:** T330, T331; **Unit 8:** T547f, T547g
Integration of Knowledge and Ideas	CC.3.Rinf.7	(7) Use information gained from illustrations (e.g., maps, photographs) and the words in a text to demonstrate understanding of the text (e.g., where, when, why, and how key events occur).	**Unit 3:** T196a, T196b, T198, SG26; **Unit 4:** SG4, SG5; **Unit 5:** T314, T315, T321, T322, T323; **Unit 6:** T366a, T366b, T366c, T369, T370, T371a, T373a, T373b, T373g, T394, SG14; **Unit 7:** T466c, T468, SG4, SG5, SG10, SG11; **Unit 8:** T540c, SG22, SG23
	CC.3.Rinf.8	(8) Describe the logical connection between particular sentences and paragraphs in a text (e.g., comparison, cause/effect, first/second/third in a sequence).	**Unit 1:** T42–43, T52, T54a, T55, SG20, SG21, SG22, SG23, SG26; **Unit 2:** T126a; **Unit 3:** T173a, T173b, T190, T198, SG16, SG17; **Unit 4:** SG22, SG23; **Unit 5:** SG20; **Unit 6:** SG4, SG5, SG20; **Unit 7:** T416a, T418, T443f, T443g, SG14, SG22, SG23; **Unit 8:** T521a
	CC.3.Rinf.9	(9) Compare and contrast the most important points and key details presented in two texts on the same topic.	**Unit 1:** T61a, T63f, T63g, SG16, SG17; **Unit 2:** T133a, SG16, SG17; **Unit 3:** T173g, T173h, T201g; **Unit 5:** T300a, T300b, T303, T304, T305a, T307f, T307g, SG14; **Unit 7:** T435q, T435r, T441a, T442, T443g, T443h, T443p, T471a, T472, T473g, T473h, SG16, SG17; **Unit 8:** T545a
Range and Level of Text Complexity	CC.3.Rinf.10	(10) By the end of the year, read and comprehend informational texts, including history/social studies, science, and technical texts, at the high end of the grades 2–3 text complexity band independently and proficiently.	**Unit 1:** T1i, T27j, T33r, T38, T41, T42–43, T47, T48, T49, T50–51, T52, T53, T53a, T54a, T55h, T56a, T56b, T57, T61a, T63a, T63f, SG5, SG11, SG17, SG20, SG21, SG23, SG26, SG27; **Unit 2:** T95j, T103r, T108, T111, T112–113, T114–115, T116–117, T121, T122–123, T126a, T127h, T128a, T128b, T129, T130–131, T133a, T135a, T135b, T135f, T135g, SG5, SG11, SG14, SG15, SG17, SG20, SG21, SG23, SG26, SG27; **Unit 3:** T141j, T165j, T173a, T173b, T173f, T173r, T178, T181, T182–183, T184–185, T186, T189, T190, T191, T192, T194a, T195h, T196a, T196b, T197, T198, T199a, SG5, SG11, SG17, SG20, SG21, SG23, SG26, SG27; **Unit 4:** T207j, T233j, T239r, T241a, T259h, T260a, T260b, SG5, SG11, SG17, SG20, SG21, SG23, SG26, SG27; **Unit 5:** T273j, T299j, T307r, T312, T315, T316–317, T326a, T327, T327h, SG5, SG11, SG14, SG15, SG17, SG20, SG21, SG23, SG26, SG27; **Unit 6:** T341j, T348, T365j, T373g, T373r, T378, T395h, T397, T398–399, SG5, SG11, SG14, SG15, SG17, SG20, SG23; **Unit 7:** T418, T436a, T437, T438, T439, T440, T441a, T443a, T443b, T443f, T443g, T448, T465j, T466a, T466b, T467, T468, T469, T470, T471a, T473a, T473b, T473f, T473g, SG5, SG11, SG14, SG15, SG17, SG23, SG26, SG27; **Unit 8:** T481j, T488, T507j, T519r, T524, T527, T528, T529, T530, T531, T533, T534–535, T539h, T541, T542–543, T547a, T547b, T547f, T547g, SG5, SG11, SG17, SG20, SG21, SG23, SG26, SG27

Grade 3 Common Core Standards

Reading, continued

Strand	Code	Standards Text	Grade 3 Units 1–8 Standards Correlations
Foundational Skills			
Phonics and Word Recognition	**CC.3.Rfou.3**	**(3)** Know and apply grade-level phonics and word analysis skills in decoding words.	**Unit 1:** T1i, T1l, T1m, T27j, T27m, T27n, T33r, T33u, T33v, T55h, T55k, T55l; **Unit 2:** T69j, T69k, T69l, T69m, T69n, T95j, T95k, T95l, T95m, T95n, T96, T96c, T103c, T103e, T103r, T103s, T103t, T103u, T103v, T127h, T127l, T127q, T128, T128c, T135c, T135e; **Unit 3:** T141j, T141m, T141n, T165j, T165m, T166c, T173r, T173u, T173v, T195h, T195k, T195l, T196, T196c, T201c, T201e; **Unit 4:** T207j, T207k, T207l, T207m, T207n, T233j, T233k, T233l, T233m, T239r, T239s, T239t, T259h, T259i, T259j; **Unit 5:** T273j, T273k, T273l, T273m, T273n, T299j, T299k, T299l, T299m, T299n, T307r, T307s, T307t, T307u, T307v, T327h, T327i, T327j, T327k, T327l; **Unit 6:** T341j, T341k, T341l, T341n, T365j, T365k, T365l, T365m, T365n, T373r, T373s, T373t, T373u, T373v, T395h, T395i, T395j, T395k, T395l; **Unit 7:** T411j, T411k, T411l, T411m, T411n, T435j, T435m, T435n, T443p, T443s, T443t, T465j, T465m, T465s, T466, T466c; **Unit 8:** T481j, T481k, T481l, T481n, T507i, T507j, T507k, T507l, T507n, T519r, T519u, T519v, T539h, T539k
	CC.3.Rfou.3.a	**(a)** Identify and know the meaning of the most common prefixes and derivational suffixes.	**Unit 3:** T196, T196c, T201c, T201e; **Unit 4:** T233s, T234, T234c, T239c, T239e; **Unit 8:** T481m, T481n, T507m, T507n
	CC.3.Rfou.3.b	**(b)** Decode words with common Latin suffixes.	**Unit 8:** T481l, T507k, T507l, T519t, T539j
	CC.3.Rfou.3.c	**(c)** Decode multi-syllable words.	**Unit 2:** T127q, T128, T128c, T135c, T135e; **Unit 3:** T165k, T165l; **Unit 4:** T207m, T207n, T233k, T233l, T233m; **Unit 5:** T273m, T299n, T307v, T327k; **Unit 6:** T341k, T341l, T341m, T365n, T373u, T395l; **Unit 7:** T443q, T443r, T465i, T465k, T465l, T465s, T466, T466c, T473c; **Unit 8:** T481m, T481n, T507m, T507n, T519s, T519t, T519u, T539j, T539k, T539l
	CC.3.Rfou.3.d	**(d)** Read grade-appropriate irregularly spelled words.	**Unit 1:** T1j, T1k, T33s, T33t, T55i, T55j; **Unit 2:** T69k, T69l, T95k, T95l, T103s, T103t, T127i, T127j; **Unit 3:** T141k, T141l, T165k, T165l, T173s, T173t, T195i, T195j; **Unit 4:** T207k, T207l, T239s, T239t, T259i, T259j; **Unit 5:** T273k, T273l, T299k, T299l, T307s, T307t, T327i, T327j; **Unit 6:** T341k, T341l, T365k, T365l, T373s, T373t, T395i, T396j; **Unit 7:** T411k, T411l, T435k, T435l, T443q, T443r, T465k, T465l; **Unit 8:** T481k, T481l, T507k, T507l, T519s, T519t, T539j
Fluency	**CC.3.Rfou.4**	**(4)** Read with sufficient accuracy and fluency to support comprehension.	**Unit 1:** T5a, T8, T12–13, T28a, T29, T31a, T33b, T35a, T38, T42–43, T56a, T57, T62, T63b; **Unit 2:** T73a, T76, T80–81, T96a, T97, T101a, T103b, T105a, T108, T112–113, T128a, T129, T134, T135b; **Unit 3:** T145a, T148, T152–153, T166a, T167, T172, T173b, T175a, T178, T182–183, T196a, T197, T200, T201b; **Unit 4:** T211a, T214, T218–219, T234a, T235, T238, T239b, T241a, T244, T248–249, T260a, T261, T266, T267b; **Unit 5:** T277a, T280, T286–287, T300a, T301, T306, T307b, T309a, T312, T316–317, T328a, T329, T334, T335b; **Unit 6:** T345a, T348, T352–353, T366a, T367, T372, T373b, T375a, T378, T382–383, T396a, T397, T404, T405b; **Unit 7:** T415a, T418, T422–423, T432, T436a, T437, T442, T443b, T445a, T448, T452–453, T457, T465, T466a, T467, T471a, T473b; **Unit 8:** T485a, T488, T494–495, T508a, T509, T518, T519b, T521a, T524, T528, T533, T539, T540a, T541, T546, T547b
	CC.3.Rfou.4.a	**(a)** Read on-level text with purpose and understanding.	**Unit 1:** T12–13, T23, T42–43, T47; **Unit 4:** T214, SG8, SG9, SG14, SG15; **Unit 6:** T397; **Unit 7:** T437, T452–453, T457, T467; **Unit 8:** T541, T547b
	CC.3.Rfou.4.b	**(b)** Read on-level prose and poetry orally with accuracy, appropriate rate, and expression on successive readings.	**Unit 1:** T1i, T12–13, T23, T27, T27i, T28a, T29, T31a, T33b, T33d, T33l, T33r, T42–43, T47, T54a; **Unit 2:** T69j, T80–81, T89, T95, T103r, T112–113, T121, T127; **Unit 3:** T141i, T141j, T152–153, T159, T164a, T165, T166a, T167, T172, T173b, T173r, T182–183, T189, T195; **Unit 4:** T207j, T218–219, T225, T233, T234a, T235, T238, T239b, T239r, T248–249, T255, T258a, T259h; **Unit 5:** T273j, T286–287, T293, T299, T307r, T316–317, T321, T326a; **Unit 6:** T341j, T352–353, T357, T365, T366a, T367, T372, T373r, T382–383, T391, T395; **Unit 7:** T411j, T422–423, T435, T436a, T437, T442, T443b, T443o, T443p, T466a, T467, T471a, T473b; **Unit 8:** T481j, T494–495, T499, T507, T507i, T508a, T509, T518, T519b, T519r, T540a, T541, T546, T547b
	CC.3.Rfou.4.c	**(c)** Use context to confirm or self-correct word recognition and understanding, rereading as necessary.	**Unit 6:** T405e; **Unit 8:** T539q, T540, T540c, T547c, T547e

Writing

Strand	Code	Standards Text	Grade 3 Units 1–8 Standards Correlations
Text Types and Purposes	CC.3.W.1	**(1)** Write opinion pieces on topics or texts, supporting a point of view with reasons.	**Unit 4:** T233b, T233c, T258, T259g, T259o, T259p, T268, T269, T270, T273; **Unit 5:** T327o, T327p, T337, T338, T339; **Unit 6:** T341i, T373g, T388–389, T403; **Unit 7:** T434, T471; **Unit 8:** T481q, T481r, T507b, T507c, T516–517, T547d
	CC.3.W.1.a	**(a)** Introduce the topic or text they are writing about, state an opinion, and create an organizational structure that lists reasons.	**Unit 4:** T259o, T259p, T268, T269, T270; **Unit 5:** T327o, T327p, T337, T338, T339; **Unit 8:** T507b
	CC.3.W.1.b	**(b)** Provide reasons that support the opinion.	**Unit 4:** T233b, T233c, T259g, T259o, T259p, T268, T269, T270, T273; **Unit 5:** T337, T338; **Unit 6:** T373g, T388–389, T403; **Unit 7:** T434; **Unit 8:** T481q, T481r
	CC.3.W.1.c	**(c)** Use linking words and phrases (e.g., because, therefore, since, for example) to connect opinion and reasons.	**Unit 4:** T242, T259o, T259p, T268, T269, T270; **Unit 5:** T337, T338; **Unit 6:** T341i; **Unit 7:** T471; **Unit 8:** T481q, T481r, T516–517
	CC.3.W.1.d	**(d)** Provide a concluding statement or section.	**Unit 5:** T327p, T337, T338; **Unit 8:** T507b, T507c
	CC.3.W.2	**(2)** Write informative/explanatory texts to examine a topic and convey ideas and information clearly.	**Unit 1:** T55g, T68, T69; **Unit 2:** T69i, T103q, T127q, T137, T138; **Unit 3:** T141i, T165j, T173q, T195g, T195h, T195o, T195p, T202, T203, T204, T205; **Unit 4:** T207j, T259h; **Unit 5:** T273j, T299q, T299r, T307i, T307j, T307k, T307l, T307q, T307r, T327g; **Unit 6:** T373j, T373k, T373l, T395h; **Unit 7:** T465i, T465q, T465r, T478; **Unit 8:** T481i, T507i, T507j, T519q
	CC.3.W.2.a	**(a)** Introduce a topic and group related information together; include illustrations when useful to aiding comprehension.	**Unit 2:** T69i, T103r, T127q, T137, T138; **Unit 3:** T141j, T165j, T173r, T195o, T195p, T202, T203; **Unit 4:** T233i, T259g; **Unit 5:** T273j, T299q, T299r, T307j, T327g; **Unit 6:** T395o, T395p, T406, T407; **Unit 7:** T435q, T435r, T465q, T465r, T478; **Unit 8:** T481i, T519q, T539a, T539b, T553
	CC.3.W.2.b	**(b)** Develop the topic with facts, definitions, and details.	**Unit 2:** T127o, T127p, T137, T138; **Unit 3:** T203, T204; **Unit 5:** T307j, T307k, T307q; **Unit 7:** T465q, T465r, T476, T476a, T478
	CC.3.W.2.c	**(c)** Use linking words and phrases (e.g., also, another, and, more, but) to connect ideas within categories of information.	**Unit 3:** T141q, T141r; **Unit 7:** T436b, T443d, T465q, T465r
	CC.3.W.2.d	**(d)** Provide a concluding statement or section.	**Unit 6:** T373k
	CC.3.W.3	**(3)** Write narratives to develop real or imagined experiences or events using effective technique, descriptive details, and clear event sequences.	**Unit 1:** T1h, T27b, T27c, T65, T66; **Unit 2:** T95b, T95c, T103q; **Unit 3:** T141q, T141r, T165a, T165b, T165c, T165d, T165q, T165r; **Unit 5:** T307q, T341; **Unit 6:** T373q, T395g; **Unit 7:** T411i, T416, T465b; **Unit 8:** T481i, T519j, T519k, T519q, T548, T549, T550
	CC.3.W.3.a	**(a)** Establish a situation and introduce a narrator and/or characters; organize an event sequence that unfolds naturally.	**Unit 1:** T1p, T1q, T27a, T27b, T27c, T55b, T65, T66; **Unit 2:** T103q; **Unit 4:** T233q, T233r, T239j, T239k; **Unit 5:** T307q; **Unit 7:** T465b; **Unit 8:** T507i, T507q, T507r, T519j, T519k, T548, T549, T550
	CC.3.W.3.b	**(b)** Use dialogue and descriptions of actions, thoughts, and feelings to develop experiences and events or show the response of characters to situations.	**Unit 1:** T27c, T27q, T27r, T33i, T33j, T33k, T55b, T65, T66; **Unit 2:** T95b, T95c, T141; **Unit 4:** T231a, T273; **Unit 5:** T273i, T273q, T273r, T290–291, T297a, T299a, T299b, T299c, T299d, T299i; **Unit 7:** T443w, T443x, T454–455, T465b, T465c; **Unit 8:** T505a, T507i, T507q, T507r
	CC.3.W.3.c	**(c)** Use temporal words and phrases to signal event order.	**Unit 1:** T1q, T55b
	CC.3.W.3.d	**(d)** Provide a sense of closure.	**Unit 1:** T1q, T66; **Unit 8:** T539o, T539p
Production and Distribution of Writing	CC.3.W.4	**(4)** With guidance and support from adults, produce writing in which the development and organization are appropriate to task and purpose. (Grade-specific expectations for writing types are defined in standards 1–3 above.)	**Unit 1:** T33i, T33j, T33k; **Unit 2:** T95i, T103i, T103j, T103k; **Unit 3:** T165a, T165b, T165c, T165d, T173i, T173j, T173k, T173l; **Unit 4:** T259g; **Unit 6:** T341i, T341r, T365b, T365q, T365r, T373i, T373j, T373k, T373l, T411; **Unit 7:** T435a, T435b, T435c, T435d, T465b, T465c, T474–475, T476, T476a, T477, T478
	CC.3.W.5	**(5)** With guidance and support from peers and adults, develop and strengthen writing as needed by planning, revising, and editing. (Editing for conventions should demonstrate command of Language standards 1–3 up to and including grade 3 on pages 28 and 29.)	**Unit 1:** T1o, T27a, T27b, T27c, T27d, T27p, T33i, T33j, T33k, T33l, T33x, T55n, T64, T65, T66; **Unit 2:** T69p, T95a, T95b, T95c, T95d, T95i, T95p, T103i, T103j, T103k, T103l, T103x, T127n, T136, T137, T138; **Unit 3:** T141i, T141p, T165a, T165b, T165c, T165d, T165p, T173i, T173j, T173k, T173l, T173x, T195n, T202, T203, T204, T205; **Unit 4:** T207p, T233a, T233b, T233c, T233d, T233p, T239i, T239j, T239k, T239l, T239x, T259n, T268, T269, T270; **Unit 5:** T273p, T299a, T299b, T299c, T299d, T299p, T307i, T307j, T307l, T307x, T327m, T336, T337, T338, T339; **Unit 6:** T341i, T365a, T365b, T365c, T365d, T365p, T373i, T373j, T373k, T373l, T373x, T395n, T406, T407, T408, T409; **Unit 7:** T411p, T435b, T435c, T435d, T435p, T465a, T465b, T465c, T465d, T465p, T476, T476a, T477, T478, T479; **Unit 8:** T481p, T507a, T507b, T507c, T507d, T507p, T519i, T519j, T519k, T519l, T519x, T539n, T548, T549, T550
	CC.3.W.6	**(6)** With guidance and support from adults, use technology to produce and publish writing (using keyboarding skills) as well as to interact and collaborate with others.	**Unit 2:** T95j, T127b; **Unit 3:** T165a, T165b, T165c, T165d, T173i, T173j, T173k, T173l, T195h, T195g, T195o, T195p; **Unit 4:** T239y, T239z; **Unit 6:** T365b, T365c, T365d, T373j, T373k, T373l; **Unit 7:** T465b, T465c, T465d

Writing, continued

Strand	Code	Standards Text	Grade 3 Units 1–8 Standards Correlations
Research to Build and Present Knowledge	**CC.3.W.7**	(7) Conduct short research projects that build knowledge about a topic.	**Unit 1:** T33q, T33z, T55a; **Unit 2:** T103y, T103z; **Unit 3:** T173q, T173y, T173z, T195a, T195b, T195h, T202; **Unit 4:** T207j, T239y, T239z, T259a; **Unit 5:** T327a, T327b; **Unit 6:** T373i, T373j; **Unit 7:** T411j, T435i, T435q, T443i, T476, T476a; **Unit 8:** T539a, T539b
	CC.3.W.8	(8) Recall information from experiences or gather information from print and digital sources; take brief notes on sources and sort evidence into provided categories.	**Unit 1:** T1i, T33q, T33z, T55a, T55h; **Unit 2:** T69j, T103r, T127a, T127b; **Unit 3:** T141i, T141j, T165i, T165j, T173q, T173r, T173y, T173z, T195a, T195b, T195h, T202, T203; **Unit 4:** T259a, T259b; **Unit 5:** T299i, T299j, T307y, T307z, T327a, T327b; **Unit 6:** T341j, T373i, T373j, T373y, T373z, T395a, T395b, T395g; **Unit 7:** T411j, T435i, T435q, T435r, T443i, T443j, T443p, T465i, T476a, T477, T478; **Unit 8:** T519y, T519z, T539a, T539b
Range of Writing	**CC.3.W.10**	(10) Write routinely over extended time frames (time for research, reflection, and revision) and shorter time frames (a single sitting or a day or two) for a range of discipline-specific tasks, purposes, and audiences.	**Unit 1:** T1h, T6, T8, T9, T21, T25, T26, T27b, T27c, T27i, T27s, T31, T31a, T33d, T33g, T33j, T33k, T33q, T34, T36, T38, T39, T44–45, T53a, T54, T55g, T56b, T60–61, T61a, T63d, T63g, T65, T66, SG8, SG9, SG14, SG15, SG20, SG21, SG26, SG27; **Unit 2:** T69i, T69q, T69r, T74, T76, T77, T86–87, T92–93, T94, T95i, T95j, T95q, T95r, T96b, T100, T101, T101a, T103d, T103g, T103i, T103j, T103k, T103l, T106, T108, T118–119, T124–125, T126, T127g, T128b, T132–133, T133a, T135d, T135g, T140, SG8, SG9, SG14, SG15, SG20, SG21, SG26, SG27; **Unit 3:** T146, T148, T149, T157, T163a, T164, T165a, T165b, T165c, T165d, T165i, T166b, T170–171, T171a, T173d, T173g, T173i, T173j, T173k, T173l, T176, T178, T179, T187, T193, T194, T195g, T195q, T196b, T199, T199a, T201d, T201g, T202, T203, T204, T205, T206, T207, SG8, SG9, SG14, SG15, SG20, SG21, SG26, SG27; **Unit 4:** T207i, T207q, T207r, T212, T214, T215, T223, T224, T233b, T233c, T233i, T234b, T237, T237a, T239d, T239g, T239j, T239k, T239q, T239r, T242, T244, T245, T253, T257, T258, T260b, T264–265, T265a, T267d, T267g, T268, T269, T270, T272, T273, SG8, SG9, SG14, SG15, SG20, SG21, SG26, SG27; **Unit 5:** T273i, T278, T280, T281, T282, T292, T298, T299a, T299b, T299c, T299d, T299i, T300b, T305, T305a, T307d, T307g, T307i, T307j, T307k, T307l, T310, T312, T313, T318–319, T325, T326, T328b, T333, T333a, T335d, T335g, T336, T337, T338, T339, T340, T341, SG8, SG9, SG14, SG15, SG20, SG21, SG26, SG27; **Unit 6:** T341i, T346, T348, T349, T354–355, T363a, T364, T365a, T365b, T365c, T365d, T365i, T365j, T366b, T371, T371a, T373a, T373e, T373i, T373j, T373k, T373l, T373q, T376, T378, T379, T380, T393, T394, T396b, T403, T403a, T405d, T405g, T406, T407, T408, T409, T410, T411, SG8, SG9, SG14, SG15, SG20, SG21, SG26, SG27; **Unit 7:** T418, T428–429, T433, T433a, T436b, T441, T441a, T443d, T443g, T443i, T443j, T443o, T446, T448, T449, T454–455, T463a, T464, T466b, T466c, T471a, T473d, T473g, T480, T481, SG8, SG9, SG14, SG15, SG20, SG21, SG26, SG27; **Unit 8:** T486, T488, T489, T497, T505a, T506, T507b, T507c, T508b, T508c, T517a, T519d, T519g, T519j, T519k, T522, T524, T525, T531, T536–537, T538, T539g, T540b, T544–545, T545a, T547d, T547g, T548, T549, T550, T552, T553, SG8, SG9, SG14, SG15, SG20, SG21, SG26, SG27

Speaking and Listening

Strand	Code	Standards Text	Grade 3 Units 1–8 Standards Correlations
Comprehension and Collaboration	CC.3.SL.1	(1) Engage effectively in a range of collaborative discussions (one-on-one, in groups, and teacher-led) with diverse partners on grade 3 topics and texts, building on others' ideas and expressing their own clearly.	**Unit 1:** T1h, T10, T26, T27i, T27s, T28c, T32, T33h, T33r, T36a, T46, T55g, T55q, T56c, T62, T63h; **Unit 2:** T69i, T88, T102, T103h, T106a, T107, T110, T120, T128c, T134, T135h, T141; **Unit 3:** T141i, T150, T165i, T165j, T166c, T172, T173q, T180, T194, T195g, T195h, T195q, T196c, T200, T201, T201d, T201h; **Unit 4:** T210, T216, T224, T232, T233, T233i, T234c, T239d, T239h, T242a, T254, T258, T259, T259g, T259q, T260c, T266, T267h, T273; **Unit 5:** T273i, T276, T277, T282, T292, T298, T299, T299i, T299j, T299s, T300c, T306, T314, T320, T326, T327, T327g, T327h, T327q, T328c, T334; **Unit 6:** T341i, T350, T356, T365s, T372, T373r, T380, T394, T395h, T396c, T404, T405d; **Unit 7:** T420, T435i, T436c, T446a, T464, T465i, T465j; **Unit 8:** T481i, T481j, T490, T506, T507s, T508c, T518, T519q, T519r, T520, T526, T539q, T539q, T540c, T546
	CC.3.SL.1.a	(a) Come to discussions prepared, having read or studied required material; explicitly draw on that preparation and other information known about the topic to explore ideas under discussion.	**Unit 1:** T63d, SG8, SG9, SG14, SG15, SG20, SG21, SG26, SG27; **Unit 2:** T96c, T106a, T127h, T140, T141, SG8, SG9, SG14, SG15, SG20, SG21, SG26, SG27; **Unit 3:** T164, T165, T165i, T173q, T201d, T201h, T206, SG8, SG9, SG14, SG15, SG20, SG21, SG26, SG27; **Unit 4:** T232, T239d, T258, T259, T266, T272, SG8, SG9, SG14, SG15, SG20, SG21, SG26, SG27; **Unit 5:** T273i, T299i, T307h, T335h, T340, T341, SG8, SG9, SG14, SG15, SG20, SG21, SG26, SG27; **Unit 6:** T373h, T395q, T405h, T410, SG8, SG9, SG14, SG15, SG20, SG21, SG26, SG27; **Unit 7:** T412, T434, T443h, T465j, T473h, T480, T481, SG8, SG9, SG14, SG15, SG20, SG21, SG26, SG27; **Unit 8:** T517a, T519h, T547h, T552, T553, SG8, SG9, SG14, SG15, SG20, SG21, SG26, SG27
	CC.3.SL.1.b	(b) Follow agreed-upon rules for discussions (e.g., gaining the floor in respectful ways, listening to others with care, speaking one at a time about the topics and texts under discussion).	**Unit 1:** T27s, T36a, T55q; **Unit 3:** T195q; **Unit 4:** T238, T239h, T267h; **Unit 5:** T327q; **Unit 7:** T411i
	CC.3.SL.1.c	(c) Ask questions to check understanding of information presented, stay on topic, and link their comments to the remarks of others.	**Unit 1:** T27s, T33z; **Unit 2:** T69i, T72, T95i, T106a, T127q, T135h; **Unit 3:** T145, T146a, T147, T165s, T207; **Unit 4:** T273; **Unit 5:** T278a; **Unit 6:** T350, T365s, T409, T410, T411; **Unit 7:** T443d; **Unit 8:** T552, T553
	CC.3.SL.1.d	(d) Explain their own ideas and understanding in light of the discussion.	**Unit 1:** T26, T40, T54; **Unit 2:** T69i, T95i, T126, T127q; **Unit 3:** T141i, T146a, T165i, T173q, T176a, T195g; **Unit 4:** T210, T240, T241, T242a, T254, T258, T259, T266; **Unit 5:** T299s, T306, T334; **Unit 6:** T372; **Unit 7:** T416a, T435s, T444, T445, T465s; **Unit 8:** T486a, T518
	CC.3.SL.2	(2) Determine the main ideas and supporting details of a text read aloud or information presented in diverse media and formats, including visually, quantitatively, and orally.	**Unit 1:** T2, T36a; **Unit 2:** T70, T127g, T135a, T135b, T135d; **Unit 3:** T142; **Unit 4:** T207i, T208, T233j, T239q, T259g; **Unit 5:** T307d; **Unit 6:** T342, T346a, T373d, T373q, T405d, T410, T411; **Unit 7:** T411i, T435j, T443p, T465i, T473d; **Unit 8:** T482, T538, T539g
	CC.3.SL.3	(3) Ask and answer questions about information from a speaker, offering appropriate elaboration and detail.	**Unit 1:** T33q, T33z, T55b, T55g, T68, T69; **Unit 2:** T127g; **Unit 3:** T145, T146a, T174; **Unit 4:** T239q, T240, T273; **Unit 5:** T307d, T310a, T327b; **Unit 6:** T341i, T344, T345, T346a, T364, T365, T365i, T395g; **Unit 7:** T465i; **Unit 8:** T481i, T484, T485, T519q, T522a
Presentation of Knowledge and Ideas	CC.3.SL.4	(4) Report on a topic or text, tell a story, or recount an experience with appropriate facts and relevant, descriptive details, speaking clearly at an understandable pace.	**Unit 1:** T1h, T4, T5, T6a, T22, T26, T33q, T34, T55b, T55g, T69; **Unit 2:** T74a, T94, T95s, T126; **Unit 3:** T158, T162, T173d, T173h, T173r, T195b; **Unit 4:** T207i, T207j, T212a, T233i, T233s, T259b, T267d; **Unit 5:** T306, T307q, T308, T327b, T327g, T334, T341; **Unit 6:** T341j, T356, T365s, T373q, T395b, T395g, T405d; **Unit 7:** T414, T415, T435j, T443j, T443p, T465j, T472; **Unit 8:** T507d, T507s, T519d, T532, T539b, T539h, T547d
	CC.3.SL.5	(5) Create engaging audio recordings of stories or poems that demonstrate fluid reading at an understandable pace; add visual displays when appropriate to emphasize or enhance certain facts or details.	**Unit 1:** T1h, T27i, T33l, T55b; **Unit 2:** T127b, T141; **Unit 3:** T195b; **Unit 4:** T207i, T239l; **Unit 5:** T273i, T299, T307r; **Unit 6:** T365d, T365i, T373q, T395b; **Unit 7:** T435j, T465j, T479, T481; **Unit 8:** T507i, T519l, T519q, T539h, T551
	CC.3.SL.6	(6) Speak in complete sentences when appropriate to task and situation in order to provide requested detail or clarification. (See grade 3 Language standards 1 and 3 on pages 28 and 29 for specific expectations.)	**Unit 2:** T78, T95i, T103q, T104, T126, T127g; **Unit 7:** T435i; **Unit 8:** T520

Grade 3 Common Core Standards

Language

Strand	Code	Standards Text	Grade 3 Units 1–8 Standards Correlations
Conventions of Standard English	CC.3.L.1	(1) Demonstrate command of the conventions of standard English grammar and usage when writing or speaking.	**Unit 1:** T1n, T1o, T27d, T27o, T27p, T32a, T33, T33l, T33w, T33x, T55m, T55n, T55o, T55p, T62a, T63, T66; **Unit 2:** T95d, T102a, T103, T103q, T103w, T103x, T127m, T127n, T134a, T135, T138; **Unit 3:** T141o, T141p, T165d, T165o, T165p, T172a, T173, T173l, T173u, T173w, T173x, T195m, T195n, T200a, T201, T204, T207; **Unit 4:** T207o, T207p, T233d, T233o, T233p, T238a, T239, T239l, T239w, T239x, T259m, T259n, T266a, T267, T270; **Unit 5:** T273o, T273p, T299c, T299o, T299p, T306a, T307, T307l, T307w, T307x, T327m, T327n, T334a, T335, T338; **Unit 6:** T341o, T341p, T365d, T365o, T365p, T372a, T373, T373l, T373w, T373x, T395m, T395n, T404a, T405, T408; **Unit 7:** T411o, T411p, T433, T434, T435o, T435p, T442a, T443, T443u, T443v, T465o, T465p, T472a, T473; **Unit 8:** T481o, T481p, T507d, T507o, T507p, T518a, T519, T519w, T519x, T539m, T539n, T546a, T547, T550
	CC.3.L.1.a	(a) Explain the function of nouns, pronouns, verbs, adjectives, and adverbs in general and their functions in particular sentences.	**Unit 1:** T1n, T1o, T27d, T27o, T27p, T33l, T33w, T33x; **Unit 3:** T173l, T204; **Unit 4:** T207o, T207p, T239w, T239x, T259m, T259n; **Unit 5:** T273o, T273p, T299o, T299p, T306a, T307w, T307x; **Unit 6:** T341o, T341p, T365o, T365p, T373l, T373w, T373x, T395m, T395n, T404a, T405; **Unit 7:** T411o, T411p, T416, T419, T435o, T435p, T442a, T443u, T443v; **Unit 8:** T481o, T481p, T539m, T539n
	CC.3.L.1.b	(b) Form and use regular and irregular plural nouns.	**Unit 3:** T165o, T165p, T172a, T173, T173l, T173w, T173x, T195n, T200a, T201, T204
	CC.3.L.1.c	(c) Use abstract nouns (e.g., childhood).	**Unit 1:** T1o
	CC.3.L.1.d	(d) Form and use regular and irregular verbs.	**Unit 4:** T233d, T239l, T239w, T239x, T259m, T259n, T266a, T267, T270; **Unit 8:** T481o, T481p, T507d, T507o, T507p, T518a, T519, T519l, T519w, T519x, T550
	CC.3.L.1.e	(e) Form and use the simple (e.g., I walked; I walk; I will walk) verb tenses.	**Unit 4:** T207o, T207p, T233o, T233p, T238a, T239, T239u, T239v, T259k, T259l; **Unit 8:** T481o, T481p, T507d, T507o, T507p, T518a, T519, T519l, T519w, T519x, T539m, T539n, T546a, T547, T550
	CC.3.L.1.f	(f) Ensure subject-verb and pronoun-antecedent agreement.	**Unit 1:** T55m, T55n, T62a, T63, T66; **Unit 4:** T207o, T207p, T233o, T233p, T238a, T259m, T259n, T266a, T267; **Unit 6:** T341o, T341p, T365d, T408; **Unit 8:** T519w
	CC.3.L.1.g	(g) Form and use comparative and superlative adjectives and adverbs, and choose between them depending on what is to be modified.	**Unit 5:** T273o, T273p, T299g, T299o, T299p, T306a, T307, T307l; **Unit 7:** T411p, T435d, T435o, T435p, T442a, T443, T443u, T443v
	CC.3.L.1.h	(h) Use coordinating and subordinating conjunctions.	**Unit 1:** T55m; **Unit 2:** T127m, T127n, T134a, T135; **Unit 3:** T141o, T141p
	CC.3.L.1.i	(i) Produce simple, compound, and complex sentences.	**Unit 2:** T95i, T103w, T103x, T127m, T127n, T134a, T135, T138; **Unit 3:** T141o, T141p, T165d; **Unit 4:** T234c; **Unit 6:** T365q, T365r
	CC.3.L.2	(2) Demonstrate command of the conventions of standard English capitalization, punctuation, and spelling when writing.	**Unit 1:** T1l, T1m, T1n, T1o, T27m, T27n, T27p, T33u, T55k; **Unit 2:** T69m, T69n, T69o, T69p, T95m, T95o, T95p, T102a, T103, T103l, T103v, T103w, T103x, T127l, T127m, T127n, T134a, T135; **Unit 3:** T141m, T141o, T141p, T165d, T165n, T165o, T165p, T172a, T173, T173l, T173u, T173v, T173w, T173x, T195l, T195n, T200a, T201; **Unit 4:** T207m, T207n, T207p, T233m, T233n, T233o, T233p, T238a, T239s, T239t, T239v, T259k, T259l; **Unit 5:** T273m, T273n, T307v, T327m, T327l, T327m, T327n; **Unit 6:** T341m, T365n, T373l, T395k, T395l; **Unit 7:** T411m, T435n, T443t, T454–455, T465m, T465n; **Unit 8:** T481m, T481n, T481o, T481p, T507d, T507m, T507n, T507o, T507p, T518a, T519, T519u, T539m, T539l
	CC.3.L.2.a	(a) Capitalize appropriate words in titles.	**Unit 2:** T69o, T69p
	CC.3.L.2.b	(b) Use commas in addresses.	**Unit 2:** T69o, T69p
	CC.3.L.2.c	(c) Use commas and quotation marks in dialogue.	**Unit 2:** T69p, T95d, T141; **Unit 4:** T273; **Unit 7:** T443w, T443x, T465c
	CC.3.L.2.d	(d) Form and use possessives.	**Unit 5:** T327m, T327n, T334a, T335, T338; **Unit 6:** T408
	CC.3.L.2.e	(e) Use conventional spelling for high-frequency and other studied words and for adding suffixes to base words (e.g., sitting, smiled, cries, happiness).	**Unit 1:** T1j, T1k, T1m, T27k, T27l, T27n, T33s, T33t, T33v, T55i, T55j, T55l; **Unit 2:** T69k, T69l, T69n, T95k, T95l, T95n, T103s, T103t, T103v, T127i, T127j, T127k, T127l; **Unit 3:** T141k, T141l, T141n, T165k, T165l, T165m, T165n, T173s, T173t, T173v, T195i, T195j, T195k; **Unit 4:** T207k, T207l, T207n, T233k, T233l, T233n, T239s, T239t, T239u, T239v, T259i, T259j, T259l; **Unit 5:** T273k, T273l, T273n, T299k, T299l, T299m, T299n, T307s, T307t, T307v, T327i, T327j, T327l; **Unit 6:** T341k, T341l, T341m, T365k, T365l, T365m, T373s, T373t, T373u, T373v, T395i, T395j, T395l; **Unit 7:** T411k, T411l, T411m, T411n, T435k, T435l, T435n, T443r, T443t, T465l, T465n; **Unit 8:** T481k, T481l, T481n, T507k, T507l, T507n, T519s, T519t, T519v, T539j, T539l
	CC.3.L.2.f	(f) Use spelling patterns and generalizations (e.g., word families, position-based spellings, syllable patterns, ending rules, meaningful word parts) in writing words.	**Unit 1:** T1j, T1k, T1l, T1m, T27k, T27l, T27m, T33s, T33t, T33u, T33v, T55i, T55j, T55l; **Unit 2:** T69k, T69l, T69m, T95k, T95l, T95n, T103s, T103t, T103u, T103v, T127i, T127j, T127k, T127l; **Unit 3:** T141k, T141l, T141m, T141n, T165k, T165l, T165m, T173s, T173t, T173u, T173v, T195i, T195j, T195k, T195l; **Unit 4:** T207k, T207l, T207n, T233k, T233l, T233n, T239s, T239t, T239u, T259i, T259j, T259k; **Unit 5:** T273k, T273l, T273m, T299k, T299l, T299n, T307s, T307t, T327i, T327j; **Unit 6:** T341k, T341l, T341m, T341n, T365k, T365l, T365m, T373s, T373t, T373u, T395i, T395j, T395l; **Unit 7:** T411k, T411l, T411m, T411n, T435k, T435l, T435m, T443r, T443s, T443t, T465l, T465m, T465n; **Unit 8:** T481k, T481l, T507k, T507l, T519s, T519t, T519u, T539i, T539j
	CC.3.L.2.g	(g) Consult reference materials, including beginning dictionaries, as needed to check and correct spellings.	**Unit 1:** T27n; **Unit 2:** T127l; **Unit 4:** T259l; **Unit 5:** T307v; **Unit 7:** T443t; **Unit 8:** T519u , T539k

Language, continued

Strand	Code	Standards Text	Grade 3 Units 1–8 Standards Correlations
Knowledge of Language	CC.3.L.3	**(3)** Use knowledge of language and its conventions when writing, speaking, reading, or listening.	**Unit 1:** T27d, T27q, T27r, T32a, T33, T33l, T62a, T63, T66, T68, T69; **Unit 2:** T95d, T95q, T95r, T102a, T103, T103l, T134a, T135, T138; **Unit 3:** T165d, T172a, T173, T173l, T200a, T201, T204; **Unit 4:** T233d, T238a, T239, T239l, T266a, T267, T270; **Unit 5:** T299d, T302, T306a, T307, T307l, T334a, T335, T338; **Unit 6:** T341q, T341r, T345a, T352–353, T359, T362, T363a, T363b, T364, T364a, T365d, T372a, T373, T373a, T373b, T373c, T373d, T373l, T404a, T405, T408, T410, T411, SG6, SG7, SG24, SG25; **Unit 7:** T411i, T411q, T411r, T435c, T435d, T442a, T443, T472a, T473; **Unit 8:** T507d, T518a, T519, T519l, T546a, T547, T550
	CC.3.L.3.a	**(a)** Choose words and phrases for effect.	**Unit 1:** T27q, T27r, T28b, T33d, T69; **Unit 2:** T95q, T95r, T103i, T103j, T103k, T141; **Unit 3:** T165q, T165r; **Unit 5:** T273i, T335e; **Unit 6:** T341q, T341r, T365a, T365b, T365c, T373a, T373b, T373c, T373d, T411; **Unit 7:** T411i, T411q, T411r, T435a, T435b, T435c
	CC.3.L.3.b	**(b)** Recognize and observe differences between the conventions of spoken and written standard English.	**Unit 1:** T55o, T55p; **Unit 3:** T206; **Unit 4:** T273; **Unit 7:** T443o, T443w, T443x, T481
Vocabulary Acquisition and Use	CC.3.L.4	**(4)** Determine or clarify the meaning of unknown and multiple-meaning words and phrases based on grade 3 reading and content, choosing flexibly from a range of strategies.	**Unit 1:** T4, T5, T6a, T7, T33a, T34, T35, T36a, T37, T55q, T56, T56c, T63c, T63e; **Unit 2:** T74a, T75, T95i, T95j, T97, T103q, T106a, T107; **Unit 3:** T146a, T147, T165s, T166, T166c, T173c, T173e, T176a, T177; **Unit 4:** T212a, T213, T231b, T232, T242a, T243; **Unit 5:** T278a, T279, T310a, T311, T328c; **Unit 6:** T346a, T347, T376a, T377; **Unit 7:** T417, T435s, T436, T436c, T443c, T443e, T444, T445, T465s, T466, T466c, T473c, T473e; **Unit 8:** T486a, T487, T522a, T523
	CC.3.L.4.a	**(a)** Use sentence-level context as a clue to the meaning of a word or phrase.	**Unit 3:** T165s, T166, T166c, T173c, T173e; **Unit 5:** T327q, T328
	CC.3.L.4.b	**(b)** Determine the meaning of the new word formed when a known affix is added to a known word (e.g., agreeable/disagreeable, comfortable/uncomfortable, care/careless, heat/preheat).	**Unit 3:** T195g, T195q, T195r, T196c, T201c, T201e; **Unit 4:** T233s, T234, T234c, T239c, T239e
	CC.3.L.4.c	**(c)** Use a known root word as a clue to the meaning of an unknown word with the same root (e.g., company, companion).	**Unit 4:** T233s, T234, T234c, T239c, T239e; **Unit 7:** T435s, T436, T436c, T443c, T443e
	CC.3.L.4.d	**(d)** Use glossaries or beginning dictionaries, both print and digital, to determine or clarify the precise meaning of key words and phrases.	**Unit 1:** T1l, T33v, T55l, T55q, T56, T56c, T63c, T63e; **Unit 2:** T69n, T95n, T103q; **Unit 3:** T141n, T165n, T173v, T195l; **Unit 4:** T207m, T207n, T233n; **Unit 5:** T273n, T327k, T307c, T307e; **Unit 6:** T365i, T395g; **Unit 7:** T435n, T465n; **Unit 8:** T481g, T507m, T519e, T540c
	CC.3.L.5	**(5)** Demonstrate understanding of word relationships and nuances in word meanings.	**Unit 3:** T166b; **Unit 4:** T259q, T260, T260c, T267c, T267e; **Unit 5:** T299s, T300, T300c, T307c, T307e, T327g, T327q, T328, T328c, T335c, T335e; **Unit 6:** T348, T349, T395q, T396, T396c; **Unit 7:** T411i, T411q, T411r, T435c, T465s, T466, T466c, T473c, T473e; **Unit 8:** T507s, T508, T508c, T519c, T519e
	CC.3.L.5.a	**(a)** Distinguish the literal and non-literal meanings of words and phrases in context (e.g., take steps).	**Unit 2:** T141; **Unit 6:** T365s, T366, T366a, T366b, T366c, T368, T370, T373a, T373c, T373e
	CC.3.L.5.b	**(b)** Identify real-life connections between words and their use (e.g., describe people who are friendly or helpful).	**Unit 6:** T345a, T358, T363a, T364a
	CC.3.L.5.c	**(c)** Distinguish shades of meaning among related words that describe states of mind or degrees of certainty (e.g., knew, believed, suspected, heard, wondered).	**Unit 5:** T328, T328c, T335c, T335d; **Unit 8:** T508c, T519c, T519e
	CC.3.L.6	**(6)** Acquire and use accurately grade-appropriate conversational, general academic, and domain specific words and phrases, including those that signal spatial and temporal relationships (e.g., After dinner that night we went looking for them).	**Unit 1:** T1h, T4, T5, T6a, T7, T10, T22, T25a, T27i, T31a, T33q, T34, T35, T36a, T37, T40, T46, T53b, T55g, T55q, T56, T56c, T61a, T63c, T63e, SG5, SG6, SG7, SG11, SG12, SG13, SG17, SG18, SG19, SG23, SG24, SG25; **Unit 2:** T69i, T72, T73, T74a, T75, T78, T88, T93a, T95i, T101a, T103q, T104, T105, T106a, T107, T110, T120, T125a, T127g, T133a, SG5, SG6, SG7, SG11, SG12, SG13, SG17, SG18, SG19, SG23, SG24, SG25; **Unit 3:** T141i, T144, T145, T146a, T147, T150, T158, T163b, T165i, T165s, T166, T171a, T173q, T174, T175, T176a, T177, T180, T188, T193a, T195g, T199a, SG5, SG6, SG7, SG11, SG12, SG13, SG17, SG18, SG19, SG23, SG24, SG25; **Unit 4:** T207i, T210, T211, T212a, T213, T216, T224, T231b, T233i, T237a, T239q, T240, T241, T242a, T243, T246, T254, T257a, T259g, T259q, T260, T260c, T265a, T267c, T267e, SG5, SG6, SG7, SG11, SG12, SG13, SG17, SG18, SG19, SG23, SG24, SG25; **Unit 5:** T273i, T276, T277, T278a, T279, T282, T292, T297b, T299i, T299s, T305a, T307q, T308, T309, T310a, T311, T314, T320, T325a, T326, T327g, T333a, SG5, SG6, SG7, SG11, SG12, SG13, SG17, SG18, SG19, SG23, SG24, SG25; **Unit 6:** T341i, T344, T345, T346a, T347, T350, T356, T363b, T365i, T366c, T371a, T373q, T374, T375, T376a, T377, T380, T390, T393a, T394, T395g, T395q, T403a, T410, T411, SG5, SG6, SG7, SG11, SG12, SG13, SG17, SG18, SG19, SG23, SG24, SG25; **Unit 7:** T411i, T414, T415, T415a, T416a, T417, T420, T430, T433a, T435i, T435j, T441a, T443o, T444, T445, T446a, T447, T450, T456, T463b, T465i, T471a, SG5, SG6, SG7, SG11, SG12, SG13, SG17, SG18, SG19, SG23, SG24, SG25; **Unit 8:** T481i, T484, T485, T486a, T487, T490, T498, T505b, T507i, T507s, T508, T517a, T519q, T520, T521, T522a, T523, T526, T532, T537a, T539d, T539q, T540, T545a, SG5, SG6, SG7, SG11, SG12, SG13, SG17, SG18, SG19, SG23, SG24, SG25

Program Features and Resources Index

I

L

M

N

O

P

R

S

T

Skills Index

Index of Authors

Index of Illustrators/ Photographers

Acknowledgements, continued

Acknowledgments, continued

Text Credits

Unit One

Candlewick Press: Excerpt from *Those Shoes* by Maribeth Boelts, illustrated by Noah Z. Jones. Text copyright © 2007 by Maribeth Boelts. Illustrations © 2007 by Noah Z. Jones. Reproduced by permission of the publisher, Candlewick Press, Somerville, Mass.

Children's Book Press: "Guardian Angel," by Francisco X. Alarcon, from *Angels Ride Bikes*. Copyright © 1999 by Francisco X. Alarcon. Reprinted by permission of the publisher, Childrens book Press, San Francisco, Calif. www.childrensbookpress.org

Highlights for Children: Excerpt from "The World's Greatest Underachiever" by Henry Winkler from *Highlights for Children*, March 2005. Copyright © 2005 by Highlights for Children. Reprinted by permission of Highlights for Children, Inc.

Unit Two

Penguin Group (USA) Inc.: Excerpt from *When the Pigs Took Over* by Arthur Dorros, illustrated by Diane Greenseid. Text copyright © 2002 by Arthur Dorros. Illustrations © 2002 by Diane Greenseid. Used by permission of Dutton Children's Books, a Division of Penguin Young Readers Group, a Member of Penguin Group (USA) Inc., 345 Hudson Street, New York, NY 10014. All rights reserved.

Walker & Company: Excerpt from *When the Wolves Returned* by Dorothy Hinshaw Patent. Text copyright © 2008 by Dorothy Hinshaw Patent. Photographs © 2008 by Dan Hartman and Cassie Hartman. Reprinted by permission of Walker & Company. All rights reserved.

Unit Three

Random House Children's Books: Excerpt from *Two Old Potatoes and Me* by John Coy, illustrated by Carolyn Fisher. Text copyright © 2009 by John Coy. Illustrations © 2009 by Carolyn Fisher. Reprinted by permission of Random House Children's Books.

Lee & Low Books: "Papaya", "Potato," and "Corn" from *Yum! ¡Mm Mm! ¡Qué rico! Americas' Sprouting* by Pat Mora. Text copyright © 2007 by Pat Mora. Illustrations © 2007 by Rafael López. Reprinted by permission of Lee & Low Books, Inc., New York, NY 10016.

Unit Four

Barefoot Books: Excerpt from *Mama Panya's Pancakes* by Mary and Rich Chamberlin. Text copyright © 2005 by Mary and Rich Chamberlin. Illustrations © 2005 by Julie Cairns. Reprinted by permission of Barefoot Books.

Unit Five

Cengage Learning, Inc.: Excerpt from *Quicksand* by Kris Hirschmann. Copyright © 2002 by Gale. Reprinted by permission of Cengage Learning, Inc. www.cengage.com/permissions.

Unit Six

Henry Holt and Company LLC: Excerpt from *Oye, Celia! A Song for Celia Cruz* by Katie Sciurba,

illustrated by Edel Rodriguez. Text copyright © 2007 by Katherina Sciurba. Illustrations © 2007 by Edel Rodriguez. Reprinted by arrangement of Henry Holt and Company LLC.

Highlights for Children, Inc.: Excerpt from "Carving Stones in Cedar" by Kristine F. Anderson from *Highlights for Children*, November 2007. Copyright © 2007 by Highlights for Children, Inc. Reprinted by permission of Highlights for Children, Inc.

Unit Seven

HarperCollins Publishers: Excerpt from *An Island Grows* by Lola M. Schaefer, Illustrated by Cathie Felstead. Text copyright © 2006 by Lola M. Schaefer. Illustrations © 2006 by Cathie Felstead. Reprinted by permission of HarperCollins Children's Books.

Shen's Books: Excerpt from *Selvakumar Knew Better* by Virginia Kroll, illustrated by Xiaojun Li. Text copyright © 2009 by Virginia Kroll. Illustrations © 2009 by Xiaojun Li. Reprinted by permission of Shen's Books.

Unit Eight

Evans Brothers Ltd.: Excerpt from *Running Shoes* by Frederick Lipp, illustrated by Jason Gaillard. Text copyright © 2007 by Frederick Lipp. Illustrations © 2007 by Jason Gaillard. First published by Zero to Ten Limited (a member of the Evans Publishing Group). Text and illustrations reproduced with kind permission of Evans Publishing Ltd., 2A Portman Mansions, Chiltern Street, London, W1U 6NR.

NATIONAL GEOGRAPHIC SCHOOL PUBLISHING

National Geographic School Publishing gratefully acknowledges the contributions of the following National Geographic Explorers to our program and to our planet.

Joseph Lekuton, 2006 National Geographic Emerging Explorer

Zeb Hogan, 2004 National Geographic Emerging Explorer

Corneille Ewango, 2007 National Geographic Emerging Explorer

Gid Simoes and Paola Segura, 2008 National Geographic Emerging Explorers

Maycira Costa, National Geographic grantee

Elizabeth Kapu'uwailani Lindsey, National Geographic Fellow

Carsten Peter, National Geographic Contributing Photographer

Constanza Ceruti, 2005 National Geographic Emerging Explorer

Photographic Credits

iv (tl) Gideon Mendel/Corbis. v (tl) Mak Remissa/epa/Corbis. vi (tr) Eric Lodde/UNESCO - World Heritage Centre. vii (tr) Emielke van Wyk/Gallo Images/Getty Images. ix (tl) Dinodia/Stock Connection. x (tl) Carsten Peter/National Geographic Image Collection. xi (tl) photo courtesy of Constanza Ceruti. xv (br) Picture Contact/Constanza Ceruti. 2-3 (UnitOp) Tim Pannell/Ivy/Corbis. 7 (bl) Don Mason/Blend Images/Getty Images. (bc) James Woodson/Photodisc/Getty Images. (tc) Robert Brenner/PhotoEdit. (tl) Ariel Skelley/Blend Images/age fotostock. (tc, tl, tr) Hola

[The text continues across multiple pages with extensive photographic and illustrator credits for pages 642, 643, and 644.]